DICKENS STUDIES ANNUAL
Essays on Victorian Fiction

DICKENS STUDIES ANNUAL

Essays on Victorian Fiction

DICKENS
STUDIES
ANNUAL

Essays on Victorian Fiction

VOLUME
38

Edited by
Stanley Friedman, Edward Guiliano,
Anne Humpherys, Talia Schaffer, and Michael Timko

AMS PRESS
New York

Dickens Studies Annual: Essays on Victorian Fiction is published in cooperation with Queens College and the Graduate Center, CUNY.

International Standard Book Number
Series: 978–0–404–18520–6 / Series ISBN-10: 0-404-18520-7
Vol. 38: 978–0–404–18938–9 / Vol. 38 ISBN:10: 0-404-18938-5

Dickens Studies Annual: Essays on Victorian Fiction welcomes essay- and monograph-length contributions on Dickens and other Victorian novelists and on the history of aesthetics of Victorian fiction. All manuscripts should be double-spaced and should follow the documentation format described in the most recent *MLA Style Manual*. The author's name should appear only on a cover-page, not elsewhere in the essay. An editorial decision can usually be reached more quickly if two copies of the article are submitted, since outside readers are asked to evaluate each submission. If a manuscript is accepted for publication, the author will be asked to provide a 100– to 200–word abstract and also a disk containing the final version of the essay. The preferred editions for citations from Dickens's works are the Clarendon and the Norton Critical when available, otherwise the Oxford Illustrated or the Penguin.

Please send submissions to The Editors, *Dickens Studies Annual*, Ph.D. Program in English, The Graduate Center, CUNY, 365 Fifth Avenue, New York, NY 10016-4309. Please send inquiries concerning subscriptions and/or availability of earlier volumes to AMS Press, Inc., Brooklyn Navy Yard—Unit #221, 63 Flushing Ave., Brooklyn, NY 11205-1005.

Manufactured in the United States of America

Contents

Preface

The richness and variety of the lives and works of Dickens and other Victorian writers of fiction continue to attract the attention of scholars and critics with diverse interests and approaches. This volume offers essays seeking both to remind us of the contexts in which earlier fiction was produced and to suggest ways in which this literature still entertains and enlightens in our trying times.

Like greeting cards celebrating holidays and anniversaries, our prefaces are given to repetition. We thank all of those who sent us submissions, and we express our gratitude to our outside readers who very generously assist our contributors and us by forwarding detailed, insightful recommendations.

We are grateful, too, to Diana C. Archibald for her valuable survey of Dickens scholarship published in 2005, and to Roger G. Swearingen for his detailed survey of biographical studies and his inclusive checklist of critical works published over the last thirty-five years on Robert Louis Stevenson (a survey and a checklist supplementing the same scholar's review in Volume 37 of *DSA* of editions of letters by Stevenson, reference works about him, and editions of his literary works).

In addition, we thank Ruth F. Glancy, who has provided an updating of her *Dickens's Christmas Books, Christmas Stories, and Other Short Fiction: An Annotated Bibliography* (New York: Garland, 1985), and we are grateful to Duane DeVries, the General Editor of The Dickens Bibliographies (now being published by AMS Press), for helping to make this bibliographical supplement available to us and for assisting with its editing. (This bibliography includes its own index.)

We also sincerely appreciate the practical assistance offered by the following administrators: President William P. Kelly; Acting Provost Linda N. Edwards; Ph.D. Program in English Executive Officer Steven F. Kruger; Marilyn Weber, Assistant Program Officer, Ph.D. Program in English; and Meghan Mehta, Assistant Program Officer, Ph.D. Program in English, all of The Graduate Center, CUNY; and President James L. Muyskens; Dean of Arts and Humanities Tamara S. Evans; and Department of English Chair Nancy R. Comley, all of Queens College, CUNY.

We again thank John O. Jordan, Director of The Dickens Project at the University of California, Santa Cruz; JoAnna Rottke, Project Coordinator for

The Dickens Project; and Jon Michael Varese, the Project's Research Assistant and Web Administrator, for placing on the Project's website the tables of contents for volumes 1–27 of *DSA*, as well as abstracts for subsequent volumes. (These materials are included in the Project's Dickens Electronic Archive.) The Dickens Project can be reached at <http://humwww.ucsc.edu/dickens/index.html>.

We thank Gabriel Hornstein, President of AMS Press, who continues to show pleasing confidence in the value of our enterprise; Jack Hopper, retired Editor-in-Chief at AMS Press, who still greatly assists *DSA*; and Ashlie K. Sponenberg, Editor-in-Chief at AMS Press, whose courtesy and resourcefulness solve many problems. In addition, we are very grateful to three skilled and devoted editorial assistants, Alyssa Pelish, Marta Bladek, and Matt Lau, who helped, respectively, with the beginning, middle, and concluding phases of work on this volume.

—The Editors

Notes on Contributors

Diana C. Archibald is Associate Professor of English and Gender Studies at the University of Massachusetts Lowell. Her book *Domesticity, Imperialism, and Emigration in the Victorian Novel* (University of Missouri Press, 2002) examines the image of the "angel in the house" in an age of mass migration from the English imperial center to New World peripheries. She is currently writing a creative nonfiction book about her immigrant ancestors.

Alan P. Barr is Professor of English at Indiana University Northwest. He divides academic interests between Victorian literature and modern drama, with occasional forays into film. His publications on the Victorians include editing *Thomas Henry Huxley's Place in Science and Letters: Centenary Essays* and *The Major Prose of Thomas Henry Huxley* and articles on Meredith's "Modern Love," D. G. Rossetti's "Jenny," and C. G. Rossetti's "Goblin Market."

Clay Daniel is Associate Professor in the English Department at the University of Texas-Pan American. He is the author of *Death in Milton's Poetry* (Bucknell, 1994), and his research also has appeared in *Milton Studies, Studies in English Literature 1500–1900, Milton Quarterly*, and *Notes and Queries*.

Ruth F. Glancy is Professor of English at Concordia University College of Alberta. Among her publication are editions of Dickens's Christmas books and stories and *"A Tale of Two Cities": A Sourcebook*.

Shari Hodges Holt is Instructional Assistant Professor of English at the University of Mississippi and has authored papers on Dickens, Gothic fiction, and film adaptations of literature. Her present research examines cinematic adaptations of Dickens's novels as critical interpretations of their literary originals that demonstrate how Dickens is "read" under varying cultural and historical circumstances. She is also the co-author of *Ouida the Phenomenon: Evolving Social, Political, and Gender Concerns in Her Fiction*, a critical study of the works of nineteenth-century novelist "Ouida" (Marie Louise Ramé), forthcoming from the University of Delaware Press.

DAVID MCALLISTER has recently completed his doctoral studies at Emmanuel College, Cambridge, during which he researched representations of the relationship between the living and the dead in Victorian literature. He is currently researching the life of F. W. H. Myers, the Victorian poet, psychologist, and founder of the Society for Psychical Research.

ALBERT D. PIONKE is Assistant Professor and Director of Undergraduate Studies in the English Department at the University of Alabama, Tuscaloosa. He is the author of *Plots of Opportunity: Representing Conspiracy in Victorian England*, and is currently working on a book-length study of Victorian elite public ritual.

THOMAS RECCHIO is Associate Professor of English at the University of Connecticut, Storrs. He has published widely in composition studies and on the work of Elizabeth Gaskell; his most recent piece, " 'Charming and Sane': School Editions of *Cranford* in America, 1905–1914'' appeared in *Victorian Studies* (Summer 2003). He has just finished editing a Norton Critical Edition of Gaskell's *Mary Barton* (forthcoming 2008). He recently was awarded a research fellowship to work on the publication history of Gaskell's *Cranford* in a book project tentatively titled *The Cultural Uses of "Cranford."*

ROGER G. SWEARINGEN is best known for his authoritative guide to the writing and publication of Stevenson's many prose works, *The Prose Writings of Robert Louis Stevenson: A Guide* (1980), as the discoverer of RLS's first published work of fiction, *An Old Song* (1877), using manuscript and other sources at Yale (1982), and as the author of the RLS entry for the third edition of the *Cambridge Bibliography of English Literature* (2000). He is currently the website architect for a major electronics firm and is at work on a full-length biography of RLS titled *Robert Louis Stevenson: Spirit of Adventure.*

LEONA TOKER is Professor in the English Department of the Hebrew University of Jerusalem. She is the author of *Nabokov: The Mystery of Literary Structures* (1989), *Eloquent Reticence: Withholding Information in Fictional Narrative* (1993), *Return from the Archipelago: Narratives of Gulag Survivors* (2000), and articles on English, American, and Russian writers. She is the editor of *Commitment in Reflection: Essays in Literature and Moral Philosophy* (1994) and co-editor of *Rereading Texts/Rethinking Critical Presuppositions: Essays in Honour of H. M. Daleski* (1996). At present she is the editor of *Partial Answers: Journal of Literature and the History of Ideas.*

"Subject to the sceptre of imagination": Sleep, Dreams, and Unconsciousness in *Oliver Twist*

David McAllister

This essay explores Dickens's recourse to sleep as a narrative event in Oliver Twist. *It does so by considering the importance of sleep and unconsciousness throughout the novel, identifying and examining a source for the two most significant descriptions of Oliver asleep, and considering the possibility that the novel's engagement with the subject is linked to Mary Hogarth's death. Dickens was fascinated by the workings of the sleeping mind throughout his career, but it is only in* Oliver Twist *that this interest plays a significant role in his fiction. Oliver's frequent lapses into unconsciousness function in different ways—to protect him from the taint of criminal guilt, for example, and as a means of escape in which the hardships of Oliver's life can be assuaged. Dickens draws several of his descriptions of different states of sleep from Robert Macnish's popular study of the subject* The Philosophy of Sleep. *I suggest that Dickens turned to Macnish's book in an attempt to understand his own nightly dreams of Mary Hogarth, which began immediately after her death in 1837, and that the nature of his engagement with Macnish is reflected in the types of sleep experienced by Oliver.*

In January 1851, Dr. Thomas Stone submitted "Dreams," the second in a series of three articles on sleep states, to Dickens's journal *Household Words*.

Dickens Studies Annual, Volume 38, Copyright © 2007 by AMS Press, Inc. All rights reserved.

Stone had no reason to expect that his paper would elicit any adverse editorial response as it was simply a précis of contemporary theories on the sources and nature of dreams; furthermore, it had been preceded by an article on "Sleep" in the same vein, which Dickens had published without any comment. "Dreams," however, did provoke a response, and Dickens sent Stone a long letter advising him to rewrite the article and proffering advice on how it might be improved. It is perhaps surprising that this advice was offered on the grounds of content rather than form—surprising because Stone was a man with medical training and he had clearly researched his article well, citing numerous scientific and medical authorities to back up his assertions, and yet Dickens still felt himself qualified to suggest that these sources were insufficient and that Stone would do better to mine another rich and as yet untapped seam of information on the subject: Dickens himself. Dickens explains to Stone that he has "read something on the subject, and . . . long observed it with the greatest attention and interest" (*Letters* 6: 276), and illustrates his expertise by detailing several personal anecdotes about dreams that he felt would make Stone's article less reliant on "conventional philosophy and belief" (276), a phrase that indicates a characteristically Dickensian privileging of personal experience over attested scientific authority. Dickens ends the letter with a piece of editorial advice that simultaneously denies that he is coercing Stone into changing his article while implying precisely the reverse:

> If you think any of these random remarks worth your consideration, I should be happy to appoint a time for discussing the subject still further with you. I shall be happy to insert the paper, as it stands, if you prefer it—but in that case I should desire to pursue it with my own hints of experience and opinion—and if we could agree we might dispatch the subject in one paper.   (277)

Dickens's threat to trump Stone's article with one of his own seems to contain an unspoken subjoinder at the end of his apparently friendly "if we could agree"; perhaps "if we could agree *that I am right*" comes close to capturing his meaning. We can assume that Stone arrived at a similar interpretation and took Dickens up on his offer to discuss the content of "Dreams" before revising the text, because when his paper was published the following month it included almost all of the "hints of experience" that Dickens had proffered. Stone's judicious incorporation of Dickens's editorial advice ensured that this threatened follow-up article never materialized, and, as a result, Dickens never again committed his thoughts on the subject of dreams to paper; but it is clear from this letter that he fostered a deep and intensely personal interest in the issues that surrounded the topics of sleep, dreams, and the workings of the unconscious mind in the mid-nineteenth century.

Dickens was fascinated with the latent potential of the mind, as his interest in mesmerism shows, and while this and the sporadic insomnia that led him on his night walks through London have received recent critical attention, his interest in sleep and dreams has elicited comparatively little comment. I wish to suggest that this is a significant omission, and that this becomes apparent when we consider the influence that his interest in sleep and dreams has on the plot development of *Oliver Twist*, a novel in which different sleep states are described in unusual detail and where they function as important sites of transformation in which the appalling circumstances of Oliver's waking life can be suddenly, almost magically, changed for the better. This patterning of sleep, dreams, and unconsciousness as transformative states relates directly to the circumstances of Dickens's own life during the years in which he wrote and published the novel. This essay examines Dickens's representation of sleep states in *Oliver Twist*, identifying the sources he used to research the different types of sleep that Oliver experiences, and considering what significance they have to the novel as a whole. It concludes with a discussion of the crucial influence of Mary Hogarth's death in initiating Dickens's fascination with dreams, and her indirect but shaping influence on the narrative of *Oliver Twist*.

Oliver Twist contains several strangely precise descriptions of sleep states that are unprecedented in Dickens's early writing, and which are not a consistent feature of his later novels. David Paroissien has noted that these taxonomic descriptions bear an overwhelming similarity to those described in *The Philosophy of Sleep* by Robert Macnish, the mid-nineteenth century's best known authority on sleep (Paroissien 101, 217). A Glasgow doctor with a literary bent, Macnish wrote articles and stories for *Blackwood*'s throughout the 1830s and 40s under the pseudonym The Modern Pythagorean and came to prominence with his first book *The Anatomy of Drunkenness* (1821), but it was his second book, *The Philosophy of Sleep*, which was a considerable popular success on publication in 1828, and went on to be reprinted numerous times and widely translated, for which he was best known.[1] Although Macnish's book concentrates on sleep, it situates the subject as one of a number of interrelated states of consciousness, which he examines in chapters on dreaming, prophetic dreams, nightmare, daymare, sleepwalking, sleeplessness, trance, spectral illusions, reverie, and abstraction. His style is digressive and anecdotal, and the book is full of personal observations, poetic descriptions of sleep, and passages that illustrate the author's inclination to lyricism:

> "Night," observes the poet Montgomery "is the time for sleep;" and assuredly the hush of darkness as naturally courts to repose as meridian splendour flashes on us the necessity of our being up at our labour. . . . That this is not the mere effect of custom, might be readily demonstrated. All nature awakes with the rising sun; the birds begin to sing; the bees to fly about with murmurous delight. The flowers which shut under the embrace of darkness, unfold themselves to

the light. The cattle arise to crop the dewy herbage; and "man goeth forth to his labour until the evening." At close of day, the reverse of all this activity and motion is observed. The songs of the woodland choir, one after another, become hushed, till at length twilight is left to silence, with her own star and her fallen dews. Action is succeeded by listlessness, energy by languor, the desire of exertion by the inclination for repose. Sleep, which shuns the light, embraces darkness, and they lie down together under the sceptre of midnight.

(3)

The Romantic influence that is apparent in the evocation of nature in this passage extends to Macnish's fascination with the role played by the imagination in sleep, and his wider conception of unconsciousness as a condition in which the imagination can hold sway. Sleep is "the intermediate state between life and death" (2), and therefore a state where "the mind is wholly subject to the sceptre of imagination" (80). For Macnish, sleep enables the individual to tap into a hidden realm that is denied to the mind under normal conditions.

Access to this imaginative realm is not automatic. Macnish argues that there are two broad categories of sleep, broken and complete, which occupy different positions on a continuum: at one end of this continuum lies absolute wakefulness, and at the other end lies the ultimate absence of wakefulness: death. This occasional subjection of the mind to the imagination does not take place in all types of sleep. It cannot, he argues, take place in a state of complete sleep, because its position close to the end of the continuum makes it "a temporary metaphysical death" (2) in which "all the mental faculties are . . . dormant, and for a short period the person exists in a state of the most perfect oblivion" (52). The more complete one's sleep, the less one dreams: the closer sleep is to the deathly end of the continuum, the greater its restorative power. Complete sleep "is the grand restorer of nature; the talisman which enables the body to recover the sensorial power expended in the waking state; the *elixir vitae* which animates with energy the corporeal and intellectual faculties" (46). It is only in broken sleep, which is caused by the continued activity of any physiological faculty, that the imagination is given free rein in the mind of the sleeper:

> When . . . one faculty, or more than one, bursts asunder the bonds which enthralled it, while its fellows continue chained in sleep, then visions ensue, and the imagination dwells in that wide empire which separates the waking state from that of perfect sleep.　　　　　　　　　　　　　　　　　　　(52)

Broken or incomplete sleep, then, is a means of entry into a world ruled by an unfettered imagination, which is "at work, while the judgement is asleep; and thereby indulges in the maddest and most extravagant thoughts, free from the salutary check of the latter more sedate and judicious faculty" (53). As a consequence, the sleeper awakes without experiencing the perfect rest and regeneration that characterizes complete sleep. This separation between complete and incomplete transforms sleep into a state of infinite and unpredictable possibility: if sleep is complete, it "invigorates, refreshes, and fills [the sleeper's] mind with new ideas" (45) when he or she wakes next morning; if it is broken or incomplete, then the sleeper's imagination is free to explore the limits of its potential throughout the course of the night: however, the sleeper is unable to predict or control which of these sleep states will occur when he or she goes to bed.

We know that Dickens read Macnish: an 1840 dual edition of *The Anatomy of Drunkenness* and *The Philosophy of Sleep* was in his library at Gad's Hill on his death; he refers to *The Philosophy of Sleep* in the letter to Stone from 1851, and in 1853 *The Anatomy of Drunkenness* was to provide him with examples of spontaneous combustion with which to rebut G. H. Lewes's criticism of Krook's death in *Bleak House*. As Paroissien has pointed out, however, the descriptions of sleep in *Oliver Twist* suggest that Dickens had read *The Philosophy of Sleep* as early as 1837. I intend to argue firstly that Macnish's writing on sleep had a wider influence on both Dickens's personal life and his literary output for a period in 1837 and 1838 than has generally been recognized, and secondly that we can date Dickens's intellectual engagement with *The Philosophy of Sleep* with some precision to May or June 1837, and thereby establish a definite link between Dickens's interest in dreams and the death of Mary Hogarth.

Oliver Twist is a novel in which the protagonist falls into states of sleep and unconsciousness with almost monotonous regularity, and it is one of the novel's curiosities that these periods of unconsciousness frequently coincide with crucial developments in the narrative. When Oliver is first rescued from Fagin's gang by Mr. Brownlow, he lies in a feverish state of semi-consciousness "for many days"[2] (86) before his illness breaks and he is made aware of the favourable change in his circumstances. Almost immediately, he falls into "that deep tranquil sleep which ease from recent suffering alone imparts; that calm and peaceful rest which it is pain to wake from" (89). Oliver's next significant lapse in consciousness occurs on the Maylies' doorstep following the robbery in Chertsey. He is brought into the house "speechless and exhausted" (231) and when Rose and Mrs. Maylie first see him he has "sunk into a deep sleep" (238). Once again, Oliver wakes to discover that he has been rescued from dire trouble during his period of unconsciousness. Lisa Rodensky has argued persuasively that, were it not for this fortuitous habit of losing consciousness at crucial moments, Oliver might come to be seen by other characters in the novel, "and perhaps by readers too," as implicated in the crimes of his sometime cohorts, Sikes and Fagin:

The rather extreme forms of protection Dickens constructs on Oliver's behalf, particularly as the novel unfolds, appear designed to keep anyone from assigning any criminal taint to Oliver. Using a kind of belt-and-suspenders strategy, Dickens not only critiques the reach of the criminal law when it latches onto Oliver, he also ensures Oliver's innocence by, in essence, making him unconscious at key moments in the text.   (72)

So despite Oliver's frequent presence when criminal events take place, his innocence is maintained by Dickens's ploy of putting him in a "state of suspended animation" (72).

This analysis certainly explains the reasons behind Oliver's collapse at Fang's court, which removes him from the magistrate's presence before he has a chance to answer for his involvement with the attempt by the Dodger and Charley to pick Brownlow's pocket, and his illness at Chertsey, which leaves Dr. Losberne to lie to the Bow Street Runners about his association with Fagin and Sikes. Rodensky rightly points to J. Hillis Miller's claim, used to support a reading of the novel that emphasizes its fairy-tale qualities, that Oliver's best course of action throughout the novel seems to be to remain as passive as possible (43). The frequency with which Oliver's unconsciousness leads to his salvation suggests a link in Dickens's thought between sleep and rescue, as if Oliver's frequent periods of unconsciousness function as physical or psychological correlatives to his general state of helplessness and symbolize the isolation and susceptibility to influence that will determine his "progress" and career. However, Rodensky's analysis does not adequately explain the two best known, and most important, episodes of sleep in *Oliver Twist*. The first of these occurs when Oliver spends his first night with Fagin's gang, while the other takes place when Fagin and Monks appear at Oliver's window outside of the Maylies' country cottage. Oliver's innocence is not under threat during either of these incidents, neither in the eyes of the law nor the mind of the reader. Significantly, as I will argue, these two descriptions of different sleep states are clearly drawn from Macnish's *The Philosophy of Sleep*, and demand a fuller explanation.

The first of the two passages with which the rest of this essay is concerned occurs at the beginning of chapter 9 in the first book, when Oliver wakes up after spending his first night asleep in Fagin's den:

Although Oliver had roused himself from sleep, he was not thoroughly awake. There is a drowsy, heavy state, between sleeping and waking, when you dream more in five minutes with your eyes half open, and yourself half conscious of everything that is passing around you, than you would in five nights with your eyes fast closed, and your senses wrapt in perfect unconsciousness. At such times, a mortal knows just enough of what his mind is doing to form some glimmering conception of its mighty powers, its bounding from earth and spurning time and space, when freed from the irksome restraint of its corporeal associate.   (67)

Although this curious passage is frequently cited by critics of the novel, few of them have attempted to explain the purpose of Dickens's digression into the behavior of the mind during sleep. Fred Kaplan has identified this passage as evidence of Dickens's interest in mesmerism, arguing that it shows that "whether or not he had attended any mesmeric sessions" by the summer of 1837, Dickens had already "taken the subject into his creative consciousness" (145). *Oliver Twist* was written at the height of what Kaplan calls the "mesmeric mania," and he is correct in asserting that there are similarities between the theories that mushroomed from the voguish pseudoscience and Dickens's suggestion here that the mind has almost limitless untapped potential. However, in his search for evidence of Dickens's interest in mesmerism, Kaplan misses the uncomfortable fact that this passage is derived from a book that is primarily concerned with sleep, one, moreover, which was written before "mesmeric mania" took hold of the nation. The book in question is, of course, *The Philosophy of Sleep*, and there is an unmistakable similarity between the description of Oliver's sleep and several passages written by Macnish. This influence is particularly apparent when Dickens describes the collapsing of temporal logic in this state between sleep and waking; the subject's ability to "dream more in five minutes . . . than . . . in five nights" closely resembles Macnish's argument that "when we are suddenly awaked from a profound slumber . . . a train of actions which it would take hours, or days, or even weeks to accomplish, sometimes passes through the mind" (61). And where Dickens describes the mind "spurning time and space," Macnish claims that to the sleeping mind "time . . . seems to be in a great measure annihilated. An extensive period is reduced, as it were, to a single point, or rather a single point is made to embrace an extensive period" (61). In this state, Macnish writes, we instantaneously "pass through many adventures, see many strange sights, and hear many strange sounds" (61). Kaplan's analysis of this passage rather misses its point: this precise, taxonomic description of a specific sleep state is surely more than simply a means by which Dickens can slip in a fashionable allusion to mesmerism; it is a source of interest in and of itself.

Dickens emphasizes the particularity of the condition he has identified, writing that Oliver was in "precisely the condition I have described" (67) and therefore subject to this collapsing of temporality and the liberation from corporeality that allows the sleeping mind to spurn time and space. This emphasis suggests that Dickens considers it important that the reader retain an awareness of the almost visionary potential of Oliver's condition, and yet if we examine what Oliver actually sees while half asleep it seems as if the "mighty powers" of his mind are rather underemployed. What Oliver sees when he opens his eyes does not necessitate the abstraction of soul from body, nor the spurning of any of life's familiar dimensions: through his "half-closed eye," he sees Fagin take from his secret store beneath the floorboards a box filled with "watches . . . rings, brooches, bracelets, and other articles of jewellery: of such magnificent materials, and such costly workmanship, that Oliver had no idea even of their names" (67). Rodensky's suggestion that Dickens here constructs a *cordon sanitaire* of unconsciousness round Oliver seems inadequate: he is in no danger of committing a crime, nor does his sleepy state protect him from the possible taint of seeing Fagin handle stolen goods—he clearly observes both the nature and location of Fagin's hidden loot, even if he is too much of an innocent to understand properly what he has witnessed. Dickens's use of Macnish here builds a sense of anticipation, and yet the passage is essentially bathetic: there is nothing visionary at work here; Oliver is simply watching as Fagin exults, with stereotypical miserly cupidity, in his horde of treasures. Why, then, does Dickens bother describing the state of sleep with such taxonomic precision that he raises in the mind of the reader the possibility that Oliver is in a condition that will allow him to see a revelatory vision?

We can discover one possible solution to this puzzle in the problems that Dickens faced as an apprentice novelist writing in a form (monthly instalments) that did not allow him to rewrite early passages of a novel in order to suit later plot developments. Burton M. Wheeler has identified this sleep scene as evidence of the ad hoc nature of Dickens's plotting in *Oliver Twist*, suggesting that it can be read as an example of Dickens's reliance on contingent planning in the years before he perfected the system of notebook chapter plans that would allow the construction of the complex plot machinery of the later novels. He argues that when Dickens allows Oliver to see Fagin pull out a trinket that seems to have "some very minute inscription on it" (*Oliver Twist* 67) he was preparing the ground for a future plot twist which, as it turned out, was never needed (Wheeler 53). The trinket anticipates the locket that turns up later in the novel, which had originally belonged to Oliver's mother Agnes. Wheeler argues that Dickens was here providing himself with a peg "upon which he could hang a plot" (53), perhaps one that might eventually explain Oliver's parentage.

This is a plausible suggestion, and would help explain why a passage that proves to have no direct significance to the resolution of the narrative is written in such a peculiar and memorable style. The description of the old man hauling treasures, "sparkling with diamonds" (67), from beneath the floor of his squalid hovel has a fairy tale quality that is heightened by Dickens's evocative description of Oliver's state of semiconsciousness. The suggestion that this moment of revelation occurs when Oliver's mind has broken free from his body emphasizes the significance of the episode, making a mundane episode of spying seem like a moment of supernatural or extrasensory revelation. If Wheeler is right, and Dickens had originally intended that Oliver would here see the location of the evidence that would eventually prove his parentage, then Dickens's adoption of Macnish's ideas about the collapse of temporal logic in sleep would make more sense: the "drowsy, heavy state" would have proved every bit as revelatory as the heightened description seems to anticipate, spanning the time between the prehistory of the novel, when Oliver's mother gives up the locket to her deathbed nurse, and the conclusion of the novel when Oliver's history is revealed. It seems likely that this first description of sleep may thus have been intended as a revelatory state in which the anxieties of the waking world (in this case Oliver's underlying concern about his parentage) are mysteriously—almost magically—resolved.

The authorial interest in the nature of sleep and, more specifically, in the ideas expressed in Macnish's *The Philosophy of Sleep* that are so clearly evident in this passage appears as if from nowhere. Considering the frequency with which Oliver's sleep is described after this point in the narrative, it seems curious that neither the highly precise and taxonomic descriptions of sleep nor the figuring of sleep as a transformative state appear in chapters 1 to 8, a period in which Oliver is clearly in need of some form of escape, however temporary, from his dreadful existence. There are numerous points in these early chapters which could have allowed Dickens to go into detail about the nature of Oliver's sleep: when he is kept in solitary confinement in the workhouse; when he arrives at Sowerberry's and is told to sleep among the coffins; when he forces himself to stay awake the night before he leaves for London. On the one occasion in these early numbers when Dickens does represent sleep as a relief, when Oliver stops on the road to London, his throwaway treatment of it has little in common with the detailed descriptions that occur later in the novel: "Being very tired with his walk, however, he soon fell asleep and forgot his troubles" (58). When compared to the complex and specific evocations of different types of sleep in the rest of the novel, this is flat, generic, and entirely incidental to the narrative, and reveals no trace of Macnish's influence.

Furthermore, these nonspecific descriptions of sleep in the early numbers of *Oliver Twist* are entirely consistent with the rest of Dickens's fictional output at this stage in his career. This nonspecificity in describing sleep is also apparent in the other novel that Dickens was writing in this period. The first number of *The Pickwick Papers* had been published in April 1836, and yet despite the comical narcolepsy of Joe, the Fat Boy, Dickens had not felt the need to write any detailed description of a specific type of sleep in more than a year's worth of monthly numbers. Joe repeatedly falls asleep in the early part of the novel but the specific nature of that sleep is never considered worthy of description. It is significant, therefore, that the first (indeed only) moment in the novel when a sleep state is described with any particularity is when Mr. Pickwick is taken to the Fleet. On his first night in prison Pickwick finds his allocated bed in a room that was evidently shared by three other debtors. When these cellmates return from the prison taproom their carousing wakes Pickwick, who "had been in a state of slumber for some time, when he had a faint perception of the drunken man bursting out afresh with the common song" (556).

Until this moment in the narrative, sleep has always been an absolute state, without any of the gradations from broken to complete that we find in *Oliver Twist*: when someone roars at the Fat Boy, or attempts to consume food in his vicinity, he instantly wakes. But here for the first time Dickens suggests that there are different types of sleep, and that in certain types the sleeper's consciousness is susceptible to encroachment by those around him: "He then once again dropped off to sleep, with a confused consciousness that Mr. Smangle was still engaged in relating a long story" (556). Admittedly this description is less detailed than those that are found in *Oliver Twist*, but there has been nothing like this recognition that degrees of consciousness exist within sleep in any of the previous fourteen numbers of the novel. The significance of this first detailed description of sleep in *Pickwick* lies in its date of composition: it comes in the July 1837 number, and was therefore written and published in the same month as the number of *Oliver Twist* that opens with the description of Oliver's dreamy state as he sleeps on Fagin's floor. This means that the first detailed descriptions of sleep states in the whole of Dickens's fiction occur simultaneously in the July 1837 numbers of *Oliver Twist* and *The Pickwick Papers*. It seems unlikely that this is coincidental, and it allows us to date speculatively Dickens's reading, or perhaps rereading, of Macnish's *The Philosophy of Sleep* to the period immediately before the publication of these two monthly numbers, in either May or June 1837.

The identification of May or June 1837 as a likely moment at which this interest was initiated suggests another possible explanation for why Dickens turned to Macnish when writing the opening paragraphs of the ninth chapter of *Oliver Twist*. There had been no June number of either *Oliver* or *Pickwick* as a result of the death of Mary Hogarth on May 7, 1837. The story of her death is well known: seventeen-year-old Mary collapsed on her way to bed in Dickens's house in Doughty Street after spending the evening at the theater with her sister and brother in law. She died in Dickens's arms later that day. Dickens was utterly grief-stricken and moved with his wife to a farmhouse in Hampstead for a month to recover from the shock of the catastrophe. When Dickens felt able to write again, he set to work on the numbers of *Oliver Twist* and *The Pickwick Papers* in which Macnish's influence first becomes apparent.

It seems highly likely that Dickens read *The Philosophy of Sleep* in the weeks that followed Mary Hogarth's death, in an attempt to gain a better understanding of his own troubled dreams. Indeed, there are several passages in *The Philosophy of Sleep* in which Macnish discusses the frequent appearances of the dead in the dreams of the living. The link between Mary's death and Dickens's sudden interest in sleep and dreams is made explicit by Dickens himself in the letter that he writes to Thomas Stone in 1851, with which this essay begins. When Dickens returns Stone's article he furnishes him with examples of notable dreams from his own life. One of these concerns a sequence of recurring dreams concerning Mary Hogarth that he claims to have had on a nightly basis for the year that followed her death. Critics have long speculated on the precise nature of Dickens's attachment to Mary, drawing various conclusions from the sole reliable fact of the matter, which is the astonishing depth and vigor of his grief. Whatever its psychological roots, the intensity with which Dickens felt her loss manifested itself in his sleep with equal if not greater intensity than when he was awake, as he explains to Stone: "I dreamed of her, every night—sometimes as living, sometimes as dead, never in any terrible or shocking aspect" (*Letters* 6: 277). These nightly dreams had such an effect on Dickens that he was evidently able to recall them with admirable precision more than a decade later.

He claims that these visitations continued for a year, during which they seem to have been keenly anticipated.[3] He tells Stone that after a year

> I lay down to sleep, in an Inn on a wild Yorkshire Moor, covered with snow. As I looked out of the window on the bleak winter prospect before I undressed, I wondered within myself whether the subject would follow me here. It did.
>
> (*Letters* 6: 277)

One of the problems with Dickens's habitual privileging of experience over authority raises its head here, for his memory of these events is not quite accurate: this snowy night in Yorkshire was actually January 31, 1838, and thus some three months short of being a year after Mary's death. We know this because the following day he wrote to Catherine and told her of the dreams:

> Is it not extraordinary that the same dreams which have constantly visited me since poor Mary died, follow me everywhere? After all the change of scene and fatigue, I have dreamt of her ever since I left home, and no doubt shall 'till I return. I should be very sorry to lose such visions for they are very happy ones—if it be only the seeing her in one's sleep—I would fain believe too, that her spirit may have some influence over them, but their perpetual repetition is extraordinary.   (*Letters* 1: 366)

It is interesting to note that until this letter in February, nine months after her death, he had kept the dreams to himself, considering it judicious not to tell Catherine: "As she had been my wife's sister, and had died suddenly in our house, I forbore to allude to these dreams—kept them wholly to myself"

(*Letters* 6: 277). There is a discernible tension in Dickens's phrasing here: the apparent self-denial of "I forbore to allude" seems ill at ease with the proprietorial, almost greedy phrasing of "kept them wholly to myself," hinting, perhaps, at a mixture of motives and raising the possibility that Dickens may have had more psychologically complex reasons for keeping the dreams to himself than the one offered here, which is simply that he wished to avoid upsetting his wife. Whatever its cause, Dickens's decision not to share his dreams seems to have resulted in their perpetuation. He acknowledges as much in his letter to Stone, linking his initial secrecy with the dream's recurrence.[4] The cessation of the dreams at the moment of their revelation to Catherine suggests that they may have been a guilty pleasure for Dickens at a time when pleasure was hard to come by in the months after Mary's death. Sleep offered Dickens a chance to resurrect his beloved sister-in-law in a state that his reading of Macnish would have reassured him was subject only to "the sceptre of imagination," and therefore at one crucial remove from the reality of his day-to-day life with Catherine. The description of Oliver asleep on Fagin's floor signals Dickens's engagement with Macnish's ideas, and suggests that it was the heightened, revelatory state of sleep that was uppermost in his mind in the immediate aftermath of Mary's death.

It is my contention that Dickens, during these nine months when he was expecting and hoping to see Mary in his dreams, transformed *Oliver Twist* into a novel in which sleep, dreams, and states of unconsciousness play a significant role in the narrative, a role that mirrors the transformative and magical role that sleep had assumed in his own life. His recourse to sleep as a significant narrative event in these months can be seen in the way he chooses to end his monthly numbers. While his dreams of Mary lasted, from May 1837 to February 1838, Dickens wrote nine numbers of *Oliver Twist*: in four of those numbers, the narrative ends on a character other than Oliver; of the other five numbers, each of which ends with a description of Oliver, the hero of the novel is either asleep or unconscious. As Dickens put each monthly number to bed, so, more often than not, he sent his little parish boy there as well, leaving him in a liminal state which was, for Dickens himself in these months, simultaneously a refuge from grief, the site of a guilty secret, and a realm in which his imagination held sway over reality and allowed him to commune with the dead.

The second of the two most significant descriptions of sleep in *Oliver Twist* lends credence to the identification of a link between Dickens's dreams of Mary Hogarth and his patterning of unconsciousness as a transformative state in the novel. It invites closer examination not only because it is the novel's final description of a specific type of sleep, but also because it is the only one of these passages that was written after Dickens's obsessive dreams of Mary ended in February 1837. It seems to be a recantation of sorts, in which, through Oliver, Dickens denies the beneficial power of that type of revelatory sleep in which the imagination holds sway over reality, which he had described in such vivid terms earlier in the novel. The description comes in the fifteenth monthly number, which was published in May 1838, exactly one year after Mary's death:

> There is a kind of sleep that steals upon us sometimes which, while it holds the body prisoner, does not free the mind from a sense of things about it, and enable it to ramble as it pleases. So far as an overpowering heaviness, a prostration of strength, and an utter inability to control our thoughts or power of motion can be called sleep, this is it: and yet we have a consciousness of all that is going on about us, and even if we dream, words which are really spoken, or sounds which really exist at the moment, accommodate themselves with surprising readiness to our visions, until reality and imagination become so strangely blended that it is afterwards a matter of impossibility to separate the two. Nor is this the most striking phenomenon incidental to such a state. It is an ascertained fact, that although our senses of touch and sight be for the time dead, yet our sleeping thoughts, and the visionary scenes that pass before us, will be influenced, and materially influenced, by the *mere silent presence* of some external object which may not have been near us when we closed our eyes, and of whose vicinity we have had no waking consciousness.   (281)

Immediately after this passage Oliver dreams himself back in Fagin's den, despite knowing "perfectly well that he was in his own little room" (281). In his sleepy state Oliver dreams that Monks and Fagin are plotting against him, and when he wakes he sees them standing at his open window, a point from which their conversation has apparently influenced his dream. There is no doubt that the men are actually there (as Monks admits in his confession to Brownlow) and that their conversation acts upon Oliver's sleeping consciousness in the manner described by Macnish, but when Oliver awakes and rouses the house to chase after the intruders they have vanished like phantoms, leaving no physical trace of their presence.

As with the earlier passage, critics have pored over this passage without seeking to explain why Dickens turns once again to Macnish for a description of a specific type of sleep. In an essay published in 1962, John Bayley suggests that this passage is so similar to the earlier description of Oliver's sleep at Fagin's that Dickens probably "repeated himself accidentally in the hurry of composition" (52). This seems unlikely, as a comparison of this passage with its source in Macnish indicates that Dickens takes pains to describe with absolute precision a sleep state that is quite different from those that have gone before it:

> When . . . the slumber is not very profound, [the sleeper] may hear music, or conversation, and have a sense of pain, hunger, and thirst; and, although not

awakened by such circumstances, may recollect them afterwards. These impressions, caught by the senses, often give rise to the most extraordinary mental combinations, and form the groundwork of the most elaborate dreams.

(Macnish 41)

This is not the broken sleep midway between sleeping and waking described earlier, although no doubt the two would be situated in close proximity on Macnish's continuum between wakefulness and death. Nor is Rodensky's analysis of sleep as a state in which Oliver is protected from evil relevant to this situation: if anything, Oliver's unconsciousness is almost his undoing here. It is only when he wakes and sees the conspirators at his window that he achieves a measure of security; while he was asleep he remained at their mercy.

As with Oliver's earlier state of incomplete sleep on Fagin's floor, Dickens's inclusion of this rather curious passage has led critics to speculate that his sense of the novel's plot was still fluid, even at this relatively late stage in Oliver's progress. John Sutherland argues that Dickens may originally have intended that Monks and Fagin attempt to snatch Oliver from the cottage (45). With this in mind, Sutherland suggests, Dickens commissioned Cruikshank to provide the illustration of Oliver slumped beside an open window that accompanies the passage, which shows Fagin and Monks lowering over him as he sleeps. Having changed his mind about this particular plot twist Dickens rather fudges the purpose of the illustration by engineering the two criminals' disappearance while Oliver is still drowsy. This suggestion is perhaps lent a little extra credence when we consider that Dickens clearly instructed Cruikshank to draw Oliver asleep: given the frequency with which Oliver is physically removed from one location to another while unconscious, it seems eminently plausible that Dickens intended that sleep would once again be a transformative experience when he instructed his illustrator. Bayley argues that that the almost phantasmic intrusion of Fagin and Monks into Oliver's dream signals their continued presence in his psyche, and that this final episode of sleep reminds the reader that Oliver can never leave his past behind him (52). Bayley's analysis, along with his suggestion that Dickens merely repeats his description of sleep from chapter 9, emphasizes stasis in Dickens's use of sleep in the novel, and thus ignores the subtle differences between this final episode and those that have gone before.

I would like to offer an alternative reading, one that takes into account both Macnish's taxonomy of sleep and the events of Dickens's own troubled year. Earlier in the novel Dickens uses sleep and unconsciousness to emphasize Oliver's isolation and vulnerability, and the providential transformations that take place during these episodes reflect Dickens's own view of unconsciousness as a state in which the vicissitudes of life can be transformed. Here, in the only description of sleep written after the dreams of Mary Hogarth had come to an end, unconsciousness is no longer represented as a wholly positive state; the transformations that occur in sleep are now seen to have the potential to be harmful as well as beneficial. Where previously Dickens had hymned a condition in which the imagination was freed to transform reality, here the imagination is made subject once again to the external world. Sleep is no longer a joyous realm of imaginative freedom, but a state that allows the existence of a morbid version of reality to intrude while the sleeper lies prostrate and helpless. Just as Dickens comes to regard the secrecy that surrounds his dreams of Mary as a corrosive intrusion of past grief into his present relations with Catherine, Oliver is threatened by the intrusion of his own dark past into an idyllic present. His response on waking is to ask for help from those around him, a decision that echoes Dickens's own recent decision to share his dreams of Mary with Catherine. Oliver summons Giles, Harry Maylie, and Mr. Losberne, tells them of his dream, and they all set off in pursuit of the interlopers. At this crucial point in the novel, Oliver rejects the unstable and erratic transformative potential of sleep and places his trust in the material, corporeal reality of his newly adopted family. It is a decision that parallels Dickens's own rejection of sleep as a transformative state, shortly before he wrote this passage, when he first told Catherine about his dreams of Mary and brought the dreams to a sudden halt.

From this point forward, sleep ceases to be a significant feature in *Oliver Twist*; there are no further episodes of unconsciousness and the parish boy progresses with his eyes wide open. The two Macnishian descriptions of sleep states that I have examined act as markers for the period of the novel during which Oliver finds himself in mortal danger. It may simply be a coincidence that they also correspond to the beginning and end of a period in which sleep and dreams played a significant role in Dickens's personal life, when he allowed imagination to dominate reality to such an extent that his nocturnal relationship with Mary threatened to corrupt his waking relationship with Catherine; if so, it is a coincidence of stunning suggestiveness. Dickens maintained a lifelong interest in sleep, dreams, and the power of the unconscious mind; but never again would his fascination with these topics spill over into his fiction,[5] or his life, with the same sustained intensity as it did during the months when he dreamt of Mary Hogarth.

NOTES

1. In *Embodied Selves*, a collection of key psychological texts from the nineteenth century, Jenny Bourne Taylor and Sally Shuttleworth write that *The Philosophy*

of Sleep "survived to become a standard reference work on the subject for the rest of the century and is cited frequently by Freud in his discussion of 'The Stimulii and Source of Dreams' in *The Interpretation of Dreams*" (102).

2. I am referring to the Penguin editions of Dickens in this article, primarily so that I can use Philip Horne's 2002 *Oliver Twist*. My argument concerns the novel as it appeared in serialization, and Horne's is the only edition to use the serial text as it was published between 1837 and 1839.

3. In a letter to Mary's mother, Dickens describes how Mary would appear in his dreams "always with a kind of quiet happiness, which became so pleasant to me that I never laid down at night without a hope of the vision coming back to me in one shape or another. And so it did" (*Letters* 3: 483–84).

4. He went on to tell the story to G. H. Lewes, who provides this account: "in the course of a quiet chat over a cigar, we got on a subject which always interested him, and on which he had stored many striking anecdotes—dreams. He then narrated, in his quietest and most impressive manner, that after Mary's death her image not only haunted him by day, but for twelve months visited his dreams ever night. At first he had refrained from mentioning it to his wife; and after deferring this some time, felt unable to mention it to her. He had occasion to go to Liverpool, and as he went to bed that night, there was a strong hope that the change of bed might break the spell of his dreams. It was not so however. That night as usual the old dream was dreamt. He resolved to unburthen his mind to his wife, and wrote that very morning a full account of his strange experience. From that time he ceased to dream of her. I forget whether he said he had never dreamt of her since; but I am certain of the fact that the spell had been broken then and there" (154). Lewes muddles some of the facts, but we must assume that his insistence on the link between Dickens's decision to tell Catherine and the cessation of the dreams reflects the weight that Dickens himself gave to this aspect of the story.

5. There are several moments in Dickens's later fiction when we can discern Macnish's influence in sleep scenes, notably in John Jasper's opium dream at the start of *The Mystery of Edwin Drood*, and when Arthur Clennam falls asleep in his Marshalsea cell and dreams of a garden, only to wake and discover that Little Dorrit has left flowers on the table in front of him as he dozed, which initiated his dream (*Little Dorrit*, ch. 29). On each of these occasions, however, the sleep scenes (and Macnish's role in them) do not seem to have any particular significance within the novel.

WORKS CITED

Bayley, John. "*Oliver Twist*: 'Things as they really are.' " *Dickens and the Twentieth Century.* Ed. John Gross and Gabriel Pearson. London: Routledge and Kegan Paul, 1962. 49–64.

Bourne Taylor, Jenny, and Sally Shuttleworth, eds. *Embodied Selves: An Anthology of Psychological Texts 1830–1890.* Oxford: Oxford UP, 1998. 102.

Dickens, Charles. *The Letters of Charles Dickens.* The Pilgrim Edition. Ed. Madeleine House et al. 12 vols Oxford: Clarendon P, 1965–2002.

————. *Oliver Twist.* Ed. Philip Horne. London: Penguin, 2002.

————. *The Pickwick Papers.* Ed. Mark Wormald. London: Penguin, 1999.

Kaplan, Fred. *Dickens and Mesmerism.* Princeton, NJ: Princeton UP, 1975.

Lewes, G.H. "Dickens in Relation to Criticism." *Fortnightly Review* 17 (1872): 141–54.

MacNish, Robert. *The Philosophy of Sleep.* Glasgow: W. R. M'Phun, 1830.

Miller, J. Hillis. *Victorian Subjects.* Durham, NC: Duke UP, 1989.

Paroissien, David. *The Companion to Oliver Twist.* Edinburgh: Edinburgh UP, 1992.

Rodensky, Lisa. *The Crime in Mind: Criminal Responsibilty and the Victorian Novel.* New York: Oxford UP, 2003.

Sutherland, John. "Is Oliver Dreaming?" *Is Heathcliff a Murderer?: Great Puzzles in Nineteenth-Century Literature.* Oxford: Oxford UP, 1996. 35–45.

Wheeler, Burton M. "The Text and Plan of *Oliver Twist*." *Dickens Studies Annual* 12 (1983): 41–61.

Nicholas Nickleby and the
Discourse of Lent

Leona Toker

This essay discusses Nicholas Nickleby *in terms of the discourse of Lent, which is regarded not as the opposite of the discourse carnival but as its second self: both stage the blurring of borderlines between the individual and his or her environment—carnival on the basis of excess and Lent on the basis of lack. The body language of Lent is that of hunger and fasting. Literary works tend to deal with corruptions of Lent, such as the enforced starvation in Squeers's school in* Nicholas Nickleby. *The novel reveals Dickens's intuitive insight into the structures of meaning around the corruption of Lent. This emerges from a number of parallels between* Nicholas Nickleby *and concentration camp memoirs, a corpus of work in which the corruptions of Lent are dealt with massively. As in these works, in Dickens's novel a partial answer to hunger is fasting, literal (the novel abounds in motifs of hunger, deferral of its satisfaction, loss of hunger, and the breaking of the fast), or figurative—a young protagonist endorses trials and privation for the sake of making it in the world. Though in the latter case the goal of the fast is pragmatic rather than spiritual, it also involves rejection of whatever interferes with one's moral integrity. The breaking of the fast (the meal that is most frequently mentioned in this novel, by contrast to Dickens's later fiction, is breakfast) is usually a convivial occasion associated with personal benevolence which is, in its limited way, responsible for the poetic justice in the novel.*

Dickens Studies Annual, Volume 38, Copyright © 2007 by AMS Press, Inc. All rights reserved.

Let us strike a keynote: Tutbury. One of the eccentric shades who haunt Mrs. Nickleby's speeches is "the Thirsty Woman of Tutbury" (605). This historical personage, Anne Moore, was a kind of "hunger artist," who for several years made a living by abstaining from food. In 1813 she was caught imbibing liquid food passed on to her by her daughter—hence the epithet "thirsty," which ironically clashed with her actual stage name, "the Fasting Woman." One may recall that the professional pride of the protagonist of Franz Kafka's short story "The Hunger Artist" involves his demand to be constantly watched—not in his house and in a curtained bed like Anne Moore but in a circus cage, and not just out of histrionic exhibitionism but in order to prove to audiences that he was not cheating.[1]

On the basis of an analysis of Kafka's "The Hunger Artist," the story of the histrionic Lent that eventually gets corrupted, Ruth Ginsburg, a Bakhtin scholar, suggested an identification between the discourse of carnival (see Bakhtin's *Rabelais*, 1968) and the discourse of Lent: Lent is not the opposite of carnival but its second self—both are opposed to normal everyday life in society. Indeed, many of the phenomena that are associated with carnival excess are also produced by lack, by deprivation. The most striking of these phenomena is the blurring of the borderlines between individuals and their natural and human environment. One might say that the proto-discourse of Lent is the Biblical Book of Job, where the protagonist's faith is tested by total deprivation. One of the last things taken away from Job is his health. His illness, apparently a skin disease, is symbolic of the loss of discreteness, the separateness of his body contours—he is afflicted with "sore boils from the sole of his foot unto his crown" (2:7).[2] It is then that Eliphaz the Temanite attempts to comfort him, among other things, by the promise of insight into the life of things: "For thou shalt be in league with the stones of the field: and the beasts of the field shall be at peace with thee" (5:23).

The traditional function of Lent, that of the purification of the soul and the body rewarded by peace, whether with God or with the beasts of the field, can only be maintained if the Lenten fast is not arbitrarily imposed and if it is *limited in time*. (Kafka's Hunger Artist fasts for the symbolic period of forty days each time; Anne Moore's fraudulent fast lasted several years; see Hollis 530–34). Fasting that is not restricted to a humanly possible term, and also hunger forced on another, do not constitute genuine Lent—they are the two major ways in which the very idea of Lent is corrupted. The discourse of Lent in literature, including parts of Dickens's *Nicholas Nickleby*, usually deals precisely with the corruptions of Lent.

The body language of Lent belongs to the overlapping semantic fields of hunger and fasting. The examples of works of fiction dominated by these motifs are not numerous—Dickens's representation of the workhouse in *Oliver Twist* and of the Yorkshire schools in *Nicholas Nickleby*, along with

Charlotte Brontë's representation of the charity boarding school at Lowood before its reform, being among the more striking examples—though one might also cite Knut Hamsun's novel *Hunger*. At the same time, as I have shown elsewhere (e.g., Toker 2000a), there exists a considerable literary corpus in which the motifs of hunger and fasting constitute a major morphological feature. This corpus is the literature of concentration camps—in particular, the memoirs of Soviet concentration camps, the so-called Gulag. Rereading Dickens's *Nicholas Nickleby* after having studied that corpus, one is struck by the way in which the intuition of a young artist of genius reveals *the deep structure* of the social evil that he attacks, a structure that repeats itself in much later social situations and in much grimmer forms, dwarfing both tragedy and farce. "Dickens Our Contemporary" might have been the subtitle of the present essay.

References to concentration or hard-labor camps ("the crucial fact of the twentieth century" [Kiš 151]) are these days all too often made, and in all too facile ways, for hyperbolic comparison with almost any abuse or injustice. It is not my purpose to make such a comparison, or to invoke the memory of those institutions merely in order to emphasize the horrors of the Yorkshire schools. My point is that the discourse of Lent is one of the features of *Nicholas Nickleby*, and a glance at the corpus of literature where such discourse is most prominent may help articulate the vaguer semiotics of Lent in this novel. I shall point out a few parallels between the Dotheboys Hall episode and camp memoirs, address two possible objections to this analysis, and then show the inroads that the discourse of Lent makes into other parts of the novel.

***

The association between prison and the Yorkshire schools, which are represented (in a manner both overstated and understated) by Dotheboys Hall, is established early in the novel when Squeers, on his recruitment expedition to London, transacts his business at the Saracen's Head in the shadow of Newgate jail. The latter is alluded to in conjunction with public executions—the spirit of carnival gone sour[3]:

> There, at the very core of London, in the heart of its business and animation, in the midst of a whirl of noise and motion: stemming at it were the giant currents of life that flow ceaselessly on from different quarters, and meet beneath its walls, stands Newgate; and in that crowded street on which it frowns so darkly—within a few feet of the squalid tottering houses—upon the very spot on which the vendors of soup and fish and damaged fruit are now plying their trades—scores of human beings, amidst a roar of sounds to which even

the tumult of a great city is as nothing, four, six, or eight strong men at a time, have been hurried violently and swiftly from the world, when the scene has been rendered frightful with excess of human life; when curious eyes have glared from casement, and house-top, and wall and pillar, and when, in the mass of white and upturned faces, the dying wretch, in his all-comprehensive look of agony, has met not one—not one—that bore the impress of pity and compassion.   (43; ch. 4)

As Dickens strongly suggests in *Great Expectations*, the prison is not only a penal institution but also a storage house for undesirables such as Magwitch. Concentration camps, since their inception by the Spanish in Cuba (see Kotek and Rigoulot 47–59) and up to their peak in the Gulag and Nazi camps, likewise performed that function, prophylactic rather than punitive, among others: they were receptacles not so much for actual opponents of the regimes but for *potential* opponents (actual opponents met a swifter fate). Nicholas Nickleby may dream about forming useful connections with young lords at Dotheboys Hall, only to find that the pupils of that institution are children from middle-class families who for various reasons are treated as dispensable—they are either illegitimate children, or stepsons of villains like Snawley, or the unloved offspring of egotistic parents, or young orphaned wards and heirs from whose death Ralph Nickleby's clients can profit (probably through post-obits). The principle on which they are kept in Squeers's institution is also the principle that underlies the economics of concentration camps[4]: maximum profit and minimum expenditure, with the basic needs of the human body redefined in ways that turn hygiene, privacy, autonomy, and nourishment into their opposites: the boys have to wash from the same trough; they are never by themselves, even sleeping four in a bed; they are subjected to beatings for which "corporeal punishment" is a euphemism; and they are not just kept on a Lenten starvation diet but are unwittingly turned into scavengers when given the meat of dead cattle. Like concentration camp inmates, the boys are not so much killed as not kept from dying—except by the partly effective means of being allowed to go grazing, that is, stealing vegetables from other people's fields in order to fight scurvy.

The starvation of the inmates in concentration camps was not only an outcome of the peculiar economics of these institutions. It was also a means of keeping the inmates subdued, reducing their capacity for thinking and initiative, stripping them of all the layers of their personalities that were not needed for stark survival. The carnival pooling of individual affects (including the affects of the audience of public executions) was here transformed into the dehumanizing erasure of individual difference. Chronic hunger would have much the same result in a boarding school like the one in *Nicholas Nickleby*.

The treatment that the boys receive in this school is thoroughly dehumanizing and deindividualizing. One may note that during Nicholas's brief stay in

Dotheboys Hall the narrative does not single out any of the boys except Smike (who is an attendant) for personal attention, although Squeers mentions the names of several boys in referring to their mail. Nicholas's first sight of these children anticipates the shocked perplexity with which new arrivals to concentration camps regard the strange creatures—the homogenized veteran victims:

> Pale and haggard faces, lank and bony figures, children with countenances of old men, deformities with irons upon their limbs, boys of stunted growth, and others whose long meagre legs would hardly bear their stooping bodies, all crowded on the view together; there were the bleared eye, the hare-lip, the crooked foot, and every ugliness and distortion that told of unnatural aversion conceived by parents for their offspring, or of young lives which, from the earliest dawn of infancy, had been one horrible endurance of cruelty and neglect. There were little faces that should have been handsome, darkened with the scowl of sullen dogged suffering; there was childhood with the light of the eye quenched, its beauty gone, and its helplessness alone remaining; there were vicious-faced boys brooding, with leaden eyes, like malefactors in jail; and there were young creatures on whom the sins of their frail parents had descended, weeping even for the mercenary nurses they had known, and lonesome even in their loneliness. With every kindly sympathy and affection blasted in its birth, with every young and healthy feeling flogged and starved down, with every revengeful passion that can fester in swollen hearts, eating its evil way to the core in silence, what an incipient Hell was breeding there!
>
> And yet this scene, painful as it was, had its grotesque features, which, in a less interested observer than Nicholas, might have provoked a smile.
>
> (97; ch. 8)

This passage may be read as anticipating Julius Margolin's account of his first glimpse of Gulag prisoners, a description complete with an opening nominal construction reminiscent of Dickens's syntax in the above passage and with an uneasy touch of the comic grotesque:

> People of mouse-gray color. All their clothes were mouse gray: some sort of jackets, hanging rags, shapeless footwear on naked feet, mouse-gray caps with ear-flaps that flew around and endowed faces with a wild expression. And the faces were also mouse-gray, earth-hued—as if all of them were covered with dust. They seemed to wear everything in a clownish fashion: things were either too wide and long or too narrow and short. They all kept together, and at their side there stuck a man with a gun who wore military dress and obviously belonged to ''a different race.''   (1952: 17; my translation)

A similar perplexity is conveyed by Primo Levi's account of his first sight of prisoners at Auschwitz:

> strange individuals . . . walked in squads, in rows of three, with an odd, embarrassed step, head hanging in front, arms rigid. On their heads they wore *comic*

berets and were all dressed in long striped overcoats, which even by night and from a distance looked filthy and in rags. . . . This was the metamorphosis that awaited us. Tomorrow we would be like them.

(1987: 26–27; emphasis added)[5]

One of the features of the dehumanizing treatment of the inmates of such institutions is seriality. In *Nicholas Nickleby* it takes the shape of Mrs. Squeers using the same "school spoon" to pour her brimstone-and-treacle concoction unhygenically down the throats of the children. Incidentally, this pseudo-prophylaxis—actually another instrument of torture emphasized by the largeness of the spoon and the demand that the children gulp its contents at once—anticipates a similar compulsory measure in Kolyma concentration camps where, at a certain period, the prisoners could only get their daily gruel on condition of imbibing the disgusting dwarf-cedar extract, which was believed—quite wrongly—to be a vitamin-rich food supplement.[6]

Another shape that the dehumanizing attitude of the perpetrators takes is turning people into would-be inanimate objects or tools, as when Mrs. Squeers, after administrating the treacle, wipes her hands on the hair of a curly headed boy (98; ch. 8)—a striking anticipation of an episode in Primo Levi's *If This Is a Man* (also published as *Survival in Auschwitz*): despite having witnessed most horrible atrocities, what the authorial persona never forgives the not particularly sadistic German Kapo Alex is an act similar to that of Mrs. Squeers:

> *Donnerwetter*, he looks at his hand black with thick grease. In the meanwhile I have joined him. Without hatred and without sneering, Alex wipes his hand on my shoulder, both the palm and the back of the hand, to clean it; he would be amazed, the poor brute Alex, if someone told him that today, on the basis of this action, I judge him . . . and the innumerable others like him, big and small, in Auschwitz and everywhere.   (113–14)

Yet, as the letter from his wife that Squeers reads in London unwittingly suggests, the dehumanization is but skin deep—the abused boys live their own individual inner lives (a point forcefully made in most camp memoirs as well[7]):

> "The pigs is well, . . . the cows is well, and the boys is bobbish. Young Sprouter has been a-winking, has he? I'll wink him when I get back. 'Cobbey would persist in sniffing while he was a-eating his dinner, and said that the beef was so strong it made him.'—very good, Coney, we'll see if we can't make you sniff a little without beef. 'Pitcher was took with another fever,'—of course he was—'and being fetched by his friends, died the day after he got home,'—of course he did, and out of aggravation; it's part of a deep-laid system. There an't another chap in the school but that boy as would have died exactly at the end of the quarter, taking it out of me to the very last, and then carrying his

spite to the utmost extremity. 'The juniorest Palmer said he wished he was in Heaven,'—I really don't know, I do not know what's to be done with that young fellow; he's always a-wishing something horrid. He said once he wished he was a donkey, because then he wouldn't have a father as didn't love him!—pretty wicious that, for a child of six! . . . There'll be an arrear of flogging as'll have to be gone through.''   (702; ch. 57)

As is clear from Squeers's reaction to the news about the named boys, the latter risk the last remnant of safety—the precarious safety in numbers—when they betray their inner lives, making themselves conspicuous. Inconspicuousness, indeed, was a necessary (though not a sufficient) condition for surviving in the camps—this was put on record by, for instance, Bruno Bettelheim (209–12) and borne out by great numbers of camp testimonies. When Squeers reads his wife's letter, he is mentally drawing a ledger of floggings: the boys whose words have attracted the attention of Mrs. Squeers will be first on his list.

***

Two features of the Dotheboys Hall episode, may, however, seem to contradict my reading of *Nicholas Nickleby* in terms of the discourse of Lent. One is that this episode, most socially influential and for many the most memorable in the novel, is actually but a small segment of the whole text. The other is that it is also funny.

Yet it is not uncommon for concentration camp literature to be funny—humorous, witty, sarcastic. In fact, the recurrence of humorous notes in Gulag literature is what largely distinguishes it from the literature of the Holocaust, though some black humor or self-irony can occasionally be found in the latter as well. The difference lies not only in the diabolical character of the atrocities of the Holocaust but also in the fact that the contrast between official propaganda and camp realities was particularly striking in the Gulag setting (in the history of the Nazi camps the two were more in line with each other). The humor of the Dotheboys Hall episode in *Nicholas Nickleby* is based on a similar disjunction—it is not at the expense of the victims. The oxymoron of the illiterate schoolmaster, the cynicism with which he sends a boy to work his garden as a ''bottinney'' (100; ch. 8) lesson, misspelling the word botany on the way,[8] the ironic dashing of Nicholas's expectations, the abuse exceeding whatever forebodings Squeers's recruiting behavior could arouse—all these are, indeed, funny, and even somehow funnier when the reader constantly finds that his or her own misgivings about Squeers's school are dwarfed by what Nicholas actually finds there. The Squeers couple's monstrousness is almost uncanny[9]—its excesses find us unprepared and yet we have to recognize them as quite logical extensions of what we have already learned about their maxims. At this point laughter may serve the purpose of "the artistic discharge of nausea of absurdity" (Nietzsche 60). However that may be, laughter also implicates the reader: it helps us to distance ourselves from the plight of the victims, to forget it for a while, just as Nicholas tries to get a time-out from his own Lent by accepting the invitation to Fanny Squeers's tea party. Eventually Nicholas leaves the school and starts living his own life, not devoid of healthy enjoyment, while the school is always in place and no one seems to care. This is also a recurrent motif of concentration camp literature: if the world around only knew, it would not allow this to go on. Ironically, however, the world around often does find out, but remains in denial or just blandly dismisses the matter. Throughout the bulk of the book, and up to the carnivalesque poetic justice wreaked on Squeers's school at the end, Nicholas is hardly ever shown having a thought to spare for the continuing suffering of its incarcerated children. Readers, who are quite relieved to follow Nicholas away from the school in chapter 13, may find themselves implicated in not responding with sufficient sensitivity and with sufficient practical conclusions to the picture of a worse misery than their own imaginations could conjure up. We have laughed too—uneasily, perhaps, and perhaps pulling ourselves up: "This is awful; why am I laughing?" A thought like this often fuels the wish to normalize the situation by taking a stand: the complexity of the effect of Dickens's comic gusto in the school episode may, in fact, have been the core of the novel's potent consciousness-raising effect,[10] all the more potent, perhaps, because of its broader appeal, in view of Victorian proprieties, than that of the accurate detailing of the abuses might have been. In the preface to the original edition Dickens confesses to elisions; the reality of the schools, he writes, involves "such offensive and foul details of neglect, cruelty, and disease, as no writer of fiction could have the boldness to imagine"—he had recently received reliable "accounts of atrocities, in the perpetration of which upon neglected or repudiated children these schools have been the main instrument, very far exceeding any that appear in these pages" (4). Each eyewitness memoirist of concentration camps likewise has an area that is too horrible for him or her to face and describe, some Orwellian room "One-Oh-One." Testimonies regarding Soviet camps for juvenile delinquents might shed light on what that room might be where Dickens fears to tread—but I shall follow his example of not entering it at the moment.

Even without the complete detail, the historical influence of the Dotheboys Hall episode was rather satisfactory since most schools like that went out of business—a fact which is sufficiently expressive of the difference between a free society, even one in need of reform, and a closed totalitarian state in which this kind of influence was not possible, if only because no subversive book would reach the general public. The effect of Dickens's novel on York-shire boarding schools is particularly striking considering what a small place the representation of the school occupies in the text—just a little more than two out of its 65 chapters. One may well ask, moreover, why it makes sense to talk about the novel's discourse of Lent if, until the normativeness of middle-class life finally triumphs,[11] most other portions of the book abound in elements of the carnival with its "transcendent lunacy of comic invention" (Schlicke 35)—crowd-scenes, long or loud harangues, reminiscences and con-fessions, tears, blood, slapstick brawls, melodramatic performances, tables loaded with food, reversals of fortune, crownings and uncrownings, eaves-dropping, theft and other transgressions: "repletion and starvation," writes Dickens in *Nickleby* (391) "[lie] them down together" (see also Bowen 128–29). However, if one thinks of *Crime and Punishment*, which, in *Prob-lems of Dostoevsky's Poetics*, is Bakhtin's main example of the carnivalesque novel and which arguably bears traces not just of Dickens's influence but, specifically, of the influence of *Nicholas Nickleby*, one will find that the discourse in that novel pertains as much to Lent as to Carnival: Raskolnikov is severely undernourished when the action starts, and shows symptoms of what in camp-literature is called *hunger neurosis*; the lives of his mother and sister and of Mrs. Marmeladov and her children pass under the sign of genteel poverty, even genteel indigence that creates a potent temptation to sell the daughters of the house (cf. Schor) to the sex trade or to abusive marriage. It is Raskolnikov's passionate protest against this temptation that makes him cut the conventional ethical anchorage of his mental freedom.

***

The precise relationship of carnivalesque discourse and the discourse of Lent in fiction still awaits theorizing. However it may be, in *Nicholas Nickleby* the episode of Dotheboys Hall is not isolated from the rest of the narrative; it is not a separate bead on a picaresque string. As John Lucas noted in 1970, what gives the novel a thematic coherence is its concern with "lives sacrificed to financial interest" (62). Dickens's "art of analogy," to adopt the title of H. M. Daleski's book, is already evident in this relatively early novel: quite a number of characters serve as exponents of this theme—in particular, Made-line Bray before her rescue. But the theme is most condensed in the represen-tation of the school: a logical extension of the patterns prevailing in the society that has produced them, this school is like the world around it—only more so. Much the same has been said about concentration camps—their difference from the society that has made them possible is, first and foremost, quantitative: they provide a geographical and moral space in which the atti-tudes prevalent in this society at large are taken to their logical conclusion.

The motif of hunger, that is likewise most concentrated in the Dotheboys Hall episode, also infuses the rest of the novel and is sometimes employed for staging coincidences. It is because of Smike's fatigue and need of refreshment that he and Nicholas stop at an inn where they meet Crummles; it is because Nicholas is hungry that he enters the restaurant where he runs into Mullberry Hawk; it is because Newman Noggs wants his dinner that he finds himself in the closet eavesdropping on Ralph Nickleby's and Arthur Gride's conspiracy. The meager fowl that Peg Sliderskew prepares for Gride's would-be wedding breakfast suggests that hunger would have been one of Madeline's trials if imprisoned in Gride's house. Ralph's suicide is causally led up to by his refusal of a handout to Brooker when the latter is hungry and shivering with cold (one might here recollect, by way of contrast, Joe's pleasure, in *Great Expectations*, at the thought of Magwitch being kept from starvation by the stock in his pantry). One of the melodramatic gestures that Nicholas teaches Smike is the touch of one's belly that signifies hunger—an ironic point, as Helena Michie notes (95), because Smike knows all, none better than himself, about what real hunger is like. Fittingly, in the Crummles theater company he is given the parts of the so-called "starved business."

Yet the motif of hunger is not the only central constituent of the discourse of Lent, whether genuine or corrupt. What turns the literature of concentration camps into the discourse of Lent is its suggestion that *the answer to hunger is fasting* (see Toker 2000b: 94–98). This suggestion is especially prominent in the works of Aleksandr Solzhenitsyn and Varlam Shalamov; it is practically formulated in a camp narrative by an Israeli Gulag survivor, Joshua Gilboa, who recollects a Jewish ex-communist prisoner's explanation of his fasting on the Day of Atonement (Yom Kippur): "I can go hungry when the NKVD wants me to so why can't I go hungry when I want to?" (87). The hunger strikes in prisons and camps belong to the same pattern: "And whosoever shall compel thee to go a mile, go with him twain" (Matthew 5:41). For Solzhenitsyn and, in particular, for Shalamov, the spirit of fasting as a response to imposed hunger expresses itself in prisoners' resisting the temptations to compromise their integrity by shameful acts, such as informing on others, for the sake of extra food.

In terms of narrative morphology, the pattern of Lent is not limited to the literal semantics of hunger and fasting, just as carnivalesque works do not necessarily represent carnival occasions. Elsewhere I have demonstrated that the main feature of a carnivalesque work is its being almost wholly devoted to a crisis situation—well beyond the standard inclusion of such a situation at the point of climax (1995: 97–99). The plot formula of the narrative of Lent consists in the protagonist's entering a period of endurance, whether as a performing Hunger Artist, a prisoner, or a young person who is beginning the world—say, a David Copperfield embracing hardship on his way to achievement, *per aspera ad astra*, even though his goal is merely making it. On first being engaged by Squeers, Nicholas endorses the need for hard work and temporary privation without complaining; nor does his sister Kate complain of the long hours at Mrs. Mantalini's or the annoyance and the tedium at Mrs. Wittiterley's. Their mother comes to terms with their exertions by comforting herself, and perhaps even them, with daydreams of these being but temporary stages in their lives, stepping stones to affluence achievable by winning powerful friends within the framework of these dead-end jobs. The fast is expected to be temporary, as any Lenten fast should be.

Mrs. Nickeby and Kate accept a reduction in their own future diet in order to prepare a good parting supper for Nicholas on the eve of his departure for Yorkshire—he tries to respond in kind by departing without breakfast the next morning in order not to disturb their sleep. Both Kate and Nicholas face temptations of improving their circumstances at the cost of their integrity; both indignantly reject such offers and actively struggle to repel them. On realizing the corruption of his uncle, on whom the bereaved family's short-lived hopes have rested, Nicholas defies him with, to use Emerson's words (29), the self-reliance of boys "who are sure of a dinner"—he is totally free from paranoia about damaging his prospects by impetuous honesty. The trouble with Madeline Bray is that her view of her own integrity does not rest on similar self-reliance: one might, indeed, see a line of development from this partially realized character to Sonia Marmeladov in *Crime and Punishment* (whom Danilo Kiš describes as "pure human suffering, a literary character in the worst sense of the term—paper, poetry, and joie de vivre" [143]). The question that her self-sacrifice for the sake of her egoistic father raises is whether natural affection and sense of filial duty belong to the life of the spirit or to indulgent natural leanings of the flesh.

Lent, indeed, enacts the supremacy of the willing spirit over the weak flesh, whether its appetites are mortified by the exertion of will power or whether, during spells of moral heightening, anxiety, or ethical compulsion, they are effectively silenced. Newman Noggs loses his appetite when he hears Ralph's conversation with Gride; when on a later occasion Ralph wishes to send him "to his dinner," out of the way of his confabulation with Squeers, Noggs is not hungry: it is too early, he says. On the day and night before Madeline and Gride's planned wedding, Nicholas wants neither food nor sleep: his psyche is totally occupied by the imperative of not leaving a stone unturned to prevent the marriage—and it is likely that his exertions would not have been much less intense even if he had not been in love with her himself. When narrative providence (which in *Nicholas Nickleby* takes the shape of perfect timing) prevents Madeline's self-sacrifice, it initiates a self-imposed emotional abstinence on Nicholas, who considers it his duty to the Cheeryble brothers ("the twin gods of morality and benevolence" [Childers 60][12]) not to claim Madeline's hand.

The period of Lent ends with restoring normality. For Nicholas and Kate the fast is broken by the end of the novel; they are both released from self-imposed restraints in love and return to the renewed, purified normality of genteel family life. Great numbers of episodes in Dickens's novels are staged around convivial occasions (see Hardy); *Nicholas Nickleby* is no exception, but it is distinguished by the prevalence not of dinners (the most prominent type of meals in Dickens's later novels) but of breakfasts: Squeer's breakfast in the Saracen's Head, the school breakfast of porridge with bread used instead of spoons, Nicholas's and Smike's breakfasts on which fellow actors intrude in Portsmouth, the Lillyvick wedding breakfast stage-managed by Crummles, Gride's aborted wedding breakfast, Ralph Nickeby's "untasted breakfast" (717) initiating his own fast unalleviated by any last-wish amenity before his suicide, and the joyous breakfast in John Browdie's house before the brimstone-and-treacle breakfast-time revolt in Squeers's school.

I started by maintaining that Lent is not the opposite of carnival but its second self. A reading of *Nicholas Nickleby*, however, suggests some modifications on this statement. Carnival, when not used as a mask for attempts to overthrow the social order, is a safety valve, a temporary suspension of the restrictions of everyday social life. It is meant to make conformity more bearable, the system underneath ("underdarkneath," as Joyce might say) the daily provision of bread, equitable or otherwise, less alienating. Lent, on the other hand, is a suspension of the amenities of everyday life, their reduction to stark physical necessities symbolized by bread (or, in the case of other classical novels, thin gruel) as a reminder that one lives not by bread alone. Yet in a realistic novel the temporary suspension of enjoyment or indulgence, resigning oneself to temporary difficulties, does not always serve spiritual goals: it is undertaken in order to rise again, in terms of social mobility rather than moral self-perfection (or moral survival, as in Gulag literature). Ultimately, however, the Lenten spirit asserts itself in a question of ways and means: rational self-interest may not be the loftiest moral value, yet the means employed can be such as do not compromise one's integrity. Nicholas insists, not always successfully, that his interests should be pursued not *at the expense* of others; but the deployment of the novel's Lenten motifs clearly shows that the breaking of the fast requires *the voluntary assistance of others*, a loving sister, a Newman Noggs, a John Browdie, a Crummles generous with crumbs, a pair of Cheeryble Brothers providing good cheer to balance the predatory Hawk, Pyke, and Pluck, or a Tim Linkinwater, who supplies both links for the plot and the proverbial beverage for a Lenten meal.

If carnival is a communal occasion, temporarily knocking down the barriers between separate social compartments, Lent is a retreat into the self. But the end of Lent, the breaking of the fast, joyfully reintegrates the self into the network of codified social relations. In *Nicholas Nickleby*, as in most of

Dickens's novels (though not in *David Copperfield*), with the help of benevolent friends the protagonists' Lent is discontinued rather earlier than planned, but this magical relief is often sadly offset by the blighted lives of secondary characters—Smike, or Jo in *Bleak House*, or little John Harmon in *Our Mutual Friend*.

NOTES

I thank Professor H. M. Daleski and participants of the 2006 Dickens Universe at the University of California, Santa Cruz, for constructive comments on earlier versions of this essay. The essay is part of a research project on the carnivalesque mode in fiction, supported by Israel Science Foundation, grant no 903/01.

1. The time references in Kafka's story suggest that the public interest in the "show" fasts, those prolonged flirtations with death, wore out several years before World War I, when death, creeping down from its proud tower, became too insidious; see Mitchell 250–51.
2. The quotations are from the King James Version of the Bible.
3. See Bernstein for a discussion of the ways in which literary works explore the violently bitter rather than the festive carnival.
4. See also Magnet 17, where the analogies are, however, not developed.
5. Bernard Roeder opens his description of the Soviet hard labor camps of 1950–1955 with a similar account of his first impression of the convicts' faces (17–19); his perplexity is soon replaced by the sense of the tragic. See also Arthur Koestler's reaction to the first sight of internees of the 1940 French camp in Le Vernet (1941: 88).
6. See Shalamov 286. Shalamov further notes that under threat of being shot for an escape attempt the prisoners were often prevented from walking over to the real source of Vitamin C—sweetbriar hips.
7. Thus, for instance, Victor Frankl observes: "In spite of all the enforced physical and mental primitiveness of the life in a concentration camp, it was possible for spiritual life to deepen" (47).
8. Eventually, Squeers will mispronounce "monument" as "monneyment" (702)—almost anticipating Joyce's word games in *Finnegans Wake*.
9. "Characters like Mr. Bumble, Wackford Squeers, Mrs. Gamp, and the Murdstones derive their peculiar imaginative vitality from their both representing an abuse and a sort of childhood horror" (Cotsell 120).
10. I am grateful to Yael Artom and Shani Abel for a fruitful discussion of the comic treatment of Squeers's school in *Nicholas Nickleby*.
11. See McKnight (71–74) on the troubling effect that the reestablishment of such normal bourgeois life produces on Smike.
12. Childers goes on to deconstruct the motifs out of which the Cheeryble brothers are spun.

WORKS CITED

Bakhtin, Mikhail. *Problems of Dostoevsky's Poetics*. Ed. and trans. Caryl Emerson. Minneapolis: U of Minnesota P, 1984.

———. *Rabelais and His World*. Trans. Helene Iswolsky. Cambridge, MA: MIT P, 1968. Repr. Indiana UP, 1984.

Bernstein, Michael André. *Bitter Carnival: Ressentiment and the Abject Hero*. Princeton: Princeton UP, 1992.

Bettelheim, Bruno. *The Informed Heart: Autonomy in a Mass Age*. New York: Free Press, 1960.

Bowen, John. *Other Dickens: Pickwick to Chuzzlewit*. Oxford: Oxford UP, 2000.

Childers, Joseph W. "Nicholas Nickleby and the Problem of *Doux Commerce*." *Dickens Studies Annual* 25 (1996): 49–65.

Cotsell, Michael. "Nicholas Nickleby: Dickens's First Young Man." *Dickens Quarterly* 5.3 (1988): 118–28.

Daleski, H. M. *Dickens and the Art of Analogy*. London: Faber and Faber, 1970.

Dickens, Charles. *Nicholas Nickleby*. Ed. Mark Ford. London: Penguin, 1999.

Emerson, Ralph Waldo. "Self-Reliance." *The Essays of Ralph Waldo Emerson*. New York: Random House, 1944.

Frankl, Victor. *Man's Search for Meaning: An Introduction to Logotherapy*. Trans. Ilse Lasch. 3rd ed. New York: Simon and Schuster, 1984.

Gilboa, Joshua. *Confess! Confess!: Eight Years in Soviet Prisons*. Trans. Dov Ben Aba. Boston: Little, Brown, 1968.

Ginsburg, Ruth. "Karneval und Fasten: Exzess und Mangel in der Sprache des Körpers." *Poetica* 21 (1989): 26–42.

Hardy, Barbara. "Food and Ceremony in *Great Expectations*." *Essays in Criticism* 13 (1963): 351–63.

Hollis, Karen. "Fasting Women: Bodily Claims and Narrative Crises in Eighteenth-Century Science." *Eighteenth-Century Studies* 34.4 (2001): 523–38.

Kotek, Joël, and Pierre Rigoulot. *Le Siècle des camps: Détention, concentration, extermination. Cent ans de mal radical*. Paris: JC Lattès, 2000.

Kiš, Danilo. *Homo Poeticus: Essays and Interviews*. Ed. Susan Sontag. New York: Farrar, Straus and Giroux, 1995.

Koestler, Arthur. *Scum of the Earth*. London: Jonathan Cape, 1941.

Levi, Primo. *If This is a Man*. Trans. Stuart Woolf. London: Abacus, 1987.

Lucas, John. *The Melancholy Man: A Study of Dickens's Novels*. London: Methuen, 1970.

Magnet, Myron. *Dickens and the Social Order*. Philadelphia: U of Pennsylvania P, 1985.

Margolin, Julius. *Puteshestvie v stranu ze/ka* [*Journey into the Country of Z/K*]. New York: Chekhov Publishing House, 1952. First published in the French translation by Nina Berberova and Mina Journot: *La condition inhumaine: Cinq ans dans les camps de concentration soviétiques*. Paris: Calmann-Lévy, 1949.

McKnight, Natalie. *Idiots, Madmen, and Other Prisoners in Dickens*. New York: St. Martin's Press, 1993.

Michie, Helena. "The Avuncular and beyond: Family (Melo)drama in *Nicholas Nickleby*." *Dickens Refigured: Bodies, Desires and Other Histories*. Ed. John Schad. Manchester: Manchester UP, 1996. 80–97.

Mitchell, Breon. "Kafka and the *Hunger Artists*." *Kafka and the Contemporary Critical Performance: Centenary Readings*. Ed. Alan Udoff. Bloomington: Indiana UP, 1987. 236–55.

Nietzsche, Friedrich. "The Birth of Tragedy." *Basic Writings of Nietzsche*. Trans. and ed. Walter Kaufman. New York: Modern Library, 1966. 3–146.

Roeder, Bernhard. *Katorga*. Trans. L. Kochan. London: Heinemann, 1958.

Schlicke, Paul. *Dickens and Popular Entertainment*. London: Allen & Unwin, 1985.

Schor, Hilary M. *Dickens and the Daughter of the House*. Cambridge: Cambridge UP, 1999.

Shalamov, Varlam. "Perhcatka, ili KR-2." *Collected Works in Four Volumes*. Ed. I. P. Sirotinskaia. Moscow: Khudozhestvennaia literatura/Vagrius, 1998. II: 279–307.

Toker, Leona. "Kafka's 'The Hunger Artist' and Shalamov's 'The Artist of the Spade': The Discourse of Lent." *Cold Fusion: Aspects of the German Cultural Presence in Russia*. Ed. G. Barabtarlo. New York: Berghahn Books, 2000a. 277–91.

———. "Représentation de la crise dans l'oeuvre de Nathaniel Hawthorne: Le Mode Carnivalesque." Trans. Christine Raguet-Bouvart. *Éclats de voix: Crises en représentation dans la littérature nord-américaine*, ed. Christine Raguet-Bouvart. La Rochelle: Rumeur des Ages, 1995. 97–109.

———. *Return from the Archipelago: Narratives of Gulag Survivors*. Bloomington: Indiana UP, 2000b.

Degrees of Secrecy in Dickens's Historical Fiction

Albert D. Pionke

This essay traces Dickens's evolving fictional strategies for distinguishing between acceptable and unacceptable forms of secrecy. Using extended close readings of Barnaby Rudge *and* A Tale of Two Cities, *supplemented by shorter readings of* Martin Chuzzlewit *and* Great Expectations, *it shows that Dickens consistently framed the issue of secrecy using binary oppositions. In* Barnaby Rudge *and* Martin Chuzzlewit, *the opposition between licit and illicit secrecy turns on intentionality, a protolegal standard of judgment connected with early Victorian debates over criminal responsibility. By contrast, in* A Tale of Two Cities *and* Great Expectations, *readers are encouraged by the forms of the novels themselves to approve of secrecy-as-privacy while condemning secrecy-as-conspiracy. In both the earlier and the later fictions, however, these oppositions begin to break down: characters like Grip and Nadgett expose the narrator's limited ability to reveal intent; or the interpenetrations of the Manette family and the Jacquerie, and of the Castle and Little Britain, render the boundary between privacy and conspiracy indistinct. Ultimately, the essay argues that Dickens may have been incapable of defining the limits of acceptable secrecy, since his own authorial technique centrally invested him in the production, transmission, and revelation of secrets.*

Published nearly twenty years apart, Charles Dickens's only two historical novels, *Barnaby Rudge* (1841) and *A Tale of Two Cities* (1859), offer readers

Dickens Studies Annual, Volume 38, Copyright © 2007 by AMS Press, Inc. All rights reserved.

a unique perspective on his evolving attitudes toward and techniques for representing secrecy. Focusing on two different historical events, the Gordon Riots and the French Revolution, and written during two distinct periods in Dickens's career, the novels share a common preoccupation with instructing readers about how to distinguish between good and bad forms of secrecy. This process of discrimination takes place in all of Dickens's fictions, but it is made especially perspicuous in *Barnaby Rudge* and *A Tale of Two Cities* by the texts' historical settings, which elevate collective, narrowly political secrecy to unusual prominence. Since organizations like the Protestant Association and the Jacquerie are grounded, however loosely, in the historical register, which is, itself, a crucial determinant of the action of the novels, they cannot be dismissed simply as "a muddle"—as trade unionism is in *Hard Times*—and therefore Dickens is forced to explain how their practices of secrecy differ from those of his favored characters. As we shall see, both his methods of explanation and his conclusions remain largely consistent in both novels; however, Dickens's justification for his conclusions does change over time and is increasingly articulated through the form of the novel itself. Moreover, the means used to differentiate between acceptable and unacceptable forms of secrecy in the historical novels may be seen as central to Dickens's fiction more generally, as I hope to show by brief readings of the secrets contained in each of the two novels published directly after, respectively, *Barnaby Rudge* and *A Tale of Two Cities*, *Martin Chuzzlewit* (1843–44) and *Great Expectations* (1860–61).

Barnaby Rudge and *A Tale of Two Cities* serve as useful markers of Dickens's evolving figuration of secrecy not merely because they are his only historical novels, but also because they enjoy such a close intertextual relationship. As a number of Dickens scholars have noted, the novels share elements of chronology, theme, and even incidents between them.[1] Both open in 1775 and continue five years later in 1780 and both double back to the 1750s to provide an original crime that motivates their plots. Just as the double murder at the Warren sets the stage for the idiocy and criminality that combines to produce the Gordon riots in *Barnaby Rudge*, so the rape and murder of Madame Defarge's sister and brother are made a prime cause of the French Revolution in *A Tale of Two Cities*. Both are thus interested not only in the theme of rebellion, but also in the domestication of rebellion and the causal relationship between personal wrong doing and social upheaval. As Jeremy Tambling argues, both novels are also heavily invested in the related theme of violence by both revolutionary and state-sanctioned means like public execution (131–32). These outbreaks of violence revolve around the unusual codependence between male madness (Barnaby and Dr. Manette) and female self-abnegation (Mary Rudge and Lucy).

Dickens even appears to have lifted at least one scene from *Barnaby Rudge* for use in *A Tale of Two Cities*. At the end of his earlier novel the representation of social disorder reaches its apex in chapter 68, in which Barnaby witnesses a masochistic orgy outside an anonymous vintner's house:

> But there was a worse spectacle than this—worse by far than fire and smoke, or even the rabble's unappeasable and maniac rage. The gutters of the street, and every crack and fissure in the stones, ran with scorching spirit, which being dammed up by busy hands, overflowed the road and pavement, and formed a great pool, into which the people dropped down dead by dozens. They lay in heaps all round this fearful pond, husbands and wives, fathers and sons, mothers and daughters, women with children in their arms and babies at their breasts, and drank until they died. While some stooped with their lips to the brink and never raised their heads again, others sprang up from their fiery draught, and danced, half in mad triumph, and half in the agony of suffocation, until they fell, and steeped their corpses in the liquor that had killed them.   (618)

On this final night of the riots, familial ties are sundered in a grotesque and bestial frenzy of Bacchanalian proportions. This scene is reproduced with certain minor modifications in book 1 of *A Tale of Two Cities* as a sort of introduction to the Defarges' wine shop:

> A large cask of wine had been dropped and broken, in the street. The accident had happened in getting it out of a cart; the cask had tumbled out with a run, the hoops had burst, and it lay on the stones just outside the door of the wine shop, shattered like a walnut shell.
>
> All the people within reach had suspended their business, or their idleness, to run to the spot and drink the wine. The rough irregular stones of the street, pointing every way and designed, one might have thought, expressly to lame all living creatures that approached them, had dammed it into little pools; these were surrounded, each by its own jostling group or crowd, according to its size. Some men kneeled down, made scoops of their two hands joined, and sipped, or tried to help women, who bent over their shoulders, to sip, before the wine had all run out between their fingers. Others, men and women, dipped in the puddles with little mugs of mutilated earthenware, or even with handkerchiefs from women's heads, which were squeezed dry into infants' mouths; others made small mud embankments, to stem the wine as it ran; others, directed by lookers-on up at high windows, darted here and their, to cut off little streams of wine that started away in new directions; others devoted themselves to the sodden and lee-dyed pieces of the cask, licking, and even champing the moister wine-rotted fragments with eager relish.   (28)

As in *Barnaby Rudge*, this scene clearly represents the process of revolution; unlike the situation in the earlier text, however, the revolution in *A Tale of Two Cities* has not yet begun, making this act of drinking the wine—symbolically rendered as "BLOOD" by Jacques Three (29)—into a premonition of the grotesque violence yet to come.[2] Such an array of intertextual connections provides a rich background on which to trace the novels' respective attempts to discriminate between positive and negative forms of secrecy.

The Ethics of Secrecy in *Barnaby Rudge*

In *Barnaby Rudge* the narrator offers readers several explicit comments on both the attractions and dangers of secrecy. Immediately after Solomon Daisy reveals to the Maypole regulars that he has just seen what he believes to be the ghost of Barnaby's father, John Willet advises, "we had better, one and all, keep this a secret. Such tales would not be liked at the Warren" (323). The narrator soon reveals that protecting the inhabitants of the Warren from distressing news may not be the men's primary motive, however: "it was solemnly resolved that it should be hushed up and kept quiet. And as most men like to have a secret to tell which may exalt their own importance, they arrived at this conclusion with perfect unanimity" (324). In the next weekly number the narrator again dwells on the attraction of secrecy, this time expanding from the importance it may confer on individuals to the attraction it has for the crowd and the ways in which institutions can use this attraction to their advantage:

> To surround anything, however monstrous or ridiculous, with an air of mystery, is to invest it with a secret charm, and power of attraction, which to the crowd is irresistible. . . .
> . . . when vague rumours got abroad, that in this Protestant association a secret power was mustering against the government for undefined and mighty purposes . . . when all this was done, as it were, in the dark, and secret invitations [were given] to join the Great Protestant Association . . . then the mania spread indeed, and the body, still increasing every day, grew forty thousand strong.   (347–48)

Perhaps the most intriguing comment on secrecy in the novel occurs in chapter 9, where the narrator briefly reflects on his own omniscient status and the privilege that grants him, and the reader, to penetrate into any secret he wishes: "Chroniclers are privileged to enter where they list, to come and go through keyholes, to ride upon the wind, to overcome, in their soarings up and down, all obstacles of distance, time, and place" (119).[3] Whether a tale told over a boiler, a plot concealed in a trunk lining, or an affection confined to "the sanctity of [Migg's] chambers," no secret is out of reach of the crowd of Dickens's readers, who, by their very attentiveness, exalt their own and the narrator's importance.[4]

The novel does warn, however, against too enthusiastically succumbing to this multidimensional allure of secrecy. Questioned by Dolly about the secret behind Mr. Haredale's going away, Gabriel Varden pinches her cheek while administering the following advice: " 'Read Blue Beard, and don't be curious, pet; it's no business of yours or mine, depend upon that' " (386). Sexually supercharged and featuring what Bruno Bettelheim has described as "the most monstrous and beastly of all fairy-tale husbands" (299), the story of Blue Beard presents secrecy in a doubly negative light: on the one hand, the content of the title character's secret—the decaying bodies of his previous wives—is, as Bettelheim rightly says, "monstrous and beastly"; on the other hand, the discovery of this secret by his most recent spouse puts her in mortal danger. Only the fortuitous return of her brothers, who kill Bluebeard, saves her from joining her predecessors. As a character with an intimate knowledge of a professional concern for locked rooms, Varden is uniquely qualified to offer this advice on the perils of secrecy. Since the locksmith is also the moral center of the novel, his cautionary allusion should carry special weight with Dickens's reader.

At the root of both the allure and the danger of secrecy in *Barnaby Rudge* is the affiliation between secrecy and power. Whether at the individual or institutional level, keeping secrets establishes an uneven distribution of power within the text, whereas revealing these same secrets confers narrative power on the novelist directly and on the reader by proxy. Varden's warning to Dolly acknowledges that such power can be dangerous, however, especially when exercised by those whose intentions, whether monstrous or just overly curious, remain suspect. The question implicitly posed in *Barnaby Rudge*, then, is how to distinguish between good and bad secrecy, and, by extension, between good and bad forms of power.[5]

Dickens answers this question by subdividing the examples of secrecy in the novel along two axes, one defined by who is keeping the secret and the other by the one for whom the secret is being kept. According to his first division, secrets can be concealed either by individuals or by institutions. As one might surmise, given Dickens's pervasive elevation of personal over collective action throughout his works, secrecy as practiced by individuals need not be bad, whereas concealment by institutions is uniformly condemned in *Barnaby Rudge*. Gordon's Protestant Association is only the most promi-nent example of an inappropriate practitioner of collective secrecy in the novel, which also directly or indirectly critiques Sim Tappertit's 'Prentice Knights/United Bulldogs, the rioters more generally, the government's spy system, and Chartism for the same reason.[6] According to Dickens's second division, individual acts of secrecy can be judged based on the keeper's intentions generally, and specifically on whether an individual keeps a secret for his or her own benefit or to protect another person. This second distinction is what allows Varden to remain the novel's moral compass despite both being a locksmith—a professional securer of secrets—and keeping numerous secrets on behalf of other characters, including not just Geoffrey Haredale, but also Mary Rudge, Joe Willet, and even John Chester.[7]

Curiously omitted from Dickens's ethics of secrecy in *Barnaby Rudge* is any consideration for either the contents or the consequences of a given secret. This self-willed ignorance allows the novel to maintain readers' sympathy for Mary Rudge, despite the fact that, by refusing to divulge that her husband yet lives, she frustrates the British judicial system and allows suspicion of fratricide to fall on Haredale. Because she keeps her secret out of a sense of wifely duty and fear, however, her intent, and therefore her secrecy, remain acceptable. By contrast, John Chester's concealment of Hugh's parentage prompts readerly disapprobation because Chester uses the secret to, among other things, preserve his social position by continuing to obscure his connection to the rioters. Of course, the riots themselves could have been greatly mitigated had Dolly Varden not kept secret that Hugh had assaulted and robbed her, thereby allowing him to spend his time at the Boot instead of inside a cell at Newgate. Her concealment remains beyond reproach, however, because her motives are pure:

> A deeply rooted dread of the man; the conviction that his ferocious nature, once roused, would stop at nothing; and the strong assurance that if she impeached him, the full measure of his wrath and vengeance would be wreaked on Joe, who had preserved her; these were consideration she had not the courage to overcome, and inducements to secrecy too powerful for her to surmount.
>
> (221)

When Sir John keeps the same secret, though, he again excites readers' disapproval by using what he knows to gain power over Hugh (239). Finally, the novel's ethics of secrecy help to explain why Haredale and Joe Willet react with such disdain to Gashford's final pleas to be "gently used":

> "I have access to all my lord's papers, Mr Haredale," he said, in a submissive voice: Mr Haredale keeping his back towards him, and not once looking round: "there are very important documents among them. There are a great many in secret drawers, and distributed in various places, known only to my lord and me. I can give some very valuable information, and render important assistance to any inquiry. You will have to answer it, if I receive ill usage."
>
> "Pah!" cried Joe, in deep disgust. "Get up, man; you're waited for, outside."
>
> (646)

When Dennis the hangman tries the same tactic six chapters later, Dickens even sacrifices historical accuracy to enforce the novel's ethical system by condemning the fictional Dennis to die (694).

Hanging Dennis the hangman is only one example of the meticulousness with which Dickens punishes those characters that have practiced illicit secrecy. Hugh, after a final humanizing plea for Barnaby's life, followed by a curse on John Chester's, is hanged alongside Dennis before the walls of Newgate.[8] Hugh's curse, that Chester "may never sicken on his bed of down, but die a violent death . . . and have the night-wind for his only mourner" (695), comes to fruition when Haredale and Chester duel among the ruins of the Warren. Like Dennis, Sim Tappertit also undergoes an ironic and precipitous descent; unlike Dennis, however, Sim remains alive to suffer. "Shorn of his graceful limbs, and brought down from his high estate to circumstances of utter destitution, and the deepest misery" (734), he becomes a shoeblack, in which capacity he is reduced to perpetually polishing the boots of members of the Horse Guards, symbols of the very authority he had once pledged to overthrow.[9]

The neatness of Dickens's distribution of punishment and mercy in *Barnaby Rudge* obscures a crucial flaw in the novel's ethics of secrecy. By privileging intentions over contents or consequences when determining whether an individual act of concealment is acceptable or not, Dickens's text enshrines the omniscient narrator as the ultimate arbiter of judgment, since it is only through the narrator's ability to transcribe the thoughts and feelings of the characters that the reader can access their intentions. There are two immediate problems with this facile solution to the problem of secrecy. First, this abdication of responsibility to the narrator runs counter to this particular novel's and Dickens's general concern in all his novels to show the power that individuals have to effect social change. Second, once they leave Dickens's fiction, readers will no longer enjoy this narrative omniscience and so will be left unable to distinguish good secrecy from bad secrecy on the basis of intentionality.[10]

Even within the confines of *Barnaby Rudge*, one can begin to see the limits of the novel's intentional approach through the figure of Grip, who is connected with the issue of secrecy throughout the text.[11] " 'He's a knowing blade!' " says Varden in the reader's first introduction to the raven in the main text. He continues, " 'I should be sorry to talk secrets before him' " (89). Soon after, Barnaby reveals Grip's secret capacity for independent agency:

> "Call him!" echoed Barnaby, sitting upright upon the floor, and staring vacantly at Gabriel, as he thrust his hair back from his face. "But who can make him come! He calls me, and makes me go where he will. He goes on before, and I follow. He's the master, and I'm the man. Is that the truth, Grip?"
>   The raven gave a short, comfortable, confidential kind of croak;—a most expressive croak, which seemed to say, "You needn't let these fellows into our secrets."   (99–100)

Grip is suspiciously privy to the other characters' secrets as well, and is not above keeping some things entirely to himself:

> Sometimes Barnaby looked in and called him, and then he came hopping out; but he merely did this as a concession to his master's weakness, and soon returned to his own grave pursuits: peering into the straw with his bill, and rapidly covering up the place, as if, Midas-like, he were whispering secrets to the earth and burying them; constantly busying himself upon the sly; and affecting, whenever Barnaby came past, to look up into the clouds and nothing whatever on his mind; in short, conducting himself, in many respects, in a more that usually thoughtful, deep, and mysterious manner.   (518)

When Barnaby is captured, Grip figures prominently again, this time in the revelation of Hugh's secret cache of stolen gold (525). To the very end of the novel Grip remains impervious to the omniscience of the narrator, who admits himself unable to explain even why the raven has kept silent for one year following Barnaby's arrest, or why he begins to speak again (738). Dickens, as author and narrator, is clearly fascinated by this mysterious bird—Grip serves as both the opening subject in the preface and the closing character in the novel—but the reader may find him frustrating. Accustomed to judge characters according to their intentions, the reader cannot judge Grip because his interior life remains a "matter of uncertainty." The predicament that Grip represents for the reader is precisely the problem that arises whenever one seeks to apply Dickens's ethics of secrecy outside the world of *Barnaby Rudge*, where omniscience is impossible and individuals' intentions are their most closely guarded secrets.

Shifting from religious hypocrisy and the Gordon Riots in *Barnaby Rudge* to more general hypocrisy and the evils of selfishness in his next novel, *Martin Chuzzlewit*, Dickens reproduces the same framework for representing secrecy, and encounters a very similar problem with using intentionality as a standard of judgment. As in his earlier work, in *Martin Chuzzlewit* Dickens opposes institutional and individual secrets, unequivocally condemning the former and further subdividing the latter according to their keepers' intentions. Thus he brings together the English and American settings by locating in each an unacceptably secretive and criminally fraudulent institution: for England, the Anglo-Bengalee Disinterested Loan and Life Insurance Company; and for America, the Eden land development scheme.[12] Individual secrets in the novel can be readily labeled acceptable or unacceptable according to the degree to which selfish intentions originally prompted them. The novel, for example, heartily approves of Tom Pinch's secret love for Mary Graham, and morally exonerates Mrs. Todgers as a result of the "secret door" in her heart for the unhappily married Mercy Pecksniff, even as it scrupulously punishes Mercy's father for his selfish and secret plot to marry Mary Graham and disinherit young Martin. Using a similar standard of judgment-by-intention, the novel makes Jonas's intended, but unsuccessful, murder of Anthony Chuzzlewit every bit as vivid to the reader as his actual murder of Tigg Montague.

As in *Barnaby Rudge*, however, in *Martin Chuzzlewit* there is also one character whose secrecy resists easy judgment. Tom Pinch's London landlord, Nadgett, straddles the divide between institutional and individual secrecy even as his intentions remain outside the novel's ethical opposition between selfishness and selflessness. On the one hand, Nadgett gathers private information on behalf of the Anglo-Bengalee, to be used by "the directors" to blackmail, or swindle its policy-holders. In fact, Tigg, attempting to blackmail Jonas into dramatically increasing his investment in the company, uses information that Nadgett has gathered implicating Jonas in his father's death (512). On the other hand, Nadgett later relies on his knowledge of Tigg's use of the same information to arrest Jonas and thereby restore the rule of law (672). In both instances, it is very difficult to determine Nadgett's intentions. He "was born to be a secret," the narrator tells us (385–86), and he is reluctant to tell even Tigg, his employer, the results of his original investigation (509). Like Grip, Nadgett keeps secrets because it is his nature to be secretive; he appears interested in neither his own gain nor someone else's protection. Additionally, because he is himself "born to be a secret" that the narrator declines to reveal, the reader cannot know his intentions. Forced to relate to Nadgett as he or she would to a real human being, the reader of *Martin Chuzzlewit* is reminded again of the perils of discriminating between good and bad forms of secrecy on the basis of individual intention.

Privacy and Conspiracy in *A Tale of Two Cities*

Like its predecessor, *A Tale of Two Cities* presents the subject of secrecy to its readers as a puzzling problem. On the one hand, secrecy is a necessary part of the human condition; as the narrator reflects early on,

> every human creature is constituted to be that profound secret and mystery to every other. A solemn consideration, when I enter a great city by night, that every one of those darkly clustered houses encloses its own secret; that every room in every one of them encloses its own secret; that every beating heart in the hundreds of thousands of breasts there, is, in some of its imaginings, a secret to the heart nearest it! (13)

In fact, in the novel it seems that nearly everyone has a secret. To name only a few of the most prominent: Jarvis Lorry holds in trust the "valuable stores and secrets" of the customers at Tellson's Bank (15); one of those customers, Dr. Manette, is similarly privy to the secret history of Madame Defarge and the Evrémonde brothers, a bit of knowledge for which he is held "in secret" in the Bastille; Charles Darnay conceals his relationship to these same brothers by adopting a false name; this strategy is also used by Solomon Pross, also known as John Barsad, who works as a spy and *agent provocateur* in both England and France; Barsad's ruse is exposed, with the aid of Jerry Cruncher, who moonlights as a resurrection man, by Sydney Carton, whose hidden love for Lucie Manette prompts him to assume the identity of Charles Darnay immediately prior to his execution, one secretly arranged by the Defarges and their Revolutionary conspiracy, the Jacquerie. Given the ubiquity of secrecy and the fact that the revelation of individual characters' secrets forms and moves the plot of novels like *A Tale*, readers are invited to tolerate, if not take active pleasure in, Dickens's representation of secrecy.

On the other hand, Victorian readers generally and Dickens's readers in particular would have been prejudiced against practices of secrecy before ever opening "the leaves of this dear book" (13). Cultural critics have long recognized the Victorians' obsession with truth-telling and their related tendency to conflate concealment of any kind with dishonesty,[13] and Dickens's own fiction is replete with lessons in the consequences of falsehood, not least the precipitous descent of Pecksniff in *Martin Chuzzlewit*. This distrust of secretive behavior appears in *A Tale of Two Cities* in chapter 19 of book 2, where, after recounting the destruction of Dr. Manette's shoemaking tools in terms well-suited for the Newgate Calendar, the narrator observes, "So wicked do destruction and secrecy appear to honest minds, that Mr Lorry and Miss Pross, while engaged in the commission their deed, and in the removal of its traces, almost felt, and almost looked, like accomplices in a horrible crime" (207). Even when practiced by two of the most virtuous characters in the novel, then, secrecy remains deeply problematic.

As he did eighteen years earlier, Dickens attempts to solve this problem by distinguishing between licit and illicit forms of secrecy, figured in *A Tale of Two Cities* as a distinction between privacy and conspiracy. This strategy offers two immediate payoffs: first, it centers the novel in the private self and, by extension, the middle-class private family, both of which are valorized by virtue of their superiority to dangerous conspiracies like that of the Jacquerie; second, it excuses the novelist's repeated incursions into the normally sacrosanct private sphere, since these otherwise inappropriate intrusions prove why privacy is an acceptable, even laudable form of secrecy. However, as Catherine Gallagher notes, there is something duplicitous about Dickens's solution to his original problem—it both effaces the fact that he, as author, is responsible for concealing and revealing the text's secrets and, in so doing, forces him to model his authorial practice not on the private family he extols but on the conspiracy he denounces. Gallagher writes, "Both the Revolution and the Dickens narrator need to transgress against the private, and, to justify their transgression, they must create a belief that dark things (plots, conspiracies, vices) lurk everywhere, needing to be revealed. The belief in secrets creates the need to expose, but the need to expose is reciprocally dependent on the invention of secret plots'' (134).[14] In other words, although the novel appears to repudiate the Jacquerie as a conspiracy, it actually relies on this organization to uphold the virtues of the private sphere, thereby confusing its primary ideological distinction between privacy and conspiracy.

This confusion of categories is exacerbated by Dickens's characteristic technique of doubling. In a nod to his own and his readers' national prejudices, Dickens aligns acceptable secrecy, privacy, with the English domestic circle surrounding Lucie Manette and unacceptable secrecy, or conspiracy, with the web of Revolution knitted in France by Madame Defarge. However, as David Marcus observes, the novel's structural motif of spatial doubling undermines ''any self-satisfied confidence in the superiority of British institutions and attitudes'' (63),[15] including the two nations' respective attitudes toward and practices of secrecy. In fact, one form of secrecy, spying, seems an important and widely practiced activity in both nations. Not only do England and France both employ spies to uphold their respective regimes, but both actually employ the same spy, John Barsad.[16] His employment by both pre-Revolution Britain and post-Revolution France allows for a simultaneous collapse of spatial and chronological distinctions, thus inviting readers to reexamine their own present assumptions about licit and illicit secrecy in light of Dickens's historical fiction.

Doubling occurs at the levels of institution and individual as well, further destabilizing the boundary between privacy and conspiracy in the novel. Consider that eminently respectable institution, Tellson's Bank, which the narrator self-consciously identifies with England when it is first presented at the beginning of book 2 (53). In addition to serving as a repository for its clients' secrets, Tellson's is noteworthy for its ability to produce anonymous and nearly identical men of business like ''the two ancient cashiers'' and the nameless ''old clerks in distant corners'' (142, 143). ''When they took a young man into Tellson's London house,'' the narrator explain, ''they hid him somewhere till he was old. They kept him in a dark place, like a cheese, until he had the full Tellson flavour and blue-mould upon him. Then only was he permitted to be seen, spectacularly poring over large books, and casting his breeches and gaiters into the general weight of the establishment'' (54–55). Even Jarvis Lorry, when he is at work, assumes the nondescript identity of Tellson's, discernible in ''a peculiarity in his manner of shaking hands, always to be seen in any clerk at Tellson's who shook hands with a customer when the House pervaded the air. He shook in a self-abnegating way, as one who shook for Tellson & Co'' (143).

Mr. Lorry's surrender of self to Tellson & Co. uneasily mirrors the more sinister collapse of discrete selfhood encouraged by the Jacquerie. This anonymity first presents itself in an oblique conversation during Mr. Lorry's initial visit to the Defarges' wine shop:

"How goes it, Jacques?" said one of these three. "Is all the spilt wine swallowed?"

"Every drop, Jacques."

"It is not often," said the second of the three, "that many of these miserable beasts know the taste of wine, or of anything but black bread and death. Is it not so, Jacques?"

"It is so, Jacques."

The last of these three now said his say, as he put down his empty drinking vessel and smacked his lips.

"Ah! So much the worse! A bitter taste it is that such poor cattle always have in their mouths, and hard lives they live, Jacques. Am I right, Jacques?"

"You are right, Jacques."   (33)

I have purposely transcribed this exchange as it would be heard, without any identifying markers, to emphasize the degree of anonymity it enforces. Not only does this use of the codeword Jacques clearly indicate the presence of a conspiracy, but by virtue of the similarity it implies between the self-abnegation at Tellson's and negation of clearly identifiable individuality in the Jacquerie, it also undermines any clear division between the secretive practices of these two institutions.

One might also compare the various moments of personal secrecy that occur in the novel. For example, Doctor Manette is held "in secret" in One Hundred and Five, North Tower, at the behest of the Evrémonde brothers, who exert their own aristocratic authority to preserve their secret criminality. When he is later "recalled to life" and released from the Bastille, Manette is concealed by Monsieur Defarge in a garret apartment behind the latter's wine shop where, despite his newfound "freedom," he remains under lock and key, surrounded by "rusted bars." Manette's secret in book 1, that although believed dead he is actually alive, makes him an uneasy double for a far less savory character in the novel, namely the spy Roger Cly, whose counterfeit funeral in chapter 14 of book 2 disappoints Jerry Cruncher in his evening occupation as an "honest tradesman." Sydney Carton later turns this disappointment to his advantage when he uses it to coerce John Barsad, who is now working for the Revolutionary Tribunal, into helping him accomplish Charles Darnay's release from La Force, where he is being held "in secret" by Madame Defarge. Carton thus employs a spy to allow him to secretly change places with Darnay, to whom he bears an uncanny resemblance; meanwhile, although deprived of independent action by his confinement, Darnay does not lose all conscious volition and identity until freed by Carton. As Cates Baldridge cannily observes, this loss of self makes Darnay and Carton doubles not just of one another but of the Jacquerie itself:

> The central irony which emerges from Carton's successful commingling with
> Darnay in prison is that Sydney's "cure" is effected in the shadow of the

novel's explicit condemnation of the very practice which heals him, for while he participates in a process whereby one man is able to transcend the suffocating barriers of the bourgeois self, the Revolution's insistence that the same is to be done for *all* men meets with nothing but scorn. . . . The obvious fact that Sydney Carton and the Jacquerie see the annihilation of the conventional barriers between individuals as the means to ends which are diametrically opposed does not weaken this irony to the extent that one might suppose.   (647)

On one level, then, Carton's act of self-sacrifice is deeply private, since it is an expression of his hidden love for Lucie and the mechanism by which her private happiness is secured. On another level, however, it is the ironic double of the novel's central conspiracy, thereby making Lucie's happiness curiously dependent on the Jacquerie.

This constant intermingling of licit and illicit forms of secrecy allows readers of *A Tale of Two Cities* to draw conclusions about the fluid boundaries between privacy and conspiracy with which Dickens himself would likely have been profoundly uncomfortable. First, if taken to their logical endpoints, the similar self-abnegation and secrecy demanded by Tellson's Bank and the Jacquerie suggest that Tellson's, and by extension the world of business that it represents, is itself a type of conspiracy. Although recent research by Mary Poovey on Victorian investments may support such a conclusion (29–32), the presence of conspiratorial secrecy as an integral element of commerce—for Victorian economists, bankers, and businesspeople generally—would call into question both the moral foundations of England's commercial success and liberal arguments that the business world could be trusted to regulate itself. Second, the implied collapse of difference between privacy and conspiracy threatens the prevailing Victorian constructions of gender and class, since both of these identity categories were to a great extent grounded in the supposed moral superiority of the middle-class private sphere.[17] As if recognizing the unstable potential of his own text, Dickens seeks to use the novel's final paragraphs to reestablish the primacy of the private by showing its longevity relative to the "long rows of new oppressors" represented by the Jacquerie (376). And yet, as we have seen, Carton's vision of future bliss is enabled by practices of secrecy not unlike those of the novel's conspirators. Moreover, this final scene is made possible only by the exposure of Carton's last, most private thoughts; thus, in a final confusion of categories, privacy as a separate, superior form of secrecy can only be secured by its own violation.[18]

Dickens's next novel, *Great Expectations*, remains just as interested in questions of secrecy as its historical predecessor. The work opens with Pip's traumatic encounter with the convict Magwitch, who terrorizes the boy into stealing a file and some food by threatening him with the horrible retribution of an unseen companion possessing "a secret way pecooliar to himself, of getting at a boy, and at his heart, and at his liver" (6). After helping Magwitch, Pip remain oppressed by the "secret burden" of his conscience and the "the weight of [his] wicked secret" (13, 23), which puts him "on secret terms of conspiracy with convicts" (77). Ultimately, this secret comes to so dominate his sense of self that he is unable to reveal it (119)—at least until he narrates it in the novel. As in *A Tale of Two Cities*, Pip's narration of his own *Great Expectations* seeks to establish a binary opposition between private, acceptable secrecy and public, criminal secrecy; and, once again, the boundary between privacy and criminal conspiracy remains uncomfortably porous.

The two clearest examples in the novel of the division between good and bad forms of secrecy are centered on Pip and Wemmick. Specifically, when he first acquires news of his fortune, Pip remains unconcerned that his expectations require him to accede to the "profound secret" of his benefactor's identity (136). Convinced that Miss Havisham has authored this "rich attractive mystery, of which [he] was the hero," Pip is content to play his part in what he believes to be a private, appropriate domestic secret. When, in the final chapter of volume 2, he learns that the money has come from Magwitch, and that therefore he remains "on secret terms of conspiracy with convicts," Pip begins to separate himself from expectations now tainted by secrets from the public sphere. A similar division between private and public forms of secrecy shapes Pip's, and by extension the reader's, perceptions of Wemmick. While in Little Britain, trafficking in the legal secrets of Mr. Jaggers's practice, Wemmick shares his employer's "air of knowing something to everybody else's disadvantage" (163). By contrast, once in Walworth with the Aged, Wemmick loses his air of unsavory public secrecy and assumes the benign role of lord of his own domestic Castle. Appealing to Pip's "good faith," Wemmick swears him to acceptably private secrecy about the existence of Walworth when in Little Britain: "No; the office is one thing, and private life is another. When I go into the office, I leave the Castle behind me, and when I come into the Castle, I leave the office behind me. If it's not in any way disagreeable to you, you'll oblige me by doing the same. I don't wish it professionally spoken about" (206). Pip readily agrees.

As the novel progresses, the barriers between the office and the Castle, between bad and good forms of secrecy, begin to break down, until, as in *A Tale of Two Cities*, the novel suggests that public, even criminal secrecy may be necessary to preserve acceptable privacy. The compromises required by the concealment of Magwitch most noticeably bring on this collapse of categories. First, Pip requires of Herbert, to whom he had earlier attributed a "natural capacity to do anything secret and mean" (175),[19] that he preserve the secret of Magwitch's return to England. Later, after returning from visiting Miss Havisham, Pip is unnerved by Wemmick's written instructions not to go home (361). Wemmick tells Pip in person the next morning that he and Herbert have hidden Magwitch at the home of Herbert's fiancée, then proceeds to instruct him in the finer points of destroying documentary evidence

(364).[20] Thus, preserving Magwitch's secret requires both an introduction of the convict into Herbert's hidden domestic circle and the use of information and rules of evidence employed in Little Britain.[21]

The form of the novel also reflects the uneasy separation of privacy and conspiracy in the novel. On the one hand, far more effectively than the third-person narrator of *A Tale of Two Cities*, the first-person narrator of *Great Expectations* elides the epistemological and ethical problems with penetrating the private self. Accustomed from the beginning to knowing Pip's innermost thoughts and conditioned by the text's confessional form, readers are unlikely to object to Pip's revelation of his own secret dreams and desires. However, in a novel so dedicated to the exposure of its main character's innermost secrets, it is somewhat jarring to find Pip in agreement with Mr. Jaggers about the positive good of preserving criminal secrets, and thus keeping from Estella the identity of both of her parents (409).

Conclusions

Ultimately, both historical novels fail in their attempts to distinguish good from bad secrecy—*Barnaby Rudge* because the criterion for judging acts of concealment relies on a fantasy of omniscience, and *A Tale of Two Cities* because the private must be exposed before it can be approved. This shared failure is highly productive, however, since it shows not only that the issue of secrecy, whether connected with political change or domestic drama, remains of central concern to Dickens throughout his career, but also that he continues to represent this concern using the same formal mechanism. Building from his own proclivity for doubling at the levels of character, incident, chronology, and location, Dickens consistently frames the issue of secrecy using binary oppositions.

His oppositional strategy does evolve somewhat from the period of his first historical novel to that of his last, though, becoming both simpler and more systematic. The ethics of secrecy in *Barnaby Rudge*—as well as of *Martin Chuzzlewit*—consist of one binary opposition (secrets kept for oneself versus secrets kept for others) inside of another (collective secrecy versus individual secrecy); by contrast, *A Tale of Two Cities* is constructed around a single opposition (conspiracy versus privacy), which is taken up again in *Great Expectations*. In the latter novels, Dickens reinforces the distinction between these two categories more self-consciously than he had earlier in his career. The famous opening of *A Tale of Two Cities* prepares readers to think in opposing pairs, a pattern that Dickens sustains in the novel's chapters themselves, which oscillate back and forth from privacy in England to conspiracy in France; similarly, the confessional narrative form of *Great Expectations* lulls readers into accepting the revelation of private secrets.

This increased attention to novelistic construction allows Dickens to replace the practically untenable rationale of intentionality with the subtler and, I would argue, more compelling standard of judgment provided by the form of the text itself. However, as Gallagher rightly observes, this increasingly simplified and systematized method does not remove the narrator from the equation. Indeed, the narrator, whether third—or first-person, remains persistently central to the reader's ability to judge the various forms of secrecy in Dickens's fictions, just as the production, transmission, and exposure of secrets continues to be crucial to readers' enjoyment of these novels. One might speculate, in fact, that by making secrets such a prominent part of the reading experience throughout his career, Dickens may have been incapable of defining the limits of acceptable secrecy, since his own practice and his readers' expectations would have required him to transgress them.

NOTES

1. See, e.g., Tambling 131–41.
2. By placing the vintner scene at the end of *Barnaby Rudge* and the broken wine cask episode near the beginning of *A Tale of Two Cities*, Dickens signals that both the motives for and the actual outbreaks of violence will be much more severe in the second novel. As T. A. Jackson observes, "Whereas in *Barnaby* Dickens' artistic exaggerations of reality were all in the direction of making the riots seem more irrational, more wantonly destructive and more criminal than in fact they were, in the *Tale of Two Cities* the reverse is the case" (29).
3. This narrative self-description makes the chronicler of *Barnaby Rudge* an excellent example of what Jonathan Arac refers to as a "commissioned spirit," one who surveys life from an impossibly all-seeing vantage in order to " 'lift . . . the roofs' to lay bare the human agents within their circumstantial shell. The writer must not only *see* society but also see *through* it, thus at once recognizing and embodying the human forces that have made society and will change it" (7).
4. Of course, readers might legitimately claim that the narrator only inconsistently exercises his privilege to overcome all obstacles of distance, time, and place. Indeed, the narrator's strategic omniscience allows him to secure his own credibility and importance by, for example, exposing Miggs's secret affection for Sim, even as he disempowers the reader by glossing over the omission for key details like the identity of the Maypole's mysterious stranger.
5. As we shall see, the novel's response to this question is predicated on the reader's not considering the question of good and bad forms of narration, since such considerations might lead back to Dickens's own strategically omniscient narrator, trust in whom is absolutely necessary to the novel's ethics of secrecy.
6. For more on Dickens's condemnation of collective secrecy and the ways in which his position relates to nineteenth-century labor history, see Pionke, esp. 7–10.

7. In its privileging of intentions the novel preserves a standard of judgment that Lisa Rodensky identifies as central to *Oliver Twist* (1837–38). According to Rodensky, who reads this earlier novel in the context of Victorian legal debates over criminal responsibility, in *Oliver Twist* Dickens protects Oliver from the taint of criminality by providing the reader with continuous access to his pure intentions, even as Dickens allows for the legally questionable prosecution of Fagin by exposing his innermost thoughts while in prison.

8. Even as he meticulously hangs the leaders of the riots, Dickens also indicts the British judicial system for meting out the same punishment to incidental participants far less deserving of death (698).

9. In what may initially seem to be a nod to readers' expectations of a happy ending, Dickens spares Barnaby from the scaffold; in light of the novel's ethics of secrecy, however, Barnaby's triumphant escape from death makes perfect sense, since his intentions remain pure by virtue of his mental deficiencies.

10. For Rodensky, it is precisely this capacity to access individual intentions that made the novel such a prescient perspective from which Victorian readers and writers could survey the limits of purely consequentialist theories of crime.

11. For more on Grip, see Buckley.

12. In addition, the names of the New York newspapers, most noticeably the *Spy*, the *Listener*, and the *Peeper* (220), also indict America for an insufficient regard for individual privacy.

13. See, for example, Kucich, *The Power of Lies* 4–17.

14. The necessary presence of secret plots for the Revolutionaries appears during Madame Defarge and Jacques Three's decision to label Lucy's innocent waving to Charles as "signals" of a dangerous plot (361).

15. See also Kucich, *Excess and Restraint* 169.

16. Spying also plays a role in *Barnaby Rudge*; Gashford, for example, ends his career with "an appointment in the honourable corps of spies and eavesdroppers employed by the government" (733).

17. See Adams; also Kucich, *The Power of Lies.*

18. The fact that Carton's final thoughts are offered by the narrator in a hypothetical mode—"If he had given any utterance to his, and they were prophetic, they would have been these" (376)—both weakens this final plea for the primacy of the private and makes awkwardly perspicuous just how unnatural such intrusions into characters' interior lives really are.

19. As it turns out, Pip is wrong about Herbert's capacity for secrecy, since Herbert is, in fact, secretly engaged (248); however, since Herbert's secret is a private one, it is absolved of the charge of meanness.

20. For more on destroying documentary evidence, see *Great Expectations* 390–412.

21. Further interpenetrations of forms of secrecy include Pip's clandestine use of both his own and Miss Havisham's tainted wealth to aid Herbert's professional aspirations, and the ultimate reliance of the existence of the Castle on Wemmick's acquisition of "portable property" from condemned felons.

WORKS CITED

Adams, James Eli. *Dandies and Desert Saints: Styles of Victorian Manhood.* Ithaca: Cornell UP, 1995.

Arac, Jonathan. *Commissioned Spirits: The Shaping of Social Motion in Dickens, Carlyle, Melville, and Hawthorne.* Morningside Edition. New York: Columbia UP, 1989.

Baldridge, Cates. "Alternatives to Bourgeois Individualism in *A Tale of Two Cities*." *SEL: Studies in English Literature, 1500–1900* 30 (1990): 633–54.

Bettelheim, Bruno. *The Uses of Enchantment: The Meaning and Importance of Fairy Tales.* New York: Vintage, 1989.

Buckley, Jerome H. " 'Quoth the Raven': The Role of Grip in Barnaby Rudge." *Dickens Studies Annual* 21 (1992): 27–35.

Dickens, Charles. *Barnaby Rudge.* Ed. Gordon Spence. Harmondsworth: Penguin, 1997.

———. *Great Expectations.* Ed. Margaret Cardwell. Introduction by Kate Flint. Oxford: Oxford UP, 1998.

———. *Martin Chuzzlewit.* Ed. Margaret Cardwell. Oxford: Oxford UP, 1998.

———. *A Tale of Two Cities.* Ed. Norman Page. London: J. M. Dent, 1998.

Gallagher, Catherine. "The Duplicity of Doubling in *A Tale of Two Cities*." *Dickens Studies Annual* 12 (1983): 125–45.

Jackson, Thomas A. *Charles Dickens: The Progress of a Radical.* London: Lawrence and Wisehart, 1937.

Kucich, John. *Excess and Restraint in the Novels of Charles Dickens.* Athens, GA: U of Georgia P, 1981.

———. *The Power of Lies: Transgression in Victorian Fiction.* Ithaca: Cornell UP, 1994.

Marcus, David D. "The Carlylean Vision of *A Tale of Two Cities*." *Studies in the Novel* 8 (1976): 56–68.

Pionke, Albert D. "Combining the Two Nations: Trades Unions as Secret Societies 1837–1845." *The Victorian Newsletter* 97 (2000): 1–14.

Poovey, Mary. "Writing about Finance in Victorian England: Disclosure and Secrecy in the Culture of Investment." *Victorian Studies* 45 (2002): 17–42.

Rodensky, Lisa. *The Crime in Mind: Criminal Responsibility and the Victorian Novel.* Oxford: Oxford UP, 2003.

Tambling, Jeremy. *Dickens, Violence and the Modern State: Dreams of the Scaffold.* London: Macmillan, 1995.

Matters of Class and the Middle-Class Artist in *David Copperfield*

Alan P. Barr

David Copperfield *presents the recollections of a young man who sur-*
vived his loss of family, initial schooling and work, and frustrations in
love and marriage to mature into a successful artist. Accompanying this
engaging journey (Dickens's "favorite child") is a sustained critique of
the mid-nineteenth-century social structure. David's encounters with
the diverse British classes and his need, eventually, to locate himself
among them, involves a substantial criticism of the recognized middle-
class virtues of marriage and family, the ethic of work and financial
success, and the comfort and even sanctity of the home. The distaste
for commercialism and getting ahead, the dysfunctional families and
their precarious habitats, a skewed and brutal educational system, and
a questioning of what real gentility is all leave David as recognized
artist and we as his readers anything but enthusiastic about the much-
lauded world of middle-class values and accomplishments. Dickens's
social criticism, so prominent in such fictions as Bleak House, Hard
Times, *and* Our Mutual Friend, *similarly, if more quietly, colors our*
response to Copperfield.

David Copperfield occupies a substantial place among Victorian novels that
scrutinized contemporary British class structure. David's retrospective conveys a skeptical and wary image of the period's social order, particularly of
its middle class.

Dickens Studies Annual, Volume 38, Copyright © 2007 by AMS Press, Inc. All
rights reserved.

Raymond Williams, in his cultural criticism, and William Palmer, as a new historicist, are among the numerous commentators who have detailed the astonishing shifts occurring in the novels of the mid-nineteenth-century—as they increasingly reflected the new uncertainties concerning rank, class, and social mobility. No Victorian novelist was more alert to these changes and exemplified a more heightened social consciousness than Dickens, as he depicted in his fictions the quotidian realities of Britain's social and economic classes.

Robin Gilmour's *The Idea of the Gentleman in the Victorian Novel* is similarly useful in appreciating the burgeoning interest in class as a subject. Gilmour is intrigued by the way Victorian social transformations (fundamental to Dickens's stories) led to a preoccupation with the image of the gentleman—its tradition, contradictions, ambivalences, and seeming accessibility: "The idea of the gentleman could never have fascinated the Victorians as it did if it had been limited by caste or by a strict science of heraldry, nor, on the other hand, if it had been a totally moralised concept, a mere synonym for the good man" (4). *David Copperfield* (1850) includes within its awareness of classes the notion of uniting the professionally successful with the genteel. Pam Morris, writing a decade after Gilmour, is still more specific about situating David within the social history of the midcentury and the problematical quest for gentility: "The narrative construction of David as moral hero and gentleman provides an imaginary resolution of the competing ideologies of gentility and progress in a struggle for hegemonic dominance between capitalist and aristocratic interests taking place at the end of the 1840s" (78).

In its general questioning of society's arrangements and assumptions, *David Copperfield* suggests that Dan Peggotty's devotion and commitment to others bespeak at least as much of the truly civilized gentleman as Mr. Spenlow's financial insouciance—which unexpectedly resembles Micawber's—or as the "gentleman" Murdstone's rectitude and firmness. With a cast comprehending the Heeps, the Murdstones, Aunt Betsey, Agnes and her father, the Steerforths, Dora and her father, and Traddles, any easy association of gentility with a particular class is variously subverted.

As the urban novelist extraordinaire, Dickens tellingly recorded the changing class markers and structures, the vainly held rigidities of society that bumped along with London traffic. A novel like *Bleak House* (1853) ranges from the worlds of Sir Leicester and Lady Dedlock to Tom-All-Alone's, making apparent Dickens's fascination with Victorian class distinctions and their inequities. *David Copperfield* projects a more incidental or en passant view, one infrequently explored. His position of evolved prose artist writing about a part of his life that ended a decade before his penning, allows David the advantage—and vantage—of interweaving within his personal account of love, tribulations, work, and maturation a subtext of observations and implied commentary about class. If, as some have remarked, the petrific Murdstone and the serpentine Uriah Heep are partly melodramatic figures, they are also part of the novel's reportage. (David, like his author, did early training as a court stenographer.)

Less concerned with mercantilism and finance than *Dombey and Son*, without the direct onslaught against the philistines of *Hard Times*, avoiding both the satire directed against the Veneerings in *Our Mutual Friend* and the sociopolitical instruction of *A Tale of Two Cities*, *David Copperfield* does betray a recurring awareness of class. It surfaces in forms of address (the way characters defer or are deferred to), the contrasting domiciles and family constellations, employments and the attitudes toward them, and, of course, the views toward money, debt, and responsibility. Chris Vanden Bossche has written about the place of class in *David Copperfield*, but the focus of his "Cookery, not Rookery: Family and Class in *David Copperfield*" is on the protagonist's migration from delusory upper-class notions ("rookery") to bourgeois pragmatics ("cookery"). The other critic who has addressed this issue specifically is Pam Morris. As the title of her chapter "David Copperfield: Alienated Writer" conveys, her purpose is to place the protagonist within an insecure, estranging world, where the "desire for gentility masks the desire for quiescence and death" (79). These arguments are certainly on target, but there remain many other knots and nuances in Dickens's tapestry.

David begins his journey as a would-be scion of the (very) minor gentry (as Vanden Bossche notes, he "claims the title of 'David Copperfield the Younger of Blunderstone Rookery,'" 31), is quickly orphaned, teased at a school that runs the gamut from Steerforth of Highgate to Mr. Mell, whose mother is ignominiously living in an almshouse, and then bolts—essentially naked and nameless (re-formable)—to Aunt Betsey at Dover. By age nine he has viewed the spread of society's classes and is apparently ready for molding. His acquiring of an identity ("Trotwood") and a social contour are not limited to but surely include abutting Britain's classes and testing himself among them. Finding a family turns out to be a class-laden venture.

The array of households that *David Copperfield* displays is striking. Domesticities are recognizable by class, and it is as if David the social sojourner has to examine them and situate himself. As a young boy, David has a home life that seemed idyllic. Although his father has died, leaving behind the illusion (or name) of a genteel existence, Blunderstone Rookery, David has his companionable mother's attention and devotion. The superficially abrupt, but ultimately down-to-earth Aunt Betsey has vacated the scene. Happily, Peggotty remains to counteract, for a time, Clara Copperfield's fecklessness. This image of domestic comfort and stability is followed by another, when David visits Yarmouth. Just as the eight-year-old boy has no experience preparing him to anticipate that life at Blunderstone is a facade about to dissolve, so, too, is he beguiled by the working-class paradise that he imagines Peggotty's landlocked boat to be. If David's lineal family is imminently to disintegrate (and Steerforth's home is to prove a fractious den), Dan Peggotty seems magnanimously to have fabricated a successful, functioning unit. David, agreeably greeted as "Sir," is charmed, and he soon devotedly loves little Em'ly.

Both of these bowers of bliss quickly implode. David returns home to confront the unimaginable: his nursery (rookery) has become alien and rejecting in the middle-class extreme. Efficiency, prudence, firmness, discipline, and self-control (emotional ossification) now reign. The Yarmouth picture of working-class simplicity and loving congeniality, centered around Emily and Dan Peggotty, will later be similarly eviscerated, when Emily elopes with Steerforth to become a lady, Dan traipses the world to reclaim her, they all (except Ham) eventually emigrate to Australia to regroup, and the house is seen more as precariously misplaced than as endearingly eccentric.

Disciplined by his "new Pa" and distanced from his mother, David is cast out. Mr. Creakle's Salem House may hardly qualify as an academic institution, but it does quickly introduce David to the realities of class. The comparatively upper-crust Steerforth (surprisingly, or not so surprisingly) is never disciplined, but dominates, as we see when David is first carried before him "as before a magistrate'" (136; ch. 6). At the lowest rung of the social ladder, the genuine teacher, Mr. Mell, is berated and discharged because of his (disgracefully) impoverished mother. "It always gave [David] pain to observe that Steerforth treated Mell with systematic disparagement," but young and in awe, he is easily enough assuaged by Steerforth's "very noble" dispensing of money as balm (147, 154; ch. 7). Between Steerforth and Mell is the ambivalently seen figure of Traddles, sometimes mocked as Miss Traddles by Steerforth, but subsequently admired—or at least wondered at—for his fortitude in establishing a household with Sophy and five of her numerous sisters. David, always well-disposed towards Traddles, alternates between a kind of impatient condescension at his unfathomably arduous trek up the road to success and honoring that eventual success. Throughout, Traddles is distinguished by his unpretentiousness; he acknowledges that he is fighting his way "against difficulties, and it would be ridiculous if I made a pretence of doing anything else" (463; ch. 27).

The order and harmony of Yarmouth, which are so devastatingly unsettled, the disorder of the Micawbers' home (a place David associates with "An indescribable character of faded gentility" [461; ch. 27]), and the fanatical focus at the Heeps' residence seem initially opposite the secure elegance of Steerforth's home in Highgate and Mr. Spenlow's place in Norwood. But Highgate and Norwood turn out, for different reasons, to be comparably vulnerable or insubstantial: one is an emotional and the other a fiscal fraud.

Setting out from Aunt Betsey's cottage at Dover and then from the satellite flat she establishes for him in London, David is in a position to visit and observe the different classes and social possibilities. The two homes he himself later fashions, the one with Dora and the other with Agnes, predictably derive from these experiences. Dora has the charming incapacities of his mother and, as it happens, the financial imprudence of her father, who both imbibed the insubstantial ether of a superficial gentility. Agnes, by contrast, has been forged by the examples of Wickfield's good nature as well as his unfortunate susceptibilities (to port wine and to the incursions of Heep—susceptibilities she does not share, but whose threat she appreciates) and of the resolute Annie Strong.

The establishment of a home was a bourgeois fixation. The physical residences themselves emblemize the possibilities and improbabilities that confront David. Blunderstone, under Murdstone, is firm beyond tolerance or tenability; its closing is both actual and symbolic for David: "it pained me to think of the dear old place as altogether abandoned" (306; ch. 17). The houseboat at Yarmouth is likewise impermanent, a visual paradox. Highgate and Norwood have already been mentioned as seductive shams. But equally hollow is the drummed-in ethic Heep adopts: be humble, work hard, and you will succeed, success, in this instance, meaning displacing the Wickfields in their house and incidentally threatening the Strongs' home. David can be taken in and launched from Aunt Betsey's cottage, but it is never suggested as an appropriate permanent residence for him. Traddles works exaggeratedly long and hard to secure his marriage quarters, which entails moving Sophy and five sisters into his workplace. Married to Dora, David is consistently thwarted in his attempts to run a sensible household. As Vanden Bossche argues, he cannot successfully import the then-popular middle-class guides, the cookery books and household manuals, into his dwelling (38–43). Betsey warns against thinking he can change Dora (632; ch. 39); Dora asks for a cookery book, but it makes her head ache and is more suitable as a toy for Jip (670; ch. 41). With Agnes, he does achieve domestic success and stability (she has long ago become adept with both the books and the keys). In a markedly unconventional way, it involves logistics the opposite of Traddles's; David imports his work into his residence.

Houses, of course, signify families and the raising of children, and the spectrum of parent-child portraits is as varied in *David Copperfield* as the buildings they inhabit. Victorian society may have made a cultural fetish of home and hearth, but Dickens's image of family life is tenuous and problematic and generally uncompelling. The profusion of orphans (David, his mother, Emily, Mr. Dick, Ham, Traddles, Martha Endell, Rosa Dartle, and, later, Dora) stands out and underscores both the opportunity and the need to locate or establish a family. For some—Dan Peggotty, the Micawbers, Aunt

Betsey, and Traddles—taking people in is almost reflexive. (Betsey's initial rejection of the "Betsey" who emerged as David frustrates too simplistic a reading; contexts and people can change.) The response of others—the Murdstones, Mrs. Steerforth, Rosa Dartle, Mr. Spenlow, and Dora (in very different ways)—is unwelcoming and exclusionary. That both Jane Murdstone and Betsey dislike boys only serves to enrich the shadings and contrasts and make us read more discriminatingly. Adoption and inclusion are associated with the working-class Peggottys and the debt-ridden Micawbers. Closed doors, tirades against "carrion" (Rosa's invective against the Peggottys), and proscriptions against misalliances are associated with the ostensibly higher echelons. Jane Murdstone's responses to the deaths of Clara and her infant are callous and steely. Betsey adopts and renames David, just as she had Mr. Dick, whose brother would have locked him up for life (260; ch. 14). Perhaps the most extreme instance of a tightly-knit, exclusionary family is the Heep twosome. Writing for a society that applauded the glorious middle-class family with its formidable entourage of offspring, Dickens is notoriously reserved in his enthusiasm (he is likely taking a sardonic glance at his own situation). At the end, we are simply told that three of David's children are present. Passionate enthusiasm for either them or Agnes is not conveyed, despite David's invocation of the elevated language of religion to convey the intensity of his love for Agnes, and despite the last wish expressed in the narrative. Some groups or classes may be *generally* more welcoming than others, but the identifications are never categorical nor unmixed; Emily bolts, and Steerforth finds limitless love insufficient or even destructive—as Rosa harangues Mrs. Steerforth.

As much a middle-class value as the family was work and the "work ethic," whether Calvinistic or secularly Utilitarian. In his evolution, David experiences and witnesses a variety of occupations of different status. After he finishes school at Canterbury, there is the inevitable question of what he will do. Aunt Betsey essentially urges upon him what we immediately recognize as the sanctioned virtues: be "A fine firm fellow, with a will of your own. With resolution. . . . With determination. With character" (332; ch. 19). That "firm" echoes Murdstone and "resolute" and "determined" describe Uriah Heep remind us of the mercurial slipperiness of what is apparently commendable.

The dangerous abyss that borders on and threatens these virtues is the lure of money. The "middle class" also encompasses an abrasive business or commercial world. Jane Murdstone, for example, personifies what Arnold would caustically denominate its philistinism: after Clara's funeral, "She was particularly proud of her turn for business; and she showed it now in reducing everything to pen and ink, and being moved by nothing" (182; ch. 9). Images of money flow like an arterial system through the class structure, emphasizing its divisions, its desperations, and its values: Steerforth's affluence, Mell's mother's poverty, Barkis's miserliness, Traddles's painstaking labors, Spenlow's public persona, Betsey's seeming ruin and the payments extorted by her estranged husband, Dora's inability to do accounts, Micawber's debts (his admirable formula linking solvency and happiness notwithstanding), Uriah's deceptions, and—most prominently—David's expensive apprenticeship, his unsuccessful attempt to inform Dora that he is a beggar, and his campaign to earn and succeed. Because money (commercial values) determines status, class, and success, the nature of the lives the characters lead, it serves as a repeated image to alert us to a core reality of this society—its much-lauded commerce and prudence (Arnold would deride it as "machinery") that could often be venal and inhumane.

David's task is to modulate or adapt the guidance of Betsey to the world he encounters. His first, shattering stint in the workplace, before escaping to Dover, is at Murdstone and Grinby's. We are only privy to David's report, but it is clear the warehouse repulsed him. He felt his "hopes of growing up to be a learned and distinguished man, crushed in my bosom" (210; ch. 11). Betraying some class snobbery, he "happily" (223; ch. 11) avoided the companionship of Mealy Potatoes and Mick Walker, soon escaping to reclaim the aunt who had rejected him at his birth. When Betsey sends him to Dr. Strong's school, he initially feels out of place, "ashamed" of his lower-class warehouse experience (285; ch. 16). At Canterbury, David witnesses a particular, skewed instance of the diligence that he is expected to demonstrate. Uriah Heep is so scrupulous about keeping to his " 'umble" place that he rejects David's offer to teach him Latin (312; ch. 17); it would be socially transgressive and provoke his betters. Heep's manner and his extreme work "ethic" are social contrivances. Late in the novel, he is explicit about how his fulsome humility is a deliberate adaptation to his class—an adaptation taught to his father and then to him at school (829; ch. 52) and desperately urged to the end by his mother. Though David and he are probably similarly disdainful of lower-class co-workers, Heep is willing to assume the unctuous trappings of a false humility, while David is distant and rejecting. When he was seventeen and heard that the elder Miss Larkins had married not a captain, but "Mr Chestle, a hop-grower," David reacted by fighting the butcher again—this time prevailing (329; ch. 18).

Settled in London, set to make his way, David is expensively articled at Mr. Spenlow's. Doctors' Commons is the very opposite of the coarse Murdstone and Grinby's. "Mr Spenlow gave me some hints in reference to my profession. He said it was the genteelest profession in the world, and must on no account be confounded with the profession of solicitor: being quite another sort of thing, infinitely more exclusive, less mechanical, and more profitable" (447; ch. 26). David should, Spenlow admonishes, dismiss from

his mind thoughts of improving the Commons as not worthy of his "gentlemanly character" (540; ch. 33). To support himself, David undertakes the
initially impenetrable study of shorthand. Later, after Aunt Betsey announces
her ruin, he adds to these labors working for Dr. Strong. Once having abandoned dandyism as his strategy to win Dora, he becomes a burlesque of the
Victorian dedication to work (the designated salvation of the middle
class—and its beleaguered Teufelsdrockhs). He reports he is up at five in the
morning, home at nine in the evening, "But I had infinite satisfaction in
being so closely engaged, and never walked slowly on any account, and felt
enthusiastically that the more I tired myself, the more I was doing to deserve
Dora" (588; ch. 36).

At the beginning of chapter 42, "Mischief," David, transcribing from his
own experience, exemplifies the approved and rewarded professional diligence:

> a patient and continuous energy which then began to be matured within me,
> and which I know to be the strong part of my character . . . I find the source of
> my success. . . . I never could have done what I have done, without the habits
> of punctuality, order, and diligence. . . . My meaning simply is, that whatever
> I have tried to do in life, I have tried with all my heart to do well; that whatever
> I have devoted myself to, I have devoted myself to completely; that in great
> aims and in small, I have always been thoroughly in earnest. . . . Never to put
> one hand to anything, on which I could throw my whole self; and never to
> affect depreciation of my work, whatever it was; I find, now, to have been my
> golden rules.   (671–72; ch. 42)

They are golden rules that would have fit comfortably into Carlyle's *Sartor
Resartus* or even Arnold's essays on culture. They were the currency of
middle-class manuals. The disruptive irony is that they do not particularly
seem to pertain to the success that David ultimately attains as an author—an
irony that would not have escaped the almost pathologically hardworking and
energetic Dickens.

Just as we can enjoy the disparity between David's very bourgeois training
and diligence and his triumph as an artist, it is purposeful to observe the
ancillary career of Micawber. His only work as such in England is the treachery for which Uriah employs him; his success is in exposing, with full dramatic flourish, Heep's malfeasances, leaving Micawber himself reclaimed,
but unemployed and in debt. Considering emigration, Mrs. Micawber asks
about Australia: " 'Now *are* the circumstances of the country such, that a
man of Mr Micawber's abilities would have a fair chance of rising in the
social scale?'. . . . 'No better opening anywhere,' said my aunt, 'for a man
who conducts himself well, and is industrious' " (833; ch. 52). There is no
appropriate employment for Micawber in England. Nor, in the novel, is there

any attractive, satisfying traditional middle-class occupation. David's final burst of diligence is in Switzerland, preparatory to his retuning as an artist—the only profession the novel appears to endorse as appealing or praiseworthy (889; ch. 58). Novels may have entertained and been supported by the Victorian middle class, but artists, including novelists, inevitably remain essentially beyond the margins of any class.

Little Em'ly, David's first infatuation, is another indicator of the way issues of class permeate *David Copperfield*. She embodies the attraction for David of Yarmouth as a paradise apart from the rest of society, but we soon sense the undertow eroding that image. Yes, Dan Peggotty, in contrast to the Murdstones, is the generously welcoming and nurturing patriarch, securing orphans from society's torrents, but his family disintegrates and its maritime residence is battered in the tempest. Emily is enchanting, but one of her earliest, revealing declarations is that she would like to be a lady: "We would all be gentle folks together, then" (85; ch. 3). This fits seamlessly into the initial fairy-tale charm of her and Yarmouth. It also quietly suggests the difference between her and David. More threateningly, it makes her vulnerable to ruin. When repeated at Omer's funeral parlor (363; ch. 21) and in her farewell letter ("If he don't bring me back a lady" [514; ch. 31]), Emily's aspiration has become ominous. It has led directly to her eloping with Steerforth. But the implications of her quest for ladylike status or gentility notably shift. Littimer (the supreme "classist"), prompted by Rosa to taunt Dan Peggotty, tells of her improvement beyond her class. She picked up local languages and customs, and he, "a very respectable person, . . . [had been] fully prepared to overlook the past." He, "who was, at least, as good as anybody the young woman could have aspired to in a regular way: her connexions being very common," had been prepared to follow Steerforth's "honourable" proposal and marry Emily (737; ch. 46).

Littimer is arrogant and psychologically and socially preposterous or hyperbolic. But his indulgent, pseudo-genteel statement anticipates the much more dramatic tirade of Rosa herself. Having tracked the returned Emily to Martha Endell's flat, she vilifies her as one of those creatures who should be whipped. David overhears Rosa mock the very idea of her presuming to love Steerforth: "She love! . . . . That carrion! And he ever cared for her, she'd tell me. Ha, ha! The liars that these traders are!" Despite her venom toward this class of fetid traders (a tag more easily associated with Murdstone and Creakle), Rosa cannot stop herself short of uttering an unimagined discovery. She had expected to find Emily a tarnished toy, but, her intended irony and derision notwithstanding, describes her as "true gold, a very lady, and an ill-used innocent" (789; ch. 50). Mrs. Steerforth, in her haughtiness, may have disdained any concern for the plight of the socially inferior, degraded, and therefore inadmissible Emily, yet despite her jealous fury and indignation,

Rosa's exclamation unwittingly recognizes her classless mettle. Her warning that Emily had thus better hide herself implies more than just the threat of Rosa's exposure. Rosa's begruding acknowledgment cannot of course alter the Victorian social reality; the "fallen" Emily would inexorably be denied lady-like status or acceptance. But surely implicit in Dickens's social and class critique is the reader's suspicion that Emily has, in fact, come back a lady—*and* is apparently most conveniently relocated, along with the Micawbers and Peggotty, in Australia.

Contrasted with the waywardness of Emily (more exaggerated in Martha), or the emotional license of Mrs. Steerforth and Rosa, is the signature middle-class concern with deportment (Arnold would try to dignify it as conduct, right acting, in *Culture and Anarchy*). This concern makes its way into the novel, exhibiting—again—anything but a simple portrait or a categorical attitude. The Murdstones, with their fanatical desire to control behavior and exhibit firmness, and Uriah Heep (as he tortuously strains to improve his status), with his duplicitous, contrived humility, presume to be exemplars of this class value, but are undressed as sorry distortions of it. When David returns from Yarmouth, he immediately hears his new father instructing his mother to control herself (93; ch. 3). The relatively carefree days of his childhood have yielded to an emotionally straitening form of middle-class deportment, behavior that will become a primary subject at Salem House, a school that surely has at least this value in common with that which trained the Heeps. Humility, as well as a paraded rectitude and piety, can be shallow covers for a dreary tyranny.

In his marriage to Dora, David collides with the opposite threat to deportment: the irresponsibility that Dora imports from her father and Norwood. She is as hopeless in dealing with servants and merchants as she is in mastering cookery books, keeping the keys, or overseeing the accounts. The Micawbers' carefree style, while refreshing, is not an antidote to the harsh demands of responsibility. Neither is Betsey's cottage fully protected against any threatening donkeys. The genuine propriety of Annie Strong's behavior does not safeguard her from being attacked for seeming breaches. There are neither safe havens nor safe conducts.

Two dinners stand out as comments on class. When David is invited to the Waterbrooks's, it is presumably the sort of affair an up-and-coming young professional would find useful and attractive, if not exactly pleasurable. The dinner, in retrospect, however,

> was very long, and the conversation was about the Aristocracy—and Blood. Mrs. Waterbrook repeatedly told us, that if she had a weakness, it was Blood.
>
> It occurred to me several times that we had should have got on better, if we had not been quite so genteel. We were so exceedingly genteel, that our scope was very limited.   (433; ch. 25)

Assuming the role of host himself and cajoling his landlady Mrs. Crupp to serve a proper dinner to his friends in his new quarters turns out even less satisfactorily for David. Sodden indecorousness replaces the tedium of gentility. Behaving middle class resembles being on a teeter-totter: you risk swinging in extreme directions. More agreeable than either of these responses is the openness and sincerity that accompany the meals shared by the Peggottys or Micawbers, where there is little concern with class or display. Betsey's readiness to forgo the accoutrements of genteel manners (including financial security) likewise demonstrates her real worth and strength.

Mr. Spenlow's reaction to David's interest in Dora also serves to expose social pretenses. He chastises David, asking, "Have you considered my daughter's station in life, the projects I may contemplate for her advancement, the testamentary intentions I may have with reference to her?" (614; ch. 38). He rejects his clerk as unsuitable for Dora, for whom he has greater expectations. (Spenlow's attitude is at base not all that different from Murdstone's, who, in his way, presumably loved Clara, but after her death has no difficulty looking to a new marriage to raise his position.) All the while, in fact, father (and then daughter) occupy a decidedly precarious position, one every bit as insubstantial as Micawber's. Spenlow's advantage is that his façade, though vacuous, postpones exposure until he dies—ironically intestate. Though the respectable, if marginally solvent, Spenlow declares how carefully he has considered his own worldly position (615), it is the irresponsible, vagabondish Micawber who manages to establish himself in Australia.

There are other passing comments in the book about class—Steerforth's patronizing remark on the quaintness of Yarmouth and those he mixes with there (376; ch. 21), Jack Maldon's callous account about the people "always being hungry and discontented somewhere" (587; ch. 36), but they only reinforce a motif that is part of the texture of the world of *David Copperfield*. Dickens is not simply determined to punctuate his novel with reflections of his audience. He is principally interested in this class, and he systematically embeds his misgivings about it in David's memoir.

Dickens conveys these misgivings by lacing the story with instructive, admonishing contrasts, some of which I have already touched on. Keys are famously iconic for having one's household under control (a good thing!), and yet: Jane Murdstone is offensive in her expropriating of them, Dora inadequate in her toying with them, and Agnes competent without ever having to mention or show them. Cookery books and manuals present a similar paradox: useless to those who need them. Murdstone's firmness is odious; David's attempt to form Dora is kindly and retreats before her reality. Jane's suspicion of servants is paranoiac; Dora's efforts are hapless to the point of corrupting them. Reading and stories can be a horror under the punishing aegis of Murdstone or a delight as told by David (young or adult).

Very like the way these images prove to be double-edged is Dickens's rendering of values traditionally associated with the middle class. The dedication to work is undercut by the examples of Uriah Heep, Spenlow, Micawber, and even David. Diligence, particularly if it happens to be honest, may get you a home, but the recommended forms of labor lack appeal or emotional satisfaction. David's art, alone, seems satisfying as a profession. And even the homes that sustained effort should earn are serially exposed as inadequate, besieged, chaotic, or, in the case of David and Agnes's, etherealized beyond earthly warmth and passion. The world of *David Copperfield* is better at lampooning passionate involvement than at affirming its value. Again, families and children are at best a mixed and tepid quantity. The money that sustains a mercantile society is also suspect. Micawber's profligacy is not only more entertaining than Murdstone's frugality or Heep's zeal to embezzle his way up the social order, it is also more acceptable than the financial pretense of Spenlow's Norwood or the corrupting effect of the way Mrs. Steerforth funds her son. Spenlow happily mills among magistrates; Steerforth is presented as if one; Micawber actually succeeds as one in Australia. Labels, surfaces, and ''virtues'' alike, largely class concerns, decompose into ambiguity.

The examples proliferate and a pattern is perceptible. There is no question of Dickens's identification with and deep interest in the middle class. That is his world. There is also no doubt of his critique. Well aware of the limitations and extremes to which this vigorous, bounding group is liable, he appears to lament the lack of a sensible, intelligent compromise or via media, one that avoided the tunnel-visioned greed and the emotional stultification that seem almost endemic across society, especially its middle ranks. David's esthetic and intellectual perspective enables him to record its foibles and vulgarities, but also to hope for some advance from all of that energy and industry. Still, Uriah Heep is not entirely wrong-headed in railing at the dishonesty of his lower-class schooling in obsequiousness (829; ch. 52), though Dickens would certainly urge other lessons than the misguided ones he draws. As Clara early discovered, it is a troublesome and uncomfortable world (95; ch. 4). Dickens, an artist solidly entrenched within an undeniably vibrant, but chafing bourgeois society, is exasperated and partially alienated by it. But, as his own vitality and humor suggest, he is tentatively hopeful that from David's artistic achievements and modest, orderly domicile progress may be made toward greater civility and emotional expansiveness. Granted, the balance is left tilting toward the side of skepticism; we have seen too much misconduct to envision a happy chastening of humankind out of its follies, including the follies of class.

WORKS CITED

Dickens, Charles. *David Copperfield*. Ed. Trevor Blount. Harmondsworth: Penguin, 1966. Rptd. 1988.

Gilmour, Robin. *The Idea of the Gentleman in the Victorian Novel*. London: George Allen and Unwin, 1981.

Morris, Pam. *Dickens's Class Consciousness: A Marginal View*. New York: St. Martin's, 1991.

Palmer, William J. *Dickens and New Historicism*. New York: St. Martin's, 1997.

Vanden Bossche, Chris R. "Cookery, not Rookery: Family and Class in *David Copperfield*." *David Copperfield* and *Hard Times*. Ed. John Peck. New York: St. Martin's, 1995, 31–57. Rptd. from *Dickens Studies Annual* 15 (1986), 87–109.

Williams, Raymond. *The English Novel; From Dickens to Lawrence*. New York: Oxford UP, 1970.

Dickens from a Postmodern Perspective: Alfonso Cuaron's *Great Expectations* for Generation X

Shari Hodges Holt

This essay examines director Alfonso Cuaron's 1998 film Great Expectations *as a cinematic "reading" that dramatizes previously unrecognized interpretive potentials of its literary source. Radically re-envisioning Charles Dickens's novel for a late-twentieth-century American audience, Cuaron's adaptation demonstrates the particular relevance of Dickens's Victorian narrative for postmodern generations. I introduce the film's postmodern aesthetics by discussing the movie's startling contemporary transformations of Dickens's plot and characters, as well as the film's bizarre pastiche of production projects (including the creation of two stylistically eclectic soundtrack CDs based on both the movie and Dickens's novel). The essay then illuminates the postmodern potential of Dickens's text that makes such a cinematic interpretation viable by detailing the similarities between Pip's narrative of disillusionment and the cultural experience of the first truly postmodern generation, "Generation X," the audience at which Cuaron targeted his film. The film's transformation of Dickens's protagonist into the aspiring Gen X artist Finnegan Bell astutely reconfigures the novel's theme of the quest for identity in terms of the postmodern crisis of representation and transmutes Dickens's critique of the Victorian gentleman into a comment on the postmodern cult of celebrity. The essay concludes that the parallels Cuaron's film evokes between Pip and Generation X allow*

Dickens Studies Annual, Volume 38, Copyright © 2007 by AMS Press, Inc. All rights reserved.

us to reinterpret Dickens's narrative from a new and uniquely contemporary perspective.

If, as film critic Neil Sinyard attests, the art of adapting literature to film concerns "interpretation more than reproduction" (117), a cinematic adaptation can be considered an interpretive reading of the original literary text, a "critical essay" in which filmmakers adapt the literary material to their own approach, thereby throwing "new light on the original" (Sinyard 117). An excellent example of such a cinematic reading that dramatizes the previously unrecognized interpretive potentials of its literary source is director Alfonso Cuaron's 1998 film *Great Expectations*, which radically re-envisions Charles Dickens's novel for a late-twentieth-century American audience, demonstrating the particular relevance of Dickens's Victorian narrative for postmodern generations.

The film updates and relocates the original tale from the English marshes and nineteenth-century London to Florida's Gulf Coast and 1990s New York. Dickens's plot and central characters undergo similar, sometimes startling, transmogrification. Miss Havisham, Dickens's mad spinster immured in the darkness of her decaying mansion since her lover jilted her on their wedding day, becomes Nora Driggers Dinsmoor (Anne Bancroft), the aging, absurdly melodramatic "drama queen" caught in a perpetual performance of "Besame Mucho," as she dances the decades away on her ruined Florida estate, Paradiso Perduto. Dickens's protagonist Pip, the blacksmith's apprentice who longs to become a gentleman and win the nonexistent heart of Miss Havisham's adopted daughter Estella, finds his postmodern reincarnation in Finn (Ethan Hawke), the poor aspiring artist from the Florida Keys who is disillusioned through his frustrating sexual encounters with Estella and his humiliating initiation into the Manhattan art world. Abel Magwitch, the criminal fugitive who becomes Pip's secret benefactor after Pip aids him in an attempted escape, is transformed into convicted mob hitman Arthur Lustig (Robert De Niro), who clandestinely finances Finn's escape from Florida and entrance into the art world only to undermine his success with the revelation that he himself purchased all the paintings in Finn's sold-out opening exhibit.

Paradoxically, these extreme alterations recall the classic text, evoking that postmodern nostalgia typical of the "crisis in historicity" (Jameson 25) that accompanied the demise of modernist concepts of realism and historical progress. As Fredric Jameson notes, for the postmodern world, the only realism left "is a 'realism' that is meant to derive from the shock of . . . slowly becoming aware of a new and original historical situation in which we are condemned to seek History by way of our own pop images and simulacra of that history, which itself remains forever out of reach" (25). Cuaron's film replaces the realism of the nineteenth-century novel with this postmodern sense of historical dislocation by relocating Dickens's narrative within a new context of wildly diverse American pop-culture references. The film recalls numerous American tales of coming-of-age and cultural disillusionment, such as *Huckleberry Finn*; De Niro's mobster films; the movies *The Graduate* (which also starred Bancroft) and *Sunset Boulevard*, both of which focused on a young protagonist's scathing encounter with an aging seductress; and *Reality Bites*, the 1990s film about young-adult angst that made Ethan Hawke the "posterboy" of Generation X (Hawke qtd. in Hobson, "Interview"), the twenty- to thirty-something audience at whom this *Great Expectations* happened to be targeted.

This "Hollywood Update" of Dickens's text (Sterritt 16) thus typifies what Fredric Jameson terms the "nostalgia film," a postmodern cinematic genre in which the "desperate attempt to appropriate a missing past is now refracted through the iron law of fashion change and the emergent ideology of the generation" (19). Nostalgia films embody a pop-culture vision (or "re-vision") of the past adapted to the cultural tastes of the current audience, whether in the form of "the fashion-plate historicist films" (Jameson xvii), those "historical picturesque" adaptations that represent a nostalgic "fetishization of authenticity" (Johnston) in their painstaking attempts to recreate the appearance of a former time and place, or the "Hollywood Updates" that appeal to current fashions by contemporizing classic narratives, incorporating the nostalgic and the experimental to appropriate and transform canonical texts into pop-culture commodities for our consumption.[1] As an updated classic, Cuaron's film fuses disparate elements into a cultural pastiche, resulting in the "erasure of the historical boundaries between high and low culture" that is characteristic of postmodern cinema (Connor 178) and postmodern aesthetics in general. And, as I shall argue, nostalgia films such as Cuaron's *Great Expectations* are often able to elucidate past texts in new and vitally creative ways.

The various production projects behind this film created an artistic hodgepodge that defied cultural boundaries with unlikely and innovative combinations. Cuaron, a Mexican filmmaker who made his Hollywood debut with a relatively faithful adaptation of Frances Hodgson Burnett's *A Little Princess* (1996), collaborated (with some input from playwright David Mamet) on the *Great Expectations* screenplay with Mitch Glazer, screenwriter for *Scrooged*, the 1988 comedic deconstruction of *A Christmas Carol* starring Bill Murray. The visual design for Cuaron's *Great Expectations* also mingled art and popular culture, utilizing new bodies of work from Italian painter Francesco Clemente and fashion designer Donna Karan. The film's musical score similarly united artists from diverse backgrounds to produce not one but *two* albums of soundtrack music—*Great Expectations: The Score*, which Patrick

Doyle, composer of film scores in the classical symphonic style, recorded with jazz and classical artists; and *Great Expectations: The Album*, for which Doyle collaborated with both unknown and famous musicians from the alternative rock world, resulting in an eclectic range of vocal and instrumental performances. The startling mixture of musical styles on both albums, however, purposely evoked themes from both the novel and the film.[2] The film also spawned its own novelization (*not* by Charles Dickens) and numerous entertainment websites, many of which bore links to downloadable e-texts of Dickens's original novel. Therefore, this film enterprise was indeed, as Cuaron described it, "an elaboration more than an adaptation" (qtd. in James), or as Gwyneth Paltrow (Estella) put it, "a classic on acid" (qtd. in Hobson, "Date").

But is this postmodern mutation of Dickens's text a soulless simulacrum or a viable interpretation of the original? Does the film merely cannibalize the text to create marketable commodities for its Generation X audience, the MTV generation who can program a VCR but supposedly can't read a book? Or does the film legitimately re-envision the original text to elucidate its themes for a new generation? To answer these questions, we must consider the postmodern possibilities inherent in Dickens's novel and how Cuaron's film renders these possibilities in cinematic terms.

The Postmodern Dickens

First, what features of Dickens's fiction make such a postmodern translation conceivable? Possible connections between Dickens and postmodernism were virtually ignored in Dickens's scholarship until recent studies by Victorianist Jay Clayton. In "Dickens and the Genealogy of Postmodernism," Clayton notes that while Dickens criticism has played a significant role in the development of various theoretical discourses, the study of Dickens and other Victorian novelists is conspicuously absent from the theorizing of postmodernism. Speculating that the recognition of postmodern features in Dickens's fiction would call into question the postmodern dismissal of "causal and developmental issues" ("Genealogy" 190), Clayton asserts, "We must recognize that postmodernism is not the dawning of a new age but the realization of certain possibilities within Western society that were salient even in the time of Charles Dickens" ("Genealogy" 195). Clayton parallels features of postmodernism with characteristics of Dickens's fiction, from his "dispersed and decentered" characters ("Genealogy" 187), to the indiscriminate energy of his work and his "relish for parody" and the "carnivalesque" ("Genealogy" 188). Clayton's book *Charles Dickens in Cyberspace: The Afterlife of the Nineteenth Century in Postmodern Culture* expands on these ideas and embarks on an exhaustive examination of the parallels between major cultural figures of the nineteenth and twentieth centuries, beginning with Dickens "as a representative of larger cultural patterns" that suggest a "hidden or repressed connection" between postmodernism and nineteenth-century culture (5).

In his essay "Is Pip Postmodern? Or, Dickens at the End of the Twentieth Century," reprinted as a chapter in *Charles Dickens in Cyberspace*, Clayton turns his attention to *Great Expectations* in particular, arguing that it "mixes cultural signs from different periods as persuasively as any postmodern text" (621). Clayton discerns within the novel

> traces of at least five different epochs, each competing with the others for cultural space: (1) the "feudal" freehold of Wemmick's castle; (2) the preindustrial capitalism of Joe's forge; (3) the "Victorian" middle-class values of Pip's mature years, with their clear connections to the fortunes of empire; (4) the "modern" alienation that splits Wemmick into twin selves; and (5) the "postmodern" world of simulacra and pastiche.   (623)

In Clayton's view, Wemmick, living in his "theme park version of feudal England" (622) with his prized collection of oddities, is the most postmodern character of *Great Expectations* because he becomes a veritable celebration of the simulacrum, whereas Pip fails to foreshadow postmodernism because he "matures into a thoroughly up-to date middle-class Victorian" (621). Wemmick responds to the alienation of early capitalism by embracing cheerfully a life of fragmentation and pastiche; Pip, on the other hand, finally reacts to the dehumanizing, isolating effects of his society's materialistic ethos by espousing the high Victorian virtues of hard work and moral earnestness. However, while Clayton correctly associates the reformed Pip with the modernist values of nineteenth-century bourgeois humanism, he disregards the striking similarities between the narrative of Pip's disillusionment and the cultural experience of the first truly postmodern generation, the generation that American sociologists and demographers have deemed "Generation X." The resemblance of Pip's story to the biography of Generation X lends Dickens's text an additional postmodern potential upon which Cuaron's adaptation capitalizes, as I shall presently demonstrate.[3]

Pip and the Postmodern Generation X

Like Pip's inverted fairy tale, the story of this supposedly "lost" generation is marked by disenchantment. The term "Generation X" was coined by Canadian novelist Douglas Coupland in his 1990 novel of the same name to denote his fictional set of "socially disengaged" characters (Coupland) whose attitudes of frustration and withdrawal seemed to encapsulate an outlook shared by many North Americans born in the early 1960s. Historians William Strauss and Neil Howe characterized the mindset of the generation to which Coupland's characters belonged (born from 1961 to 1981) as distinguished by disillusionment and pragmatism (*Generations* 322) in contrast to the narcissism, self-satisfaction, and optimistic progressivism of the previous "Baby Boomer" generation (11, 30).[4] While Boomers grew up enjoying the prosperity and stability of the '50s and the euphoric idealism of the '60s, "Gen Xers," raised in an era of fragmented families, multi-media bombardment, and multi-cultural diversity, spent their formative years in a profoundly postmodern milieu.

Coming of age in the '70s and '80s "at a time when the consumption of drugs and alcohol was at its highest, when divorce rates seemed to signify the end of the institution of marriage, when large numbers of pregnancies ended in abortion," and when layoffs and corporate downsizing indicated severe economic recession (Cheung 106), Generation X responded to cultural instability with defensive strategies—irony, sarcasm, self-mockery (Hornblower)—that utilized the parody, hyperbole, and self-referential qualities of postmodernism as a means of daily survival. Perceived in consequence as "whiners" and "slackers," and stereotyped as a generation of "low expectations" (*Generations* 12), they in fact became "street-smart survivalists clued into the game of life the way it really gets played, searching for simple things that work in a cumbersome society that offers little to them" (Strauss and Howe, *Retry* 11). But what does this generation of caustic, bitterly sophisticated youth have in common with a Dickensian protagonist who would ultimately evince patient industriousness, endurance, and self-denial?

Both Pip and the postmodern Generation X incurred substantial psychological damage in the formative years, resulting in eventual disillusionment, followed by a renewed but pragmatic hope for the future. In particular, the childhood years of Dickens's protagonist resemble the early experiences of many Gen Xers. A generation frequently labeled as "throwaways," facing "a Boom-driven culture quick to criticize or punish them but slow to take the time to find out what's really going on in their lives" (Strauss and Howe, *Generations* 332), could perhaps identify with Pip's childhood scenario of being "brought up by hand" by distant, disparaging elders who label him "naterally wicious" (*GE* 57; ch. 4). Pip asserts, "I was always treated as if I had insisted on being born, in opposition to the dictates of reason, religion, and morality, and against the dissuading arguments of my best friends" (*GE* 54; ch. 4), a complaint with which Gen Xers might easily sympathize. As Strauss and Howe note, no other group of young Americans in the twentieth century experienced such a "collective sense of missionlessness—of feeling worthless, wasted, even despised as a group. Of wondering why they were even born" (*Retry* 85).

Gen Xers confronted a hostile, fear-filled world made desolate by the blunders of a previous generation. Like Pip spending his childhood amidst the splendid decay of Satis House, paying the price for Miss Havisham's ruined romance, Generation X matured amidst the wreckage of the passing Boomer culture to become "the fall guy for mistakes made by others" (Strauss and Howe, *Retry* 32). Strauss and Howe's generalizations about Generation X, while sometimes overstated, echo cultural sentiments common in 1990s America: "Every phase-of-life has been fine, even terrific when Boomers entered it—and a wasteland when they left," and all Gen Xers "ever get to see are the ruins" (Strauss and Howe, *Retry* 43). Attendance at Miss Havisham's rotting wedding feast permanently scars Pip's and Estella's lives, just as a late arrival at the Boomers' cultural party left many Gen Xers feeling permanently encumbered with the mess created by their self-indulgent guardians.

Gen Xers tended to respond to their disappointment as Dickens's protagonist does—by becoming increasingly materialistic. With the attitude that "money means survival" (Strauss and Howe, *Retry* 320), many Gen Xers turned to mindless acquisition as a means of deadening the pain of low self-esteem and obscuring the prospect of an uncertain future. Thus, Gen Xers embraced the postmodern identity of the individual as consumer. Postmodern commodity culture offered them the attractions of a superficial environment in which material possessions could temporarily block out the emotional emptiness of their world. Pip, longing to escape his "coarse and common" existence, indulges in dreams of a wealthy benefactor who will provide him with gentlemanly leisure; young Gen X adults, unable to survive in a harsh economic environment, "boomeranged" back to the comfort of their parents' homes to take refuge in the ephemeral paradise of a subsidized existence and enjoy the luxury of possessions they could not afford on their own. They, like Pip, became trapped in the expectations of an affluence they would never truly experience.

Gen Xers also looked to the false glamor and hyperreality of mass media for escape, turning off the real world to turn on the TV, VCR, and PC. The hollow fictions offered by the "hypermodern" environments late-twentieth-century technology created are not dissimilar to the deceiving fancies of Pip's great expectations. A postmodern generation so awash in "virtual reality," nurtured by television as a replacement for broken family relationships, could find peculiar relevance in Pip's fascination with Dickens's "virtual woman" Estella, the pretty picture without substance. And a generation of youth who immersed themselves in virtual worlds and video games "in fantasized quest of fortune or death" (Strauss and Howe, *Generations* 323) would have experienced Pip's self-deluding fantasy of doing "all the shining deeds of the young Knight of romance, and marry[ing] the Princess" (*GE* 253; ch. 29).

Ultimately, however, Generation X was forced to admit that such longings are insubstantial, evasive fancies. But in a hyperreal world in which modernist concepts of reality no longer have any power, in a world that has deconstructed the subject and deflated the modernist ideal of individualism, how is it possible to establish a sustaining lifestyle and create a constructive identity? Generation X turned to what Albert Borgmann describes as an emerging postmodern alternative to the failed model of "rugged individualism"—"informed cooperation" (65). Recognizing the need for a more concrete, constructive course of action based upon pragmatics rather than impractical ideals or escapist dreams, Gen Xers determined to rebuild their society by bolstering interpersonal relations, a goal most apparent in their commitment to re-strengthen the family (Strauss and Howe, *Retry* 221). Seared in childhood by the effects of parental divorce and the devotion of their workaholic parents to careers over family, many Gen Xers worked hard "to shield their marriages from the risk and stress of their work lives" (Strauss and Howe, *Retry* 221).[5] Just as Pip, leaving the ruins of Satis House with the reformed Estella, sees "no shadow of another parting from her" (*GE* 493; ch. 59), Gen Xers, escaping the debris of the past, attempted to "ward off the darkness that has fallen over the relationship between the sexes and reinfuse it with something that really matters" (Strauss and Howe, *Retry* 148).

Gen Xers' pragmatic focus upon renewing personal relationships as a means of counteracting the enervating effects of postmodern hyperreality and restructuring a shattered world is not far removed from Dickens's ideology of personal benevolence as a means of combating the cruelties of early industrial capitalism. Following the failure of his expectations and his unsuccessful attempt to marry Biddy and return to Joe's forge, the chastened Pip is finally reunited with Herbert and his wife to work at an Egyptian branch of a British firm, a denouement that does evince " 'Victorian' middle-class values" with "clear connections to the fortunes of empire," as Jay Clayton attests ("Pip" 623); but it is also significant to note that Pip joins the company in Egypt not to fulfill imperialist dreams of fortune (Pip notes the company was never "a great House" and did not make "mints of money" [*GE* 489; ch. 58]), but to work with Herbert and witness the fruition of the one selfless act he had performed during the period of his expectations (Pip secretly financed Herbert's promotion and his marriage with Magwitch's and Miss Havisham's money). His industriousness is based as much upon his love for his friend as upon a newfound bourgeois work ethic. Thus, the mature Pip has more in common with a postmodern population than Clayton's study admits.

Generation X had to admit the hollowness of the American dream, just as Pip is forced to confront the emptiness of the Victorian gentlemanly ideal, but Gen Xers determined to replace that dream with better alternatives. Gen Xers came "to see there are many different alternatives, all equally valid" and consequently developed "a less judgmental, more expansive opinion of the various ways people choose to be" (Smith and Clurman 87). The "X" label of the undefined generation therefore came to signify the myriad possibilities of postmodern identity which offer renewed, if ambiguous, hope in the quest for selfhood.

While Pip ultimately turns to bourgeois values to recover a foundation for his existence, "the discourse of subjectivity," for the postmodern generation, "has been cut loose from its moorings in bourgeois individualism" (Huyssen 215). Still, the quest for identity in the era of advanced capitalism shares significant features with the quest of Dickens's protagonist during the early capitalist phase. Generation X proceeded through a similar process of dream, disillusionment, and resurrected aspiration based in part on empathy with others. This shared pattern made it possible for Cuaron's late-1990s adaptation of Dickens's text to address postmodern concerns. Cuaron's *Great Expectations* is able to use Dickens's nineteenth-century bildungsroman as a template for a late-twentieth-century tale of self-discovery, a story that examines the difficulties a contemporary generation faces in the construction of a postmodern self.

Cuaron's *Great Expectations*

How does Cuaron's adaptation translate Pip's coming-of-age narrative into specifically postmodern terms? The film's transformation of Dickens's protagonist into the artist Finnegan Bell reconfigures the novel's theme of the quest for identity in terms of the postmodern crisis of representation. The postmodern experience of identity as a fiction constructed from multiple images is introduced at the film's opening when the adult Finn announces, "I'm not gonna tell the story the way it happened. I'm gonna tell it the way I remember it." The announcement occurs as we watch the child Finn sketching his impressions of his Florida surroundings. The peaceful child is then suddenly accosted by the escaped convict who will become a central figure in his art and life. Following this galvanizing encounter, Finn turns from sketching his surroundings to depicting human figures, as he struggles to capture his memories and construct his own identity by painting the various characters who have impact on his life. Susan Johnston notes "the seemingly endless layers of re-creation that characterize this film," visualizing Finn's ongoing attempts to recreate himself and his relationships with others through the images of his art. And as the eccentric, exaggerated characters in Dickens's text highlight and critique features of Pip's more complex personality, the characters who appear most often in Finn's paintings similarly call into question Finn's endeavors at self-definition.

The most striking example is the mad Miss Dinsmoor, who dramatizes the hyper-real extreme of Finn's postmodern quest for identity. Abandoned by her lover years ago, Dinsmoor, in her heavy make-up and retro fashions, like Miss Havisham in her faded wedding gown, attempts to stop time and immortalize her heartbreak; but she does so in a manner that robs her experience of emotional validity. She has become a hideous, painted simulation of lost youth who threatens to seduce the hero into her world of broken-hearted impotence.

As a child Finn first encounters her when she invites him to her ruined estate, Paradiso Perduto, to dance. When Finn enters her room, he notices a record player on a table littered with innumerable records of "Besame Mucho." The turntable spins relentlessly, playing one version of the song after another as Miss Dinsmoor madly dances with the bewildered boy. She later hires Finn to dance each week with Estella: a passionless exercise for the girl, but an agonizing delight for Finn; and as they spin through Dinsmoor's ruined ballroom year after year—surrounded by the strains of "Besame Mucho" and encouraged by Dinsmoor's wildly melodramatic cries to "Feel it! Feel it!"—their routine becomes a never-ending satiric repetition of the relationship that destroyed Dinsmoor's life.

Anne Bancroft's deliberately campy performance as Miss Dinsmoor thus depicts her as forever trapped in parodic self-dramatization. A later scene shows Dinsmoor applying her clownish makeup while seated at a vanity surrounded by mirrors—a potent image of postmodern simulation and fragmentation. Finn, now an adult, has come to thank her for financing his first art show in New York (a totally erroneous assumption on his part). The scene stresses the falsity of Dinsmoor's identity and motives. As she turns to meet Finn, her face is revealed as a garish, painted mask framed by bright red hair—"I've gone red!" she proudly declares. The surrounding mirrors distort her image with an almost fun-house effect, as one cleverly angled shot makes it appear that Finn is addressing the reflection rather than the woman. Another shot pictures Finn reflected in the mirror beside Dinsmoor, suggesting how false and ephemeral his own identity has become under her influence. And like Miss Havisham, who supports Pip's self-deception, deliberately appearing to be his fairy godmother rather than the witch who has cursed his life, Miss Dinsmoor relishes the false role Finn's hollow aspirations have assigned to her. "I expect an invitation to your opening—your show," she minces, as she applies a fake beauty mark to her face while gazing at her ridiculous reflection.

From the beginning of their relationship, Miss Dinsmoor works to sabotage Finn's artistic attempts to establish a productive identity. When they first meet, she tries to initiate Finn into her sterile parody of emotion by asking him to draw her emotionless niece Estella, whom she is training to break men's hearts.[6] Flippantly ripping a piece of wallpaper from the decaying walls of her bedroom, Miss Dinsmoor hands it to Finn to act as his canvas, an action that belittles his art and symbolizes how, from this moment, he will base his art and his quest for selfhood upon a decaying foundation. Estella reluctantly sits for the portrait, not bothering to conceal her contempt for Finn's artistic abilities, but still projecting an alluring aura, while Miss Dinsmoor continually calls Finn's attention to Estella's beauty in a deliberate attempt to provoke his desire. As Finn draws the girl, the film progresses through a montage of rapidly edited shots depicting fragments of Estella's features, while "Besame Mucho" crescendos in the background.

This scene employs a traditional cinematic means of depicting the female body, in the words of feminist critic Laura Mulvey, "stylized and fragmented by close-ups . . . [as] the direct recipient of the spectator's look" (835), a means of representation that objectifies the woman, dividing her into delectable pieces for male consumption. The sequence echoes a scene in the novel in which Miss Havisham places expensive jewels on Estella's breast and hair, thereby displaying her to Pip as a valuable object to be desired and possessed (*GE* 118; ch. 11). Similarly, Miss Dinsmoor exhibits Estella as an object for Finn's artistic consumption, foreshadowing the dangerous commodification of self upon which Finn will base his expectations in the Manhattan art world.

Later in a teasing encounter when the two protagonists are adolescents, Estella introduces the idea that Finn should take his art to Manhattan, the setting that will typify the superficial lifestyle of hypermodernity. Leaving a cocktail party to go "slumming" on a whim, Estella visits Finn's house where she discovers numerous examples of his art (dominated by portraits of herself). After telling him that he must go to New York, "the center of the art world," if he wants to avoid ending up "painting coconuts for tourists," Estella then initiates a frustrating sexual encounter of masturbation which she abruptly terminates by walking out haughtily before the climax. The image of simulated sex surrounded by simulations of the beloved in the portraits of Estella that adorn Finn's bedroom walls suggests the emotionally barren foundation upon which Estella will lead Finn to ground his artistic attempts at self-definition. When he discovers the next day that Estella has moved to Paris, Finn abandons his art, giving up further attempts to connect with the world through his paintings, until years later an offer from an anonymous, wealthy patron tempts Finn into resuming his art in preparation for a Manhattan gallery exhibition.

The novel's critique of bourgeois materialism and Victorian class conflict translates surprisingly well into the film's satire on the New York art scene. While Pip travels to London to be educated as a gentleman and enter bourgeois society, Finn travels to Manhattan, in his words, "to reinvent" himself through the powers of what sociologist John Hannigan has termed the postmodern "Fantasy City," the revitalized city of the 1980s and 1990s that

embraced the worlds of art and entertainment to create a pastiche of popular
and high culture attractions, a spectacle of simulated experience offered to
the consumer in a manner that indelibly blurred "the boundaries of commerce
and culture" (55). The film's imagery emphasizes that Finn is being born
into such a hyperreal space when he leaves Florida for New York. The camera
follows Finn at the airport as he travels in slow motion down the entry
corridor to the airplane, leaving Joe, his impoverished childhood guardian
behind him. A piece of visual trickery makes us believe we see the plane
take off, but the camera pulls back to reveal we are watching Finn play with
a toy plane, simulating his flight to New York as he now sits in a dirty subway
car. We see the city as a landscape of extremes as Finn traverses rain-swept,
dangerous streets to his dingy hotel room where, dwarfed by an extreme
long shot, he looks from his tiny window onto a paradoxically glamorous,
glittering vista.

Just as Pip attempts to cloak the squalor of his London lodgings with his
expectations of future fortune by making gentlemanly purchases that lead
him deeper into debt, Finn camouflages the squalor of his immediate surroundings in fantasies of future celebrity, wrongly imagining that Miss Dinsmoor
has financed his journey so that he will become a rich and famous artist and
"have it all." Finn narrates: "And I looked out on the great city, which held
it all, and it was that close, and it was mine."

But Finn has not entirely relinquished his artistic quest to the artificial
promise of the Fantasy City. As he begins to create pieces in preparation for
his gallery show, he finds that he can still construct a worthwhile reality for
himself through his art. He sits in Central Park, sketching the people and
objects he sees and discovers, "I could still draw. Nothing had lessened it,
as much as I'd abused it, as much as I'd abandoned it. It was a gift, and it
was still mine. And everything else was less real. What could it mean, that
picture of the world? But when it's true, we recognize it—in ourselves, in
others, we recognize it." However, just as Finn begins to recover an emotional
significance for his art and rediscover "the world of eloquent things" (Borgmann 6), Finn's false muse re-enters his life.

Suddenly appearing in the park where Finn has been sketching, Estella
surprises him with an invitation to a club to meet her friends, wealthy art
patrons. The club is a postmodern rendition of the gentleman's club Pip
joins in London—"The Finches of the Grove," an organization with an
"object . . . I have never divined," Pip admits (*GE* 292; ch. 34), providing a
pastime for the idle rich that totally lacks constructive purpose. The Finches
congregate only to demonstrate their lavish lifestyles—to "dine expensively
once a fortnight, to quarrel among themselves as much as possible after
dinner, . . . to cause six waiters to get drunk on the stairs" (*GE* 292; ch. 34),
and to argue over women as if they were possessions. When Bentley Drummle, Estella's wealthy but brutal suitor, dares to toast her name at one of the

group's meetings, Pip defies him, claiming Drummle has no right to claim a connection with Estella, only to be humiliated later when Estella sends a note to the club acknowledging the acquaintance. The so-called "gentleman's" club of Dickens's text thus satirizes the materialistic values of the society Pip has entered and emphasizes Estella's connection with those values.

The sequence at the art club in Cuaron's film similarly stresses the mercenary principles of the New York art scene and demonstrates how Estella is directing Finn back towards such superficial standards. As Finn enters the club, rapid edits of an elaborately painted ceiling, ornate carvings, and classical sculptures reveal the lavish, overbearing, and emotionally empty style of art that the club members patronize; art is a commodity valued only as an indication of wealth and social status. While Finn meets Estella's companions, we hear one of them (whom Finn later discovers to be Estella's rich lover) telling a story of how Michelangelo realized his artistic talent *only* because he secured a wealthy patron. After Estella introduces Finn as her "first love" and compliments him on the portrait he drew of her when they were children, Finn gathers courage to offer to paint Estella again, a proposal that represents Finn's desire to establish a legitimate relationship with Estella, just as the paintings of his childhood signified Finn's attempts to make meaning from his relationships with others. Estella immediately undermines Finn's overture, however, by turning to her companion Walter, the man Finn now perceives is Estella's boyfriend, and declaring, "What do you think, darling?" Cruelly invalidating her previous acknowledgment of an emotional connection between herself and Finn, she belittles his art by offering the proposed portrait as a commodity for the consumption of Finn's wealthy rival.

Throughout the scene, dialogue intimating how Finn is expected to "prostitute" his art to achieve success in New York further underscores the degradation of Finn's artistic enterprise. As a club member describes how she once slept with a famous artist who painted her, a story that she now apparently circulates only for the status it brings her in the art community, Walter asks Finn if he will charge "by the inch, or by the hour" for painting Estella's portrait. When Finn, shocked and confused, reveals he has actually never sold a painting, an immediate cut to the club's exterior shows Finn leaving alone, his humiliation highlighted by a long shot of the building's ostentatious facade towering over him. The crowning insult occurs when the maitre d' follows him to retrieve the club jacket that Finn forgot to leave behind.

The blatantly mercenary basis of artistic standards among the art patrons and the comparisons of artistic creation to prostitution and empty sexual relations suggest how the art scene of the postmodern Fantasy City will sabotage Finn's endeavors to create worthwhile human relationships through art. Finn participates in this degradation of his work when he joins Erica Thrall, the gallery owner who will sell his paintings, in an intense publicity campaign to market himself and his art that results in Finn's becoming famous before his art is even exhibited. Thus, Finn plays upon what John Hannigan sees as a central feature of the 1990s Fantasy City, the exploitation of celebrity as a cultural commodity for asserting status and identity (68–70). In this manner, the film transmutes the Victorian concept of the gentleman critiqued in the novel into the postmodern cult of celebrity, revealing both to be empty constructs founded upon shallow materialism.

Two corresponding scenes from the novel and film expose the damaging results of such superficial self-constructs. In the novel, when Pip visits the office of the criminal lawyer who is his London guardian, the office clerk, Mr. Wemmick, exhibits for Pip the death masks of two famous murderers who were the lawyers' clients, and proudly displays valuable mourning brooches and rings that these clients presented to him before their executions. Revealing that he has taken many such gifts from the condemned, he cheerfully notes his motto: "Get hold of portable property" (235; ch. 24). The masks and mourning jewelry, grim simulations of death and grief, portend Pip's association with the inherent criminality of a capitalist culture that is built upon the sufferings of poor wretches such as the criminal Magwitch, who is the secret author of Pip's wealth.

In a corresponding scene in the film, Erica Thrall, while nonchalantly closing the sale of a Picasso over her cellphone, leads Finn on a tour through her gallery's latest exhibit, which consists of rows of tall boxes, each with a hole in the center through which protrudes an enormous pregnant belly. Stopping by one of the boxes, she whacks the side, shouting, "Bellies out!" The resulting movement and groans from within the boxes reveal that the pregnant bellies are in fact real women trapped in an artistic simulation exhibited for the gallery patrons' consumption. Just as the death masks and mourning jewelry, fragmentary simulations of death, suggest in Dickens's text the dehumanization of the human subject at the dawning of commodity culture, the pregnant bellies, fragmentary simulations of life, suggest the fate of the subject in a postmodern culture in which identity is fragmented, commodified, and consumed in media images. The exhibit thus parodies Finn's own birth as a simulated subject in the hyperreal Manhattan art scene, foreshadowing how his very life, transmuted into the art by which he has constructed his identity, will be denigrated into a commodity.

Such mercenary standards of value lead to the phenomenon Fredric Jameson has termed the "waning of affect" in postmodern art, the loss of feeling caused by the commodification of the human subject (10–11). An excellent example of the "waning of affect" in Finn's art and the "tensions between commodification and essentialization" (Johnston) that dominate Finn's artistic endeavors throughout the film is the transformation of his painting of his Uncle Joe into a commodity used to gain wealth and celebrity. In a sequence structured on multiple layers of simulation, the painting that had once been an emotionally meaningful representation of Finn's admiration for Joe becomes instead a mercenary tool that Finn callously employs to enhance his fame and fortune. The sequence opens with Finn reciting his life story into a tape recorder for an interview that will promote his New York exhibit. As he exaggerates and sensationalizes the events of his life, the setting changes to Finn's Manhattan studio, where he is now telling the same story to a girl (evidently his date) in an effort to impress her. Throughout his tale, he shows her the portraits of people from his life that will appear in his exhibit, inventing new identities for the subjects that enhance the celebrity effect of his own biography. When she asks about the painting of Joe, instead of praising his uncle for his unfailing, loving support, Finn lies and tells the girl that he was a notorious drug smuggler who contributed to Finn's childhood unhappiness and finally died of an overdose.

After Finn has in effect "murdered" his childhood friend by commodifying him in his art, Joe embarrasses Finn by unexpectedly returning to life at the opening of Finn's exhibit. Finn has attempted to divest his art of its humanity but finds that the human subject returns like an avenging ghost. In a scene that approximates Joe's visit to Pip's London lodgings in chapter 27 of the novel, Finn's uncle shows up without warning at the gallery reception foolishly clad in a green-ruffled rental tux but full of pride for Finn's achievements. Upon recognizing him, Finn's date and the other gallery patrons realize Finn's fabrication of his life story, but the deception ultimately does not matter to the gallery because the painting of Joe and all the other pieces in the exhibit sell. However, Joe's love for Finn and his inherent dignity despite the embarrassing nature of the situation reveal all the noble human qualities that Finn's success has sacrificed. And Finn's shame at his loving friend's humble appearance and awkward behavior denotes the degree to which he has internalized the values of the New York art scene. Finally, like Joe in Dickens's text, who realizes that "I'm wrong out of the forge, the kitchen, or off th' meshes" (*GE* 246; ch. 27), Finn's uncle recognizes that he does not belong in the setting of Finn's new existence and retreats with a blessing, leaving behind an impression of his own solid worth and the hollow sham of the world Finn has adopted in his place.

Throughout his New York adventure, however, Finn never completely loses the longing for a human basis to his art. His undying desire to unite his art with meaningful human interaction is revealed ironically in his continuing relationship with the "inhuman" Estella. In a scene that echoes the portrait session from Finn's childhood, Estella comes to Finn unannounced and demands that he paint her portrait. As she displays herself before him, this time in the nude, the film again utilizes musical crescendo and rapid edits of her body parts as Finn consumes her, pouring his passion onto the canvas, with the result that the portrait session becomes a simulated sexual encounter. When Estella waltzes out in the middle of the session, the frustrated Finn races after her, demanding, "What is it like not to feel anything?" The question intimates that despite his temporary seduction by the shallow glamor of the commercial art world, Finn is still attempting to use his artistic simulations to establish emotional intimacies with others.

Claiming that "Estella appears in his [Finn's] drawings the way he wants her to be—not the way she is," Michael K. Johnson interprets this scene as Finn's refusal to acknowledge Estella's self-definition; according to Johnson, the portraits visualize Finn's attempt to objectify Estella for his own pleasure. On the contrary, Finn's frustration in the portrait scene indicates that in his relationship with Estella, Finn wants not to consume an object, but to interact with a person. Estella, however, objectifies herself. While Finn offers her emotional validity through his paintings, Estella views the portrait session as a means of commodifying herself to entrap men in emotionless relationships. We later learn that Estella has used the portrait session, not only to tease Finn, but also to arouse the jealousy of her noncommittal boyfriend and pressure him into a loveless marriage. In thus substituting a barren representation of herself for actual intimacy, the cinematic Estella embodies the heartlessness of Dickens's heroine in terms relevant to a postmodern generation scarred by divorce and failed relationships, a generation that came of age in a multi-media environment that encouraged the replacement of human relationships with hyperreal forms of experience.

However, Estella's response to Finn's question, "What is it like not to feel anything?" intimates that she recognizes her own behavior as a defense mechanism that has profoundly damaged her. In a rare manifestation of feeling, with tears in her eyes and a genuinely pained expression, she describes her situation to Finn: "Let's say there was a little girl. And from the time she could understand, she was taught to fear—let's say she was taught to fear daylight. She was taught that it was her enemy—that it would hurt her. And then one sunny day you ask her to go outside and play, and she won't. You can't be angry at her, can you?" Finn replies, "I know that little girl, and I saw the light in her eyes, and no matter what you say or do, that's still what I see." But Estella responds with a sad fatalism: "We are who we are. People don't change."

In this exchange, both Estella and Finn act as representatives of the postmodern Generation X, Estella expressing the angst and pessimism of late-twentieth-century youth who have been taught by the unsuccessful relationships of their parents to fear love and commitment, and Finn bespeaking the pragmatic hopes of this generation by suggesting that despite suffering and disillusionment, we can be self-inventing. Johnson interprets Finn's remarks as another indication of his denial of Estella's independent self, but rather than revealing the limitations of self-delusion, the scene allows Finn to present Estella with an alternative self laden with positive possibilities. While Johnson admits Estella's inability to "convey a concrete alternative portrait of who she is," Finn's construction of her is a revitalizing vision of warmth, growth, and transformation, a liberating option to the unproductive simulation of emotional life that Miss Dinsmoor has imposed upon her. His determination to view Estella as the little girl "with light in her eyes" and his continuing attempts to depict her in this manner through his paintings offer hope for Estella's eventual reformation. Pip's vain belief throughout his London sojourn that he will eventually "awaken the heart" within Estella (*GE* 265; ch. 29), a belief born of his notion that Miss Havisham has intended them for each other, reflects the self-deluding nature of his expectations; but Finn's belief in the possibility of constructing an emotionally fulfilling relationship suggests a viable alternative to the emptiness of postmodern existence.[7]

The film intimates Estella's movement toward this alternative through the light symbolism Cuaron employs in delineating her character. Her comparison of herself to the child who was taught to fear sunlight plays upon the light imagery from Dickens's text—Miss Havisham's refusal to allow the sunlight into Satis House and Pip's consequent association of her ward with the frosty stars that show "no help or pity in all the glittering multitude" (*GE* 80; ch. 7). Cuaron's imagery similarly envisions Estella's emotional sterility and lack of self-definition in terms of an aversion to daylight and warmth. The film continually depicts Estella as moving toward the clarity of brilliant light in moments of intimacy but then retreating into darkness. For instance, the first kiss Finn and Estella share as children in Miss Dinsmoor's mansion appears brilliantly backlit at a golden fountain to create a sensuous haze, followed by Estella's sudden retreat up the stairs into the mansion's shadows to become a dark silhouette on the landing. In the New York portrait scene, Estella, standing in a halo of sunlight in front of an open window, reveals her body to Finn, but only minutes later she is engulfed into the hotel's dingy darkness as she abruptly walks out of the session. When she tells Finn that she is going to marry Walter, Estella leads Finn from the brightness of a sunny day in Central Park into the darkness beneath a bridge where the two characters lose definition to be reduced to black silhouettes against the sunlit landscape beyond. After her revelation, Finn leaves Estella beneath the bridge, the camera tracking with him as he walks back into the sunlight while Estella's image disintegrates into a dark blur in the background.

The most striking contrast of light and dark imagery in relation to Estella's character occurs during the final sexual encounter between Finn and Estella in New York. Feeling that Estella's revelation about her intended marriage may have been a cry for help, a plea for Finn's assistance in redefining herself as an emotionally significant entity, Finn decides to make a last attempt to prevent the marriage and reconstruct Estella as a being of light and intimacy. He follows Estella and Walter to a restaurant, interrupts them at dinner, and takes Estella away to his studio where they make love. As they consummate their relationship, an overexposure dissolves the scene into a brilliant blaze of light. When Finn awakens, however, the darkness has returned. Estella leaves the bed and stands in front of the window with her back to Finn while looking out on the rainy night. A long shot portrays her naked body, once again a dark silhouette, as Estella tells him that she is leaving New York to visit her aunt. Although she promises that she will return for the opening of his exhibit, the imagery of the scene belies her, suggesting that she has again retreated from emotional commitment. When we next see her, she is leaving New York with Walter, flying away aboard a jet that disappears into the night sky.

Estella and Finn, however, eventually show signs of recovering from emotional impoverishment as they come to value human relationships, however fragile and painful, over the shallow self-constructs encouraged by the postmodern world. Finn is disillusioned with the glamorous identity he has attempted to construct when he realizes it has left him spiritually bankrupt. When Estella fails to attend his art opening, Finn discovers she has eloped with his rival, and his exhibit becomes a success only because Lustig, the mobster who financed it, buys out the entire show. However, while Lustig's revelation of himself as Finn's benefactor undermines Finn's artistic celebrity, it simultaneously affirms the emotional and relational power of his art. The fugitive has risked his life to return and witness the success of the child whose art inspired him. When Lustig is the victim of a mob hit and lies dying in Finn's arms, he reveals that he has kept Finn's childhood sketchbook as a token of the boy who befriended him. As Lustig lovingly caresses the sketches with bloodstained fingers, Finn's art regains the emotional value that it lost as a consumer commodity. When we next see Finn several years later, he has fulfilled Lustig's dream for him by going to Paris to continue his artistic endeavors with a more sober understanding of their human worth.

Estella evinces a similar realization of the importance of nurturing human relationships when she meets Finn in a final encounter that captures both the ambivalence and the hope of the novel's conclusion. Dickens originally ended the novel by allowing the protagonists to go their separate ways; his revised conclusion, however, ambiguously implies the possibility of a future union between them. They meet on Miss Havisham's ruined estate, where Estella reveals that the sufferings of her abusive marriage have taught her to appreciate the love Pip once offered. As they leave the estate, although Estella offers to "continue friends apart," Pip takes her hand, seeing "in all the broad expanse of tranquil light, . . . no shadow of another parting from her" (*GE* 493; ch. 59).

The film uses a similar contrast of light and shadow to imply the possible emotional rejuvenation of Finn and Estella. When Finn again encounters her at Paradiso Perduto, Estella now appears in a brilliant blaze of light. Tempered by motherhood and divorce, she has brought her daughter to view the ruins of her childhood home. When she asks Finn if he can forgive her, he replies, "Don't you know me?" He then narrates, "She did know me, and I knew her. . . . And the rest of it, it didn't matter. It was past. It was as if it had never been. There was just my memory of it." As Finn takes Estella's hand, there is no retreat into darkness; instead while dark clouds hover over them, they look out over a brightly sunlit sea suggesting the amorphous nature of their relationship and the numerous, if uncertain, possibilities of their future.[8]

As the conclusion of Dickens's novel offered readers a limited hope for affirming their humanity within the confines of Victorian England's dehumanizing, materialistic society, Cuaron's film implies for postmodern viewers that the contemporary quest for identity does not necessarily have to be an emotionally empty project. While acknowledging that we live in a world in which the self has become a fiction, Finn's final words suggest that the very indeterminacy of postmodern identity contains a world of expectations. The "X" of Generation X may signify lost hope and emotional withdrawal, but it also encompasses countless possibilities for human experience. By reenvisioning Dickens's tale of the ambiguous nature of human expectations from the perspective of this postmodern generation, Cuaron's film leaves us with the implication that perhaps we no longer need be determined by the empty endeavors of the Dinsmoors and Havishams of past generations, but can reinvent ourselves in more fulfilling ways.

NOTES

1. This type of nostalgia film (termed "counterpicturesque" by Susan Johnston) proved particularly popular with young audiences at the turn of the twentieth century, as evidenced by such films as *Clueless* (1995), the "valley-girl" adaptation of Austen's *Emma*, and the many Shakespeare adaptations transposed to contemporary settings and starring actors popular with Gen X audiences (e.g., the 2000 Ethan Hawke production of *Hamlet* and the 1999 teenaged-version of *The Taming of the Shrew*, *Ten Things I Hate About You*, with Julia Stiles and Heath Ledger). Johnston, proposing the "counterpicturesque film as a model for heritage adaptations" as opposed to the "historical picturesque" film that engages with the past only through a superficial "fidelity to appearance," attests that both types of adaptation emphasize "the role of connoisseurship in questions of fidelity," rewarding the "cultivated few" who are knowing enough to recognize the historical accuracy of visual detail in the picturesque adaptation or the

allusions to classic literature in the counterpicturesque. But Johnston ignores that the central target audience of the counterpicturesque film is not the "cultivated few" but a particularly young audience with a sophisticated knowledge not of past classics but of contemporary pop-culture media. The popularity of the counterpicturesque film in the late 1990s arose from the predominance of the visual image over the written word for those postmodern generations who grew up in a media-saturated environment. Particularly for Gen X and post-Gen X audiences, film has become a primary means of experiencing the arts and a popular medium for appropriating and commenting on elements of our cultural history.

2. Atlantic Records's promotional materials for the album and score deliberately emphasized the element of pastiche while stressing the thematic unity of the projects. The press release on Atlantic Records's official website described the genesis of the two soundtracks: "The filmmakers set out to enlist a diverse assortment of songwriters, with the priority that the musicians' creations mesh with the film's message." *Great Expectations: The Album* "includes all-new material from a number of today's hottest and most vital artists," including famous alternative rock musicians such as Tori Amos, Chris Cornell, and Stone Temple Pilots's Scott Weiland (accompanied by Sheryl Crow on the accordion, the website proudly asserts), and relative unknowns, such as the Verve Pipe, Poe, and Mono. "As if that weren't enough," the promotion declares, "*Great Expectations: The Album* features classic tracks from the Grateful Dead and Iggy Pop which also play into this retelling of Dickens' tale." The accompanying soundtrack, *Great Expectations: The Score*, is advertised as "an evocative and quirky score . . . highlighted by a cast of performers from the worlds of opera, classical, world-music, and jazz, including saxophonist James Carter, pianist Cyrus Chestnut, singer Cesaria Evora, guitarist John Williams, and famed soprano Kiri Te Kanawa." The press release concludes that this musical project is "pointing the way to a new ideal for future filmmakers interested in combining modern musical moods with traditional scores."

3. Historians William Strauss and Neil Howe initially identified Generation X as a segment of the United States population but later expanded their definition to cut across national and cultural boundaries. Still, the term "Generation X" is primarily associated with late-twentieth-century *American* youth. Similarly postmodernism has a "specifically American character" (Huyssen 190). Theorist Andreas Huyssen notes that postmodernism originated in the United States in the 1960s (the period that for Strauss and Howe also marked the birth of Generation X) at a time when Europe was experiencing a revival of modernism stemming from a more extensive recovery process following World War II (190–91). The shared origins of postmodernism and Generation X make the adaptation strategy of Cuaron's film particularly appropriate. The relocating and updating of Dickens's novel to 1990s America and the inclusion of Generation X protagonists are ideal adjustments for producing a postmodern reading of the text.

4. The same year that Coupland's book was published, Strauss and Howe proposed a generational theory of American history as a continuously repeating pattern of interaction among generations with distinct "peer personalities"—collective

mindsets determined by shared cultural experience. They distinguished four generational ''peer personalities'' that have followed each other throughout American history: the ''Idealist Generation'' (e.g., Baby Boomers), indulged in their
youth, then idealistic and self-absorbed in adulthood; the ''Reactive Generation''
(e.g., Generation X), under-protected and criticized in youth and pragmatic in
reaction to life's difficulties in adulthood; the ''Civic Generation,'' protected in
youth and dedicated to civic action in adulthood; and the ''Adaptive Generation,''
over-protected in youth and emulative of their elders in adulthood (*Generations*
8–9). Generation X's ''reactive'' personality would fit Dickens's protagonist in
Great Expectations; Pip is largely passive, reacting to the problems that confront
him rather than initiating heroic action.

5. The 2000 Jobtrak.com nationwide survey of Gen X college students and graduates
showed that the job benefit Gen Xers most desired was ''flexible hours,'' a finding
borne out by previous surveys (Lang E1). Richard White, career center director
at Rutgers University, reported that Generation X was experiencing an ideological
shift away from a materialistic ethic: ''Student values are changing. No longer
do they value monetary benefits—it is free time that is important to them. After
watching their parents' generation sacrifice time for their careers, the current
generation has decided that they would rather have free time to spend with friends
and family'' (qtd. in Lang E1).

6. Estella first appears to Finn in the garden of Paradiso Perduto, clad in a green
sheath dress, a costume that associates her with the serpent/seductress but likewise reflects the ambivalence of her character by suggesting life and growth. In
fact, the color green, which dominates the film's costuming and set design, combined with the sumptuous cinematography, undercuts the characters' initial emotional sterility to give the film a haunting lushness, a magical sense that it is
presenting a rich world pregnant with possibilities. For instance, while Dickens's
novel describes Miss Havisham's garden as ''rank'' and ''overgrown with tangled
weeds'' (*GE* 93; ch. 8), the garden of Paradiso Perduto is frightfully wild but
verdant and full of light and life. Cuaron's film places the remnants of Miss
Dinsmoor's wedding banquet in the garden, populated by croaking frogs and
humming insects that captivate Finn with their beauty and activity. Thus, the
ruined garden in Dickens's text represents modernist alienation and sterility,
while the green garden of Cuaron's film symbolizes the hyperactivity of the
postmodern experience that can result either in meaningless excess or rich fulfillment.

7. Pamela Katz's interview with director Alfonso Cuaron reveals that this conversation between Finn and Estella was added to the film after preview audiences
indicated that they did not understand Estella's motivations and demanded a more
''sympathetic'' character. Katz complains that the scene ''doesn't belong'' and
deems it ''one of those last-minute script Band-Aids,'' a misguided ''attempt to
sum up the psychology of a complex character in four lines of dialogue'' (100).
But I argue that the scene's power arises precisely from its epiphanous effect—it
encapsulates the emotional experience of a generation within the brief conversation of the two leading characters.

8. Throughout the film, the sea acts as a symbol of the fluidic quality of existence that offers endless possibilities for human subjectivity. An image of the ambiguous nature of identity in the postmodern world, the ocean in Cuaron's film is threatening, uncertain, but full of promise. The film opens and closes with sea imagery that is distinctly connected to the question of identity. The opening credits show Finn's paintings of the central characters with the name of each actor washing over the respective painting like a wave. The opening scene then depicts the child Finn watching fish at the seaside and sketching them in his book, the book that will inspire in Lustig "great expectations" of his own. The convict who will open Finn's eyes to the possibilities of a larger world then springs from the sea and later returns to the sea when Finn helps him escape. On the other hand, Miss Dinsmoor reveals that she seldom leaves her seaside mansion to look at the ocean, signifying her determination to prevent change and deny other opportunities for her life. When Finn as an adult leaves Florida to move to New York, he leaves behind the real and natural, if risky, world associated with the ocean for the hyperreal, artificial, controlled world of the city. After Lustig's death and his revelation of the true human quality of Finn's art, Finn returns to the sea; the film depicts him walking in the water, covered in sunlight, just before we learn that he has gone to Paris to rediscover the significance of his work. The sea in this instance suggests cleansing and rebirth. And as Finn and Estella look out on the sea in the closing shot, the imagery implies a similar hope for rejuvenation.

WORKS CITED

Atlantic Records. "Great Expectations." Album Press Release. 20 Oct. 1999 <http://www. atlantic-records.com/nonframes/Artists_Music/ biography.html? artistID=391>.

Borgmann, Albert. *Crossing the Postmodern Divide*. Chicago: U of Chicago P, 1992.

Cheung, Edward. *Baby-Boomers, Generation X and Social Cycles*. Toronto: Longwave P, 1994.

Clayton, Jay. *Charles Dickens in Cyberspace: The Afterlife of the Nineteenth Century in Postmodern Culture*. New York: Oxford UP, 2003.

———. "Dickens and the Genealogy of Postmodernism." *Nineteenth-Century Literature* 46.2 (Sept. 1991): 181–95.

———. "Is Pip Postmodern? Or, Dickens at the End of the Twentieth Century." *Great Expectations*. By Charles Dickens. Ed. Janice Carlisle. Boston: St. Martin's P, 1996. 607–24.

Connor, Steven. *Postmodernist Culture*. Oxford: Basil Blackwell, 1991.

Coupland, Douglas. "Generation X'd." *Details*. June 1995. 24 April 2000 <http://home.pix.za/gc/gc12/papers/p2011.htm>.

Cuaron, Alfonso, dir. *Great Expectations*. Perf. Gwyneth Paltrow and Ethan Hawke. 20th Century Fox, 1998.

Dickens, Charles. *Great Expectations*. Ed. Angus Calder. New York: Penguin, 1985.

Hannigan, John. *Fantasy City: Pleasure and Profit in the Postmodern Metropolis*. New York: Routledge, 1998.

Hobson, Louis B. "Date with Greatness." *Jam Movies*. 25 Jan. 1998. 20 Oct. 1999 <http://www.chl.ca/JamMoviesArtistsP/paltrow-gwyneth.html#250198>.

———. "Interview with Ethan Hawke." *Jam Movies*. 20 Oct. 1999 <http://www.chl.ca/ JamMoviesArtistsH/hawke_ethan.html>.

Hornblower, Margot. "Great Xpectations: Slackers? Hardly. The so-called generation X turns out to be full of go-getters who are just doing it—but their way." *Time* 149.23 (9 June 1997) 10 Oct. 1999 <http://www.pathfinder.com/eezD9bKgU-AOdFX1Jan/time/magazine/1997/dom/970609/society.great_xpectat.html>.

Huyssen, Andreas. *After the Great Divide: Modernism, Mass Culture, Postmodernism*. Indianapolis: Indiana UP, 1986.

James, Steve. "Gwyneth Paltrow's 'Great Expectations.' " *Reuters*. Online. AOL. 27 Jan. 1998.

Jameson, Fredric. *Postmodernism, or, the Cultural Logic of Late Capitalism*. Durham: Duke UP, 1991.

Johnson, Michael K. "Not Telling the Story the Way It Happened: Alfonso Cuaron's *Great Expectations*." *Literature/Film Quarterly* 33.1 (2005): 62–78. *Academic Search Premiere*. EBSCOhost. J. D. Williams Lib., The University of Mississippi. 16 Nov. 2005 <http://www.epnet.com>.

Johnston, Susan. "Historical Picturesque: Adapting *Great Expectations* and *Sense and Sensibility*." *Mosaic: A Journal for the Interdisciplinary Study of Literature* 37.1 (March 2004): 167–83. *Academic Search Premiere*. EBSCOhost. J. D. Williams Lib., The University of Mississippi. 16 Nov. 2005 <http://www.epnet.com>.

Katz, Pamela. "Directing Dickens: Alfonso Cuaron's 1998 *Great Expectations*." *Dickens on Screen*. Ed. John Glavin. Cambridge, UK: Cambridge UP, 2003. 95–103.

Lang, John. "Gen-Xers' Time vs. Money." *Chattanooga Times/Chattanooga Free Press* 18 Feb. 2000: E1+.

Mulvey, Laura. "Visual Pleasure and Narrative Cinema." *Film Theory and Criticism: Introductory Readings*. Ed. Leo Braudy and Marshall Cohen. 5th ed. New York: Oxford UP, 1999. 833–44.

Sinyard, Neil. *Filming Literature: The Art of Screen Adaptation.* London: Croom Helm, 1986.

Smith, J. Walker, and Ann Clurman. *Rocking the Ages: The Yankelovich Report on Generational Marketing.* New York: Harper Business, 1997.

Sterritt, John. "Time Has No Meaning in Hollywood Updates." *Christian Science Monitor* 30 Jan. 1998: 16.

Strauss, William, and Neil Howe. *Generations: The History of America's Future, 1584–2069.* New York: Quill, 1991.

———. *13th* Gen: Abort, Retry, Ignore, Fail? New York: Vintage Books, 1993.

Jane Eyre's *Paradise Lost*

Clay Daniel

Rochester and Jane's love affair is a comprehensive rewriting of the love of Adam and Eve in Paradise Lost. *Rochester (as Adam) has been ruined by an errant love for a fallen mate, the congenitally mad Bertha (earth-birth/Eve). Jane (a new Eve) then arrives in the blighted Eden. These identifications become more explicitly Miltonic when Jane discovers Rochester's fall. As she strives to emulate the Son of God, Jane takes over the role of unfallen Adam in* Paradise Lost, *confronted with a fallen mate. However, Jane remains faithful to divine law. This will enable her to return as a Christian (and Miltonic) heroine—free from the Calvinist, misogynistic limitations that infuriated Brontë—to redeem Rochester. These limitations are embodied in St. John Rivers, who also offers marriage. But, given a choice between obedient but loveless rectitude and erring but profoundly Christian love, Jane with divine guidance chooses love. Jane's feminist myth locates the primary model of Christian love in a marriage that is based on the notion of a redemptive woman. Yet Brontë subtly suggests the limitations of that myth.*

Readers of *Jane Eyre* are often vexed by the novel's unstable discourses on religion and gender. Though *Jane Eyre* "raised the ire of high-minded Christians of her time (and of ours as well)" (Franklin 479), many readers, then and now, have found in *Jane Eyre* the perspectives to be expected from the daughter of an Evangelical Anglican clergyman: "powerful, moral, vigorous, healthy, fresh, true, improving, pure, sound, straightforward, and comprehensible" (Vargish 58). Yet, according to Gilbert (and many readers), Brontë in

---

Dickens Studies Annual, Volume 38, Copyright © 2007 by AMS Press, Inc. All rights reserved.

her novel angrily attacks many of the anti-feminisms of a patriarchal Christianity. Others, perceiving a less radical message, argue that Brontë draws on several contemporary versions of Christianity to write a "Christian feminist bildungsroman" (Gallagher 67). But how feminist is a novel that concludes with the argument that a woman's deepest fulfillment is through marriage enabled by the death of another, possibly exploited woman? And then, perhaps most puzzling, there is the farewell salute to a model of the Victorian patriarch.[1]

These critical frictions are often read in relation to Brontë's reaction(s) to "Milton's bogey." But Jane's story does not simply echo, provocatively interrogate, or sporadically rewrite *Paradise Lost*. Rochester and Jane's love affair is structured by a comprehensive rewriting of the love of Adam and Eve in *Paradise Lost*. Shirley, in an acute assessment of Milton's anti-epic, avers that Milton

> saw Heaven: he looked down on Hell. He saw Satan, and Sin his daughter, and Death their horrible off-spring. Angels serried before him their battalions: the long lines of adamantine shields flashed back on his blind eyeballs the unutterable splendor of heaven. Devils gathered their legions in his sight: their dim, discrowned, and tarnished armies passed rank and file before him. Milton tried to see the first woman; but, Cary, he saw her not.   (*Shirley* 359)

Instead, Shirley explains, Milton saw in Eve his cook—and she could have added, his gardener in Adam, as part of his argument for an anti-classical, Christian, and middle-class epic heroism. However radical (and feminist) these arguments had appeared to the seventeenth—and eighteenth-century reader, by the 1840s Milton was fast becoming a monument to dead ideas—or to ideas that should be dead, especially in regard to women, according to many mid-Victorian Anglo-American feminists.[2] Ironically, characteristics with which Milton endowed Eve to counter centuries of misogyny were often precisely those that were most objectionable for many mid-Victorian feminists: sweetness, coy grace, and submissive yet majestic charm. Brontë herself located many of women's cultural disruptions in Milton's humble, winning Eve: "In *Shirley* she specifically attacked the patriarchal Miltonic cosmology, within whose baleful context she saw both her female protagonists sickening, orphaned and starved by a male-dominated society" (Gilbert and Gubar 193). Moreover, "Shirley obviously presents her vision of a new Eve in an attempt to challenge and subvert the power of the patriarchal version of the Genesis myth put forward by St. Paul and Milton" (Lawson 415). Milton's purportedly incomplete Eve is transformed into "a new feminine divinity" that is "powerful and godlike" and "pure" (Lawson 415; Gilbert and Gubar 195). This mother of Titans is "heaven-born": " . . . vast was the heart whence gushed the well-spring of the blood of nations; and grand the undegenerate head where rested the consort-crown of creation. . . . That Eve was Jehovah's daughter, as Adam was his son" (*Shirley* 360–61).

Brontë takes major, but cautiously circumscribed, steps towards this radical myth (re)making in *Jane Eyre*, engendering perspectives that alternately suggest that mid-Victorian Anglican Evangelical Christianity—especially as Brontë perceived that it derived from readings of *Paradise Lost*—is being rejected, rivaled, reformed, and/or endorsed. These perspectives are brilliantly complicated by "a dialogue between the conflicting, open-ended worldviews of the younger and older Jane" (Beaty 502). But equally significant are the conflicted worldviews of author Brontë and character-author Jane. Brontë seems to have most closely identified with the radically anti-Miltonic arguments of *Shirley*, which empower women with the attributes of a divinity. However, in her first published novel, Brontë less boldly, but more skillfully, creates an author who, whatever her challenges to patriarchal authority, is compellingly domestic and genuinely Evangelical—and then allows her to create a Miltonic narrative that is profoundly subversive yet uncannily Christian. Yet, as author Jane exorcises "Milton's bogey," author Brontë subtly observes and comments upon the limitations of creating any feminist myth within a contemporary Miltonic context. This narrative construct not only allows Brontë to distance herself from the inner turbulence that perhaps characterized her own intense engagement with Milton (and which pervades Jane's autobiography) but to disrupt and deflect the reactionary criticisms of contemporaries who were stung by "Currer Bell's" plucking "the mask from the face of the Pharisee" ("Author's Preface," *Jane Eyre* 1).

Jane's autobiography rewrites Adam and Eve's relationship in *Paradise Lost*. Rochester (as Adam) has been ruined by an errant love for a fallen mate, the congenitally mad Bertha (earth-birth/Eve). Jane (a new Eve/Eyre/Err) arrives in the blighted Eden ("Thornfield Hall—this accursed place" [*Jane Eyre* 256]). These basic identifications become more explicitly Miltonic when Jane discovers the dark secret of Thornfield, where "she is to be crowned with thorns" (Gilbert and Gubar 347; Lamonica 260). As she strives to emulate the Son of God, Jane takes over the role of unfallen Adam in *Paradise Lost*, confronted with a fallen mate. Unlike Milton's man, however, Brontë's woman remains faithful to divine law, heeding the divine voice that commands her to flee perdition. This will enable her to return as a Christ(ian)/Miltonic hero—free from the misogynistic Calvinist limitations that infuriated Brontë—to redeem Rochester. These limitations are embodied in St. John Rivers, who also offers marriage. But, given a choice between obedient but loveless rectitude and erring but profoundly Christian love, Jane with divine guidance chooses love and returns to marry Rochester. Jane's autobiography, then, inhabits the liminal spaces between "redefining the will of God" (Jenkins 74) and restating the will of God according to a rewritten myth that is deeply informed with the assumptions and contexts of its original, in this case Milton's poem. This new feminist myth locates the primary model of Christian love in marriage that, though in many ways impeccably mid-Victorian, is based on the heretical, unsettling notion of a redemptive woman. Yet, as Jane's autobiography concludes, Brontë quietly suggests the limitations of Jane's literary achievement. Brontë implies that those who successfully rewrite *Paradise Lost*, a commendable and necessary labor, are rewarded with their very own domestic sphere.

As has been documented, Jane's autobiography is shaped by both a "providential aesthetic" and by "the central narrative and imagery of the Eden myth" (Vargish; Jenkins 71).[3] In Jane's account, Rochester is frequently defined by his flaws, and his flaws are those that are endemic to the human race. "We can none of us help our nature," as Mrs. Fairfax comments on Rochester (108–09). Rochester prefaces his first confession to Jane by emphasizing that he is a fallen human rather than a fallen angel: "I am not a villain: you are not to suppose that—not to attribute to me any such bad eminence" (116). "High on a Throne of Royal State," Satan was "by merit rais'd / To that bad eminence" (*PL* 2.1–6). Rochester instead is the old Adam under Satan's sway. In Milton's works, sin often appears as an intenser form of stupidity. Rochester confesses that he lacked "the originality to chalk out a new road to shame and destruction, but trod the old track with stupid exactness not to deviate an inch from the beaten centre" (120). He tells Jane, "Nature meant me to be, on the whole, a good man" (116). He like Adam is "for contemplation . . . form'd" (*PL* 4.297): "I might have been as good as you—wiser, almost as stainless" (115). But he has become "a trite commonplace sinner" because of a mysterious "error" (116–17).

The mystery deepens when Rochester declares his shadowy sin to be an inspiration: "And who talks of error now? I scarcely think the notion that flitted across my brain was an error. I believe it was an inspiration rather than a temptation. . . . It is no devil, I assure you; or if it be, it has put on the robes of an angel of light" (117). Rochester apparently clears the mystery of his error by confessing his affair with Céline Varens. But his error has an earlier, and more profound, genesis. Rochester's (un)original sin embodies itself in his original mate. She has fallen in his luxuriant, steamy, corrupted "garden" (263) in the New World, to keep falling, everywhere, ever after:

> What crime was this, that lived incarnate in this sequestered mansion, and could neither be expelled nor subdued by the owner?—What mystery, that broke out, now in fire and now in blood, at the deadest hours of night? What creature was it, that, masked in an ordinary woman's face and shape, uttered the voice, now of a mocking demon, and anon of a carrion-seeking bird of prey? (179)

Rochester's "capital error" has linked him forever with this "crime . . . incarnate,"

> one whose consequences must follow you through life and taint all your life and taint all your existence. Mind I don't say a *crime* . . . my word is *error*. The results of what you have done become in time to you utterly insupportable. . . . You are miserable; for hope has quitted you on the very confines of life; your sun at noon darkens in an eclipse [traditional time and image for Fall and Crucifixion]. . . . Bitter and base associations have become the sole food of your memory: you wander here and there, seeking rest in exile: happiness in pleasure—I mean in heartless, sensual pleasure. . . . (185–86)

Rochester's distinction between error and crime evokes Adam's decision to fall with Eve, an error motivated not by his condoning her crime but supposedly by his profound love for her. Indeed, anticipating Rochester, Adam and Eve interpret their fall as inspired by an "angel of light," as part of a "glorious trial of exceeding Love" (*PL* 9.961) such as those common in Petrarchan courtly romances and their Victorian/Gothic derivatives. Their daring, they claim, will gain them a God-granted divinity, enabling them to partake of pleasure not "known till now," a belief embodied in, and discredited by, the fallen sex that immediately ensues (*PL* 9.935–37, 961, 1023). The degraded Rochester wanders in dissipated exile—angel-less as he later points out (221)—not unlike Milton's Adam, whose "wand'ring steps and slow" lead him from angel-guarded paradise into a world that was soon to succumb "to luxury and riot, feast and dance,/Marrying or prostituting, as befell,/Rape or Adultery" (*PL* 12.648, 11.715–17).[4] When Rochester defends his autonomous pursuit of pleasure (ironically, recalling Milton's divorce tracts), Jane counters with an Augustinian argument that was central to Milton's representations of evil: "Then you will degenerate still more, sir" (116). She concludes by restating a major theme in *Paradise Lost*: "The human and fallible should not arrogate a power with which the divine and perfect alone can be safely entrusted" (118).

Jane's autobiography repeatedly characterizes its author as an "original" (229) who shades into savior. She is "stainless . . . without blot or contamination . . . pure" (115–16). She has a mind "not liable to take infection" (122). These qualities enable her to rescue Rochester three times. First, when riding from Millcote to Thornfield with his dog Pilot, Rochester falls from his horse, if not with a thud, at least with a pun (96–99). Then, in an act characterized as a baptism, Jane rescues slumbering Rochester from Bertha's flames; and Rochester himself characterizes Jane as his savior (126–30). This characterization is most explicit after Jane rescues Mason, which is prefaced by her third rescue of Rochester ("Can I help you, sir?—I'd give my life to serve you [174]). The "ministrant spirit" revives the "seemingly lifeless" Mason, watched by the "heads of the twelve apostles . . . while above them at the top rose an ebon crucifix and a dying Christ" (174, 178–79).

Rochester, seeking redemption, finds it in Jane, "fresh . . . without taint. Such society revives, regenerates: you feel better days come back—higher wishes, purer feelings; you desire to recommence your life, and to spend what remains to you of days in a way more worthy of an immortal being" (186). Jane perceives the religious implications of Rochester's avowals. Jane responds, "Sir . . . a wanderer's repose or a sinner's reformation should never depend on a fellow-creature" (186). Her response indicates the extent to which Jane is shaped by Milton's concept of Christian heroism. Adam and Eve's fall is determined by their profound, and profoundly Renaissance, yearning to exchange humanity for divinity (an exchange with which Brontë apparently sympathized). Adam and Eve will be "putting off / Human, to put on gods" (9.713–14; 935–37). Milton often attacked these divine pretensions as part of his argument for a Christian / middle-class / anti-epic heroism. This heroism finds potent expression in little, plain Jane who outshines the rich and beautiful, who "by small / Accomplishing great things, by things deem'd weak / Subverting worldly strong, and worldly wise / By simply meek" demonstrates "that suffering for Truth's sake / Is fortitude to highest victory, / And to the faithful Death the Gate of Life" (*PL* 12.566–71). Jane delights in her mundane status. Speculating on his and Jane's honeymoon in Europe, Rochester says that he "shall revisit it healed and cleansed, with a very angel" (221). In sharp contrast to Eve (or Shirley), Jane derides his words as a flattering delusion: "I am not an angel . . . and I will not be one till I die: I will be myself. Mr. Rochester, you must neither expect nor exact anything celestial of me." She adds, "I had rather be a *thing* than an angel" (223). Jane, as Milton's Adam and Eve should have, will achieve positive mythic status not by superseding divine law, but by acting according to the humane knowledge that "to obey [God] is best" (*PL* 12.561).

The novel's vigorous Miltonic subtext is spotlighted on an "eve of separation" (214) as Rochester prepares to fall again with a woman in the Eve-Bertha tradition, Blanche Ingram.[5] Rochester laments his separation from Jane: "It is as if I had a string somewhere under my left ribs, tightly and inextricably knotted to a similar string situated in the corresponding quarter of your little frame" (215). These lines are clearly indebted, not simply to Genesis, but to Milton's descriptions of Adam's choice to remain with Eve (his left rib) rather than to obey God:

> Should God create another *Eve,* and I
> Another Rib afford, yet loss of thee
> Would never from my heart; no no I feel
> The Link of Nature draw me: Flesh of Flesh
> Bone of my Bone thou art, and from thy State
> Mine never shall be parted, bliss or woe.   (*PL* 9.911–16; also 955–59)

Yet, where this link binds Adam to disaster, it draws Rochester to salvation.

Escaping the mindless Blanche, Rochester commits his soul to the intelligent, fascinating, and Evangelical Jane. Jane's vehement despair then is transformed, as is Eve's, when her Adam's talk of ribs precedes an announcement of eternal devotion. Assured by Rochester that he loves her as his "own flesh" (217), Jane rejoices that she has been "called to the paradise of union" (218). Rochester, on the other hand, realizes the true nature of the situation, which again reworks the gender circumstances of *Paradise Lost*: his role is that of Milton's Eve (who in turn resembles Milton's Satan), who seduces an unwary Adam. Rochester again echoes Eve's exalting Adam's ruin into a "glorious trial of exceeding Love" (9.961) that will lead to "Life / Augmented" (9.984–85): "Is there not love in my heart, and constancy in my resolves? It will expiate at God's tribunal" (218).

Succumbing to Rochester's seduction, Jane's fall echoes that of Milton's Adam ("Was shee thy God?" [*PL* 10.145]): "He stood between me and every thought of religion. . . . I could not, in those days, see God for his creature: of whom I had made an idol" (234). Jane then echoes Milton's description of nature's immediate reaction to Adam's fall (Chard 201). A thunderbolt had descended as a form of divine enmity that also portends her "crucifixion" (Jenkins 73): " . . . a livid, vivid spark leapt out of a cloud . . . and there was a crack, a crash, and a close rattling peal" (218). The next morning, Jane learns of the destruction of "their tree of knowledge" (Jenkins 72): " . . . the great horse-chestnut at the bottom of the orchard had been struck by lightning in the night, and half of it split away" (219). Equally ominous, Rochester continues the satanic rhetoric that defines his Eve as a "goddess humane" (*PL* 9.732): Jane is sylph and angel (221), sprite and fire-spirit (223), fairy (228), elf (234). Jane on the other hand thinks of Rochester in connection with "Hercules and Samson with their charmers" (222). These "charmers" are noted models for the negative aspects of Milton's Eve (*PL* 9.1060). Rochester tells Jane, "Don't long for poison—don't turn out a downright Eve on my hands!" (223). Yet, again, the gender roles are reversed: it is Rochester who functions as the fallen seducer rather than the "original" Jane. Jane scorns a woman like Milton's errant Eve who will "coax, and entreat—even cry and be sulky if necessary for the sake of a mere essay of . . . power." Within Jane's myth of "feminist freedom," it is Rochester who coaxes, entreats, and cries as he is gradually "brought into the 'female' world of love and morality, out of the 'masculine' universe of power" (Moglen 143).

In accord with these role reversals, Jane is tempted to imitate Adam. On the eve of her wedding, Jane "strayed through the orchard, gathered up the apples" (236). Jane's comments on the split chestnut tree indicate that, as many readers of *Paradise Lost* have felt, Adam's last uncorrupted act was to remain faithful to the fallen Eve:

"You did right to hold fast to each other," I said: as if the monster-splinters were living things, and could hear me. "I think, scathed as you look, and charred and scorched, there must be a little sense of life in you yet; rising out of that adhesion to the faithful, honest roots: you will never have green leaves more—never more see birds making nests and singing idylls in your boughs; the time of pleasure and love is over with you; but you are not desolate: each of you has a comrade to sympathise with him in his decay."

Despite his sympathetic treatment of the fallen lovers, Milton clearly indicates Adam's guilt in clinging to his fallen mate. It is this love that, according to many readings of *Paradise Lost*, predetermines failed marriages, failed class-relations, indeed, a great many failed things, especially, perhaps, as they appeared to be failing in mid-Victorian England. "Human beings never enjoy complete happiness in this world," says Jane, unable to accept the reality of her identity as Jane Rochester (220).

Jane and Charlotte Brontë appear to be one in their intense displeasure with the position that human happiness in this world had been forfeited forever by a man's love for a woman. Brontë's "woman-as-goddess" response to this culture-curse is more fully articulated in *Shirley*. But Jane's autobiography provides a provisional solution. Jane and Rochester's marriage cannot take place until Milton's matrimonial narrative is transformed into a feminist myth of the redemptive love of a divinely inspired "helpmeet." Rochester had admonished Jane, "You have no right to preach to me, you neophyte, that have not passed the porch of life, and are absolutely unacquainted with its mysteries" (117). This accusation is essentially valid: within the context of the novel's "mysteries," Jane Rochester "did not exist" (235; 244). Rochester might have mythically fallen, but Jane has not been archetypically tempted. Only after she has successfully engaged with the central temptation of the Genesis myth can she become, if not a titan or an angel, a new Eve who can unite/ingraft with Rochester as his redeemer. Only then will she be not Jane Eyre/err, but Jane (and, in some ways, Edward) Rochester.

Jane's imminent temptation, like Eve's, is presaged in a terrifying dream. Jane dreams she falters in pursuit of Rochester through cold, rain, and darkness, with a baby in her arms. Jane has become the stereotypical fallen woman. This status becomes more explicit in the subsequent dream. Thornfield is a "dreary ruin . . . of all the stately front nothing remained but a shell-like wall" (241). Rochester and Jane's paradisial but guilty love has proven to be as ruinous and unsubstantial as Adam similar love for Eve. Attempting to gain one last glance of Rochester, Jane says that "the wall crumbled" and she "fell, and woke" (241). The airy Eve, too, in her dream thought she "could not but taste" the tempting fruit, before she "sunk down, / And fell asleep" and "wak'd / To find this but a dream!" (*PL* 5.86, 91–93). Of course, subsequent events prove that this experience was not "but a dream,'' despite Adam's disclaimer. Rochester, too, breezily avers ''incredulity beforehand'' (241). Yet he cannot deny material proof of ''crime . . . incarnate.'' Awaking, Jane finds not her Adam but his Bertha. Bertha cavorts among Jane's wedding attire, suggesting the disastrous consequences of the marriage if Jane were to step into Bertha's shoes—and trample on the veil as one more fallen woman (243).

Bertha functions as Jane's ''avatar'' or ''alter ego'' (Gilbert and Gubar 359), as Jane (and Brontë) reified an unconscious rage at the Evangelical priorities that shaped a mid-Victorian woman's life. Moreover, Bertha embodies Brontë's more conscious anger as Jane inscribes herself as a Milton's Christian hero instead of Brontë writing herself as a Titan: Bertha haunts Jane's myth as a character within her autobiography as Brontë haunts it as the author of Jane's character within Brontë's novel. Nevertheless it is Jane's myth that is foregounded in Brontë's novel. And creating Jane's myth, Brontë could not expect the ''Gentle Reader'' to accept a new myth/novel/social document, deliberately argued, based on the rhetoric of justifying the consequences of woman as a thwarted goddess-turned-beast: sensuality, violence, attempts at murder, arson, blood-lust, insanity. Indeed, the novel proved to be controversial enough. Instead, Brontë appropriates the rhetoric of official discourse, especially official Miltonic discourse, to disguise the subversiveness of Jane's text. And within the Miltonic discourses of Jane's autobiography, Bertha is a living nightmare, especially for women. She is the defining, limiting other—a ''crime incarnate'' that society uses to imprison/confine/watch all women but especially those who are unconventional. Little wonder that Bertha's manifestations coincide with ''an experience (or repression) of anger on Jane's part'' (Gilbert and Gubar 360). Bertha-as-Eve-as-Woman is precisely what Jane and Brontë are attempting to reinscribe.

Jane confronts this ''crime . . . incarnate'' in a fire-lit room, attended but not eradicated by Grace Poole, ''that mystery of mysteries'' with her Bible and porter (173). Here Rochester's fall is at last clearly sounded: '' . . . faith was blighted—confidence destroyed! Mr. Rochester was not to me what he had been. . . . The attribute of stainless truth was gone from his idea'' (252–53). The ''idea'' of Rochester is blighted not so much by his marriage to Bertha as by his attempting—unlike Adam—to abandon his guilty partner. He confesses, ''I am little better than a devil at this moment; and, as my pastor would tell me, deserve no doubt the sternest judgements of God,—even to the quenchless fire and deathless worm'' (249). Rochester conflates the fallen Eve's fears if Adam should remain obedient (''then I shall be no more'' [*PL* 9.827]) with Adam's loving decision to remain with his erring Eve (''How can I live without thee?'' [*PL* 9.908]): ''All happiness will be torn away with you. What then is left?'' (270). Coaxing, entreating, even crying, he attempts to seduce Jane into sin, a sin without which he will ''die accursed'' and alone (270).

But Jane, by all appearances, has read *Paradise Lost,* several times, and has embraced many of its more mainstream Christian messages. Here love is obedient, wise, and pointed with the self-regard that Raphael recommends to Adam. Confessing an over-fondness for Eve, Adam is told that "nothing profits more / Than self-esteem, grounded on just and right / Well manag'd": "Love refines / The thoughts, and heart enlarges, hath his seat / In reason, and is judicious" (8.571–73, 589–91). Or, as Rochester with Jane's (and Milton's) "own tongue" articulates her thoughts, "I need not sell my soul to buy bliss. I have an inward treasure, born with me, which can keep me alive if all extraneous delights should be withheld; or offered only at a price I cannot afford to give. The forehead declares, 'Reason sits firm and holds the reins . . . ' " (171). This self regard is the source for that "paradise within thee, happier far" with which Michael solaces Adam after the Fall (*PL* 12.587). Or, again as Rochester admiringly phrases Jane's thoughts, "I have a rosy sky, and a green flowery Eden in my brain; but without, I am perfectly aware, lies at my feet a rough tract to travel, and around me gather black tempests to encounter" (267). This self-regard generates Jane's, as it should have Adam's, rejection of the errant lover: "Still indomitable was the reply—'I care for myself. The more solitary, the more friendless, the more unsustained I am, the more I will respect myself. I will keep the law given by God; sanctioned by man' " (270). Jane's parting counsel to Rochester echoes Michael's admonition to Adam when he sees the fatal consequences of "ungovern'd appetite" (*PL* 11.517; 553–54): "I advise you to live sinless; and I wish you to die tranquil. . . . We were born to strive and endure—you as well as I: do so" (270).

Jane then fulfills her role as a new Eve by enacting another of Milton's favorite arguments: to obey God is to rebel against the "man of the world." Yet this Christian piety subverts Milton's narrative even as it confirms Jane's Miltonic heroism. Jane chooses obedience to a supernatural and feminine divine authority rather than wifely and evil submission to her male companion: "My daughter, flee temptation!" "Mother, I will" (272). Milton's Eve separates from her mate to encounter temptation, to disobey God, and to imperil her soul. Jane's Eve departs her "temporary heaven" (273) to flee temptation, to obey God, and to save her (and her mate's) soul. Yet, shaped by Jane's priorities of love, this separation is a definitive agony. Cupid's arrow, hallowed by divine fire, becomes a "barbed arrow-head" in her breast: "Gentle reader, may you never feel what I then felt!" (274). Fleeing Thornfield, Jane is beset by a yearning to save Rochester, "be his comforter—his pride; his redeemer from misery; perhaps from ruin" (274). In Rochester's own words, life with Bertha "is hell! this is the air—those are the sounds of the bottomless pit!" (262). Rochester adds, "I have a right to deliver myself from it if I can." Yet Rochester can no more save himself than the fallen Adam and Eve could redeem themselves. That role must be filled by an unfallen redeemer. To become Rochester's savior, Jane symbolically experiences what for many Christians is the highest configuration of love, suffering, redemption, and obedience to God: crucifixion, another version of the "pedestal of infamy" (57) on which she learned the Christian virtues exemplified by Helen Burns at the purgatorial Lowood.[6]

After two days of suffering, during which "God must have led" her through a "solitary way" (274), Jane arrives at "Whitcross . . . a stone pillar" (275). She departs from this stone pillar (traditionally, a form of the cross) on a journey that is "measured by . . . weary trembling limbs" (275) and on which is to be expected "mistrust, rejection, insult" (276). In the midst of this "torture," she, like Jesus on his cross, pities and longs to redeem the source of her suffering. Her heart "plained of its gaping wounds, its inward bleeding, its riven chords. It trembled for Mr. Rochester and his doom . . . impotent as a bird with both wings broken, it still quivered its shattered pinions in vain attempts to seek him" (276). "Crossing a field" (279), Jane makes her way to a church spire (traditionally, another form of the cross) at Mort(e?)on. Rejected here, she by "crossways and bypaths" stumbles in agony toward "the hill" (281). On this hill, she sees "at one dim point . . . a light" (281–82). "Having crossed a marsh" she heads toward "a trace of white over the moor" (282): "Some calls it Marsh End" (291). At this house of mourning, she is all but condemned to die. Jane then commends her spirit to God: " 'I can but die,' I said, 'and I believe in God. Let me try to wait His will in silence' " (286).

Yet this place contains inhabitants other than Christians who condemn a suffering though faithful servant to more suffering: "Some calls it Moor House" (291). St. John, Mary, and Diana and their "evangelical charity" (296) are "a different soart to them 'ats gone" (and not gone, or not gone far enough)—"t'old stock" of the "ancient" family of Marsh End (285). These Moor/more people, safely removed from Morton, recall especially St. John the Divine and the Virgin Mary at the Crucifixion. St. John Rivers also evokes the herald of the new era, St. John the Baptist. True to his name, St. John attempts to revive the "mere spectre" who was as "white as clay or death" by performing a kind of baptism (287), a sacrament that often was identified with crucifixion. The scene also evokes the raising of Lazarus: "Young woman, rise, and pass before me into the house" (286). And, with St John's help, Jane at last "crossed the threshold" into the house of a new life (287).

Jane spends two more death-like days "in a small room, and in a narrow bed" to which she "seemed to have grown . . . motionless as a stone" (288). She begins to recover "on the third day" (289). Blurring the herald's baptisms with the apostle's vision, the revived Jane compares herself to one cleansed by apocalyptic tribulations (289–90; Revelation 7:13–14). And, as she explains to St. John and his sisters, because (and not despite) of her punishing ordeal, she is "as free from culpability as any one of you three" though the "catastrophe which drove" Jane from "paradise was of a strange and direful nature" (296).

Though a perfect complement to the women (especially "Die"), Jane eventually clashes with St. John, a confrontation that climaxes in a marriage proposal. St. John demands a "sole helpmeet" (346) who will conform to "a cherished Evangelical model of female piety—one based directly on Milton's portrayal of Eve in *Paradise Lost*" (Lamonica 247). St. John would appear to be a perfect mate for many mid-Victorian Evangelical women and even for Jane (Lamonica 250). He is an Adam who withstands the temptation of his own Eve, the "charming," "vain," beautiful and light-headed Rosamond Oliver. He refuses to "relinquish, for the elysium of her love, one hope of the true, eternal Paradise" (313–14). Yet Jane and Brontë momentarily unite their voices to ask, "What sort of man would abandon his mate to death and hell in order to fulfill his moral priorities? And what is the ghastly nature of such moral perfection?" Such a man is St. John Rivers, in whom Jane embodies the concept of Milton that Brontë would have recognized as the dominant contemporary version, especially perhaps among Evangelicals. The "stern . . . Calvinistic" (300) St. John strongly anticipates Shirley's description of Milton, quoted above: "To me, he was in reality become no longer flesh, but marble; his eye was a cold, bright, blue gem; his tongue, a speaking instrument—nothing more" (350). Shirley will ask, "Milton was great; but was he good? His brain was right; how was his heart?" (359). Rivers "is good and great, but severe; and for" Jane "cold as an iceburg" (378). Alluding to the famous line in Milton's Sonnet 7 ("How Soon Hath Time" 14), Jane at her studies regrets "the influence of the ever-watchful blue eye" of St. John (338), who, as if "speaking Greek," lectures Jane on one of Milton's favorite themes, the parable of the talents (333). Men enacting such ideals are venerated but they are not loved except as brothers and by women such as Jane. And they themselves love only as they "*can* love," which is indeed a very limited enterprise (378). When Diana asks if he loves her, Jane responds, "No, Die, not one whit" (353)—"whit" and "Die" evoking Jane's own suffering at Whitcross.

St. John's offer of marriage tempts Jane to become with St. John an official saint in Evangelical culture. Deftly critiquing this Evangelicalism, Brontë presents this spiritual temptation as an even more perilous one than Rochester's fleshly attempt at seduction. Jane admits that, in marrying her cousin, she would only "abandon" half of herself (344). Indeed, Jane's intensely Miltonic heroism reveals why St. John would choose her rather than Rosamond Oliver and why she wholeheartedly consents—despite the protests of

"insupportable—unnatural—out of the question!"—to accompany St. John
to India as his sister-helpmeet.[7] But she resists a loveless marriage that is
justified by contemporary readings of *Paradise Lost*. Significantly, the passage that describes Jane's final wavering in St. John's power vividly anticipates Shirley's assessment of Milton ("Angels serried before him. . . .' '):
"Religion called—Angels beckoned—God commanded—life rolled together
like a scroll—death's gates opening, showed eternity beyond: it seemed, that
for safety and bliss there, all here might be sacrificed in a second" (356–57).
Jane though recognizes that to marry St. John would be "an error of judgment"—to act rightly according to St. John's myth of Eve and the Fall, where
to have married Rochester would have been "an error of principle"—to have
acted wrongly according to her own myth of the Fall (356).

Jane here also betrays the limitations of her revision of Milton's story—of
her engaging with Milton on his own terms. To resist the Miltonic St. John,
Jane draws upon intensely Miltonic values. "Angels serried before" Milton
and "Devils gathered their legions in his sight" often to be ridiculed, admonished, or condemned, as representatives of the false, satanic activity of humanity's "heroes—Christian and Pagan—her lawgivers, her statesman, her
conquerors"—in short, her St. Johns (335). Though St. John apparently labors as one of Milton's Christian heroes, Jane's language conveys her skepticism as he reveals his more authentic character. Though "Christian and
Pagan" might aptly summarize Brontë's feminist heroic, it is a rhetorical
firework within a Miltonic context, discrediting St. John (and anybody else,
presumably male) as either a Christian or Pagan hero. St. John is further
ironically praised as one of Life's heroes, "whether they be zealots, or aspirants, or despots." "Aspirants" would seem to have little hope among this
unholy company as it charges into the valleys of death (356).[8] And to sacrifice
"all" here or anywhere for "safety and bliss"—even in Heaven—is self-
centered and unchristian. There are more pleasant and positive Christian
ways to phrase giving one's life to God. The allusion to the Book of Revelation, "death's gates," "eternity beyond," a "dim room . . . full of visions"—the passage clearly points to death. And the offer itself comes from
one who, within a mythic context, acts as he who "brought death into the
world and all our woe (1.3). Clearly, St. John is "killing" her with his version
of love (351).

In perhaps the sharpest comment of all on the potency of Jane's revision
of Milton, Jane cannot resist St. John without divine intervention, a *deus ex
machina* even. Rochester's cry of "Jane! Jane! Jane!" (381) is directed by
God to Jane, who then makes a three-day journey to resurrect-save Rochester.
Thornfield, without Jane, has fulfilled the prophecy of its name: "The lawn,
the grounds were trodden and waste: the portal yawned void. . . . And there
was the silence of death about it" (362). Rochester, in his own words, has

been "forced to pass through the valley of the shadow of death. *His* chastisements are mighty; and one smote" him "which has humbled" him "for ever" (380). He is as dead as one can be without literally being dead: " . . . many think he had better be dead" (365). He, by all appearances, is "the late Mr. Rochester" (362). His stricken circumstances are a consequence of his devotion to his fallen mate, even in the fires of paradise-turned-hell: " . . . there was a great crash—all fell" (365). His life is preserved by a "beam" (with its evocation of the cross) (365). He, however, is blinded and crippled, a symbolic death if not a symbolic crucifixion, " . . . all to him was void darkness" (367). Rochester groans, "On this arm I have neither hand nor nails" (371). Worse, his second Eve has apparently proved to be as fatal as the first. The caretaker relates a story of "a young lady, a governess at the Hall, that Mr. Rochester fell in—" (363). The blank is unfilled, indicating a partner who did not fall. Discussing Jane's flight, the caretaker evokes a blighted Eden and a crucified Adam: "He would not cross the door-stones of the house; except at night, when he would walk like a ghost about the grounds and in the orchard as if he had lost his senses" (364).

But "humbled" Rochester's blindness, caused by his final selfless devotion to Bertha, has been balanced by his new spiritual insight. He, like Milton's Adam, repents his "wrong": "I began to see and acknowledge the hand of God in my doom. I began to experience remorse, repentance; the wish for reconcilement to my Maker . . . grief replaced frenzy—sorrow, sullenness" (380). In response to Adam's prayers of "sorrow unfeign'd, and humiliation meek" (*PL* 10.1104), Michael arrives to supervise the fall's aftermath. Rochester's repentance is more problematic: he cries out to "the Alpha and Omega" of' his "wishes" during a prayer to God to alleviate his "desolate, afflicted, tormented" condition, to allow him "to taste bliss and peace once more" (381). "Alpha and Omega" is Christ in Revelation (1:11, 21:6, 22:13). But Rochester's love-filled blasphemy is less objectionable than St. John's loveless rectitude. And his redemption again is furthered by his self-sacrificial love: his cry was seeking death from God so as to be reunited with Jane, whom he believed to be dead.

Within the context of Jane's rewriting of Milton's epic, this love is more than enough to compensate for Rochester's "effeminate slackness" (*PL* 11.634). The returned Jane reassures Rochester in terms that recall Jesus with his disciples after the resurrection. She is "not cold like a corpse . . . vacant like air" or "dead in some ditch under some stream" (369–70). In a variation of Adam's dream (*PL* 8.478–90), Jane had been to Rochester a vision to which he "always woke and found it an empty mockery" (370). Now Jane assures him that she is a real, "independent woman" (370)—and more. Suggesting her thoroughly Christian and domestic "titanism," Jane's narrative characterizes its author as the new Eve, a type of Mary (369, 381), a faithful semblance of her maker ("I am" [370]). [9] This humble and "beneficent spirit" (373) can, in the form of an ordinary Christian woman, enact Michael's solacing of the tormented but repentant and praying Adam and Eve (*PL* 11.1–125). Adam, hearing of the Son's love, responds, "full of doubt I stand, / Whether I should repent . . . or rejoice" [12.473–75]). Rochester, reunited with Jane, "swells with gratitude to the beneficent God of this earth" for preserving Jane from his despoliation and even for his punishment (380). Jane, in ironic contrast to the last lines of *Paradise Lost,* will lead her mate to, rather than accompany him from, paradise: "Then he stretched his hand out to be led. I took that dear hand, held it a moment to my lips, then let it pass round my shoulder: being so much lower of stature than he, I served both for his prop and guide. We entered the wood, and wended homeward" (382). Milton had rewritten classical epic heroism as Christian heroism based upon the regenerate individual: humble, patient, long-suffering, obedient to God and therefore at odds (even to the point of rebelling against) the worldly great ones. This, of course, is little Jane. But to create herself as a Christian/Miltonic "anti-heroine," Jane has subverted "the old mythology," enabling a fusion of feminism, Evangelical Christianity, love, and heroism (Moglen 106–07). Indeed, Jane, through her intensely Miltonic heroism, has rehabilitated a concept that Milton had destroyed with his epic argument for Christian heroism: the concept of woman as divine savior (that Milton had located in aristocratic court culture).

Nowhere is this concept more clearly evident than in Jane's marriage, which is an apotheosis of her roles as a humble healer/care-giver/wife: "I hold myself supremely blest . . . because I am my husband's life as fully as he is mine. No woman was ever nearer to her mate than I am; ever more absolutely bone of his bone and flesh of his flesh" (384). Jane's statement is not merely indebted to Genesis 2.23; it alludes to Adam's purported decision to disobey God because of his love for Eve: "Flesh of Flesh, / Bone of my Bone thou art, and from thy State / Mine never shall be parted, bliss or woe" (*PL* 9.914–16). In Milton's poem, these lines signal disaster, for man but especially for "woman." Jane rewrites them to celebrate Christian, feminine love. Jane nourishes rather than destroys Eden because of her willingness to die for a fallen mate, yet dying in obedience rather than in defiance of God's law. Bertha's Thornfield has been supplanted by Jane's paradise. Now under Jane's supervision, Ferndean, " 'quite a desolate spot' " (367) and "of considerable antiquity" (366), re-blossoms into another Eden (the name itself is embedded with Eden). Rochester, "no better than the old lightning-struck chestnut in Thornfield orchard" (378), had acknowledged that the male is saved by attaching himself to the female: "We must become one flesh without any delay. . . . The third day from this must be our wedding" (380). Because of his union with Jane, the stricken Rochester/tree/cross will be transformed into a "green and vigorous" one about whose roots all types of vegetation will flourish (378–79). Jane will "be eyes and hands" (370) that will "rehumanise" Rochester (371). Jane actually becomes Rochester's "vision" as he is born again: (" . . . the sky is no longer a blank to him—the earth no longer a void"): "Literally, I was (as he often called me) the apple of his eye. He saw nature—he saw books through me; and never did I weary of gazing for his behalf. . . . Never did I weary of reading to him: never did I weary of conducting him where he wished to go" (384). Though this resolution has appeared unpleasantly restrictive to many readers, within the context of her revision of *Paradise Lost*, Jane's marriage represents a triumphant acquisition of freedom that is unavailable through either privileged economic status (her inheritance) or imperial heroics (her marriage to St. John Rivers). Wealth, power, social status, and even Jane's self-effacing Christian virtues are dead ends without more fundamental changes to the conventional domestic spaces created by the contemporary reading(s) of Adam and Eve's love in *Paradise Lost* (Moglen 143; Lamonica 260).

Nevertheless, the work does conclude with an unsettling open-endedness that is created by Brontë firmly circumscribing Jane's feminist myth in anticipation of the more radical feminism that she will sketch in *Shirley*. This circumscription is centered on the character of St. John, spotlighted in the novel's conclusion. Jane escapes from the tall, erect, Grecian, "Pagan and Christian" St. John. Brontë's Titan-Woman would not have escaped from St. John—nor would he have escaped from her. Where Jane's St. John is essentially a Victorian/Evangelical Milton (at least in relation to marriage), he seems to have been for Brontë a Romantic/Byronic-satanic Milton who has been tragically thwarted in mid-Victorian England.[10] He, under the tutelage of Brontë's Titan-Woman, would have made a splendid, promethean god. And his useless death, from Brontë's perspective, makes St. John a victim of the hegemonous Miltonic myth—and even of that myth as it is revised by Jane.

Yet Jane is similarly victimized. The concluding description of Jane's marriage to Rochester indicates that Jane's intense engagement with Milton, especially in relation to marriage, has resulted in her marriage to Milton. And it is not to St. John's titanic Milton, or even to the sometimes Byronic-Satanic Rochester of Jane's early acquaintance, but to the domesticated, emasculated Milton of the blinded Edward Rochester. Milton, notoriously, saw Nature through books read to him, according to popular report, by disgruntled, exploited daughters, who, unlike Jane, grew very tired of their duties. Indeed, the description of Jane reading to Rochester is the culmination of a narrative pattern that has consistently blurred Rochester with Milton: his female household, "fine voice" for singing (154), connection to Marston Moor (and the names Fairfax and Rochester), "impetuous republican answers" (239), victimization by a marriage that involved a financial ruse (for Milton, the Powell debt), blindness, "blind ferocity" (367), talk of the "hireling" (372), and subtle contempt of "good and great" men such as "this St. John Rivers" (378). The blindness of this "sightless Samson" (367)—a figure again popularly identified with Milton—is not God's judgment on him for writing regicide tracts but for acting in accord with the arguments of Milton's divinely inspired divorce pamphlets: "Some say it was a just judgment on him for keeping his first marriage secret, and wanting to take another wife while he had one living" (365). Rochester, citing spiritual incompatibility, had harkened to a divine inner voice that had announced Bertha was no longer his wife (263). Imitating Milton's pursuit of "Miss Davis," he then sought a true soul mate, a search that culminates in his marriage to a much younger woman (for Milton, his third wife). And Jane, having as a woman fulfilled Milton's ideal (though perhaps especially of a male), will spend the rest of her life contentedly reading to a semi-blind older (if not old) man who envisions a new Eve when he thinks of his cook (Milton's third wife ousted the amanuenses-daughters in his will reputedly because of her cooking). Jane becomes his eyes, his reading, his framework of nature/reality—yet they are his, which is perhaps the reason why she does not read Brontë's novel to him. This is the inevitable result of Jane having defined herself in Miltonic terms, from embodying Milton's concept of heroism, perhaps perceiving it as *the* Christian heroic, to defining her idea of marriage in opposition to the restrictive traditions that she located in Milton's Eve.

While one of Jane's Milton-figures is domesticated, the other is destroyed in an account that serves as Jane's "culminating act of self-definition" (Williams 244). This act, rather than one of fear and rage (Williams 246), is Jane's final repudiation of St. John's dialectic—God/man/obedience/duty/life opposed to Satan/woman/disobedience/love/death—in favor of her own polarities of God/woman/obedience/love/life versus Satan/man/disobedience/lust/death. This repudiation, rather than destabilizing Jane's feminist argument, extends it to the novel's last words, taken from the Book of Revelation. Jane subverts this book's ferocious, apocalyptic rhetoric, a perennial favorite with Calvinists, to resonate with the novel's insistence on the primacy of love. In the Book of Revelation, virgins flee temptation to emerge from "the great tribulation" in "washed . . . robes"; "white in the blood of the Lamb," they are resurrected as God's unearthly bride (Revelation 7:13–17; 14:1–4). After fleeing her own temptation, Jane is "resurrected" and similarly cleansed: "My very shoes and stockings were purified and rendered presentable" with "no speck of the dirt, no trace of the disorder I so hated, and which seemed so to degrade me" (289–90). Yet Jane's cleansed clothing is not the "pearl-coloured robe" (235) she was wearing as another daughter of Eve on the threshold of social respectability in a society that was about mercilessly to observe her death. Instead it is the Lowood "black silk frock" that is identified with her social defiance. Jane's "supremely blest" marriage, instead of marking a mystical apocalypse, is defined by the happiness of daily living in this world, another of Jane's ideals that is heavily indebted to Milton's concept of Christian heroism. And when she does look towards death, Jane, like Helen Burns, "makes Eternity a rest—a mighty home, not a terror and an abyss" (49). She doubtlessly will enjoy "a gentle wafting to immortal Life" (*PL* 12.435).

St. John, as his name suggests, is the spiritual heir of the turbulent, often horrific theologies that have evolved from this dark, misogynistic book. After Jane had initially rejected his marriage proposal, St. John had selected scripture from this book "for the evening reading before prayers": " 'He that overcometh shall inherit all things; and I will be his God, and he shall be my son. But,' was slowly, distinctly read, 'the fearful, the unbelieving, &c. shall have their part in the lake which burneth with fire and brimstone, which is the second death.' Henceforward I knew what fate St. John feared for me" (355). Where Jane at her "heart's core" (255) forgives her intended husband for attempting to ruin, to kill, and even to damn her, St. John through "duty" (351) menaces his intended wife with the forgiveness of Revelation, "banished and banned . . . not by malice, but on principle"—his principle (350).

But, in another of the novel's inversions-subversions, St. John is banished to India. St. John's concept of marriage kills him, just as it would have killed Jane or anyone, man or woman. St. John's fatal concept of marriage interlocks with his imperial religion. His initial experience as a minister ends in misery: "I considered; my life was so wretched, it must be changed, or I must die" (308). So he becomes a missionary, to die in India, among "rocks and dangers" (385). There he "labors" not for the Indians but "for his race" (385). Despite his much touted virtues and his incredible but self-controlled ambition, St. John apparently achieves nothing except his own death. Yet St. John—Lycidas-like (indeed, like St. John)—envisions himself as a Bride of the Lamb, whose appearance "before the throne of God" (Rev. 7:15) precedes the horrors that attend the opening of the Seventh Seal. St. John's ideal of marriage, which has been created by his loveless, joyless, sexless life (all of which Milton heartily condemned), causes him "eagerly" to implore not only his own death but the death, and consignment to hell, of most of the human race, including Jane (though he "trusts" that Jane is "not of those who live without God in the world, and mind only worldly things," this is not encouraging from a Calvinist [383]). In this he confirms himself as "a fallen seraph of the abyss"—Jane's "eternal enemy" (351)—from whom Jane was rescued by her ability to discern the voice of "a messenger from the eternal throne" (117). This throws a lurid shadow over the tears of "Divine joy" shed by Jane for the man that she meets on death's doorstep (her death, his doorstep) and leaves on death's doorstep (385). His death, like Scrooge's, has produced only happiness, and this in turn links him with that other dark creation of British colonialism, Bertha Mason. Just as Bertha's death frees Rochester, so St. John's imminent death lifts a shadow from Jane's marriage.

In the concluding lament for St. John, Jane's triumphant voice mingles almost imperceptibly with the more complex tones of Charlotte Brontë who has already signaled that Jane is as much a victim of Jane's myth-making as St. John. The citation of Revelation signals a claim to prophecy that is more explicitly asserted in Brontë's Preface. She acts as Micaiah to those who, because they ignore her messages, will be annihilated by "bloody death" (*Jane Eyre* 2). Though ostensibly these Ahabs were a "carping few," the novel's complex narrative strategies indicate that Brontë expected pervasive misunderstanding and/or hostility to her arguments on gender and religion. And, indeed, this cultural resistance more or less ensues. Readers who would have opened themselves to Jane's rewriting of *Paradise Lost* would have recognized that St. John's loveless, failed perfection is irreconcilably opposed to, and defeated by, Jane's triumphant perfection of human love. And those readers who would have perceived the faint imprint of Brontë's own feminism in St. John's fate would have sensed the author's lament for the tragic waste of structuring a life according to Evangelical-Imperial priorities. But, as Brontë feared, the concluding paragraphs on St. John are read as the tribute that they are according to the hegemonous Christian-Miltonic myth. And the cultural disasters to be experienced by the heirs of these gentle but misreading readers are, astonishingly, not unlike those sounded in the Preface as well as in the ominous rumbling of St. John's disquieting death-wish. India was soon bitterly to demand its independence, Evangelicalism was to be increasingly derided in England and abroad, and the Modernists will banish Milton from the drawing-rooms to the universities. Indeed, "Victorianism" itself was soon to disintegrate in the aftermath of a war that many have seen as the punishing culmination of Victorian Europe's imperialism, racism, exploitive economic policy, sham religion, wrong gender relations, and sexual dysfunction—all, of course, major concerns of Charlotte Brontë in *Jane Eyre*.

NOTES

1. Lamonica (245–46) and Vargish (58–60) rehearse perpectives on Christianity and feminism in the novel. Gordon comments on how the "explosion of praise" that greeted the book was mixed with reservations about the dangers of such a book being written by a woman (161–63).
2. Revealingly, Walter Raleigh in 1900 made his famous comment in defense of Milton: "The *Paradise Lost* is not the less an external monument because it is

a monument to dead ideas'' (85). Modern scholars have tended to argue that the deadness was not in Milton's ideas but in Victorian interpretations of Milton's ideas. As Cass points out, Milton was hardly a misogynist (193–94). Yet "in the hands of the Victorians *Paradise Lost* was newly theologized and conventionalized, and . . . Victorian women were now responding less to Milton's poem than to current readings of it" (Wittreich 40).

3. Jenkins writes that "freely trading roles without warning, Rochester and Jane take on aspects of every character in the Eden Myth" (72). He also notes Brontë's use of the Passion and Resurrection in "an extended cluster of death and resurrection imagery" in which Rochester is characterized as Christ and Pilate, and Jane displaces Christ (72–73). Imlay, in arguing Brontë's rejection of Platonism, also comments on elements of the Passion and Resurrection (155–57) and Jane as Eve (38, 91), as well as pointing out that Rochester, Jane, and their son form a concluding "trinity" (204).

4. Rochester, able and unable to repent, also pursues a dissipated "pleasure" not unlike Satan's pleasurable evil (Brontë 116; Moglen 118). He also echoes Satan's "All Good to me is lost" (*PL* 4.109) and "let it" (*PL* 9.173). And when Rochester asks, "By what instinct do you pretend to distinguish between a fallen seraph of the abyss and a messenger from the eternal throne—between a guide and a seducer?" (117), Jane responds that she had read pleasure-seeking Rochester's "countenance" as clearly as Uriel reads the evil-pursuing Satan's "looks" (*PL* 4.570).

5. Prior to this, the Miltonic is perhaps most evident in Jane's much-commented upon water-colors. Jane's water-color pictures boldly enact her rewriting of Milton. The first picture includes "a half-submerged mast, on which sat a cormorant, dark and large" (107). This recalls Satan's initial entry into the Garden of Eden, where "the first grand Thief . . . on the Tree of Life . . . sat like a Cormorant" (4.192–96). The "fair arm" of "a drowned corpse" suggests the "rash hand" (9.780) of Eve that plucked the forbidden fruit and "brought Death into the World, and all our woe" (1.3). The third picture is "a colossal head" with a crown, which is characterized with lines that describe Death in *Paradise Lost* (2.666–73). The second picture disrupts this Miltonic sequence with Brontë's vision of the redeeming female.

6. This "crucifixion" also recalls Jane's symbolic burial and rebirth at the Reeds (11–16). Chapter 26, in which Jane discovers Rochester's marriage to Bertha, concludes with quotations of Psalms 22 and 69, scripture often identified with the crucifixion of Jesus.

7. It would be in keeping with the character of Jane that she was aware of the savage, cynical policies of British imperialism that were defended by an argument that was also used by authorities to justify her own suffering as a poor orphan and a governess: the suffering of the powerless is a providential consequence of Divine Appointment. She would have been alerted to the evils of imperialism by, if no one else, Milton, who is nowhere as satiric about epic/military heroics as when they are aligned with pride, power, politics, egotism, statecraft, religion, and exploitation of the weak. She would also have learned from Milton of the dangers of a state church, especially as an instrument of repression. But even Milton,

perhaps because of his thorough appropriation as "St. John" into mid-Victorian ideology, cannot help Jane to resist the British imperial imperative.

8. "Currer Bell" refers to himself to be "an obscure aspirant" to authorship in the Preface to the second addition of the novel (*Jane Eyre* 1).

9. Lamonica argues Jane's identification with the redemptive Virgin Mary "as a Mediatrix for Rochester" (256–57).

10. Which "Milton" Brontë herself credited as the more authentic—contented Victorian Grandfather, triumphant neo-Puritan Patriarch, tragic Romantic devil, or something else—is difficult to determine. But clearly she had a high regard for Milton's art. She admonishes a friend in an 1834 letter to read only "first rate" poetry, and in the list of authors that follows Milton is first (qtd. in Peters 37). Also see Pfeiffer for Brontë's intense engagement with Milton—an engagement that indicates the urgency of Brontë's search for her own creative space.

WORKS CITED

Beaty, Jerome. "St. John's Way and the Wayward Reader." *Jane Eyre.* Ed. Richard J. Dunn. 3rd. ed. New York: Norton, 2001. 491–503.

Brontë, Charlotte. *Jane Eyre.* Ed. Richard J. Dunn. 3rd. ed. New York: Norton, 2001.

———. *Shirley.* Ed. Herbert Rosengarten and Margaret Smith. Oxford: Clarendon, 1979.

Cass, Jeffrey. "Miltonic Orientalism: *Jane Eyre* and the Two Dalilas." *Dickens Studies Annual* 33 (2003): 199–213.

Chard, M. Joan. " 'Apple of Discord': The Centrality of the Eden Myth in the Novels of Charlotte Brontë." *Brontë Society Transactions* 19 (1988): 197–205.

Franklin, J. Jeffrey. "The Merging of Spiritualities: Jane Eyre as Missionary of Love." *Nineteenth-Century Literature* 49 (1995): 456–82.

Gallagher, Susan. "*Jane Eyre* and Christianity." *Approaches to Teaching Brontë's* Jane Eyre. Ed. Diane Hoeveler and Beth Lau. New York: MLA, 1993. 62–68.

Gilbert, Sandra, and Susan Gubar. *The Madwoman in the Attic: The Woman Writer and the Nineteenth-Century Literary Imagination.* New Haven: Yale UP, 1979.

Gordon, Lyndall. *Charlotte Brontë, A Passionate Life.* London: Chatto and Windus, 1994.

Imlay, Elizabeth. *Charlotte Brontë and the Mysteries of Love: Myth and Allegory in* Jane Eyre. Hemel Hempstead, New York: Harvester Wheatsheaf, 1989.

Jenkins, Keith. "*Jane Eyre*: Charlotte Brontë's New Bible. *Approaches to Teaching Brontë's* Jane Eyre. Ed. Diane Hoeveler and Beth Lau. New York: MLA, 1993. 69–75.

Lamonica, Maria. "Jane's Crown of Thorns: Feminism and Christianity in *Jane Eyre*. *Studies in the Novel* 34 (2002): 245–63.

Lawson, Kate. "Imagining Eve: Charlotte Brontë, Kate Millett, Hélène Cixous." *Women's Studies* 24 (1995): 411–26.

Moglen, Helene. *Charlotte Brontë: The Self Conceived*. New York: Norton, 1976.

Milton, John. *Complete Poems and Major Prose*. Ed. Merritt Hughes. New York: Odyssey, 1957.

Peters, Margot. *Unquiet Soul: A Biography of Charlotte Brontë*. New York: Doubleday, 1975.

Pfeiffer, Julie. "John Milton's Influence on the Inspired Poetry of Charlotte Brontë." *Brontë Society Transactions* 28 (2003): 37–45.

Raleigh, Walter. *Milton*. New York: Putnam, 1900.

Vargish, Thomas. *The Providential Aesthetic in Victorian Fiction*. Charlottesville: UP of Virginia, 1985.

Williams, Carolyn. "Closing the Book: The Intertexual End of *Jane Eyre*." *Jane Eyre*. Ed. Heather Glen. New York: St Martin's, 1997. 227–50.

Wittreich, Joseph. *Feminist Milton*. Ithaca: Cornell UP, 1987.

Toward a Theory of Narrative Sympathy: Character, Story, and the Body in *The Mill on the Floss*

Thomas Recchio

This essay explores the narrative function of a pattern of negation associated with Maggie Tulliver that produces a tension on three levels: formally, in Maggie's opposition to various narratives within which other characters attempt to constrain her; psychologically, in the repeated frustration of Maggie's efforts to develop a life that remains consonant with what we might call her bodily attunement to the material world; and socially, between Maggie's personal desires and the social roles available to her for their realization. Readers' experience of these tensions and their lack of resolution produce a reader-based narrative sympathy. Drawing on George Poulet's discussion of the double-consciousness that characterizes the interiority of reading, and weaving together literary, Bakhtinian, and anthropological theories of sympathy that all, in one way or another, exphasize the simultaneous separation and tension between character (or individual) and story (narrative or social script) that is most visible in forms of resistance associated with the materiality of the body, the essay argues that sympathy is a form of frustration that results from a collision between individual desire (in novelistic character and in actual reader) and a limited set of available social narratives that are incommensurate with that desire. The author develops the argument by offering a Kristevan reading that emphasizes the semiotic function of Maggie Tulliver as character.

Dickens Studies Annual, Volume 38, Copyright © 2007 by AMS Press, Inc. All rights reserved.

> "... she writhed under the demonstrable truth
> of the character he had given to her conduct, and
> yet her whole soul rebelled against it as unfair
> from its incompleteness."
>
> —Book Fifth, Chapter 5 (446)

At the end of the first chapter of Book V ("Wheat and Tares") of *The Mill on the Floss*, Philip Wakem and Maggie Tulliver exchange the following words:

> "Ah Maggie," said Philip almost fretfully, "you would never love me so well as you love your brother."
> "Perhaps not, " said Maggie simply; "but then, you know, the first thing I ever remember in my life is standing with Tom by the side of the Floss while he held my hand; everything before that is dark to me. But I shall never forget you, though we must keep apart." (322)

Simple as that moment may seem, with Philip "almost" expressing his impatience with Maggie's blindness to her significance to him, a blindness confirmed by Maggie's apparent matter-of-fact assertion of the priority of family ties, it is, nonetheless, perplexing. The simplicity of Maggie's response to Philip is out of proportion to the complexity of motive and desire implicit in the exchange. That lack of proportion gives Maggie's response a non sequitur quality, for it does not necessarily follow that Maggie's earliest family memory should function as an obstacle to the extension of her feelings beyond the family. The quality of Maggie's response in its syntactic disruption, however, enacts in miniature the way in which Eliot presents Maggie throughout the novel as resistant to the social and cultural logic that figures the patterns of behavior and meanings of Maggie's life in advance of her living it and in opposition to her own desires for it. Maggie's response is, in addition, unambiguously a refusal, and Maggie's character from the very beginning of the novel has been defined in some measure by her capacity for refusal. Maggie's first words in the novel are, in fact, a refusal: " 'Oh, mother,' said Maggie in a vehemently cross tone, 'I don't *want* to do my patchwork' " (18). Rather than exploring Maggie's refusals as a pattern of negation that reveals the internal contradictions within Maggie as a character, I would like to consider the narrative function of Maggie's refusals as the production of a set of tensions that resonate on three levels: formally, in the tension generated by Maggie's opposition to the various narratives within which other characters attempt to constrain her; psychologically, in the tension generated by the repeated frustration of Maggie's efforts to develop a life that remains consonant with what we might call her bodily attunement to the material world in her precognitive, preoedipal state; and socially, in the tension generated between Maggie's personal desires and the social roles available to her for their realization. Further, I would like to suggest that it is in the reader's experience of these tensions and their irresolution that what I am calling narrative sympathy emerges. But, first, what is it really that Maggie refuses? What role does that refusal play in the narrative? And what, finally, might the effect of Maggie's refusal be on readers?

A brief answer to those questions will sketch out my argument. First, what Maggie refuses, I think, is to allow other characters' stories or social discourses more generally to be imposed on her experience. Second, the narrative effect of that refusal is to call into question the explanatory power, that is, the authority, of the various narratives and social discourses deployed in the novel, thereby establishing a tension-filled gap between character and narrative. That gap suggests that there is always some degree of noncorrespondence between character and narrative situation, that an aspect of novelistic character escapes containment in stories and social discourses. Third, readers' perceptions of the gap between character and narrative, the noncorrespondence between character and situation, produces a sense of sympathy for character. This sympathy, which is part self-recognition, part self-projection, and part intersubjective community, results from readers' awareness of the inadequacy of social discourses and the stories others tell about them to represent their experience fully. There is always something missing in any explanation about the relations among experience, narrative, character, and reader. And that something missing is tied to inarticulate bodily sensation and expression.

The contemporary literature on sympathy is extensive,[1] but Audrey Jaffe's *Scenes of Sympathy: Identity and Representation in Victorian Fiction* (2000) is most relevant to my concerns in this essay because of Jaffe's emphasis on the relationship between identity and social placement. Arguing that Victorian novels "repeatedly stage sympathy as representation," Jaffe explores how the self—because it is presented inevitably "*as* image"—can be perceived by readers as fundamentally "an effect of social determinants" (10). Here is how she summarizes that part of her argument:

> The scene of sympathy opens up a space between self and representation which gives way to a perception of the self as representation; imagining the self as occupying another's space is only a step away from imagining the self as merely occupying its own. What "place" signifies, then, is cultural possibility: a negative or, conversely, idealized image of identity. Sympathy in Victorian culture . . . is sympathy both for and against images of cultural identity.   (10)

But "images of cultural identity" are not necessarily merely place holders that define and isolate static social positions. And novelistic images of personal identity, as Jaffe's fine reading of Elizabeth Gaskell's *Ruth* amply demonstrates, are not necessarily stable, for Ruth's "official" identity through much of the novel is a disguise. "That sympathy should manifest itself as disguise,'' Jaffe claims, ''brings out, not least, the way both involve an imaginative transgression of the boundaries of social identity'' (78–79). Associating sympathy and disguise with imaginative transgression places the novelistic character's effort to shape a personal identity against the social narratives that would provide personal identity in advance. In Ruth's case, the social marker ''fallen woman'' provides that identity, an identity that she simultaneously confirms and undermines through her death (see Jaffe 92–94).

The deaths of female characters such as Ruth, Thomas Hardy's Tess, and, of course, Eliot's Maggie have been read as evasions of the political issues set in motion by the novels since the deaths evoke feelings of sympathy for the individual peculiarities of the characters' situations and fates, essentially erasing the social contexts evoked in the characters' stories. ''Sympathy thus conceived,'' explains Jaffe, ''grounds the self in the dissolution of the social, doing away with representation in order to reach a common ground of feeling—as if the only escape from social difference were in a common humanity attained in dissolution and death'' (15–16). There is another way to read how the ''dissolution of the social'' in novels may provide a common ground for beginning to imagine the possibility of restructuring the social rather than escaping from it, for ''dissolution and death'' are physical phenomena. When we read about a character's death in a novel, our sense of our own mortality is activated; we are reminded of the frailty of our own bodies and our own frustrations in trying to finds ways to realize ourselves through the social forms that we perforce must find a way to live into and through. We have to project in some form this question: how will the end of my own life make sense in relation to the social order in which my death occurs? Is every one's life—because we all die—an evasion of the social? My short answer to that question is no. Fictional deaths, I would argue, become available to our individual consciousness through a fundamentally relational activity: the encounter of two historically specific subjectivities through reading is simultaneously a formal (i.e., literary), a psychological, and a social event.

In *Nobody's Story* (1994) Catherine Gallagher reads David Hume's *Treatise on Human Nature* in order to argue for the peculiar connection between sympathy and fiction: ''Hume's *Treatise* reveals why fictional characters were uniquely suitable objects of compassion. Because they were conjectural, suppositional identities *belonging* to no one, they could be universally appropriated. A story about nobody was nobody's story and hence could be entered, occupied, identified with by anybody'' (168). Gallagher's argument is based on a model of reading where the reader is active, the text passive, offering a narrative that readers can ''occupy.'' Making the narrative conform to their own desires, readers consume the subjectivity embodied in the text and make the text a version of themselves. As Gallagher notes, quoting Hume, ''In sympathy there is an evident conversion of an idea into an impression. This conversion arises from the relation of objects to our self. Our self is always intimately present to us'' (168–69). ''Sympathy, then,'' Gallagher explains, ''is not an emotion about someone else but is rather the process by which someone else's emotion becomes our own'' (169).

George Poulet's well-known and provocative ''Criticism and the Experience of Interiority'' offers a useful corrective to what may be taken as the rather aggressive singularity of the reader's activity in Gallagher's gloss on Hume. Rather than emphasizing how readers enter into the stories they read, Poulet explores what happens when, as he emphatically puts it, ''I deliver myself, bound hand and foot, to the omnipotence of fiction'' (43). As partial answer, he explains, ''When I am absorbed in reading, a second self takes over, a self which thinks and feels for me'' (45). ''Who,'' he then asks, ''is the usurper who occupies the forefront? Who is the mind who alone all by himself fills my consciousness and who, when I say I, is indeed that I?'' (46). He first suggests that that mind is the author's but quickly shifts to arguing that the work itself has a mind of its own, a mind that Poulet, as reader, ''summon[s] back into existence by placing [his] own consciousness at its disposal'' (47). Every reader might then say with Poulet that when we give ourselves to reading a fictional text, ''the work thinks itself in me'' (47). ''Everything happens . . . as though, from the moment I become prey to what I read, I begin to share the use of my consciousness with this being whom I have tried to define and who is the conscious subject ensconced at the heart of the work. He and I, we start having a common consciousness'' (47).

In her gloss on Poulet in *Schools of Sympathy*, Nancy Roberts argues that Poulet describes what she calls the social work of the novel, ''the creation of this subject-effect,'' which is for her a ''confusion of roles'' that results from our inability ''to tell ourselves from the character or the author'' (26). What Roberts ignores, of course, is how, for Poulet, what begins as a confusion of roles becomes ''a common consciousness,'' and that common consciousness, I would argue, is central to the way in which readers experience narrative sympathy, for while sympathy in social life and in visual culture (painting and the theater) may be informed by forms of spectacle and be fueled by the effort of the viewer to overcome the separation between self and other through imaginative projection, novelistic narratives come to life in the consciousness of readers; narratives inhabit readers just as much as readers inhabit narratives. And in novels that concern themselves with the inner life of characters, readers experience that inner life as both an invasion and a possession. One result is a peculiar sense of sympathy that emerges in opposition to or a surplus of narrative as such.

Mikhail Bakhtin's discussion of the development of the novelistic ''hero'' in his ''Epic and Novel,'' and Victor Turner's concept of ''communitas'' as articulated in his *The Ritual Process: Structure and Anti-Structure* provide a strong basis for making a distinction between a reader's sense of novelistic character that is in excess to the narratives through which character moves, in the former case, and, in the latter case, between the idiosyncratic specificity of the people we encounter in the world and the social frames and cultural stories within which they (and we) are all placed. Bakhtin argues that "An individual cannot be completely incarnated into the flesh of existing socio-historical categories." For novelistic heroes, then, "There always remains an unrealized surplus of humanness; there always remains a need for a future, and a place for this future to be found. . . . Reality as we have it in the novel is only one of many possible realities; it is not inevitable, not arbitrary, it bears within itself other possibilities" (37). Bakhtin seems to be arguing that the "unrealized surplus of humanness" of novelistic character is available to readers through a sense of readers' own unfinished, unrealized, yet to be lived out humanness. As character lives in the consciousness of readers, the open-ended possibilities set in motion by the narrative share a common momentum with the open-ended possibilities of readers' own lives. In the midst of reading, the future of character and the future of readers are both open questions. When narratives end, however, "other possibilities" for novelistic character are closed off; readers are left with a sense of the gap between the possibilities suggested by character and the sense of incompleteness that results from narrative closure. Readerly frustration—consider the long history of complaints about the arbitrariness of novelistic endings—may manifest itself, then, as a sense of sympathy for character that has been weirdly intensified by the inevitable limitations of narrative. The withdrawal of half of the consciousness that readers experience as "common" with their own consciousness in reading feels like a death.

If the withdrawal of common consciousness that I have been trying to describe feels like a figurative death, we might say then that our experience as readers is analogous to our experience of encountering other people in their historical specificity in the world since reading texts and engaging with other people are both inter-subjective experiences. Each is what Victor Turner calls "an inward experience of existential communitas" (132). For Turner, "communitas is a relationship between concrete, historical, idiosyncratic individuals," who are not yet "segmentalized into roles and statuses," and whose relationship can be characterized as a "direct, immediate, and total confrontation of human identities" (131–32). This full recognition of the common humanness of a radically unique other is unstable, however, although it is the basis, according to Turner, for the development of "norm-governed relationships between social personae" (132). Within social norms, nonetheless, a residual sense of existential communitas remains and can be seen as the stimulus for various models of social reform designed to realize more completely the full humanness of each person. Such a desire for social reform

Turner calls "ideological communitas," which he defines as follows: "Ideological communitas is at once an attempt to describe the external and visible effects—the outward form, it might be said—of an inward experience of existential communitas, and to spell out the optimal conditions under which such experiences might be expected to flourish and multiply" (132). Victorian novels in general, and *The Mill on the Floss* in particular, it seems to me, do not spell out "optimal conditions" for revolution or reform, but they do more than merely describe the effects of existential communitas; they provide the intersubjective experience that is existential communitas itself insofar as they enable readers to experience another subjectivity in a way that feels presocial or asocial (despite all the specific social markers within the novels themselves) through the common consciousness produced by reading.

The Mill on the Floss does more than provide such an experience, however. In its nearly obsessive concern with Maggie's inner life, *The Mill* sustains Maggie's integrity through the paradox of keeping her suspended in a preoedipal version of existential communitas, fully aware of an "other" (her brother Tom) and fully resistant to the necessary fall into normative, role governed social structure, a version of which is embedded within the symbolic order of language itself. One of the things Maggie refuses to do, then, is to allow herself to be defined by a social order and a patriarchal language that would sever her sense of self from her bodily experience. Maggie refuses, then, to surrender her surplus of humanness as a character to social narratives that can only diminish her. By keeping Maggie's body (and her psyche) always poised on the border between a preverbal, presocial integrity and a distorting social and symbolic order, Eliot offers what I find to be her most powerful critique of Victorian culture as a whole, for by presenting the social as continually frustrating Maggie's desires (desires that readers experience as their own), the social, economic, and moral narratives upon which the culture is based are continually called into question. There is no place for a woman (or a man, for that matter) to be fully human in the culture where too often social scripts and individual desires are incommensurate.

Water and the Semiotic as Refusal

The Mill on the Floss opens in a dream of embracing waters: "A wide plain, where the broadening Floss hurries on between its green banks to the sea, and the loving tide, rushing to meet it, checks its passage in an impetuous embrace" (53). That opening strikes a note of concord and discord, of movement and stasis as the Floss, clearly defined "between its green banks," is, in effect, obliterated by the "impetuous embrace" of "the loving tide." Clarity of line and direction are erased in a rush of water, a rush that is enacted in the language as the relative clause beginning "where the broadening Floss" overwhelms the main clause, interrupting it, leaving "a wide plain" a mere fragment, a syntactic disruption on the sentence level that is analogous to the non sequitur disruption with which this essay began. There is movement of other water as the opening develops. "Just by the red-roofed town the tributary Ripple flows with a lively current into the Floss. How lovely the little river is, with its dark, changing wavelets! It seems to me like a living companion while I wander along the bank and listen to its low, placid voice, as to the voice of one who is deaf and loving" (53). Here the narrator announces herself, projecting desire onto the water, which "seems . . . like a living companion," "loving" though "deaf" and implicitly oblivious to the narrator's desire. The opening evokes currents and counter-currents, figuring desire as a kind of negation with images of submersion. "I am," the narrator enthuses, "in love with moistness, and envy the white ducks that are dipping their heads far into the water . . . ". And, again, deafness. "The rush of the water and the booming of the mill bring a dreamy deafness. . . . They are like a great curtain of sound, shutting one out from the world beyond" (54). The "curtain of sound" becomes a circle of water at the end of the opening when the narrator describes "[t]hat little girl" who "has been standing on just the same spot on the edge of the water" watching the "unresting" mill "wheel sending out its diamond jets of water" (54).

"That little girl," of course, is Maggie Tulliver, whose image, framed by the circle of water—the culmination of the series of associations of water with currents and flow, a "loving deafness," and submersion—becomes the focus of the narrator's identification of desire with the muting of sense and the suppression of language. In other words, the opening of the narrative *The Mill on the Floss* is dominated by images that simultaneously evoke the flow of narrative (the desire to tell) and resist that flow (the knowledge that no telling can ever be adequate), redirecting the narrative energy into a circle—movement with no direction, desire that goes nowhere.

Such a reading of the opening of the novel has a certain formalist force since the novel ends with Maggie and Tom drowning in a flood, a flowing obliteration of sense and language if there ever was one and an echo of the water image with which the opening ends; the novel comes full circle imagistically. But without embracing a formalist reading and without rejecting the claims of realism and the psychologizing of character that realism implies, I would like to read *The Mill on the Floss* in response to the quality of the imagery and language of its opening in order to demonstrate how those qualities provide both the ground for and an aesthetic of narrative sympathy. Julia Kristeva's distinction between the semiotic and the symbolic, the two "modalities of the same signifying process" (24) as she puts it, will help me in that task for that distinction addresses how literary language achieves significance in a way that accounts for issues of narrative form, social discourse, and individual subjectivity, and it is the breaks or fissures between and among form, discourse, and subjectivity that generate the experience of narrative sympathy I have sketched out. After clarifying the distinction between the semiotic and the symbolic, I will demonstrate how Maggie Tulliver is consistently associated with images of the semiotic which are placed in opposition to structures of the symbolic. The semiotic/symbolic tension is figured most forcefully in Maggie's relationships to the men in the novel, relationships which, in the cases of Tom Tulliver, Philip Wakem, and Stephen Guest, are animated by Maggie's refusal to accept the terms of definition for those relationships insisted upon by the men. Through those relationships the novel consistently places qualities associated with the semiotic in opposition to various social discourses (versions of the symbolic); that opposition produces narrative moments where a prediscursive desire is recatalyzed in Maggie and, because that desire of necessity must be rendered in language, it is thwarted over and over again. Maggie's character as a result seems suspended at the moment of what Kristeva would call the "thetic break," the moment that makes visible the deep structure of the narrative sympathy that I'm arguing for.

The thetic marks the point of intersection between the semiotic and symbolic, the moment when each becomes visible or, perhaps, merely apprehensible in an originating experience of self-consciousness, the separating out between self and the not-self. In order for a human being to be a human subject—that is, to "have" subjectivity—the human being must already be positioned within the symbolic order; that does not mean, however, that the semiotic is left behind for the semiotic is not a psychological, developmental stage. It is always in a dialectic with the symbolic. "Because the subject is always *both* semiotic *and* symbolic, no signifying system he produces can be either 'exclusively' semiotic or 'exclusively' symbolic, and is instead necessarily marked by an indebtedness to both" (24).

In this formulation, the semiotic exists always in relation to the symbolic; in a sense, it cannot be conceptualized without the symbolic, and as Kristeva points out, the part of the semiotic that "precedes" the symbolic is "only a *theoretical supposition* justified by the need for description." Consequently, the semiotic "exists in practice only within the symbolic and requires the symbolic break to obtain the complex articulation we associate with it in musical and poetic practices" (68). Kristeva identifies this "complex articulation" with art, which she then defines as "the semiotization of the symbolic" (79). In this way she places art in opposition to or in dialectic with the systems of discourse that shape the social order. Art thus becomes for Kristeva asocial, but its asociality has, potentially, social effects since art as it is realized in "the signifying process" can produce a "different kind of subject": "[T]he

signifying process, as it is practiced by texts—those 'truly free works'—transforms the opaque and impenetrable subject of social relations and struggles
into a subject in process/on trial. Within this apparent asociality, however,
lies the social function of texts: the production of a different kind of subject,
one capable of bringing about new social relations . . . '' (105), in short, the
transformation of individual consciousness through reading.

   Even though Kristeva's next move is to constrain the possibilities of ''new
social relations'' by relegating those relations to ''the process of capitalism's
subversion'' (105), approvingly quoting Marx on how a ''new subject'' in the
''realm of freedom . . . will enter into the process of immediate production''
(105–06), it is not necessary, it seems to me, to tie the semiotic to a Marxist
teleology, which is, after all, at the service of a definitive symbolic order, a
finalized sociality. Rather the power of Kristeva's concept of the semiotic
resides in its asociality, its resistance to the symbolic order, its persistence in
a refusal to be contained, controlled, directed. In such resistance, Kristeva's
semiotic has affinities with Turner's ''existential communitas'' and Bakhtin's
''surplus of humanness,'' for all three concepts place the unspecified, un-
formed, unstructured, and unpredictable quality of consciousness, bodily
awareness, and the persistent desire for harmony between the two at the base
of utopian hope and artistic expression. Kristeva puts this latter point somewhat hyperbolically: ''In 'artistic' practices the semiotic—the precondition
of the symbolic—is revealed as that which also destroys the symbolic'' (50),
through, perhaps, the return of the repressed? Taking a cue from Margaret
Homans, who in *Bearing the Word* argues that Kristeva presents the semiotic
as something repressed and thus ''capable of a dangerous return'' (19), I
would argue that what Homans restricts to a ''mother-daughter language''
can be extended to human subjectivity more generally where the desire for
an inviolable, pre-social/a-social expressiveness ''is continuous from childhood . . . [and] is . . . socially and culturally suppressed and silenced'' (19).
In such a formulation, we can argue that the semiotic both sustains and
destabilizes rather than destroys the symbolic. ''Through themes, ideologies,
and social meanings, the artist introduces into the symbolic order an asocial
drive, one not yet harnessed by the thetic'' (70–71). The asocial energy of
the semiotic is manifest in the language of the text and in the relation between
the text and reader. In the case of *The Mill on the Floss*, the images, themes,
and social meanings associated with Maggie Tulliver enact an asocial drive
that resists the pre-established social discourses that others would impose on
Maggie as subject. Such an asocial drive thrives on the particularity of bodily
experience attuned to the sounds, rhythms, and sensations of the natural
world. So contra Homans, who characterizes ''a seductively beautiful version
of the narrative pattern of Maggie's life'' as the movement from a drive
toward self-transcendence to ''a return to particularity,'' her increasing ''liter-
alizing life'' becoming a form of regression (130) (rather, might the cultural

suppression and silencing of Maggie's desires be at work here?), I would argue that Maggie's silences are forms of resistance that find their power less in the themes of the novel and more in the experience of the reader. So while Maggie's "vital resistance (willful or unconscious) to feminine submissiveness" may fail on the level of story, Maggie's "complete passivity as a reader" (125) is counterbalanced by the activity of Eliot's readers who may find Maggie's passivity a function of her silencing. So while Homans argues that when "Maggie does at last determine what her own words would be" (in response to Stephen's request for her to summon him), "but they 'find no utterance but in a sob' " (125) as a mark of her "vanished" capacity for "original invention and self expression" (125), one could argue that the "sob" is Maggie's final refusal to complete someone else's narrative, to resist with her body rather than words.

Tom and Maggie

As Maggie's words to Philip in the Red Deeps indicate, her earliest memory is of her brother Tom at that delicately poised moment that marks a transition from the semiotics of prediscursive significance to the symbolic order, a kind of fall into discourse where one's subjectivity becomes defined by social relations through the assumption of a social position. The position that Maggie, quite clumsily as the text makes clear, falls into is structured by family relations, Maggie being the youngest of two children and only daughter of a provincial English family during the early years of the nineteenth century. Maggie's position is defined through a discourse of "nature," a discourse more or less unquestionably shared by the people of St. Oggs and environs which Maggie seems "naturally" (i.e., in her bodily form) to defy. Here is how Maggie is introduced in a dialogue between her parents:

> "It seems a bit of a pity, though," said Mr. Tulliver, "as the lad should take after the mother's side instead o' the little wench. That's the worst on't wi' the crossing o'breeds; you can never justly calkilate what'll come on't. The little un takes after my side, now; she's twice as 'cute as Tom. Too 'cute for a woman, I'm afraid," continued Mr. Tulliver, turning his head dubiously first on one side and then on the other. "It's no mischief much while she's a little un, but an over-'cute woman's no better nor a long-tailed sheep—she'll fetch none the bigger price for that."
>
> ....
>
> "You talk o' 'cuteness, Mr. Tulliver," she [Mrs. Tulliver] observed as she sat down, "but I'm sure the child's half an idiot i' some things; for if I send her upstairs to fetch anything, she forgets what she's gone for, an' perhaps 'ull sit down on the floor i' the sunshine an' plait her hair an' sing to herself like a Bedlam creatur', all the while I'm waiting for her downstairs. That niver run

i' my family, thank God, no more nor a brown skin as makes her look like a
mulatter. I don't like to fly i' the face o' Providence, but it seems hard as I
should have but one gell, an' her so comical.''

''Pooh, nonsense!'' said Mr. Tulliver. ''She's a straight black-eyed wench
as anybody need wish to see. I don't know i' what she's behind other folks's
children, and she can read almost as well as the parson.''

''But her hair won't curl all I can do with it, and she's so franzy about having
it put i' paper, and I've such work as never was to make her stand and have it
pinched with th' irons.''

''Cut it off—cut it off short,'' said the father rashly.   (59–60)

That passage reflects a series of very recognizable gender specific oppositions,
the most obvious being between the male/mind and the female/body. Those
oppositions, however, function in a very unstable way in the passage. Maggie's acuteness is transformed in her mother's perception to a form of insanity
because that quality has crossed the ''natural'' lines of gender, rendering
Maggie an idiot, insane (''a Bedlam creature''), and comical. That violation
of the ''natural'' lines of gender is, however, the natural result of, in Mr.
Tulliver's words, ''the crossing o' breeds,'' which would be, based on the
logic of the passage, any offspring of a nonincestuous relationship. In the
passage, then, the construction of the ''natural'' through a cultural discourse
is called into question by the physical results of a natural process; the nondis-
cursive materiality of Maggie Tulliver is a physical check on the claims of a
gender specific discourse. Maggie, as an ''embodiment'' of the semiotic,
poses a challenge to the symbolic, an argument that can be reinforced by
quite conventional literary tropes, in this case the trope of a woman's unruly
hair as a mark of her insanity. Ophelia serves well as an analogue.

With that in mind, Mr. Tulliver's ''cut if off short'' can be read as a
response to Mrs. Tulliver's reading of Maggie. The only conceivable response
to the conflict between the discursively ''natural'' and the physically natural
is to destroy the physical, to destroy that which cannot be contained within
discursive forms of significance. In other words, discourse has somatic effects
on the body and on the mind which can be traced on the surface of the body.
That latter point is most evident when Maggie, with Tom's help, cuts off her
own hair in response to the pressures of social disapproval from her family.
Maggie thus partly embodies an ''other'' against which normative discourses
can be seen, measured, and found wanting. Since she is not literally destroyed
(until the end of the novel in any event), Maggie has a double function: she
enables discursive meaning even as she resists containment in that meaning.
She enacts what Kristeva calls ''the text's semiotic distribution,'' which functions as follows: ''when instinctual rhythm passes through ephemeral but
specific theses, meaning is constituted but is then immediately exceeded by
what seems outside meaning: materiality, the discontinuity of real objects''

(100). Within the "text" of *The Mill on the Floss*, Maggie serves as a metaphor for the semiotic that necessitates an emphasis on her physicality, her materiality, her body, creating an illusion of her human subjectivity that exceeds her role as a character in a novel. In that way in the experience of a reader, Maggie takes on the status of a "real object." Maggie, as a "real object" for the reader (a reading effect that depends on the reader's sense of Maggie as a "real" subject to herself), resists and exceeds the social discourses that would represent her.

What generates sympathy in the novel, then, is not the particulars of any painful situation in which readers find Maggie as the novel unfolds; rather it is the consistent sense of the discontinuity between Maggie and the stories others in the novel construct for and about her. Narrative sympathy in this formulation depends on a resistance shared between character and reader to the shutting down of semiotic desire for the sake of narrative clarity and closure. Such sympathy is akin to the kind of inarticulate frustration and resistance one feels for one's self when one becomes the object of rumor and speculation, where the narrative details of the rumor have a certain surface discursive logic but the narrative closure projected through those details is wildly misrepresentative. The effect of such speculation is to negate the real sense of lived experience in the subject of the speculation; the discourse of rumor replaces unfinalized experience with narrative clarity, placing the full range of bodily awareness produced by the interactions among intellect, emotion, and physical sensation in opposition to discourse. Eliot's barely suppressed rage at "the world's wife" upon Maggie's return to St. Oggs registers this narrative sympathy born of frustrated feeling,[2] which she captures with exquisite precision soon after Tom discovers Maggie's secret meetings with Philip. He accuses her of disobedience and deceitfulness, of throwing "away her own respectability by clandestine meetings with the son of a man that has helped to ruin her father" (359); he then accompanies her to what he insists is the last meeting. On their way, the narrator comments: "Tom had this terrible clutch on her [Maggie's] conscience and her deepest dread; she writhed under the demonstrable truth of the character he had given to her conduct, and yet her whole soul rebelled against it as unfair from its incompleteness" (361). "Unfair from its incompleteness" indeed characterizes the social discourse, extended innumerable times in dialogues among the Gleggs, Pullets, and Tullivers, that Tom imposes most emphatically on Maggie. That imposition effaces over and over again the semiotic significance of Maggie's loving desires.

Through much of the first half of the novel, Tom provides the focus for Maggie's hunger for love, a hunger he intermittently gratifies but mostly denies. His denial of love to Maggie is usually an effect of what he perceives as his social placement; first, as older brother, he takes it as his place to judge and to punish, and later, as head of the family, he takes control of Maggie's life, determining where she lives and what she does until she comes of age. In both cases he subordinates Maggie's need for love and his own loving impulses to the social discourse and values of provincial, middle class, mercantile propriety represented by his maternal aunts and uncles. Early in the novel, however, he does reveal a capacity for love which is rendered in images that associate love with prediscursive significance. After Tom decides to punish Maggie for having neglected his rabbits—by asserting that he does not love her and then refusing to take her fishing the next day as he had promised (88)—his father orders him, " 'And be good to her, do you hear? Else I'll let you know better' " (90). So Tom searches Maggie out, and when he finds her, the narrator comments:

> . . . Maggie and Tom were still very much like young animals, and so she could rub her cheek against his and kiss his ear in a random, sobbing way; and there were tender fibres in the lad that had been used to answer to Maggie's fondling, so that he behaved with a weakness quite inconsistent with his resolution to punish her as much as she deserved; he actually began to kiss her in return and say, "Don't cry, then, Magsie—here, eat a bit o' cake."
> Maggie's sobs began to subside, and she put out her mouth for the cake and bit a piece; and then Tom bit a piece, just for company, and they ate together and rubbed each other's cheeks and brows and noses together while they ate, with a humiliating resemblance to two friendly ponies.   (91–92)

Love in this scene is expressed in sound (kissing in a "sobbing way") and in gesture (rubbing cheeks, brows, and noses together), images associated with the semiotic which, for the moment, undercuts the demands of the symbolic (Tom's "resolution to punish"). The eating of the cake adds an overtone of communion, introducing a psychic component to the physical scene. The prediscursive bond illustrated in the scene extends to the next day when Tom takes Maggie fishing after all. "It was," the narrator tells us, "one of their happy mornings" (93), and the reason for that happiness, I would argue, is in large part because of the absence of language.

Here is how the narrator characterizes Maggie's experience of fishing, a time spent mostly sitting quietly by the "Round Pool," "which the floods had made a long time ago": "There was nothing to mar her delight in the whispers and the dreamy silences when she listened to the light dipping sounds of the rising fish and the gentle rustling, as if the willows and the reeds and the water had their happy whisperings also. Maggie thought it would make a very nice heaven to sit by the pool in that way and never be scolded" (93). Heaven, for Maggie, means being away from the sound of a socially inflected human voice, the carrier of a discourse of positionality and judgment. Sound in the passage is muted, the rustlings and whisperings presented as "dreamy silences." In the paragraph that follows, Maggie and Tom are shown trotting, sitting, seeing, hearing, playing, and gathering reeds together but not speaking; the mill is booming, the spring-tide "like a hungry monster" is rushing, and the "Great Ash" they gaze upon "had once wailed and groaned like a man" (93). The inarticulate sounds, silences, and rushings of water echo the burden of the opening chapter of the novel where the desire to tell a story, to render significance within the symbolic order, is suspended by a counter-desire to render significance semiotically in images evocative of movement without direction, sound without articulation, significance without meaning.

That counter-desire—"the semiotization of the symbolic" that Kristeva claims "represents the flow of jouissance into language" (79)—in the pattern of imagery I have been tracing here includes allusions to death. "Maggie," we are told at the end of the passage cited above, "when she read about Christiana passing 'the river over which there is no bridge,' always saw the Floss between the green pastures and the Great Ash" (93–94). Such allusions permeate the novel, from Mrs. Tulliver's fears of Maggie's drowning (a leitmotif in book 1), to the legend of St. Oggs and stories of the local floods, to the climactic death of Maggie and Tom in the final flood. Those allusions provide a context within which *jouissance*, with its connotations of orgasm and the mobile fluidity of female pleasure, can be read in the language of *The Mill on the Floss* as animating the old literary trope variously rendered in the binaries love and death, death and desire, sex and death and so on, suggesting that Maggie and Tom's drowning is a kind of incestuous *liebestod* (Gilbert and Gubar 494, Polhemus 168–95). Rather than pursue the implications of that reading, however, a reading which, through its emphasis on the dramatics of the final death scene, ultimately avoids the painful texture of the dispersed effects of a *jouissance* consistently in conflict with the symbolic demands of narrative closure, I would like to suggest that the thwarting of *jouissance* by way of the demands of the symbolic order transforms *jouissance* from the pursuit of bodily pleasure in the isolation of the amorphous desires of the body to the realization of one's primal, pre-discursive humanness in relation to an "other" or others. In short, *jouissance*, although Kristeva would most likely object to such a formulation, is inseparable from what Turner calls "spontaneous communitas" and what others might call love. The following brief scene at the end of book 2, when Maggie fetches Tom from his school at the Stellings with the news of their father's losing the law suit and his subsequent illness, illustrates the sort of thing I have in mind.

Tom and Maggie were standing on the door-step, ready to set out, when Mrs. Stelling came with a little basket which she hung on Maggie's arms, saying,

"Do remember to eat something on the way, dear." Maggie's heart went out towards this woman whom she had never liked, and she kissed her silently. It was the first sign within the poor child of that new sense which is the gift of sorrow, that susceptibility to the bare offices of humanity which raises them into a bond of loving fellowship, as to haggard men among the icebergs the mere presence of an ordinary comrade stirs the deep fountains of affection.

(269)

Although "the gift of sorrow" is presented as a "new sense" born of experience, the qualities of that gift have affinities with the qualities associated with the semiotic. Note, for example, the emphasis on silence and physicality in the scene with Maggie kissing Mrs. Stelling "silently"; the image of the men in the closing simile whose "mere presence" with each other "stirs the deep fountains of affection" seems in the same key as Maggie's earliest memory of being with Tom on the banks of the Floss. The "bare offices of humanity" efface the divisions of human relations that result from social positioning; Maggie "had never liked Mrs. Stelling" largely because of Mrs. Stelling's obsession with her social position and self-presentation in terms of that position. "The gift of sorrow," however, disrupts positionality; it reinvigorates the desires at play just prior to the thetic break, the fall into discourse. There is pain in Maggie's sorrow to be sure, but there is also the pleasure of communion, the primal and physical bond with others. *Jouissance* is a protean pleasure, and in a gentle way in the scene above, it becomes the ground of human connectedness as it transforms sorrow into union. That transformation, an aspect of the semiotic challenge to the symbolic, is only momentary, though, a prelude to more division, coming as it does at the moment of parting. The Stellings immediately return to their social roles, and Tom and Maggie return home to begin "their new life of sorrow" (270).

That new life of sorrow is characterized more by division than union. It is but a slight exaggeration to claim that the mildest residual experiences of a protean, loving *jouissance* in Maggie's relations to others, mainly her father and Tom, are brutally squashed by the discursive pressures of family reputation and social position. Consider in this regard the way Eliot characterizes Maggie's return home after her father's loss of the lawsuit and subsequent stroke. Mr. Turnbull, the doctor, tells her that her father had been asking for her. "Keep as quiet as you can," he says; "take off your things and come upstairs with me." Maggie, we are told, "obeyed with that terrible beating of the heart which makes existence seem simply a *painful pulsation.*" Upon entering the room, she "rushed towards him and clasped him with *agonized kisses.*" Eliot then comments:

Poor child! It was early for her to know one of those *supreme moments in life* when all we hoped or delighted in, all we dread or endure, falls away from our regard as insignificant—is lost like a trivial memory in that simple, *primitive love* which knits us to the beings who have been nearest to us, in their times of helplessness or anguish.   (278, all italics added)

The boundary between pleasure and pain, desire and fear, frustration and satisfaction is almost indistinguishable in the language of the passage. Cognition, rendered as those things we hope or delight in, dread or endure, is suspended and absorbed by pulsations, kisses, and "primitive love." The bond of father and daughter, is figured as prediscursive as Mr. Tulliver takes "infantine satisfaction in Maggie's near presence—such satisfaction as a baby has when it is returned to the nurse's lap" (278–79). The psychological complexity of that bond—Maggie, the daughter, taking on the role of wet-nurse for her father—is, in my reading, less significant than its elemental physicality, the simple need of the presence of an "other" who is experienced fundamentally as "not other." The desire associated with the semiotic, the gestural, rhythmical, pulsational energies of prediscursive significance resist, in the quoted passage, the distinction making pressures of the symbolic.

Tom, in contrast, though briefly responsive at his father's sickbed (285), later at his deathbed (465), and finally in the boat with "Magsie" in the flood (655) to the elemental physicality and rhythm of feeling associated with Maggie and the semiotic, reacts to the social pressures of the symbolic order by embracing those pressures. Tom sets out on a course of action to repay the family debts, to restore the family's good name, and ultimately to reacquire the family home and mill, reestablishing the family's social position. In embracing so completely the demands of the symbolic order, Tom, who "had very clear prosaic eyes, not apt to be dimmed by mists of feeling or imagination" (368), brooks no opposition.

Laudatory as Tom's efforts eventually turn out to be, and Eliot takes pains to indicate the real good that Tom does (456), his single-mindedness dehumanizes him and isolates Maggie. In her isolation, Maggie's "conflict between the inward impulse and outward fact" (367) becomes an exclusively internal struggle. Consequently, the dialectic between pre-discursive, passional significance and the discursive forms of human social relations enacted in earlier encounters between Maggie and Tom becomes an inner conflict wherein Maggie searches for a substitute authority (another social discourse) to place against her own desires. In other words, she searches for an authority through which she can see herself and against which she can define herself. That search takes the form of an opposition between music and discourse, passion and explanation. In book 4, "The Valley of Humiliation," chapter 3, we are told: "Every affection, every delight the poor child had had was like an aching nerve to her. There was no music for her any more—no piano, no harmonized voices, no delicious stringed instruments with their passionate

cries of imprisoned spirits sending a strange vibration through her frame''
(378). The physical delight of passionate sound has become pain, ''an aching
nerve.'' What Maggie wants is ''some explanation of this hard, real life.''
Affection and intellect split apart as Maggie and Tom split apart, for central
to Maggie's struggle is ''the cruel sense that Tom didn't mind what she
thought or felt.'' Maggie, then, feels compelled to find a position for herself, to
establish a ground ''that would enable her to understand, and in understanding
endure, the heavy weight that had fallen on her young heart'' (379).

This fissioning of Maggie's life and her turn inward are strongly inflected
by gender. ''If she had been taught 'real learning and wisdom, such as great
men knew,' she thought she should have held the secret of life'' (379). Eliot
renders this gendering of Maggie's inward turn quite starkly in the following
exchange between Maggie and Tom which takes place just after Tom has put
a stop to Maggie's secret meetings with Philip at the Red Deeps.

> ''You are nothing but a Pharisee. You thank God for nothing but your own
> virtues; you think they are great enough to win you everything else. You have
> not even a vision of feelings by the side of which your shining virtues are
> mere darkness!''
> ''Well,'' said Tom with cold scorn, ''if your feelings are so much better than
> mine, let me see you show them in some other way than by conduct that's
> likely to disgrace us all, than by ridiculous flights first into one extreme and
> then into another. Pray, how have you shown your love that you talk of either
> to me or my father? By disobeying and deceiving us. I have a different way of
> showing my affection.''
> ''Because you are a man, Tom, and have power, and can do something in
> the world.''
> ''Then, if you can do nothing, submit to those that can.''   (450)

Quite simply, Maggie has no choice but to internalize the conflict between
her inward condition and external circumstances because her relation to those
circumstances is defined in gendered terms and regulated by the men in her
life. Tom stands in as representative of the law, the family, the father, the
controller of discourse while Maggie is constructed as a vehicle of extreme
and dangerous feelings, a potential source of embarrassment at best and disgrace at worst. And disgrace, of course, is really a question of the disposal
of Maggie's body: who, in the end, will possess her? The paternal anxieties
associated with that question necessitate that Tom cut off any avenue of
action for Maggie in the world; her body must remain in the control of Tom
as surrogate father. Maggie has been resisting others' physical control of her
her whole life, a resistance confirmed by numerous episodes in her childhood
from her cutting off of her own hair to her pushing her cousin Lucy in the
mud and running away to the gypsies. When Maggie tries to submit to Tom's
demands, then, her submission does not change the psychic energy of her

resistance; it redirects it in what John Kucich has defined as "Victorian repression."

For Kucich, Victorian repression "transforms assertive energy into self-negating energy" (23), and in Eliot's work that form of repression marks a moral failure based on Eliot's characters' and her own fear of dependence.[3] Certainly in *The Mill on the Floss*, a fear of dependence is a problem, but such a fear cannot be addressed apart from the question of gender: who, after all, is dependent on whom? Although Eliot does not announce gender as an explicit concern, gender is at the heart of her characterization of Maggie, undeniably one of the many "special circumstances that mark the individual lot" (521). For Eliot, there is no way for a thoughtful and sensitive mind to separate social circumstances from the individual lot. Her social vision, then, is never comprehensive, her sense of the real interdependence among people too complex to be reduced to a single, totalizing picture, however detailed. A "fellow feeling with all that is human" (521) of necessity includes a sympathetic response to the particular cultural pressures on women whose bodies too often become sites of male desire and social conflict in ways that generate a fractured sense of their own wholeness. In *The Mill on the Floss*, the possession of Maggie's body becomes the focus of social conflict between the Tullivers and the Wakems (most notably, perhaps, in the conflation of the legal battle over control of the water that drives the mill and Maggie's possible marriage with Philip) and between Maggie and all the men who desire to possess her.

Viewed in that light, Maggie's internalization of the conflict between inward condition and external circumstances is an inevitable extension of social conflict, a conflict which Maggie as a woman and object of desire (not just as desiring subject) experiences in a fundamentally different way than any of the men do. The repression Kucich describes need not be merely an "autonomous, inward version of altruistic feeling" (181) that readers and Eliot herself have wrongly rationalized as satisfying "both the needs of individuals and the needs of relationship" (181); such repression, inflected by gender, can be equated with what Kristeva calls in "About Chinese Women" "masochistic *jouissance*," a kind of *jouissance* that results from a woman's effort to participate in "the symbolic paternal order." Here is Kristeva's explanation: " . . . if a woman is not a virgin, a nun, and chaste, but has orgasms and gives birth, her only means of gaining access to the symbolic paternal order is by engaging in an endless struggle between the orgasmic maternal body and the symbolic prohibition—a struggle that will take the form of guilt and mortification, and culminate in masochistic *jouissance*" (*Reader* 147). Despite the fact that Maggie never gives birth, her difficulties with maintaining a chaste orientation in her relationship with Stephen Guest and her capacity for orgasm are never in doubt. There is, then, a psychological aptness in Kristeva's explanation applied to Maggie for the ways in which others, from Maggie's parents to Stephen Guest, respond to Maggie's body (both her appearance and the materiality of her flesh) determines to a large extent how Maggie experiences her own body. From the extremity of Maggie's self-negation in her response to reading Thomas à Kempis's *Imitation of the Life of Christ*, a book she reads partially as a reaction to Tom's dismissal of her physical significance since she cannot work to earn much money, to the other extremity of her pleasure in the secret meetings with Philip, meetings in which Philip draws attention over and over again to her physical beauty, Maggie's internal contradictions reflect those competing external constructions of her physicality. The contradictions of those competing constructions disrupt Maggie's ability to come to terms with the potential pleasures and real powers of her "orgasmic maternal body," cutting off any avenue for the realization of Maggie's desire. Such constructions mask a fundamental patriarchal fear of the female body when it is not completely constrained by male dominated social formations; the desire of the men to control Maggie's body expresses their fear of the semiotic. By placing Maggie within a narrative, a symbolic discourse, each male character can try to control her body and mitigate his own fear of the semiotic. As I have already shown, Tom, as representative of the family, places Maggie within a discourse of the dutiful daughter who must submit to family demands. Try as she might, Maggie cannot be contained within such a narrative; Maggie experiences the ill fit between narrative and character as emotional and physical suffering, a pattern of suffering established early on in the novel through the attic scenes where Maggie drives nails into her doll "fetish" (79). A variation on that pattern occurs when Maggie returns alone from her "boat trip" with Stephen Guest, only to have Tom falsely construct her as a fallen woman, reinforcing the novel's insistence on the gap between character and story.[4]

Although it would seem that Maggie's relationships with Philip Wakem and with Stephen Guest provide ways out of the trap of her family situation, enabling her to construct her own narrative and thereby close the gap between her sense of her self (her "character") and the narrative unfolding of her life (her "story"), the gap between the semiotic grounding of her embodiment and her placement in the symbolic order, and the gap between her body and its power as a vehicle for her attunement to and fulfillment in the world, those gaps remain because the social terms available to close them are all determined by male desire. And the only way that Maggie can sustain any genuine sense of her integrity in the world—the integrity of her own body—is to resist the determinations of male desire, even at times, as in the case of Stephen, when male desire seems closest to her own. Maggie remains throughout the novel an embodiment of the semiotic, rather than a case of truncated psychosexual development as readings that emphasize the incestuous qualities of her relationship with Tom would have it. The problem is not Maggie's development as such but of the socially available narratives about what her development should be and mean. In that sense, the painful intractability of Maggie's refusal to live others' stories about her and her partial and flailing efforts to live alternatively evokes the situation of most women at the time, a point reinforced by the autobiographical readings of the novel and by Eliot's comment in a letter to John Blackwood that her trip to Rome "will at last chase away Maggie and the Mill from my thoughts; . . . for she and her sorrows have clung to me painfully" (Letters 244). Maggie's "sorrows" are Eliot's sorrows; they are, in part, every Victorian woman's sorrows, and they become the readers' sorrows, male or female. The nonunfolding of her life in *The Mill on the Floss* is, in the end, a powerful critique of Victorian patriarchy that is extended through the work of readers' experience of sympathy into a critique of patriarchy more generally. I will develop this latter point by looking at the terms of Maggie's relationships with Philip and Stephen with a particular emphasis on the paradoxical discourse of nature that frames those relationships. As is the case with the discourse of nature that frames Maggie's introduction in the novel, a discourse that renders Maggie inexplicable and invisible, Maggie's "great temptation" is to erase herself under the belief that she is realizing her own desire. In the end, her "great temptation" is not the possibility of wounding Philip and betraying Lucy by running off with Stephen. Her "great temptation" is marriage itself.

Maggie, Marriage, and the Discourse of Nature

After Tom discovers Maggie's and Philip's meetings at the Red Deeps and brutally wrings a promise from Maggie to stop seeing Philip, the narrator describes Maggie's reaction as "almost like a sharp bodily pain" and closes the chapter with these words: "And yet—how was it that she was now and then conscious of a certain dim background of relief in the forced separation from Philip? Surely it was only because the sense of deliverance from concealment was welcome at any cost?" (451). Of that quoted passage, Dorothea Barrett notes, "The concluding question mark leaves the question open, and the reader recalls the end of the previous chapter" (59). By reading the question as open and referring back to the scene where Maggie promises to marry Philip in "one of those dangerous moments when speech is at once sincere and deceptive" (437) Barrett points toward an answer: Maggie's relief is related to her being spared from her "promised" marriage that could not offer her sexual fulfillment, a potential marriage that Stephen Guest later characterizes thrice as "unnatural" (569, twice and 570 once) and "horrible" (569). And in the terms of the novel, he is right. Note, for instance, the narrator's description of Philip in his request for a kiss to seal Maggie's tacit promise: his face was "pale" and "full of pleading, timid love—like a woman's" (438). There is a kind of mutual feminine recognition between Maggie and Philip born of the limitations of their independent spheres of action, Philip's truncated by his deformity and Maggie's by her gender. What is peculiarly painful in Maggie's recognition of the "sacrifice in this love" for Philip is Philip's role in awakening Maggie's awareness into her sexual maturity on the one hand (cf. his patient courtship through his sharing of novels and music) and his inability to satisfy the desires associated with that maturity on the other (cf. most simply, his physical limitations). In courting Maggie, Philip sets a narrative in motion that he cannot sustain; there is an ill fit between Philip and the masculine role the courtship narrative requires of him. The gap between his character and the narrative he constructs for himself and attempts to impose upon Maggie generates sympathy akin to the sympathy the novel stimulates for Maggie: in both cases the semiotic qualities associated with the feminine disrupt and elude containment within narratives of masculine desire. Maggie's measured consent to marry Philip ("Yes, Philip:" she says, "I should like never to part; I should like to make your life very happy" (437)) becomes an extension of her self-renunciation in "The Valley of Humiliation": a sacrifice of the "orgasmic maternal body." Maggie chooses a form of martyrdom by choosing a form of chastity, something less than the full extension of her sexuality.

Maggie's choice to marry Philip as a form of renunciation—a version of her cutting off her hair as a child—is opposed by Tom and by Maggie's own desires. Those desires, associated as they are with her attachment to Tom and the Floss (brother and the flow of water) have been read as incestuous, implying, as I noted earlier, that Maggie's psychosexual maturity simply does not develop, that Maggie's parents' early assessment of her as going against the natural order of things is somehow accurate. As Robert M. Polhemus puts it in *Erotic Faith*, "the image of Tom blots out Philip and leaves the way open for Stephen, whose force resembles Tom's" (184). In this reading, rather than Maggie's post-adolescent desire for Stephen being a mature extension of and breaking away from her pre-adolescent desire for unity with Tom, her desire for Stephen is her desire for Tom. "The girl [Maggie]," Polhemus writes, "has no way out of her bind. The pattern of her life, formed on the model of incestuous desire and taboo, is relationship followed by renunciation; . . . The early relationship is so strong that it stimulates erotic feelings, floods them with guilt, and paralyzes other relationship" (186). The psychological determinism of such a reading ignores two crucial points: the distinction between pre-adolescent physicality and post-adolescent sexuality and the equally determining pressures of social structures and modes of perception as articulated by preexisting social narratives. The sexualization of pre-adolescent physical expressiveness (the pre-lingual, presymbolic expressiveness of sound and touch that Kristeva calls the semiotic) appropriates the semiotic into the symbolic; narrative sexualizes pre-symbolic human bonds. In this context, psychological patterns and social norms both become forms of symbolic determination.

Consequently, the psychological, incestuous reading should include a social reading; in other words, the patterns of imagery in the novel that imply a thread of incestuous desire are not one thing and the depictions of social life and attitudes something else. The evidence for incest in the novel, most notably the often discussed *liebestod* drowning in the end, is an effect of the social, which I read as addressing the question of what are the potentially most damaging effects of a social structure that closes off every opening for a woman's growth into full, autonomous maturity. The short answer the novel suggests to that question is that such a woman (Maggie) refuses to participate in the social narratives that would determine her life, and *the* narrative for any Victorian woman is the story of her movement from daughter to wife and mother. Thus, when Maggie refuses to marry Stephen, she refuses to accept her role in the central Victorian woman's narrative. Maggie's "will," the narrator writes, "was fixed unswervingly on the coming wrench [parting with Stephen]. She had made up her mind to suffer" (600). In a slightly different context, Polhemus argues that in *The Mill* Eliot "expresses an almost desperate longing for an existence in which sexuality would not have to be renounced" (187). Maggie's refusal to marry is her way of renouncing her sexuality, and the necessity for such a renunciation in the novel concerns the way sexuality becomes denatured through social narratives. Maggie's moment of greatest happiness with Stephen takes place as they float down river in a scene reminiscent of Maggie's fishing at the "Round Pool" with Tom when they were children. Both scenes freeze time and silence social voices. In both scenes, "Memory was excluded" (589).

> They glided rapidly along, to Stephen's rowing, helped by the backward-flowing tide, past the Tofton trees and houses—on between the *silent*, sunny fields and pastures which seemed filled with a *natural* joy that had no reproach for theirs. The breath of the young, unwearied day, the delicious rhythmic dip of the oars, the fragmentary song of a passing bird heard now and then as if it were the overflowing of brim-full gladness, the sweet solitude of a two-fold consciousness that was mingled into one by that grave untiring gaze which need not be averted—what else could there be in their minds for the first hour? Some low, subdued, languid explanation of love came from Stephen from time to time, as he went rowing idly, half automatically: otherwise *they spoke no word*; for what would words have been but an inlet to thought? And thought did not belong to that enchanted haze in which they were enveloped—it belonged to the past and the future that lay outside the haze. Maggie was only dimly conscious of the banks, as they passed them, and dwelt with no recognition on the villages[.]   (italics added, 589)

The echo from Keats's nightingale ode—the song of the "passing bird . . . overflowing of brim-full gladness"—the presentation of "joy" as "natural" and thus having "no reproach" for whatever the human circumstances are, and the emphasis on silence and particularly the lack of speech all point to a repetition of the "heaven" Maggie dreamed of as a child at the Round Pool: "Maggie thought it would make a very nice heaven to sit by the pool . . . and not be scolded" (47). Again, as in the opening of the novel, we have inarticulate sound and the rushing/flowing of water; we also have consciousness in suspension and thought held at bay, a repetition of that moment just prior to the thetic break, the fall into consciousness and into the determinations of the symbolic order. But since Maggie and Stephen are past adolescence, fully sexual and involved in a set of complex and contradictory social relations, the stakes are higher in their eventual return to consciousness and social relations. The stakes concern who ultimately will control Maggie's adult, sexual body, and Stephen makes his case for possession through a discourse of nature.

Stephen makes his case most succinctly soon after the narrator notes Maggie's determination to suffer. In response to Maggie reminding him that they had already resolved to part, Stephen says: " 'We have proved that the feeling which draws us towards each other is too strong to be overcome. That natural law surmounts every other, —we can't help what clashes with it' " (601). Natural law here, of course, is sexual attraction/selection, and the force of that law at this point in the novel emerges through the repeated physical discontinuities asserted about Maggie and Philip and the essential easy, superficiality of the implicit engagement between Stephen and Lucy, aspects of what Stephen earlier refers to as "unnatural bonds" (590). It also contrasts with Maggie's parents' presentation of her as against nature as well. In the novel, then, two discourses of nature emerge: an early one that imposes socially constructed "natural" categories against the realities of the body and this later one that claims the body as the ground of nature itself, with the latter functioning as a corrective to the former and for Maggie offering vindication and fulfillment. The natural law Stephen asserts seems simply to be true, and especially in the context of Darwinian natural selection verified by contemporary science. Maggie's chance to live in harmony with and through her body, to be attuned (cf. the novel's emphasis on how music provides Maggie with a feel for the possibilities of a fully physical life) to the world is neither moral nor immoral. It simply is.

For Maggie to accept Stephen, then, she would have to accept an amoral vision of the world, and that is something that neither she nor George Eliot can accept. To say there is natural law that functions by demanding conformity or extinction is to erase the peculiarity of the individual lot, to efface the significance of individual choice, and to ignore the complexities of social arrangements on every level. As Maggie notes soon after she realizes that she and

Stephen have drifted well past their landing point, "You [Stephen now and later his natural law argument] have wanted to deprive me of any choice" (591). Given the peculiar circumstances of Maggie's lot, the only way she can exercise her choice is to say no. Her integrity depends on her capacity for refusal.

At the end of Chapter 2 in "The Final Rescue," the narrator makes her plea for the necessity of "sympathy," which she defines as that "wide fellow-feeling with all that is human" (628). She contrasts the sympathetic imagination with minds that "lace themselves up in formulas, . . . minds that are guided in their moral judgment solely by general rules" (628). Eliot's effort to generate narrative sympathy in *The Mill on the Floss* is grounded in her undercutting of "general rules," which are expressed most consistently in pre-set social narratives that she puts in motion and then disrupts through a continual series of collisions between those narratives and Maggie's bodily experience. Those collisions always leave Maggie where she started in that first moment of consciousness standing on the bank of the Floss hand-in-hand with Tom. As an emblem of patriarchy, Tom most completely represents those powerful cultural discourses that control the female body. The *liebestod* ending, then, is not an incestuous consummation; it is a return to the starting point of the narrative of Maggie's life, a narrative that never develops, and thus Maggie's experience is never effaced by the generalities of preestablished narrative coherence. Maggie emerges separately from the stories that surround her (Eliot remembers Maggie and "her sorrows" not her story). The flood is not a metaphor of narrative closure; it is a repetition of the representative image of an individual female life. The sympathy readers feel is a form of frustration that depends on their recognition of the inevitability of narrative misrepresentation of individual lives, including their own.

NOTES

1. For an overview of the philosophy and science of sympathy that ranges from David Hume (1711–1776) to Charles Darwin (1809–1882) and William McDougall (1871–1938) and that includes such topics as "The Roles of Imagery and Mimicry in Sympathy," see Wispe. For a philosophical exploration of sympathy in the work of Hume with an emphasis on ethics, see Mercer. For a sociological view of sympathy that includes discussion of the role of novel reading in the development of the capacity to be sympathetic, see Clark, especially "Research Strategies" 263–67. For an ambitious analysis of the relations among theater, reading novels, and sympathy as an aesthetic and moral problem, see the two volumes by Marshall. For a reading of sympathy in the context of Anglo-American literary and visual culture, see Hinton. Almost every one of the above texts

addresses the role of Hume and Adam Smith in the development of the modern concept (and modern problem) of sympathy. They all also emphasize in one way or another the role of spectacle and the pleasures/dangers of aestheticizing the suffering of others. My interest in this essay is to explore the intersection between concepts of sympathy and a theory of reading. Consequently, I do not address the role of spectacle or the problem of sympathy disconnected from sympathetic actions. See Mercer on that latter point.

2. I am grateful to an anonymous reviewer for *Dickens Studies Annual* for this particular connection.

3. In that formulation, Maggie's turn inward, which has been forced upon her by her family situation and her brother's explicit demands, takes on a life of its own, separate from Maggie's social circumstances; the energy of Maggie's resistance to the social definitions and discourses that would determine her sense of self and control her actions becomes a pleasurable source of self-negation. "Eliot's novels," Kucich argues, "are in pursuit of self-conflict through repression for its own sake. They seek to organize this self-conflict as an inward dialectic of desire, rather than as an outward one, a dialectic in which the impersonal, negative energies of the self come to replace the fusional energies of collectivist impulse" (121). The effect of this shift from social context to personal struggle in Eliot's novels according to Kucich is Eliot's failure to "[grapple directly] with what she believed to be social inadequacies" (136). "What is missing in Eliot," Kucich concludes, "is not fulfilled desire or passion, but the truly social, interdependent vision she tried hard to create" (200). In other words, Eliot's novels fail to provide a discernible domain and plausible goals for the application of a wider sympathy.

   Kucich's criticism of Eliot's failure to offer explicit remedies for the social ills so apparent in her novels amounts to a charge that Eliot is finally unable to articulate a renovative, revolutionary political program for her culture; she has no consistent principles upon which to base a "*truly* social, interdependent vision" (italics added). Her failure, in short, is a moral failure based on her fear of dependence (Kucich 181).

4. Of course, Maggie's return is an ironic and subversive response to her childhood desire to know the subsequent history of the prodigal son after his return: " . . . and she wished much that the subsequent history of the young man had not been left a blank" (83). That wish calls into question the assumed self-evident meaning of the story, and when we draw Maggie's wish together with her own enactment of the prodigal's story—the "prodigal" daughter returns after the father dies and is at the mercy of the older brother—we have, similar to her non sequitur reply to Philip and the syntactic disruption of the opening sentence of the novel, another example of how Maggie's bodily reality and the fluidity of water associated with it destabilize what we might call the grammar of her culture.

WORKS CITED

Bakhtin, Mikhail. "Epic and Novel." *The Dialogic Imagination*. Austin: U of Texas P, 1981.

Barrett, Dorothea. *Vocation and Desire: George Eliot's Heroines*. London: Routledge, 1991.

Clark, Candace. *Misery and Company: Sympathy in Everyday Life*. Chicago: U of Chicago P, 1997.

Eliot, George. *The Mill on the Floss*. London: Penguin Books, 1985.

Gallagher, Catherine. *Nobody's Story: The Vanishing Acts of Women Writers in the Marketplace, 1670–1820*. Berkeley: U of California P, 1994.

Gilbert, Sandra and Susan Gubar. *The Madwoman in the Attic: The Woman Writer and the Nineteenth Century Literary Imagination*. New Haven: Yale UP, 1985.

Haight, Gordon, ed. *Selections from George Eliot's Letters*. New Haven: Yale UP, 1985.

Hinton, Laura. *The Perverse Gaze of Sympathy: Sadomasochistic Sentiments from Clarissa to Rescue 911*. Albany: State UP of New York, 1999.

Homans, Margaret. *Bearing the Word: Language and Female Experience in Nineteenth-Century Women's Writing*. Chicago: U of Chicago P, 1986.

Jaffe, Audrey. *Scenes of Sympathy: Identity and Representation in Victorian Fiction*. Ithaca: Cornell UP, 2000.

Kristeva, Julia. *Revolution in Poetic Language*. New York: Columbia UP, 1984.

———. *The Kristeva Reader*. Ed. Toril Moi. New York: Columbia UP, 1986.

Kucich, John. *Repression in Victorian Fiction: Charlotte Brontë, George Eliot, and Charles Dickens*. Berkeley: U of California P, 1987.

Marshall, David. *The Figure of Theater: Shaftsbury, Defoe, Adam Smith, and George Eliot*. New York: Columbia UP, 1986.

———. *The Surprising Effects of Sympathy: Marivaux, Diderot, Rousseau, and Mary Shelley*. Chicago: U of Chicago P, 1988.

Mercer, Philip. *Sympathy and Ethics: A Study of the Relationship between Sympathy and Morality with Special Reference to Hume's Treatise*. Oxford: Oxford UP, 1972.

Polhemus, Robert M. *Erotic Faith: Being in Love from Jane Austen to D. H. Lawrence*. Chicago: U of Chicago P, 1990.

Poulet, Georges. "Criticism and the Experience of Interiority." *Reader Response Criticism: From Formalism to Post-Structuralism*. Ed. Jane Tompkins. Baltimore: Johns Hopkins UP, 1980.

Roberts, Nancy. *Schools of Sympathy: Gender and Identification through the Novel.* Montreal: McGill-Queen's UP, 1997.

Turner, Victor. *The Ritual Process: Structure and Anti-Structure.* Ithaca: Cornell UP, 1969.

Wispe, Lauren. *The Psychology of Sympathy.* New York: Plenum Press, 1991.

Recent Dickens Studies—2005

Diana C. Archibald

This review essay examines over 100 books and articles published in 2005, offering an overview of their ideas, arguments, and topics; summarizing findings; and providing direct quotations when possible. Almost thirty books are discussed, and articles from the three major outlets for Dickens scholarship—The Dickensian, Dickens Studies Annual, and Dickens Quarterly—are all included, as well as many essays from other publications. The materials are arranged according to topic, including the following: Latin America, Gender, Urban Life and Literature, Health, Education, Science, Interdisciplinary Approaches in the Humanities and Social Sciences, Visual and Print Culture, Style, Sketches by Boz, Pickwick Papers, Oliver Twist, Nicholas Nickleby, The Old Curiosity Shop, Christmas Books and Christmas Stories, Dombey and Son, David Copperfield, Hard Times, Little Dorrit, Great Expectations, Our Mutual Friend, and Influence and Afterlife.

A few months after I began working on this review, I had the pleasure of meeting a life-long Dickens hobbyist who was downsizing and wished to give his extensive collection of Dickens books, both primary and secondary sources, to me to keep or donate to the University of Massachusetts Lowell library as I saw fit. My husband and I drove up to Maine one blustery day to have lunch with Ray and his wife and collect the hundred or so books he had acquired through the years. Ray had first encountered Dickens when, as a boy, he lost his mother and a brusque but insightful priest handed him a copy of *David Copperfield* and told him to stop moping. That gift initiated decades of enjoyment of Dickens. Among the boxes Ray gave me that summer, I found, in addition to the novels that one would expect, first editions of *Household Words* and the *Mudfog Papers*, a handsomely bound copy of *The Life of Our Lord*, a beautifully illustrated edition of Dickens's children's tales *Captain Boldheart* and *The Magic Fishbone*, perhaps every biography of Dickens ever written, and a heap of scholarly classics. Unpacking the boxes, I found myself squealing and grinning like a child on Christmas morning. Perhaps I ought not to admit this, but it's true. I was grateful not only to Ray for this wonderful gift but also to the many fine scholars who have exercised their intellect, engaged their imagination, and spent their whole careers studying and sharing insights. Seeing those books reminded me of the long history of Dickens criticism, of the many distinguished scholars who have chosen this field as their life work.

Nevertheless, reading some past *Dickens Studies Annual* reviewers' laments about the current state of scholarship, I worried, briefly, about what I would encounter in considering the scholarship published in 2005. I was, however, pleasantly surprised. As each book arrived in the mail, I was very seldom disappointed with what I discovered. While I found some studies difficult to enjoy, most of the 115 or so books and articles that I read seemed to offer something worthwhile. Resisting the urge to scold those whose language is inaccessible and jargon-filled or lambaste critics whose arguments are simplistic and overdone, I have elected to summarize the main points of these works, offering direct quotations frequently, both to clarify argument and to provide readers with clues to an article's style and approach. I have arranged these materials according to topic, with the inevitable agonizing over where to put that wonderful article on *Dombey* that belongs equally to the part dedicated to individual works of fiction and to the long segment on gender criticism. While I can't claim to have included everything in this review that was published in a year in which Dickens scholars were particularly productive, I did make a fair attempt to survey as much as possible, with the goal of providing readers with an overview of ideas, arguments, and topics.

The year 2005 was, indeed, busy. Not only did *Dickens Studies Annual* release an extra volume, but also a special issue of *Critical Survey* was published on "Dickens and Sex," and almost 30 books appeared in which Dickens was the sole or partial subject. This year was also the centenary of *The Dickensian*, the "Magazine for Dickens Lovers," as the first issue was dubbed. Published by The Dickens Fellowship, *The Dickensian* has served as a mainstay for generations of readers. The centennial issue of the journal begins, appropriately, with reminiscences by past editors and novelist A. S. Byatt, who writes of her first encounter with Dickens as a child and her continued recognition of his genius. When Leavis declared, "Dickens was

not literature and was not part of the Great Tradition,'' she knew that Dickens
"was one of the very great. . . . He made things and people so memorable
that they inhabited the reader's brain forever, thus changing his or her world"
(6). As the first academic to serve as editor, Michael Slater was well aware
of readers' concerns that the journal would become "professionalized, " and
so he set the wise "editorial policy of choosing . . . those [articles] that
. . . enlarged our knowledge and understanding of Dickens the man, and of
the historical, biographical and bibliographical background to his writings''
(7). Andrew Sanders, who served from 1978 to 1986, reminds us of the trials
of publishing in the days of "movable type" when "both typesetters and
editors worked without the aid of a computer'' (11), a recollection likely to
give any of us working on large projects a shudder. Finally, Margaret Reynolds ends with her own memories of encountering Dickens in her twenties
and the part that the Fellowship played in this "affair.'' Alan Watts had once
told her that "reading old copies of *The Dickensian* was like eating peanuts:
'once you'd started, you couldn't stop'. Now I know that it is true,'' she
remarks (13). Certainly after 100 years of publication, *The Dickensian* does,
indeed, continue to provide food for thought. While the first issue of the year
opened by celebrating 100 years of *The Dickensian*, the year closed with a
note from the newly elected president of the Fellowship, Gerald Dickens,
great-great-grandson of Charles. He wrote of the death of his father, David,
who passed on the very same day that Gerald had given a speech to the
Fellowship at its Annual Conference. An obituary written by Thelma Grove
appears in the end of the issue honoring his legacy.

Also recognizing the centenary of *The Dickensian*, Leon Litvack offered
Dickens Quarterly readers a brief history of the publication in *''The Dickensian*: Editors, Contributors and Readers, 1905–2005.'' After a quick discussion of the publication's editors—B. W. Matz, Walter Dexter, Leslie Staples,
Michael Slater, Andrew Sanders, Margaret "Peggy" Reynolds, and Malcolm
Andrews—Litvack provides a splendid comparison of the three main publications devoted to Dickens, elucidating both differences and overlapping terri-
tory. Throughout the piece, we find interesting anecdotes such as one of the
period during World War II when Dexter worked on *The Dickensian* "with
gas mask and steel helmet at the ready'' (71), or when Slater had to reserve
a certain number of pages for an article by a well known contributor "with
no forewarning on the article's subject'' or even a title for the forthcoming
essay (72). Litvack's description of the challenges writers for and editors of
The Dickensian face with an audience of both lay enthusiasts and academics
reminds me a great deal of the times I have spent at the Dickens Universe at
UC Santa Cruz, sponsored by The Dickens Project. At that week-long Dickens
"summer camp'' I have met both honored scholars and also lovers of Dickens's tales from all walks of life, and I have learned equally from both.

Litvack, like Slater above, explains that editors must remember their audience includes both "academic subscribers" and "a host of others: sociable people who love to discuss Dickens in company, book-club readers, movie makers and writers of radio dramas, collectors of books and memorabilia, popular biographers, and those who love a good comedy or mystery" (75). Like *The Dickensian*, Ray's gift reminded me that as Dickens scholars we write not only for our fellow academics and our students but also for many others whose interest in the ongoing critical conversation about Dickens's life and works leads them to "listen in." I offer up this survey of 2005, then, for a wide range of readers in the hopes that it may prove useful. The materials are arranged according to topic, including the following: Latin America, Gender, Urban Life and Literature, Health, Education, Science, Interdisciplinary Approaches in the Humanities and Social Sciences, Visual and Print Culture, Style, *Sketches by Boz, Pickwick Papers, Oliver Twist, Nicholas Nickleby, The Old Curiosity Shop, Christmas Books* and Christmas stories, *Dombey and Son, David Copperfield, Hard Times, Little Dorrit, Great Expectations, Our Mutual Friend*, and Influence and Afterlife.

Latin America

In Uruguay in the summer of 2003, a conference was held on Dickens in Latin America: Views from Montevideo. Readers of *Dickens Studies Annual* 36 will find a special section collected by Beatriz Vegh with nine essays that emerged from that conference. Together these essays offer a fascinating glimpse into Latin American scholarly readings of Dickens. While not fully representative of the great diversity of Latin American criticism, their responses to Dickens remain instructive. As Vegh's introduction reminds us, "Latin America is a big wor(l)d which has never referred at all . . . to any true unity, either of language . . . or of culture" (266).

The first two essays, Tomás de Mattos's "A Borgesian Clue to Dickens's Characterization in *Pickwick Papers*" and Jean-Philippe Barnabé's "Borges as a Reader of Dickens," link Boz with Jorge Luis Borges (1899–1986), acclaimed and prolific Argentinean poet, essayist, and short fiction writer, known for his great contribution to Latin American literature: magical realism. In a class on Dickens, Borges once said, "Dickens was not really interested in the plot, . . . [which] is just a mechanical means to enable the development of the action. *There isn't really any development of their* [his characters'] *personality*" (274). De Mattos's essay takes issue with that claim, showing, in the case of Jingle and Pickwick that these characters *do* reflect "reality." He contends that in the beginning Dickens lacks control of his story, making Pickwick seem at first "ridiculous, rather foolish, and quite unlovable'' (277). But as Dickens learns his craft and gains command over his story, Pickwick changes and develops into a character not only true to life but full of ''heart'' (283). Barnabé, also interested in Borges and Dickens, examines a different novel, *The Mystery of Edwin Drood*, translated into Spanish by Borges in 1951. Citing Borges's lectures, just published in 2000, Barnabé remarks upon Borges's claim that ''almost at the exact moment when he is about to reveal who the murderer is, God ordains [Dickens's] death, and so we will never know the real secret'' (289). What is curious here is that Borges focuses on the drama of Dickens himself, rather than the novel; indeed, what Barnabé means by his title is ''Borges as a reader of the story entitled Charles Dickens.'' The essay shows that such an approach is ''an eminently Borgesian idea'' (290) and that to Borges, Dickens's death just as he is ''discovering a new identity as a writer'' is the most important story.

The next pair of essays analyzes the highly original illustrations of a Spanish translation of *Hard Times*. Miguel Battegazzore's ''A Cubo-Futurist Reading of Dickens: Rafael Barradas's 1921 Illustrations to *Hard Times*'' examines the relationship between these illustrations and the Cubist movement. The Uruguayan Barradas ''readily subscribed to [Daniel-Henri] Kahnweiler's idea that Cubism had inaugurated a new path for painters that made painting an equivalent to writing'' (299). The essay explains how the ''structural conception of pictorial language'' (301) played out in the illustrations, as Barradas used repetition of commonplace objects such as chimneys and circus tents as ''leitmotifs'' encouraging readers to see the interplay between illustration and text in ''a new dialectic'' where ''the visual and literary texts . . . work in parallel on the reader and viewer'' (303). Illustrations need not represent the text literally, but can offer interpretive images that deviate substantially from the plot or description, as when Barradas portrays Louisa looking out the window rather than at the fire. Beatriz Vegh, in ''Dickens and Barradas in Madrid, 1921: A Hospitable Meeting'' also examines the connection between these illustrations and the text, though she does not focus on the influence of Cubism but rather explores how the illustrations influence the reader's understanding of the novel. For example, she notes that Barradas's illustration of Sissy portrays ''the circus girl'' as ''an avant-garde figure of naturalness and colorful fantasy'' (309), a freer version of Sissy than appears throughout much of Dickens's text. ''Barradas,'' Vegh suggests, ''seems to modulate the text, destabilizing what is linear, detailed, and minutely rendered'' (310). The accompanying plates of Barradas's illustrations are an unusual treat for those interested in artistic interpretations of Dickens's work.

Two essays compare Uruguayan novelist Armonía Somers's *Un retrato para Dickens* (*A Portrait for Dickens*) with *Oliver Twist*. Somers imagines a female Oliver-like heroine in her novel, which takes place in Montevideo.

María Cristina Dalmagro demonstrates, in her essay "The Reversal of Innocence: Somers, Dickens, and Shared Oliver," how Somers rewrites Dickens's happy and fantastical ending for Oliver by making her heroine "orphaned again" at the end of her novel and facing "an uncertain future" (327). The fact that part of the novel is also narrated by a parrot further "subverts all the possibilities to hold on to reality and to all the realistic versions of the different narrative lines in the text" (326). Somers, Dalmagro asserts, sees Dickens as "another milestone in the story of evil in the world and of the suffering of innocent children" (328), but a figure with limited tools to represent such injustice. Alicia Torres focuses on identity in the two novels. In her essay "Dickens's Oliver and Somers's Orphan: A Traffic in Identities," Torres remarks on the curious fact that Somers does not name or describe the orphan protagonist of her novel, especially surprising since this author is known generally for her "many strange names." The orphanage director tells us that her name "reminded him of something related to 'a certain weeping bundle wrapped in newspapers which has to be given a name somehow' " (333), which mirrors Bumble's hasty naming of Oliver Twist. In fact, Torres argues, "Oliver is the fraternal other, the twin, . . . a double who has been born not of him but at his side" (324) though on another continent in another time. Ultimately, Somers's work diverges from Dickens's in significant ways, despite the fact that "they have both been constructed from the pain and the pity aroused by the social helplessness of children marginalized by societies both in the North and in the South" (337).

The next two essays discuss the theater and Dickens. Leticia Eyheragaray's "*The Strange Gentleman*: Dickens on the Uruguayan Stage" considers a 1946 Montevideo staging of Dickens's *The Strange Gentleman* (1836), one of only four plays Boz wrote and the only one "considered successful" (341). Dickens later tried to disown his text, claiming he would give a thousand pounds for the comedy to be "forgotten" (343). Though reviews were mixed, the show ran more than sixty nights. The Montevideo performance made use of a Spanish translation, probably the 1943 version by Francisco Madrid, who noted the extreme difficulty of translating comedy into another language. Still, Eyheragaray claims that the translation follows the original closely and argues that the play's excellent reception one hundred years after its creation came from the audience's delight at the novelty of such a play by a favored author. Verónica D'Auria, in "Spectacle and Estrangement in Dickens," claims that her fellow Uruguayans see Dickens very differently from the way those in the northern hemisphere read him. For Latin American readers, Dickens's novels are not "picturesque image[s] of an industrial past that has been already overcome" (350). Rather, these novels are reflections of the spectacle of misery around them. By applying Brecht's terminology, she shows that *Great Expectations*, for example, uses the techniques of modern theater to distance the reader/audience from the narrative and the narrative from the formulaic happy ending they expect. Dickens "transforms this narration by using doubles, self-parody, and the exchange of traditional roles" (351).

In the last essay, "Dickens in Latin America: Borrioboola-Gha Revisited," Lindsey Cordery summarizes her view of the author's connection to the continent: "Dickens is a . . . creative artist of genius, whose powerful treatments of universal themes of kindness and cruelty, greed and generosity, and the need for parental love, are still current today . . . [but] another question must be considered: not why we read Dickens, but *how* we read Dickens in Latin America today, and in answering it, I believe that we cannot disregard contexts: the context of the Victorian Empire and the present context of globalization" (360). Cordery offers a quick overview of the following historical and literary contexts in her essay: Disraeli's concept of "Two Nations," the Great Exhibition of 1851, the Chartist movement and Carlyle's response to it, Dickens's Mrs. Jellyby and her African Borrioboola-Gha project, American slavery as depicted in *American Notes*, racist remarks in Dickens's 1853 article for *Household Words* entitled "The Noble Savage," the Indian Mutiny in 1857 and the Jamaican rebellion in 1865, imperialist commerce in several Dickens novels, and postcolonial critics' assessments of European literature. She contends that due to this imperialist context, Latin American readers must read Dickens "against the grain, subversively, . . . appropriating narratives" in order to forge "a clearly defined identity, where past and present are integrated" (360). It is fitting that the special section of this volume of *Dickens Studies Annual* end on such a note, reminding us that Dickens, as a respected yet ideologically bound author, must and will be read differently depending on readers' own worldviews.

Another essay from the Montevideo conference appeared in *Dickens Quarterly*. Lee Williams, in "Telling as Denouement in Dickens's *Great Expectations* and Roberto Arlt's *El juguete rabino* [*Mad Toy*]," compares these two novels and argues that "neither is a *Bildungsroman*." Comparing the protagonists, Pip and Silvio, he claims that their "redemption is not found in the stories they relate, [but] rather in the relation of their stories," where "each of these 'defeated' narrators wrests control of an abject past, paradoxically, by way of demoralizing memoirs" (19). Similar, in part, to Tyson Stolte's essay (discussed below), Williams's article sees "the narration itself" as Pip's "final vindicating act" (29). Williams diverges, however, in his use of the "narratological topology of Gérard Genette" (19). He differentiates between the young Pip, seen as a "focalizing agent," that is, "the prism through which a novel's events are provided" (20), and Pip, the older narrator. The essay offers several points of comparison between Dickens's and Arlt's very different novels, especially the narrators' shared "discursive habits." Ultimately, however, Williams argues that "Dickens's Pip remains a mild-mannered precursor to Arlt's radicalized Silvio of the twentieth century" (30).

Gender

"Dickens and Sex," a conference held in March of 2004 at the Institute of English Studies in London, generated an important reconsideration of the ways in which scholars approach this topic. As guest editors Holly Furneaux and Anne Schwan remark in their introduction to a special issue of *Critical Survey*, the seven essays included offer "new readings of Dickens's writings" with explorations of "the wider political and theoretical investments at play in current debates about both Dickens and sexuality." The editors suggest that "conventional criticism" generally downplays the ways Dickens transgresses the boundaries of "respectable' fiction" (1), but that their collected essays "demonstrate the fruitfulness of a dialogue between different critical perspectives" (3).

William A. Cohen, in "Interiors: Sex and the Body in Dickens," employs a cultural phenomenological approach, paying "close attention to embodied experience, to affects, emotions, and senses, to bodily transformations across dimensions of time and space, all the while understanding such experience to be socially, culturally, and historically situated" (7). Cohen examines "how Dickens imagines sexual desire" through the way that he portrays "the bodies of characters both as containers for interiority—be that interior the mind, soul, heart, or viscera—and as outer forms, which serve as the means of interacting with objects in the world, including other bodies" (7). The essay focuses on one "especially vivid . . . embodied relation between interior and exterior" (8), the keyhole. Cohen suggests that we read such scenes not as "narrative allegories of omniscience" (9) but as places where, through the physical senses, encounters between bodies are often sexualized. For example, of the many scenes in *The Old Curiosity Shop* of keyhole spying, Cohen cites the moment when Dick Swiveller and the Marchioness at last meet. According to Cohen's argument, "The bodily connections between Dick and the Marchioness—which include looking, touching, feeding, playing and, presumably, maritally sanctioned sexual congress as well—are both initiated and condensed in the figure of the keyhole" (13). In *David Copperfield*, too, the keyhole offers an avenue by which language (in Peggotty's whispers) becomes a material thing to be swallowed (by David, who forgets to move his mouth away from the keyhole). Cohen argues that after ingesting her kind words, David feels a "fierce, nearly erotic attachment" (14) for his nursemaid, and this "language of absorption and ingestion sets the pattern for Copperfield's future expressions of intense feeling" (15).

Vybarr Cregan-Reid begins "Bodies, Boundaries and Queer Waters: Drowning and Prosopopoeia in Later Dickens" with a discussion of the Victorian "cultural anxiety over the status of water as a live, conscious and capriciously dangerous agent" (20), as evidenced by a famous court case of an industrial flood. The essay notes that about thirty characters in Dickens drown—all of these men, a fate usually reserved in Victorian fiction for women guilty of sexual sin. In Dickens's later fiction, in particular, these drownings are often some of the most gruesome deaths he creates for his characters, though we still find examples in the earlier works of drowning as "an opportunity to mete out the most terrible punishments," as in the case of Quilp (24). With James Steerforth's offstage death, we see a more ambivalent portrait: "Steerforth dies with some dignity, but still he suffers the effeminizing death of those who have the mark of sexual impropriety." Cregan-Reid reads this death by drowning as highly sexualized and argues that Steerforth's "sexual deviance" leads to a "subtle effeminisation" (28) that makes his death by drowning seem appropriate. In the instance of Rogue Riderhood's and Bradley Headstone's double drowning, the essay argues that this death is not only a punishment for sexual impropriety (as well as general "criminality and immorality"), but it is also "a permanent embrace" (29). Citing Dickens's reaction to the Paris Morgue and subsequent public bathing, the essay contends that "Dickens's fears and anxieties become commingled with a disgust of same-sex desire" (31).

Taking issue with such critics as Cregan-Reid and Eve Sedgwick, who emphasize Dickens's homophobia and fail to recognize same-sex desire not linked to violence in the novels, Holly Furneaux in " 'It Is Impossible to Be Gentler': The Homoerotics of Male Nursing in Dickens's Fiction" seeks to counter this overstatement by pointing to, in particular, "the Victorian sexualisation of nursing" (34). Focusing on male nursing in *Martin Chuzzlewit* and *Great Expectations*, Furneaux offers an excellent close reading of a few key scenes that ably demonstrate her contention that "the extremely tender expressions of same-sex desire offered in Dickens's scenes of male nursing provide an alternative frame of interpretation to that passed forward by the homoerotic violence thesis" (45). Countering Sedgwick's assertion that "an absence of violence signals an absence of desire" (35), Furneaux begins by pointing to Herbert's care for Pip, noting the "gentle physicality of Herbert's nursing" (36) and how their "alleged heterosexual interest" (36) in women being discussed at the time is constantly interrupted by tender touching and eroticized physical closeness. The essay argues that nursing, to the Victorians, was "a more culturally visible form of erotic contact than fisticuffs" because through nursing, "male characters [could] legitimate their physical contact and express their excitement at such intimate touching" (38). In *Martin Chuzzlewit*, the Martin-Mark pairing can be read as an exploration of same-sex intimacy, and even desire, as expressed through mutual nursing. Furneaux ably supports her claim that "interpretations of Dickens as 'homophobic' " (45) are insufficient, providing an alternate view of Dickens as author of literary spaces that enable tender and eroticized male touching.

In " 'Red-Headed Animal': Race, Sexuality and Dickens's Uriah Heep" Tara MacDonald discusses "Uriah as a scapegoat figure on a grand scale," the character on whom "David displaces many of his own class, gender and sexual anxieties" (48). In this first-person narrative, David writes of Uriah, an Englishman, in highly racialized language, "mark[ing] him as 'other' " (48). In particular, the "codes through which he is represented are similar to anti-Semitic representations of Jews" (49); MacDonald is not saying that Uriah is supposed to be a Jew, but she does show that his association with anti-Semitic stereotypes is an important key to understanding both Uriah and David. Anti-Semitic representations of Jews in Victorian England included the following characteristics: "economic parasite" (50), "lack of masculine self-discipline" supposed to manifest itself in "a dangerous, savage sexuality that was a threat to Victorian women" (50), "lust for money" (51), "degenerate" and animal-like (52), red hair (53), and a "feminisation of the Jewish male body" (56). MacDonald further argues that David's "fascination for Uriah arises because he *fears* he is like him" (57). When David fantasizes about running Uriah through with a red-hot poker, MacDonald claims, "this moment is filled with homoerotic suggestions" (58). What is most important, she argues, is that David's violent fantasy aligns him more closely to the " 'savage' Uriah" (58) because David is dangerously close to losing his manly self-control, hallmark of the British gentleman. The novel presents Uriah as the contaminating influence that endangers the hero, dread of "contamination" by other races being a prevalent fear.

Jenny Hartley's "Undertexts and Intertexts: The Women of Urania Cottage, Secrets and *Little Dorrit*" shows the connections between Dickens's activities at Urania Cottage, the home for fallen women that he helped to administer, and one of the novels he was writing at the time. The institution was, as Hartley puts it, "part theatre, part Big Brother social experiment, part reform colony, and part data bank" (64). As the administrator, Dickens had "privileged access into women's secret histories" that he wrote down "in a casebook now probably lost" (65). These "back-stories, . . . of women's sexual histories in particular" connect to *Little Dorrit*'s theme of "the locked or secret story" (65) through Dickens's reticence to portray these characters too explicitly. Women's stories in the novel are always getting "suppressed, diverted, opened, [and] shut up again" (66), like Arthur's birthmother's letters, Mrs. Clennam's speeches (unheard by the one person—Arthur—who most needs to listen to her), and Miss Wade's self-disclosing history. For example, Dickens writes of Miss Wade that he had "observed [her] in real life," and that he knew "the character to be true in every respect" (70), clearly referencing this source, where an "atmosphere of high female emotion" (71) reigned. Unlike his friend Wilkie Collins, however, Dickens was "ever mindful of his 'family' image" (72) and exercised considerable caution, in the case of *Little Dorrit* "censoring himself and desexualizing his female characters" (73). All the women except Flora Finching are "shut up, silenced" (73), but Flora's verbal flood, Hartley adds, "alert[s] us to the presence of female desire" (74) and through her and through untold secrets, we see the inspiration the women of Urania Cottage offered to their bene-factor.

Kristina Aikens, in "The Daughter's Desire in *Dombey and Son*," argues that critical dismissal of "Florence as a passive, victimized sexual object" overlooks the complexity of this character. Aikens sees "subtle, often vexed traces of Florence's sexual agency" (77), which mark her as "a heroine who simultaneously exemplifies and deviates from the sexual vacancy she represents" (78). For example, the essay provides evidence that Florence's "childhood [was] sexualized and her womanhood eventually sanctified as sexually innocent through the purifying effect of maternity" (78). Noting Florence's situation in the "oedipal narrative of replacing the mother" (78) as well as her "sexually coded," though not necessarily overtly incestuous relationship with her brother, Aikens argues that "all of [Florence's] sexual desires play out under the apparently innocent cover of the family" (81), perhaps especially her relationship with her stepmother, Edith. The essay offers an intriguing discussion of Florence's ordeal when she is kidnapped, citing six-year-old Florence's unbound hair as a loosely veiled code for unbri-dled sexuality. That Walter and Florence are both attracted to one another during this episode, despite the repeated assurances of the narrator that they are innocent, is especially clear from Aikens's analysis. In the case of Flore-nce and Edith, Aikens argues that their "desire is homoerotic, making it more disruptive to, but less sustainable within, the 'family romance'" (82). Again Aikens reads the appearance of loose hair when they are together as code for Victorian imagery of sexual licentiousness and deviance. Unlike the other women in the novel, however, Florence has a "sexuality ... repeatedly protected or concealed" (84) by the men in her life, and this "covering" of the book's heroine "marks her possession by the patriarchal order," "further eroticises her within that order [,] *and* marks her own denied, potentially disruptive desire" (84).

Co-Editor Anne Schwan ends the special issue with her article, "The Limi-tations of a Somatics of Resistance: Sexual Performativity and Gender Dissi-dence in Dickens's *Dombey and Son*." For Schwan "contemporary critical practice" (103)—especially cultural phenomenology—is limited because it is "a critique of social experiences that is conceptualized through attention to individualized, or intersubjective, corporeal practices," and thus may end up supporting "a political agenda that privileges the bourgeois concept of individuality over that of collectivity" (93). Though examining the ways in which characters embody resistance can yield insight into texts, she argues this approach alone is not enough. To illustrate her point, she looks at "two forms of sexual deviance, enacted by the figures of Paul and Edith Dombey" (93). While these characters resist patriarchal gender identities that are foisted on them, ultimately the text fails "to imagine a systemic transformation" (93) of that patriarchal system. Gender critics have often ignored Paul Dombey, Jr., but Schwan sees his importance in his use of an alternate, or "deviant," gender identity as his "mode of resistance" (95). The essay argues that Paul is "coded" as "masturbatory" (98), "feminine" (99), and perhaps "an early representation of homosexuality" (100)—not that Paul *is* those things but that "he is coded as such" (100). Edith's embodied resistance, as well, leads only to her banishment, not a reformation or revolution of society. Edith, like Paul, "is coded as sexually deviant" (101), "depicted through a language of sensuality and sexuality that associates her with sexual fallenness and hysteria" (101). The essay sees the pair's "separation" as revealing "Dickens's inability in this novel to fully envision new, intersubjective relationships in a collective context that would truly explode the social order" (102). Whether Dickens had any such interest is not a part of Schwan's discussion, but, that said, her caution against the limits of contemporary critical approaches is a point well taken.

"Flogging and Fascination: Dickens and the Fragile Will" appeared in the summer issue of *Victorian Studies*, offering a complex and nuanced analysis. Natalie Rose begins by discussing the flogging of children and adults in Victorian life and literature. She notes that while flogging children was "tolerate[d] . . . flogging of adults had become increasingly unacceptable" (505). Indeed, flogging children was seen as a necessary means of shaping their character. Through an extensive discussion of flogging practices in England, the essay analyzes the "kinds of manliness and the models of the self that flogging was seen to produce or threaten" (505). For example, flogging boys was sometimes viewed as a means of imposing self-discipline through external and violent means, indicating a belief that manliness can only be formed through the agency of others, with "self-control" springing from "submission" (509). In other cases, we see instances of flogging sailors portrayed as a cruel and sadistic, sexualized act perpetrated on passive victims. Rose notes the "debates about whether flogging [men] makes or unmakes manliness, and whether it secures or threatens the individual's self-control" (514). The essay analyzes various characters whom Rose sees as exemplifying "fascination": Heep, Steerforth, Magwitch, Miss Havisham, Estella, Lammle, and Fledgeby, and it suggests that "fascinated characters in Dickens's later novels" reveal "anxieties about the will and the fragility of autonomy and self-determination" (505) that become visible in flogging scenes.

In *Bleak Houses: Marital Violence in Victorian Fiction,* Lisa Surridge provides a superb analysis of domestic abuse in Victorian life and literature.

Carefully explaining the relationship between the laws that Parliament debated and enacted and the information the public gained through various print media, including newspapers, journals, and fiction, she contends that "realist fiction and the newspaper" played a key role in "bringing marital violence into the public eye" (12). Indeed, this book provides ample evidence through examples from newspapers, court records, and her insightful readings of Victorian fiction in which abuse figures prominently. Surridge begins with two chapters devoted to Dickens and then explores texts by Anne Brontë, George Eliot, Wilkie Collins, Anthony Trollope, Mona Caird, and Conan Doyle, but throughout her book, she frequently refers to Dickens's corpus. Chapter 1 examines most closely *Oliver Twist*, but also discusses *Sketches by Boz*, *Pickwick Papers*, *The Old Curiosity Shop*, and *Martin Chuzzlewit*. These texts, according to Surridge, "responded to and participated in the new prominence of marital assault in the public press" and revealed "an enormous anxiety concerning the new visibility of wife assault" (17). Dickens was writing these early works soon after the 1828 Offenses Against the Person Act, which opened a floodgate of working-class petitions for public intervention in what had previously been deemed a private matter: martial assault.

Comparing cases published in the *Times* or *Morning Chronicle* with Dickens's abused characters, Surridge reveals Dickens's "deep ambivalence concerning public intervention" in private domestic life (27). Dickens "creates sympathy for the battered woman, but simultaneously implies that women who defend themselves or others are unworthy of sympathy" (29), for these victims must display qualities held in high esteem by the middle class to be seen as figures in need of protection by male medical, legal, or journalistic institutions. The second chapter tackles *Dombey and Son*, arguing that the novel is Dickens's "full anatomy of failed manliness" (45). Surridge notes that in the early years of public debate, marital assault was seen as a men's problem. If men are the "natural protectors" of the weaker sex, logic dictates that a man who beats his wife exhibits a failure of manliness. When Mr. Dombey strikes Florence, the act seems to lead to the loss of "his business, his home, and his very identity" (45) because he has forgotten his primary role as protector, a core value of Victorian manhood. Of particular note in this chapter is Surridge's discussion of the ways in which the text portrayed middle-class marital violence in the period after the Cochrane decision of 1840, which reinforced the "doctrine of coverture," insisting that men held complete authority over their wives. Surridge's reading of the novel and newspaper suggests a close relationship between the two.

Britta Zangen, in *Our Daughters Must Be Wives: Marriageable Young Women in the Novels of Dickens, Eliot, and Hardy* discusses an extensive list of their novels. Her book is interested in how both non-fictional and literary texts responded to and affected debate on the Woman Question. Zangen discusses numerous literary examples of marriageable young women heroines in the novels of those authors considered by their contemporaries to be the "greatest . . . novelists" (89) of the Victorian age. While the sections devoted to literary analysis contain mostly plot summary, it is useful to have all such characters in Dickens listed in one place. The two chapters of socio-historical context provide some interesting and less well-known information about public debates on the Woman Question, along with references to respected earlier studies. Ultimately, Zangen seems to argue that the image of woman and the necessity of her being married becomes more complex as the century progresses. Further, she writes: "Just as non-fictional texts presented the protection and support of and dependence on a husband as essential and natural for the well-being of a woman, so did Dickens'[s] novels. How then could a young female reader not believe that the message was correct?" (346). How, indeed?

Beth Harris, editor of *Famine and Fashion: Needlewomen in the Nineteenth Century*, has collected an exceptional anthology of essays analyzing images of seamstresses ranging from paintings, penny dreadfuls, and politics to songs, the sex trade, and shop windows. Two essays in the volume, in particular, are directly relevant to Dickensians, though the volume is worth examining as a whole, too. In " 'Let Herself Out to Do Needlework': Female Agency and the Workhouse of Gender in Charles Dickens's *Little Dorrit*," Joellen Masters examines Amy Dorrit's work as a needlewoman. To Masters, Amy's "employment, denied by other characters, holds up the myth of a privileged family structure in which a lady need not work" (53). Amy is often invisible in the novel, just as a needlewoman's labor was supposed to be hidden from the view of her rich clientele. And she holds the plot of the book together, as the act of sewing binds what would be separate without the pattern of the thread—supporting without being seen. Masters calls Amy "a textual helpmeet" who "preserves . . . the rotten fabric of patriarchy" and "constructs the hero's consciousness" (54). Amy's work allows her "the freedom to traverse borders" between public and private spaces and "cross a variety of thresholds" from the debtor's prison to the upper-class household, but this freedom amounts to little—literally, it amounts to Little Dorrit's very brief story, which "makes her as invisible as possible" (55). Amy actually appears in only 22 of the novel's 68 chapters, and when she does appear, she is often merely "one of many . . . , a supporting player" (56). To Masters, Little Dorrit is Arthur Clennam's "vanishing point, . . . that place beyond a picture's frame, . . . that area where parallel lines converge, something, which by definition, they cannot do, so that by implication, Dickens's seamstress portrays a curiosity of identity" (59). She is always in the process of diminishing without ever disappearing completely, an "invisible support of male authority" (63).

Ian Haywood, in "The Retailoring of Dickens: *Christmas Shadows*, Radicalism, and the Needlewoman Myth," discusses what he dubs "a forgotten minor Victorian novel" (82), *Christmas Shadows*, an anonymous book published in 1850. The essay discusses how this minor novel employed Dickens's *Christmas Carol*, *The Chimes*, and "The Story of the Goblins who stole a Sexton" from *Pickwick*. In essence, Haywood argues that this "clever pastiche of Dickens's first two Christmas books in which the Scrooge figure is replaced by an employer of needlewomen" (67), provides a "fantasy of class revenge" in which the "employer-father" (69), Cranch, sees a horrifying future in which his own two daughters must work as needlewomen when he loses his business. Their resulting destitution and slippage into sexual sin terrify him into becoming a "model employer" (71), paying a living wage and offering medical benefits. Haywood sees this 1850 reworking "as liberating the political unconscious of Dickens's text" and "foreground[ing] an important aspect of the 'woman question' " (73). In *The Chimes*, Trotty Veck's vision of his daughter Meg's fall centers on her becoming a destitute needlewoman. In the end this disaster is averted and Meg is set to be married, but Dickens's plot line "distance[s] the problem of needlework from contemporary reality" by making the problem part of a "Dantean future, not the curable present" (77). Likewise, Haywood points to *Nicholas Nickleby* wherein the reader is relieved when Kate is fired from her job as a needlewoman and becomes a companion instead, thus "emerg[ing] unscathed to rejoin the marriage plot" (78). In contrast to Dickens's use of needlewomen, *Christmas Shadows* offers a stronger critique by showing "that respectable feminine virtue is a fragile asset which soon crumbles under economic pressures" (82).

Ironically, I first learned of Martin A. Danahay's study *Gender at Work in Victorian Culture: Literature, Art and Masculinity* in a bibliography where it appeared as *Men at Work in Victorian Culture*, which could easily serve as an alternate title. Danahay "examine[s] the history of the construction of 'gender at work' as a literary and visual trope in the Victorian period and examine[s] the ways in which 'men' and 'work' were used as virtual synonyms and the possibility of female labor excised" (1). Classifying his work as "second wave masculinity studies" (3), Danahay offers in his introduction a thorough and clear summary of the critical context for his argument. The book includes analyses of Ford Maddox Brown, Munby and Cullwick, Ruskin, and Gissing, with an early chapter on "Dickens, Work and Sexuality." While Dickens's novels are filled with "workers" of various persuasions, Danahay focuses on two novels in which "work is a more than usually explicit subject": *Hard Times*, which "represents labor not in terms of the worker but in terms of the regulation of female sexuality," and *Bleak House*, which, through Esther, "examines the status of all kinds of work carried out

in the home, including writing'' (67). Danahay contends that the threat of
"effeminization" that "literary men who worked at home" faced (74) exposes "the contradictions inherent in the Victorian division of labor along
gender lines" (75). Both Louisa Gradgrind and Esther Summerson "enact
Dickens'[s] difficulties with defining the status of his own work" (67). In
both characters "issues of work are translated into issues of feminine consciousness and sexuality," thus turning them into "representatives of excluded or repressed [male] desires" that do not fit easily into "the world of
masculine work" (84).

I turn finally in this section to a book I enjoyed immensely. From *Dinner
for Dickens: The Culinary History of Mrs. Charles Dickens's Menu Books,*
by Susan M. Rossi-Wilcox, I learned that Catherine Dickens recommended
fish as a first course three times as often as soup, but not plaice or halibut,
considered food for the working classes. In addition to the particulars of
Catherine's suggested "bills of fare" in her 1851 cookbook and four chapters
about Victorian food, this book includes a wealth of commentary and analysis,
with chapters on the *Menu Book*'s publication history, a brief biography of
Catherine Thomson Hogarth Dickens, a discussion of the Dickenses' experience of world cuisine, and details of how the Dickens household was run,
with special sections on dining at their home and their amateur theatricals.
While the volume's meticulously researched and thorough explanations of
food and Dickens will prove interesting to scholars and enthusiasts alike, I
agree with Lillian Nayder, who writes in her "Foreword" that Rossi-Wilcox
has helped us to see Catherine Dickens not as portrayed by critics who "often
overlooked or denied" her, but rather through "Catherine's own self-portrait,
in the pages of her book" (10). Drawing upon multiple sources, including
letters, Rossi-Wilcox sees Catherine Dickens's book as a "period piece that
unwittingly chronicle[s] attitudes towards food that are cultural, regional,
socio-economical, and idiosyncratic" (77). Further, through this volume we
meet a Catherine who is "a personable, intelligent woman holding her own
in a diverse social milieu" (305).

Urban Life and Literature

Unlike many previous critical works addressing the changing urban landscape
of the modern period, Robert Alter's new book does not attempt to show
how novels reflect the reality of city life. Instead, *Imagined Cities: Urban
Experience and the Language of the Novel* undertakes an examination of
"the intersection of . . . a new urban reality" and "the subtle deployment of
experiential realism," by which he means the narration technique in which
readers see solely through an individual character's "sensory, visceral, and

mental'' experience (x). Alter spends two chapters on Dickens, also discussing Flaubert, Andrei Bely, Woolf, Joyce, and Kafka. He maintains that Dickens, although keeping: ''quite unswervingly to an external and omniscient point of view'' and thus not generally engaging in ''experiential realism,'' nevertheless manages to ''convey the feel of life in this new urban reality'' (45) in unique and powerful ways. In particular, Alter argues that Dickens's use of surprising and powerful figurative language enables his descriptions of cityscapes to elicit strong feelings in readers. Part of Dickens's power lies in his ability to employ *''archaic vision''*: he describes scenes in order to ''trigger certain primal fears and fantasies,'' thus revealing ''the troubled meanings of the new urban reality'' (47). Alter demonstrates through several examples how Dickens creates ''metaphors and similes [that] are vividly original, often startling,'' and appear to be the result of ''improvisation'' (48). Especially in his later novels, this strategy allows him to express his concerns about ''crowded urban life in the industrial age, . . . alarmingly clogged and polluted'' (61) while still maintaining belief in the possibility of ''a small sustaining community of the kindhearted within the urban wasteland'' (50). Pointing to the language of apocalypse that surfaces in *Our Mutual Friend*, Alter reads that novel, especially, as evincing ''certain forebodings as to the price that may be exacted for . . . alienation from the natural world'' (71). A Victorian novel detailing all manner of dirt, from human-made waste to naturally produced grime, must, necessarily, engage with the issue of ecological responsibility, and Dickens's use of powerful metaphors reaches an audience as no simple catalogue can.

The essay collection, *Babylon or New Jerusalem? Perceptions of the City in Literature*, edited by Valeria Tinkler-Villani, offers 20 essays on a number of topics, from Volpone to jazz, all linked together through their analysis of the way that urban landscapes are figured in literature. A considerable portion of the book is devoted to nineteenth-century authors, with two chapters on Dickens. Alan Shelston, in ''Dickens and the Burial of the Dead,'' examines the way that Dickens's ''interest . . . in burial . . . has a dimension that goes beyond the fictional,'' that the manner of burial adopted in urban spaces ''focus[es] anxieties for Dickens's generation and indeed for his successors on the London scene about what might really be involved in the passage from this life to the next'' (78). While recognizing that Dickens's fascination with death may arise from a personal, ''morbid sensibility'' (79), Shelston contends that burial practices were a matter of serious national concern and debate. For example, in 1843 a Parliamentary Commission was charged with investigating interment practices in England's growing towns and cities, where the rising population made standard burial practices difficult to maintain. Shelston reads Little Nell's death in this context, contending that Nell's burial place is ''the countryside, and a country churchyard, not as it is but as the weary Londoners need it to be'' (83). Interpreting various illustrations, such as Phiz's portrait of Lady Dedlock at the gates of the cemetery, and using other Dickens scenes such as the Parisian morgue in *The Uncommercial Traveller* and *A Tale of Two Cities*, the essay asserts ''the frailty of traditional religious consolations'' (85) in an age of urban congestion.

Robert Druce, like Shelston, finds in the Victorians' and Dickens's image of the city much anxiety. In ''Charting the Great Wen: Charles Dickens, Henry Mayhew, Charles Booth,'' Druce discusses the ''enduring image'' of London, first suggested by William Cobbett, of the city as a '' 'monstrous wen'—a disfiguring and ceaselessly-growing tumour . . . which was deforming the body of England by sucking into itself and its corrupt and corrupting tissues the peoples and the prosperity of the country and her empire'' (93). The essay contends that Dickens, Mayhew, and Booth all ''set out to anatomize the city, to chart its relentless growth'' (94) through different means, whether fiction, journalism, or blue book reports. After a brief overview of the growth of London, the essay launches into an analysis of the three writers' reaction to the St. Giles, Seven Dials, and Soho area, noting Dickens's particular response: ''attraction of repulsion,'' as Forster put it, to the area (101). The essay includes an ample selection of long quotations from the three writers, providing readers with access to lesser-known source material.

With urbanization came a professional police force. Linda Strahan takes as the subject of her article the first ''positive'' representation of a policeman in British literature: Inspector Bucket of *Bleak House* (57). Writing for a journal on detective fiction, Strahan asks in ''There's a Hole in the (Inspector) Bucket: The Victorian Police in Fact and Fiction,'' if ''Dickens has distorted or preserved the actual policeman of Victorian London'' (57). Dickens was well acquainted with the Metropolitan Police but was not writing a history lesson, of course. But Strahan argues that since Bucket (along with Wilkie Collins's Sergeant Cuff) has been so influential in contributing certain stereotypical qualities of the police in detective fiction, an examination of the ways in which Dickens chose to stray from ''the actual'' is warranted. The essay claims that Inspector Bucket, though he is certainly a fictional creation who diverges upon occasion from the ''legislated rules of conduct'' (61), is a largely accurate ''historical artifact, preserved forever'' (62).

Finally, I include here Richard Jones's book *Walking Dickensian London: Twenty-Five Original Walks Through London's Victorian Quarters* primarily because it provides excellent color photos and maps of various neighborhoods featured in Dickens's corpus. Arranged into 23 chapters of city walks and 2 in the countryside, the book offers in each a relatively short tour through a particular area, with relevant quotations from the novels interspersed and careful directions included. Jones frequently adds information about other relevant figures when the walks take readers past a pertinent site like, for example, a pub patronized by William Hogarth just minutes from Church House, 10 South Grove, "believed to have been the 'old brick house at Highgate on the very summit of the hill', where the Steerforths lived'' (62). The close proximity of so many points of interest gives readers a keen sense of the many layers of London and of the interconnectedness of its history and literature.

Health

Though *A Medical Companion to Dickens's Fiction* makes no claim to providing literary criticism, scholar Joanne Eysell does supply a valuable resource for those wishing to understand, in historical context, Dickens's views on medical practitioners, the types of diseases and remedies portrayed in his texts, and the role of public health. While many have written about Dickens's use of illness as metaphor, few have examined what Eysell calls Dickens's "medical realism," that is, the "quality of his medical descriptions" (10). The book argues, "Dickens was an astute observer of morbid physical states" (9) and amply proves its point through painstaking research drawing upon not only Dickens's whole corpus but also medical texts available to him, medical articles published in *Household Words* and *All the Year Round*, and many medical journal articles written up to the present, revealing "the reception of his works by the profession" (11). Combining the techniques of "retrospective diagnosis" with "historical interpretation, based on examination of medical texts available in Dickens's day" (11), Eysell has identified over twenty-six diseases appearing in minor characters or playing a minor role in the novels and four illnesses which play a significant role in the novels: epilepsy, stroke, tuberculosis, and smallpox. Unlike most of his contemporaries, Dickens describes even the most minor of characters' ailments with precise realism. Throughout the book, Eysell amply demonstrates that Dickens understood much about the symptoms and treatments of his day, even describing with considerable precision illnesses and syndromes not yet named at that time. From the first chapter, devoted to Dickens's medical practitioners, to the extensive appendices with lists of medical books in Dickens's libraries and relevant medical articles and speeches, this companion is filled with useful information. What this revised dissertation lacks in elegance, it more than makes up for in thoroughness and clarity.

While Eysell is interested primarily in the realism of Dickens's medical scenes, setting aside symbolic and metaphorical interpretation, Allan Conrad Christensen, in *Nineteenth-Century Narratives of Contagion: "Our feverish contact,"* is focused on contagious disease as metaphor with minor attention to disease in actuality. Taking his cue from Matthew Arnold's narrator, who warned the scholar-gypsy to keep away from "this strange disease of modern life" (1), Christensen argues that "the distinction between literal and metaphorical is blurred" when "literal episodes of contagion are [so often] compared to military aggression" and other "power struggles" (7). The book interweaves analyses of eight novels, of which Dickens's *Bleak House* is one. To suggest the notion of a "single larger text," Christensen constantly moves from text to text to "emphasize the permeability of the individual novels" (10). Depending on how familiar readers are with such works as Ruffini's *Lavinia* and Manzoni's *I promessi sposi*, to name two, this constant shifting between works within paragraphs may prove difficult to follow. *Narratives of Contagion* does offer some nuggets for readers of *Bleak House*, however. For instance, Christensen's analysis of Voles's money laundering reveals the metaphorical connection between "dirty money" and contagion, asserting that when the "dirty money" is "laundered" in the Vale of Taunton, "it corrupts the innocence of the idyllic Vale" and demonstrates "the morally tainting sordidness of most financial transactions" (279). On our ability to reconstruct history, whether we are looking for an accurate understanding of the role of contagious diseases or some other topic, Christensen declares, "[H]istory occurs more convincingly in the secondary narratives than in the primary records of historical archives" (292).

Middle-class Victorians were understandably anxious about "filth," remarks Pamela K. Gilbert in the opening paragraph of "Medical Mapping: The Thames, the Body, and *Our Mutual Friend*." Indeed, urban growth and poor sanitation had resulted in rampant disease and frequent epidemics, which often was rightly attributed to "decomposing waste, especially [improperly disposed of] animal and human feces" (78). Gilbert argues, "Dickens uses the mid-century sanitary iconography of London's water supply to elaborate his representation of the urban, social body as well as the individual body in *Our Mutual Friend*" (81). Contending that Bradley Headstone, who cannot control his bodily fluids, "pollutes the river with blood and the fluid excess of his desire" (82), Gilbert sees such characters as embodying an "iconography of leakage versus containment" (84). Like Robert Druce, Gilbert also looks at Mayhew and Booth, and also John Snow, who mapped correspondences between the city's water supply and disease outbreaks. Dickens was very concerned about sanitation reform, as many scholars have noted; what this essay argues is that Dickens also takes issue with the notion that the suburbs and city are disconnected. Headstone's decomposing body pollutes the rural river, which is connected to the city, thus demonstrating the "interdependence between city and suburb" and the "deceptiveness" (94) of the appearance of water purity. In the end, Gilbert maintains, *Our Mutual Friend* is a more conservative novel than *Bleak House*, which blamed a "sick government" and "systemic corruption" for disease rather than the "individual incontinence . . . mapped directly onto the body of the city'' (99) in *Our Mutual Friend*.

The heart of Natalie Schroeder and Shari Hodges Holt's argument in ''The Gin Epidemic: Gin Distribution as a Means of Control and Profit in Dickens's Early Nonfiction and *Oliver Twist*'' is the contention that Dickens uses gin consumption and distribution as a ''metaphor for social control,'' with ''gin consumption among England's poor . . . [being] a symbol of . . . the abuse of the impoverished working classes by an increasingly callous, materialistic society'' (2). To Dickens, those who advocated total abstinence missed the point of the gin problem—that drunkenness among the poorer classes was a symptom and not necessarily a cause of social ills, ''that poverty and the government's indifference to the horrors of poverty are responsible for such scenes'' (6) as shown in Cruikshank's *Low Sunday*, an engraving depicting ''the spectacle of working-class drunkenness'' (7). The essay claims that Dickens believed ''temperance propaganda was dangerously misdirecting the impulse for social reform away from root causes'' (8), and in response, his novels portrayed these underlying societal ills. Gin, rather than being a cause of social ills, ''serve[s] as an agent . . . of dehumanizing and criminal activities throughout the novel [*Oliver Twist*]'' (14). The essay examines three characters, among others: Mrs. Mann, who ''uses her parochial stipend to buy gin for her own consumption'' (15); Mrs. Thingummy, who, ''made bold by gin, . . . steals the gold locket'' and pawns ''Oliver's future'' (15); and Mrs. Corney, who uses gin to attract Bumble's attention and secure financial gain for herself (16). With these three women, ''alcoholism's perversion of the nineteenth-century womanly ideal . . . typifies poverty's detrimental effect on treasured human values'' (17). Gin is everywhere in the novel and, the essay argues, alcohol abuse is meant to be taken as ''symptomatic of a greater social problem, a philosophy'' of capitalist and utilitarian ideologies ''that perpetuated poverty, ignorance, and crime'' (28).

Nostalgia—that is, homesickness—was once considered a disease to be treated medically. Tamara S. Wagner, in *Longing: Narratives of Nostalgia in the British Novel, 1740–1890*, examines how nostalgia is figured in novels by Austen, Dickens, Charlotte Brontë, Gaskell, and Collins. Nostalgia is often much maligned, seen as the result of overblown emotion and sentimentality, and critics have tended to follow this track in their scholarship, seldom questioning the negative perception of nostalgia. Wagner reveals ''the positive and creative, indeed hopeful, aspects of nostalgia'' (12). At the heart of her argument is the claim that ''nostalgia creatively fosters an imaginative and personal memory'' (22). For Dickens she notes that nostalgia is generally linked to ''childhood memories or . . . children and their homes or homelessness'' (125). Characters can even feel nostalgic for a home or childhood they never had, as in the case of Oliver Twist, Esther Summerson, John

Harmon, Florence Dombey, and Arthur Clennam. In such instances, Wagner claims, "the good home is present through its absence" because "its negation asserts the need for it more vigorously than the praise of a realized ideal could" (125). These characters use their imaginations, mostly unconsciously, to create a memory of and nostalgia for an ideal home in order to deal with their harsh reality, and, in this sense, Wagner sees "the nostalgic imagination as a survival strategy" (126) and a positive force. These acts of creation produce happiness in an otherwise bleak existence. Through their function as a "softening influence" (159), nostalgic musings also keep characters from developing resentment towards those who mistreat them, making them happier but perhaps less appealing characters, at least to a modern audience. A clear and carefully supported argument, *Longing* provides a new perspective on homesickness.

Education

At the "Dickens and America" conference held in Lowell, Massachusetts, in 2002, I heard an early version of David Paroissien's "Monsters in the Classroom: Dickens's Case Against Industrial Education" and was therefore delighted to find a portion published recently in *The Dickensian*. Paroissien here focuses his discussion on "Dickens's responses to primary school policies introduced in the 1850s in the spirit of aggressive modernization and improvement" (101–02). While Ruskin suggested that Dickens was "a pure modernist" (101), key passages in *Hard Times* and *Our Mutual Friend* reveal "skepticism and hostility to innovations designed to upgrade existing educational practices" (102). Clearly, Dickens understood that reform was necessary, but he objected to "the new breed of teachers and the schools that evolved under the direction of Kay-Shuttleworth and other reformers" (109), whose Utilitarian bent Dickens found disagreeable, if not dangerous. Kit Polga begins "Dickens and the Morality of Imagination" with a summary of a recent article in the *Sunday Times Magazine* featuring a British elementary school noted for its excellence. Linking the modern-day school environment to Dickens's *Hard Times*, Polga goes beyond mere surface connections to uncover what is at the heart of Dickens's concern about an educational system that inhibits imagination: "the suppression of the imagination" as threat to "moral development" (173). Simply stated, "Putting oneself in the place of another requires imagination" (173), and any educational endeavor that squelches imagination must destroy empathy—the basis for Dickens's moral code of the Golden Rule. Dickens believed that it was the "Christian duty" of every adult in "society . . . to promote" empathy (175). Like Molly Clark Hillard, in an essay discussed below with other studies of *The Old Curiosity*

Shop, Polga suggests that Dickens saw fairy tales, in particular, as "humanly useful" and was interested in "protecting fairly tales in their original form" in order to "nurture the imaginative faculty in the young" (176). Whether through such tales or through other means, Dickens calls on us all to "become more compassionate and moral citizens" through exercising our imaginations (177).

Science

" 'Lost in the vast worlds of wonder': Dickens and Science," Jude Nixon's ambitious and extensive survey of Dickens's "direct, oblique, and metaphoric engagement" (271) with science, provides a good overview of scholarly output on this topic as well as descriptions of relevant primary materials. Noting the relative lack of direct references to science in Dickens's novels, Nixon nevertheless demonstrates how Dickens was genuinely interested in the scientific discoveries and advancements of his day. After an overview in which Nixon makes some general claims about Dickens and science and provides a few examples, like a partial list of the scientific books in Dickens's library, the essay discusses references to science in the correspondence, claiming that for the most part "the letters show a consistent albeit superficial engagement with science" (273). Next, the essay surveys a sampling of critical works dealing with this topic, summarizing their findings. The third section covers a few notable instances of engagement with science in the novels, arguing that while "the general neglect of science in the novels" can be attributed to Dickens's belief that "the novel should be about—the social. . . . Still, one finds in the fiction a sustained though subtle interest in science" (287). The essay cites examples from *Hard Times*, *Great Expectations*, and *Dombey and Son*, through which Nixon demonstrates Dickens's engagement with problems of industrialism, the theory of evolution, and the ways in which "natural phenomena [seem to] comment on human events" (288). The major contribution of this essay lies with its discussion of science in *Household Words* and *All the Year Round*, where we see a much more profound appreciation of science than in any other place in Dickens's oeuvre. Three-dozen articles on science from *Household Words* are categorized into several groups and discussed in the essay, and Nixon shows that "Dickens's scientific interest in *Household Words* continued in its sequel," *All the Year Round*—"both important forums for serious scientific discussion and debate" (318). While Dickens was generally receptive to and curious "about the new world science is opening to us," he remains "guarded" (322) as well, cognizant of the potential evils of science without morality or imagination.

Interdisciplinary Approaches in the Humanities and Social Sciences

James Buzard writes in *Disorienting Fiction: The Autoethnographic Work of Nineteenth-Century British Novels* of the "nineteenth-century novel as a determinedly self-interrupting form . . . devoted to the performance of a 'metropolitan autoethnography' " (7). An ethnography—"a study of a people's way of life centering on the method of 'immersion' in extensive field work and raising the issue of how, and how far, the outsider can become a kind of honorary insider in other cultures" (8)—includes a "Participant Observer" (10), who is both an insider and outsider in a "culture." This observer's awareness of the ways in which culture cannot be contained within narrative leads to the self-interruption characteristic of the mid-Victorian novel. Buzard is particularly concerned with "autoethnographic thinking as it might apply to the imperial center" (15), which he sees as neglected in these terms. The book attempts "to show how the novel puts its own fictions of English or British culture *on* show, committing itself to the skeptical questioning and testing of its own nation-making and culture-making procedures" (44). The chapter on Dickens focuses on *Bleak House* as an autoethnographic response to the Great Exhibition. The novel, Buzard contends, "responded to the triumphant universalism of 1851 by exhibiting, not the works of industry of all nations, but the neglected human by-products of the national anticulture" (156). Through the device of the double narrator, Dickens gives "formal embodiment to the ambivalence residing in the conception of culture he reaches for. Each voice forestalls the possibility of the other's having free reign or gathering too much discursive momentum" (122). Thus the narration enacts the interplay between the Participant Observer's status as simultaneous insider and outsider, revealing the difficulties of autoethnography. Ultimately, this ambivalence, Buzard claims, makes the text a "narrative of modernity" (156). Through close readings of novels by Scott, Dickens, Charlotte Brontë, George Eliot, and William Morris, Buzard offers his response to the "decentering approaches" (18) of cultural studies, but the book may prove difficult for some readers as it employs a considerable amount of specialized vocabulary.

With the expansion and development of British imperial power came suspicion and fear of colonized peoples, often enacted in representations of "savage" threats. *Outlandish English Subjects in the Victorian Domestic Novel*, by Timothy L. Carens, examines such representations, tracing their prevalence and varying manifestations within Victorian evangelicalism and the new discipline of anthropology, where, Carens contends, we can find the root of imperial anxiety. Like Buzard, Carens is interested in "domestic autoethnography" and, in particular, "novels in which ethnographic language and narrative structures infiltrate description of the English state and subject" (21). The book argues that the "universal human family" espoused by anthropology as well as evangelicalism made it possible for colonial "others" to establish themselves and their supposedly "inferior" "impulses, beliefs, and practices" (22) inside the English imperial center—the home itself. Dickens, Carens suggests, uses ethnographic descriptions of Africa in *Bleak House* to comment on the Condition of England Question and advocate that the English should "redirect the civilizing mission to the urban metropolis" (116). At the same time, his creation of a "colony" that abandons the city "also indicates an inability to solve the problems that have eroded distinctions between the imperial metropolis and the Niger delta" (116). Discussing other novelists such as Charlotte Brontë, Wilkie Collins, and George Meredith, this readable volume offers a well-considered corrective to those who argue that "Victorian domestic novels advance imperial aims" (20).

Two works examine Dickens through the lens of religious studies. A slim volume published by Hon's Penguin, *Revivalism and Conversion Literature: From Wesley to Dickens*, by Takashi Terauchi, contains three short essays on evangelicalism. The first essay, from which the volume takes its name, presents a short history of evangelicalism and views several literary works in this context, of which Dickens's *A Tale of Two Cities* and *Great Expectations* form the greatest part. Terauchi reads Carton as "the ideal [that was] erected by the Revival and Evangelical Movements" (21) of one who follows the teachings of Christ in sacrificing himself for the safety of others. Of *Great Expectations*, the essay claims somewhat less convincingly that "all four main characters are converted" (21): Miss Havisham, Magwitch, Pip, and Estella. Though some readers may disagree with Terauchi's assertion that Dickens "was an Evangelist novelist," his reminder about the prevalence of the trope of "instantaneous conversion" (24) stressed by evangelism seems pertinent. The other two essays link Dickens and Longfellow through their mutual use of the motto "Excelsior," seen by Terauchi as a motto of reform and progress in keeping with the spirit of evangelicalism.

Gary L. Colledge undertakes the important task of examining in "*The Life of Our Lord* Revisited" what this neglected text can tell us about "not only Dickens's religious beliefs, but also the larger Dickens corpus" (125). The first section of the essay offers a discussion of the work in the "context of other theological literature" (125). As "a paraphrased selective juvenile harmony" of the Gospels (127), *Life* used Dickens's own words except in direct discourse, which are taken from the King James Bible. Dickens chose to include only some events and sayings that were best suited to achieve his ends, leaving other sections out. For instance, Dickens chooses to harmonize Luke's Good Samaritan account with "the controversy stories of Matt. 22:34–40 and Mark 12:28–34" (130) in which Jesus states that loving God is the greatest commandment, followed by loving one another. Colledge explains that Dickens's choice to harmonize these sections stems from the desire "to emphasize what he saw as a central aspect of the teaching of Jesus and a central lesson he would want his children to learn" (131)—that is, the Golden Rule as exemplified by the Good Samaritan. The essay argues that for Dickens religion meant "a practical or ethical Christology" rather than "theological formulation or conjecture" (126), and it was this view of Christianity as a religion centered on the person and teachings of Jesus that he was attempting to teach his children.

Concerned with the philosophical question of how to promote moral behavior, Natalie B. Cole in "Dickens and the Act of Gardening" shows that Dickens's fictional gardens reveal "the moral discipline of his characters" (244). Cole discusses many examples from a variety of novels, showing how "gardening seems most consistently a way Dickens conveys the remarkable resilience of his characters' emotional lives" (253). Among the many characters discussed are urban gardeners such as Tim Linkinwater and Smike in *Nicholas Nickleby*, as well as Jenny Wren and Lizzie Hexam in *Our Mutual Friend*. Cole notes the importance of gardening to "celibate characters, disappointed in love, or sacrificing romantic love for familial ties" (249): Betsey Trotwood in *David Copperfield*, Miss Tox and Harriet and James Carker of *Dombey and Son*. The essay briefly touches also on "Dickens's 'Wasteland' gardeners, those who show no patience, wait through no fallow seasons, and coax no seeds" (251) and ends with a discussion of *The Mystery of Edwin Drood*. Dickens, surrounded in his "small glass conservatory" by "the scarlet geraniums [he] loved" (252), fully enjoyed the fruits of gardening and was reminded of the beneficial "moral discipline" (253) of the enterprise.

Weaving "the ideological history of theology and political economy, the literary history of the novel, and the commodity history of the serial into a single sociological narrative of developments in religion, social theory, and literary culture" (ix), David Payne's *The Reenchantment of Nineteenth-Century Fiction: Dickens, Thackeray, George Eliot, and Serialization* covers the years of "Dickens's literary production, from . . . 1836 to . . . 1870." Payne shows how "the literary forms" of Dickens, Eliot, and Thackeray connect to "religious and economic ideologies" as well as the "serial novel's status as literary commodity" (13). Dickens and Eliot, Payne argues, undertake "the task of atoning for modernity" (19) by adopting "an ideology of restoration" (x) when faced with the "overwhelming nature of historical change" (18) and the disenchantment of modernity. In a chapter focusing on *Little Dorrit*, Payne highlights the many personal changes Dickens experienced from 1856 to 1858, including separating from his wife and starting his affair with Ellen Ternan, the end of *Household Words* and beginning of *All the Year Round*, and Dickens's new role as "theatrical public reader in pursuit of profit" (11). Amidst these changes, *Little Dorrit* emerged with its "profusion of literary innovations" published in the archaic "commodity form" of the monthly serial (11). Showing how *Little Dorrit* recalls *Pickwick* "in the prison cell," Payne contends that Dickens holds out the possibility "of a joyful and hilarious rather than agonized and grieving knowledge" (93) of the past.

Employing the strategies of the New Economic Critics, Gail Turley Houston examines a range of Victorian novels, *Villette, Dracula*, and *Dr. Jekyll and Mr. Hyde*, as well as *Little Dorrit*, revealing connections between the language of economics and Gothic tropes. *From Dickens to Dracula: Gothic, Economics, and Victorian Fiction* begins with a discussion of "economic panic," which Houston claims was "normalized" by "Victorian capitalism" to the point where panic came to be seen as "necessary to a so-called healthy economy" (10). The novels she analyzes create "narratives in which economic panic is a deep structure; . . . model[ing] means of managing and sublimating panic in order to achieve fiscal success; . . . [and] encourag[ing] unlimited desire while also relying upon crisis and permanent panic in order to contain that desire" (10–11). Houston includes a brief overview of "the historical record on Victorian economic panic(s)" (13), with a particularly useful description of common discourse on the business cycle and the inevitabilities of repeated collapse and stagnation. The book's fourth chapter, " 'The Whole Duty of Man': Circulating Circulation in Dickens's *Little Dorrit*," elucidates how this "novel about debtors' prison, a banking crash, and the circumlocutionary ineptitude of government as agent of business, portrays the rough cycle of trade" (71). Political economist Henry Dunning Macleod wrote in 1855 of the capitalist's duty to circulate currency and to push others to do so as well. Houston notes the startling similarities between Macleod and the "fictional Panck's own business philosophy . . . [of] circulation and duty" (76). Dickens's portrait of capitalists fulfilling that duty, Houston claims, reveals a high degree of personal anxiety about "constantly increasing one's output" (79)—that is, feeling "imprisoned" by the need to write. Throughout the novel, we see an increase in this anxiety about the need to circulate, finally dramatized in the haunted house as an extended metaphor for the private Clennam bank's "impending economic collapse" (86).

Ready to Trample on All Human Law: Financial Capitalism in the Fiction of Charles Dickens, like Houston's book, is interested in financial panics but focuses entirely on Dickens's works as both "reflections of the evolution of [the financial] system, and as attempts to shape and influence, . . . public opinion" (1–2). Paul Jarvie examines "elements of Dickens's work that form a critique of financial capitalism" based on the "difference between productive circulation and mere accumulation" (2). Jarvie starts with *Nicholas Nickleby*, where "the distinction between use-value and exchange-value drives much of the moral action of the story" (3). Next follows a chapter on *A Christmas Carol*, which "proposes a change of heart as the solution to the problems of living under financial capitalism'' (4). The third chapter tackles *Little Dorrit*, Dickens's fullest articulation ''of the problem of financial capitalism'' (6), and the final chapter discusses *Our Mutual Friend*, in which Dickens ''plunges beneath the obvious outward representations of the capitalist system to grapple with the process . . . at its heart'' (6), attempting to show ''alternatives . . . [to] succumbing to capitalism's powerful shape-shifting process'' (7). This revised dissertation is a readable book with extensive endnotes.

Visual and Print Culture

While many reviews of film and television adaptations of Dickens texts appeared in 2005, and I am not including them here, I will mention Michael Eaton's survey of hundreds of issues of *The Dickensian*, read to assess the journal's helpfulness in identifying early cinematic adaptations of Dickens's works. ''*The Dickensian* goes to the Cinematograph'' finds the journal lacking by not providing ''regular and reliable judgment upon . . . features made in the 1920s'' (238–39). The essay is very helpful, however, in identifying notable early adaptations of Dickens.

In *Realist Vision* Peter Brooks offers a new look at the realist project's fascination with the visual. Readers will find discussions of texts written by Balzac, Dickens, Flaubert, Eliot, Zola, and Woolf; paintings by Courbet, Manet, Caillebotte, Tissot, and Lucian Freud; and even the strange new medium of so-called ''reality TV.'' Stating that ''[w]e thirst for a reality that we can see, hold up to inspection, understand'' (1), Brooks proceeds to show the ''case for realism'' (19) through literature and art. The chapter on Dickens focuses on *Hard Times*, admittedly an odd choice, but to Brooks an excellent example for both what it does and does not do well. The ''narratorial language'' (42) describing Coketown is highly metaphorical, escaping through imagination the oppressive system it describes. Dickens's description, in fact, ''refus[es] to see'' in the way that ''realism tends to be intensely visual'' with frequent recourse to ''inventories of the real'' (43). Instead, in *Hard Times*, all facts are transformed into ''questions of style'' and the novel becomes ''a drama of opposed styles'' (44). Ultimately, Brooks refuses to omit this novel from the canon of realism despite the fact that ''it cannot be counted a persuasively full effort to represent industrial England'' (53). He sees the ''very incoherences and failures of representation'' in the novel as a welcome ''disruption in a smoother understanding of Dickens'' (53).

Several articles in 2005 investigated print culture and the materiality of writing. Ivan Kreilkamp examines how advances in secretarial technology reveal ''the fear that the human voice may be somehow diminished or destroyed by writing and modern print culture'' (28) in his essay ''Speech on

Paper: Charles Dickens, Victorian Phonography, and the Reform of Writing.'' The essay provides a brief history of writing technology with particular attention to G. Bradley's 1842 *A Concise and Practical System of Stenography, of Short-Hand Writing*. Bradley's claim was that his system of capturing "voice" would enable writing to maintain the "vocal" instead of imposing writing "whole cloth on speech" (15). Kreilkamp notes that Dickens mastered shorthand as a reporter and "boast[ed] of his shorthand expertise many years after he gave it up," and this facility with the technique may have contributed to "Dickens's characteristic style, the vivid immediacy of his characters' voices" (19), a claim made earlier by Steven Marcus, which Kreilkamp builds upon. Through a careful reading of David Copperfield's attempts to learn shorthand as a path to gaining Dora, the essay argues that shorthand is the "site of an impossible effort to control language and one's own body" (25) and stands for a "model of masculine authority that is later rejected: one of straightforward mastery, where the woman is simply the object of desire to be earned by the husband's labor" (26).

Lorna Huett, winner of the 2004 Van Arsdel Prize for her essay, "Among the Unknown Public: *Household Words, All the Year Round*, and the Mass-Market Weekly Periodical in the Mid-Nineteenth Century," offers a detailed discussion of the implications of Wilkie Collins's unsigned 1858 article in *Household Words*, "The Unknown Public." Contending that through his article, in part, Collins was seeking to construct a "stable, superior identity . . . for the journal . . . [by] simultaneously addressing and creating a middle-class audience" (61), Huett argues that such an effort to define the identity of a publication is "part of the writing, editing, design and marketing of every journal," and this goal affects even "format, printing, illustration and advertising" (62). In the case of Collins's portrait of the Unknown Public, Huett contends that his article has "highly significant implications for the understanding of the identity and nature of *Household Words* as a whole" (62). One of the essay's strengths lies in its analysis of the significance of Dickens's journal within the realm of the nineteenth-century literary marketplace, with special attention to comparative circulation numbers and audience demographics. The attention to details such as how the size of a journal (double crown quarto versus royal octavo) affected its public image provides Dickens scholars with useful insights into how the material production of literature is connected to perception and reception.

Along similar lines, rather than seeing publications as " 'derived' from the period marked by the rise of modern nations and nationalism,'' Olga Stucherbrukhov suggests in "The 'Nation-Less' State of Great Britain and the Nation-State of France in *Household Words*'' that Dickens's journal was "an active participant in the formation of Victorian national consciousness" (392). In particular, she asserts that Dickens and his contributors "use France and its state and cultural practices to promote their own middle-class idea of a nation'' (392). The French were portrayed as a model of ''the advantages of state control'' but also potentially dangerous with their ''collectivist'' and protectionist inclinations, whereas England is portrayed as ''individualistic'' and erratic and in need of more balance between ''order'' and ''culturally and emotionally satisfying communal life'' (393). Stucherbrukhov analyzes several examples from *Household Words*, showing that Dickens saw France as a ''well-balanced nation-state'' because it was not ruled by the retrograde forces of the aristocracy or by the hyper-modernism of industrialized capitalism.

While many scholars, according to Daniel Hack in *The Material Interests of the Victorian Novel,* have claimed that the material conditions of writing were hidden or ignored by Victorian novelists, Hack argues that authors such as Dickens, Eliot, Thackeray, and Collins used themes emerging from these conditions to enrich their work. Indeed, Hack claims, ''No Victorian novelist devotes more attention to the physical materiality of writing and signs than does Charles Dickens'' (37), and none of his novels is so thoroughly ''a document about the materiality of documents and the interpretation of that materiality'' (38) as *Bleak House*. Examining both the literary text and advertisements that appeared alongside the serialized novel, Hack argues that the ''materialities'' of both kinds of writing ''authorize . . . the efforts of a writer such as Dickens to describe and analyze the workings of the body in particular and the natural world in general'' (40), for the body and writing are inextricably connected. Take for instance, Lady Dedlock's recognition of her presumed dead lover's handwriting on a legal document, the discovery of which ''reminds Lady Dedlock of her experience of forbidden physical passion and results in an experience of vulnerable embodiedness'' (41). The adjacent advertisements, as well, demonstrate a similar interest in the materiality of writing, warning readers/consumers about swindlers, who can only be discovered through careful attention to labels' font styles and ink colors. Such advertisements look as though they ''were scripted by Dickens himself,'' as if they were a part of *Bleak House* ''rather than an adjunct to it'' (61).

Style

One might think that previous scholars have already unearthed all there is to be said about Dickens's mode of composition, but Herbert Foltinek manages to add to the subject in *Imagination All Compact: How Did Charles Dickens Compose His Novels?* Foltinek views Dickens as operating in two modes: the first is the ''traditional, or constructive'' approach based on a ''ground-plan'' in which the author ''tentatively lay[s] out a line of progress,'' and the second is based on "the impulse of an immensely fertile imagination" (5). He sees the second mode as "centrifugal," that is "reaching out for directions and patterns that tend to widen the significance of the narrative work" (8). Rather than being a sign of an undisciplined compositional style, sections of his novels composed in this mode can be seen as "imaginative flights, which he [could later choose] to rein in or expand" (10), depending on his readers' responses to his serialized numbers. Foltinek's analysis of the uncertainties of Dickens's planning notes for *Martin Chuzzlewit, David Copperfield,* and the *Mystery of Edwin Drood,* in particular, indicates the impossibility of making a "precise investigation into the genesis of . . . individual works" (14). Showing how the practice of serialization enabled "infinitely inventive" Dickens a wider range of options (15), Foltinek argues against the notion that Dickens's "lack of decisiveness is a flaw" (16). Rather, he attempts to illuminate the various worlds Dickens was contemplating, however fleetingly, as he wrote.

Focusing his attention on the power of naming in literature, John R. Reed argues in "Dickens and Naming" that Dickens's approach to naming is incompatible with the conventions of realism, which use naming to link real and fictional worlds. Reed examines "the ways in which Dickens exploits a wide range of possibilities in the naming of characters" (183). He sometimes names characters to highlight their "comic qualities" (184), while other times names have "connotative value only" or "associational power" (185). Then again, some names are overtly "denotative . . . as with Bradley Headstone" (185) or "directly borrowed" or allude "satirically to real names" (185). Of particular importance to Reed, however, is "those instances where characters call attention to the act of naming and, in doing so, signal Dickens's own ultimate authority as the source of all such naming" (185). Reed notes that Garret Stewart has pointed to "Dickens's complicated naming activity" in *The Old Curiosity Shop,* where Dick Swiveller, perhaps an analogue for Dickens himself, "effectively brings the [Marchioness] . . . into being" (185) by naming her. And in *Our Mutual Friend,* Stewart discusses Jenny Wren's renaming of herself and the power of that act. Reed adds that it is ultimately Dickens himself who has named Fanny Cleaver and given her permission to rename herself. Throughout Reed's argument, he shows how Dickens inserts himself into various texts in order to call "attention to his own authority in the act of naming" (187). Dickens, he contends, is not interested in having his names—of people, of places—sound real, creating "an easy flow between fiction and reality" and maintaining "the illusion of transparency to which realism aspires" (192). He enjoys the power of naming too much.

Rodney Stenning Edgecombe's essay "Dickens and the Comedy of Abbreviation" offers a fascinating look at Dickens as precursor of Modernist "unprepared transitions and bricolage" (80). Noting that when "aesthetic developments'' first appear, they often provoke laughter, Edgecombe contends that ''Dickens, sensing that suddenness and abbreviation were foreign to the Victorian idea of craft, chose to include them in his repertoire of comic effects'' (81). This essay offers numerous excerpts of characters' speech to demonstrate how this technique is applied. Mr. Jingle's ''fragmentary speech'' (81) can sometimes be made out, but other times ''the gaps of signification become too wide to bridge'' (82). Voluble Flora Finching, while a seeming opposite to the dash-ridden Mr. Jingle, is also ''born of wholesale excisions'' (84). Her speech, made nearly opaque by the lack of end punctuation, is somewhat decipherable, however, when one compares it with Mr. F's Aunt, whose ''narrative abbreviation . . . is too severe to permit the retrieval of anything'' (85). Citing further examples from *Our Mutual Friend*, *Bleak House*, and *Little Dorrit*, Edgecombe argues that the sort of ''omissions and elisions'' found in Modernist literature ''were to be found in Dickens's art long before the modern era,'' but in his hand, they became ''a source of merriment'' that was ''quickly resolved into the rhythms of conventional narrative'' (90).

Sketches by Boz

Ian Wilkinson in ''Performance and Control: The Carnivalesque City and Its People in Charles Dickens's *Sketches by Boz*'' notes the two typical approaches to *Sketches by Boz*, examining the text's '' 'fidelity' of representation'' or searching for traces of ''Dickens's talents as a novelist'' (2), as well as some critics' work on the connection between *Sketches by Boz* and the theater. Wilkinson claims that the sketches are largely about Londoners at play, and as such Bakhtin's theory of the carnivalesque should be applied. He suggests that Dickens ''represents London through its people, rather than through topographical descriptions, and notes the performances in Londoners' everyday lives'' (2). Countering D. A. Miller's argument that in *Sketches* ''Dickens's bourgeois fear at the proliferation of the masses'' (15) surfaces, Wilkinson contends that Dickens's use of the carnivalesque reveals a much more egalitarian view as well as a strong appreciation for the energy of the individual. The essay's treatment of ''The Pawnbroker's Shop'' reads Mrs. Tatham as a skilled performer who uses comic ''verbal banter'' and well-placed allusions to family troubles to acquire the money that she needs for her family's survival. Wilkinson sees her as ''typical of the struggling poor as they are portrayed in the sketches'' because of how she, ''despite her dire circumstances,'' retains ''the ability to perform her part with energy that fills out her character'' (4). She is ''not a victim'' but rather effectively resists the established order of things through humor, contributing to the spirit of carnival in the text. Wilkinson notes how in "Greenwich Fair" and "Astley's" Boz determines to observe spectators as performers in a show where "class, gender, and even the distinction between adult and child are obscured" (9). The streets, too, contain a "subversive life-force," for Boz "rejoices in the underdog's rebellion against the symbols of authority" (12) such as the police. Those who belong on the street, whether criminals or working-class pedestrians, seem not to notice the performance; rather it is the outsider who can appreciate the "street theater" (15) of real life. This text, Wilkinson claims, is an intimate and appreciative portrait of heterogeneous London.

Paul Schlicke has been working on an authoritative edition of *Sketches by Boz*, and in 2005 shared some of his findings in two articles. In " 'Risen like a Rocket': The Impact of *Sketches by Boz*" he notes that, in general, critics have held *Sketches by Boz* in "low esteem," taking their cue from Dickens's own estimation of his first book. Schlicke questions this "critical consensus" (3) and proves unequivocally, to my mind, the importance of this frequently neglected work, by "systematically [demonstrating] how enthusiastically they [the sketches] were received on their first appearance" (4) and proving that Dickens had already risen to fame before the success of *Pickwick*. For example, the sketches were published individually "in their entirety, or virtually unabridged, in *at least 140 different locations* in newspapers and periodicals" (5), not including pirated copies in other countries. Numerous "spin-offs," both in theater and in print, further "served to contribute to public awareness of the sketches" (7). In reviews of the time, Schlicke found "thirty-six excerpts, taken from twenty-two different sketches, on display in fourteen different papers and magazines" (7), all contributing to a sense in the reading public of the great "range of Dickens's subjects and the variety of tones" (8). Clearly, Dickens's contemporaries saw much to praise, as "fully eighty-seven per cent of the sketches were identified as being of particular merit" (12). While a handful of negative remarks did appear in reviews, by far the majority praised the collection and identified the young Dickens as an up-and-coming star. In "Revisions to *Sketches by Boz*," Schlicke notes that Dickens revised all sixty collected sketches. He discusses a few of these, comparing the originals published in periodicals with the revised book versions in order to "consider the gains and losses" that the changes effected. Schlicke asserts, "The sketches as originally published were often racier, more topical, more politically outspoken, and less concerned with Dickens's emerging role as a popular family author, than the later versions" (29).

Pickwick Papers

John Bruns, in "Get Out of Gaol Free, or: How to Read a Comic Plot," responds to Chesterton's and other critics' assessment that *Pickwick* is, respectively, not a novel or is a failed novel. Bruns suggests, "*Pickwick* is a book that teaches us to read comically, not novelistically'' (26). He sees the main difference between these ways of reading as the dictate that the reader of novels ''must always be moving endward, . . . towards resolution'' versus the view that ''the reader [of comic plots] must always be moving somewhere, . . . anywhere'' (27). A comic character does not need to grow and change, develop in some linear progression, or even be understood. All that a comic character must do is move. Our ''failure to read [Pickwick] comically'' (28) is in large part due to an Aristotelian conception of plot, based on tragedy not comedy. Bruns advocates for a ''comprehensive resignification of *Pickwick*'' (29) through a close reading of scenes such as the hunting episode of Chapter 7, the awakening in the ''Pound,'' and, of course, the trial and imprisonment in the Fleet, among other passages. This essay was published in the *Journal of Narrative Theory*, and thus it addresses directly theories of narratology. Bruns argues that ''traditional narratology, with its emphasis on paradigmatic structures, fails to take into consideration the dynamics of reading'' (45)—that is, the ways in which readers themselves construct plot. If one reads expecting a novel (because such is our habit), one might well miss what this book has to offer.

Paul Goetsch, in ''Charles Dickens's *The Pickwick Papers* and *Don Quixote*,'' sees Cervantes's tale as ''less [of a] concrete source for the characters and episodes of Dickens's novel than a general model'' (143). Though there are certainly similarities between Pickwick and the Don—both ''elderly men on various journeys'' (145) who are not really changed by what they experience—Goetsch points out their seeming differences as well, placing Pickwick as an inverse of the Spanish hero. Pickwick, ''far from being a would-be hero of romance'' is more often ''a comic elderly gentleman caught by circumstances''; however, the two characters do both become ''objects of ridicule'' (149), who eventually capture the affection of readers ''because of the values they so ridiculously represent'' (143). While the two heroes' trusty servants also share some commonalities, they are more ''distant cousins,'' with Sam Weller sharing more in common with the ''witty servants of traditional stage comedies'' (153). Goetsch accounts for the differences in the two texts in their historical contexts, noting that in Dickens's case, he ''does not allow contemporary reality to invade and destroy Pickwick's idyllic circles'' (155) as Cervantes does to Don Quixote. On a side note, if readers are interested in how well Dickens translates into Spanish, Pilar Orero has written ''The Translation of Wellerisms: The Spanish Case'' in which she argues that due to the ''peculiar structure—which contains wordplay and truncated idioms'' (266) of Wellerisms, they have not been adequately translated into the Spanish editions of *Pickwick* which she examined. There are ''no subversive comments, no word-play, no humor'' and the ''reminiscence of the tandem Sancho-Quijote is also lost'' (268).

Oliver Twist

In 2005 Roman Polanski's adaptation of *Oliver Twist* was released, so that a flurry of reviews were published. The best, by Juliet John, is "Fagin, The Holocaust and Mass Culture: or, *Oliver Twist* on Screen," which examines the use of Dickens in the film industry. Claiming that "from its inception the film industry has seen Dickens as a short cut to both cultural respectability and to the mass market" (205), the essay summarizes the long history of film adaptations of *Oliver Twist*, the most featured of all of Dickens's works on film (with *Christmas Carol* topping the list of television adaptations). Dubbing the novel a " 'culture-text': that is, a text that permeates the cultural consciousness" (207), John notes the absence of a study of the wider cultural life of the novel and points to literary critics' post-Holocaust reluctance to discuss anti-Semitism in canonical authors as the "major reason" (207). John discusses some of the many film versions that have been produced and argues that after David Lean's controversial film in 1949, "Fagin on screen has seldom subsequently been both very Jewish and very evil" (213). Of special interest for this review is John's discussion of Polanski's film, in which Sir Ben Kingsley plays a Fagin whose Jewishness is never mentioned, a "comic, camp and gauche rather than omnipotent and otherworldly" villain (215). Finally, the essay notes that Dickens's "upward cultural mobility" (218) and his "continued presence in modern mass culture" (220) are largely due to his popularity on screen.

Asking why Dickens did not do more to purge his revised version of *Oliver Twist* of its anti-Semitism, Susan Meyer offers an answer in "Antisemitism and Social Critique in Dickens's *Oliver Twist*." Meyer sees Dickens's Christianity as pertinent to his mode of representing Fagin. Dickens begins the novel by representing the "unchristian . . . behavior of the English toward the poor" but then introduces the "distinctly non-Christian Fagin," who is eventually killed off in a symbolic purging of the "novel's representative of the absence of Christianity, . . . preparing the way for a vision of a purified England in the idyllic village, with the church at its moral center" (241). Once the early examples of unchristian behavior (like Bumble) are replaced by solid middle-class Christians such as Mrs. Maylie, "unchristian evil in the novel is centered in the figure of the Jew" (244). Meyer points out that with Fagin's execution, the world of the novel is "purged" of its "anti-Christian Jew," so there is no need "to punish the many English townspeople who have behaved in an unchristian way toward Oliver in the past" (248). The novel is successful at least in part because it uses Christian rhetoric to make its case against the terrible treatment of the poor, and anti-Semitic stereotyping is an "inextricable" part of this approach (250).

David L. Gold offers a thorough and meticulously researched argument in "Despite Popular Belief, the Name Fagin in Charles Dickens's *The Adventures of Oliver Twist* Has No Jewish Connection." Some scholars have argued that Fagin is an English spelling of the East Ashkenazaic name Feygin, but Gold demonstrates that the name was most likely not found in England before May 1837. Further he surmises that even if it did exist in England, Dickens would have been unlikely to have heard it, and he offers compelling evidence that Bob Fagin, Dickens's supposed companion in the Blacking Factory, was not Jewish. Peter Rowland provides the results of his investigation into the death records at the Family Record Centre in "No Sich a Person? The Hunt for Fagin." Rowland explains that most likely Dickens's childhood friend Bob Fagin, actually spelled his surname "Fagan," a much more commonplace name with multiple entries in the Register.

Finally, Holly Furneaux takes issue with previous critics' separation of *Oliver Twist* into two separate sections—the first half filled with "social criticism of the workings of the New Poor Law" and the second half a "more plot-driven . . . 'Newgate' narrative style" (213). In " 'Worrying to Death'—Reinterpreting Dickens's Critique of the New Poor Law in *Oliver Twist* and Contemporary Adaptations" Furneaux shows, through analysis of several adaptations of *Oliver Twist*, that the novel provides a "carefully sustained critique" (213) of the this new law. In particular, the essay shows how our examination of various stage adaptations makes more explicit to us Dickens's implicit "link between pauperism and crime" (219). His contemporaries, and particularly his adaptors, Furneaux argues, saw clearly the interconnectedness of what twentieth-century readers separate into two sections of the novel.

Nicholas Nickleby

In "Nickleby, Flanerie, Reverie: The View from Cheerybles' " Michael Hollington counters George Eliot's famous claim that the psyches of Dickens's characters were far less realistically drawn than their "external traits" (22). Applying the concept of the flaneur, this essay examines *Nicholas Nickleby*—not generally seen as having much "psychological depth" (22). Hollington claims that the "figure of the flaneur" is "noticeably present . . . in a number of forms, especially if we broaden the concept sufficiently to include all those who perambulate the streets of London" (22). As Dickens's characters walk the streets fantasizing, the reader may glimpse their psychological states and make-up. For Hollington, Nicholas, the novel's primary flaneur, walks London at all hours, aimlessly fantasizing or daydreaming, and his "indoor thoughts are simply reproduced as the rhythm of the walk outdoors takes over'' (26). He suggests that Nicholas's "compulsion to motion" (27) leads to useful discoveries and is clearly necessary for the character to "think things out" (29). The essay further argues that Dickens understands "metropolitan psychology, not just of Nicholas, but of how a whole class of solitary people, isolated from each other, think and behave as they move through the throng of the streets" (30). He calls Smike, Miss La Creevy, Kate, and, surprisingly, Ralph, flaneurs. Perhaps the essay's most useful insight is how flanerie provides structure for this novel—generally thought to be "among the most episodic and loosely organized" of Dickens's works (42). Flanerie provides "a quasinaturalist device that can serve as a means of transition, of linking or reintroducing characters through chance encounters on the street" (32).

The Old Curiosity Shop

Eileen Cleere playfully begins her essay, " 'Implicit Faith in the Deception': Misanthropy, Natural History and *The Old Curiosity Shop*,'' by recalling a career services computer program that listed puppeteer as the third best career for English majors. Her anecdote then segues to an insightful analysis of Codlin and Short, the two antithetical puppeteers in *The Old Curiosity Shop*. Short, she asserts, is seemingly a philanthropist, "an even-tempered, happy-go-lucky friend" to Nell and her grandfather, though this later proves to be untrue. Codlin, on the other hand, is "a misanthrope, suspicious of his fellow wanderers from the beginning" (47). In the novel, "misanthropy is perpetually figured as imagination disappointed, or as curiosity curtailed" (51). Codlin is "a cultural emblem of the embattled intellectual" whose attitudes derive from the necessity of maintaining illusion for the audience. Cleere sees the misanthropy with which Codlin is identified as the result of "a declining faith in the positivist illusions of anthropocentrism" (49). Nell, too, is resignedly complicit "in a series of fictions that inspire faith and trust in the positivist illusion of human freedom, morality, and goodness" (52). She is "privy to disappointing backstage contrivances" (52), whether it be flaccid puppets behind a screen, Mrs. Jarley's waxwork figures' morphing identities for different audiences, or the way that the Bachelor's graves contain "only good people" (59). The illusion many are seeking to maintain is the primacy and progress of human beings, yet the novel appears as "a land of giants, dwarfs, and monsters" (55), like Quilp. Noting that in mid-nineteenth-century Britain "deformity" was perceived to be a physiological response to industrialization and appeared to be on the rise, Cleere argues that Nell's death may represent "the disappearing ideal of bodily coherence and human perfectibility" (58), but it need not propel us into "misanthropy or monastic gloom" (60). Rather, we can follow Dick Swiveller's creed and believe in life's "harmless enabling fictions" (60), allowing curiosity and imagination to replace both misanthropy and philanthropy.

Molly Clark Hillard, in "Dangerous Exchange: Fairy Footsteps, Goblin Economies, and *The Old Curiosity Shop,*" reads the novel through the lens of fairy legend, noting the numerous parallels between characters and Victorian sanitized versions of fairies, the terrifying fairies of folk tales, hobgoblins, and laboring house sprites. Hillard employs Marxist theory to show how "Dickens's 'fairy plots' guide a powerful critique of England's post-industrial political economy" (64). Noting the Victorian association of fairies with a vanishing rural past, Hillard sees the novel as a "vital example" of Victorians' sense of collectively "bearing witness to the death of old traditions" (65). Nell is a "fairy as middle-class English authors wished [fairies] to be" (69)—the idealized, girlish, and delicate casualty of "encroaching modernity" (66). Quilp is closely aligned with the fairies of oral culture, "slippery folk, artful shape-shifters and expert grifters" (69). He is malevolent, quixotic, inexplicably alluring, and "stands for the corrupting influence of money" (75). Nell's grandfather's financial deal with the hobgoblin Quilp and its disastrous results are natural consequences of engaging in commerce with fairy creatures, always a dangerous proposition in folk tales. Quilp's drowning and Nell's death by wasting away signify that "nothing as good as Nell nor as evil as Quilp can survive in Dickens's England" (77). As Hillard ably demonstrates, the novel's third fairy figure, the Marchioness, is "an amalgam of the other two" (77), whose qualities correspond to the "laboring house sprite" (78) of fairy tradition who is ultimately transformed into a housewife.

Rosemary Coleman's feminist reading, "Nell and Sophronia—Catherine, Mary, and Georgina: Solving the Female Puzzle and the Gender Conundrum in *The Old Curiosity Shop,*" brings Herbert Sussman's work on Victorian masculinities as well as biographical information to bear on this early novel. Coleman likens the central dilemma of the novel to what Sussman identifies as the main problem in the practice of male sexuality in the Victorian period: how to "regulate" male "energy and "aggressions" (35). The essay argues that the novel deals with this problem three ways: first, through "physical punishments enacted on [male] bodies" (35), second through metaphorical "radical surgeries performed on the . . . bodies" of Nell and the Marchioness, and third "in the text's happy ending" where Dickens "constructs both a masculine plot and a marriage plot in which Dick Swiveller can thrive and prosper" (36). Many critics have commented on Nell's child-like innocence as well as her eroticism, and Coleman builds on these earlier appraisals. The essay argues that Dickens's way to contain Nell, a source of temptation for male energy, is to make her body become "reconstructed as ethereal memory" (47). Nell's "slow decline," rather than a particular illness, "ensures that her body is simultaneously ethereal, desirable, and unavailable'' (40). The Marchioness, on the other hand, became the ''opportunity for fulfillment of the marriage plot denied to Nell'' (41), but only through undergoing a radical transformation. When Dick renames her Sophronia Sphinx and sends her to finishing school to acquire middle-class manners and values, ''the shrewd, daring girl'' undergoes ''educational surgery'' to become ''an efficient and domesticated Angel-in-the-House'' (44). She never speaks in the novel again. Coleman attributes the further fact that she has no children to Dickens's desire to sanitize her and minimize her ''sexual side'' (45). The essay ends by showing the connection between the three Hogarth sisters, and ''sexually enticing Nell . . . , idealized, romanticized Nell in heaven, [and] a sororal, domestic, companionate Sophronia'' (49).

Christmas Books **and** Christmas Stories

Exceptionally well researched and written in an accessible style, *Christmas and Charles Dickens* will be of great use to those interested in Dickens and Christmas. Though David Parker's antipathy to postmodern literary theory and practice, which emerges forcefully in his conclusion, will undoubtedly put off some, there is no denying that the painstakingly and meticulously gathered evidence of his early chapters fully supports his claims about Dickens and Christmas and provides an essential resource. The purpose of the book is straightforward: to counteract the prevailing myth that Dickens ''invented Christmas.'' Parker draws mainly on historical evidence for his first three chapters, beginning with a discussion of festivals in ancient cultures and wending his way through discussions of the Christmas festival as practiced in the early church through mid-Victorian England. Parker follows this thorough history of Christmas with four chapters dedicated to Dickens's writings on and for Christmas, with chapters on the early texts, a full chapter on *A Christmas Carol*, another explicating the other Christmas books and stories, and a final chapter discussing Dickens's later relationship to Christmas. Parker's conclusion attempts to answer why the myth of Dickens's invention of Christmas has persisted. Parker's most valuable contribution is his explanation of how social class is a key factor in the way the festival was celebrated. For example, with the Puritan Interregnum and the elevation of the ''preparation of Christmas pies . . . [to] a punishable offence,'' the festival came under considerable attack. But it was mostly the upper class—those most visible—that had to abstain from Christmas festivities or face severe penalties. The majority continued to celebrate, though ''switch[ing] from hall to hearth.'' With this movement of ''festive customs'' (40) into the home, Christmas ceased to be ''an occasion for male networking'' in the lord's hall and became a festival identified with the domestic space and family. The elite who had abandoned Christmas did not take it up again with the Restoration, since it had become associated with coarse, plebian revelry and excess. Most writers, Parker notes, followed the fashion of these elite and either omitted all reference to the festival or wrote of it disparagingly.

For generations, however, Dickens's family had engaged in Christmas merrymaking; therefore, what Dickens accomplishes in his writings, especially in *A Christmas Carol*, is to acknowledge his enjoyment of the season and proclaim unabashedly that this unfashionable practice ought to be embraced by all. "Without apology, he was extolling the plebian and bourgeois Christmas, celebrated at that time around the family fireside by most English men, women, and children" (161), and the popularity of the *Carol*, at least in part, arises from the public's recognition that Dickens was speaking to their own experience. Dickens did not invent Christmas, then, so much as validate what most people already did and help make the festival fashionable for the upper classes.

Three pieces appeared in 2005 in *The Dickensian* concerning Dickens's Christmas narratives. While clearly *A Christmas Carol* is one of the most frequently adapted of Dickens's works today, scholars have maintained that after a short burst of dramatizations right after publication, there was a lull in *Carol* productions. Allan Sutcliffe, however, in "Pepper's Ghost and *A Christmas Carol*," reveals that there were actually many performances of a stage adaptation in which new technology was used to create ghostly images reflected on plate glass. Sutcliffe shows that, in fact, on the basis of the high numbers of these "Pepper's Ghost" performances, "the accepted view that there were few dramatic performances of *A Christmas Carol* [in the last 25 years of the nineteenth century] cannot be substantiated" (232). Nicholas Clark had written at the time of a "great might-have-been . . . , an operatic version of *A Christmas Carol*" suggested by Eric Crozier to Benjamin Britten. Unfortunately, no response survives, and so we are left with more questions than answers about the vision for such an adaptation. Michael Hollington, in " 'The Perils of Certain English Prisoners': Dickens, Collins, Morley and Central America," takes a different approach than most critics who see this Christmas tale "almost exclusively as a statement about India" (198). Hollington offers contextual evidence, particularly a number of articles from *Household Words*, to suggest that the Latin American setting was, indeed, important to Dickens. Largely agreeing with Lillian "Nayder's critical account of the underlying wishful thinking and social fantasies of this text" (208), Hollington disagrees on several minor details, such as the level of artistry.

Philip V. Allingham offers a much-needed reconsideration in "The Illustrations in Dickens's *The Haunted Man and the Ghost's Bargain*," which examines a Christmas tale often ignored or maligned by critics. This extended essay excels in its discussion of the importance of illustrations, especially the interplay between text and image. What is unusual about this Christmas tale is the way in which the illustrations are not full-page plates that stand alone, but rather appear with text on the same page. Allingham asserts that when a full-page plate appears at the beginning of a text, it "dominate[s] our thoughts as we begin reading," but with the illustrations and text combined, "the reader is simultaneously reader and viewer of both text and illustration on the same page, experiencing one message in two media" (77). The result is a much richer experience, with the plates becoming "not mere visual translations of specific textual moments but interpolated elaborations of . . . social issues" (76). Allingham suggests that Dickens directed "the mixed-media project" with sensitivity, "always suggesting and pointing through praise, but never directly commanding his colleagues," in essence treating the book as "a collaborative artistic endeavor rather than a mere commercial, money-making venture" (93). The illustrations highlight "the professional and specifically male expertise of the protagonist . . . juxtaposed with the essentially feminine knowledge of domesticity and personal relationships" (82), the latter of which ends up being stronger, both according to the text and the images integrated into text. In fact, taken together, text and images convey the idea that a happy childhood in a stable and loving home is more important than any other factor in producing responsible and successful men in the public sphere. In effect, Dickens "asserts the emotional and personal superiority of [the feminine] sphere in *The Haunted Man*" (116), questioning "the validity of the generally accepted assumption that the female sphere is necessarily inferior to the male" (117).

Simon Cooke shows in "Anxious Travelers: A Contextual Reading of 'The Signalman' " how the original readers of this tale would not have seen it as a disorienting and macabre tale of indeterminacy and "ambiguity" (101). Rather, Dickens's contemporaries would have read the story in light of recent railway disasters "such as those at Helmshore in Lancashire . . . , Kentish Town . . . , and Staplehurst in Kent" (102). The essay shows convincing connections between details of "The Signalman" crash and the Clayton tunnel accident in 1861. Further, quotations from contemporary articles about the railway reveal a high level of public anxiety about rail safety, much of which was due to a concern that workers such as signalmen could not be trusted. Their stressful jobs, in unhealthy working conditions with a high degree of responsibility, were thought to cause instability in such workers, who also sometimes suffered from the effects of what would later be named Post-Traumatic Stress Disorder. Cooke, arguing that Dickens's signalman seems to have PTSD, remarks, "The Signalman sees the specter after the accident" (105) and goes on to state that this character "pitifully grapples with a haunting which, he fails to understand, is the product of his traumatic experience'' (106). While I agree that he suffers recognizable psychological damage, the argument of causality is questionable, since the signalman sees the ghost for the first time a full six hours before the accident occurs. That important fact noted, Cooke's argument still holds much merit, as his contribution of the context of railway disasters alone makes this an important essay for those studying this tale.

Dombey and Son

Ella Westland examines the use of sea stories and nautical tropes in *Dombey and Son*. While the novel is full of well-noted references to the sea, Westland's "Dickens's *Dombey* and the Storied Sea" focuses on less obvious elements. For example, she discusses how the "comic excess" of Walter and Uncle Sol's "virtuoso performance on the theme of shipwreck" is a "celebration of the plentitude of the storied sea" (88). Other such scenes in the book, including those with Captain Cuttle, contrast the collaborative nature of sea story-telling, emerging from a strong sense of community and shared experience, with the solitariness of the middle-class Victorian family. As Westland puts it, the novel allows Florence to escape "from the repressive coldness of a patriarchally controlled bourgeois household to the relaxed warmth of an extended family" (89) at Solomon Gill's shop. The essay offers a unique reading of Walter, "routinely dismissed" (90) as uninteresting. Dickens's alignment of Walter with the midshipman, despite the fact that he is not in the navy, summons up a wealth of audience expectations, including the notion that Walter will engage in "youthful adventures and career success . . . and marry his lady love" (92) in the end. In Dickens's original conception of Walter, however, he had planned to have "the promising lad . . . go to the dogs" (95), in the tradition of the midshipman with a woman in every port. The novel is filled with references that Victorian readers would likely recognize, which the essay traces to a variety of sea stories, showing how Dickens uses them to add interest to Walter's plot line without disappointing his readers' desire for a happy ending.

Michal Peled Ginsburg argues, in "House and Home in *Dombey and Son*," that by the conclusion of the novel "the house/home can no longer be a symbol, nor even the container, for home/family" (59). Central to her argument is that in the nineteenth-century idealized home and family, "happiness is seen as static and stable, . . . beyond time and change" (57). Therefore, familial relationships and the feelings of comfort derived from a home could not be portrayed as requiring effort and time; instead, they appeared almost magically in fixed form. Many critics have pointed out Dombey's subordination of his family and home to his business or "house"; what Ginsburg adds is an exploration of how the novel's growing "representation of the home/ house as subject to time and therefore in need of care becomes gradually incompatible with the creed that family feelings do not depend on any labor for their reproduction since they are spontaneous and indestructible" (59). Through a close reading of the many scenes in which the old house is described, Ginsburg reveals why, ultimately, Dickens chooses to end with no visible home for Mr. Dombey. For example, after Dombey goes bankrupt, the empty house at last shows him what he has missed: "family ties" (70). Instead of recognizing that to establish and maintain such ties takes effort and time, Dombey "concludes that he should have invested his attention in something which was not subject to time and change: his daughter Florence who 'alone had never changed' " (70). While familial bonds, thus, are maintained as unchanging, the house as home has become an object in need of care. Only when Dickens deprives the house "of all materiality" by emptying it of all possessions and putting it out to let can it be an "idealized" (71) space.

David Copperfield

"Benevolence or Manipulation? The Treatment of Mr. Dick," by Akiko Takei, reexamines *David Copperfield*'s "insane character" in light of Victorian psychiatry, "assess[ing] Mr. Dick's psychosis and his relationship with Betsey in terms of the socio-medical climate in those days" (116). Takei describes the shift that took place from treatment in the home by family members to treatment in institutions by professionals. That Mr. Dick should be cared for by a relative stranger, Betsey Trotwood, in her home, was certainly surprising, and Betsey's treatment of her charge shows kindness but also manipulation. David's application of what was known as "moral treatment" (129)—expecting patients to not only behave in a decent fashion but also to be productive members of society—is more effective than Betsey's use of the technique because he gives Mr. Dick meaningful work as a copyist. Ultimately, Takei argues, the novel "signals Dickens's optimistic view of curing the insane" (130).

While David Copperfield is praised as "the ideal literary man," Micawber as a letter writer is "arguably the novel's most memorable writer," says Laura Rotunno in "The Long History of 'In Short': Mr. Micawber, Letter-Writers, and Literary Men." While critics generally diminish Micawber as merely a comic character, Rotunno suggests that his writings lead the reader to question "whether the literary standards embodied in David's writing should be unequivocally privileged" (415). Providing a short history of letter-writing manuals and an analysis of Micawber's "familiar letters," the essay shows how Dickens "link[s] Victorian letter writing with social aspirations" (419). When critics read the novel as a "portrait of an artist as a young man," they tend to dismiss Micawber as relatively unimportant. But Rotunno argues, "Micawber's writing—specifically its connection to popular culture and social status—is an integral influence in David's authorial career" (423), an influence which ultimately he rejects, as in chapter 64, when "in almost funereal description, David retreats from his friends [and] family" (425).

Kevin Ohi, in "Autobiography and *David Copperfield*'s Temporalities of Loss," points out the "incompatibility" of the novel's "claimed power to recover the past and . . . lost loved ones" and the way in which exercising this power "proves curiously disruptive to its narration" (435). Building on D. A. Miller's and Rosemarie Bodenheimer's discussions of the novel, Ohi claims, "David's difficulty inhabiting his name, be he hero or not—he arrives bearing a name not his own, that names a father who died six months before his birth—beyond being a peculiarity of his situation, figures a structural difficulty for the narrative voice in autobiography." Ohi sees autobiography as "unsettling" because "one cannot be until after one has written what one was" (438). Demonstrating various instances throughout the text of such confusion of temporalities, the essay highlights the problems of narration Dickens faced in this novel.

Hard Times

David M. Wilkes, in " 'This Most Protean Sitter': The Factory Worker and Triangular Desire in *Hard Times*," surveys a number of schema used by critics to make sense of the "muddle" (158) of relationships in *Hard Times*. He then turns to "the relational geometry of René Girard's model for triangular desire" (158). Girard attempts to examine the interrelationships among figures through triangles in which each set of corners represents "a *mediator* (as model/obstacle), a *subject* (as disciple/rival), and an *object* (as 'means of reaching the mediator')" (158). The mediator chooses an object that the subject pursues. Wilkes creates two triangles with Rachael as mediator and Stephen as subject, and alternately Mrs. Blackpool or Slackbridge as objects, and he reads several scenes in light of Girard's triangulation. For example, when Stephen meets Rachael outside the factory in book 1, chapter 10, Wilkes labels the exchange as "the mediator-as-model . . . predetermining the type of desire that Stephen-as-subject will pursue, namely, to maintain the constancy of their friendship" (159), since he is still married to his drunkard-as-object wife. Citing several critics' reactions to Stephen's enigmatic decision to stay outside of the union, Wilkes offers "the emotional logic of triangulated desire" (169) as the reason for his choice.

Little Dorrit

Joel J. Brattin offers yet another of his excellent studies based on careful attention to manuscript evidence in ''The Failure of Plot in *Little Dorrit.*'' Brattin's examination of the ''densely revised manuscript'' (111) and Dickens's ''almost incoherent private notes'' (114) reveals that Dickens himself had trouble constructing and justifying the plot of *Little Dorrit*. It is unclear, for example, why ''a man might plausibly leave a substantial legacy to his brother's son's lover's former friend's brother's youngest daughter'' (111). Brattin advises that Dickens's ''real interests lay elsewhere'' than in the plot, and ''ours—as sensitive readers of Dickens—should lie elsewhere also'' (114).

Great Expectations

Four essays in *Dickens Studies Annual* 35 centered on *Great Expectations*. Utilizing his knowledge of Victorian law, Randall Craig in ''Fictional License: The Case of (and in) *Great Expectations*'' explores how the concept of legal ''suppositional narratives'' is applied in two key instances in the novel, demonstrating how these scenes were connected to real disputes between Dickens and lawyers. In 1840 Dickens wrote a letter to the editor of the *Morning Chronicle* criticizing ''license of counsel, the freedom of trial attorneys to use suppositional narratives to cast doubt upon the testimony of witnesses or the interpretation of opposing counsel'' (110). James Fitzjames Stephen later launched a similar attack, claiming that novelists, especially Dickens, ought not to include ''fictional caricatures of the serious business of the law,'' not only because of their ignorance of it but because to do so is ungentlemanly and unpatriotic (111). Craig is particularly interested in how both sides of this debate used similar or even identical arguments about practitioners in separate domains best knowing their conventions and practices, and his essay explains how this debate made its way into *Great Expectations*. For example, Jaggers consistently uses license of counsel in court and is known as a skillful practitioner of the tactic, but it is his use of this approach in defense of those he knows to be guilty, like Molly, that Dickens finds particularly despicable (both in Jaggers and in real lawyers of his day). Craig shows how Jaggers's power derives from his narrative skill—the power of his fiction making. This power is revealed as particularly strong when Jaggers tells Pip and Wemmick Estella's story. Jaggers spins a tale that, despite its inconsistencies, keeps both Pip and Wemmick silent about Estella's parentage, thus protecting himself and keeping Estella ignorant. Craig points to the uncritical acceptance of "Jaggers's exercise of license of the bar" as "eloquent testimony to his narrative power" (120). Through Jaggers in *Great Expectations*, Dickens exposes the dangers of fictional narrative in the wrong hands.

Sue Zemka begins her essay "Chronometrics of Love and Money in *Great Expectations*" by declaring, "The game of making profits is a waiting game" (133). Her essay explores this notion's basis in theories of political economy and its application to *Great Expectations*. Much of the novel occurs in a "state of postponement" (134), and the so-called "epiphanic or frozen moments" that critics favor do not "provide an aesthetic liberation from the regimented consciousness of clock time" but rather "convey a sense of trauma and a poignantly disturbed state of desire" (134). Happiness lies instead in the "blank duration" (147), long periods of time glossed over by the text but containing the only true satisfaction for Pip. Magwitch has perfectly internalized the idea of delayed gratification. When Pip discovers that the source of his wealth is Magwitch's labor and not "genteel capital," however, he is "confronted with the reality of alienated human labor within and behind the material comforts of his brief bourgeois existence" (150). In contrast to Magwitch, rich Miss Havisham "extravagantly and melodramatically wastes her time" (146), but Zemka rightly points out that they both are "psychologically enveloped within the structuring of time as deferral" (146)—Magwitch in patiently making a gentleman of Pip and Miss Havisham in manipulating Estella. It is only through long labor in Herbert's firm that Pip finally moves from the "temporal alienation of the idle spendthrift to that of the hardworking and modestly compensated clerk" (146), thus achieving happiness through the long duration and not the epiphanic moment.

Aaron Landau's essay "*Great Expectations*, Romance, and Capital" also uses Marxism to contend that the novel's romance "conventions are given an additional ironic twist that transforms their latent and often conservative concern with society into an overall, penetrating, and quite radical exploration of Victorian class relations and the dynamics of nineteenth-century capitalism" (158). Landau shows that both Marx and Dickens use "the figurative language of fantasy and romance" to undermine commodity fetishism (160) by exposing their embodied labor. For example, when Estella's parentage and Pip's patron are revealed, the connection of their wealth to labor becomes visible and the failure of romance is clear. Victorians generally held to the belief that for a person to achieve and maintain genteel status, he or she must not engage in manual labor. Landau shows how the novel offers an "extended critique" (163) of this anti-labor preoccupation. The novel's inverted romance pattern "establishes vital economic links . . . between all characters, high and low" (168) and thus debunks the notion that gentlemen are cut off from labor. Magwitch certainly recognizes the fallacy of such a notion, for he has bought himself a gentleman "in order to demonstrate his own superiority" (168). Further, Satis House, as the "enchanted castle" of romance, is shown to be "an unwholesome retreat from the productive vitality of the market into the eccentricity and sterility of hoarding, shutting oneself up from the world, and cutting short any commerce with society" (161). While the novel can, at times, offer "profound insights into the workings of capitalism" (171), ultimately, Landau argues, Dickens's own middle-class worldview keeps the elements of that critique from coalescing into a more radical criticism of capitalism itself.

Central to Tyson Stolte's "Mightier than the Sword: Aggression of the Written Word in *Great Expectations*" is the reminder that the novel's author is Pip and not Dickens, that the entire book is supposed to be this character's creation. While many scholars have noted Pip's aggressive behavior in the early chapters, most "insist that he attains a degree of maturity" by the end (180) or, alternately, that he "undergoes a sort of spiritual regeneration" (181). Stolte shows that Pip's aggression continues up until the last page since the very act of writing the book is "a means of exacting his vengeance" (180). The essay outlines three means of aggression that Pip discovers and attempts to employ in order to take revenge on those responsible for his abused childhood. Magwitch represents the first model: "the possibility of the free expression of aggression" (183) so antithetical to Joe's emasculated passivity. Pip identifies with the man he calls "my convict"—both isolated and mistreated—and by feeding Magwitch, he is, in effect "feeding . . . his own aggression" (185). Following Magwitch's example, however, is untenable for someone as young, physically weak, and submissive as Pip. His time at Satis House provides an alternate model, "the effectiveness of social class as a means of exacting the revenge he desires" (187). Once he learns of his expectations, he immediately begins using his newly acquired rank to exact revenge on his abusers through class snobbery, with Joe being "the most frequent target of Pip's aggression" (189). Most critics claim that Pip then undergoes a transformation, but Stolte reminds us that the act of penning this supposedly penitential confession is itself an act of aggression. Not only does Pip often justify or excuse his reprehensible actions through the narrator's voice, but he also makes people look ridiculous. Stolte concedes that Pip may, indeed, be deceiving "himself as much as he deceives his readers" (197), yet he points to several excellent examples of Pip's authorial aggression, the best of which is Pip's revelation to the reader of Estella's parentage, which he has sworn to keep secret—a final revenge on the woman who tortured him for so long.

Our Mutual Friend

In "Darwinian Sexual Selection and Dickens's *Our Mutual Friend*" Ernest Fontana argues that "the darker Darwinian plot of sexual selection struggles against the romance plot'' and is ''the source of the novel's originality and power'' (37). Fontana reads the Lammle/Fledgby and Wrayburn/Headstone rivalries ''in light of Darwin's theory of sexual selection'' and sees the Boffin/ Harmon/Bella Wilfer plot as ''more conventional'' (37) and tied to romance. Of particular interest is the discussion of Bradley Headstone's ''unfitness to procreate . . . underlined by Dickens's repeated references to Headstone's seizures, his epileptic-like loss of physical and mental control'' (40). I was reminded here of Eileen Cleere's discussion of deformity as byproduct of industrialization. For Fontana, Headstone, in Darwinian terms, lacks ''fitness,'' but it would be interesting to add industrialization into the mix here, as well, to consider whether it may, too, be a source of Headstone's unfitness. Wrayburn's disfigurement, unlike Headstone's ailment, is necessary in order to turn Wrayburn from a seducer into a husband since ''for Dickens male procreative power must be channeled into the institution of marriage'' (41). Wrayburn must be made vulnerable in order to undergo this transformation. This essay brings a new perspective to bear on the tangled relationships of characters in the novel, offering an intriguing explanation of ''this darker, often more violent plot of sexual selection that is . . . at the center of *Our Mutual Friend*'' (42).

In ''Dickens and the Scattered Identity of Silas Wegg,'' Goldie Morgentaler begins by discussing ''Dickens's understanding of how identity is related to corporeal integrity'' (92). Whether it be by decapitation, dissection, or dismemberment, the body which is not whole, to Dickens, in some way loses its identity (92). Wooden legs were common enough in Dickens's day, mostly due to accidents, but in literature one rarely finds a ''positive, stout-hearted'' (93) character with a wooden leg—perhaps a prosthetic arm, like Captain Cuttle, but not a wooden leg. In the case of Silas, ''an unmitigated scoundrel—sly, mercenary and calculating—without a single redeeming feature'' (94), Dickens paints him as ''a man in search of himself'' (95). Morgentaler explains the significance of Silas's lost leg in terms of ''both identity and caste'' (95), and she notes how his wooden leg becomes more himself than his living body. ''Dickens,'' the essay asserts, ''insists that Silas's real identity resides in the artificial part of him, in the add-on, in the false limb that stands for the false man'' (97). In a novel with themes of mistaken identity and commodification of the body, ''Silas's scrambled self fits in perfectly'' (97). The essay offers an interesting argument that could be applied to *A Tale of Two Cities* as well, with its threat of decapitation and the identity theme.

Jamieson Ridenhour's '' 'In that Boney Light': The Bakhtinian Gothic of *Our Mutual Friend*'' claims that *Our Mutual Friend* is a gothic novel, not because it slavishly observes strict conventions of a genre but because it is written in the Gothic ''mode'' with ''Gothic's primary narrative'' form: ''the story of the ignorant, violent past being subdued and banished by modernity''

(157). For example, the schoolmaster Bradley Headstone 's "struggle between the savagery of the past [represented by his obsessive desire to murder Wrayburn] and the refinement of civilization" (166) represents "the most overt element of the Gothic in *Our Mutual Friend*, and savagery's victory with Headstone sharply undermines the neat wrapping up Dickens effects in the other plot lines" (167). Headstone, whose "speech is forcibly restrained and 'half-choked' " (167), is one of several characters whom Ridenhour points to as comprising the *heteroglossia* of the text. He also shows how the narrator engages in three main forms of discourse, centered on death, dirt, and money. The essay asserts that we need not read the Gothic merely in terms of the psychological but that an historical/Bakhtinian approach is warranted, and the essay's many examples from the text as well as references to critics of the novel and of the Gothic seem to indicate the fruitfulness of this approach.

James D. Mardock reinterprets the character of Mr. Riah in *Our Mutual Friend* as a response to Shakespeare's anti-Semitic Shylock, rather than merely a stick figure apologia for Dickens's stereotypically wicked Fagin. While other scholars (e.g., John Gross, and Deborah Heller) have discussed Riah's connection to Shylock before, Mardock sees *Our Mutual Friend* as being much more deeply engaged with *The Merchant of Venice*, noting several overlaps in plot and characterization throughout the two texts. Setting aside the question of whether Charles Dickens, the man, was an anti-Semite, this essay focuses mainly on showing the ways in which Riah and Shylock mirror one another yet diverge. The essay argues that "Dickens uses his anti-Shylock to critique his own society's depiction of the stage Jew" (1), to expose the ways in which England "abuse[d] . . . Shylock as an anchor for English attitudes toward Jews" (5). Ultimately, Mardock contends that *Our Mutual Friend* is a "Dickensian adaptation of *The Merchant of Venice*" (16).

Influence and Afterlife

A few articles in 2005 discussed influences on Dickens. Rodney Stenning Edgecombe offered two instances of influence this year. In "Dickens, Hunt and the Waiter in Somebody's Luggage" he shows the similarities between Leigh Hunt's depiction of "London waiters as men of few words" (25) and Dickens's use of the trope in his *American Notes*, *Little Dorrit*, and "Somebody's Luggage." In a brief note in *The Dickensian*, Edgecombe demonstrates the connection between "Dickens and Hood's 'Ode to Rae Wilson, Esq,' " contending that Thomas Hood's 1837 poem is "the source of two characteristic conceits" (211) in *Hard Times* and *Little Dorrit*. Masako Uchida, in "The Activities of the Chancery Reform Association and Dickens's Writing of 'A December Vision': Part II," traces the portrayal of Chancery in *Bleak House* back to Dickens's article "A December Vision," published in 1850 in *Household Words*. Uchida shows the article's genesis in William Carpenter's *Lecture*, "a slim pamphlet of 28 pages, . . . [and a] very handy manual for Chancery reformers" (47). The essay ends by questioning why Dickens omits the "Chancery prisoners" (55) so prominent in Carpenter's work, leaving the answer for Part III. Finally, in "Dickens's *Bleak House*" Myron C. Noonkester points out Dickens's surprising use of "classical allusion" (42) in his descriptions of the Dedlocks' townhouse after Lady Dedlock leaves. The essay shows the connection to Virgil's *Aeneid* (book 4, lines 173–174), noting the ways in which Dickens echoes the Latin text's reference to personified "Rumour," swiftly running through the city.

A few other articles explore Dickens's influence on others. Dale Nelson suggests in "Little Nell and Frodo the Halfling" that Dickens was more important to Tolkien than has been generally acknowledged. One has only to think about "the weary Frodo, 'bound' to a whining, undependable, addicted and dangerous Gollum, making his way across the blighted landscape of Mordor whilst being pursued by an implacable enemy" (245–46) to see the similarities, not to mention Tolkien's and Dickens's shared "horror of the industrial spoliation of the English countryside" (247). Michael Klotz writes in "Two Dickens Rooms in 'The Yellow Wall-Paper' " of Charlotte Perkins Gilman's admiration for Dickens, the only male author excepted from her 1911 critique of patriarchal culture. Klotz points out the similarities between Gilman's story and two scenes from Dickens: Pip's wakeful night in the room at the Hummums in Covent Garden and Phil Squod's circling of George's Shooting Range, making his mark upon the wall. An avid reader of Dickens, Gilman seems to have built upon these images in her own work. Gabrielle Malcolm has transcribed a heretofore unpublished "Introduction to a 'Costly' Edition of *Little Dorrit*," written by Mary Braddon, popular author of *Lady Audley's Secret*. Dickens exerted a profound effect on Braddon, who repeatedly acknowledges "the inspiration and influence that his fame and writing held for her" (15). Her introduction to the novel was intended to be published in an American edition never completed, due to the death of its general editor, F. G. Kitton. Braddon seems most concerned in her introduction with "the structure and reception of Dickens's work," with some attention to themes such as "childhood and loss of innocence" and "portrayal of parental figures" (17). On the other side of the globe, Australian Peter Carey also seems to have found Dickens's work inspiring, with the construction of *Jack Maggs* (1997), which Annegret Maack notes is a blend of "the historical novel, fictional biography and metafiction with an intensively marked intertextuality, borrowing characters and plot elements from Charles Dickens's *Great Expectations*" (229). In "Peter Carey's *Jack Maggs*: An Aussie Story?" Maack "explores Carey's debt to Dickens, his re-creation of historical London, and his metafictional blending of narratives" (229). The essay argues that in this novel Carey is successful in creating "an authentic Australian version" (242) of *Great Expectations* through its movement of Mags/Magwitch to the center. In the same collection, Barbara Schmidt-Haberkamp suggests in "The Writing-Back Paradigm Revisited: Peter Carey, Jack Maggs, and Charles Dickens, *Great Expectations*" that *Jack Maggs* "seems to be a pure and perfect example of the writing-back paradigm"(248) described by Bill Ashcroft, Gareth Griffiths, and Helen Tiffin in their ground-breaking post-colonial book, *The Empire Writes Back*. Yet her essay, which includes much commentary on Dickens's text, ultimately argues that Carey's novel also "exposes the weaknesses" of this paradigm that relies on "opposing essentialisms like pitting a (post)colonial text against an imperial one" (260).

Though K. M. Newton's "Revisions of Scott, Austen, and Dickens in *Daniel Deronda*" is concerned primarily with George Eliot's use, revision, and rejection of romance and realism in *Daniel Deronda*, the portion devoted to her interaction with Dickens's work merits some attention. Since Eliot criticized Dickens for not offering enough psychological realism in his fiction, many critics have come to see the writers as opposites or antagonists, but in fact Eliot admired Dickens as a "great novelist" and "the exemplar of the novelist as social critic" (256). Newton sees setting, plot, and character parallels between *Little Dorrit* and *Daniel Deronda*. The essay demonstrates parallels between several pairings: Arthur Clenam and Daniel Deronda, Henry Gowan and Henleigh Grandcourt, Amy Dorrit and Mirah Lapidoth, Pet Meagles or Miss Wade and Gwendolen Harleth. Newton also contends that Eliot "historicizes and psychologizes the character types she has drawn" from Dickens (261). Further, the essay tackles the issue of Eliot's "use of coincidence and improbability in *Deronda*" (260), for which critics fault her. Newton claims that Eliot's coincidences are not as farfetched as Dickens's and that "narratives that eliminate coincidence totally are not driven by realism" but instead "undermine" it (260) because "reality" includes coincidence as well as randomness. Eliot, Newton argues, tries "to adapt Dickensian plot and narrative structure in order to reconcile them with her form of realism" to be able to "achieve something of the imaginative range and scope of Dickens's panoramic novels" (261).

Along with Chesterton, Gissing is often considered one of the most important early Dickens scholars, known by his contemporaries as a "Dickens expert" (8). When Chapman and Hall asked Gissing in 1901 to write a new biography of Dickens, he presented a counteroffer to abridge and edit Forster's lengthy *Life of Dickens* instead. Gissing claims in his preface to the 1902 abridgement, "Many who would like to make acquaintance with Forster's work are deterred by its length" (25). In her introduction to the 2005 reissue of *Forster's Life of Dickens Abridged and Revised by George Gissing*, editor Christine DeVine draws a connection between turn-of-the-century readers' desire for a " less cumbered version of the *Life*" (17) and the demise of the Victorian triple-decker. What Gissing left out of his version of Forster's massive biography was much of the personal information about Dickens, Forster's critical commentary on the novels, and almost all of the old-fashioned first-person narrator. The result was "a paired-down Dickens, a determined and dedicated writer, with the flourishes painted out" (3). By "pruning out the personal details and Dickens's anecdotes," Gissing offers the reader "a tighter view of the author at work" (5), a "writer's writer" (6). DeVine notes how Forster followed what was considered the premier model for biography in his day, James Boswell's *Life of Johnson* (1791). Close friends of the famous, as eyewitnesses, were seen as the most reliable sources for biography. Gissing never met Dickens, and his version of Forster's *Life* reveals the shift in the early twentieth century towards more objective biography. The reissue of this abridgment offers readers an opportunity to see "in a new light" not only Dickens but also Gissing himself, as well as evidence of "the changing theory of biography" (19). For those who still find Forster's brilliant but lengthy biography daunting, Gissing provides a good alternative, and this edited version offers excellent context and commentary.

Like the Gissing edition of Forster's *Life of Dickens*, the publication in 2005 of a heretofore unknown manuscript written by Harry Furniss provides readers with a fascinating glimpse of early twentieth-century readers' views on Dickens's life and work. In the case of *An Edwardian View of Dickens and His Illustrators: Harry Furniss's "A Sketch of Boz"* and editor Gareth Cordery's introduction, we find an excellent resource for understanding why interest in Dickens revived in the Edwardian period. Cordery's argument, in brief, suggests that Furniss's popular lecture on Dickens and his illustrators, first given in 1905 and available in printed form for the first time in this volume, contributed to the Dickens revival by reaffirming Britain's "sense of identity" in the face of real and perceived threats. With the end of British imperialist power, signaled most overtly by the Boer War (1899–1902), and with the rise of Irish nationalism, the suffragette movement, the increasing power of trade unions, and a host of other so-called threats to "the political and social stability that characterized so much of the Victorian age" (16), "the human, moral and cosily domestic Dickens . . . carefully promoted by the Fellowship and by Chesterton, became a rallying call" (17) for Britain. Cordery offers plenty of evidence, not least of which is the text of Furniss's lecture itself, to suggest that Dickens was appropriated in this way. Cordery also provides an accessible overview of the artists with whom Dickens collaborated. Furniss, an illustrator and caricaturist, was "the only artist to have 'illustrated an entire series of Dickens's completed works' " (2), having created 500 plates for the eighteen-volume 1910 Charles Dickens Library Edition.

In a two-part series, appearing in *Dickens Quarterly,* Cordery also presents "A Special Relationship: Stiggins in England and America." In both parts, Cordery seeks to show how Dickens "was used and transformed by a later culture for sometimes opposing political objectives" (135). The essays show how Furniss appropriated the character Stiggins, "the canting minister of Ebenezer chapel and consumer of large quantities of spirits" (136), from *The Pickwick Papers,* in order first to combat teetotalism and later to defend "England against American cultural imperialism" (135). In "Part One, Stiggins in England," Cordery shows how Furniss, "an avid Dickensian, . . . exploited a readily available and well known text and iconography" (136) to counter the anti-drink Strength of Britain Movement founded in 1916 to protect the country during time of war from the evils of alcohol. Sharing many of Dickens's concerns, Furniss saw the need for "moderation" as the "ideal" (142), which he advocated in a forty-eight-page satire of the movement called *Deceit?* (1917). In Part Two Cordery examines a later tract published during American prohibition, *Stiggins! His Appearance, His Disappearance, and His Reappearance* (1920). Furniss appropriated both Dickens's and Phiz's Stiggins in order to oppose both "Prohibition and Americanization" (225). In fact, the essay has a great deal to say about anti-Americanism, building on Dickens's own opinions of America seen in his letters and *American Notes.* Stiggins, after his rejection in Britain, immigrates to America where he becomes a popular figure. When this "Little Yankee Stiggins" later returns to Britain with "his bags stuffed with American dollars" (232), he attempts to persuade his native land to engage in "whole hoggism" (227) and reject all alcohol outright. Citing "Dickens's notoriously ambivalent responses towards America" (236), Cordery presents a fascinating picture of later appropriation of Dickens's life and work.

Conclusion

As I draw this essay to a close, I end with a mention of those works I most admire, knowing full well the level of perseverance required to complete such work. I speak first of Robert R. Garnett's fine extended review of Dickens scholarship in 2003 for *Dickens Studies Annual* 35. Not only to read so much but also to produce an engaging and discerning essay is no small task. Next, I mention editors Angus Easson and Margaret Brown, who have provided another supplement to Dickens's collected letters in *The Dickensian.* As always, the notes are superb, and this painstaking work is much appreciated by those of us who study Dickens's life and times. Finally, I applaud David Paroissien, who has performed an invaluable service for scholars in producing his "*Oliver Twist*: An Annotated Bibliography Supplement I—1984–2004," an update of the 1986 volume published in the Garland Dickens Bibliography series, edited by Duane DeVries. With well over 200 entries, this supplement is an impressive achievement. After a brief introduction, Paroissien presents his annotated bibliographic entries in two parts. Part I (Text) includes 42 entries on editions of the novel; Dickens's reading adaptations; stage adaptations; film, musical, radio and television adaptations; and prose adaptations for children. Part II (Studies) includes one hundred and seventy-one entries, most of which appear under the heading "Criticism," others of which are listed under *Oliver Twist* and the Newgate Novel; Special Studies: Dickens, Cruikshank, and the illustrations; Fagin and anti-Semitism; literary parallels, sources, and influences; and topographical studies. Paroissien's entries are clear and succinct, demonstrating a remarkable breadth of knowledge. I found the cross-referencing of works both in the supplement and the original 1986 bibliography particularly useful. Certainly scholars will continue to find all of these works indispensable for years to come. It is my hope that my own essay here will contribute something useful as well. In any case, now that I have finished with 2005, I will finally have time to get back to Ray's boxes.

WORKS CITED

Aikens, Kristina. "The Daughter's Desire in *Dombey and Son*." *Critical Survey* 17.2 (2005): 77–91.

Allingham, Philip V. "The Illustrations in Dickens's *The Haunted Man and the Ghost's Bargain*: Public and Private Spheres and Spaces." *Dickens Studies Annual* 36 (2005): 75–123.

Alter, Robert. *Imagined Cities: Urban Experience and the Language of the Novel.* New Haven: Yale UP, 2005.

Barnabé, Jean Philippe. "Borges as a Reader of Dickens." *Dickens Studies Annual* 36 (2005): 285–97.

Battegazzore, Miguel Angel. "A Cubo-Futurist Reading of Dickens: Rafael Barradas's 1921 Illustrations for *Hard Times*." *Dickens Studies Annual* 36 (2005): 299–306.

Brattin, Joel J. "The Failure of Plot in *Little Dorrit*." *The Dickensian* 101.2 (Summer 2005): 111–15.

Brooks, Peter. *Realist Vision.* New Haven: Yale UP, 2005.

Bruns, John. "Get Out of Gaol Free, or: How to Read a Comic Plot." *Journal of Narrative Theory* 35.1 (2005): 25–59.

Buzard, James. *Disorienting Fiction: The Autoethnographic Work of Nineteenth-Century British Novels.* Princeton, NJ: Princeton UP, 2005.

Byatt, A. S., Michael Slater, Andrew Sanders, and Margaret Reynolds. "Centenary Reminiscences: Dickens and *The Dickensian.*" *The Dickensian* 101.1 (Spring 2005): 5–14.

Carens, Timothy L. *Outlandish English Subjects in the Victorian Domestic Novel.* Basingstoke, UK: Palgrave Macmillan, 2005.

Christensen, Allan Conrad. *Nineteenth-Century Narratives of Contagion: "Our feverish contact."* London: Routledge, 2005.

Cleere, Eileen. " 'Implicit Faith in the Deception': Misanthropy, Natural History and *The Old Curiosity Shop.*" *Dickens Studies Annual* 35 (2005): 45–62.

Cohen, William A. "Interiors: Sex and the Body in Dickens." *Critical Survey* 17.2 (2005): 5–19.

Cole, Natalie. "Dickens and the Act of Gardening." *Dickens Quarterly* 22.4 (2005): 242–54.

Coleman, Rosemary. "Nell and Sophronia—Catherine, Mary, and Georgina: Solving the Female Puzzle and the Gender Conundrum in *The Old Curiosity Shop.*" *Dickens Studies Annual* 36 (2005): 33–55.

Colledge, Gary L. *"The Life of Our Lord* Revisited." *Dickens Studies Annual* 36 (2005): 125–51.

Cooke, Simon. "Anxious Travelers: A Contextual Reading of 'The Signalman.' " *Dickens Quarterly* 22.2 (2005): 101–08.

Cordery, Gareth, ed. "Introduction." *An Edwardian View of Dickens and His Illustrators: Harry Furniss's "A Sketch of Boz."* Greensboro, NC: ELT Press, 2005. 1–22.

———. "A Special Relationship: Stiggins in England and America (Part One)." *Dickens Quarterly* 22.3 (2005): 135–52.

———. "A Special Relationship: Stiggins in England and America (Part Two)." *Dickens Quarterly* 22.4 (2005): 224–41.

Cordery, Lindsey. "Dickens in Latin America: Borrioboola-Gha Revisited." *Dickens Studies Annual* 36 (2005): 355–61.

Craig, Randall. "Fictional License: The Case of (and in) *Great Expectations.*" *Dickens Studies Annual* 35 (2005): 109–32.

Cregan-Reid, Vybarr. "Bodies, Boundaries and Queer Waters: Drowning and Prosopopoeia in Later Dickens." *Critical Survey* 17.2 (2005): 20–33.

Dalmagro, María Cristina. "The Reversal of Innocence: Somers, Dickens, and a 'Shared Oliver.' " *Dickens Studies Annual* 36 (2005): 319–30.

Danahay, Martin A. *Gender at Work in Victorian Culture: Literature, Art and Masculinity.* Aldershot, England: Ashgate, 2005.

D'Auria, Verónica. "Spectacle and Estrangement in Dickens." *Dickens Studies Annual* 36 (2005): 349–54.

DeVine, Christine, ed. "Introduction." *Collected Works of George Gissing on Charles Dickens, Volume 3: Forster's Life of Dickens, Abridged and Revised by George Gissing.* Grayswood, England: Grayswood, 2005. 1–24.

Dickens, Gerald. "From the New President of the Fellowship." *The Dickensian* 101.3 (Winter 2005): 195–96.

Druce, Robert. "Charting the Great Wen: Charles Dickens, Henry Mayhew, Charles Booth." Tinkler-Villani. 93–111.

Easson, Angus, and Margaret Brown. "The Letters of Charles Dickens: Supplement V." *The Dickensian* 101.2 (Summer 2005): 134–58.

Eaton, Michael. "*The Dickensian* goes to the Cinematograph." *The Dickensian* 101.3 (Winter 2005): 233–40.

Edgecombe, Rodney Stenning. "Dickens and Hood's 'Ode to Rae Wilson, Esq.': Two Points of Contact." *The Dickensian* 101.3 (Winter 2005): 211–12.

———. "Dickens and the Comedy of Abbreviation." *Dickens Quarterly* 22.2 (2005): 80–91.

———. "Dickens, Hunt and the Waiter in Somebody's Luggage." *Victorian Newsletter* 107 (2005): 25–28.

Eyheragaray, Leticia. "The Strange Gentleman: Dickens on the Uruguayan Stage." *Dickens Studies Annual* 36 (2005): 341–48.

Eysell, Joanne. *A Medical Companion to Dickens's Fiction.* New York: Peter Lang, 2005.

Foltinek, Herbert. *Imagination All Compact: How Did Charles Dickens Compose His Novels?* Wien: Verlag der Österreichischen Akademie der Wissenschafen, 2005.

Fontana, Ernest. "Darwinian Sexual Selection and Dickens's *Our Mutual Friend.*" *Dickens Quarterly* 22.1 (2005): 36–42.

Furneaux, Holly. " 'It Is Impossible to Be Gentler': The Homoerotics of Male Nursing in Dickens's Fiction." *Critical Survey* 17.2 (2005): 34–47.

———. " 'Worrying to Death'—Reinterpreting Dickens's Critique of the New Poor Law in *Oliver Twist* and Contemporary Adaptations." *The Dickensian* 101.3 (Winter 2005): 213–24.

Furneaux, Holly, and Anne Schwan. "Introduction: Dickens and Sex Special Issue." *Critical Survey* 17.2 (2005): 1–4.

Furniss, Harry. *An Edwardian View of Dickens and His Illustrators: Harry Furniss's "A Sketch of Boz."* Ed. Gareth Cordery. Greensboro, NC: ELT Press, 2005.

Gaile, Andreas, ed. *Fabulating Beauty: Perspectives on the Fiction of Peter Carey.* Amsterdam, Netherlands: Rodopi, 2005.

Garnett, Robert R. "Recent Dickens Studies—2003." *Dickens Studies Annual* 35 (2005): 335–95.

Gilbert, Pamela K. "Medical Mapping: The Thames, the Body, and *Our Mutual Friend.*" *Filth: Dirt, Disgust and Modern Life.* Ed. William A. Cohen and Ryan Johnson. Minneapolis: U of Minnesota P, 2005. 78–102.

Ginsburg, Michael Peled. "House and Home in *Dombey and Son.*" *Dickens Studies Annual* 36 (2005): 57–73.

Gissing, George. *Collected Works on Charles Dickens.* Vol. 3. *Forster's Life of Dickens Abridged and Revised by George Gissing.* Ed. and Introduction by Christine De-Vine with Afterword by James A. Davies. Grayswood, UK: Grayswood Press, 2005.

Goetsch, Paul. "Charles Dickens's *The Pickwick Papers* and *Don Quixote.*" *Cervantes in the English-Speaking World: New Essays.* Ed. Darío Fernández-Morera and Michael Hanke. Kassel, Germany: Reichenberger, 2005. 143–57.

Gold, David L. "Despite Popular Belief, the Name Fagin in Charles Dickens's *The Adventures of Oliver Twist* Has No Jewish Connection." *Beiträge zur Namenforschung* 40.4 (2005): 385–423.

Grove, Thelma. "Obituaries: David Kenneth Charles Dickens." *The Dickensian* 101.3 (Winter 2005): 284–85.

Hack, Daniel. *The Material Interests of the Victorian Novel.* Charlottesville: U of Virginia P, 2005.

Harris, Beth, ed. *Famine and Fashion: Needlewomen in the Nineteenth Century.* Aldershot, England: Ashgate, 2005.

Hartley, Jenny. "Undertexts and Intertexts: The Women of Urania Cottage, Secrets and *Little Dorrit.*" *Critical Survey* 17.2 (2005): 63–76.

Haywood, Ian. "The Retailoring of Dickens: *Christmas Shadows*, Radicalism, and the Needlewoman Myth." In: Harris. 67–86.

Hillard, Molly Clark. "Dangerous Exchange: Fairy Footsteps, Goblin Economies, and *The Old Curiosity Shop.*" *Dickens Studies Annual* 35 (2005): 63–86.

Hollington, Michael. "Nickleby, Flanerie, Reverie: The View from Cheerybles'." *Dickens Studies Annual* 35 (2005): 21–43.

———. " 'The Perils of Certain English Prisoners': Dickens, Collins, Morley and Central America." *The Dickensian* 101.3 (Winter 2005): 197–210.

Houston, Gail Turley. *From Dickens to Dracula: Gothic, Economics, and Victorian Fiction*. Cambridge, UK: Cambridge UP, 2005.

Huett, Lorna. "Among the Unknown Public: *Household Words*, *All the Year Round*, and the Mass-Market Weekly Periodical in the Mid-Nineteenth Century." *Victorian Periodicals Review* 38.1 (Spring 2005): 61–82.

Jarvie, Paul. *Ready to Trample on All Human Law: Financial Capitalism in the Fiction of Charles Dickens*. New York: Routledge, 2005.

John, Juliet. "Fagin, The Holocaust and Mass Culture: or, *Oliver Twist* on Screen." *Dickens Quarterly* 22.4 (2005): 204–23.

Jones, Richard. *Walking Dickensian London: Twenty-Five Original Walks Through London's Victorian Quarters*. Northampton, MA: Interlink, 2005.

Klotz, Michael. "Two Dickens Rooms in 'The Yellow Wall-Paper.' " *Notes and Queries* 52.4 (2005): 490–91.

Kreilkamp, Ivan. "Speech on Paper: Charles Dickens, Victorian Phonography, and the Reform of Writing." *Literary Secretaries/Secretarial Culture*. Ed. Leah Price and Pamela Thurschwell. Aldershot, England: Ashgate, 2005. 13–31.

Landau, Aaron. "*Great Expectations*, Romance, and Capital." *Dickens Studies Annual* 35 (2005): 157–77.

Litvack, Leon. "*The Dickensian*: Editors, Contributors and Readers, 1905–2005." *Dickens Quarterly* 22.2 (2005): 70–79.

Maack, Annegret. "Peter Carey's *Jack Maggs*: An Aussie Story?" In Gaile. 229–43.

MacDonald, Tara. " 'Red-Headed Animal': Race, Sexuality and Dickens's Uriah Heep." *Critical Survey* 17.2 (2005): 48–62.

Malcolm, Gabrielle. "Mary Braddon, Literary Critic: Introduction to a 'Costly' Edition of *Little Dorrit*." *The Dickensian* 101.1 (Spring 2005): 15–26.

Mardock, James D. "Of Daughters and Ducats: *Our Mutual Friend* and Dickens's Anti-Shylock." *Borrowers and Lenders: The Journal of Shakespeare and Appropriation* 1.2 (2005): [no pagination].

Masters, Joellen. " 'Let Herself Out to Do Needlework': Female Agency and the Workhouse of Gender in Charles Dickens's *Little Dorrit*." Harris. 53–66.

Mattos, Tomás de. "A Borgesian Clue to Dickens's Characterization in *Pickwick Papers*." *Dickens Studies Annual* 36 (2005): 273–83.

Meyer, Susan. "Antisemitism and Social Critique in Dickens's *Oliver Twist*." *Victorian Literature and Culture* 33.1 (2005): 239–52.

Morgentaler, Goldie. "Dickens and the Scattered Identity of Silas Wegg." *Dickens Quarterly* 22.2 (2005): 92–100.

Nelson, Dale. "Little Nell and Frodo the Halfling." *Tolkien Studies: An Annual Scholarly Review* 2.1 (2005): 245–48.

Newton, K. M. "Revisions of Scott, Austen, and Dickens in *Daniel Deronda*." *Dickens Studies Annual* 35 (2005): 241–66.

Nixon, Jude V. " 'Lost in the Vast Worlds of Wonder': Dickens and Science." *Dickens Studies Annual* 35 (2005): 267–333.

Noonkester, Myron C. "Dickens's *Bleak House*." *Explicator* 64.1 (2005): 35–38.

Ohi, Kevin. "Autobiography and *David Copperfield*'s Temporalities of Loss." *Victorian Literature and Culture* 33.2 (2005): 435–49.

Orero, Pilar. "The Translation of Wellerisms: The Spanish Case." *Proverbium* 22 (2005): 263–71.

Parker, David. *Christmas and Charles Dickens*. New York: AMS, 2005.

Paroissien, David. "Monsters in the Classroom: Dickens's Case Against Industrial Education." *The Dickensian* 101.2 (Summer 2005): 101–10.

———. *"Oliver Twist*: An Annotated Bibliography Supplement I—1984–2004." *Dickens Studies Annual* 35 (2005): 397–514.

Payne, David. *The Reenchantment of Nineteenth-Century Fiction: Dickens, Thackeray, George Eliot, and Serialization*. Basingstoke, England: Palgrave Macmillan, 2005.

Polga, Kit. "Dickens and the Morality of Imagination." *Dickens Quarterly* 22.3 (2005): 172–78.

Reed, John R. "Dickens and Naming." *Dickens Studies Annual* 36 (2005): 183–97.

Ridenhour, Jamieson. " 'In That Boney Light': The Bakhtinian Gothic of *Our Mutual Friend*." *Dickens Quarterly* 22.3 (2005): 153–71.

Rose, Natalie. "Flogging and Fascination: Dickens and the Fragile Will." *Victorian Studies* 47.4 (Summer 2005): 505–33.

Rossi-Wilcox, Susan M. *Dinner for Dickens: The Culinary History of Mrs. Charles Dickens's Menu Books, Including a Transcript of "What Shall We Have for Dinner?" by "Lady Maria Clutterbuck."* Totnes, UK: Prospect, 2005.

Rotunno, Laura. "The Long History of 'In Short': Mr. Micawber, Letter-Writers, and Literary Men." *Victorian Literature and Culture* 33.2 (2005): 415–33.

Rowland, Peter. "No Sich a Person? The Hunt for Fagin." *The Dickensian* 101.2 (Summer 2005): 132–34.

Schlicke, Paul. "Revisions to *Sketches by Boz*." *The Dickensian* 101.1 (Spring 2005): 29–38.

————. " 'Risen Like a Rocket': The Impact of *Sketches by Boz.*" *Dickens Quarterly* 22.1 (2005): 3–18.

Schmidt-Haberkamp, Barbara. "The Writing-Back Paradigm Revisited: Peter Carey, Jack Maggs, and Charles Dickens, *Great Expectations.*" In Gaile. 245–62.

Schroeder, Natalie, and Shari Hodges Holt. "The Gin Epidemic: Gin Distribution as a Means of Control and Profit in Dickens's Early Nonfiction and *Oliver Twist.*" *Dickens Studies Annual* 36 (2005): 1–32.

Schwan, Anne. "The Limitations of a Somatics of Resistance: Sexual Performativity and Gender Dissidence in Dickens's *Dombey and Son.*" *Critical Survey* 17.2 (2005): 92–106.

Shelston, Alan. "Dickens and the Burial of the Dead." Tinkler-Villani. 77–92.

Stolte, Tyson. "Mightier than the Sword: Aggression of the Written Word in *Great Expectations.*" *Dickens Studies Annual* 35 (2005): 179–208.

Strahan, Linda. "There's a Hole in the (Inspector) Bucket: The Victorian Police in Fact and Fiction." *Clues: A Journal of Detection* 23.3 (2005): 57–62.

Stucherbrukhov, Olga. "The 'Nation-Less' State of Great Britain and the Nation-State of France in *Household Words.*" *Victorian Periodicals Review* 38.4 (2005): 392–413.

Surridge, Lisa. *Bleak Houses: Marital Violence in Victorian Fiction.* Athens: Ohio UP, 2005.

Sutcliffe, Allan. "Pepper's Ghost and *A Christmas Carol.*" *The Dickensian* 101.3 (Winter 2005): 225–32.

Takei, Akiko. "Benevolence or Manipulation? The Treatment of Mr. Dick." *The Dickensian* 101.2 (Summer 2005): 116–31.

Terauchi, Takashi. *Revivalism and Conversion Literature: From Wesley to Dickens.* Yamagata, Japan: Hon's Penguin, 2005.

Tinkler-Villani, Valeria, ed. *Babylon or New Jerusalem? Perceptions of the City in Literature.* Amsterdam, Netherlands: Rodopi, 2005.

Torres, Alicia. "Dickens's Oliver and Somers's Orphan: A Traffic in Identities." *Dickens Studies Annual* 36 (2005): 331–40.

Uchida, Masako. "The Activities of the Chancery Reform Association and Dickens's Writing of 'A December Vision': Part II." *The Dickensian* 101.1 (Spring 2005): 46–57.

Vegh, Beatriz. "Dickens and Barradas in Madrid, 1921: A Hospitable Meeting." *Dickens Studies Annual* 36 (2005): 307–13.

————, ed. "Dickens in Latin America: Views from Montevideo." *Dickens Studies Annual* 36 (2005): 265–361.

Wagner, Tamara S. *Longing: Narratives of Nostalgia in the British Novel, 1740–1890.* Lewisburg: Bucknell UP, 2005.

Westland, Ella. "Dickens's *Dombey* and the Storied Sea." *Dickens Studies Annual* 35 (2005): 87–108.

Wilkes, David M. " 'This Most Protean Sitter': The Factory Worker and Triangular Desire in *Hard Times.*" *Dickens Studies Annual* 36 (2005): 153–81.

Wilkinson, Ian. "Performance and Control: The Carnivalesque City and Its People in Charles Dickens's *Sketches by Boz.*" *Dickens Studies Annual* 35 (2005): 1–19.

Williams, Lee. "Telling as Denouement in Charles Dickens's *Great Expectations* and Roberto Arlt's *El juguete rabioso* [*Mad Toy*]." *Dickens Quarterly* 22.1 (2005): 19–35.

Zangen, Britta. *Our Daughters Must Be Wives: Marriageable Young Women in the Novels of Dickens, Eliot, and Hardy.* New York: Peter Lang, 2005.

Zemka, Sue. "Chronometrics of Love and Money in *Great Expectations.*" *Dickens Studies Annual* 35 (2005): 133–56.

Recent Studies in Robert Louis Stevenson: Survey of Biographical Works and Checklist of Criticism—1970–2005

Roger G. Swearingen

This essay completes my survey of publications since 1970 on the life and works of Robert Louis Stevenson (1850–1894). The first three parts were published in Volume 37 of Dickens Studies Annual *(2006) and covered Letters, Reference Works, and Texts. The present essay covers Biography, in detail, and includes a list of Works Cited. After this, I provide a checklist of criticism that I have tried to make as complete as possible. Unfortunately, the large number of such works does not allow room for descriptive and evaluative commentary. My goal has been the same as in the previous sections: to create a reliable and inclusive guide that will be useful to scholars and to ordinary readers alike. Almost all of the publications surveyed are in English, however, and much good work has been published in other languages. And, since there are valuable works in English that I have not been able to consider or may have overlooked, there is plenty of room for a sequel. The work of the many scholars and other writers whose efforts have come under review in the present undertaking makes it likely that we will not have to wait another 35 years for the next review of research on Stevenson. Serious work has begun and will continue.*

As in the previously published parts of my survey, Stevenson's letters are quoted from and are cited by letter number, date, and recipient, in the authoritative edition, *The Letters of Robert Louis Stevenson*, ed. Bradford A. Booth and Ernest J. Mehew (8 vols., New Haven: Yale UP, 1994–95), referred to here as the Yale Letters. References to materials in the Beinecke Rare Book and Manuscript Library, Yale University, are identified as "Beinecke" and followed by the item number if they are listed in the catalogue by George L. McKay, *A Stevenson Library* . . . (6 vols., 1951–64). Other such items are identified simply as "Yale." Items offered in the three-part sale at the Anderson Galleries, New York, 1914–16, are identified as Anderson, followed by the part and item number in the catalogues of this sale. References to Graham Balfour's biography are to the English edition, *The Life of Robert Louis Stevenson*, 2 vols., London: Methuen, 1901. Quotations from Stevenson's published works follow the first book-form edition and are identified by title and date of first publication. Page references for quotations are usually omitted except in the case of book-length studies.

Biography

Some preliminary remarks may be helpful before we look in detail at work produced since 1970. The best short biography of Stevenson is Ernest Mehew's concise, judicious, detailed entry for the *Oxford Dictionary of National Biography* (2004). The best full biography is in the Yale *Selected Letters* (1997), more than 500 pages in which RLS's own brilliant and engaging statements are selected and then qualified, balanced, and placed in context by Mehew's Introduction, linking summaries, and annotations.

Among regular, full-length biographies, those by RLS's cousin Graham Balfour (2 vols., 1901) and J. C. Furnas, *Voyage to Windward* (1951), remain the standard by which all such works must be judged. What can be offered, now, that is not already present in Balfour or in Furnas? Both had access to nearly all of Stevenson's letters, manuscripts, and notebooks. They were not limited to the published selections and versions, as almost all other biographers have been, and as a result they both wrote from a knowledge of Stevenson's letters and manuscripts that could not readily be approached until recently. Although the publication of the Yale Letters (1994–95) made the correspondence accessible, other materials remain difficult to consult. Balfour, moreover, had Stevenson's manuscripts and notebooks as Stevenson left them, not, as many of the manuscripts and all but a few of RLS's notebooks are today, divided into pieces as short as a page or two, removed from the context of other pages in the same notebook, and scattered among various libraries. He also had his own firsthand acquaintance with his cousin and continuing personal access to Stevenson's family and friends.

It is clear today that William Ernest Henley's denunciation of Balfour's biography as depicting a "Seraph in chocolate, [a] barley-sugar effigy of a real man" (*Pall Mall Magazine*, Dec. 1901), reveals chiefly the depth of Henley's own bitter feelings of loss—his conviction that RLS had outgrown him, had chosen his wife over his friend, and had eventually cast him off entirely to enjoy, instead, the poisoned fruits of wealth, popularity, and world-wide acclaim. For Henley, as he wrote in his review, there were "two Stevensons: the Stevenson who went to America in '87; and the Stevenson who never came back. The first I knew, and loved; the other I lost touch with, and, though I admired him, did not greatly esteem." Henley's "old, riotous, intrepid, scornful Stevenson" is not absent from Balfour's biography, however. He lives, as he must, between rather than in the lines of a narrative in which almost all of the persons of Stevenson's own generation were then still living. For the same reason, the quarrel and estrangement between Henley and RLS in 1888 over Fanny Stevenson's story "The Nixie" is also not mentioned in Balfour, nor is the fact that it was Henley about whom RLS cautioned prudence in giving him much money: "if I gave him more, it would only lead to his starting a gig and keeping a Pomeranian dog" (RLS to Charles Baxter, 15 July 1894, Letter 2759; qtd. in Balfour, *Life*, II, 181). As J. C. Furnas noted, Henley's dwelling on this passage in his review shows that he surely realized who was meant (*Voyage to Windward* [1951], 258–59; see also Ernest Mehew's note to Letter 2759 quoting Baxter's remark in a letter to Lord Guthrie, 4 April 1914, that the quotation was "an intentional slight" by Fanny, who was "much too clever not to know how it would wound," and that it was surely "the match that set fire to Henley's explosion"). Understood in context, Balfour proves to be a remarkably shrewd and discerning biographer, omitting much but within his limits writing accurately and, although with reticence, without distortion. His biography also remains the only published source of much autobiographical material, early and late, by RLS himself.

J. C. Furnas, writing 50 years later, was able to speak openly about Stevenson's younger days, the quarrel with Henley, and about many other matters, and he also got rid of legends such as the idea that the "Claire" in some of Stevenson's early poems was a real young woman in Scotland rather than, as was actually the case, merely a name that RLS had given to Mrs. Sitwell for poetical purposes. Furnas was also able to benefit from the generosity of Edwin J. Beinecke in giving him access to his own collection, at that point, not yet at Yale, and from the deposit in the National Library of Scotland of RLS's letters to Mrs. Sitwell and of a second group of letters, on the quarrel with Henley. Furnas was thus the first biographer after Balfour who was able to work with anything like the complete record of Stevenson's letters and manuscripts.

Among the many full-length biographies since Furnas's, two stand out: those by Jenni Calder (1980) and by Claire Harman (2005), both of which are discussed below. Others include David Daiches's *Robert Louis Stevenson and His World* (1973), which combines a good short biography with a first-rate collection of pictures; Nicholas Rankin's *Dead Man's Chest: Travels After Robert Louis Stevenson* (1987), the best of the then-and-now travel books, containing much good research and many shrewd insights about Stevenson as well; and Ian Bell's *Robert Louis Stevenson: Dreams of Exile* (1992), among the few studies to do justice to RLS's Scottishness.

The following survey is divided into five sections. "General Essays" covers short studies of Stevenson, including his life in Edinburgh, his religious views, and what his voice and accent may have sounded like. Also included are a few items that are hard to classify: essays about the biographies by Balfour and J. C. Furnas (the latter written by Furnas himself), and accounts of the collections now in the RLS Silverado Museum and in the Beinecke Rare Book and Manuscript Library at Yale. "Books and Essays on Special Topics" covers, in the chronological order of the period in Stevenson's life to which they apply, the many studies of individual periods and topics, from his family background as the son and grandson of Scottish civil engineers, to his years in the South Pacific. "Stevenson's Health" examines contributions on this much-discussed subject. "Book-Length Biographies" discusses such studies in the chronological order of their publication. The last section, "Fanny Stevenson and Isobel Strong," reviews reprints and work on RLS's wife and her daughter Belle, two of the most important women in his life.

General Essays

Ernest Mehew's entry in the *Oxford Dictionary of National Biography* (2004) is a masterpiece of detail, compression, and relevance. "A turning point in Stevenson's life came in the summer of 1873 at Cockfield rectory, in Suffolk, the home of Professor Churchill Babington, whose wife was Stevenson's cousin Maud," he writes of RLS at the age of 22.

> There he met Professor Sidney Colvin and his friend Mrs Frances Sitwell, a beautiful woman of thirty-four (living apart from her clergyman husband), whom Colvin would much later marry. They recognized his potential and did all they could to help him. Colvin became Stevenson's literary mentor and closest friend. Stevenson fell in love with Mrs Sitwell, and for the next two years poured out long diary-letters to her; they constitute a touching record of his emotional dependence on her and of his growth to maturity. Mrs Sitwell began as 'Claire' (the name wrongly applied to the imaginary Edinburgh prostitute) and progressed to being his 'Madonna'—a goddess and mother figure.
>
> (599)

Every word counts in this narration: Mehew manages to remind us of all of the key details as well as their general context. At the end, Mehew provides a short list of source materials and archives and a list of 50 likenesses: portraits, sketches, and photographs. That there are so many of these reminds us that thanks to RLS's living in an era of photography and illustrated magazines he is among the most familiar of authors visually.

In his contribution to the "God and the Novelists" series in the journal *The Expository Times* (1999), Ernest Mehew offers a concise but detailed account of RLS's religious experiences, of the religious influences upon him from the Covenanters and his nurse Alison Cunningham to his father and Herbert Spencer, and of his religious views from early childhood onward. "On the evidence of his letters and essays," Mehew writes, "he [Stevenson] can best be described as an agnostic with strong Christian undertones."

> His Scottish Presbyterian background deeply influenced his life and thought: he was concerned about the moral principles upon which man should conduct his life and his novels and short stories show his preoccupation with the ambiguities in human nature and the problem of evil. Because of his upbringing he was well versed in the Bible and the Metrical Version of the Psalms and his letters and other writings are full of biblical allusions.

According to Mehew, the clearest statement of RLS's mature views on God and religion is in a long and angry letter scolding his young friend and protégé Adelaide Boodle "when she told him that on the advice of a friend she had decided that she could not visit him in Samoa because she would be unable to obtain there the consolations of the Anglican Church." Stevenson strongly asserts, in response: "God is no churchman, my dear lady; and no clergyman. The world is great and rough: he is nearest to the right divinity who can accept that greatness and that roughness. . . . Face the gross facts: if you be pure, you will be the more pure; if you be brave, the more courageous" (Letter 2294).

Mehew observes that two of Stevenson's essays, "Pulvis et Umbra" (which in a letter at the time of its writing RLS called a "Darwinian Sermon"—RLS to Sidney Colvin, 20 November 1887, Letter 1944) and "A Christmas Sermon," both first published in *Scribner's Magazine* in 1888, offer more public statements of his views. On 23 August 1893 he wrote to Sidney Colvin: "I believe in an ultimate decency of things; ay, and if I woke in hell, should still believe it!" (Letter 2624).

Robert Kiely, author of the critical study *RLS and the Fiction of Adventure* (1964), contributes, in a reference compilation, a presentable and well-illustrated short account of RLS's life and literary career. Especially notable is a seldom-reproduced pencil sketch by RLS of his childhood nurse Cummy (Alison Cunningham), probably done sometime in the 1880s, when RLS was in his thirties and she had left the employ of the family. (This is now in the Berg Collection, New York Public Library.)

For Richard Dury (2000), RLS was a Scot, but—very much more than that—he was an Edinburgh Scot. The few firsthand accounts that survive suggest that RLS's accent was Edinburgh Scottish as spoken by the professional classes. That he was a Scot would have been apparent, but it would not have been difficult for Englishmen or Americans to understand him. Sandra Marwick's attractive, large-format (A4), 32–page pictorial compilation on RLS is one of three such guides produced by the Edinburgh City Museums department on the three writers honored in the Writers' Museum in Edinburgh, Burns and Scott being the others. Marwick offers some 60 well-chosen quotations from Stevenson's works and letters and from reminiscences of him, chiefly on his early years as a child and as a student in Edinburgh. Also included are 18 black-and-white photographs of RLS, his family, and the places he lived, a chronology, and a list of RLS's works. My own pocket-sized guide to places in and around Edinburgh associated with RLS (2001) is also produced by the Edinburgh City Museums. Illustrated with contemporary photographs and drawings and a map, it consists of quotations from his own letters and essays and from anecdotes and recollections by people who knew him. It is remarkable how many places in Edinburgh have RLS associations, and how little has changed about many of them.

In a contribution to the collection *Stevenson and Victorian Scotland* (ed. Jenni Calder, 1981), Graham Balfour's son Michael tells again the fascinating story that he had first told in letters to the *Times Literary Supplement* in early 1960, of how his father came to write the authorized biography of his second-cousin, RLS, published in two volumes in 1901. Henley was RLS's first choice. But as early as 1885 RLS was having second thoughts, and after he and Henley quarreled irrevocably in the spring of 1888, RLS wrote a letter to be opened after his death stating that he wished Sidney Colvin to produce, if Colvin were willing, "a sketch of my life" but to urge him to do it promptly. When RLS died at the end of 1894, Charles Baxter and Graham Balfour brought his papers and manuscripts back to Colvin in London, and Baxter also got together as many letters as he could. But as RLS had feared, Colvin was overwhelmed by other work, including the Edinburgh Edition, and by early 1899 Colvin had written little more than three chapters and the introductory and linking comments that he eventually used in the letters. On 14 April 1899, Lloyd Osbourne, acting on behalf of himself and his mother, and mentioning their great patience, finally took the project away from him. Michael Balfour suggests that Fanny and Lloyd probably already had in mind approaching his father. They knew him well from his residing off and on at Vailima, and of course Balfour felt much more positively about the whole affair of the South Seas than Colvin ever had. On 4 June 1899 Fanny asked him to take on the task, and by mid-August an agreement had been reached. For a time, by his own account to Balfour's wife many years later, Colvin resented bitterly that the job had been taken away from him. But in the end he found Balfour's account "very, *very* good. . . . [O]f course he knew Samoa, and he *was* the right person for that. But what I am now struck with, is that he has done the earlier part so well: the part he didn't know about personally."

In an aptly titled memoir, *My Life in Writing: Memoirs of a Maverick* (1999), J. C. Furnas tells with his usual charm and modesty the story of his own biography of RLS, including his proving that "Claire" was a fictitious character, one of various names that RLS had invented for Mrs. Sitwell, to whom he was addressing poems: "A pity to treat an attractive girl so ruthlessly, but my exorcising her gave me not only great pleasure but also my chief claim to scoring a coup in scholarship" (287). Furnas recalls, with great affection, the informality and generosity of Edwin J. Beinecke (1886–1970), whose collection was then not at Yale but in his home in Connecticut.

Vincent Giroud, who in 2004 was coming to the end of his service as Curator at the Beinecke Rare Book and Manuscript Library, Yale University, draws upon a wealth of unpublished records and correspondence to paint a lively insider's portrait of Edwin J. Beinecke, whom he rightly calls "[the] greatest of all Stevenson collectors" (42). Giroud writes of the role of Beinecke's personal librarian, Gertrude Hills, in organizing and cataloguing the collection; of Beinecke's own active pursuit of materials not only inside but far away from the auction room; and of the importance of Yale librarian James T. Babb's personal influence in securing the collection, originally intended for the New York Public Library, and later the Beinecke Rare Book and Manuscript Library building itself, as a benefaction to his own and Beinecke's alma mater. Five years after the Beinecke Library opened, another important collector, Norman H. Strouse, founded the museum now known as the Robert Louis Stevenson Silverado Museum in St. Helena, Napa Valley, California. This was in 1969, not long after his retirement as Board Chairman of the J. Walter Thompson advertising firm. Strouse offers a good survey of high points and of his pleasure in building the collection. Having decided many years earlier to found the museum, he writes, "I began to collect Stevenson in quite a different way. I began to search for Stevenson material, 'as if we *had* a museum.' " Strouse's discussion also shows the important role that booksellers can have in building major collections.

Books and Essays on Special Topics

"Whenever I smell salt water," Stevenson wrote when he was 29, "I know I am not far from one of the works of my ancestors. The Bell Rock stands monument for my grandfather; the Skerry Vhor for my Uncle Alan; and when the lights come out at sundown along the shores of Scotland, I am proud to think they burn more brightly for the genius of my father'' (''Memoirs of Himself,'' 1880). Stevenson was proud to be part of a distinguished family of civil engineers, whose history and his own relations to it are traced in three excellent and quite different accounts. Craig Mair (1978) draws upon previously unavailable family and business papers, photographs, paintings, and portraits—many of them now in the National Library of Scotland—to offer a wonderfully readable, detailed, and insightful history. Mair is particularly good on the evolution of the Stevenson firm as a private business working chiefly on public projects of all kinds, not only on lighthouses; on the family's highly practical approach to engineering—the Stevensons were builders, not only designers; and on the strong emphasis that the Stevensons placed on learning through apprenticeship, not only academic study, on hard work and meticulous attention to detail, and on absolute integrity. RLS is in all of these respects very much a Stevenson. Mair includes a list and map of all of the Stevenson lighthouses in Scotland, and 28 excellent, mostly contemporary, photographs and other illustrations. Bella Bathurst (1999) is much more interested in the personalities, the driving and driven temperaments, that one finds in the Stevensons, than she is in the business or in the engineering. Her account is really of Robert Stevenson and his three engineering sons (RLS's grandfather, father, and two of his uncles), and for practical purposes it ends with RLS's father's work building the Dhu Heartach lighthouse (1867–72) and the new harbor at Wick (1868), both of them projects in which RLS himself participated. Most of the two-dozen illustrations are from contemporary engravings of the finished lighthouses or details of their construction.

Professor Roland Paxton, a noted historian of civil engineering at Heriot-Watt University, Edinburgh, is a lifelong student of the work of RLS's grandfather Robert Stevenson, on whom he contributed the entry in the most recent *DNB* (2004). Jean Leslie is the granddaughter of RLS's first cousin Charles Alexander Stevenson and, following in the footsteps of her father D. Alan Stevenson, is the family historian. Each chapter in their collaboration has two sections, ''Family recollections'' by Jean Leslie and ''A professional aspect'' by Professor Paxton, and there are dozens of illustrations both in the text and in a separate additional section of pictures (150–74). Almost all of these are previously unpublished or unpublished since their original publication, usually in technical books, reports, and journals, and they do much to convey a sense of what it must have been like to grow up a Stevenson. Professor Paxton's contributions bring alive the engineering work of all of the Stevensons, and he also traces the often bitter conflicts over money and partnership shares in dividing the income from the firm, in some of which

RLS was an agonized, unhappy bystander. Paxton also notes, as Craig Mair does, the fact that the Stevensons were not only lighthouse engineers. For example, in 1821 RLS's grandfather Robert Stevenson did the engineering and construction of the 140-foot-high, 1,500-ton Melville Column in St. Andrew Square that is still an Edinburgh landmark. RLS's father Thomas Stevenson was an inventor as well as an engineer, among his inventions being a marine dynamometer to measure the force of waves as they struck, lenses and other lighthouse apparatus, and a louvered box for protecting thermometers from sunlight—a design still in use and known as a Stevenson screen. Jean Leslie also quotes from a few previously unpublished family papers, mostly describing life among the David Stevensons, RLS's uncle and cousins. In addition, the book includes an annotated list of publications by the Stevensons, including RLS's several engineering papers, a complete list of the Stevenson lighthouses in Scotland, and a short genealogical table.

Ernest Mehew, in "Glimpses of Stevenson's Childhood" (2000), adroitly pulls together and quotes reminiscences of Stevenson's childhood by RLS himself, in his works and letters, and by others. Mehew notes that even though Stevenson's early childhood was "dominated by his ill-health" and he was "soaked in religion," nonetheless "[his] memories of his childhood were happy ones and he loved to recall them in his writings. As late as 1893 in his unfinished essay, 'Rosa Quo Locorum' we find him remembering the books read to him in his childhood, whose plots he re-enacted in his play, and the imagery called up in his mind from local scenes before he was seven by the reading of the metrical version of the twenty-third psalm."

RLS's life-long love affair with France is illuminated by three inclusive studies, as well as by several works related to his time in the Cévennes in 1878 discussed later. Although Stevenson is mentioned only in passing, John Pemble shows in a fascinating study based on contemporary sources, *The Mediterranean Passion: Victorians and Edwardians in the South* (1987), that in the 1860s RLS's parents (and others in the family) were entirely typical of their social class and wealth in spending the severest months of the winter at Nice and Mentone, as they did twice, in 1863 and 1864. Mentone was especially favored by British visitors seeking health, thanks to the tireless enthusiasm of Dr. James Henry Bennet (1816–1891), who had settled there for his own health in the winter of 1859–60. Bennet's *Mentone and the Riviera as a Winter Climate* (1861) reached a fifth English edition under the title *Winter and Spring on the Shores of the Mediterranean* (1875). RLS was 12 and 13 during the family's two stays during the 1860s and thoroughly enjoyed them; and he was himself entirely typical when, a decade later, at the end of 1873, he was sent by Dr. Andrew Clark to winter again at Mentone, to recover his mental as much as his physical health, owing to the extreme stress of disagreements over religion at home and his new-found passion for

Mrs. Sitwell. His residence at Hyères during 1883 and 1884 reflects the same mixture of motives that Pemble finds among many British visitors at the time: a climatological theory of disease, in which climate, in the sense of "psychological, biological, and environmental" conditions more so than the air or temperature as such—ambiance rather than treatments or drugs—was thought to bring about palliation or cure; and a renewed Romantic feeling that the south was a place of tolerance, simplicity, and freedom, a refuge from the frantic pace of modern urban life.

Louis Stott gives us a detailed, informative guide to the places in France that RLS visited or lived in, with a short introductory chapter on RLS's reading in French literature. It is well illustrated with period and contemporary photographs and quotations from RLS's works and letters and those of his friends. Maps at the end show what's where in Mentone, Barbizon, and Grez, and along the routes of *An Inland Voyage* (1878) and *Travels With a Donkey* (1879). Robin Hill's compilation is not the equal of Louis Stott's in detail or illustrations. But there are notes on French Polynesia and many gleanings from Hill's own visits to RLS places in France.

RLS's years as a student at the University of Edinburgh are greatly illuminated by Gillian Cookson and Colin A. Hempstead in a splendid short biography of RLS's teacher, mentor, and friend, Professor Henry Charles Fleeming Jenkin (1833–1885). It is an invaluable complement to RLS's own "Memoir of Fleeming Jenkin" (1887), written over the space of two years after Jenkin's death on 12 June 1885 at the age of 53. RLS naturally concentrated on Jenkin's personal qualities and character—on their friendship. Cookson and Hempstead discuss, also, Jenkin's remarkable education, which besides the Edinburgh Academy included almost five years residence abroad, with tutors and university study in Frankfurt, Paris, and Genoa; his engineering work on electrical measurements for submarine telegraphy; his effective advocacy of a new approach to engineering education, in which theoretical science both preceded and followed an interval of practical training; and, as Stevenson also does, the extraordinary breadth of Jenkin's interests both in science and in the arts, especially drama. Cookson and Hempstead also depict the vibrant scientific, engineering, and academic milieu of Edinburgh during the 1870s, in which RLS and his father both participated also, although in different ways, and they explain lucidly Jenkin's role in the refinement and clarification of Darwin's thought that led to Darwin's high praise and thanks in the fifth edition of *Origin of Species* (1869). Jenkin's textbook, *Electricity and Magnetism* (1873), they note, "was the first book on electricity written with students in mind, in a modern style, and was a huge success." RLS's copy is at Yale (Beinecke 2545). There are complete lists of Jenkin's publications and patents, a valuable list of secondary works on the range of Jenkin's interests, and two dozen well-chosen pictures, including photos of Jenkin and his wife

Anne at the time RLS would have known them and a charming sketch of Jenkin in his laboratory in 1884 by William Hole, Stevenson's friend and contemporary, who illustrated *Kidnapped*, *The Master of Ballantrae*, and *The Wrecker*.

An amusing footnote to all this is provided by Gordon K. Booth in his essay on RLS and William Robertson Smith (1846–1894). Although the story was never mentioned by either of the principals, RLS was apparently much given to distracting Smith from his duties as a laboratory assistant in Professor P. G. Tait's class in Natural Philosophy (1868–70) by engaging him in theological discussions. Smith was himself a student, at the New College of the Free Church of Scotland, and upon completing his studies there was appointed to the Chair of Hebrew and Old Testament Exegesis at the Free Church College in Aberdeen, where he took up his duties in November 1870. There is no evidence that RLS and Smith ever met again, although they both contributed to the ninth edition of the *Encyclopædia Britannica* (1875) and RLS mentions him in the postscript of a letter to his mother in July 1879, possibly only in response to newspaper accounts of a Free Church inquiry into Smith's religious views (Letter 634). RLS also glances at him in his reference to "Smith o' Aberdeen" in "The Scotsman's Return from Abroad" (1880).

RLS was 24 when he first met William Ernest Henley (1849–1903). This was on 9 February 1875, when Leslie Stephen, then editor of the *Cornhill Magazine*, who was lecturing in Edinburgh, took RLS to see Henley at the Edinburgh Infirmary, during Henley's convalescence after receiving antiseptic surgical treatment from Professor Joseph Lister for tuberculosis in his foot. Edward H. Cohen, the author of a valuable monograph, *The Henley-Stevenson Quarrel* (1974), which is discussed later in this section, provided in 2004, the first publication of draft versions of 14 additional hospital poems that Henley wrote under the collective title "Lazarus" during his convalescence in June and July 1875 at Portobello, near Edinburgh. Cohen gives an excellent summary of the evolution of the whole sequence and of RLS's continuing support and enthusiasm for this second group of poems even though efforts to find a publisher were unavailing. "R. L. S. thinks the 'Hospital Moments' a work of genius—perverse, misdirected, bad; but genius all the same," Henley wrote to Anna Boyle on 23 April 1877 about the "Lazarus" poems under their then-current title. "Our ways lie apart, my Dear, but *he* will recognise me, if none other does" (MS, Yale). In an earlier article (1995) discussing the reception of Henley's hospital poems, Cohen quotes from an unspecified page in one of Henley's manuscripts (J. Pierpont Morgan Library, New York) RLS's marginal comment: "Good man! that's what I *do* call realism, and yet like."

RLS met Fanny Vandegrift Osbourne, the American woman whom he married three and one-half years later in California, at Grez at the end of

September 1876—a meeting that RLS affectionately recalled in a letter to Fanny in mid-May 1888, looking forward to their eighth wedding anniversary on 19 May (Letter 2087). In *The Passionate Kindness: The Love Story of Robert Louis Stevenson and Fanny Osbourne* (1974), Alanna Knight gives an astonishing account of their love and marriage, freely combining surmise, speculation, and invention with quotations from letters and secondary sources in producing an account that only a true fan could love. She invents dialogue, muddles facts, embellishes scenes, and ignores rough places—all with boundless and uncontrollable energy.

In the title of *A Quixotic Companionship: Fanny and Robert Louis Stevenson* (2nd ed., 1997), Elaine Fitzpatrick recalls Lloyd Osbourne's comment on RLS's reading *Don Quixote* during one of their Pacific cruises. "Suddenly he looked up," Graham Balfour reports Lloyd recalling, "and, with an air of realisation, said sadly, as if to himself, 'That's me' " (II, 178). Fitzpatrick all but completely ignores the sadness, however, and spends her time enthusiastically retelling the story of the love, marriage, and married life of Fanny Osbourne and RLS—from their meeting in France in 1876 to Fanny's death in California in 1914. The story is all high points and foreground, however: a completely unskeptical collection of colorful anecdotes, as often as not consisting of speculations (and errors) drawn from secondary sources. We hear little about what each person might have seen in or drawn from the other, or how their relationship might have changed or grown; little of their conflicts with one another, or of Fanny's with Stevenson's friends. Henley, for example, is never mentioned, nor his accusation that Fanny plagiarized "The Nixie" (1888) from a story by RLS's cousin Katharine DeMattos. RLS's heated response, which other commentators have found both quixotic and uxorious, led to the permanent estrangement of the two men. "My marriage was hugely in the teeth of what my parents wanted," RLS commented to one of his oldest friends when he was 42. "And now, as I look back, I think it was the best move I ever made in my life" (RLS to Anne Jenkin, 5 December 1892, Letter 2505). No doubt Fitzpatrick would agree. The trouble is that there is nothing in her cheerful treatment of the matter to answer those, from the Samoan trader Harry J. Moors and Fanny's one-time stepson Joe Strong to George S. Hellman and Frank McLynn—not to mention Henley himself—who think, or thought then, exactly the opposite: that Stevenson was deluded in his belief, oppressed and driven to an early grave by a neurotic wife and her feckless, greedy, and demanding children. Only part of the story, the positive side, is being told by Fitzpatrick.

Travels With a Donkey in the Cévennes (1879) is RLS's account of the 12–day, 140-mile walking tour that he took in France from Le Monastier-sur-Gazielle to St.-Jean-du-Gard in 1878. Richard Holmes, now known as a biographer of Shelley and of Samuel Johnson's friend Richard Savage, says that it was Stevenson who inspired him to become a writer. When he was 18, Holmes retraced RLS's steps in the Cévennes:

> For Stevenson . . . the whole Cévennes experience was a kind of initiation cere-mony: a grappling with physical hardships, loneliness, religious doubts, the influence of his parents, and the overwhelming question of whether he should take the enormous risk of travelling to America and throwing his life in with Fanny's. . . . Stevenson was making a pilgrimage into the recesses of his own heart . . . asking himself what sort of man he should be, what life-pattern he should follow.   (65, 38)

Holmes also maintains that RLS's four essays under the general title "Virgini-bus Puerisque" (1876–80) "are evidently drawn from his passion for Fanny, and they represent an entirely new note in his work and outlook": RLS was "genuinely frightened" by marriage because it seemed to threaten "to kill the boy in him" (45–46).

The centenary of RLS's visit to the Cévennes was celebrated in 1978 by a conference and exhibition at Alés and the publication of Gordon Golding's edition of RLS's journal, now in the Huntington Library, on which see the comments in the section on Texts in the first part of this survey (*DSA* 37, 2006). RLS's route was first seriously marked for walkers then, and in her *National Geographic* article Caroline Bennett Patterson tells of her own ad-ventures following RLS's route 99 years after he did. The chief value of her article is in the photographs and also in the juxtapositions of RLS's own notebook sketches of people and places with their counterparts today.

Two excellent trail guides have appeared. Alan Castle's 1992 contribution to the Cicerone series of walking guides divides the journey into eleven one-day stages, on each of which he gives details on distances and elevations, accommodations, points of interest, RLS's experiences, and a detailed practi-cal commentary on the route. General maps and color and black-and-white photographs also help to re-create RLS's experiences. Jacques Poujol and others associated with the Club Cévenol created in 1994 a beautifully pro-duced, portable, and durable walking guide that traces in detail route GR 70, "Le Chemin de Stevenson," by means of informative color photographs and watercolors, detailed topographical maps, and practical and historical comments. It is an inspiring, useful, and informative complement to Alan Castle's more practical guide to the same trail.

RLS's year-long stay in California in 1879–80 was, until the mid-1960s at least, the subject of much popular attention. Charles Warren Stoddard's "Stevenson's Monterey" (*National Magazine*, Dec. 1905) was followed by *Stevenson in California* (1911), written by Lloyd Osbourne's estranged wife Katharine Durham Osbourne. Other accounts appear in Fanny's sister Nellie Sanchez's "In California with Robert Louis Stevenson" (*Scribner's Maga-zine*, Oct. 1916), substantially assimilated into her *Life of Mrs. Robert Louis*

Stevenson (1920), and in Fanny's daughter Belle's California chapters in *This Life I've Loved* (1937). Book-length studies appeared by Anne Benson Fisher on RLS in Monterey (1946), and Anne Roller Issler on RLS's time in the Napa Valley (1939) and in San Francisco and Oakland (1949); these were followed by Issler's well-researched article, "RLS in Monterey" (*Pacific Historical Review*, Aug. 1965). Possibly because of these many studies, Roy Nickerson's 1982 account was the first in many years. Unfortunately, it is an adequate but wholly external summary that relies uncritically on earlier accounts and on my own chronological summary prepared in 1980 for the RLS Silverado Museum. There is nothing original or searching, only a repetition of received details, including many that are wrong or of doubtful accuracy.

The goat ranchers' cabin where RLS nearly died in September 1879 (Letters 652, 653) is now a ruin, all but the fireplace and chimney. It is at the end of present-day Robinson Canyon Road, in the Carmel Valley, inland from Monterey. My own short essay uses land records in the Monterey County Courthouse, Salinas, to show that in RLS's time the ranch on which this cabin was located belonged to a partnership formed in April 1877 between Jonathan Wright and Anson Smith. The partnership ended in 1886 when Smith sold his "undivided half interest" in the 178-acre ranch and "1000 goats (more or less), three head of cattle, one wagon, farming implements and household furniture" to Bradley V. Sargent.

Arthur W. Orton takes up a later part of the California story in a wonderfully detailed illustrated pamphlet, *Reconstructing the Robert Louis Stevenson "Silverado Squatters" Cabin* (1980, 1993). Orton reproduces all three versions of Joe Strong's frontispiece sketch in *The Silverado Squatters* (from the English and American first editions, 1883 and 1884, and the Edinburgh Edition, 1895) and explains how these sketches, combined with references in the book, allowed him to create the scale model of the bunkhouse now on display in the RLS Silverado Museum. Possibly his most interesting insight is that Joe Strong's sketch is almost certainly a composite. RLS and Fanny would not have brought the kitchen table and its jugs and bottles upstairs to the sleeping quarters. Joe has artfully combined two views.

Using on-the-spot examination of surviving buildings, as well as nineteenth-century newspapers, guidebooks, and maps, Lawrence Popplewell, in *The Search for Bonallie Tower: R. L. S. in Branksome Park* (1996, 2000), has determined for the first time the exact location of the house called Bonallie Tower, in which RLS and Fanny lived for six months, from early November 1884 until mid-April 1885, and very much else besides. Fanny, RLS, and Lloyd (who was to attend school there) arrived in Bournemouth on 12 July 1884, and Popplewell gives a detailed account of their various resting places in Bournemouth after that, some of which survive. Still hoping to find a house to buy and still without a permanent residence, on Monday, 3 November

1884, RLS and Fanny moved into the newly-built house Bonallie Tower, No.
1 Burton Road, in Branksome Park, Westbourne, about a mile to the west of
the town center of Bournemouth and just south of the Poole Road. No doubt
an important factor in their choice was that the rent was only £4 a month.

> [Situated on the] still very wild, western edge of newly founded Westbourne
> [the area] was mainly a district of pine, sand and furze, essentially a place
> lonely and long unspoiled. Aside from a few smuggler's tracks nearby, there
> existed only a handful scattering of large houses, all in substantial grounds the
> exact boundaries of which were scarcely even clearly or properly laid out.

Although Popplewell does not mention this fact, it was at Bonallie Tower, in
December 1884, that RLS first read *Huckleberry Finn* and first sat for John
Singer Sargent, who was much taken aback that RLS insisted upon having
the novel read aloud during their sittings (RLS to Mark Twain, 12 April 1888,
Letter 2064). He does note that Herbert Beerbohm Tree also visited and left
a short account of the house. Tree's first visit was on 1 February 1885, among
other things to hear RLS read parts of *Macaire*, on which see Letter 1389.
Unfortunately, no photograph or drawing of Bonallie Tower survives, and
the house itself was torn down, probably in the early twentieth century.

In "The Squire and the Gamekeeper: RLS and Miss Adelaide Boodle,"
Olena M. Turnbull adds nothing to Adelaide's own memoir of RLS and Fanny
at Bournemouth, *RLS and His Sine Qua Non: Flashlights from Skerryvore*
(1926), or to RLS's rather stern letters to her during the 1890s in the Yale
Letters. But she does provide a good case study of the friendships that RLS
often inspired with people much younger than himself.

In the late autumn of 1886, Auguste Rodin sent to RLS a plaster version
of his sculpture *Le Printemps* (1884), inscribed in a special panel on the base:
"A R. L. Stevenson | au sympathetique | Artiste au grand | et cher poète |
A Rodin." It is now in the Philadelphia Museum of Art, beautifully reproduced in color on the cover of John L. Tancock's authoritative catalogue
(1976). Tancock also discusses the sculpture and its development in detail,
with a black-and-white photograph and reference to other versions (241–47).
The copy that Rodin sent to RLS was always on display in the so-called
Great Hall at Vailima and it remained with the Stevensons until after Fanny
Stevenson's death in 1914, when it was sold (for $1,500) as Anderson I, 484,
in the catalogue of which sale *Le Printemps* is the frontispiece photograph.

Edward Cohen, in *The Henley-Stevenson Quarrel*, reviews the now-famous
correspondence that began with Henley's accusation, in a letter to RLS dated
9 March 1888, that Fanny Stevenson plagiarized her story, "The Nixie,"
then just published in *Scribner's Magazine* (March 1888), from a story, never
published and seemingly abandoned by her, by RLS's cousin Katharine De-
Mattos (Letter 2032). This led to a correspondence that eventually consisted

of some two dozen letters chiefly among RLS, Henley, and Charles Baxter as a friend to both. Although Cohen is covering ground that for the most part had been considered before, he adds one letter not previously published, (Baxter's response on 31 May 1888 to a letter from Fanny Stevenson [Beinecke 4055, now Letter 2100; Cohen 64]), and a few other previously unpublished letters of indirect interest. Among these is a very late comment by Sidney Colvin acknowledging the deep division between Fanny Stevenson and Henley during the Bournemouth period over what she saw as Henley's reckless indifference to Stevenson's health (Beinecke 8371; qtd. 91–92). Cohen quotes at length from Henley's review of Balfour's biography (77–82), but this has since become available complete in Jenni Calder's *Robert Louis Stevenson Companion* (1980). Several additional letters, now at Yale, turned up in 1980, and, of course, all of the quarrel letters—replies and correspondence among the other principals included—are now available in the Yale Letters (Letters 2032 and following), with Ernest Mehew's valuable annotations and his own judicious summary not only of the quarrel but of what preceded and followed it, this last in his introductory biographical sketch of Henley (I, 59–60).

Cohen's analysis of the quarrel is not particularly searching, and he carefully avoids deep speculation: both men were at fault and let stress and their emotions run away with them. He gives a very good depiction of their friendship and of some of the later reactions of both men to their quarrel—for example, in Henley's "De Amicitia" ("Friends . . . old friends . . . / One sees how it ends," *Scots Observer*, 6 April 1889; qtd. 74) and RLS's undated fable "The Man and His Friend" (qtd. vi). He also gives details about the manuscript versions of two of Henley's poems on RLS. The first is Henley's well-known sonnet on RLS later titled "An Apparition" ("Thin legged, thin chested, slight unspeakably") of which there are three slightly differing early manuscript versions and a fourth manuscript from early 1888, the very time of the quarrel, all of these in the J. Pierpont Morgan Library, New York (13–15, 71–72). The sonnet was written during the winter of 1875–76 in the first year of their friendship, and in February 1876 Henley sent a copy to RLS (Beinecke 7242); Cohen discusses this version briefly and quotes RLS's mother's letter of thanks and Henley's reply (Beinecke 5616, 4691; qtd. 13–15). Cohen also publishes, for the first time, a much racier portrait dated 22 April 1882, "Ballade R. L. S." (Beinecke 7243), of which the first stanza follows:

> An Ariel quick through all his veins
>   With sex & temperament & style;
> All eloquence & balls & brains;
>   Heroic—also infantile;
> Without the faintest touch of guile

> Yet living but to plot & plan;
> Behold him, bubbling into bile,
> A bald and cullidheaded man! (qtd. 18)

Cohen also notes RLS's early and continuing high regard for Henley's poetry.

RLS's month-long stay on the New Jersey coast in May 1888, after the winter that he spent at Saranac Lake, New York, is summarized by Bridget Falconer-Salkeld from the Yale Letters and the well-known published accounts by Will H. Low (*A Chronicle of Friendships*, 1908, 405–29) and Charlotte Eaton (*A Last Memory of Robert Louis Stevenson*, 1916, expanded as *Stevenson at Manasquan*, 1921). Falconer-Salkeld also gives the text of a never-before-reprinted newspaper article, "Pleasantly Recalled Is R. L. Stevenson's Brielle Stay," *Asbury Park Evening Press*, New Jersey, 1924 [no more precise date is given], brought to her attention by John E. Belding, borough historian of Brielle, NJ (41–42); a 1909 sketch of catboats of the type that RLS was fond of sailing (42); and a reproduction of a postcard showing the "Union House, Brielle, New Jersey" (43). The 1924 article draws upon recollections of various local residents. The hotel proprietor Henry W. Wainwright, with whom Will H. Low had arranged the Stevensons' stay, was by then dead, and the hotel had burned down "ten years ago." But his wife and daughter were still living. They recalled that RLS usually wore a poncho, spent the remarkable sum of $8.00 on a telegram to Fanny in San Francisco, and was visited by the sculptor Augustus Saint-Gaudens to model his hands for the medallion begun the previous autumn in New York City. A four-line poem by RLS on the daughter's early-morning piano playing is quoted, no doubt from the copy that RLS gave to her:

> Little girls should take and tackle their pianos Early in the morning, as I like to hear you do; Stick to early rising, and the various other virtues Looking out for early folks, will come and stick to you.

A somewhat different version of this poem, "Early in the morning I hear on your piano," also four lines, probably from a draft in one of RLS's notebooks, first appeared in *Poems Hitherto Unpublished*, ed. George S. Hellman (2 vols., Boston Bibliophile Society, 1916) II, 32. It is poem CXXXIV among the "New Poems" in the Tusitala Edition *Poems* (1924) II, 181.

Falconer-Salkeld herself gives a history of Union House, which had been built shortly before the American Civil War by a local sea captain and mariner, John Maxon Brown, and was in Stevenson's time owned and run by Brown's daughter Adelaide and her husband, Henry Wainwright. The hotel accommodated 100 guests during the summer, and Wainwright also ran "a combined store and post office." The actual location was Union Landing, in the borough of Brielle, however, not Manasquan, which was close nearby.

Manasquan was probably used in giving the location (by Will H. Low, RLS, and others) as it was better known.

Three of the essays originally given at meetings of the Social Science Association of Hawaii and compiled to celebrate its centenary (1982) are on RLS. Frank Pleadwell's "The Cruise of the Silver Ship" (1 Dec. 1947) offers a detailed account of RLS's first South Seas cruise, aboard the *Casco* from June 1888 to January 1889. (Pleadwell's annotated typescript, with many of his working materials, is in the Hamilton Library, University of Hawaii–Manoa.) O. A. Bushnell's " 'Our Good Friend Mr. Stevenson' " (6 Oct. 1980), quotes previously unpublished recollections of RLS's visit to the leper settlement at Molokai in May 1889 by one of the nuns who lived there. Also included is an essay by Harold W. Kent, "Charles McEwen Hyde" (1 Feb. 1954), anticipating his book-length study published in 1973.

In this book, a well-researched biography and defense, *Dr. Hyde and Mr. Stevenson: The Life of the Rev. Dr. Charles McEwen Hyde including a discussion of the Open Letter of Robert Louis Stevenson*, Kent examines details of Hyde's career, of Father Damien and the leper settlement at Molokai, and of RLS's impassioned open letter of denunciation and its aftermath. RLS and Hyde met in Honolulu in 1889, and Hyde at that time wrote on RLS's behalf in aid of a scheme, later abandoned, to continue their Pacific travels on the missionary ship the *Morning Star*. Kent summarizes and quotes at length from this correspondence. He also quotes from the private journal of Dr. Nathaniel B. Emerson, president of the Board of Health in Honolulu, opposing RLS's wish to visit the leper settlement at Molokai—"once we make exception to him others will want to also go over and play tourist"—and describing King Kalakaua's asking him, as a personal favor, to let RLS go because of the good publicity that RLS could generate for their efforts. Emerson acceded to this request, and RLS visited the settlement from 22 May to 28 May 1889.

Hyde's comments on Father Damien, in a private letter of 2 August 1889, were in answer to questions from a fellow-minister H. F. Gage, who published them in a religious newspaper without Hyde's knowledge or permission, with a few comments of his own explaining the context; Hyde sent a similar letter to the American Board of Commissioners for Foreign Missions, in Boston. His comments attracted little attention outside the religious press. Several months later, they were reprinted in the Sydney *Presbyterian* for 26 October 1889, without Gage's comments, and it was in this form that they came to RLS's attention in Sydney in February 1890.

In discussing RLS's letter on Father Damien, Kent concerns himself almost entirely with individual points of fact rather than with larger questions of outlook, ethos, or attitude. Not surprisingly, therefore, he finds Stevenson wrong about both Hyde and Father Damien, and in almost every detail. This was the same position that Hyde himself took in his own reply to RLS,

"Father Damien and His Work," in the *Congregationalist*, published in Boston on 7 August 1890 (included here as an appendix). Although RLS may not by then have seen Hyde's reply in its entirety (and may have changed his mind when he did), RLS, in a letter to Andrew Chatto (2 December 1890, Letter 2284—first published in 1995 in the Yale Letters and thus unknown to Kent) outlined a wish to put out a new edition of his open letter, at his own expense, and to include in it Hyde's reply and a letter from the United States vice-consul in Honolulu published at the same time. "It was my single object to defend the character of Damien," RLS planned to say in the preface, and Hyde's reply is "a conclusion to [the] controversy not more gratifying than it is unusual." Nothing came of this plan, however.

R. L. S. in the South Seas: An Intimate Photographic Record (1986) is a compilation by Alanna Knight of excerpts chiefly from RLS's letters and *In the South Seas* on the voyages of the *Casco*, the *Equator*, and the *Janet Nichol* interspersed with more than 90 photographs of RLS and the people and places that he saw. The photographs are very poorly reproduced, however, probably because they come from published versions rather than the original prints. One reproduction even includes the caption in the prior publication. Details of date, place, and persons depicted are generally lacking, as is any indication of source more specific than the Edinburgh City Libraries. The placement of the photographs is occasionally haphazard: pictures from Hawaii and Samoa appear amidst the text on Tahiti, for example.

Lowell D. Holmes (2001) retells the stories of the cruises of the *Casco*, the *Equator*, and the *Janet Nicoll*, chiefly from the well-known accounts by RLS, Fanny, T. M. MacCallum (*Adrift in the South Seas*, 1934), Belle (*This Life I've Loved*, 1937), and Lloyd (*An Intimate Portrait of RLS*, 1924). Oddly, Holmes makes little use of RLS's works or letters, and, although they were by then available, he neither cites nor uses the Yale Letters. As a result, his is a largely external account. Holmes leaves mostly unexamined the effect of the South Seas on RLS's writing or imagination and his place in the literary, political, and cultural cross-currents of the 1890s, in the Pacific and elsewhere. A major contribution is Holmes's detailed history of each vessel and the splendid reconstructions of the hull, deck, and sail plans by the maritime historian and artist Raymond Aker (249–65). Holmes also presents a physician friend's analysis of RLS's health, arguing that he probably did not have tuberculosis but the chronic bronchial condition known as bronchiectasis (247–48).

After a cruise from Hawaii and a long stay in the Gilbert Islands (now Kiribati), RLS, Fanny, her son Lloyd Osbourne, and Fanny's then son-in-law Joe Strong arrived in Samoa aboard the trading schooner *Equator* on Saturday 7 December 1889. Practically the first person they met was the colorful American merchant and trader in Samoa, Harry J. Moors

(1854–1926). As Moors recalled in his book on RLS, *With Stevenson in Samoa* (1910), he had heard from Joe Strong about six months earlier (the *Equator* party sailed from Honolulu on 24 June 1889) that they might call at Samoa. Little more than a month after their arrival, RLS had bought land and was arranging with Moors to have a house built. In two wonderfully informative, illustrated articles based chiefly on family sources among Moors's descendants in Samoa and in Germany, Joseph Theroux adds much to our knowledge of Moors's background and his more than 50 years residing in Samoa.

Born in Detroit, Moors graduated from high school in San Francisco in 1870 and took a job there as a mechanic at the Union Iron Works. But by 1875, at the age of 21, he had found his way to Samoa, where he was to reside for the rest of his life. In Samoa, Moors worked briefly in agriculture before securing an appointment from the Hawaiian Board of Immigration as an agent attempting to supervise the labor recruiting trade, much of it illegal and nearly all of it deceptive and exploitive, in the Gilbert and Wallis Islands. "He learned the languages, picked up stories and later wrote two novels about blackbirding [a deceptive labor practice that amounted virtually to kidnapping]: *Tapu*, and *The Tokanoa, or the Wizard Doctor of Marakei*." (Neither novel was published, and both manuscripts are still in family hands. But microfilm copies are in the Pacific Manuscripts Bureau, National Library of Australia, Canberra, under slightly different titles from those recalled by the family for Theroux: "Tapu: A Tale of Adventure in the South Seas," and "The Tokanoa: A Plain Tale of Some Strange Adventures in the Gilberts." Both are assumed by the library to have been written some time after 1910.)

By the early 1880s Moors had given up the labor trade and entered into what proved to be a short-lived partnership (of three years) with the German trader E. A. Grevsmühl, a partnership that RLS mentions in recalling Grevsmühl as "the most infamous trader in these waters, the man who is accused of paying natives with whist counters" (RLS to Charles Baxter, 20 March 1890, Letter 2219). Theroux plausibly suggests that Grevsmühl's practices (and notoriety) led both to Moors's withdrawing from their partnership and to RLS's comment a few years later on Moors's seemingly far from spotless background—this, and RLS's also not understanding that it was not as a blackbirder but as a government agent that Moors had been involved in the labor trade.

On 10 July 1883 Moors married the niece of the Samoan wife of "a Scotsman named Johnson." Her nickname was Nimo, she was then 20 years old, and she had spent the previous five years in Scotland with her aunt and her aunt's Scottish husband Johnson before their return to Samoa. "Moors was smitten at once with her looks and recently acquired Scottish brogue." The attraction was mutual, and after a series of teas, "Moors, in his forthright

American way, exploded, 'Marry me, Nimo! I love you. You will never regret it.' '' They were married 43 years; six children were born to them, of whom five survived to adulthood; and Moors died in Nimo's arms at the age of 72. His last words were: ''Oh, Nimo, how I have loved you!'' Moors's two sons from liaisons earlier, Kane and Mark, were always acknowledged and were part of the family from the start.

By the time that the Stevensons arrived in Samoa for the first time six years later, at the end of 1889, Moors had created a substantial and flourishing business:

> His general store [in Apia] carried garden tools, canned goods, vegetables and fruits from his gardens, and clothing. He bought copra from the traders on Savaii [the largest of the Samoan islands], a rough lot known in those days as the Savaii Squires which included such notables as Crooked-Neck Bill (so-called because he had survived a hanging in England and looked as if he had), Spanish Mike, Monkey Jack Stowers and Petelo Dick. He made his calls in his own boat, sailing into lagoons on much more agreeable errands than in Gilbertese days.

From the moment that the Stevenson party arrived, Moors took them under his personal supervision. He found them accommodation, showed RLS and Fanny the land that they eventually bought at Vailima, and was their general contractor for building there. RLS and others recalled Moors, who was 35 when they met, as a wonderful talker, with a wide and deep knowledge of the South Seas (and of Samoa in particular) that made him an invaluable and accurate source for RLS's *A Footnote to History* (1892). He was also, says Theroux, ''a voracious reader'' and the ''overflowing bookshelves [of his library] . . . included hundreds of volumes of well-thumbed Dickens, Thackeray and Shakespeare.'' From a previously unpublished manuscript presumably still in the Moors family, Theroux quotes Moors's own recollection how ''evening after evening we [Moors and RLS] lay side by side in lounge chairs, a bottle of whiskey between us, and we discussed British and American literature from its earliest beginnings with Fielding and Smollett.''

In 1892, taking up the suggestion of ''a wandering actor and ex-Rough Rider named Charles Mason Mitchell,'' Moors sent to the Polynesian Village exhibit at the Chicago World's Fair in 1893 a group of Samoans, hiring Joe Strong (whom Belle had divorced bitterly in July 1892) to manage the group and take it on tour elsewhere in the United States after the World's Fair closed. Moors himself took the show on the road again various times, including a trip to the Louisiana Purchase Exposition in St. Louis in 1904 and an eighteen-month-long tour after that. Theroux here follows J. C. Furnas's account in his *Anatomy of Paradise* (1948), 419–21, and he reproduces from Furnas the wonderful 1904 advertisement of ''Moors Picturesque South Sea

Islanders . . . 50-MEN AND GIRLS-50 . . . Novel, Original, Highly Instructive and Very Attractive.''

Whatever may have been his relations with Fanny Stevenson earlier, from mid-1892 onward Moors seems to have made no secret of the fact that he took Joe's side in the divorce; and in his book 15 years later Moors made it clear that in his opinion RLS was continually oppressed by the women at Vailima, by Fanny Stevenson above all. He was also concerned that Stevenson was being misrepresented, as he says in a previously unpublished letter quoted by Theroux: ''I was surely Mr Stevenson's earliest friend in Samoa and probably his most useful one. It annoys me just as it would worry him to see him set up in various quarters as a kind of Saint, and I assure you that he never made any such pretensions.'' According to Theroux, RLS left to Moors ''a photo of himself,'' now owned by his grandson Oliver, ''and his Caligraph typewriter . . . [which] has been lost.''

Moors was not only Stevenson's principal builder. Before, during, and long after Stevenson's five years in Samoa, he was also deeply involved in Samoan politics, in various roles including spy, arms smuggler, and self-appointed emissary to Washington. After the partition of Samoa in 1899, the German governor Dr. Wilhelm Solf ''repeatedly asked Moors to be a member of the newly-formed Government Council,'' an appointment that he declined, as he also did, in the same year, a high chiefly honor from Mata'afa. In the worldwide influenza epidemic that reached Samoa in 1918, the New Zealand colonial governor Robert Logan did not quarantine the ship *Talune* even though it had been quarantined in Fiji, this because (according to Theroux) Logan ''had friends he wanted to invite ashore.'' The result was that 8,000 natives died in Samoa, more than one-fifth of the population. Moors looked after as many as he could, and he lost his son Mark in the epidemic. Moors soon afterwards ''documented Logan's abuses and mismanagement [not only in this crisis but generally] and sent the details to Wellington, saying: 'Believe me, these papers come from a determined man, who fears no official, governor, or diplomat, and who will pursue his course to a finish and on schedule.' '' Logan was soon afterwards removed.

From Moors family sources, Theroux reproduces three previously unknown and unpublished items: a portrait of Moors as a (very handsome) young man in his mid-twenties, about the time that he arrived in Samoa; a 1920 photograph made in New Zealand of his wife, Nimo; and the opening lines of Moors's manuscript account of his self-created diplomatic mission to Washington in 1892 and his brief career as an arms smuggler. From *The Cyclopedia of Samoa, Tonga, Tahiti, and the Cook Islands* (Sydney: McCarron, Stewart, 1907; facsimile rpt. Papakura, NZ: R. McMillan, 1983), he reproduces photographs of Grevsmühl and of Moors's two-story wood-frame store in Apia around 1900, ''with railway line down to the waterfront and the family home upstairs,'' this juxtaposed with a recent photograph of the same building and a matching companion building beside it, also built by Moors.

All of these details vindicate Theroux's belief that Moors was ''something more than a footnote.'' More important, they remind us what an odd, remote, and un-classifiable place Samoa, no doubt like the rest of the South Pacific, must have been in the early 1890s when Stevenson was there. He had no need to invent memorable characters such as John Wiltshire in ''The Beach of Falesé'' (1892), although he did. They were everywhere around him.

Taking as his title the name by which Harry J. Moors and his stores were known, Misimoa—Mr. Moors—Damon Salesa offers a readable, accessible summary chiefly of the information in Paul Theroux's articles and Moors's own *With Stevenson in Samoa* (1910). This is augmented from other sources by some additional details on the 1893 World's Fair and on the more recent history of the family. Salesa also includes from his own copy of *The Cyclopedia of Samoa* . . . (1907) a reproduction of the photo first published there of Moors's store in Apia.

Neil Macara Brown describes RLS's copy of *The Journal of Sir Walter Scott From the Original Manuscript at Abbotsford*, 2 vols. (Edinburgh: David Douglas, 1890), now in his collection. In a letter to the bookseller James Bain, 6 October 1890, RLS asked to be sent ''as soon as it comes out, Douglas's new edition of Scott's diary'' (Letter 2256). Both volumes have RLS's Athenaeum Club visiting card as a bookplate, the covers are varnished, and there is one mark, a line in the margin beside Scott's comment on his *Life of Napoleon*: ''Better a superficial book, which brings well and strikingly together the known and acknowledged facts, than a dull and boring narrative, pausing to see further into the mill-stone at every moment than the mill-stone admits'' (I, 60).

Girolamo Pieri Nerli (1860–1947) was an Italian-born painter who became a major figure in the artistic life of Australia and New Zealand during the 1880s and 1890s. He spent 13 weeks in Samoa, from 12 August to 9 November 1892, and during the three weeks from 15 September to 4 October (RLS finished writing *David Balfour* on 26 September) he painted his now famous portrait of RLS. Greatly refining and extending the 1988 catalogue by Peter Entwisle and his associates, described later in this review, Roger Neill (1997) suggests, convincingly, that the version painted from life is the one now in the Scottish National Portrait Gallery, Edinburgh, and that there are four copies, not two as had previously been believed: at Yale, in the Writers' Museum, Edinburgh, in a private collection, and in the Edinburgh Academy. This last copy is unsigned and may be a reference copy that Nerli painted to help him with the others. All of the copies were made after RLS's death, the last of them probably in 1910. Neill also discusses the pastel and watercolor portraits, Nerli's Samoan landscapes, and his use of photographs as source material. A real high point is Neill's discovery, also at the Edinburgh Academy, of a splendid watercolor portrait of RLS: "a fine, energetic work, spontaneous in its brushwork, very much like a sketch." It is "possibly the earliest of any of the RLS portraits by Nerli—an exploratory study, with, in its bottom right-hand corner, a tiny vignette of a Samoan girl in a landscape setting, quickly painted to try out an effect" (50). A black-and-white reproduction is one of the 20 illustrations in this attractive little book of 75 pages, the first reproduction of this watercolor except (at postage-stamp size) in a RLS tourist brochure published in 1989.

Two recently discovered letters from the Australian artist Arthur Streeter to the photographer Henry Walter Barnett, 18 January and 9 February 1910, are presented by Roger Neill ("Mr. Nerli," 2000) and strengthen his previous guess that "the majority of Nerli's 'Samoan' paintings were produced over a short period of time around 1910 in one or another of Barnett's [studio] properties in Knightsbridge" and that Nerli and Barnett had not known each other before then. For example, the two very similar pastel portraits of RLS, at Princeton and in the Scottish National Portrait Gallery, both "[s]eem to be based on a photograph of Stevenson taken by Barnett in Sydney in 1893—the year after Nerli's visit to Samoa" and thus were probably done in London much later. Although they are signed and dated 1892, Nerli's seven watercolors of Samoan landscapes and three portraits of native Samoans are unknown until "years after that date."

Peter Entwisle, Michael Dunn, and Roger Collins's *Nerli: An Exhibition Of Paintings and Drawings* (1988) is a beautifully produced catalogue of an important, inclusive, major exhibition of Nerli's work. It is augmented with a detailed survey of Nerli's life and career and a detailed and informative initial catalogue raisonné listing and describing more than 204 of his works. Of these, 21 date from Nerli's visit to Vailima in 1892, although as Roger Neill has shown many of them, including versions of his portrait and his pastel sketch of RLS, were executed much later, in Australia and in London (items 74–93; 125–41).

Roger Neill's beautifully produced exhibition catalogue, *Legends: The Art of Walter Barnett* (2000), offers an authoritative short survey of the career of the Australian photographer Henry Walter Barnett (1862–1934). Barnett's innovation as a portrait photographer was in lighting: "Barnett introduced dramatic sidelights, emphasising bone structure and skin texture, allowing his sitters' individual personalities to shine through." He also took many more photographs than was usual in a given sitting, and in a variety of poses, and in his portraits of men he used as little retouching as possible. Barnett began by working for (and learning from) other photographers, notably I. W. Taber in San Francisco and William Downey in London. In 1885 he returned to Australia and opened the Falk Studios, where he photographed RLS in Sydney in 1893. In 1898, Barnett moved to London and spent the rest of his career there. In 1910, he helped Nerli sell to Lord Guthrie in Edinburgh paintings and watercolors based on Nerli's visit to RLS at Vailima in 1892. These are now in the Writers' Museum, Edinburgh. More than 30 of Barnett's photographs are reproduced, including RLS (1893), Mark Twain (1896), Elinor Glyn (1903), Dame Nellie Melba (1903), Ignaz Jan Paderweski (1904), Auguste Rodin (1904), Sarah Bernhardt (1910), and Thomas Hardy (ca. 1909).

British-born sculptor Allen Hutchinson (1855–1929) is the subject of an excellent article by Elizabeth C. MacPhail. Hutchinson followed his interests in sculpture and in faraway cultures and races to Canada, the United States, and in 1888 to Hawaii. He shared a studio with Jules Tavernier (1844–1889) and became friends also with Joe Strong. During RLS's stay in Hawaii in 1889, RLS commissioned, and persuaded King Kalakaua to sit for, a life mask by Hutchinson. RLS took it with him eventually to Samoa, where it was displayed at Vailima. After RLS's death it was kept by Fanny Stevenson and in turn by her daughter Belle (who sold almost everything else) and it is now in the Stevenson House Collection, Monterey State Historic Park, California.

During his second visit to Hawaii, in September and October 1893, RLS sat for a bust of his head by Hutchinson, who also made a plaster cast of his right hand. "I am being busted here by a party named Hutchinson. Seems good," RLS wrote to Sidney Colvin on 23 October 1893, Letter 2641. Hutchinson's own account is in his article, "Stevenson's Only Bust from Life: Recollections of the Sittings at Waikiki," *Scribner's Magazine*, 80 (Aug. 1926): 140–43. The bust, in clay, was first shown in Honolulu in the first exhibition of the Kilohana Art League, which opened 5 May 1894. It was offered at $35.00 and did not sell. Early in 1895, shortly after RLS's death, Hutchinson took the bust of RLS's head and other works of his to London. The bust was exhibited at the New Gallery, London, in 1895; a photograph of it, from this exhibition, appears in the *Book-Buyer*, New York, June 1897. The bust was then stored for more than 30 years, until 1926, at Hutchinson's brother's home in England. From this original, Hutchinson then had five or more bronze copies made, these known copies now being at Yale, the Honolulu Academy of Arts, the Huntington Library, the National Portrait Gallery (London), and the RLS Silverado Museum. Hutchinson then sold the original bronze to the Stevenson Society of America. It was formally presented by him at the Society's annual meeting at Saranac Lake, on 27 August 1927, and it remains in the collection there. Hutchinson sent the plaster cast of RLS's hand to his brother in 1901. It is now at Yale.

In *A Dream of Islands: Voyages of Self-Discovery in the South Seas* (1980), Gavan Daws, a major historian of Hawaii and the Pacific, offers lively, informed narratives of the South Seas experiences of the missionary John Williams, Herman Melville, the political dreamer Walter Murray Gibson, RLS, and Paul Gauguin. Of RLS's politics in Samoa he writes:

He was no real politician; there remained too much of the naughty boy or the impressionable romantic in him. Just the same, after he was dead, it turned out that he had been as right as any politician about the situation in Samoa. . . . He was right on the incompetence of the treaty officials, right on the idea that a three-power regime was unworkable, right in predicting that one nation would eventually rule (it turned out to be Germany, of which he would not have approved), and right on Mata'afa, who was eventually brought back from exile by the Germans to be what all along he maintained he was, "king of the Samoans."   (206–07)

Taking up his central theme, Daws brings out with balance and insight the all-important meaning that RLS's way of life in Samoa had for him, "a poor, sad, fantastic young man who had grown older, more stable, richer, happier, come into his kingdom in this great house on the mountain":

Stevenson made it the work of decades to disinherit himself from his father's profession, from his own forced choice of a career in the law, from his family's Calvinism, from middle-class respectability, from Edinburgh, then from England, then from Europe. All this took him as far as Samoa. And once there, he began reconstituting this inheritance in a way that suited him: the household at Vailima, patriarchy, property, political responsibilities, prayers in the great hall, collected works to go on the library shelves. His mother lived with him, and all around the wall of the great hall were family faces—a portrait of his grandfather, a bust of his father, Stevenson and Fanny painted together by the American John Singer Sargent, Saint-Gaudens's bronze medallion.   (208–09)

(The bust was actually of RLS's grandfather Robert Stevenson, one of several copies including the one at Bell Rock lighthouse, removed late in the 20th century when the light was automated. The portrait of RLS's father by Sir George Reid is now in the Scottish National Portrait Gallery.)

As Daws observes, "Everything came back to family, which figured in Stevenson's last years both as millstone and bedrock. He talked of wanting to retire but being unable to because his family depended on him. Yet he depended on them, drew sustenance from them" (214). Surrounded as he now was by multiple families—of blood, marriage, and an acquired Samoan household—and the head of all of them, RLS finally took up writing the history of his own family, able at last to count himself as an equal and taking pleasure in the mere sense of connectedness: "I see like a vision the youth of my father, and of his father, and the whole stream of lives flowing down there far in the north, with the sound of laughter and tears, to cast me out in the end, as by a sudden freshet, on these ultimate islands. And I admire and bow my head before the romance of destiny" (Dedication of *David Balfour*, 1893).

Kenneth Starr Mackenzie's dissertation, "Robert Louis Stevenson in Samoa, 1889–1894" (Dalhousie University, Canada, 1974), is based on amazingly thorough research in the records and correspondence of the British

Foreign Office and the Colonial Office, from which unpublished sources he quotes at length, and in other archives from the London Missionary Society to the Turnbull Library, Wellington, New Zealand. RLS was considerably more respected, and considerably more a subject of concern, than it appeared at the time or from the outside. Mackenzie's research has been fully assimilated, both for the background as well as for specific points, into the annotations of the Yale Letters. But his study remains worth reading for his presentation of the whole picture, including RLS's political views earlier than in Samoa, and for details that do not come up in the letters.

Two of the most important of these are the following:

(1) RLS's friend E. W. Gurr eventually became the Associated Press representative in Samoa, and on his retirement in 1927 Gurr recalled that throughout "the latter end of 1894" he and RLS, both of them "advocates for the preservation of the Samoan race and its institutions," collaborated on a general plan for Samoa. The central point was the union of the "rival royal factions in Samoa"—a point that, as Mackenzie notes, "was the one thing that RLS had advocated consistently from the start" (409). The result survives as a three-page draft beginning of a letter to the British consul Berry Cusack-Smith, in the hand of Isobel Strong, offering their plan as a possible solution to "the present deadlock of Samoan affairs" (Beinecke 3121, quoted complete in Mackenzie, 470).

(2) In a full-page article in the *British Weekly*, 20 October 1898, the then-former British consul in Samoa Berry Cusack-Smith, never a friend of RLS, blamed RLS's "meddling" for encouraging rebellion and warfare in Samoa and depicted him as an unwitting traitor to his friend, the Samoan chief Mata'afa Iosefo. According to Cusack-Smith, RLS had encouraged Mata'afa to fight rather than accept another chief, Malietoa Laupepa, as the supreme native chief in Samoa, as had in effect been mandated by the Berlin Act in 1887. In May 1891, Mata'afa had moved to the village of Malie, symbolically asserting his own claim. But in July 1893, having considerable support of his own, Mailetoa chose to attack Malie and other villages sympathetic to Mata'afa, in an attempt to settle the question. After some delay, the consuls finally intervened. Mata'afa and his supporters had retreated to the nearby Samoan island of Manono, and the consuls, themselves aboard, sent three warships in support of Malietoa's own attacking forces and compelled Mata'afa to surrender to the captain of the British warship *Katoomba*. Mata'afa and ten of his chiefs were exiled to the island of Jaluit, in the Marshall Islands, under German control, and were not allowed to return to Samoa until after Malietoa's death in 1898. This was, of course, after RLS's death much earlier, at the end of 1894. (For details, see especially Ernest Mehew's notes to Letters 2331, 2595, and 2606.)

Although letters of refutation appeared in the next few weeks from Graham Balfour, Sidney Colvin, and the Rev. W. E. Clarke, Mackenzie has also found and quotes extensively from an even better source, an interview with Mata'afa himself by the American reporter A. W. Pickard, "A Defense of RLS by his Friend King Mata'afa," *Saturday Evening Post*, 22 April 1899. RLS always urged him against war, Mata'afa said, "[but] my people would not let me. . . . Before I went to Malie I met Malietoa secretly, and asked him to let the people choose one of us for King, promising to stand by the result. He would not give me an answer." Cusack-Smith's accusations about RLS are entirely false, says Mata'afa. "He was my dear friend, I loved him, and to hear such things said of him makes me feel as bad as I felt the day the news of his death came to me in Jaluit. Do not let the American people believe this about Tusitala [RLS]" (qtd. in Mackenzie, 426–27).

Mackenzie's excellent short study (1979) complements his dissertation in focusing on Stevenson's aims and actions locally in Samoa, in which RLS's letters to the *Times* and his correspondence with the Foreign Office were a part, but not the only one. Stevenson locally was practical, adaptable, and focused on developing policies that benefited Samoans, Mackenzie writes. "His . . . was a clear and level-headed attempt to obtain for the Islanders as much autonomy as he thought possible within the framework of what he recognised as the irresistible juggernaut of Western civilisation." Especially notable was his determination, by the time he first reached Samoa at the end of 1889, "never again to be a silent onlooker at [imperialism's] apparently inexorable march," as he felt that he had been at times during the 1880s. Now, he wanted to shape it.

Although at first he echoed "the anti-missionary tenor of much of contemporary ideas," RLS soon found the missionaries essential in his anthropological research and, as his personal acquaintance with them and their work grew, he became a sympathetic and active ally. Of the older "pioneer" generation RLS became acquainted with George Brown, James Chalmers, and S. J. Whitmee. Of their younger colleagues he was especially fond of the Rev. W. E. Clarke, "a man I esteem and like to the soles of his boots; indeed, I prefer him to any man in Samoa and to most people in the world" (RLS to Sidney Colvin, 15 June 1892, Letter 2415; qtd. 161).

Politically, RLS quickly realized that nothing good would, or could, happen for the Samoans without an end to the divided form of whites-only government imposed by the Berlin Act and the incompetence of the officials who comprised it. German, British, and American consuls governed together with an appointed President of the Municipality of Apia, a Chief Justice of the Supreme Court, and three Land Commissioners who were to investigate and settle claims. In late 1891, RLS rushed to complete *A Footnote to History* (1892) in time for it to be ready for a hoped-for review of the Berlin Act of 1889 that it had been agreed could occur at any time from mid-1892. This review did not occur, but as a result of his activity RLS came to prominence locally and successfully brought agreement at a meeting of European and American residents devoted to the same end. In April and May 1892 he worked hard, and according to Mackenzie "very nearly succeeded," in securing the participation of the rival chiefs Mat'afa Iosefo and Malietoa Laupepa jointly in a new government of Samoa. The fact that the opposition of the European officials prevailed convinced RLS, Mackenzie says, "that if he was to have a voice in Samoan affairs he too needed some sort of official position." Through Sidney Colvin, who later downplayed RLS's interest, and others in London, RLS tried hard to be appointed British Consul, but, despite rumors over the next couple of years, the British government does not seem to have considered him seriously for the position.

In early 1893, Mackenzie writes, "as part of an increasing usurpation of authority by the three Consuls" it seemed likely that new regulations were to be implemented, by force if necessary, and that they might cause "a general uprising." RLS responded, this time, by writing directly to Lord Rosebery, and he found that compared to his letters to the *Times*, "his letters and deeds were heeded by the Foreign Office to a far greater extent than by the public at large." The plans were dropped, probably in part due to RLS's activity, but by April it was apparent that Mata'afa's supporters were planning a revolt against the officially backed head of state, Malietoa. Once more, RLS was not successful, either in his active personal engagement urging immediate British intervention to prevent bloodshed or, later, as a mediator between the Samoan chiefs. War came, briefly, in July, leading to Mata'afa's defeat and enforced exile. At this point, Mackenzie notes, RLS might well have given up in frustration or disgust, but he did not. In Honolulu in October 1893 and throughout what proved to be the last year of his life, 1894, he continued actively to mediate between the chiefs and a new set of officials; and at the time of his death he was working with E. W. Gurr on a comprehensive general plan for Samoa. This plan, discussed in Mackenzie's dissertation, is summarized in my previous entry. As Mackenzie notes of this plan in "The Last Opportunity," "[s]eventy years later, when Western Samoa became independent, the path it followed was startlingly similar to the plan of union [RLS] had espoused."

Derek W. Ferguson's main point in his M.A. thesis, "Robert Louis Stevenson and Samoa: A Reinterpretation" (1980), is that RLS favored British annexation of Samoa, on which subject he mentions a note in Fanny's journal on 17 November 1891 (cited to Neider, ed., *Our Samoan Adventure* [1956], 117, but this reference is incorrect), RLS's letter to the *Times* published 4 April 1893 (Letter 2537), and his letter to Poultney Bigelow, 16 July 1893 (Letter 2603). Ferguson doubts that the purported interviews with RLS published in Arthur Johnstone, *Recollections of RLS in the Pacific* (1905), 90, 92, ever took place. Johnstone was editor of the *Pacific Commercial Advertiser* in

Honolulu at the time of RLS's second visit to Hawaii in September and October 1893. On 21 September 1893, he published a summary of an interview with RLS that he said had taken place the day before, the day of RLS's arrival in Hawaii. Ferguson thinks, apparently on the grounds of its contents alone, that it is "highly unlikely that this interview ever occurred" (204). The second interview appears only in Johnstone's book, not in any of the newspapers at the time. Both purported interviews, in Ferguson's opinion, are in fact paraphrases of remarks in RLS's letter to the *Pall Mall Gazette*, a letter written in July and published on 4 September 1893.

Chapter 20 in Deryck Scarr's engaging *Viceroy of the Pacific: The Majesty of Colour: A Life of John Bates Thurston* (1980) is titled "Deport all novel writers" and refers to Thurston's wonderful comment, made facetiously and privately in a letter, 11 May 1892, touching on the many difficulties that existed in Samoa. And it shows that RLS was on his mind at least six months before Thurston published, as British High Commissioner, Western Pacific, his ill-fated "A Regulation . . . for the Maintenance of Peace and Good Order in Samoa," 29 December 1892. Thurston's view, developed over time, was that RLS was mostly interested not in Samoa but in boosting his own personal reputation in England—a view with which his superiors found that they did not agree—and he was chiefly provoked less by RLS than by the part-Samoan William Yandall (or Yandell), who was urging Samoans to pay no taxes to Malietoa, a campaign in which RLS himself was active behind the scenes, although Thurston never knew this. In addition, Thurston was anxious to find a means of punishment less drastic than deportation. Scarr quotes letters from Thurston to RLS in 1893 and 1894, after the Regulation and its withdrawal, that show an effort on both sides to compose their differences and to work together toward the same ends—as Thurston did, for example, in trying to have Mata'afa (then still a prisoner) moved from the Marshall Islands to the less alien locale of Fiji. Scarr's detailed biography is a valuable supplement to the thorough treatment of the affair in the Yale Letters (Letter 2537 especially) and in the work of Kenneth Starr Mackenzie.

In his "John Bates Thurston: Grand Panjandrum of the Pacific" (1979), Scarr offers an excellent short account of Thurston. "He knew the South Sea Islands from the viewpoint of trader, Consul, planter, labour recruiter," Scarr writes. "Most of all, though, he was a far-sighted, highly individual man who hated cant-theories of white supremacy. He thought that the racism of his fellow European settlers towards Islanders would bring both white and black to ruin. Fiji and the Western Pacific were not white men's countries" (95).

My own discussion, *Robert Louis Stevenson and Samoa After 100 Years* (1999), is a detailed and annotated expansion of a talk given at Vailima, 3 December 1997, on Stevenson's political and social views about Samoa. Four themes stand out: (1) Samoans must recognize the present day as a time of crisis, a time when the very survival of the Samoan people really is at stake. (2) They must also learn that there is such a place as Samoa, as a distinct entity, and that it must be competed for, lest non-Samoans take it away, as they surely will if Samoans do nothing. (3) Samoans must become less lazy. The arena of competition is the land, and it is no longer enough merely to inhabit the land: one must cultivate it actively. (4) Finally, Samoans must recognize and act strongly, decisively, and together, as a society, against the genocidal dangers of disease—including leprosy, which had come to the Pacific centuries earlier, possibly from China, and venereal diseases, which had come to the Pacific in the last century from Europe and the Americas. Hawaii was a sad example of what might soon occur in Samoa. RLS wished to see (and believed was possible) an end to the "horrid white mismanagement" of Samoa that had come from the Berlin Act of 1887—in the short run, by means of a British protectorate and reconciliation between Mata'afa and Malietoa—and eventually in the emergence of Samoan self-government based on *fa'a Samoa*, the indigenous laws and customs of the people.

In a very thoroughly researched discussion, *Robert Louis Stevenson and the Colonial Imagination* (2004), Ann C. Colley finds Stevenson's political and other views during the six and one-half years that he lived in the Pacific so rooted in the particulars of each situation as to make generalizations all but impossible. A term such as imperialism, she maintains, is often used in a manner that "weighs down the nuance and topples the delicate and shifting freight of life and thought" (7). "No slide show, not even a dissolving representation in which one representation blended into another, could represent the multiple perspectives and ambiguities of Stevenson's Pacific fiction," she writes at the end of her own first chapter, on Stevenson and missionaries (44). At the end of a 35–page chapter titled "Stevenson's Political Imagination" (135–78), almost half of which is devoted to a minute account of RLS's difficulties with the Rev. Arthur Claxton (153–70; see Letters 2463 and 2466, and Ernest Mehew's detailed annotations), Colley offers little more than the cheerful observation that studying Stevenson's politics in Samoa "gives one a sense of a personality who can be described adequately only through a long list of incompatible adjectives . . . volatile, tenacious, generous, authoritarian, playful, and legalistic" (171).

Colley has a highly commendable and all but unshakeable determination to stick to the facts—to engage the details rather than speculate on larger questions—and this is at once the strength and a considerable limitation of her book. She teases from an amazingly thorough study of the Yale Letters, from previously unpublished letters by others chiefly at Yale, from letters and records in the London Missionary Society, and from other sources, detailed and interesting separate chapter-length essays on Stevenson and missionaries, native and colonial dress, memory, photography and magic-lantern shows, politics, and missionary magazines aimed at children. More than two dozen illustrations from a wide range of sources are also included, nearly half of them previously unpublished photographs still in the original albums now in the Writers' Museum, Edinburgh, taken mostly by Lloyd Osbourne during RLS's several Pacific voyages and in Hawaii and Samoa.

This is a major contribution of information, pictures, and detail. The trouble is that the next step is not taken. The details are never brought together into conclusions, or even proposals. Stevenson's relation to what we now think were among the leading issues of his time—imperialism, race, gender, and primitivism—comes across, in Colley's account, as having been so specific to situations and so variable as perhaps to vindicate the charge (made at the time and possibly reinforced inadvertently by the Yale Letters showing the great seriousness with which Stevenson took his own every move) that in Samoan politics, at least, he never amounted to anything more than an egotistical dilettante meddling, on no fixed or predictable principles, in matters that he did not understand. Colley does not argue this view, but on the other hand she never engages it, either in support or refutation.

Colley's literary comments are few, and they are only lightly supported by detailed readings. Her preference is to offer figurative generalizations that are meant to link the works with her chosen topics.

> In a sense the choice to go without shoes makes its mark in many of Stevenson's South Seas tales where he seems, for a moment, to abandon the romantic story telling and adventure traditions of his Scottish fiction . . . [to] feel the sand and the sting of the island cultures' complexities with the nakedness of his bare feet. He walks through these tales unshod, more open to the rough edges of experience and to the realities of life on the beach.   (57)

Thus Colley writes at the end of her first chapter, on Stevenson and missionaries. To the extent that there is a literary conclusion here at all, it is supported only by half a dozen insightful but sketchy pages on *The Ebb-Tide* and "The Beach of Falesá," and these are only partly related to the missionary theme at hand.

In the last chapter, an attempt is made to connect *A Child's Garden of Verses* (1885) with missionary magazines aimed at children, of which (as Colley concedes) there is no indication that Stevenson ever read. He also knew plenty of real children in foreign lands—his Balfour cousins—and had no need of magazines to become aware of them. This attempt is soon given up, however, in favor of a much more interesting general discussion of the ways in which the missionary enterprise influenced home perceptions of primitive peoples. So impressive are Colley's energy and her passion for detail—her book is full of interesting information, much of it new—that one can only regret that she is unwilling to take the next step and advance and defend some general conclusions. (Colley is also the author of *Nostalgia and Recollection in Victorian Culture* [1998], in which some of the topics in the present book are anticipated and two of the chapters are about RLS. Both of these are chiefly critical rather than biographical, however, and are therefore included in my Checklist of Criticism.)

After 20 years as a foreign news correspondent, Gavin Bell spent nine months in 1992–93 visiting places in the western Pacific where Stevenson had lived or visited (Australia and New Zealand are not covered), gathering material for what is now a pleasant, engaging travel book (1994). RLS is more pretext than subject, of course, Bell's focus being on his own adventures, but he brings in RLS's experiences often and well. Bell notes how little seems to have changed in the natural landscape since Stevenson's time, and how much in ways of life and social conditions, not always for the better. Suicide among young people is a major problem in Samoa, for instance, and all over the western Pacific local economies and indigenous cultures are struggling. Bell visited Samoa just as work was beginning on the repair and restoration of Vailima after catastrophic hurricanes in two successive seasons, and he gives a good brief depiction of the damage that has now been remedied in a spectacular restoration.

Between the chapters of a once-over-lightly, almost gossipy, popular biography of RLS, Hunter Davies intersperses accounts of his own visits to many of the places that RLS lived in or visited, writing these in the form of letters to RLS. Like Gavin Bell, Davies arrived in Samoa just as work was beginning on the restoration of Vailima, and he gives informative sketches of the people, plans, and project that then lay ahead. Davies also tells of meeting (in Honolulu) Robert Van Dyke, a collector of Hawaiiana and RLS, and he passes on, without comment, a number of Van Dyke's claims about his collection (262–69). Among these are a claim of having 173 letters by RLS and 225 by Fanny, including one to her sister Cora telling of giving birth, at Vailima, to a stillborn boy at seven months whose remains they buried in a tin box below the cellar (265). Van Dyke also told Davies that he had "the original version of the cable which Fanny sent to Louis" asking him to come to California in 1879. "I do not wish to reveal the details, as I will probably publish it myself some day," Van Dyke said (266). He also showed Davies what he said was some of Fanny's personal jewelry, some of it supposedly authenticated by its appearance in photographs of Fanny (267). Robert Van Dyke died in Honolulu in August 2004, but none of the artifacts that he told Davies (and others, including myself) that he owned has been found among his effects. As far as I can tell, only the jewelry (which I have also seen) and possibly Isobel Field's annotated copy of her autobiography, *This Life I've Loved* (1937), was ever seen by anyone—and the location of these items too is now unknown.

Sarah Gadd's digital manipulations of nine photographs from Stevenson's residence and travels in the South Pacific show an astonishing command of reflections, textures, perspectives, colors, and light. As exhibited at the Scottish National Portrait Gallery, the images were each considerably more than a meter wide and comparably high, and each is beautifully reproduced in the catalogue of the exhibition (2003). Duncan Forbes comments in his introduction to the catalogue that in juxtaposition with the originals they "[draw] special attention to the visual legacy of Stevenson's travels" and "the dense interdependence between photography and tourism during the nineteenth century. . . . There is a sense in which these photographs provide both the most reliable, and most fantastic, traces of Stevenson's life in the South Seas." Elaine Grieg contributes a good sketch of Stevenson's travels and of the photographs themselves. All of the photographs are in the Writers' Museum, Edinburgh, and two are published here for the first time. Grieg also includes, in color, the beautiful engraved map showing RLS's travels that was first published in vol. 20 of the Edinburgh Edition (1896) and, slightly modified, in Balfour's *Life* (1901), II, facing 41, from which source it appears here.

Stevenson's Health

In an article in the *Journal of the American Medical Association* (5 April 1971) Myron Schultz notes that during the summer and autumn of 1885, in the months just before *Dr. Jekyll and Mr. Hyde* was written, cocaine was being hailed in Britain (and America) as a wonder drug. An editorial in *The Lancet*, July 1885, remarked that "the value of this wonderful remedy seems only beginning to be appreciated" and commented on its use to treat hay fever and asthma. In September, the use of cocaine in a solution applied to the larynx was described, also in *The Lancet*. (Fanny Stevenson is said to have been a devoted reader of *The Lancet*, possibly at this time as well as later, but there are no exact references.) This article, Schultz suggests, "could have decided the issue" and caused RLS's physician at Bournemouth, Dr. William Bodley Scott, to begin treating RLS with cocaine—at the very time that he was conceiving and then writing *Dr. Jekyll and Mr. Hyde*. Side effects of a great increase in physical energy and "the syndrome of lilliputian hallucinations" may also be present in RLS's very hard, rapid work on the story and in his attributing to his "Brownies" a major role in creating both this story and "Olalla," written in November and December. Nevertheless, Schultz concedes, there is no mention of cocaine either in Scott's writings or in Stevenson's letters, and its addictive properties did not become known for another year, after both stories had been published.

Commenting on Schultz's article in "The Star-Spangled Powder: Or, Through History with Coke Spoon and Nasal Spray" (*Rolling Stone*, 17

August 1982), Charles Perry doubts that *Dr. Jekyll and Mr. Hyde* has any relation to cocaine use—by RLS or in the story. Neither RLS nor Dr. Scott mentions cocaine, only morphine, and in the story the changes are chiefly in appearance, not personality, energy level, or metabolism. Neither RLS nor Arthur Conan Doyle fits the pattern of a heavy user of cocaine.

According to the Jungian commentator Barbara Hannah, *Dr. Jekyll and Mr. Hyde* was not only a story. It could have given RLS ''an extraordinary insight into his own split and suffering psyche, if only he could have seen the connections.'' ''It is quite clear that the fatal end of the story was the direct result of an *unwillingness to suffer*'' on Jekyll's part—''also a mistake of Stevenson himself.'' In *Weir of Hermiston*, the younger Kirstie is ''the novel's anima figure *par excellence*.'' But unfortunately, ''for some reason which we cannot possibly know, an answer seem[ed] demanded of him [RLS]. Apparently it was too much for him, further than he could go.'' He was ''confronted with that most difficult task for all men: having it out with the anima.'' And so he died, with the book unfinished.

In *The Strange Case of Robert Louis Stevenson*, Richard Woodhead, a retired physician, imagines in first-person reminiscences what five of RLS's physicians (Andrew Clark, Karl Ruedi, Thomas Bodley Scott, E. L. Trudeau, and Bernhard Funk) would say recalling their acquaintance with Stevenson as a patient. He chose this approach, Woodhead says, because early on

> I came to realise that it would be impossible to prove or disprove a diagnosis of tuberculosis, and that a factual account of Stevenson's illness would be unsatisfactory and inconclusive. By that stage, I knew that the exact diagnosis was less important than the way the illness was perceived by Stevenson, by his family, and by the many doctors who treated him. As a physician myself, I was particularly interested in the personality, attitudes, and prejudices of the doctors. (x)

Woodhead makes good use of the Yale Letters and sticks closely to the very limited information that RLS's doctors left behind. In fact, much must simply be gathered from what Stevenson and others reported that the doctors said. Woodhead's re-creations have some life, and he puts in as many details as he can about his five physicians, from a good list of sources that he includes at the end. Nevertheless the result, on purpose, is more a series of character sketches than a study of RLS's medical history. Woodhead does not offer, even as an appendix, an illness-by-illness medical chronology, although given his medical knowledge and his research on RLS he would have been well placed to do so. This would also have helped demonstrate his assertion that ''[t]he story of Stevenson's illness offers more questions than answers.''

Commenting on a remark earlier in the journal *Science* on the correlation between fourth-digit length and psychiatric depression and the suggestion that RLS was an example, Thomas M. Daniel notes that RLS was very seldom depressed even though his long fingers do fit the description. Against the suggestion that RLS had bronchiectasis but not tuberculosis, Daniel remarks that "bronchiectasis is commonly associated with clubbed fingers, which Sargent's portrait demonstrates Stevenson did not have; tuberculosis is not or only rarely associated with clubbed fingers." Daniel comments elsewhere on RLS, in his *Captain of Death: The Story of Tuberculosis* (1997).

Consisting of 253 pages, including 28 pages of index, M. A. Banfield's self-published collection of what he calls health biographies (2001) is a gathering of biographical details about RLS's and Fanny's illnesses, and about their general health, with comments by the author and quotations from older and current general medical books. The book is a scrapbook rather than an argument, however. It is hard to tell what conclusions, if any, we are meant to draw, and the reliance on secondary sources (often unreliable or distant ones) for health data is troubling. Diagnoses are always implicit in the descriptions in secondary accounts. The evidence itself, moreover, is rarely clear and is never written in our own medical language. Nor do we have any actual medical records, only what Stevenson, Fanny, and sometimes others such as RLS's uncle Dr. George Balfour reportedly said to lay persons at the time, describing their opinions of the problem. Although Stevenson's mother noted during his childhood that he had several attacks of "croup," that word is not mentioned. Nor is the fact that the official medical definition was at that very time changing because of the range of conditions to which it was being applied. Nothing is said about the author's own medical knowledge except that he is the author of a lengthy study called *Posture Theory*. And he seems to have overlooked Fanny Stevenson's remark in 1905, prefacing *A Child's Garden of Verses*, quoted by Ernest Mehew in the Yale Letters: "When the child [RLS] . . . took after cold, antimonial wine [sherry containing tartrated antimony] was administered continuously for a period extending into months; 'enough' said [RLS's uncle] Dr George Balfour, 'to ruin his constitution for life' " (Letter 814, annotating RLS's comment that "I had too much of the latter [antimonial wine] when a child").

According to Alan E. Guttmacher, MD, and J. R. Callahan, RLS's medical history "suggests the possibility" that rather than tuberculosis or bronchiectasis he and his mother both had Hereditary Hemorrhagic Telangiectasia (HHT), a genetic abnormality of the blood vessels that causes "persistent respiratory complaints, recurrent pulmonary hemorrhage, and cerebral hemorrhage." Unfortunately, there is "no clear evidence" that either RLS or his mother exhibited such characteristic symptoms of HHT as frequent nosebleeds (epitaxis) or red or purple lesions of the skin and mucous membranes (telangiectasis), or that either suffered from cerebral or gastrointestinal hemorrhages in addition to their respiratory complaints—unless, of course, one includes the apparently isolated cerebral hemorrhage from which RLS died. The fact that RLS's mother's diary contains no entries in the last five months of 1867 (and that some entries in early 1868 are in the opinion of these authors incoherent or are written in a wobbly hand) is taken by as proof of "his mother's hitherto unreported but apparent stroke, at age 38 years"—and this is then taken to show that she probably had HHT. With this analysis contrast RLS's own comment at the time in a letter to his cousin Bob, 29 December 1867, Letter 39: "Mamma has been anything but well. A *very* bad sore throat. We were in quite a fright about her; but I am glad to say that she is a good deal better now." Her illness was diagnosed as diphtheria (there is no reference to or evidence of a stroke), and during intervals from his first-year classes at the University of Edinburgh RLS spent much time helping her in a long convalescence. So much for the all-important idea that she had a stroke. The authors conclude: "Although it appears possible that Stevenson had HHT, currently available information is insufficient to prove the diagnosis." Given that Stevenson's mother did not have a stroke in 1867, the case is clearly much weaker than that.

Book-Length Biographies

Because so much has been added, year by year, to published knowledge of Stevenson during the last 35 years, above all by the publication of the Yale Letters (1994–95) but also by reference works such as my own *The Prose Writings of Robert Louis Stevenson: A Guide* (1980) and by new editions and other studies, book-length biographies are here taken up in the order of their publication, from David Daiches's *Robert Louis Stevenson and His World* (1973) to Claire Harman's *Robert Louis Stevenson: A Biography*, published in the United States as *Myself and the Other Fellow: A Life of Robert Louis Stevenson* (2005).

David Daiches's earlier short study (1947) on RLS remains a landmark in Stevenson criticism, and in *Robert Louis Stevenson and His World* (1973), he offers a fine brief biography of RLS illustrated with more than 100 well-chosen and well-reproduced photographs, sketches, and portraits. There are a few errors, generally traceable to other sources. The manuscript page from *Weir of Hermiston* is in Belle's hand, not RLS's; Fanny and RLS met after, not before, the canoe trip described in *An Inland Voyage*; and her divorce was granted in December 1879, not in the spring of 1880. But this book is on the whole an immensely useful and engaging contribution—the only short biography of RLS until Ernest Mehew's contribution to the *Oxford Dictionary of National Biography* (2004) that rivals Janet Adam Smith's insightful biographical sketch in 1938.

The list of 16 titles "by the same author" facing the title page of what proved to be James Pope-Hennessy's last book shows the breadth of his interests. These ranged from the West Indies to Richard Monckton Milnes, from Queen Mary to Hong Kong, and from there to Anthony Trollope. Pope-Hennessy's well-written account of RLS (1974) is sympathetic and insightful, and he brings in many details from letters and other sources that were, in the early 1970s when he did his research, accessible only by going to the libraries that held them. The text lacks the author's final revisions and corrections—the pioneer of antiseptic surgery Joseph Lister is always called Liston, for example—and there are also no annotations. Among the illustrations are attractive sketches of the Stevenson family home at 17 Heriot Row (33, 37) and the cottage at Swanston (78) done expressly for this book by John Knight.

In *Journey to Upolu: Robert Louis Stevenson, Victorian Rebel* (1974) Edward Rice offers a pleasant although not always accurate short biography of RLS greatly enhanced by more than 50 photographs and other illustrations, almost all of them from photographs, sketches, books, and other materials in the Beinecke Rare Book and Manuscript Library at Yale. (A copy of Rice's book, annotated by a member of the library staff with catalogue numbers for the Yale items, is on reference shelf in the reading room at Beinecke.) Among the most notable are sketches by Belle of scenes during the fighting in Samoa in 1893, illustrating articles by her (112, 132), and previously unpublished sketches, from Belle's notebook, of RLS (122) and Fanny (123) at Vailima. The sketch of Fanny is captioned "The critic on the hearth listening to the reading of *St. Ives*" and is dated Vailima, 20 October 1894. Rice also juxtaposes, on facing pages, John Singer Sargent's April 1887 painting of RLS seated in a wicker armchair (Taft Museum of Art, Cincinnati) and a photograph of RLS by Hawker, Bournemouth, showing him in almost the identical dress and pose, also seated in a wicker armchair—a resemblance that is so close as to suggest that Sargent may have relied heavily on the photograph for his painting (96–97).

The most remarkable feature of Paul Binding's regrettably bland and often ill-informed extended lecture about RLS (1974), seemingly aimed at adolescents, is that he spends fewer than one-tenth of his pages on the six and one-half years of Stevenson's life after he left Saranac Lake in April 1888. As it happened, these years amounted to almost one-third of Stevenson's short life after his first paid publication, "Roads," in 1873—the years that he spent in the Pacific, as a celebrity, trouble-maker, head of a household, and as Tusitala. Somehow these years, too, should have been brought more fully into the depiction. There is no index, nor are there footnotes or illustrations apart from decorative chapter headings.

Jenni Calder's *Robert Louis Stevenson: A Life Study* (1980) is a detailed, thorough, and painstaking biography, and she makes good use of the information in RLS's letters: especially those at Yale and in the National Library of Scotland (many of them, at the time that she wrote, unpublished or available otherwise only in Sidney Colvin's edition), and also those in *RLS: Stevenson's Letters to Charles Baxter*, ed. DeLancey Ferguson and Marshall Waingrow (1956). The story of RLS's life is here, but unfortunately not much of the excitement. For example, about the map that RLS says that he drew at Braemar that led to *Treasure Island* we do not hear his own words: "it was elaborately and (I thought) beautifully coloured; the shape of it took my fancy beyond expression; it contained harbours that pleased me like sonnets; and with the unconsciousness of the predestined, I ticketed my performance *Treasure Island*" ("My First Book," 1893). Nor do we hear, from RLS's first letter to Henley about the book, of which RLS had by then written only two chapters: "If this don't fetch the kids, why, they have gone rotten since my day.... [T]he trouble is to work it off without oaths. Buccaneers without oaths—bricks without straw" (24 August 1881, Letter 843). "Louis received £100 for it," Calder says of the book-form publication. RLS told his parents the same thing on 5 May 1883, but in the following words: "I have had a great piece of news. There has been offered for *Treasure Island*—how much do you suppose? ... A hundred pounds, all alive, oh! A hundred jingling, tingling, golden, minted quid" (Letter 1098). Nor do we learn that when the map for the frontispiece went astray it was redrawn in the Stevenson engineering office in George Street, Edinburgh, or that (in RLS's words) "my father himself brought into service a knack he had of various writing, and *forged* the signature of Captain Flint and the sailing directions of Billy Bones" ("My First Book," 1893). Instead we have two paragraphs by Calder trying to state the importance of the book in Stevenson's career—"It was in more than one respect a breakthrough for Louis to have written an adventure story with a juvenile audience in mind. It was his first full-length piece of fiction." (172)—and in literature: "*Treasure Island* has lasted as a children's adventure story. It rests uneasily in that genre. It has always been a story that adults have relished perhaps more than children" (173).

Dr. Jekyll and Mr. Hyde is treated in a similarly distant and abbreviated manner (220–23): without, for example, RLS's own remark to his wife on the need for money, that "I drive on with *Jekyll*, bankruptcy at my heels" (20 October 1885, Letter 1472); or his similar comment to F. W. H. Myers that "the wheels of Byles the Butcher drive exceedingly swiftly, and *Jekyll* was conceived, written, rewritten, re-rewritten, and printed inside ten weeks" (1 March 1886, Letter 1567); or his comment in "A Chapter on Dreams" (1888), prompted by journalists' questions about the story, that "I had long been trying to write a story on this subject, to find a body, a vehicle, for that strong sense of man's double being which must at times come in upon and overwhelm the mind of every thinking creature" ("A Chapter on Dreams," 1888).

Kidnapped, chiefly written the following spring and early summer, is dispatched in four sentences, having been the subject of a brief but strictly literary discussion earlier comparing it to *The Black Arrow* (1883)—a discussion that most readers, I think, will unfortunately take to mean that *Kidnapped* was written in 1883 and 1884 (188–91). In her later comment Calder says only this:

> The serialisation of *Kidnapped*, again in *Young Folks*, in the summer of 1886 brought solidity to Louis's reputation. The published edition soon followed. The quality of the book was recognised at once, though Louis was not entirely happy about it and shook his head over public gullibility. If the public liked something, he complained to Gosse, it was a sure sign that it was bad. (224).

RLS is so good at telling the story of his own life, so anxious (as it were) is he to take control of the narrative, that biographers must indeed be careful not to become mere editors of the autobiography that he was always writing in his letters and essays. Calder, I think, has gone too far the opposite way, controlling almost the whole story herself, chiefly but not only by paraphrasing what might well have been quoted and by letting RLS himself speak only sometimes, and rarely or never in his own most exuberant, colorful, and self-celebrating moments.

Nicholas Rankin's *Dead Man's Chest: Travels After Robert Louis Stevenson* (1987) tells the story of his following RLS, roughly a century afterwards, from Edinburgh across the United States to the South Seas. But it is considerably more than an engaging then-and-now travel book. It is that, of course, but Rankin also tells the story of RLS's own experiences, and he does so insightfully, for the most part accurately, and well. He has done his research, and with skills no doubt developed in his work as a features journalist for the BBC, Rankin presents it unobtrusively and yet in depth throughout. He has even stolen a march on Stevenson scholars in being the first to ask if the New York Public Library had the passenger list of the *Devonia*, on which RLS first travelled to the United States in 1879. The original is in the National Archives in Washington, DC, but from the microfilm in New York Rankin gives for the first time an account other than RLS's own of his fellow passengers: 51 in the Saloon; 22 in the Second Cabin, where RLS was ("fifteen Scots including six women, four Norwegians, a Dane, a Swede and an Irishman") and 183 in the Steerages ("Scots, Irish, German, Scandinavian, one Russian"), these with a great range of occupations from brewer, carpenter, and chemist, to watchmaker, weaver, and wife (123–24). Full disclosure also obliges me to state that among the Stevenson specialists Rankin writes about in telling of his own travels, now just over 20 years ago, is myself.

Ian Bell's *Robert Louis Stevenson: Dreams of Exile* (1992) is a vigorous, readable, and personal book. A journalist and native of Edinburgh who, like RLS, attended the University of Edinburgh, Bell obviously likes his subject and enjoys writing about him. His book is personal, too, in the sense that it is RLS's temperament and personality—and his Scottishness—that command center stage. The works are inseparable from the life, and both are inseparable from RLS's Scottish environment and background. Swanston, for example, where RLS's family leased a cottage from the City of Edinburgh throughout the years of his late teens and twenties, was not only a pleasant retreat in the foothills of the Pentlands:

> Swanston was good for his health and his imagination. He read Dumas there, explored the places where the Covenanters had camped, and grew to know the shepherds and the farmers. The road to the cottage took him past Hunters' Tryst and its inn, familiar to Walter Scott and Allan Ramsay. . . . Swanston was important, too, for tuning his ear to the speech of the countryside, the old speech of the Lothians that was to give him his version of Scots.   (68–69)

The old shepherd John Todd, recalled by RLS in "Pastoral" (1887), was a Swanston companion and friend. "Todd's speech survived, if nowhere else, in *Weir of Hermiston*," Bell writes, "but there were many more like him around Swanston" (69). *Dr. Jekyll and Mr. Hyde* is in a rich literary tradition of books about doubles—Bell mentions, appropriately, works by E. T. A. Hoffman, James Hogg, Poe, Dostoevsky, and others—but it also comes from, and is in large part about, his own Scottish background:

> Louis had had first-hand experience of Victorian hypocrisy in Edinburgh; he had grown up in a divided city; he had often stepped out of the respectable New Town into the disinhibited, amoral semi-underworld of the Old. He knew well enough that respectable "burgesses" haunted the brothels. He understood the emblematic nature of a figure like Deacon Brodie in his own city, and he knew how Calvinism divided the world into the elect and the damned. In the play, Brodie calls his nocturnal self "my maniac brother who has slipped his chain."   (191)

Bell's focus on RLS and, to a lesser extent, on Fanny, and on their mutual relations as husband and wife, causes him to say less than he might have said about RLS's immediate, contingent social milieu. His religious views and his thoughts on such topics as primitive cultures, missionaries, politics, and government are simplified rather than probed. And his importance in, and shaping by, the rapidly-changing late-Victorian literary scene makes its appearance here almost only in RLS's friendship with Henry James. These, however, are minor defects in a thoughtful and engaging biographical study.

Frank McLynn's biography of RLS (1993) was among the first of many works occasioned by the centenary of Stevenson's death in 1994. It is, unfortunately, an unpleasant, tiresome book, chiefly because of McLynn's nonstop denunciation of the motives and behavior of almost everyone who was on intimate terms with Stevenson, starting with his mother and continuing through everyone else after that. No turn, as they used to say in vaudeville, is left unstoned. No good deed, no matter how well-intentioned, goes unpunished by McLynn's relentless negative commentary. "While Thomas was away on business," he writes of Stevenson's parents during his childhood, "Maggie herself was often *hors de combat* with illness and she suffered particularly badly from ill-health during 1850–62—the precise time when her son most needed her" (13). RLS's nurse Cummy, for all her kindness, "was also a religious maniac . . . forever frightening him with stories of ghosts, body-snatchers, and Covenanters . . . careless, ignorant and superstitious talk that exacerbated the child's night horrors." "Her good intentions led straight to Hell in the most direct sense," McLynn concludes generously, "but perhaps to understand her benighted inadequacy is to forgive all" (14–15, 17). "The 'problem' with Lloyd's eyes (doubtless an inability to focus on engineering books) which led Fanny to express fears that he might eventually go blind were soon cleared up when his mother suggested he go on a tour of the West Indies to recuperate—at RLS's expense, of course" (272). "Those who had studied Fanny closely would have been able to predict the next stage: psychosomatic illness. After working with gusto throughout October, almost immediately after her 5 November diary entry she began to complain of blinding headaches and took to her bed; by Christmas 1890 the headaches had become earache. Louis went back to supervising the labour gang" (386). It doesn't take long to perceive that the misbehavior is almost entirely attributed—a feature less of the deeds or persons themselves, whose motives might have been quite otherwise, than of McLynn's own perspective. Self-serving, RLS-victimizing motives—Colvin's "treacherous, venal and unscholarly attitude" (414), Lloyd's "leech-like battening on Stevenson" (440)—are the only motives that McLynn ever seems willing to infer.

McLynn's account is also unpleasant for the number of times that he misunderstands and thereby misrepresents the actual record of what occurred. It is not only his interpretations but his facts that are wrong. Ernest Mehew commented on a great many of McLynn's errors in a long article in the *Times Literary Supplement*, "The True Stevenson," 2 July 1993, 15–16, recalling in his title McLynn's spiritual ancestor George S. Hellman, to whom all smoke meant fire, every silence was a suppression, and everyone was taking advantage of RLS. J. C. Furnas, "SOS for RLS," *American Scholar*, 63 (Autumn 1994), 619–22, added his own list, remarking also that McLynn's was a "tendentious, ill-tempered book." McLynn's lapses are more annoying than Hellman's, however, because they so often come wrapped in the appearance of scholarship.

"[I]t is clear that Stevenson contracted syphilis in these years," McLynn writes of the early 1870s, in a bold, confident passage not even commented upon by Mehew. "[RLS] speaks of 'the unblushing daughters of Venus' who 'did him a lasting injury' and boasts that no woman of easy virtue could ever resist him'' (56). A lengthy footnote citing sources, seemingly of these and other remarks, is attached (519, n.27). But neither the quoted words nor the assertion that ends this sentence appear in any of the sources that McLynn cites, in this note or elsewhere. RLS never used the phrase ''unblushing daughters of Venus''; and when he did use a phrase like it, in an entirely unrelated context, his phrasing was ''The French have a romantic evasion for one employment, and call its practitioners the Daughters of Joy'' (''Letter to a Young Gentleman Who Proposes to Embrace the Career of Art,'' 1887). Nor did he use the phrase ''a lasting injury'' done to himself (or anyone else), or anywhere say or imply that he ever had syphilis. The actual source of these memorable words about the Daughters of Venus is not RLS but J. A. Steuart, another spiritual ancestor of McLynn's. ''What quality, what feminine grace and charm in 'Claire' caught and held his roving and rather volatile affection?'' Steuart asks about the young RLS. ''In those sordid resorts there were other girls, unblushing 'daughters of Venus,' ready enough with their appeal to primitive man, and some of them did Stevenson a lasting injury. But 'Claire' alone inspired and kept his love'' (*Robert Louis Stevenson Man and Writer: A Critical Biography*, [2 vols., 1924], I, 131). RLS's remark on his irresistibility, for which there is also no citation in McLynn, actually exists, in a letter of early 1880, but it has nothing to do with whether he contracted syphilis, or when, or how (RLS to Sidney Colvin, mid-February 1880, Letter 688).

Brendan Bevan's *Robert Louis Stevenson: Poet and Teller of Tales* (1993) is a businesslike, uncritical recital of familiar facts and anecdotes pulled together chiefly from well-known published sources. Bevan has visited most of the places where Stevenson lived or visited in Scotland and the United States, but he says little about them. He rarely quotes Stevenson and rarely ventures beyond the obvious in his assessments. His annotations (184–90) are imprecise and often wrong. The National Library of Scotland, in Edinburgh, is more often than not called the ''National Library of Edinburgh''; there is only one manuscript leaf of ''An Old Song,'' which was first published, anonymously, in 1877, and the correct name of its location is the Edwin J. Beinecke Collection; the manuscript of ''The Enchantress'' is there also. The 12 pages of mostly familiar black-and-white photographs, chiefly from the Writers' Museum, Edinburgh, are large and well reproduced.

''There has been no shortage of books about Stevenson, and they keep coming,'' Philip Callow remarks in the first sentence of the foreword to his *Louis: A Life of Robert Louis Stevenson* (2001). ''What is the fascination?'' (ix). Unfortunately, Callow never answers his own question, either in his own voice or by letting Stevenson's fascination shine on its own. Although he describes the Yale Letters as ''exemplary'' and as constituting ''a biography in itself, with its annotations and linking commentary'' (311), Callow actually quotes Stevenson's letters—and his works—only rarely, and he shows no hesitation in disregarding the letters and their annotations whenever he likes. For example, Ernest Mehew's annotation of a letter in November 1879 mentioning ''difficulties about Belle'' is that ''[t]he 'difficulties' must have been the discovery of Belle's marriage to [Joe] Strong'' (Letter 665, n.2). Earlier, Mehew gives the actual date of their marriage, 9 August 1879, and he mentions that there is a copy of the marriage certificate at Yale (Letter 643, n.3). Callow, however, prefers the version of Frank McLynn. He scoffs at ''those who maintain that Belle was already married'' by the time that RLS arrived in Monterey at the end of August, and with McLynn he also prefers Lloyd's second wife Katharine (not Katherine, as Callow spells it) Osbourne's statement in 1922 that the commotion in November, or whenever it was, occurred because Belle proposed marriage to RLS, which according to McLynn's speculation occurred at Monterey (138).

Instead of a portrait of Stevenson, in Stevenson's own words and those of people who knew him, or a biography based on a fresh reading of the letters, works, and recollections, we are offered a narrative in which Stevenson is always a figure in the middle distance, a person about whom Callow is telling us interesting things that he has heard somewhere: for example, that Stevenson arrived in Monterey by stage, wearing ''a blue serge suit and a bowler hat'' (130); in fact, he arrived by train and no one knows what he was wearing; or that a collaborative novel with Fanny Stevenson called *The Dynamiters* influenced Jack London's *The Star Rover* (198). *More New Arabian Nights: The Dynamiter* is not a novel, but a joint collection of linked stories; and why the influence on Jack London matters is never explained. The result is a middle-of-the-road compilation of interesting tidbits and biographical opinions (and errors) from others. ''The definitive biography is now surely the splendid book by Frank McLynn,'' Callow writes, in an odd comment from a fellow biographer. ''One cannot imagine it being surpassed in the forseeable future'' (311).

John Cairney is a professional actor who has played RLS many times, and this fact is no doubt the source equally of the strengths and the weaknesses of his book, *The Quest for Robert Louis Stevenson*. Stevenson is a character, in all senses of the word, and he is brought to life in a brisk narrative full of anecdotes. ''I have thought myself so vividly into the life of Robert Louis Stevenson,'' Cairney remarks, ''that he lives in my imagination like an old friend'' (187). Cairney has done his homework, albeit rather uncritically, and he has a fine eye for the picturesque and memorable. For example, during Sidney Colvin's Christmas visit to RLS at Mentone in 1873, Colvin recalled in his headnote to one letter, RLS

had no adequate overcoat, so it was agreed that when I went to Paris I should try and find him a warm cloak or wrap. I amused myself looking for one suited to his taste for the picturesque and piratical in apparel, and found one in the style of 1830–40, dark blue and flowing and fastening with a snake buckle.
(Letter 213, n.1)

Cairney slightly abridges and rewrites this comment, to emphasize the piratical style and the snake buckle. RLS commented at length on the cloak after it had arrived, in two letters to his mother (13 February, 20 March 1874, Letters 240, 253)—not, as Cairney says in a harmless mistake, in a letter ''to his father'' (44). Cairney deftly combines RLS's comments in these letters into one quotation, as if both came from the same letter. He omits RLS's comments on his health, his request to be sent some Scottish sheet music, and his remarks on his general frugality, to which the cloak is of course a great exception. From RLS's remarks in the second letter he drops the last sentence and all but the second clause of the first sentence, to end his quotation on the high note: ''it is a fine thought for absent parents that their somn possesses simply THE GREATEST VESTMENT in Mentone'' (Letter 253). The result is a fast-moving, upbeat narrative—almost the script for a one-man show—unfortunately at the expense of being, also, a portrait with any depth or balance. Everything is foreground.

Stevenson's work is also missing, as if the fact that he was a writer was all that needed to be said. *Dr. Jekyll and Mr. Hyde* is discussed in a page consisting of one paragraph on the Edinburgh cabinetmaker Deacon Brodie as the historical source and a shorter on one on the writing of the book at the end of 1885, its reception, and its importance:

> To achieve this masterpiece, Stevenson put his own contradictions under the aesthetic microscope and in creating the monster out of himself, he at last spat out the devil of hypocrisy that had been tormenting him since adolescence. The novel marks the maturing of Robert Louis Stevenson.   (110)

This eloquent and unelaborated comment is immediately followed by Cairney's telling of the death of RLS's father in May 1887, more than a year after *Dr. Jekyll and Mr. Hyde* was published, and the further comment that ''by this time, *Jekyll and Hyde*, his 'bogie tale', was taking the United States by storm and he [RLS] was eager to go there and taste his new celebrity'' (110). The comment itself is not quite accurate. But what is really astonishing about this passage is that the year 1886, in which *Kidnapped* was written and published, is missing altogether, not only here but anywhere other than in three lines in a reference chronology at the end of the book. Unless there are anecdotes to be had, or memorable remarks to be quoted, there is apparently no need to say anything. There are also many errors—the main street in

Monterey is actually spelled Alvarado, and Fanny's lawyer friend Timothy Rearden had nothing to do with her divorce, least of all as a visitor to RLS in Monterey—and there are neither notes nor an index. There is, however, a good selection of photographs from the collection in the Writer's Museum, Edinburgh.

William Gray's *Robert Louis Stevenson: A Literary Life*, despite its title, is not a biography but work of criticism. For this reason, I have commented on it in my Checklist of Criticism only.

Claire Harman's *Robert Louis Stevenson: A Biography* is not a break-through study, nor is it meant to be. But it is of great importance nevertheless. Harman presents the known facts capably, accurately, and well, with apposite quotations and thoughtful but prudent comments of her own. Although she seldom strays from the well-trodden pathways, she has read the Yale Letters carefully and completely and has had the courage to follow them where she thinks they lead. It is not as if others have not seen or used the letters, unpublished though they may have been at the time. The difference is that all of the letters, whether at Yale or in Sydney or known only through an auction catalogue, are now readily accessible, between hard covers, for reading and rereading, correctly dated and unabridged, and with Ernest Mehew's detailed and useful annotations. Harman's is the first full-length biography to show the good effects of this fact.

The results are sometimes breathtaking, as if a window has been opened or a corner has suddenly been turned. No one has ever before suggested, for example, that in going to California RLS was putting into effect, on his own and unaided by Fanny or anyone else, ''a plan which had been simmering for a long time, to set off for America and try to sort out the situation with Fanny once and for all'':

> There is a tradition that his precipitate departure was triggered by a telegram from California, but the truth seems to have been rather less romantic than that, and though he understood Fanny to be ill, rushing to nurse her does not seem to have been his primary motivation. . . . It was his own misery that he wished to curtail, and the endless passive waiting.   (170)

Although Harman maintains that it is only ''a tradition'' that Stevenson's departure was due to his receiving news that Fanny was desperately ill, no one in a position to know ever suggested otherwise, and the story was told and retold often in the 30 years after Stevenson's death. In his first letter to Sidney Colvin from the United States he adds a postscript, the following day, on the state of Fanny's health as he now knew it from a letter or telegram that was waiting for him in New York and that he called for; and he does so as if Colvin already knew that Fanny's health was in danger (18 August 1879, Letter 643). Harman herself immediately backs away from her own contention, however, revising her initial statement about the simmering plan by saying that "though he understood Fanny to be ill" this was not his "primary" motivation in departing. Harman also finds herself obliged to offer a weak cause (his parents were about to be "safely out of the way in Cumberland") in place of a strong one (Fanny, or someone, asked for help) and to impose a hierarchy among the motivations—a book to be written, Fanny's health, the chance of resolving at last the impasse in their relations—where there was probably only a jumble, in which no one of the motivations would have sufficed.

In Harman's account, for the first time, and thanks to the completeness and detail of the Yale Letters, a biographer has kicked free, albeit only for moments here and there, of the romance and the counter-romance alike. In Harman's biography, the facts are beginning again to speak for themselves, and the story that they tell is a richer, subtler, truer, more complicated, and much more convincingly human story than has been told hitherto—at least since Balfour, Masson, Janet Adam Smith, and J. C. Furnas all told the same complex story, for other generations, years ago.

Harman is willing to speculate: for example, when she suggests (I think wrongly) that Fanny may have been pregnant with RLS's child when she returned to San Francisco, and to her husband Sam Osbourne, in August 1878 (159, 253–56). That Fanny was still unable to ask Sam for a divorce more than a year later, and probably would not have done so had RLS not gone to California, suggests that confrontation was the very last thing that she would have sought. In a very labored discussion elsewhere (211–15), Harman suggests that while RLS "seems never to have had any homosexual experiences whatever," even so "[he] can't have been unaware of the homo-erotic forcefield he generated, that 'power of making other men fall in love with him' " to which Andrew Lang referred in a tribute after his death. Harman here seems to me confusing sexual attractiveness with charisma or personal magnetism. But Harman tries to base her speculations on facts and shows a desire to make sense of them, avoiding innuendoes or dark hints.

Although there are some minor errors of detail, it is a tribute to Harman's care that nearly all of them have been corrected in the paperback editions. Henley's racier version of his lines on RLS (qtd. 117), "Ballade R. L. S." (Beinecke 7243), for example, is no longer referred to as unpublished. It first appeared in Edward Cohen, *The Henley-Stevenson Quarrel* (1974), 18, from which source I have quoted the first stanza in my comments on Cohen's monograph elsewhere in this survey. One picture caption unfortunately remains incorrect. As the bars on the windows remind us, the picture of Jules Simoneau and Jules Tavernier conversing is not of "Simoneau's peeling and ramshackle hostelry in Monterey" (after 172) but of the disused jail nearby.

Harman's 16 pages of black-and-white illustrations are well chosen and very well reproduced.

Fanny Stevenson and Isobel Strong

In a short introduction to a reissue of the biography of Fanny Stevenson by her younger sister Nellie Sanchez, her niece Ysabel Matney corrects from family sources a number of minor errors. The text itself is the same as in the original edition.

Although written more than 40 years after the events and demonstrably more faithful to the spirit than to the letter, *This Life I've Loved* (1937), by Fanny's daughter Belle (by then Isobel Field) captured much of the footloose Bohemian atmosphere of Grez and of San Francisco in the 1870s and early 1880s, of Hawaii in the last decade of the monarchy, and of Vailima as she experienced and liked to remember it. The new edition (2005) corrects some typographical errors in the original and includes some helpful annotations identifying people. (There is, unfortunately, no annotation for the American sculptor Ernest Pardessus nor any correction of his name from the erroneous first-edition version Pasdesus. And Joe Strong and Belle were married on 9 August 1879, not in November.) The new version includes a color photograph of Belle in later life, on the cover, and 22 well-reproduced illustrations, among them a charming sketch of Belle's from 1876, now among many such items in the RLS Silverado Museum: ''Adventures at Grez. Only amusements painting and fishing'' (96). It shows her mother painting and her younger brother Lloyd, then known as Sam, fishing, only weeks before Fanny and RLS met.

Writing in the journal of the Santa Barbara Historical Society, Katherine E. Marriott gives an excellent account, based on local sources, of Fanny's purchase and remodeling of Stonehedge, a spacious house in Montecito in the hills behind Santa Barbara, California, and her residence there from 1907 until her death in 1914. Stella Haverland Rouse, in the same journal, reprints an interview with Isobel Field at her home, Monte Serena, on the Pacific coast just south of Santa Barbara. It was first published in a publication for librarians in 1938, and though it has almost no new information it conveys a sense of Belle's life as a celebrity long after the death of RLS and of her mother.

Alexandra Lapierre's *Fanny Stevenson: Entre passion et liberté* is a work of great energy and much information seriously harmed by its presentation in an overwritten, semi-fictional narrative that must be described as, on the whole, only loosely based on fact. As Jean-Pierre Naugrette wrote of the original edition, in French, there is so much imagined reconstruction, and it is all given to us in "[s]o many fake, stereotyped bits of dialogue, which sound like part of a poor screenplay or bad (comic) movie," that very soon we end up wondering about *everything* Lapierre says (253). The book also lacks either an index or footnotes.

A good example of Lapierre's approach is the scene—the book is not so much a narrative as a series of scenes—in which Lapierre has Henley, Gosse, and Colvin all meeting around a table at the Savile Club in mid-December 1879, RLS then being in America (English version, 283–85). No matter that Colvin was then actually in Paris, or that Henley's remarks were made in a letter to Colvin almost a fortnight later, or that almost the only comment that she quotes from Gosse comes from a third letter written more than a month earlier. Henley, whiskey at his elbow, begins an emphatic speech in much the same words as he used in his letter to Colvin. The unwary might think that Lapierre is quoting, or paraphrasing, as she is in the first several sentences. But a sentence or two later, at the end of the same quoted paragraph, in Lapierre's version, Henley denounces Fanny as a "damn slut" (285)—words that there is no evidence that he ever used, about anyone. This drifting between fact and fiction occurs throughout Lapierre's account and consistently robs it of credibility. "It had been raining incessantly in San Francisco since November," Lapierre tells us a few pages later about Stevenson's arrival there from Monterey in 1879. "A searing wind blew off the sea. The newspapers spread the alarm for respiratory patients" (291). No doubt this is how it ought to have been. But not until 26 January, more than a month after he came to San Francisco, did RLS himself comment on the weather, and then it was to remark that after "weeks of lovely warm weather . . . [i]t is today bitter cold" (RLS to Charles Baxter, 26 January 1880, Letter 683; also in *RLS: Stevenson's Letters to Charles Baxter*, ed. DeLancey Ferguson and Marshall Waingrow [1956], 75). Respiratory patients were indeed urged to avoid cold and drafts, but this was a couple of months later and hardly amounted to spreading the alarm.

About Fanny Stevenson herself, Lapierre says that letters in the Bancroft Library at the University of California-Berkeley, prove beyond a doubt that in the late 1890s, after Stevenson's death, Fanny (who was then in her late fifties) had a passionate sexual love-affair with Gellett Burgess. She describes a "packet of letters" there, letters that according to Lapierre refer to "pleasure given and received" (492) and that "leave no doubt" that Fanny and Burgess had sexual relations (507). Although they are, or were, identified in the catalogue as having been written by Fanny Stevenson, the letters themselves show that this attribution is incorrect. The handwriting is not Fanny Stevenson's; the dates and places don't match where we know that Fanny Stevenson was during 1898; and what is said in the last of the four letters, 8 July 1898, makes it clear that Burgess's correspondent was a music teacher who, at least then, divided her time between New York City and Great Neck, New York, on Long Island. So anxious is Lapierre to find a story that she pays no attention to what she should have known about her subject's handwriting, whereabouts, and travels.

A notable discovery of Lapierre's is that Fanny's husband Sam Osbourne visited Paris a second time during her lengthy residence there with the couple's children, Belle and Sam (as Lloyd was then still known), a year after he had come for the heart-rending death of their youngest child Hervey in Paris on 5 April 1876. This was for about fortnight, from the very end of May until 10 or 11 June 1877—after the relationship between RLS and Fanny had begun—and the family spent most of this time in Grez. The evidence is in hotel receipts and other souvenirs in a scrapbook of Sam Osbourne's in the RLS Silverado Museum. Lapierre's account of the visit (198–207) mixes fact and fiction, however, and she is mistaken as to the date that the visit ended, but it is an important discovery nevertheless. RLS was in Edinburgh the whole time, but he knew of Sam's visit and had written nervously and rather cryptically to Baxter about it in March or April: "The man with the linstock is expected in May; it makes me sick to write it. But I'm quite insane; and when the mountain does not come to Mahomet, Mahomet will to the mountain" (Letter 468). Lapierre's notes on sources (507–42) are themselves often in error, but mention is made of a number of lesser-known accounts of some value. In addition, her eight pages of black-and-white illustrations (after 528) include a number of previously unpublished early photographs and sketches.

WORKS CITED

Balfour, Michael. "The First Biography." *Stevenson and Victorian Scotland*. Ed. Jenni Calder. Edinburgh: Edinburgh UP, 1980. 33–47.

Banfield, M. A. *The Health Biographies of Alexander Leeper, Robert Louis Stevenson and Fanny Stevenson*. Modbury, South Australia: [self-published], 2001.

Bathurst, Bella. *The Lighthouse Stevensons*. London: HarperCollins, 1999.

Bell, Gavin. *In Search of Tusitala: Travels in the Pacific after Robert Louis Stevenson*. London: Picador, 1994.

Bell, Ian. *Robert Louis Stevenson: Dreams of Exile*. Edinburgh: Mainstream, 1992.

Bevan, Brendan. *Robert Louis Stevenson: Poet and Teller of Tales*. London: Rubicon Press, 1993.

Binding, Paul. *Robert Louis Stevenson*. London: Oxford UP, 1974.

Booth, Gordon K. "The Strange Case of Mr Stevenson and Professor Smith." *Aberdeen University Review* 59 (Spring 2001): 386–97. Online as "Robert Louis Stevenson and William Robertson Smith: A Study In Contrast." <http://www.gkbenterprises.fsnet.co.uk/papers/rlswrs.htm>

Brown, Neil Macara. "Ex Libris RLS: Much Travelled Books." *Scottish Book Collector* 4 (Nov. 1994): 5–6.

Cairney, John. *The Quest for Robert Louis Stevenson*. Edinburgh: Luath, 2004.

Calder, Jenni. *Robert Louis Stevenson: A Life Study*. London: Hamish Hamilton, 1980.

Callow, Phillip. *Louis: A Life of Robert Louis Stevenson*. Chicago: Dee, 2001.

Castle, Alan. *The Robert Louis Stevenson Trail: A Walking Tour in the Velay and Cévennes, Southern France*. Milnthorpe, Cumbria: Cicerone, 1992.

Cohen, Edward H. "Henley's *In Hospital*, Literary Realism, and the Late-Victorian Periodicals Press." *Victorian Periodicals Review* 28 (Spring 1995): 1–10.

———. *The Henley-Stevenson Quarrel*. U of Florida P, 1974.

———. "The Second Series of W. E. Henley's Hospital Poems." *Yale University Library Gazette* 78 (Apr. 2004): 128–50.

Colley, Ann C. *Robert Louis Stevenson and the Colonial Imagination*. Aldershot: Ashgate, 2004.

Cookson, Gillian, and Colin A. Hempstead. *A Victorian Scientist and Engineer: Fleeming Jenkin and the Birth of Electrical Engineering*. Aldershot: Ashgate, 2000.

Daiches, David. *Robert Louis Stevenson and His World*. London: Thames and Hudson, 1973.

Daniel, Thomas M. "Stevenson's Fingers." *Science* 286 (8 Oct. 1999): 239.

Davies, Hunter. *The Teller of Tales: In Search of Robert Louis Stevenson*. London: Sinclair-Stevenson, 1994.

Daws, Gavan. "Robert Louis Stevenson." *A Dream of Islands: Voyages of Self-Discovery in the South Seas*. Honolulu: Mutual, 1980. 162–215.

Dury, Richard. "The Spoken Words." In the collection by Steele 10–13.

Entwisle, Peter, Michael Dunn, and Roger Collins. *Nerli: An Exhibition of Paintings and Drawings*. Dunedin, NZ: Dunedin Public Art Gallery, 1988.

Falconer-Salkeld, Bridget. "Manasquan Re-Visited." In the collection by Steele 45–49.

Ferguson, Derek W. "Robert Louis Stevenson and Samoa: A Reinterpretation." M.A. Thesis. U of Saskatchewan, 1980.

Field, Isobel. *This Life I've Loved: An Autobiography*. Ed. Peter I. Browning. Lafayette, CA: Great West, 2005.

Fitzpatrick, Elaine Wareing. *A Quixotic Companionship: Fanny and Robert Louis Stevenson*. 2nd ed. Monterey: Old Monterey Preservation Society, 1997.

Furnas, J. C. *My Life in Writing: Memoirs of a Maverick*. New York: Morrow, 1999.

Gadd, Sarah. *Navigating Stevenson: Digital Artworks by Sarah Gadd*. Ed. Elaine Grieg, James Lawson, and Catherine Moriarty. Edinburgh: Scottish National Portrait Gallery, 2003.

Giroud, Vincent. "E.J.B. and R.L.S.: The Story of the Beinecke Stevenson Collection." *Journal of Stevenson Studies* 1 (2004): 42–59.

Gray, William. *Robert Louis Stevenson: A Literary Life*. Basingstoke: Palgrave Macmillan, 2004.

Guttmacher, Alan E., MD, and J. R. Callahan. "Did Robert Louis Stevenson Have Hereditary Hemorrhagic Telangiectasia?" *American Journal of Medical Genetics* 19 (2000): 62–65.

Hannah, Barbara. "Robert Louis Stevenson." *Striving Toward Wholeness*. New York: C. G. Jung Foundation for Analytical Psychology, 1971. 38–71.

Harman, Claire. *Robert Louis Stevenson: A Biography*. London: HarperCollins, 2005. Published in the United States as *Myself and the Other Fellow: A Life of Robert Louis Stevenson*. New York: HarperCollins, 2005.

Hill, Robin A. *R. L. S., Francophile*. Edinburgh: privately printed, 1993.

Holmes, Lowell D. *Treasured Islands: Cruising the South Seas with Robert Louis Stevenson*. Dobbs Ferry, NY: Sheridan, 2001.

Holmes, Richard. "1964: Travels." *Footsteps: Adventures of a Romantic Biographer*. London: Hodder and Stoughton, 1985. 11–69. Originally: "In Stevenson's Footsteps," *Granta 10: Travel Writing* (Harmondsworth: Granta Publications, 1984): 192–251.

Kent, Harold Winfield. *Dr. Hyde and Mr. Stevenson: The Life of the Rev. Dr. Charles McEwen Hyde Including a Discussion of the Open Letter of Robert Louis Stevenson*. Rutland, VT: Tuttle, 1973.

Kiely, Robert. "Robert Louis Stevenson." *Victorian Novelists after 1875*. Ed. Ira B. Nadel and William E. Fredeman. Detroit: Gale, 1983. 268–88. Dictionary of Literary Biography series.

Knight, Alanna. *R. L. S. in the South Seas: An Intimate Photographic Record*. Edinburgh: Mainstream, 1986.

————. *The Passionate Kindness: The Love Story of Robert Louis Stevenson and Fanny Osbourne*. Glasgow: Molendinar Press, 1974 [rpt. 1980].

Lapierre, Alexandra. *Fanny Stevenson: Entre passion et liberté*. Paris: Pierre Lafont, 1993. English trans., *Fanny Stevenson: A Romance of Destiny*. Trans. Carol Cosman. New York: Carroll and Graf, 1995.

Leslie, Jean, and Roland Paxton. *Bright Lights: The Stevenson Engineers 1752–1971*. Edinburgh: published by the authors, 1999.

Mackenzie, Kenneth Starr. "Robert Louis Stevenson in Samoa, 1889–1894." Diss. Dalhousie U, 1974. Microfilm lending copy: National Library of Canada, Ottawa.

Mackenzie, Kenneth. "The Last Opportunity: Robert Louis Stevenson and Samoa, 1889–1894." *More Pacific Island Portraits*. Ed. Deryck Scarr (Australian National UP, 1979), 221–47.

MacPhail, Elizabeth C. "Allen Hutchinson British Sculptor (1855–1929)." *Journal of San Diego History* 19 (Spring 1973): 21–38.

Mair, Craig. *A Star for Seamen: The Stevenson Family of Engineers*. London: John Murray, 1978.

Marriott, Katherine E. "Fanny Stevenson, Mistress of Stonehedge." *Noticias* 23 (Fall 1986): 47–53, photo on front cover.

Marwick, Sandra. *Capital Writers: Edinburgh and Robert Louis Stevenson*. Edinburgh: City of Edinburgh Museums and Art Galleries, [1997].

McLynn, Frank. *Robert Louis Stevenson: A Biography*. London: Hutchinson, 1993.

Mehew, Ernest. "Glimpses of Stevenson's Childhood." In the collection by Steele 5–9.

————. "God and the Novelists: 12. Robert Louis Stevenson." *The Expository Times* [Edinburgh: T. and T. Clark] 110 (1999): 312–16.

————. "Robert Louis Stevenson (1850–1894)." *Oxford Dictionary of National Biography*. Ed. H. C. G. Matthew and Brian Harrison. Oxford: Oxford UP, 2004. 52: 597–606.

Naugrette, Jean-Pierre. Rev. of *Fanny Stevenson: Entre passion et liberté* by Alexandra Lapierre. *Studies in Scottish Literature* 28 (1993): 250–53.

Neill, Roger. *Legends: The Art of Walter Barnett*. Canberra: [Australian] National Portrait Gallery, 2000.

————. "Mr Nerli, Canty Kerlie." In collection by Steele 18–20.

————. *Robert Louis Stevenson and Count Nerli in Samoa: The Story of a Portrait*. Banbury, Oxfordshire: Red Lion Press, 1997.

Nickerson, Roy. *Robert Louis Stevenson in California: A Remarkable Courtship*. San Francisco: Chronicle Books, 1982.

Orton, Arthur W. *Reconstructing the Robert Louis Stevenson "Silverado Squatters" Cabin*. St. Helena, CA: [Silverado Museum], 1980; 2nd ed. 1993, rpt. 2007.

Patterson, Caroline Bennett. "Travels With a Donkey—100 Years Later." *National Geographic* 154 (Oct. 1978): 535–61.

Pemble, John. *The Mediterranean Passion: Victorians and Edwardians in the South*. Oxford: Clarendon, 1987.

Perry, Charles. "The Star-Spangled Powder: Or, Through History with Coke Spoon and Nasal Spray." *Rolling Stone*, 17 August 1982: 24–26.

Pope-Hennessy, James. *Robert Louis Stevenson*. London: Jonathan Cape, 1974.

Popplewell, Lawrence. *The Search for Bonallie Tower: R. L. S. in Branksome Park*. Revised edition. Bournemouth: Melledgen Press, 2000. Originally published 1996.

Poujol, Jacques, et al. *Le Chemin de Stevenson: Le Puy/Le Monastier/Florac/St-Jean-du-Gard/Alès*. Paris: Fédération Française de la Randonnée Pédestre/Clermont-Ferrand: Chamina, 1994.

Rankin, Nicholas. *Dead Man's Chest: Travels After Robert Louis Stevenson*. London: Faber, 1987.

Rice, Edward. *Journey to Upolu: Robert Louis Stevenson, Victorian Rebel*. New York: Dodd, Mead, 1974.

Rouse, Stella Haverland. "Isobel Field." *Noticias* 23 (Fall 1986): 53–57, photo inside front cover.

Salesa, Damon. "Misimoa: An American on the Beach." *Common-place*, 5:2 (Jan. 2005). 28 November 2006. <http://www.historycooperative.org/journals/cp/vol-05/no-02/salesa/index.shtml>.

Sanchez, Nellie Vandegrift. *The Life of Mrs. Robert Louis Stevenson* (1920). Intro. Ysabel Matney. Whitefish, MT: Kessinger Publishing, 2004.

Scarr, Deryck. "John Bates Thurston: Grand Panjandrum of the Pacific." *More Pacific Island Portraits*. Canberra: Australian National U, 1979. 95–114.

———. *Viceroy of the Pacific: The Majesty of Colour: A Life of John Bates Thurston*. Canberra: Australian National U, 1980.

Schultz, Myron G. "The 'Strange Case' of Robert Louis Stevenson." *JAMA: Journal of the American Medical Association* 215 (5 April 1971): 90–94.

Social Science Association of Hawaii. *A Centenary Celebration, 1882–1982: Representative Essays*. UP of Hawaii, 1982.

Steele, Karen, ed. *The Robert Louis Stevenson Club 150th Birthday Anniversary Book.* Edinburgh: Robert Louis Stevenson Club, [2000].

Stevenson, Robert Louis. *Selected Letters of Robert Louis Stevenson.* New Haven: Yale UP, 1997.

Stott, Louis. *Robert Louis Stevenson & France.* Milton of Aberfoyle: Creag Darach, 1994.

Strouse, Norman H. "Dream and Realization: Collecting RLS." *PNLA Quarterly* 35 (Oct. 1970): 4–17.

Swearingen, Roger G. *The Prose Writings of Robert Louis Stevenson: A Guide.* Hamden, CT: Archon, 1980.

———. "Robert Louis Stevenson & the Goats: Monterey County Ranch Discovered." *Quarterly Newsletter, Book Club of California* 46 (Summer 1981): 65–67.

———. *Robert Louis Stevenson and Samoa After 100 Years.* Apia, Samoa, and Phoenix, Arizona: Robert Louis Stevenson Museum/Preservation Foundation, Inc., 1999.

———. *Robert Louis Stevenson's Edinburgh: A Concise Guide for Visitors and Residents.* Edinburgh: City of Edinburgh Museums and Galleries, 2001.

Tancock, John L. *The Sculpture of Auguste Rodin.* Philadelphia: Philadelphia Museum of Art, 1976.

Theroux, Joseph. "Rediscovering 'H. J. M.', Samoa's 'unconquerable' Harry Moors." *Pacific Islands Monthly* 52:8 (Aug. 1981): 51–57; and "HJM: Showman, Author, Farmer—and Crusading Politician." *Pacific Islands Monthly* 52:9 (Sept. 1981): 59–64.

Turnbull, Olena M. "The Squire and the Gamekeeper: RLS and Miss Adelaide Boodle." *Robert Louis Stevenson Reconsidered: New Critical Perspectives.* Ed. William B. Jones, Jr. Jefferson, NC: McFarland, 2003. 215–27.

Woodhead, Richard. *The Strange Case of Robert Louis Stevenson.* Edinburgh: Luath, 2001.

Checklist of Criticism

The following checklist of studies from 1970 on has four sections.

(1) "Influences and Successors" lists discussions of Stevenson's relations to Walter Pater and George Moore, his views on George Macdonald and George Eliot, RLS's influence on Henry James's story "The Pupil" and on Gissing and Frazer's *The Golden Bough*, his remarkable importance to Oscar

Wilde, his influence and the publication of his work in the Netherlands, Russia, France, and elsewhere, the editing and production of the early collected editions of his works, and comments by and discussions of the lines of influence and admiration between and among RLS and Joseph Conrad, G. K. Chesterton, Jack London, T. S. Eliot, D. H. Lawrence, John Steinbeck, Graham Greene, Jorge Luis Borges, Wallace Stevens, and Vladimir Nabokov. It ends by citing an essay on the relations of the recent feature film *Fight Club* (1999) to *Dr. Jekyll and Mr. Hyde* (1886) and to James Hogg's *Private Memoirs and Confessions of a Justified Sinner* (1824).

(2) "General Studies" lists discussions of Stevenson's work as a whole or that consider more than a few of his works. These general contributions are listed in the order of their dates of publication.

(3) "Individual Works" lists discussions of only one or a few of Stevenson's works. These are presented in the order of the earliest work or works by Stevenson with which they are mainly concerned. Within such groups, the discussions are then taken up in the order of their date of publication. Subheadings indicate the main focus of each subdivision in this section, although some overlapping cannot, of course, be avoided.

(4) "Collections of Essays" lists collections of critical essays on Stevenson that have appeared since 1970, with a few words on the special contents or focus of most of these volumes. Individual contributions in these collections are listed in the preceding sections, however, even when their first appearance was in one of these collections.

When it is not apparent from the title what the subject is or which works are under discussion, I have added a note of explanation or summary, as I have also done, occasionally at some length, when the studies themselves are difficult to obtain.

1. Influences and Successors

Costello, Peter. "Walter Pater, George Moore and R. L. Stevenson." In collection by Liebregts and Tigges 126–38.

Gray, William. " 'Amiable Infidelity, Grim-faced Dummies and Rondels': Robert Louis Stevenson on George MacDonald." *North Wind: Journal of George MacDonald Society* 23. [not seen]

Mooneyham, Laura. "Robert Louis Stevenson and the 'High . . . Rather Dry Lady'." *George Eliot-Henry Lewes Studies* 22–23 (Sept. 1993): 61–68. [not seen]

Tintner, Adeline R. "James Writes a Boys' Story: 'The Pupil' and R. L. Stevenson's Adventure Books." *Essays in Literature* 5 (1979): 61–73.

Crawford, Robert. "Frazer and Scottish Romanticism: Scott, Stevenson, and *The Golden Bough.*" *Sir James Frazer and the Literary Imagination: Essays in Affinity and Influence.* Ed. Robert Fraser. London: Macmillan, 1990. 18–37. "Frazer was a keen reader of Stevenson, particularly in the late 1880s, when he was working on the First Edition of *The Golden Bough.*" According to Crawford,

> we should see Stevenson, one of the descendants of Scott in the Scottish Romantic novel, and Frazer, one of the descendants of Scott in the Scottish tradition of anthropological assemblage—or even epic—as connected parts of one cultural tradition whose roots stretch back into the Scottish Enlightenment, but whose work also points forward towards modernism. (32–33)

Hoefnagel, Dick. "George Gissing and Robert Louis Stevenson," *Gissing Newsletter*, 20 (1984): 22–26. [Not seen]

Murray, Isobel. "Strange Case of Dr Jekyll and Oscar Wilde," *Durham University Journal*, 79 (June 1987): 311–19. Wilde's high regard for Stevenson and his particular interest in *Dr. Jekyll and Mr. Hyde* are especially apparent in his criticism and other works during the late 1880s and early 1890s. Wilde's story "The Fisherman and His Soul" (1891) and *The Picture of Dorian Gray* (1890), "can be seen as both in part 'criticisms' of *Strange Case of Dr Jekyll and Mr Hyde*":

> Wilde was not converted to an interest in dualism by *Jekyll and Hyde*: he was already familiar with it and attracted to it, but Stevenson's novella seems to have provided him with various accidentals to react to—or against. (311)

The many affinities between *The Picture of Dorian Gray* and *Dr. Jekyll and Mr. Hyde* were recognized at once and pointed out by many reviewers. Extending an observation made by Rodney Shewan, *Oscar Wilde: Art and Egotism* (London: Macmillan, 1977), 212, Murray suggests that Wilde may have been taking up a challenge implicitly made by Andrew Lang in his article "Literary Plagiarism," published in the *Contemporary Review* in June 1887. Situations, incidents, even poetic meters, are the common property of all writers, Lang asserted, with the result that plagiarism is "easy to prove, and almost impossible to commit." What one must avoid is echoing anything too recent or well known: a minister's confession, which can only bring to mind *The Scarlet Letter*, or the meter of *In Memoriam*. Lang continues:

Again, double personality is a theme open to all the world: Gautier and Poe and Eugène Sue all used it; but it is wiser to leave it alone while people have a vivid memory of Dr Jekyll and Mr Hyde. It is not inconceivable that an author might use the old notion as brilliantly and with as much freshness as Mr Stevenson has done; it is certain that if he tries, he will be howled at by the moral mob.   (qtd. 315)

Although his use of the meter of *In Memoriam* in "The Sphinx" seems to have occurred already, Wilde shows his familiarity with and echoes the wording of Lang's essay in his account of art criticism among the Greeks in the first part of "The Critic as Artist." In *The Picture of Dorain Gray*, Murray writes,

I suggest that Wilde deliberately takes up Lang's challenge, and echoes *Dr Jekyll and Mr Hyde*, and that at the same time he has a very different story to tell, a story that is central to his own theories of art, life, egotism and individualism, and very different in its essence from Stevenson's grim sermon about an evil that seems gratifyingly horrible and untempting to all but the unfortunate Henry Jekyll.   (316).

van Eeden, Frederik. "Frederik van Eeden on Stevenson and Pater." Trans. Wim Tigges. In collection by Liebregts and Tigges 271–75. This is the first translation into English of comments on Pater and Stevenson by the Dutch writer and psychotherapist Frederik van Eeden (1860–1932), in a paper titled "New English Prose" (Sept. 1891; collected, 1894). Five paragraphs are on RLS, advancing the idea that RLS is essentially an entertainer: "one of the best writers in a genre which [is] nowadays not held in very high esteem. . . . He is the writer for pastime . . . a very deserving author. Only, he is not a great artist" (271).

Alblas, Jacques B. H. "The Early Production and Reception of Stevenson's Work in England and the Netherlands." In collection by Liebregts and Tigges 209–19.

Diakonova, Nina. "Robert Louis Stevenson in Russia." *Scottish Slavonic Review* 10 (1988): 207–24.

Houppermans, Sjef. "Robert, Alexandre, Marcel, Henri, Jean et les Autres: R. L. Stevenson and his 'French Connections.' " In collection by Liebregts and Tigges 188–207. Houppermans offers an engaging and informative survey of French writers influenced by RLS, from Marcel Schwob (1867–1905) to Jean-Marie Le Clézio (b. 1940) and Jean Echenoz (b. 1947).

" 'The Dead Should Be Protected From Their Own Carelessness': the Collected Editions of Robert Louis Stevenson." *The Culture of Collected Editions.* Ed. Andrew Nash. Basingstoke: Palgrave Macmillan, 2003. 111–27. Drawing chiefly on the Yale Letters and the Chatto and Windus archive at the Reading University Library, Nash tells the story of the six collected editions of RLS's works published in England from his death in 1894 through the launching of the Tusitala and Skerryvore editions in 1924 and 1925. Printed from the same plates, these two editions were the first in England not limited as to numbers, and the Tusitala edition was the first in a small format. They were created in anticipation of RLS's works passing into unrestricted copyright thirty years after his death, as they did in December 1924. RLS participated actively in the initial planning of the first such edition, the Edinburgh edition, the completed first volume of which Charles Baxter was bringing with him to Samoa when RLS died on 3 December 1894. It looked like a good opportunity financially, and he was also tempted by the possibility of revising various works and adding prefaces to others. RLS also had strong views that the edition was to be selected, not all-inclusive: for example, he wanted to have both "The Story of a Lie" and "The Misadventures of John Nicholson" omitted and "The Body-Snatcher" and *Moral Emblems* both included. (As Nash observes, the opposite was done in three of the four instances, and *Moral Emblems* was long delayed.) But by June 1894, for practical reasons and due to a renewed interest in current work, RLS put Sidney Colvin and Charles Baxter solely in charge of the contents, arrangement, and editorial details. He objected strongly, therefore, to a slip that Colvin proposed to insert (and did insert) in the first volume stating that "additions, omissions, and corrections (other than those merely of press) have the sanction and approval of the author."

> Really, if you consider your letter of this month and the various corrections which you here indicate it must appear to the meanest capacity that you *are* the editor, and that I *did not* make all excisions, alterations, and additions.   (RLS to Colvin, 4 November 1894, Letter 2797; see also RLS to Baxter, 4 November 1894, Letter 2805)

RLS's two letters were received too late to prevent the proposed insertion from appearing, and no doubt the misleading claim that RLS had overseen the edition contributed to making it the huge success that it was. The Edinburgh edition was fully subscribed in two months and brought a profit of £10,000 to the publishers. Subsequent editions were also limited, and also in sumptuous format, and in the sometimes odd distribution of material into volumes they were influenced by the fact that RLS's copyrights were spread among four publishers, each wanting to keep their own works together, for accounting purposes. The texts generally reprinted the Edinburgh Edition text or, for previously unpublished or uncollected material, texts prepared by Colvin or Lloyd Osbourne. The Vailima edition, launched in 1922 under Lloyd Osbourne's sole supervision, was criticized (by Edmund Gosse and Sidney Colvin, among others) for including so much previously unpublished material, including fragments and drafts, many of which RLS himself was known to have held in low esteem. But by then RLS's manuscripts and notebooks had been dispersed at auction and were beginning to appear in print anyway.

Watts, Cedric. "*The Ebb-Tide* and *Victory.*" *Conradiana* 28 (1996): 133–37. Joseph Conrad's *Victory* (1914) appeared twenty years after the last novel that RLS completed during his lifetime, *The Ebb-Tide* (1894). Commenting on its sources, Watts notes that *Victory* "resembles an amalgam of literary materials borrowed from many locations and fused in an unstable combination"—and that to the list one must surely add *The Ebb-Tide*. "There are no close verbal parallels," he writes, but there are "intermittent resemblances in aspects of plot, location, and characterization."

Hetzler, Leo A. "Chesterton and Robert Louis Stevenson." *Chesterton Review* 17 (May 1991): 177–87. Reading RLS's essays, including "Pulvis et Umbra" (1888), helped Chesterton personally to overcome what Hetzler calls "[a] dark mood of solipsism and morbidity" in 1894. Chesterton recalls this in his dedicatory poem to *The Man Who Was Thursday* (1908). He also revived the spirit of RLS's New Arabian Nights stories in his own *The Club of Queer Trades* (1905). Of Chesterton's two books on RLS Hetzler notes that in his 1903 contribution to the Bookman Booklets series, Chesterton is mainly trying to separate RLS from the Aesthetes. In his 1927 book, despite disclaiming an interest in biography, Chesterton writes chiefly about RLS's personal outlook, which he greatly admired.

Petersen, Per Serritslev. "The Jekyll and Hyde Motif in Jack London's Science Fiction: Formula and Intertextuality in 'When the World Was Young.'" *Jack London Journal* 3 (1996): 105–16. [Not seen]

Briggs, Grace B. "Stevenson's *The Ebb-Tide* and Eliot's *The Hollow Men.*" *Notes and Queries* 24 (1977): 448–49. [Not seen]

Satpathy, Sumanyu. "An Allusion to Stevenson in *The Waste Land.*" *Papers on Language and Literature* 31 (Summer 1995): 286–90. In Eliot's line, "Or under seals broken by the lean solicitor" (408), the lean solicitor "could well be 'Mr. Utterson the lawyer' in *Dr. Jekyll and Mr. Hyde.*"

Ricks, Christopher. "A Note on 'The Hollow Men' and Stevenson's *The Ebb-Tide*." *Essays in Criticism* 51 (Jan. 2001): 8–17. Remarking on T. S. Eliot's high regard for Stevenson both in an undergraduate essay "The Defects of Kipling" (1909) and in his review of Chesterton's study (*Nation and Athenaeum*, 31 Dec. 1927), Ricks presents many verbal as well as thematic echoes—even a similar juxtaposition of nursery rhymes and horror—that connect the next-to-last chapter of *The Ebb-Tide* with "The Hollow Men" and with other poems by Eliot. "[E]ven though little should be claimed for Stevenson as important to Eliot, *The Ebb-Tide* may well have been among the prompters of 'The Hollow Men' (1925), there with the imperial writings usually adduced, those of Kipling and Conrad" (9).

Sagar, Keith. "D. H. Lawrence and Robert Louis Stevenson." *D. H. Lawrence Review* 24 (Summer 1992): 161–65. Personal resemblances between RLS and D. H. Lawrence include, besides the fact that each died not long after his 44th birthday, chronic respiratory troubles, including convalescence in Bournemouth at about the same age, rebellion against "a puritanical upbringing . . . respectability and 'getting on,' " marriage to an older woman with children, residence abroad, and writing in a wide range of genres including travel literature. *Treasure Island* was among Lawrence's favorite books as a boy, and he reread it with Jessie Chambers along with *Kidnapped* and *The Master of Ballantrae* when he was an adolescent.

Simmonds, Roy S. "John Steinbeck, Robert Louis Stevenson, and Edith McGillcuddy." *San Jose Studies* 1 (Nov. 1975): 29–39. According to Simmonds, Steinbeck seems to have drafted his story, "How Edith McGillcuddy Met Robert Louis Stevenson" (*Harper's Magazine* 183 [August 1941] 252–58), in late 1932 or early 1933, just before he began *Tortilla Flat* (1935), his first great success. As Steinbeck noted in a limited edition printed for the Rowfant Club, Cleveland, in 1943, he was drawing upon the recollections of a family friend in Salinas, Mrs. Edith Wagner, who in 1879, at the age of twelve, had attended a funeral in Monterey and was then taken by other children to meet a strange long-haired young man and his cigarette-smoking lady friend who were having tea together in the garden of an adobe. Steinbeck quotes a letter of appreciation for the story from Mrs. Wagner stating that with three trifling exceptions "that is the way it happened." For reasons unknown, Simmonds says, Steinbeck did not try to publish the story at the time of its writing, and during the later 1930s he seems to have forgotten it altogether. He reworked it for publication "sometime during 1940 or early 1941." Steinbeck's draft is in the Humanities Research Center Library, University of Texas, Austin. Although it differs only slightly from the published version, Simmonds quotes several interesting passages side by side for comparison. In his account of the story, Jackson J. Benson, *The True Adventures of John Steinbeck, Writer* (New York: Viking, 1984), 218–20, suggests that Steinbeck probably wrote it in early 1934, after he had completed the first draft of *Tortilla Flat*, and that in June 1934 he had his agents cease offering it for publication when he learned from Mrs. Wagner's response to the draft that he sent her that she was then trying to publish her own account in *Reader's Digest*. Only when she did not succeed in this effort did Steinbeck continue, with Mrs. Wagner's permission. On the last page of a copy of the story as it appeared in *Harper's Magazine* (Beinecke 2387), Edwin J. Beinecke's librarian Gertrude Hills wrote caustically: "Insufferable bilge. Had this been written by an unknown author, it would have gone into the scrapbasket. Steinbeck knows absolutely nothing of RLS's true life in Monterey, or he could not have written this absurdity."

Greene, Graham. *Conversations with Graham Greene*. Ed. Henry J. Donaghy. Oxford: UP of Mississippi, 1992. In an interview with Robert Osterman (*Catholic World* 170 [Feb. 1950], 356–61), Greene was asked about his plans to write a biography of RLS. Greene's reply was: "Yes, I've thought about it. But I think I'll wait until after the centenary. . . . There's an American preparing a biography. If he does a complete job of it, then there'd be little point in my writing another one" (27). Greene refers to the centenary of RLS's birth, in 1950, and to J. C. Furnas, whose *Voyage to Windward* was published in 1951. Nicholas Rankin, *Dead Man's Chest* (1987), 74–77, fills in the details, including Greene's advertisement for information (*Times Literary Supplement*, 24 June 1949) and a list of some of the people to whom Greene wrote as he was getting started. Greene's mother was a second cousin of RLS and Greene did, in fact, give up his thoughts of writing a biography of RLS to leave a clear path for J. C. Furnas.

———. Greene/Majoribanks Collection, Georgetown University, Washington, DC. The collection consists of nine letters and Greene's manuscript of "A Weed Among the Flowers," an essay on a 1957 visit to China (*The Times*, London, 1985; rpt. *Graham Greene: Reflections*, ed. Judith Adamson, 1990), 308–15. In 1985, Greene donated the manuscript to the RLS Trust to be sold to benefit the creation of an RLS Memorial in Edinburgh. It was bought, along with the correspondence about it, by Georgetown University. Greene remarks in passing that he admires some of RLS's poems, much of his prose, and still reads with pleasure *Weir of Hermiston*, *Dr. Jekyll and Mr. Hyde*, and *The Master of Ballantrae*. "I think it was Stevenson's method of describing action without adjectives or adverbs which taught me a good deal" (Green to Sir James Majoribanks, 12 November 1985).

———. "In Memory of Borges" (1984). *Graham Greene: Reflections*. Ed. Judith Adamson. London: Reinhardt; New York: Viking Penguin, 1990. 306–07. In a talk at the Anglo-Argentine Society, London, in 1984, Greene recalled walking with Borges to lunch with a mutual friend in Buenos Aires: "Borges talked about the influence G. K. Chesterton had had on him and the influence of Robert Louis Stevenson had had on his later stories. He spoke of the prose of Stevenson as a great influence." At this point Greene remarked that RLS "did write at least one good poem": the verses on his family "Say not of me that weakly I declined" (*Underwoods*, I, 38). "It was a very noisy, crowded Buenos Aires street," Greene continues. "Borges stopped on the pavement and recited the whole poem to me, word perfect."

Balderston, Daniel. "Borges's Frame of Reference: The Strange Case of Robert Louis Stevenson." Diss. Princeton U, 1981. Balderston shows that Borges was considerably more than an admirer of Stevenson. To Borges, Stevenson was not only an influence but an admired predecessor, almost a collaborator, working along many of the same lines. The two writers share much in their theories of literature, narrative techniques, and thematic preoccupations. To both, "fiction is abstract and artificial rather than representational and mimetic" (269). Both examine the theory as well as the practice of their art, and they offer similar conclusions. Both write about literature as consisting chiefly of moment-by-moment effects on readers, effects that are consolidated into visually striking scenes, rather than as something that has instrumental value toward philosophic or moral ends; both look back to the uninhibited reading habits of childhood as an ideal. Both are narrative and descriptive minimalists. They prefer salient, visually striking details and scenes to voluminous realistic particularity. They show characters chiefly from the outside, as other characters might see them, rather than trying to capture the inner flow of consciousness. Illusions, delusions, ambiguity, doubles, and identity fascinate them both, as do marginal literary forms in which to explore these matters—forms such as the fantastic tale and the detective story.

Borges's fiction itself has been "profoundly affected by Stevenson's explorations of romantic, episodic narrative, use of the sensational visual scene, and attention to details which open up 'whole vistas of secondary stories'" (273). In chapter 3, for example, "The Short Sketch: Selection, Exaggeration, Caricature," 99–144, Balderston takes up Borges's collection of sketches of rogues and villains, *Historia universal de la infamia* (1935), in particular Borges's account, "El impostor inverosímil Tom Castro". This is a retelling of the story of the Tichborne Claimant, a celebrated inheritance case with which Stevenson too was familiar, tried both as a civil and then as a criminal matter in two lengthy proceedings in the early 1870s. For his facts, Borges himself credits chiefly Thomas Seccombe's article in the eleventh edition of the *Encyclopædia Britannica*. But for the manner in which Borges tells the story, especially his use of what Stevenson calls "epoch-making scenes," Balderston credits Stevenson:

> "[A]ll four of the 'epoch-making scenes' in the story—Orton helping Bogle across the street, Bogle throwing open the curtains when Orton meets Lady Tichborne, Bogle's walk in London under a honey-colored moon, and the death of Bogle—are unknown to history (and to Thomas Seccombe, Borges's source), and strikingly similar to dramatic moments in Stevenson's fiction, or at least close to the idea of the sensational scene proclaimed in 'A Gossip on Romance.' " (137).

> Borges's habits are Stevenson's habits: "an intensification of the original story, [and] a tendency toward condensation, exaggeration and caricature" (137).

Appendix I (278–322) is a chronological list quoting the references to RLS in Borges's criticism, interviews, and reviews, a total of 106 of these from December 1920 through August 1980. Appendix II (323–71) consists of edited transcripts of six conversations about Stevenson that Balderston had and recorded in Buenos Aires in 1978: three with Borges, in English, two with Bioy Casares, and one with José Bianco, in Spanish. These interviews are among the many sources of Balderston's own arguments in the main body of the text.

Brogan, Jacqueline Vaught. "Stevens and Stevenson: the Guitarist's Guitarist." *American Literature* 59 (May 1987): 228–45. In his journal, 7 July 1899, the young Wallace Stevens, then between his second and third years at Harvard, commented on RLS's story "Providence and the Guitar" (1878), which he had read that afternoon:

> I felt thoroughly how carefully the story had been written and how artificial it was. Leon Berthelini is a paper doll and entirely literary, patly illustrating the difference between literary creations and natural men. Out in the open air with plenty of time and space I felt how different literary emotions were from natural feelings.
> (*Souvenirs and Prophecies: The Young Wallace Stevens*, ed. Holly Stevens [New York: Knopf, 1976], 41–42; qtd., 229)

The influence of RLS's story on Stevens's work, Brogan suggests, was "both subtle and pervasive, informing first his prose, then later a number of poems, including, most notably, 'The Man with the Blue Guitar' " (228). RLS's story helped Stevens refine his own thinking about art and nature and the differences between "literary emotions" and "natural feelings." In addition, the figure of the guitarist became for Stevens "even in the earliest of his mature poetry one of the central figures for his own art" (233). Brogan brings out the many ironies and complexities of RLS's story and notes that Stevens seems to have missed or ignored them, incorrectly seeing himself as writing chiefly in opposition to RLS's point of view.

Feldman, Jessica. *"Prince Otto* in *Pale Fire*: 'A Wrench, a Rift.' " *Gender on the Divide: The Dandy in Modernist Literature.* Ithaca, NY: Cornell UP, 1993. 261–68. Nabokov's *Pale Fire* (1962) has "mirrorings, coincidences, [and] echoes [of *Prince Otto*] too numerous to discuss at length. . . . Stevenson's novel provides Nabokov with Kinbote's homosexuality and the means of interpreting it. Otto himself, not a homosexual, is a rather impotent fellow. . . . What is whispered in *Prince Otto* is spoken in *Pale Fire*.' " Feldman also notes (77) Wallace Stevens's liking, as a young man, for *The Silverado Squatters*, citing Holly Stevens, *Souvenirs and Prophecies: The Young Wallace Stevens* (New York: Knopf, 1976), 77.

Stirling, Kirsten. " 'Dr Jekyll and Mr Jackass': *Fight Club* as a Refraction of Hogg's *Justified Sinner* and Stevenson's *Dr Jekyll and Mr Hyde*." *Refracting the Canon in Contemporary British Literature and Film.* Ed. Susana Onega and Christian Gutleben. Amsterdam and New York: Rodopi, 2004. 83–94. Postmodern Studies, 35. Stirling presents many affinities between David Fincher's film *Fight Club* (Twentieth Century Fox, 1999; screenplay by Jim Ulhs, starring Brad Pitt as Tyler Durden; based on the novel of the same name by Chuck Palahniuk [New York: Henry Holt, 1996]) and *Dr. Jekyll and Mr. Hyde* and James Hogg's *Private Memoirs and Confessions of a Justified Sinner* (1824). The affinities are much greater with Hogg's novel than with *Dr. Jekyll and Mr. Hyde*, she writes, both because Hogg has much more interest than Stevenson does in "the role of society in determining the nature of the individual" and because, in the film, as in Hogg, the interactions between the narrator and his double are shown in detail and are much more complex. *Fight Club* is not an attempt to "rewrite" either of these earlier works: "it is more a brand of twentieth-century gothic that strongly recalls aspects of both . . . [a] highly modern reworking of the theme of the *Doppelgänger*."

2. General Studies

Welsh, Alexander. "Theories of Science and Romance, 1870–1920." *Victorian Studies* 17 (Dec. 1973): 135–54.

Saposnik, Irving S. *Robert Louis Stevenson*. New York: Twayne, 1974. Twayne's English Authors Series. In addition to chapters on other works, Saposnik reprints his essay "The Anatomy of *Dr. Jekyll and Mr. Hyde*," *Studies in English Literature* 11 (Autumn 1971): 715–31.

Hart, Francis Russell. *The Scottish Novel From Smollett to Spark*. Cambridge: Harvard UP, 1978.

Furnas, J. C. "Stevenson and America." In collection by Calder, *Stevenson and Victorian Scotland* 94–104. Lothian Lecture, University of Edinburgh, 1979.

Daiches, David. "Stevenson and Scotland." In collection by Calder, *Stevenson and Victorian Scotland* 11–32.

Royle, Trevor. "The Literary Background to Stevenson's Edinburgh." In collection by Calder, *Stevenson and Victorian Scotland* 48–61.

Gifford, Douglas. "Stevenson and Scottish Fiction." *Stevenson and Victorian Scotland*. Ed. Jenni Calder. Edinburgh: Edinburgh UP, 1981. 62–87.

Harvie, Christopher. "The Politics of Stevenson." In collection by Calder, *Stevenson and Victorian Scotland* 107–25.

Furnas, J. C. "Stevenson and Exile." In collection by Calder, *Stevenson and Victorian Scotland* 126–41.

Good, Graham. "Rereading Robert Louis Stevenson," *Dalhousie Review* 62 (Spring 1982): 44–59.

Calder, Jenni. "Cash and the Sex Nexus." *Sexuality and Victorian Literature*. Ed. Don Richard Cox. Knoxville: U of Tennessee P, 1984. 40–53. Tennessee Studies in Literature, 27.

———. "Robert Louis Stevenson: The Realist Within." *Studies in Scottish Fiction: Nineteenth Century*. Ed. Horst W. Drescher and Joachim Schwend. Scottish Studies, 3. Frankfurt: Peter Lang, 1985. 253–70.

Simpson, K. G. "Realism and Romance: Stevenson and Scottish Values." *Studies in Scottish Literature* 20 (1985): 231–47.

Gifford, Douglas. "Myth, Parody, and Dissociation: Scottish Fiction 1814–1914." *The History of Scottish Literature: Volume III, Nineteenth Century*. Ed. Douglas Gifford. Aberdeen: Aberdeen UP, 1988. 217–58.

Hart, Francis R. "Robert Louis Stevenson in Prose." *The History of Scottish Literature: Volume III, Nineteenth Century*. Ed. Douglas Gifford. Aberdeen: Aberdeen UP, 1988. 291–308.

Keating, Peter. *The Haunted Study: A Social History of the English Novel 1875–1914*. London: Secker and Warburg, 1989.

Angus, David. "Robert Louis Stevenson: The Secret Sources." *Studies in Scottish Literature* 28 (1993): 81–91. Many characters in Stevenson's Scottish novels have the names of real people whose gravestones RLS might have seen. For example, there is an Ephraim Mackellar in the graveyard at Kirkmichael.

Swearingen, Roger G. " 'A Scotsman of the World': Robert Louis Stevenson after 100 Years," *Edinburgh University Journal*, 36 (June 1994): 158–63. Stevenson is an entirely typical member of the first post-Darwininan generation in Britain, a generation that never knew a time when the Darwninian explanation was not only well known but intellectually dominant.

Calder, Jenni. "Story and History: R. L. Stevenson and Walter Scott." *Cahiers Victoriens et Edouardiens* 40 (Oct. 1994): 21–34. RLS special issue, ed. Jean-Claude Amalric.

Hubbard, Tom. *Seeking Mr Hyde: Studies in Robert Louis Stevenson, Symbolism, Myth and the Pre-Modern*. Frankfurt am Main: Peter Lang, 1995. Scottish Studies, Johannes Gutenberg U, Mainz, 18.

Sandison, Alan. *Robert Louis Stevenson and the Appearance of Modernism: A Future Feeling*. Basingstoke: Macmillan, 1996.

Cowan, Edward J. " 'Intent upon my own race and place I wrote': Robert Louis Stevenson and Scottish History." *The Polar Twins*. Ed. Edward J. Cowan and Douglas Gifford. Edinburgh: John Donald, 1999. 187–214.

Linehan, Katherine. "Revaluing Women and Marriage in Stevenson's Short Fiction" *English Literature in Transition 1880–1920* 40 (1997): 34–59.

Calder, Jenni. "The Eyeball of the Dawn: Can We Trust Stevenson's Imagination?" In collection by Jones 7–20.

Jones, William B., Jr. "Forty-Eight Pages and Speech Balloons: Robert Louis Stevenson in *Classics Illustrated*." In collection by Jones 228–37. A shorter version of this essay appears in the collection by Steele 25–30.

Lumsden, Alison. "Postmodern Thought and the Fiction of Robert Louis Stevenson." *Of Lion and of Unicorn: Essays on Anglo-Scottish Literary Relations in Honour of Professor John MacQueen.* Ed. R. D. S. Jack and Kevin McGinley. Edinburgh: Quadriga, 1993. 115–38.

Colley, Ann C. *Nostalgia and Recollection in Victorian Culture.* Basingstoke: Macmillan, 1998. Two of the chapters are on RLS: "R. L. Stevenson's Nationalism and the Dualities of Exile" and "R. L. Stevenson and the Idea of Recollection."

Jolly, Roslyn. "Stevenson, Robert Louis" and "Samoa." *Literature of Travel and Exploration: An Encyclopedia.* Ed. Jennifer Speak. 3 vols. London: Routledge, 2003.

Arata, Stephen. "On Not Paying Attention." *Victorian Studies* 46 (Winter 2004): 193–205.

———. "Stevenson Reading." *Journal of Stevenson Studies* 1 (2004): 192–200.

Mishra, Sudesh. "No Sign is an Island." *Journal of Stevenson Studies* 1 (2004): 201–11.

Gray, William. *Robert Louis Stevenson: A Literary Life.* Basingstoke: Palgrave Macmillan, 2004. Gray offers capable, informed commentaries on most of Stevenson's works, suggestively grouped by place rather than chronologically: "The English Scene," "The French Connection," "Forever Scotland," "America," and "The South Seas."

Bloom, Harold. Introduction. *Robert Louis Stevenson.* Philadelphia: Chelsea House, 2005. Bloom's Modern Critical Views series.

Reid, Julia. *Robert Louis Stevenson, Science, and the* Fin de Siècle. Basingstoke: Palgrave Macmillan, 2006. Along with much additional matter, Reid reprints, with revisions, her "Robert Louis Stevenson and the 'Romance of Anthropology.' " *Journal of Victorian Culture* 10 (Spring 2005): 46–71.

3. Individual Works

Early Writings

Dölvers, Horst. *Fables Less and Less Fabulous: English Fables and Parables of the Nineteenth Century and Their Illustrations.* Newark: U of Delaware P;

London: Associated University Presses, 1997. Included is a revised and expanded version of Dölvers's article, " 'Quite a serious division of creative literature': Lord Lytton's *Fables in Song* and R. L. Stevenson's Prose Fables." *Archiv für das Studium der neueren Sprachen und Literaturen* 230 (1993): 62–77.

Mulholland, Honour. "Robert Louis Stevenson and the Romance Form." In collection by Noble 96–117. Mulholland discusses RLS's early fable "The House of Eld" (*ca.* 1874), "The Merry Men" (1882), and "The Beach of Falesá" (1892).

Farr, Liz. "Surpassing the love of women: Robert Louis Stevenson and the pleasures of boy-loving." *Journal of Stevenson Studies* 2 (2005): 140–60. Farr comments on RLS's essays, "Notes on the Movement of Young Children" (1874), "Child's Play" (1878), and "The Lantern-Bearers" (1888), and also on *A Child's Garden of Verses* (1885).

Pollin, Burton R., and J. A. Greenwood. "Stevenson on Poe: Unpublished Annotations of Numerous Poe Texts and a Stevenson Letter." *English Literature in Transition 1880–1920* 37 (1994): 317–49. The letter is RLS's reply, mid-January 1875, to John H. Ingram's letter taking issue with his criticism of the many errors in rendering French and German words in the first two volumes of Ingram's four-volume edition, *The Works of Edgar Allan Poe* (1874–75). RLS's review appeared in *The Academy*, 2 January 1875. RLS's letter, which Pollin and Greenwood think may be a draft that RLS recopied before sending, now appears as Letter 352 in the Yale Letters. Stevenson's review copy of the edition, and the letter, were sold as Anderson, I, 473, and are now in the Berg Collection, New York Public Library, from which source all of his more than 100 marks in these volumes are listed. The authors also suggest that there are many specific reminders of Poe in Stevenson's own work.

Short Stories

Campbell, Ian. Introduction. *Selected Short Stories of R. L. Stevenson.* Edinburgh: Ramsay Head, 1980. 7–22.

Shaw, Valerie. *The Short Story: A Critical Introduction.* London: Longmans, 1983. Shaw devotes a key early chapter to RLS, discussing "A Lodging for the Night" (1877), "Will o' the Mill" (1877), "The Merry Men" (1881), "Thrawn Janet" (1881), "Markheim" (1885), and *Dr. Jekyll and Mr. Hyde* (1886).

Gelder, Kenneth. Introduction. *Robert Louis Stevenson: The Scottish Stories and Essays*. Edinburgh: Edinburgh UP, 1989. Gelder's collection and introduction are discussed in the section on Texts in the first part of this survey (*DSA* 37, 2006).

Menikoff, Barry, ed. Introduction. *The Complete Stories of Robert Louis Stevenson: Strange Case of Dr. Jekyll and Mr. Hyde and Nineteen Other Tales*. New York: Random House, 2002. This Modern Library edition augments and thereby supersedes Menikoff's earlier collection, *Tales from the Prince of Storytellers* (1993), from which the glossary and notes are also taken. Menikoff's first-rate critical introduction is also kept, with a few small changes.

Egan, Joseph J. "Dark in the Poet's Corner: Stevenson's 'A Lodging for the Night,' " *Studies in Short Fiction*, 7 (1970): 402–08.

Walt, James. "Stevenson's 'Will O' the Mill' and James's 'The Beast in the Jungle.' " *Unisa English Studies* 8 (1970): 19–25.

Cornwell, Neil. "Two Visionary Storytellers of 1894: R. L. Stevenson and Anton Chekhov." In collection by Liebregts and Tigges 171–85. Cornwell compares RLS's "Will o' the Mill" (1878) with Chekhov's "The Black Monk" (1894).

Menikoff, Barry. "*New Arabian Nights*: Stevenson's Experiment in Fiction." *Nineteenth-Century Literature* 45 (1990): 339–62.

Honaker, Lisa. "The Revisionary Role of Gender in R. L. Stevenson's *New Arabian Nights* and *Prince Otto*: Revolution in a 'Poison Bad World.' " *English Literature in Transition 1880–1920* 44 (2001): 297–319.

Dury, Richard. "The Campness of the *New Arabian Nights*." *Journal of Stevenson Studies* 1 (2004): 103–25.

Warner, Fred B., Jr. "The Significance of Stevenson's 'Providence and the Guitar.' " *English Literature in Transition 1880–1920* 14 (1971): 103–14.

Essays and Travel Writings

Wilson, James. "Landscape with Figures." In collection by Noble 73–95. Wilson discusses RLS's early landscape essays and his travel books through *The Silverado Squatters* (1883).

Clunas, Alex. " 'Out of My Country and Myself I Go': Identity and Writing in Stevenson's Early Travel Books." *Nineteenth-Century Prose* 23 (1996): 54–73.

Hirsch, Gordon. "Robert Louis Stevenson (13 November 1850–3 December 1894)." *British Travel Writers, 1876–1909.* Ed. Barbara Brothers and Julia Gergits. Detroit: Gale Research Company, 1997. 268–22. Dictionary of Literary Biography series.

———. "The Travels of RLS as a Young Man," *Victorian Newsletter* 99 (Spring 2001): 1–6. RLS's two earliest travel books differ most in that *An Inland Voyage* (1878) is about personality and *Travels with a Donkey* (1879) is about a relationship.

Farr, Liz. "Stevenson's Picturesque Excursions: The Art of Youthful Vagrancy." *Nineteenth-Century Prose* 29 (2002): 197–225.

Pierce, Jason A. " 'The Damned Thing in Boards and a Ticket on Its Behind': Stevenson's First Book, *An Inland Voyage*." In collection by Jones 127–39.

Swearingen, Roger G. " 'Essays on the Enjoyment of the World': The Place of *Travels with a Donkey* in Stevenson's Work and Literary Career." *Cahiers Victoriens et Edouardiens* 8 (April 1979): 25–38.

Raban, Jonathan. "Introduction." *The Amateur Emigrant*. London: Hogarth P, 1984.

Phillips, Lawrence. "Robert Louis Stevenson: class and 'race' in *The Amateur Emigrant*." *Race & Class* 46 (2005): 39–54.

Gelder, Kenneth. "Stevenson and the Covenanters: 'Black Andie's Tale of Tod Lapraik' and 'Thrawn Janet'," *Scottish Literary Journal* 11 (December 1984): 56–70.

McCracken-Flesher, Caroline. "Thinking Nationally/Writing Colonially? Scott, Stevenson and England" *Novel: A Forum on Fiction*: 24 (1990/91): 296–318. Stevenson's "Thrawn Janet" (1882) and *Kidnapped* (1886) are both discussed.

Egan, Joseph J. " 'Grave Sites and Moral Death: A Reexamination of Stevenson's 'The Body Snatcher.' " *English Literature in Transition 1880–1920* 46 (1970): 9–15.

Shearer, Tom. "A Strange Judgement of God's? Stevenson's *The Merry Men*." *Studies in Scottish Literature* 20 (1985): 71–87.

Gifford, Douglas, Sarah Dunnigan, and Alan MacGillivray, eds. "Robert Louis Stevenson: *The Merry Men, Dr Jekyll and Mr Hyde* and *The Master of Ballantrae*." *Scottish Literature in English and Scots*. Edinburgh: Edinburgh UP, 2000. 403–33 (criticism), 1080–84 (reading list).

Treasure Island

Hardesty, William H., III, and David D. Mann. "Historical Reality and Fictional Daydream in *Treasure Island.*" *Journal of Narrative Technique* 7 (Spring 1977): 94–103.

Blake, Kathleen. "The Sea-Dream: *Peter Pan* and *Treasure Island.*" *Children's Literature* 6 (1977): 165–81.

Hardesty, William H., III, and David D. Mann. "*Treasure Island* in the OED." *American Notes and Queries* 16 (May 1978): 94–103.

Fowler, Alastair. "Parables of Adventure: The Debatable Novels of Robert Louis Stevenson." *Nineteenth-Century Scottish Fiction: Critical Essays.* Ed. Ian Campbell. Manchester: Carcanet, 1979. 105–29. Fowler writes chiefly about *Treasure Island* and *The Ebb-Tide.*

Pickering, Sam. "Stevenson's 'Elementary Novel of Adventure.'" *Research Studies* 49 (June 1981): 99–106.

Hardesty, William H., III, and David D. Mann. "Stevenson's Method in *Treasure Island*: 'The Old Romance, Retold." *Essays in Literature* 9 (Fall 1982), 180–93.

Mackenzie, Mary Louise, Sister. "The Toy Theatre, Romance, and *Treasure Island*: The Artistry of *Treasure Island.*" *English Studies in Canada* 8 (Dec. 1982): 409–21. [not seen]

Robson, W. W. "The Sea Cook: A Study in the Art of Robert Louis Stevenson." *The Definition of Literature and Other Essays.* Cambridge: Cambridge UP, 1982.

Usher, Robert G. "RLS and 'the man in the Bible' " *Studies in Scottish Literature.* 23 (1988): 273. In the fifth paragraph from the end of ch. 2 in *Treasure Island*, Dr. Livesey's warning to Billy Bones that if Bones takes any more drink, he will "die, and go to your own place, like the man in the Bible" refers to Judas (Acts 1:25). The reference is identified, but without mention of Judas, in Wendy R. Katz's edition (Edinburgh UP, 1998), 215.

Gannon, Susan. "Robert Louis Stevenson's *Treasure Island*: The Ideal Fable." *Touchstones: Reflections on the Best in Children's Literature.* Vol. 1. Ed. Perry Nodelman. West Lafayette, IN: Children's Literature Association, 1985. 242–52.

Jackson, David. "*Treasure Island* as a Late-Victorian Adults' Novel." *Victorian Newsletter* 72 (Fall 1987): 28–32.

LeVay, John. "Stevenson's *Treasure Island*." *Explicator* 47 (Spring 1989): 25–29.

Nelson, Claudia. "Sex and the Single Boy: Ideals of Manliness and Sexuality in Victorian Literature for Boys." *Victorian Studies* 32 (1989): 525–50. Although she does not discuss Stevenson, Nelson suggests that beginning in the work of G. A. Henty (1832–1902) and then throughout the last three decades of the nineteenth century, boys' books in England present an ideal of manliness that consists chiefly of physical strength and courage rather than, as earlier, unselfish generosity and largeness of spirit.

Loxley, Diana. "Slaves to Adventure: The Pure Story of *Treasure Island*." *Problematic Shores: The Literature of Islands*. New York: St. Martin's Press, 1990. 129–69.

Moore, John D. "Emphasis and Suppression in Stevenson's 'Treasure Island': Fabrication of the Self in Jim Hawkins' Narrative." *CLA Journal* 34 (June 1991): 436–53.

Bristow, Joseph. "The Art of Fiction: *Treasure Island*." *Empire Boys: Adventures in a Man's World*. London: Harper Collins Academic, 1991. 109–26.

Sutton, Max. "Jim Hawkins and the Faintly Inscribed Reader in *Treasure Island*." *Cahiers Victoriens et Edouardiens* 40 (Oct. 1994): 37–47. RLS special issue, ed. Jean-Claude Amalric.

Hardesty, William H. "Odds on *Treasure Island*," *Studies in Scottish Literature* 29 (1996): 29–36.

Riach, A. "*Treasure Island* and Time." *Children's Literature* 27 (1996): 181–93.

Alexander, Doris. "The Real Treasure in *Treasure Island*." *Creating Literature Out of Life: The Making of Four Masterpieces: Death in Venice, Treasure Island, The Rubiyat of Omar Khayyam, War and Peace*. University Park, PA: Pennsylvania State UP, 1996. 23–43.

Wood, Naomi J. "Gold Standards and Silver Subversions: *Treasure Island* and the Romance of Money." *Children's Literature* 26 (1998): 61–85.

Colebatch, Hal. "A 'Treasure Island' Mystery: What Are We To Make of It?" *Quadrant* 32 (Jan.–Feb. 1988): 85–87.

Seelye, John, ed. "Introduction." *Treasure Island*. Harmondsworth: Penguin, 1999. vii–xxvi.

Peck, John. "Adventures at Sea." *Maritime Fiction: Sailors and the Sea in British and American Novels, 1719–1917*. Basingstoke: Palgrave Macmillan, 2001. 149–64. In a section on *Treasure Island* (153–59), Peck argues that "in the process of reinventing the sea story . . . Stevenson also contributes to its demise." *Treasure Island* "seems to embody more than one aspect of a change of mood in Britain that can be dated from the early 1880s."

Gibson, Brian. "One Man is an Island: Natural Landscape Imagery in Robert Louis Stevenson's *Treasure Island*." *Victorian Newsletter* 101 (Spring 2002): 12–21.

Honaker, Lisa. " 'One Man to Rely On': Long John Silver and the Shifting Character of Victorian's Boys' Fiction." *JNT: Journal of Narrative Theory* 34 (Winter 2004): 27–53.

Kaighin, Errol D. "The Sea Cook." *Quadrant* 46 (Jan. 2002): 77–80.

Buckton, Oliver S. " 'Faithful to his Map': Profit and Desire in Robert Louis Stevenson's *Treasure Island*." *Journal of Stevenson Studies* 1 (2004): 138–49.

Essays and Criticism

Katz, Wendy R. " 'Mark, Printed on the Opposing Page': Robert Louis Stevenson's *Moral Emblems*." *Emblematica* 2 (Fall 1987): 337–54.

Richardson, Ruth. "Silent Pirates of the Shore: Robert Louis Stevenson and Medical Negligence." *The Lancet* 356 (23 Dec. 2000): 2171–75. RLS's comic poem, "Robin and Ben: or, the Pirate and the Apothecary" (1882), derives perhaps from his visiting "a chemist's in Broadway, a great temple near the Post Office" in New York when he arrived there in August 1879. RLS was "examined and prescribed for by a fine gentleman in fine linen" and sold useless remedies for his skin rash. "He might as well have given me a cricket bat and a copy of Johnson's dictionary" (*The Amateur Emigrant*, 1880). Richardson finds RLS condemning "the arrogance of malignant unconcern."

Swearingen, Roger G. "Notes on the Port of St. Francis (1951)." *Quarterly Newsletter, Book Club of California* 69 (Spring 2004): 35–41. *Notes on the Port of St. Francis* (1951) is a black-and-white nonfiction descriptive film by Frank Stauffacher, narrated by Vincent Price, in which all but one or two of the words are from RLS's essay on San Francisco, "A Modern Cosmopolis" (1883).

Graham, Kenneth. "Stevenson and Henry James: A Crossing." In collection by Noble 23–46.

Dekker, George. "James and Stevenson: The Mixed Current of Realism and Romance." *Critical Reconstructions: The Relationship of Fiction and Life.* Ed. Robert M. Polhemus and Roger B. Henkle. Stanford: Stanford UP, 1994. 127–49.

Jolly, Roslyn, " 'A whole province of one's imagination': On the Friendship between Henry James and Robert Louis Stevenson." *HEAT*: 5 (Giramondo Publishing Company for the School of Language and Media, U of Newcastle: Callaghan, NSW, Australia, 2003): 177–94.

Ambrosini, Richard. "The Art of Writing and the Pleasure of Reading: R. L. Stevenson as Theorist and Popular Author." In collection by Jones 21–36.

———. "R. L. Stevenson and the Ethical Value of Writing for the Market." *Journal of Stevenson Studies* 1 (2004): 24–41. RLS's "A Gossip on Romance" (1882), "Popular Authors" (1888), and "A Letter to a Young Gentleman Who Proposes to Embrace the Career of Art" (1888) show him trying to reconcile popular appeal with artistic integrity and achievement.

Fiction, Drama, and Essays of the 1880s

Comanzo, Christian. "L'imaginaire dans *Prince Otto* de R. L. Stevenson: Merveilleux et érotisme," *Cahiers Victoriens et Edouardiens* 7 (Nov. 1978): 55–65.

Sandison, Alan. "A World Made for Liars: Stevenson's *Dynamiter* and the Death of the Real." In collection by Jones 140–62.

Cairney, John. "Helter-Skeltery: Stevenson and Theatre." In collection by Jones 192–208.

Gilbert, Elliot L. "In The Flesh: *Esther Waters* And The Passion For Yes." *Novel: A Forum on Fiction* 12 (Fall 1978): 48–65. RLS's story "Olalla" (1885) offers "a naturalistic universe . . . [in which] all choice is overruled by necessity." Yet the principal character has choices and chooses affirmatively not to continue her bloodline. In this respect, RLS looks ahead to Moore's affirmative yet naturalistic fiction.

Beattie, Hilary J. "Dreaming, Doubling and Genre in the Work of Robert Louis Stevenson: The Strange Case of 'Olalla.' " *Journal of Stevenson Studies* 2 (2005): 10–32.

Gelder, Kenneth. "R. L. Stevenson's Scottish Christmas Story: 'The Misadventures of John Nicholson', The Free Church, and the Prodigal Son." *Studies in Scottish Literature* 23 (1988): 122–35.

Louit, Robert. "Robert Louis Stevenson: Un roman de Dumas." *L'Arc* [Aix-en-Provence] 71 (1978): 70–75. This is not a critical essay but a translation by Louit of RLS's essay "A Gossip on a Novel of Dumas's" (1887).

Norquay, Glenda. "Ghost Writing: Stevenson and Dumas." *Journal of Stevenson Studies* 1 (2004): 60–74. RLS's essay "A Gossip on a Novel of Dumas's" (1887) presents "what we might call a performative analysis of the act of reading . . . [and] a piece of text which ensures that the reader will seek a return to the words of not one, but two writers."

Buckton, Oliver S. "Reanimating Stevenson's Corpus." *Nineteenth-Century Literature* 55 (June 2000): 22–58. Rpt. in collection by Jones 37–67. According to Buckton, corpses brought back to life have a central role not only in *The Wrong Box* (1889) but in *Treasure Island* (1883), *The Master of Ballantrae* (1889), and *The Ebb-Tide* (1894).

Poetry

Morgan, Edwin. "The Poetry of Robert Louis Stevenson." *Scottish Literary Journal*, 1 (1974), 29–44. Rpt. in his *Crossing the Border: Essays in Scottish Literature*. Manchester: Carcanet, 1990. 141–57.

Lukens, Rebecca. "Stevenson's *Garden*: Verse is Verse." *Lion & Unicorn*, 4 (Winter 1980–81): 49–55.

Stamm, Rudolf. " 'To an Air of Schubert': R. L. Stevenson's 'The Vagabond' Re-considered." *English Studies* 64 (Feb. 1983): 36–40.

Lewis, Joanne. "How Far From Babylon? The Voices of Stevenson's Garden." *The Voice of the Narrator in Children's Literature: Insights from Writers and Critics*. Ed. Charlotte F. Otten and Gary D. Schmidt. New York: Greenwood P, 1989. 239–51.

Rosen, Michael. "Robert Louis Stevenson and Children's Play: The Contexts of *A Child's Garden of Verses*." *Children's Literature in Education* 26 (1995): 53–72.

Hollander, John. "On *A Child's Garden of Verses*." *The Work of Poetry*. New York: Columbia UP, 1997. 129–41.

Colley, Ann. " 'Writing Towards Home': The Landscape of *A Child's Garden of Verses*." In collection by Jones 174–91.

Dr. Jekyll and Mr. Hyde

Nabokov, Vladimir. "Robert Louis Stevenson (1850–1894)," in his *Lectures on Literature*, ed. Fredson Bowers (London: Weidenfeld and Nicolson, 1980), 178–205. Published here for the first time are the lecture notes on *Dr. Jekyll and Mr. Hyde* that Vladimir Nabokov used in undergraduate lectures at Wellesley College, 1941–48, and later at Cornell University. Besides the text, this edition includes several of Nabokov's hand-drawn diagrams, used in his lecture, and his own hand-drawn cover wrapper for his copy of the book.

Jefford, Andrew. "Dr. Jekyll and Professor Nabokov: Reading a Reading." In collection by Noble 47–72.

Philmus, Robert. "Jekyll and Hyde: A Faustian Mystery," in his *Into the Unknown: The Evolution of Science Fiction from Francis Godwin to H. G. Wells* (Berkeley: U of California P, 1970): 90–99.

Rogers, Robert. *A Psychoanalytic Study of the Double in Literature*. Wayne State UP, 1970.

Tymms, Ralph. *Doubles in Literary Psychology*. Cambridge: Bowes and Bowes, 1971. A long excerpt appears in Harry M. Geduld, ed. *The Definitive Dr. Jekyll and Mr. Hyde Companion* (New York: Garland, 1983): 77–94.

Smith, Ralph. "Jekyll and Hyde and Victorian Science Fiction." *Sphinx: a Magazine of Literature and Society* 4 (1975): 62–70.

Reed, John R. "Disguise." *Victorian Conventions*. Athens: Ohio UP, 1975. 289–361.

Sontag, Susan. "Dr. Jekyll." *I, Etcetera*. New York: Vintage, 1978. 187–232.

King, Stephen. "Introduction." *Frankenstein, Dracula, and Dr. Jekyll and Mr. Hyde*. New York: New American Library, 1978. v–xiii.

Punter, David. *The Literature of Terror: A History of Gothic Fictions from 1765 to the Present Day*. 2nd ed. 2 vols. London: Longmans, 1996. First published, 1980. Ch. 9 on *Dr. Jekyll and Mr. Hyde*. [not seen]

Welsch, Janice R. "The Horrific and the Tragic." *The English Novel and the Movies*. Ed. Michael Klein and Gillian Parker. New York: Frederick Ungar, 1981. 165–79. Welsch compares RLS's story in detail with the 1932 film version directed by Rouben Mamoulian and starring Frederic March.

Fraustino, Daniel V. "*Dr. Jekyll and Mr. Hyde*: Anatomy of Misperception," *Arizona Quarterly* 38 (Autumn 1982): 234–40.

Block, Ed, Jr. "James Sully, Evolutionist Psychology, and Late Victorian Gothic Fiction." *Victorian Studies* 25 (Summer 1982): 443–67.

Berman, Barbara. "The Strange Case of Dr Jekyll & Mr Hyde." *Survey of Modern Fantasy Literature*. Ed. Frank N. Magill. 5 vols. Englewood Cliffs, NJ: Salem Press, 1983. 4: 1834–39.

Fraustino, Daniel J. "The Not So Strange Case of Dr. Jekyll and Mr. Hyde." *Journal of Evolutionary Psychology* 5 (1984): 205–09.

Thorpe, Douglas. "Calvin, Darwin, and the Double: The Problem of Divided Nature in Hogg, MacDonald, and Stevenson," *Victorian Review: Newsletter of the Victorian Studies Association of Western Canada* 11 (Spring 1985): 6–22. [not seen]

Berger, Dieter A. "Robert Louis Stevenson's *The Strange Case of Dr. Jekyll and Mr. Hyde* Reconsidered." *Studies in Scottish Fiction: Nineteenth Century*. Ed. Horst W. Drescher and Joachim Schwend. Frankfurt: Peter Lang, 1985. 217–31. Scottish Studies, Johannes Gutenberg U, Mainz, 3.

Miller, Karl. *Doubles: Studies in Literary History*. Oxford: Oxford UP, 1985. Ch. 11, "Queer Fellows," comments on RLS (209–16), W. S. Sharp (Fiona Macleod), Henry James, Wilde, and others.

Sedgwick, Eve Kosofsky. *Between Men: English Literature and Male Homosexual Desire*. New York: Columbia UP, 1985.

Heath, Stephen. "Psychopathia Sexualis: Stevenson's *Strange Case*." *Critical Quarterly* 28 (1986): 93–108.

Gaughan, Richard T. "Mr. Hyde and Mr. Seek: Utterson's Antidote." *Journal of Narrative Technique* 16 (1987): 184–97.

Baldick, Chris. "Dangerous Discoveries and Mad Scientists: Some Late-Victorian Horrors." *In Frankenstein's Shadow: Myth, Monstrosity, and Nineteenth-Century Writing*. Oxford: Clarendon, 1987. 141–62 (RLS, 144–46).

Harrington, Anne. *Medicine, Mind, and the Double Brain*. Princeton: Princeton UP, 1987. [not seen]

Labarrére, André. "Onamastique, structure et dédoublement dans le cas étrange du Docteur Jekyll et de Mister Hyde." *Hommage à Claude Digeon*. Ed. Claude Faisant. Paris: Belles Lettres, 1987. 303–13.

Koestenbaum, Wayne. "The Shadow on the Bed: Dr. Jekyll, Mr. Hyde, and the Labouchere Amendment," *Critical Matrix: The Princeton Journal of Women, Gender, and Culture*, 1 (31 March 1988): 31–55.

Gates, Barbara T. "Monsters Of Self-Destruction: Robert Louis Stevenson's *The Strange Case of Dr. Jekyll and Mr. Hyde*." *Victorian Suicide: Mad Crimes and Sad Histories*. Princeton, NJ: Princeton UP, 1988. [not seen]

Oates, Joyce Carol. "Jekyll/Hyde," *Hudson Review*, 40 (Winter 1988): 603–08.

Garrett, Peter K. "Cries and Voices: Reading *Jekyll and Hyde*." In collection by Veeder and Hirsch 59–72. A revised and expanded version of this essay appears in Garrett's *Gothic Reflections: Narrative Force in Nineteenth-Century Fiction* (Ithaca: Cornell UP, 2003).

Thomas, Ronald R. "The Strange Voices in the Strange Case: Dr. Jekyll, Mr. Hyde, and the Voices of Modern Fiction." In collection by Veeder and Hirsch 73–93. This essay also appears as "In the Company of Strangers: Absent Voices in Stevenson's *Dr. Jekyll and Mr. Hyde* and Beckett's *Company*." *Modern Fiction Studies* 32 (Summer 1986): 157–73.

Veeder, William. "Children of the Night: Stevenson and Patriarchy." In collection by Veeder and Hirsch 107–60.

Hogle, Jerrold E. "The Struggle for a Dichotomy: Abjection in Jekyll and His Interpreters." In collection by Veeder and Hirsch 161–207.

Hirsch, Gordon. "*Frankenstein*, Detective Fiction, and *Jekyll and Hyde*." In collection by Veeder and Hirsch 223–46.

Lawler, Donald. "Reframing *Jekyll and Hyde*: Robert Louis Stevenson and the Strange Case of Gothic Science Fiction." In collection by Veeder and Hirsch 247–61.

Brantlinger, Patrick, and Richard Boyle. "The Education of Edward Hyde: Stevenson's 'Gothic Gnome' and the Mass Readership of Late-Victorian England." In collection by Veeder and Hirsch 265–82. In revised form, this essay is part of Brantlinger's "The Educations of Edward Hyde and Edward Reardon," *The Reading Lesson: The Threat of Mass Literacy in Nineteenth-Century British Fiction* (Bloomington: Indiana UP, 1998): 178–81.

Wexman, Virginia Wright. "Horrors of the Body: Hollywood's Discourse on Beauty and Rouben Mamoulian's *Dr. Jekyll and Mr. Hyde*." In collection by Veeder and Hirsch 283–307.

Manlove, Colin. " 'Closer Than an Eye: The Interconnection of Stevenson's *Dr. Jekyll and Mr. Hyde.*" *Studies in Scottish Literature* 23 (1988): 87–103.

Doane, Janice, and Devon Hodges. "Demonic Disturbances of Sexual Identity: The Strange Case of Dr. Jekyll and Mr/s Hyde." *Novel: A Forum on Fiction* 23 (Fall 1989): 63–74.

Herdman, John. "The Double in Decline." *The Double in Nineteenth-Century Fiction.* Basingstoke: Macmillan, 1990. 127–52 (RLS, 127–37).

Oates, Joyce Carol. Foreword. *The Strange Case of Dr. Jekyll and Mr. Hyde.* By Robert Louis Stevenson. U of Nebraska P, 1990. ix–xvii. [not seen; probably a reprint from *Hudson Review*, 1988]

Showalter, Elaine. *Sexual Anarchy: Gender and Culture at the Fin de Siècle.* New York: Viking, 1990. Showalter devotes a chapter, "Dr. Jekyll's Closet," to RLS, *Dr. Jekyll and Mr. Hyde*, and the book's later adaptations, chiefly in films, during the twentieth century (105–26).

Tropp, Martin. "Dr. Jekyll and Mr. Hyde, Schopenhauer, and the Power of the Will." *Midwest Quarterly* 32 (Winter 1991): 141–55.

Shaw, Marion. " 'To Tell the Truth of Sex': Confession and Abjection in Late-Victorian Writing." *Rewriting the Victorians: Theory, History, and the Politics of Gender.* Ed. Linda M. Shires. London: Routledge, 1992. 87–100.

Kreitzer, Larry. "Robert Louis Stevenson's *Strange Case of Dr. Jekyll and Mr. Hyde* and Romans 7:14–25: Images of the Moral Duality of Human Nature." *Journal of Literature and Theology* 6 (June 1992): 125–44.

Leps, Marie-Christine. *Apprehending the Criminal: The Production of Deviance in Nineteenth-Century Discourse.* Durham, NC: Duke UP, 1992. 205–20.

Hendershot, Cyndy. "Overdetermined Allegory in *Jekyll and Hyde*." *Victorian Newsletter* 84 (Fall 1993): 35–38.

Block, Edwin F., Jr. "The Psychomythic Tale and Stevenson's *Strange Case*" and "The Enchanted Family: Robert Louis Stevenson's 'Olalla.' " *Rituals of Dis-Integration: Romance and Madness in the Victorian Psychomythic Tale.* New York: Garland P, 1993. 3–30, 135–61.

Danahay, Martin A. *A Community of One.* Albany: State U of New York at Albany P, 1993. 135–45.

Clunas, Alex. "Comely External Utterance: Reading Space in *The Strange Case of Dr. Jekyll and Mr. Hyde.*" *Journal of Narrative Technique* 24 (Fall 1994): 173–89.

Persak, Christine. "Spencer's Doctrines and Mr. Hyde: Moral Evolution in Stevenson's 'Strange Case.' " *Victorian Newsletter* 86 (Fall 1994): 13–18.

Campbell, Ian. "Jekyll, Hyde, Frankenstein and the Uncertain Self." *Cahiers Victoriens et Edouardiens* 40 (Oct. 1994): 51–62. RLS special issue, ed. Jean-Claude Amalric.

Foss, Chris. "Xenophobia, Duality, and the 'Other' Side of Nationalism: A Reading of Stevenson's *Jekyll and Hyde.*" *Cahiers Victoriens et Edouardiens* 40 (Oct. 1994): 63–76. RLS special issue, ed. Jean-Claude Amalric.

Naugrette, Jean-Pierre. "*The Strange Case of Dr. Jekyll and Mr. Hyde*: essai d'onomastique." *Cahiers Victoriens et Edouardiens* 40 (Oct. 1994): 77–95. RLS special issue, ed. Jean-Claude Amalric.

Dollar, J. Gerard. "Addiction and the 'Other Self' in Three Late-Victorian Novels." *Beyond the Pleasure Dome: Writing and Addiction from the Romantics.* Ed. Sue Vice, Matthew Campbell, and Tim Armstrong. Sheffield: Sheffield Academic P, 1994. 268–74.

Wright, Daniel L. " 'The prisonhouse of my disposition': A Study of the Psychology of Addiction in 'Dr. Jekyll and Mr. Hyde.' " *Studies in the Novel* 26 (Fall 1994): 254–68.

Frayling, Christopher. "*Dr. Jekyll and Mr. Hyde.*" *Nightmare: The Birth of Horror.* London: BBC Books, 1996. 114–61.

Arata, Stephen D. *Fictions of Loss in the Victorian 'Fin de Siècle.'* Cambridge: Cambridge UP, 1996. The book assimilates Arata's essay, "The Sedulous Ape: Atavism, Professionalism, and Stevenson's 'Jekyll and Hyde,' " *Criticism* 37 (Spring 1995): 233–60.

Williams, M. Kellen. " 'Down With the Door, Poole': Designating Deviance in Stevenson's *Strange Case of Dr. Jekyll and Mr. Hyde,*" *English Literature in Transition 1880–1920* 39 (1996): 412–29.

Jagoda, Susan Heseltine. "A Psychiatric Interpretation of Dr Jekyll's 'Case'." *Victorian Newsletter* 89 (Spring 1996): 31–33.

Rose, Brian A. Jekyll and Hyde *Adapted: Dramatizations of Cultural Anxiety.* Westport, CT: Greenwood P, 1996. Contributions in Drama and Theatre Studies, 66.

Kabel, Ans. "The Influence of Walter Pater in *Dr Jekyll and Mr Hyde* and *The Picture of Dorian Gray.*" In collection by Liebregts and Tigges 139–47.

Mack, Douglas S. "Dr Jekyll, Mr. Hyde, and Count Dracula." In collection by Liebregts and Tigges 149–56.

Youngs, Tim. "Stevenson's Monkey-Business: *The Strange Case of Dr Jekyll and Mr Hyde*." In collection by Liebregts and Tigges 157–70.

Sutherland, John. "What does Edward Hyde look like?" *Is Heathcliff a Murderer? Puzzles in 19th-Century Fiction*. Oxford: Oxford UP, 1996. 184–88.

Hurley, Kelly. *The Gothic Body: Sexuality, Materialism, and Degeneration at the Fin de Siècle*. Cambridge: Cambridge UP, 1996. Except for a few passing references, RLS is not considered in this study, which is chiefly concerned with works of the 1890s and later, among them H. G. Wells's *The Island of Dr. Moreau* (1896) and *The Time Machine* (1895), Richard Marsh's *The Beetle* (1897), and Arthur Machen's *The Great God Pan* (1894) and *The Three Impostors* (1895).

Rosner, Mary. " 'A Total Subversion of Character': Dr. Jekyll's Moral Insanity." *Victorian Newsletter* 93 (Spring 1998): 27–31.

Phelan, James E. "Freudian Commentary on the Parallels of the Male Homosexual Analysand to Robert Louis Stevenson's *The Strange Case of Dr Jekyll and Mr Hyde*." *Journal of Evolutionary Psychology* 19 (1998): 215–22.

Beattie, Hilary. "A Fairbairian Analysis of Robert Louis Stevenson's *Strange Case of Dr. Jekyll and Mr. Hyde*." *Fairbairn, Then and Now*. Ed. Neil J. Skolnick and David E. Scharff. Hillsdale, NJ: Analytic P, 1998. 197–211.

Brantlinger, Patrick. "The Educations of Edward Hyde and Edward Reardon." *The Reading Lesson: The Threat of Mass Literacy in Nineteenth-Century British Fiction*. Bloomington: Indiana UP, 1998. 166–91 (RLS, 166–81). This is a revised version of Brantlinger's essay in collaboration with Richard Boyle, "The Education of Edward Hyde: Stevenson's 'Gothic Gnome' and the Mass Readership of Late-Victorian England," in the collection by Veeder and Hirsch 265–82.

Hendershot, Cyndy. "The Animal Within: Darwinism and Masculinity." *The Animal Within: Masculinity and the Gothic*. Ann Arbor: U of Michigan P, 1998. 97–119. Hendershot comments on *Dr. Jekyll and Mr. Hyde* and "Olalla."

Goh, Robbie. "Textual Hide and Seek: 'Gentility,' Narrative Play, and Proscription in Stevenson's *Dr. Jekyll and Mr. Hyde*." *Journal of Narrative Theory* 29 (1999): 158–83.

Hennelly, Mark M., Jr. "Stevenson's 'Silent Symbols' of the 'Fatal Cross Roads' in *Dr. Jekyll and Mr. Hyde*." *Gothic* 1 (1999): 10–16.

Towheed, Shafquat. "R. L. Stevenson's Sense of the Uncanny: 'The Face in the Cheval-Glass,' " *English Literature in Transition 1880–1920* 42 (1999): 23–38.

Mighall, Robert. *A Geography of Victorian Gothic Fiction: Mapping History's Nightmares*. Oxford: Oxford UP, 1999. Mighall devotes parts of the fourth and fifth chapters of his study to *Dr. Jekyll and Mr. Hyde*: "Atavism: A Darwninan Nightmare" (130–65), and "Unspeakable Vices: Moral Monstrosity and Representation" (166–209).

Cookson, Gillian. "Engineering Jekyll and Hyde." *Notes and Queries*: 46 (Dec. 1999): 487–92. "Most of the characters in *Jekyll and Hyde* bear the names of engineers, some of them well-known, others less so." Cookson's essay is reprinted in the collection by Steele 21–24.

Edwards, Owen Dudley. "Stevenson, Jekyll, Hyde and all the Deacon Brodies." *Folio* [National Library of Scotland] 1 (Autumn 2000): 9–12.

Haggerty, George E. " 'The end of history': Identity and Dissolution in Apocalyptic Gothic." *Eighteenth Century: Theory and Interpretation* 41 (Fall 2000): 225–48.

Smith, Andrew. "Freud's Uncanny Sublime." *Gothic Radicalism: Literature, Philosophy, and Psychoanalysis in the Nineteenth Century*. New York: St. Martin's, 2000. 166–73. In a section on RLS (166–73), Smith describes similarities between Kant's and (especially) Freud's views of subjectivity, the sublime, and the uncanny (*unheimlich*), and RLS's renderings of these in *Dr. Jekyll and Mr. Hyde*.

McNally, Raymond T., and Radu R. Florescu. *In Search of Dr. Jekyll and Mr. Hyde*. Los Angeles: Renaissance Books, 2000.

Beattie, Hilary. "Father and Son: The Origins of *Strange Case of Dr Jekyll and Mr Hyde*." *Psychoanalytic Study of the Child* 56 (2001): 317–60.

Hubbard, Tom. *Édimbourg-La-Mort: The Fantastic in Charles Dickens and Robert Stevenson*. Grenoble: Université Stendhal, 2001. Études ecossaises series, 7.

Mighall, Robert. Introduction and "Diagnosing Jekyll: The Scientific Context to Dr Jekyll's Experiment and Mr Hyde's Embodiment." *The Strange Case of Dr Jekyll and Mr Hyde and Other Tales of Terror*. Ed. Robert Mighall. London: Penguin, 2002. ix–xlii, 145–61.

Abi-Ezzi, Nathalie. "Robert Louis Stevenson." *The Double in the Fiction of R. L. Stevenson, Wilkie Collins and Daphne du Maurier*. Bern: Peter Lang, 2003. 67–120. In addition to *Dr. Jekyll and Mr. Hyde*, Abi-Ezzi covers *Kidnapped*, *The Master of Ballantrae*, and various shorter works.

Dryden, Linda. " 'City of Dreadful Night': Stevenson's Gothic London." *The Modern Gothic and Literary Doubles: Stevenson, Wilde and Wells*. Basingstoke: Palgrave Macmillan, 2003. 74–109.

Garrett, Peter K. "*Dr. Jekyll and Mr. Hyde*." *Gothic Reflections: Narrative Force in Nineteenth-Century Fiction*. Ithaca: Cornell UP, 2003. 103–22. This is a revised and expanded version of Garrett's essay "Cries and Voices: Reading *Jekyll and Hyde*," In collection by Veeder and Hirsch 59–72.

Mills, Kevin. "The Stain on the Mirror: Pauline Reflections in *The Strange Case of Dr. Jekyll and Mr. Hyde*." *Christianity and Literature* 53 (Spring 2004): 337–49.

Dalrymple, Theodore. "Mr. Hyde & the Epidemiology of Evil." *The New Criterion* 23 (Sept. 2004): 24–29.

Walker, Richard J. "He, I say—I Cannot Say I: Modernity and the Crisis of Identity in Robert Louis Stevenson's *Strange Case of Dr Jekyll and Mr Hyde*." *Journal of Stevenson Studies* 1 (2004): 77–102.

Linehan, Katherine, ed. "Sex, Secrecy, and Self-Alienation in *Strange Case of Dr. Jekyll and Mr. Hyde*." *Strange Case of Dr. Jekyll and Mr. Hyde*. Ed. Katherine Linehan. New York: Norton, 2003. 204–13. Revised from the original version: " 'Closer Than A Wife': The Strange Case of Dr. Jekyll's Significant Other," in the collection by Jones 85–100.

Dury, Richard. "The Hand of Hyde." In collection by Jones 101–16.

Cookson, Gillian. "Engineering Influences on *Jekyll and Hyde*." In collection by Jones 117–23.

Clayson, Sara. " 'Steadfastly and securely on his upward path': Dr Jekyll's spiritualist experiment." *Journal of Stevenson Studies* 2 (2005): 51–51.

Dury, Richard. "Strange Language of *Dr Jekyll and Mr Hyde*." *Journal of Stevenson Studies* 2 (2005): 33–50.

Gray, William. "A Source for the Trampling Scene in Jekyll and Hyde." *Notes and Queries* 52 (2005): 493–94. RLS may be remembering the wooden men in George MacDonald's *Phantastes: A Faerie Romance* (1858), to which he refers in a letter to his cousin Bob, October 1872 (Letter 112).

Nash, Andrew. "Walter Besant's *All Sorts and Conditions of Men* and Robert
Louis Stevenson's *The Strange Case of Dr Jekyll and Mr Hyde*." *Notes
and Queries* 52 (2005): 494–97. This familiar phrase is used in the second
chapter of *Dr. Jekyll and Mr. Hyde*, where it is said that the houses in the
square in which Jekyll lived were mostly "let in flats to all sorts and
conditions of men: map-engravers, architects, shady lawyers and the agents
of obscure enterprises." As Richard Dury notes in his edition (Edinburgh:
Edinburgh UP, 2004: 91), it appears in the Book of Common Prayer (1662)
as well as in the title of Besant's popular novel of 1882. Besant's novel,
Nash argues, "deals explicitly with the idea of the double-nature of London in the late nineteenth century," Besant there describing East London
as an "immense forgotten great city." RLS "might have been thinking
of Jekyll's house as being on the east side of the city."

Miller, Renata Kobetts. *Recent Reinterpretations of Stevenson's* Dr. Jekyll
and Mr. Hyde: *Why and How This Novel Continues to Affect Us*. Lewiston,
ME: Edwin Mellon P, 2005. Studies in British Literature, 101. Miller
includes a chronology of adaptations of *Dr. Jekyll and Mr. Hyde* on the
stage, and in film, television, and other media, including print, through the
year 2002 (43–62). Slightly more than two-thirds of her book (63–224)
consists of transcripts of her interviews in 1992 with the authors of three
recent renditions of the Jekyll and Hyde story, together with Miller's own
comments on their interviews and books: Emma Tennant, author of *Two
Women of London: The Strange Case of Ms. Jekyll and Mrs. Hyde* (London: Faber, 1989); Valerie Martin, author of *Mary Reilly* (New York:
Pocket Books, 1990); and David Edgar, author of *The Strange Case of Dr.
Jekyll and Mr. Hyde* (London: Nick Hern Books, 1992).

Kidnapped

Lascelles, Mary. *The Story-Teller Retrieves the Past: Historical Fiction and
Fictitious Adventure in the Art of Scott, Stevenson, Kipling, and Some
Others*. Oxford: Clarendon, 1982. Lascelles chiefly discusses *Kidnapped*
(1886), *The Master of Ballantrae* (1889), and *Weir of Hermiston*
(1892–94).

Calder, Jenni, ed. Introduction. *Kidnapped*. Edinburgh: W. and R. Chambers,
1980. ix–xxi. Chambers Centenary Edition.

Robson, W. W. "On *Kidnapped*." In collection by Calder, *Stevenson and
Victorian Scotland* 88–106. Rpt. in Robson's *The Definition of Literature
and Other Essays*. Cambridge: Cambridge UP, 1982. 97–118.

Beer, Patricia. *"Kidnapped." Children's Literature in Education* 14 (Spring 1983): 54–62.

Stewart, Ralph. "The Unity of *Kidnapped." Victorian Newsletter* 64 (Fall 1983): 30–32.

von Zahren, W. M. *"Kidnapped*: Improved Hodgepodge?" *Children's Novels and the Movies.* Ed. Douglas Street. New York: Frederick Ungar, 1983. 81–91.

Noble, Andrew. "Highland History and Narrative Form in Scott and Stevenson." In collection by Noble 134–87.

Gannon, Susan R. "Repetition and Meaning in Stevenson's David Balfour Novels." *Studies in the Literary Imagination* 18 (1985): 21–33.

Federico, Annette. "Books for Boys: Violence and Representation in *Kidnapped* and *Catriona." Victorians Institute Journal* 22 (1994): 115–33.

Sorensen, Janet. " 'Belts of Gold' and 'Twenty-Pounders': Robert Louis Stevenson's Textualized Economies," *Criticism* 42 (Summer 2000): 279–97.

Noble, Andrew. "Highland History and Narrative Form in Scott and Stevenson." In collection by Noble 134–87.

Menikoff, Barry. *Narrating Scotland: The Imagination of Robert Louis Stevenson.* U of South Carolina P, 2005. Menikoff shows Stevenson's deep indebtedness in *Kidnapped* (1886) and its sequel *Catriona* (1893) to half a dozen primary historical sources on the Scottish Highlands during the eighteenth century.

Nimmo, Ian. *Walking with Murder on the* Kidnapped *Trail.* Edinburgh: Birlinn, 2005.

The Master of Ballantrae

Craig, David M. "The Closed Form of *The Master of Ballantrae." Interpretations* 12 (1980): 40–52.

Gifford, Douglas. "Stevenson and Scottish Fiction: The Importance of *The Master of Ballantrae.*" In collection by Calder, *Stevenson and Victorian Scotland* 62–87.

Mills, Carol. *"The Master of Ballantrae*: An Experiment with Genre." In collection by Noble 118–33.

Naugrette, Jean-Pierre. "*The Master of Ballantrae*: Fragments d'un discours aventureux." *Études anglaises* 43 (1990): 29–40.

———. "Jacobus, Jacob, James: Historicité et onomastique dans *The Master of Ballantrae* de Robert Louis Stevenson." *Études écossaises* 1 (1992): 293–301.

Clunas, Alexander B. " 'A Double Word': Writing and Justice in *The Master of Ballantrae.*" *Studies in Scottish Literature* 28 (1993): 55–74.

Eigner, Edwin M. "*The Master of Ballantrae* as Elegiac Romance." *Cahiers Victoriens et Edouardiens* 40 (Oct. 1994): 99–106. RLS special issue, ed. Jean-Claude Amalric.

Jumeau, Alain. "*The Master of Ballantrae*: Roman d'aventures ou tragédie?" *Cahiers Victoriens et Edouardiens* 40 (Oct. 1994): 107–18. RLS special issue, ed. Jean-Claude Amalric.

Amalric, Jean-Claude. "*The Master of Ballantrae*: Un conte d'hiver? Note sur un sous-titre." *Cahiers Victoriens et Edouardiens* 40 (Oct. 1994): 119–25. RLS special issue, ed. Jean-Claude Amalric.

Orel, Harold. "Stevenson and the Historical Romance" and "Robert Louis Stevenson and *The Master of Ballantrae.*" *The Historical Novel from Scott to Sabatini: Changing Attitudes toward a Literary Genre, 1814–1920.* London: Macmillan, 1995. 37–41, 42–49. Stevenson's contribution was to liberate the historical novel from the tyranny of facts and the burden of moralizing. *The Master of Ballantrae* (1889) is "a notable example of the New Historical Novel."

Fielding, Penny. *Writing and Orality: Nationality, Culture, and Nineteenth-Century Scottish Fiction.* Oxford: Clarendon, 1996. Fielding has three chapters chiefly or only on Stevenson. "Bookmen: Orality and Romance in the Later Nineteenth Century" (132–52), is on Stevenson and Andrew Lang. It is followed by separate chapters on *The Master of Ballantrae* (153–78) and *Weir of Hermiston* (179–97).

Sutherland, John. "Who is Alexander's father?" *Is Heathcliff a Murderer? Puzzles in 19th-Century Fiction.* Oxford: Oxford UP, 1996. 189–95. In *The Master of Ballantrae* it is just possible that James Durie is the father of the second child born to Alison Durie, a son named Alexander who was born on 17 July 1757 (ch. 6).

Massie, Eric. "Robert Louis Stevenson and The Private Memoirs and Confessions of a Justified Sinner." *Studies of Hogg and His World* 10 (1999): 73–77.

Pearson, Nels C. "The Moment of Modernism: Schopenhauer's 'Unstable Phantom' in Conrad's *Heart of Darkness* and Stevenson's *The Master of Ballantrae*." *Studies in Scottish Literature* 31 (1999): 182–202.

Kucich, John. "Melancholy Magic: Masochism, Stevenson, Anti-Imperialism." *Nineteenth-Century Literature* 56 (Sept. 2001): 364–400. Kucich chiefly discusses *The Master of Ballantrae*.

Massie, Eric. "Scottish Gothic: Robert Louis Stevenson, *The Master of Ballantrae*, and *The Private Memoirs and Confessions of a Justified Sinner*." In collection by Jones 163–73.

Watson, Roderick. " 'You cannot fight me with a word': *The Master of Ballantrae* and the Wilderness beyond Dualism." *Journal of Stevenson Studies* 1 (2004): 1–23.

South Seas Writings—General Studies

Charlot, John. "The Influence of Polynesian Literature and Thought on Robert Louis Stevenson." *Journal of Intercultural Studies* [Osaka, Japan] 14 (1987): 82–106.

Edgecombe, Rodney Stenning. "Dickens, Robert Louis Stevenson and South Sea Idols." *Victorian Newsletter* 105 (Spring 2004): 27–28. RLS's mention of the two stone statues from Easter Island that once stood outside the British Museum, in his poem "To S. C." (1889; *Songs of Travel*, XXXVII), was preceded by Dickens, who mentions them in *Little Dorrit* (1855–57). Annotating RLS's letter sending him the poem, 2 December 1889, Sidney Colvin remarks: "The allusion is to the two colossal images from Easter Island which used to stand under the portico to the right hand of the visitor entering the Museum, were for some years removed, and later restored to their own place" (*Letters*, Tusitala Edition, 3, 272; Letter 2191). RLS would have known them from his visits to Colvin at his residence at the British Museum beginning in 1884, when Colvin became Keeper of the Department of Prints and Drawings.

Hillier, Robert Irwin. *The South Seas Fiction of Robert Louis Stevenson.* Bern: Peter Lang, 1989. The first two chapters reprint Hillier's "*In the South Seas*," *Studies in Scottish Literature*, 23 (1998), 104–21, and "Folklore and Oral Tradition in Stevenson's South Seas Narrative Poems and Short Stories," *Scottish Literary Journal*, 14 (Nov. 1987), 32–47. The other chapters are on *The Wrecker* (1892), *The Ebb-Tide* (1894), and "The Beach of Falesá" (1892).

Menikoff, Barry. " 'These Problematic Shores': Robert Louis Stevenson in the South Seas." *English Literature and the Wider World—Volume 4, 1876–1918, The Ends of the Earth.* Ed. Simon Gatrell. London: Ashfield, 1992. 141–56. Menikoff finds the chapters on the Marquesas that make up the earliest of RLS's nonfiction writings on the South Seas "representative both in style and substance of the entire work" (150).

Harris, Jason Marc. "Robert Louis Stevenson: Folklore and Imperialism." *English Literature in Transition 1880–1920* 46 (Fall 2003): 382–400.

Rennie, Neil. *Far-Fetched Facts: The Literature of Travel and the Idea of the South Seas.* Oxford: Clarendon, 1995. Rennie comments briefly (208–18) on RLS's *The South Seas* (begun 1890) and "The Beach of Falesá" (1892), in comparison with Melville, R. M. Ballantyne, and the French sailor and novelist Julien Viaud (1850–1927), who wrote as Pierre Loti.

Jolly, Roslyn. "Robert Louis Stevenson and Samoan History: Crossing the Roman Wall." *Fictions of Empire: Complete Texts with Introduction, Historical Contexts, Critical Essays.* Ed. John Kucich. Boston: Houghton Mifflin, 2003. 126–33. Originally published in *Crossing Cultures: Essays on Literature and Culture of the Asia-Pacific.* Ed. Bruce Bennett, Jeff Doyle, and Satendra Nandan. London: Skoob Books, 1996.

Edmond, Rod. *Representing the South Pacific: Colonial Discourse from Cook to Gauguin.* Cambridge UP, 1997. In a chapter titled "Taking up with kanakas: Robert Louis Stevenson and the Pacific" (160–93), Edmond discusses *The South Seas* (1890), "The Beach of Falesá," *The Ebb-Tide* (1894), and Stevenson's experiments in native poetic forms in *Ballads* (1890).

Smith, Vanessa. *Literary Culture and the Pacific: Nineteenth-Century Textual Encounters.* Cambridge Studies in Nineteenth-Century Literature and Culture, 13. Cambridge UP, 1998. Smith devotes more than half of her book to Stevenson, offering him as a case study of literate, European, "metropolitan" interaction with the South Seas: in his role as a political figure and traveller as well as a fiction-writer and historian.

———. "Robert Louis Stevenson: Belated First Contact." *Exploration & Exchange: A South Seas Anthology 1680–1900.* Ed. Jonathan Lamb, Vanessa Smith, and Nicholas Thomas. Chicago: U of Chicago P, 2000. 299–301. Smith offers a brief introduction to selections from RLS's account of his stay at Ho'okena, in Hawaii, and at Apemama. The same collection also includes Fanny Stevenson's letter to Sidney Colvin, written at Tai-o-hae in the Marquesas, August 1888, lamenting that he is writing ethnography rather than first-person romance.

Tulloch, Graham. "Stevenson and Islands: Scotland and the South Pacific." In collection by Jones 68–82.

Menikoff, Barry. "Prayers at Sunset." In collection by Jones 209–12.

South Seas Writings—Fiction

Hirsch, Gordon. "The commercial world of *The Wrecker*." *Journal of Stevenson Studies* 2 (2005): 70–97.

McLaughlin, Kevin. "The Financial Imp: Ethics and Finance in Nineteenth-Century Fiction." *Novel: A Forum on Fiction* 29 (1996): 165–83. In his essay on Thoreau (1880) and in "The Bottle Imp" RLS is engaged with ethical questions about having and using money, as Kant and Bentham also were.

Gray, William. "The incomplete fairy tales of Robert Louis Stevenson." *Journal of Stevenson Studies* 2 (2005): 98–109. Gray comments on "The Bottle Imp" (1890), "The Isle of Voices" (1892), and "The Waif Woman" (1892) and their debts to European *märchen*, or fairy-tales.

Scheick, William J. "The Ethos of Stevenson's The Isle of Voices." *Studies in Scottish Literature* 27 (1992): 143–49.

South Seas Writings—The Beach of Falesá

Gilmour, Peter. "Robert Louis Stevenson: Forms of Evasion." In collection by Noble 188–201. Gilmour answers in the negative his own question whether "The Beach of Falesá" and *The Ebb-Tide* "stand comparison with Melville ["Benito Cereno"] and Conrad [*Heart of Darkness*]" (190).

Brantlinger, Patrick. *Rule of Darkness: British Literature and Imperialism, 1830–1914*. Ithaca: Cornell UP, 1988. Brantlinger comments on "The Beach of Falesá" as a critique of imperialism (39–42) and, in passing, on RLS and Andrew Lang's affinity with "[t]he three principal themes of imperial Gothic . . . individual regression or going native; an invasion of civilization by the forces of barbarism or demonism; and the diminution of opportunities for adventure and heroism in the modern world" (230–33).

Linehan, Katherine. "Taking Up With Kanakas: Stevenson's Complex Social Criticism in 'The Beach of Falesá,' " *English Literature in Transition 1880–1920* 33 (1990): 407–22.

Dixon, Robert. *Writing the Colonial Adventure: Race, Gender and Nation in Anglo-Australian Popular Fiction, 1875–1914*. Cambridge: Cambridge UP, 1995. [not seen]

Warner, Marina. "Siren, Hyphen; or, The Maid Beguiled: R. L. Stevenson's 'The Beach at [sic] Falesá.' " *A Talent(ed) Digger: Creations, Cameos, and Essays in Honour of Anna Rutherford*. Ed. Hena Maes-Jelinek, Gordon Collier, and Geoffrey V. Davis. Amsterdam: Rodopi, 1996. 211–15. Cross/Cultures: Readings in the Post/Colonial Literatures series, 20.

Jolly, Roslyn. "Stevenson's 'Sterling Domestic Fiction': 'The Beach of Falesá,' " *Review of English Studies* 50 (1999): 463–82.

The Beach of Falesá in Context: A Collection of Essays. Ed. Graham Tulloch. Adelaide: English Department, Flinders U, 1999. [not seen]

Jackson, Darren. "*The Beach of Falesá* and the Colonial Enterprise." *Limina* 6 (2000): 72–84.

Jolly, Roslyn. "South Sea Gothic: Pierre Loti and Robert Louis Stevenson." *English Literature in Transition 1880–1920* 47 (2004): 28–49. RLS's "The Beach of Falesá" (1892) "contemplates, but explicitly rejects, gothic modes of imagining the Polynesian woman" (34)—modes of the sort embodied notably in the final one-third of Pierre Loti's *The Marriage of Loti* (1880).

Connell, Liam. "More Than a Library: The Ethnographic Potential of Stevenson's South Seas Writing." *Journal of Stevenson Studies* 1 (2004): 150–71. Connell suggests that in its original context of *The Illustrated London News* (1892) "The Beach of Falesá" was construed not only as a story but as ethnographic reporting.

Mack, Douglas. " 'Can the Subaltern Speak?': Stevenson, Hogg, and Samoa." *Journal of Stevenson Studies* 1 (2004): 172–91. Mack suggests that both "The Beach of Falesá" (1892) and *Weir of Hermiston* (1892–94), "in their different ways, grow out of Stevenson's response to his encounter with the operations of Empire in the South Seas."

Kramer, Jürgen. "Unity in Difference—A Comparative Reading of Robert Louis Stevenson's 'The Beach of Falesa' and Joseph Conrad's *Heart of Darkness*." *Journal of Stevenson Studies* 2 (2005): 110–39.

South Seas Writings—Later Novels

Calder, Jenni, ed. "Introduction." *Catriona*. Edinburgh: W. and R. Chambers, 1980. ix–xx. Chambers Centenary Edition.

Turnbull, Olena M. " 'All life that is not mechanical is spun out of two threads'; Women Characters in Robert Louis Stevenson's *Catriona* (1893)." *Journal of Stevenson Studies* 1 (2004): 126–37.

Osborn, Marijane. "Stevenson's Heavenly Island." *Scottish Literary Journal* 3 (1976): 43–50. Commenting on the description of Attwater's island at the beginning of ch. 7 of *The Ebb-Tide* (1894), Osborn calls attention to the many echoes of RLS's own description of Fakarava, in the Paumotus, at the beginning of the second chapter of his account of that island in *The South Seas* (1890).

Koestenbaum, Wayne. *Double Talk: The Erotics of Male Literary Collaboration*. New York: Routledge, 1989. Koestenbaum spends half a dozen pages on RLS and his stepson Lloyd Osbourne, chiefly on *The Ebb-Tide* (1894), in a section of the last chapter titled "Stevenson's Queer Yarns" (145–51).

Derry, Stephen. "*The Island of Doctor Moreau* and Stevenson's *The Ebb-Tide*." *Notes and Queries* 43 (Dec. 1996): 437.

Davidson, Guy. "Homosocial Relations, Masculine Embodiment, and Imperialism in Stevenson's *The Ebb-Tide*." *English Literature in Transition 1880–1920* 47 (2004): 123–41.

Scott, Anne MacNicol. "The Images of Light in Stevenson's *Weir of Hermiston*." *English* 19 (Autumn 1970): 90–92.

Simpson, K. G. "Author and Narrator in *Weir of Hermiston*." In collection by Noble 202–27.

Zenzinger, Peter. "The Ballad Spirit and the Modern Mind: Narrative Perspective in Stevenson's *Weir of Hermiston*." *Studies in Scottish Fiction: Nineteenth Century*. Ed. Horst W. Drescher and Joachim Schwend. Frankfurt: Peter Lang, 1985. 233–53. Scottish Studies, 3.

Sutherland, John. "What is Duncan Jopp's crime?" *Is Heathcliff a Murderer? Puzzles in 19th-Century Fiction*. Oxford: Oxford UP, 1996. 224–27.

Babb, Genie. "Where the Bodies are Buried: Cartesian Dispositions in Narrative Theories of Character." *Narrative* 10 (Oct. 2002): 195–212. Babb develops a taxonomy of representational techniques and, as a case study, examines their use in *The Ebb-Tide* (1894).

Collections of Essays

Calder, Jenni, ed. *The Robert Louis Stevenson Companion.* Edinburgh: Paul
Harris Publishing, 1980/*Robert Louis Stevenson: A Critical Celebration.*
New York: Barnes and Noble, 1980. Calder reprints essays by Colvin,
Gosse, Low, Barrie, Henley, and James, with 40 well-known pictures,
chiefly photographs of people and places, from the collection in the Writers' Museum, Edinburgh. Calder's introduction is an excellent biographical sketch of RLS, with good comments on the various essays. *Choice*,
March 1981, 953, complains rightly, however, about the "careless editing,
proofreading, and hit-or-miss arranging of black-and-white illustrations."

Calder, Jenni, ed. *Stevenson and Victorian Scotland.* Edinburgh UP, 1981.

Noble, Andrew, ed. *Robert Louis Stevenson.* London: Vision Press; New
York: Barnes and Noble, 1983. Critical Studies series.

Veeder, William, and Gordon Hirsch, eds. *Dr. Jekyll and Mr. Hyde after One
Hundred Years.* Chicago: U of Chicago P, 1988. In addition to Veeder's
pioneering but now superseded transcriptions of the surviving portions of
RLS's notebook and final manuscripts, this collection includes a survey
of book illustrations and stage and screen versions.

Knight, Alanna, and Elizabeth Stuart Warfel, eds. *Bright Ring of Words.*
Nairn: Balnain, 1994. Compiled as a "Centennial Celebration" of RLS,
this collection consists of 21 short personal thoughts from various writers
and fans including David Daiches, Jenni Calder, Nicholas Rankin, and
others. Also included are reprints of "Stevenson's Infancy" from the
Vailima Edition (1926), these being entries tracing ultimately to his mother's diary, and chapters from Lloyd Osbourne's *An Intimate Portrait of
RLS* (1924). As the comments are personal rather than critical or biographical—they are about the authors, not RLS—I have not considered any of
them separately in this survey.

Liebregts, Peter, and Wim Tigges. *Beauty and The Beast: Christina Rossetti,
Walter Pater, R. L. Stevenson and their Contemporaries.* Amsterdam and
Atlanta: Rodopi, 1996. 126–38. Studies in Literature 19.

Steele, Karen, ed. *The Robert Louis Stevenson Club 150th Birthday Anniversary Book.* Edinburgh: Robert Louis Stevenson Club, [2000].

Jones, William B., Jr., ed. *Robert Louis Stevenson Reconsidered: New Critical
Perspectives.* Jefferson, NC: McFarland, 2003. This collection has 16 critical essays, five of them given at an "RLS 2000" conference in Little

Rock, Arkansas, in November 2000, the others solicited or chosen for reprinting by the editor.

Bloom, Harold, ed. *Robert Louis Stevenson*. Philadelphia: Chelsea House, 2005. Bloom's Modern Critical Views series. This collection consists of eleven essays, mostly chapters of books or essays published in the last 25 years, and a very brief introduction by Bloom. The earlier items are G. K. Chesterton's chapter, "The Style of Stevenson" (1927), Leslie Fiedler's introduction to the Rinehart Edition of *The Master of Ballantrae* (1954), and the chapter by Robert Kiely, "The Aesthetics of Adventure" (in his *Robert Louis Stevenson and the Fiction of Adventure*, 1964). Unfortunately, in the production of this volume of reprints there are very many indications of imperfect optical scanning of the originals not corrected due to careless editing. For example, "clone" appears for "done" in the text of Leslie Fiedler's essay, and the reprint of George Dekker's article includes such slips as "Jones" for "James" in the third sentence, "die direction" for "the direction," and "a lean should draw" for "a man should draw," in the footnotes.

Dickens's Christmas Books, Christmas Stories, and Other Short Fiction

An Annotated Bibliography, Supplement I: 1985–2006

Ruth F. Glancy

*Works annotated in this supplement include the Christmas Books (*A Christmas Carol, The Chimes, The Cricket on the Hearth, The Battle of Life, *and* The Haunted Man*), the Christmas numbers of* Household Words *and* All the Year Round *and Dickens's portions of them (described by Dickens as Christmas Stories), and four stories that were originally published separately: "To Be Read at Dusk," "Hunted Down,"* Holiday Romance, *and "George Silverman's Explanation." Included are editions that contain new introductory or explanatory material, abridgments, and children's versions. Stage, film, reading, and sound adaptations are included only if a print or audiovisual (CD, DVD, VHS) version has been produced, or if there have been very few adaptations of a particular work; thus some of the many stage and television adaptations of* A Christmas Carol *are not included. This supplement offers a reasonably complete survey of criticism and studies published between 1985 and 2006, but foreign language studies, translations of stories, and dissertations are excluded. The arrangement of entries follows the 1985 bibliography, with some smaller sections amalgamated. Items are numbered consecutively, taking up where the 1985 volume,* Dickens's Christmas Books, Christmas Stories, and Other Short Fiction: An Annotated Bibliography, *left off. Cross-reference numbers appear in bold print in parentheses, and numbers between 1 and 2001 refer to the 1985 bibliography. This supplement includes its own index.*

Dickens Studies Annual, Volume 38, Copyright © 2007 by AMS Press, Inc. All rights reserved.

Dickens's Christmas Books, Christmas Stories, and Other Short Fiction

An Annotated Bibliography, Supplement I: 1985–2006

Ruth F. Glancy

Contents

Christmas Stories

Part III: Separately Published Short Fiction

Part IV: Mixed Editions and Guides,
Indexes and Compendiums

Preface

How to Use This Bibliography

The stories covered in this supplement are arranged chronologically, from *A Christmas Carol* (1843) to "George Silverman's Explanation" (1868). The Christmas Books are dealt with individually and then as a collection. Similarly the Christmas Numbers are dealt with individually and then in their collected form as Christmas Stories. At the end of the supplement the reader will find a listing of "mixed editions." This section lists collected editions that contain a variety of stories, or stories bound with other works by Dickens or other writers. The annotations in this section do not always provide complete lists of contents; usually they list only the works covered by this supplement. A final section lists compendiums or other reference books that deal briefly with some or all of the stories. Not included are dissertations, foreign language studies, and translations of stories.

The "Studies" sections of the collected Christmas Books and Christmas Stories contain works that deal with several pieces together, although extended studies of a particular story may appear within the "Studies" section of that story as well. The reader is referred to the Index to find all items pertaining to a particular story. Numbers in the Index refer to entry numbers in the supplement, as do bracketed numbers within the entry (printed in bold). Cross-reference numbers between 1 and 2201 refer to items contained in the original bibliography: *Dickens's Christmas Books, Christmas Stories, and Other Short Fiction: An Annotated Bibliography* (Garland, 1985). Because many works have multiple entries, a full bibliographic description appears only once. All other entries provide only the author's name, the title, and the relevant page numbers, with a cross-reference to the main entry. Within sections devoted to individual works, entries are arranged alphabetically by author unless accompanied by the subheading "Chronological Listing" as in sections on editions and adaptations.

Acknowledgments

Duane DeVries, bibliographer extraordinaire, has once again provided invaluable advice, editing help, and encouragement throughout the compilation of this update. Dr. DeVries has overseen the production of the Dickens bibliographies since their inception in the late 1970s while preparing his own remarkable contributions to the series, and his professionalism and kindness have never flagged. I would also like to thank Concordia University College of Alberta for funding research trips to the British Library. The Concordia librarians, in particular Wilda Campbell, have been endlessly patient and diligent in their search for rare materials through interlibrary loans. Christopher Stilson helped to compile the Index.

Introduction

Preparing this update of my 1985 Garland bibliography has brought home to me most forcibly the power and extent of the tidal wave of technological change on which we have all been surfing (or sinking) for the past twenty years. Looking back at the entries in that early volume, I remember vividly, as my co-editors will, the days when "cut and paste" meant real scissors and real glue, when "delete" often meant retype the whole page or section, when "put in alphabetical order" meant cover every available square inch of floor with file cards and shuffle them around. And what of the search for entries? Never in our wildest dreams could we have imagined Google, the IMDB, Worldcat, listserves, and all the other wonders of the Internet that allow us to explore the world's resources from anywhere in that world. In those days, finding the treasures contained at the British Library meant long hours beneath the dome at the British Museum, poring over the huge catalogue books, their yellowed and finger-blackened pages a romantic reminder of generations of previous readers, including, of course, Dickens himself.

There was much to be said for that system, of course (quite apart from the thrill of working in a room filled with ghosts); even better was having access to a library's shelves and cruising them for gems that only a particular human eye could detect as relevant. For most of us, a quick tour through a book's index still beats an electronic search in an e-book any day. But would we return to the methods of an earlier time, when having an electric typewriter with a built-in correction tape seemed the height of sophistication? I don't think so. While cruising Google, however, it did often occur to me that at least in those days there was a limit to what one could reasonably expect to uncover. One book inevitably led to another, but at a leisurely pace. Now we can Google Dickens's *A Christmas Carol* and in seconds we are facing 1,230,000 entries. The young ladies who attended the Miss Crumptons' illustrious school in *Sketches by Boz* acquired "a smattering of everything, and a knowledge of nothing." We can only hope that technology isn't returning us to a similar state of affairs.

A Christmas Carol has never relinquished its unique hold over the minds and hearts of the general public and the scholarly community, despite Philip Bolton's prediction that 1984 was "the crest of a wave" for *Carol* productions (**2312**). While stage versions continue to be popular in Great Britain (including a musical production starring, of all unlikely people, Tommy Steele [**2289**]), film and television versions appear to be largely a North American obsession. Fred Guida's excellent survey of film adaptations of the *Carol* (**2373**) lists around 110 North American appearances of the story—from full-length feature films to a variety of spin-offs in television series such as *Beavis and Butt-head* (**2352**)—between 1908 and 1998, whereas only 37 are listed for Great Britain for the same period. And most of the British productions appeared prior to 1974; Guida lists only four British versions between 1985 and 1998, to North America's 31. In the theater, the *Carol* continues to attract new generations of producers, actors, and audiences worldwide. A ballet version (**2288**) with music by Carl Davis, first staged in England in 1991, reopened this year after a three-year hiatus. John Mortimer's highly successful 1994 production (**2296**) with the Royal Shakespeare Company has been adopted by theater companies on both sides of the Atlantic, as has Neil Bartlett's adaptation for the Lyric Theatre, Hammersmith, in 2002. The prize for longest-running dramatization probably goes to North Carolina's Theatre in the Park at Raleigh, where 2006 marked the thirty-second year of their *Carol*. Edmonton, Canada, is typical of the North American fascination with Scrooge's story: for the past seven years, Edmontonians have been able to enjoy at least three *Carols* during the Christmas season—a stage production, a rock-and-roll version, and the CBC's annual nationwide reading for charity (**2411**). When one of the child actors was asked this year if he wasn't tired of performing in the Citadel Theatre's annual play, he replied, "Who would get tired of *A Christmas Carol?*" Who indeed? According to John Irving (**2523**), even illiterate circus children in India share this young actor's enthusiasm for a story that is truly universal in its appeal.

Scholars and amateur researchers have not tired of the *Carol* either, and they continue to puzzle over the unprecedented appeal of the book while tracking its popularity. Several significant publications specifically on the *Carol* have appeared in the past 20 years, including Guida's comprehensive guide to screen adaptations. Michael Patrick Hearn's updated and expanded *Annotated Christmas Carol* (**2224**) contains a wealth of information as well as illustrations and photographs, the whole attractively bound in red and printed in black and green. A similar edition also intended for more general audiences is Simon Callow's *Dickens' Christmas* (**2221**); it, too, sports a bright red cover, as do many of the books on Dickens and Christmas. Modern publishers are as conscious as was Dickens (when he wanted the first edition of *A Christmas Carol* to look festive) that appearance is important. Another red book is Paul Sammon's amusing *The Christmas Carol Trivia Book* (**2381**), modest, but useful to anyone interested in the adaptations. Before we leave red covers, however, we must mention the most important book to appear on the subject of Christmas and Charles Dickens: David Parker's 2005 study of that name (**2546**). Every Christmas, dozens of small articles are published on this topic (most of them not included in this bibliography because they appear in newspapers and popular magazines), but Parker's authoritative study is essential (and entertaining) reading, insightful not just on *A Christmas Carol* but on the history of the English Christmas and Dickens's unique relationship to the season.

Another seminal book about *A Christmas Carol* appeared in 1990. Paul Davis's tour de force, *The Lives and Times of Ebenezer Scrooge* (**2503**), traces the evolution of the story from its beginnings as an overnight best-seller to its remarkable position as a defining icon of the modern Christmas. Davis gave the world the phrase "culture text," referring to *A Christmas Carol* in its protean adapted forms, and the *Carol*'s status as cultural event has been foremost in literary criticism since 1990. In his introduction to a recent limited edition of the *Carol* (**2211**), Davis points out that the book is memorable not just because it is stylistically energetic and elastic (as Parker and J. Hillis Miller [**2536**] ably demonstrate), but also because it is rich in visual images. Davis sees these images as essentially religious, and in likening the *Carol*'s iconography to Dickens's description of Christ's ministry and miracles in "A Christmas Tree" he reminds us that for Dickens, Christmas "called up the whole life of Jesus in a magic lantern of the mind." Audrey Jaffe (**2524**), Emily Walker Heady (**2656**), and Karen Petroski (**2549**) are among several scholars who have looked closely at the complex relationship involving Scrooge, the reader, and the images provided by the ghosts.

In 1996, Joseph Cusumano (**2500**) credited his psychoanalytical reading with being the next stage in Paul Davis's cultural evolution of the *Carol*. Certainly fashionable is Cusumano's diagnosis of Scrooge's ailment as dysfunctional chakras, as is his gloomy prediction that North American children are growing up neglected and angry. In viewing Dickens as being able to diagnose and treat Scrooge's ailment, Cusumano is one of several commentators to take this tack, although opinions differ as to the source of Scrooge's problems. Was it faulty toilet training, as argued by Natalie Shainess (**2557**), or is he perhaps a walking zombie (**2490**)? The debate will no doubt continue as Scrooge's redemption is taken up by succeeding generations of readers.

Scrooge as economic man rather than psychologically damaged case study was first fully argued by Edgar Johnson in his influential 1952 biography of Dickens (**575**), but economic theories continue to inform studies of the *Carol*. For Lee Erickson (**2512**), Dickens was a Keynesian economist, intuitively (and correctly) urging consumer spending as the solution to the depression of the 1840s. But Marxist readings continue to flourish as well, with Paul A. Jarvie (**2525**) finding the book at odds with itself for both criticizing and maintaining capitalism, and Andrew Smith (**2560**) regretting that Scrooge merely becomes a better capitalist.

Every year, a host of new editions of *A Christmas Carol* appear, many in gift book format with elaborate illustrations. Most editions are designed for children, and there are surely few other books that can be marketed to appeal to people from the ages of two (picture pop-up editions) through school-age (teaching editions with study questions and activities—approved of, no doubt, by Dickens's dreaded Mr. Barlow, grim tutor of young Sandford and Merton) to adult readers. Many of these abridged and edited editions are listed in this bibliography. Another large section is devoted to "Miscellaneous Adaptations and Imitations." Here we can see the astonishing influence that the *Carol* has had on western culture as year after year writers adopt Dickens's characters for their own purposes. *A Christmas Carol* has become a kind of shorthand for writers wishing to tell a story of redemption, especially at Christmas time. What has to be redeemed varies because Scrooge has undergone some remarkable transformations—popular is the cranky CEO or equivalent who neglects family and friends in the pursuit of power and wealth. The ghosts are often attached to computers of course, variations on the ghost in the machine. But there have also been physics lessons (**2452**), anti-tax rants (**2460**), and socialist tracts (**2461**). Most of these adaptations range from the banal to "loathesome trash," as Fred Guida succinctly described the *Beavis and Butt-Head* television adaptation. While Guida, Davis, Michael Pointer (**2380**), and Philip Bolton (**2312**) have exhaustively and authoritatively recorded the many screen and stage adaptations, this bibliography has deliberately focused more on published versions of this remarkable story.

The other four Christmas books have remained in the shadows of their illustrious forebear. As early as 1913, the master bibliographer John C. Eckel (**28**) apologized for relegating *A Christmas Carol* to the category of "secondary books" but explained that it was hard to detach it from the inferior work of the other four. In the most recent critical edition of the Christmas Books (**2858**), editor Robert Douglas-Fairhurst concurs with Eckel's view and has little to say about them. It is common now to find selections of Dickens's Christmas writings—taken from a variety of sources such as *Pickwick Papers* and the Christmas stories—published with one or two of the Christmas books. (See Michael Slater's fine 2003 Penguin edition, for example [**2857**]). In her 1999 Everyman edition of the Christmas Books (**2638**), Sally Ledger stresses the centrality of a domestic ideal in them, a topic taken up by other recent critics such as Catherine Waters (**2676**). There have been a few excellent studies of individual books, of course, such as Scott Moncrieff's (**2603**) on marriage in *The Cricket on the Hearth*. But the most wide-ranging and perceptive reading of the artistry of the five Christmas books to date is provided in an (unfortunately) hard-to-obtain study by the Russian critic Tatiana A. Boborykina (**2644**). Dickens would have been delighted by this little book, roughly the same size as his first edition Christmas books, with a cover (designed by Boborykina) of stars in a night sky and Daniel Maclise's "The Spirits of the Bells" from *The Chimes*. Boborykina's analysis is informed by an extensive knowledge of European culture, and she is able to make illuminating comparisons between Dickens and the art, music, and literature of the Continent.

The 1845 Christmas book, *The Cricket on the Hearth*, has attracted the attention of scholars in disability studies, who examine Bertha and her relationship to the other characters with regard to other depictions of blindness in the nineteenth century. Elisabeth Gitter (**2601**), Martha Stoddard Holmes (**2602**), Julia Miele Rodas (**2605**), and Mary Klages (**2663**) all argue that Bertha's exclusion from marriage and family life is typical of the Victorians' fear of the disabled. In being his daughter's "eyes," Caleb is seen as the able-bodied mediator who condescendingly deprives the disabled person of free will (a charge some of the critics level at Dickens as well). Tiny Tim in *A Christmas Carol* has also been the subject of much comment in the disabled community, where he is seen as the "poster child," representing everything that is wrong with Victorian (and contemporary) attitudes of pity and self-righteousness. Tiny Tim was created, it is argued, to allow other people to be charitable and kind-hearted, and his hold on the public imagination perpetuates this view of the disabled as feeble and dependent. In these readings, Tiny Tim is smug and arrogant (**2551**), a very different child from the familiar one first suggested by Sol Eytinge, when he drew Tim on his father's shoulder in an 1867 American edition of the *Carol*. Martin F. Norden (**2377**) has examined the influence of film versions on this view of Tiny Tim.

The Christmas Stories have fared rather better than the Christmas Books. From their previous obscurity, they are becoming more widely known, partly through on-line editions, but also through the 1996 Everyman edition (**2785**), and the publication of the (sometimes) complete Christmas numbers by Hesperus Press in London. This small press is dedicated to publishing little-known works, an admirable goal, but their quality is uneven. Some editions are complete, with useful introductions—the Lirriper collection, for example, which contains both Lirriper numbers (**2731**)—while others, such as *The Haunted House* (**2717**), have been carelessly edited. Although the important sketch "A Christmas Tree" (written in 1850) has received the attention it merits in recent years (see, for instance, David Parker), "The Signalman" remains the most popular and critically acclaimed of the Christmas Stories. Ghost stories never seem to fall out of favor, and there are any number of collections in which one can find Dickens's ghost stories reprinted. "The Signalman" is undoubtedly the most complex of these, and it has attracted a considerable following among European scholars. (Japanese readers also enjoy ghost stories; see Toru Sasaki for an interesting explanation of ghosts and spirits in Japanese literature [**2555**].) Research by Simon Cooke (**2764**), Jill Matus (**2771**), and Norris Pope (**2772**) sheds interesting light on "The Signalman's" topicality as a response to railway accidents, common in the 1860s, and the stress involved in being a signalman. Other recent articles take up the ongoing debate about the relationship between the narrator and the signalman (are they doubles?) and the nature of the haunting. Is the signalman suffering from a mental illness, as Graeme Tytler suggests (**2774**)? Helmut Bonheim (**2761**) and Allessandro Vescovi (**2776**) examine the complex structure of the story in its use of repetition and cyclicity, and the importance of this structure to the reader's understanding of the paranormal events. Louise Henson (**2657**, **2796**), and Tore Rem (**2806**) have recently examined Dickens's role in the wider Victorian debate over science and the supernatural.

The topic of Dickens as editor and especially Dickens as collaborator has turned critical attention to the Christmas numbers in recent years. There is still much work to be done on the collaborative fiction (John Drew's recent book, *Dickens the Journalist* [**2610**], hardly mentions the Christmas numbers), but Lillian Nayder (**2696**) Laura Callanan (**2701**), and Grace Moore (**2705**) are among several scholars to re-examine the working relationship of Dickens and Wilkie Collins, particularly in *The Perils of Certain English Prisoners*. This story has made its way into several books about the empire, such as Linda Colley's 2002 study, *Captives: Britain, Empire and the World, 1600–1850* (**2702**), and it usually serves as an example of Victorian racist attitudes (Dickens's contributions in particular; Collins fares much better, especially in Nayder's account). Gill Gregory (**2626**) and Fran Baker (**2721**) consider the resistance of Adelaide Procter and Elizabeth Gaskell respectively to Dickens's authorial control in their contributions to the Christmas numbers.

Recent historical studies of the Christmas stories often incorporate essays from the journalism of the day, including *Household Words* and *All the Year Round*. Nayder examines *The Wreck of the Golden Mary* in relation to labor unrest among British sailors, while Anthea Trodd (**2697**) sees it in terms of other sea narratives, such as Frederick Marryat's. Trodd also sheds light on *A Message from the Sea* in her discussion of the use of messages in bottles by the Admiralty and Reuters. Laura Peters (**2709**) considers *The Perils of Certain English Prisoners* in relation to the attitudes towards Empire in *The Illustrated London News*, while Michael Hollington (**2703**) provides a useful defense of this Christmas number by relating it to Henry Morley's articles about Latin America in *Household Words*. *No Thoroughfare* has also been the subject of study, especially as a collaboration between Dickens and Collins, where again Nayder finds Collins at odds with Dickens's patriarchal attitudes (**2782**). Jenny Bourne Taylor's discussion of the London Foundling Hospital (**2783**) includes an examination of identity in the story, and the ever-original Michael Hollington (**2781**) sees *No Thoroughfare* as a link between Collins's *The Moonstone* and Dickens's *The Mystery of Edwin Drood* and a clue to the older writer's murderous designs on his younger (and now success-ful) protégé. In another biographical essay, John Bowen (**2790**) finds evidence in the later Christmas numbers that while in France, Ellen Ternan gave birth to Dickens's child. David Parker speculates more generally that Dickens stopped writing stories and sketches about the domestic celebration of Christ-mas when his broken marriage made such pieces seem hypocritical.

Also included in this update are the four stories originally published sepa-rately. "To Be Read at Dusk" remains obscure, but "Hunted Down" has been published in a selection of Dickens's detective stories, edited by Peter Haining (**2811**). The story continues to attract little attention (in his biography of Thomas Griffiths Wainewright, Andrew Motion claims that "it is difficult to see Dickens doing much in his story except make money" [**2817**]), but Jennifer Ruth usefully compares the story to *A Tale of Two Cities* in marking the rise of the professional as public servant rather than businessman (**2818**). Philip Allingham, who has written several articles on the Christmas books and stories, discusses the unreliable narrator in "Hunted Down" (**2814**). Allingham (**2825**) has also written about the illustrations in *A Holiday Ro-mance*, Dickens's late collection of stories for children which appeared in the Everyman edition in 1995, edited by Gillian Avery (**2823**). Anita Moss (**2829**) has compared it to E. Nesbit's *The Story of the Treasure Seekers* in the use of a child narrator, but she finds Nesbit's novel more convincing. Claudia Bacile di Castiglione strongly defends *A Holiday Romance*, however, finding it "perhaps the most concise and brilliant of Dickens's texts" (**2827**).

For Harry Stone, expert miner of Dickens's dark corners, the prize for most concise and brilliant of Dickens's texts goes to "George Silverman's Explanation." Stone's fine edition of the story was published in 1984 (**2832**), too late for inclusion in the last bibliography, and the long introduction to that edition has been expanded in his exhaustive 1994 study of Dickens, *The Night Side of Dickens: Cannibalism, Passion, Necessity* (**2845**). For Stone, the story is hauntingly autobiographical, solid evidence that two years before his death, Dickens was paralyzed by a lifelong guilt that arose in the blacking factory and became obsessive as a result of his hidden relationship with Ellen Ternan. Peter Ackroyd, Dickens's most recent biographer, takes a less gloomy view, seeing the story as Dickens's life "if it had gone altogether wrong" (**2834**).

The extensive work of the many scholars documented in the following pages, and the long listings of editions and adaptations, indicate that while the stories (*A Christmas Carol* always excepted) may still be considered the ''small beer'' of a writer whose forte was indisputably the novel, there is still much to uncover, explore, and enjoy in these pieces that were so close to Dickens's heart. In the past, access to the stories, particularly the Christmas numbers, was difficult, but Dickens's portions are now readily available on the Internet, and a move is afoot to make all of *Household Words* and *All the Year Round* electronic, thus opening up to scholars a greater opportunity to place the stories in their Victorian context and to examine the relationship between Dickens and his contributors. The scholarship of the last 20 years has proven that when it comes to a genius like Dickens, each generation finds a new way of reading him, a fresh insight into understanding him, and a continued respect for one of the world's most extraordinary writers.

Part I. Christmas Books

1. A CHRISTMAS CAROL

A *Christmas Carol* in Progress

2202. *A Christmas Carol: A Facsimile Edition of the Autograph Manuscript in the Pierpont Morgan Library.* Intro. John Mortimer. New York: The Pierpont Morgan Library; New Haven: Yale UP, 1993. xxx +139.
This attractive edition was produced to mark the 150th anniversary of *A Christmas Carol*, whose manuscript is stored at the Morgan Library and is put on display every Christmas. The red cover and gold wreath decoration replicate the original. A transcription faces each page of the manuscript; where the manuscript is illegible, the first edition was used. Deletions are not transcribed, but an appendix reproduces Dickens's cancelled passages which appeared on the backs of pages 16, 18, 25, 26, 31, 42, and 63. Leech's color prints are reproduced, but not the black-and-white vignettes. Leech's preliminary sketches are also included. For commentary on the illustrations see Tatham (**2205**). A foreword (pp. vii–viii) by Charles E. Pierce, Jr., director of the library, explains how the manuscript came to be in the Morgan collection. Pierce correctly recommends the edition as bringing readers "back to the *Carol*'s particularity as the remarkable creation of a great mind." Noting that the book has become almost a folktale, "timeless and authorless" because of the many adaptations of it, Pierce observes that the manuscript is an important reminder of *A Christmas Carol* as the work of Dickens. Introduction by John Mortimer (**2540**).

COMMENTARY ON THE MANUSCRIPT, PUBLICATION, TEXTUAL MATTERS, ILLUSTRATIONS

2203. Kinnane, John. "Facsimile of 'A Christmas Carol' Manuscript." *Antiquarian Book Monthly* 20 (December 1993): 22.

Describes the 1993 facsimile edition (**2202**), thinking it the first. Kinnane is apparently unaware that there have been several facsimile editions including a 1967 Pierpont Morgan edition (**7**).

2204. Hancher, Michael. "Reading the Visual Text: *A Christmas Carol*." *The Yale University Library Gazette* 74 (October 1999): 21–40.

After providing an excellent description of the cover and opening pages of the *Carol*, Hancher concentrates on the layout of the illustrations and the close relationship between text and illustration that the layout provided in the original edition (and that was missed in later editions such as the 1946 Penguin). Hancher notes that this relationship extended even to the full-page color illustrations. At the end of p. 77 of the first edition, the reader reads that the Spirit of Christmas Present's lamp light fell on Scrooge "as he came peeping round the door." At that point the reader turns the page (peeps round the door) to find the full-page illustration of the ghost. The article includes all the illustrations as well as photographs of the cover and title pages. It also provides interesting insights into Victorian publishing methods.

2205. Tatham, David. "John Leech's Illustrations." In *A Christmas Carol: A Facsimile Edition of the Autograph Manuscript in the Pierpont Morgan Library* (**2202**). xv–xxiii.

This excellent article begins by discussing the original drawings that are now in Harvard's Houghton Library. These "roughs," he notes, preserve the "liveliness" of Leech's hand in ways that the final copper or wood cuts cannot. Noting that the Ghost of Christmas Past's feet are visible under the extinguishing cap in the original drawing but are not in the woodcut, Tatham suggests that the change shifted the emphasis from the feet to the light of memory released by the ghost and which Scrooge cannot now extinguish. While Dickens "almost certainly" specified the subjects, this alteration may have been Leech's idea. Tatham provides a very useful account of the process involved in making woodcuts, as well as some information on William James Linton, the engraver. In his sensitive discussion of Leech's illustrations, Tatham argues that they convey a warmheartedness not present in Leech's work for *Punch*. Leech's Scrooge is never grotesque and never beyond redemption, and the ghosts are full of humanity.

SUBSEQUENT EDITIONS CONTAINING NEW INTRODUCTIONS

Chronological Listing

2206. Dickens, Charles. A Christmas Carol *Christmas Book*. New York: IBM, 1984. 162.

This edition concludes with *A Christmas Carol*, illustrated by Leech's preliminary sketches and his final color plates. Five sections written by Tim Hallinan precede the text. "*A Christmas Carol*: A Story in Pictures" tells the story through photos taken during the filming of the George C. Scott version in Shrewsbury (**2340**). This was the first adaptation to be filmed in color entirely on location. Section Two, "Mr. Dickens and Christmas," surveys the writing of the book and provides a short history of the celebration of Christmas, with good accompanying pictures. Section Three, "Christmas By Hand: Victorian Holiday Crafts and Traditions," offers ideas for recreating a Victorian family Christmas. Section Four, "Feasts and Revels," gives a short history of Christmas dinners and drinks, and provides recipes and games. Section Five contains a history of Christmas carols. Section Six contains the unabridged *A Christmas Carol*. Photography for the book is by David James.

2207. ———. *A Christmas Carol*. Harmondsworth, Middlesex: Puffin; New York: Viking Penguin, 1985. 134.
Illustrated by Michael Foreman. In a good, brief introduction (pp. 11–14) Leon Garfield suggests that Dickens did not invent Christmas, but he "dragged [it] out of the cold churches and solemn monasteries" and into the world's homes. He sees the story as a sermon on the limitations of cleverness and reason.

2208. ———. *A Christmas Carol*. Illustrated by Michael Cole. London: Pagoda Books; Woodbury, NY: Barron's, 1985. 81.
This unusual and clever edition narrates the story in frames with the dialogue appearing, cartoon-style and in script, in balloons while the narrative is inset in typescript. Interspersed are full-page and double-page illustrations.

2209. ———. *A Christmas Carol*. In *The Annotated Dickens*. Ed. Edward Guiliano and Philip Collins. Vol. 1. London: Orbis, 1986. 824–83.
An excellent introduction (pp. 824–26) discusses Dickens and Christmas, the origins of the *Carol*, and its reception, as well as analyzing the book as echoing the "contrast central to the idea of Christmas" in the Bible and the early church: the humble birth of the Son of God at midwinter. The text of the *Carol* is fully annotated, and there are numerous photographs from film versions and illustrations from various editions as well as the manuscript.

2210. ———. *A Christmas Carol*. Saxonville: Picture Book Studio, 1988; New York and London: North-South Books, 2000. 67.
This large-format book with fine full-page illustrations by Lisbeth Zwerger was first published in Switzerland under the title *Ein Weihnachtsmärchen*.

2211. ———. *A Christmas Carol in Prose: Being a Ghost Story of Christmas*. San Francisco: Arion Press, 1993. 115.

Illustrated by Ida Applebroog, this limited edition of 226 copies, each signed by the illustrator, was issued on the 150th anniversary of the *Carol*. In an excellent introduction, Paul Davis draws attention to the visual strength of the *Carol*, noting that the book has become our iconography of Christmas. He provides a very abbreviated summary of his remarkable 1990 study of the *Carol*'s history (**2503**). This edition is beautifully produced on fine paper, but Applebroog's illustrations (produced from polymer plates) are somewhat stark.

2212. ———. *A Christmas Carol*. Ed. Geoff Barton. Harlow, Essex: Longman, 1994. xviii + 107.

A senior school textbook containing helpful background information and study questions. "The Writer on Writing" provides background on the writing of the *Carol*, using Dickens's letters. "Readers' Reactions" quotes from Forster, Thackeray, and Carlyle. A seven-page introduction discusses Victorian Christmases and everyday life in the 1840s. Barton points out that while we remember the scenes describing an abundance of food and jollity, in the book these scenes are a part of a dream that vanishes. Dickens's message is that perfect Christmases have to be created through generosity and love. A glossary follows the text, which is complete and with the original spelling. An excellent Study Programme contains such exercises as having to arrange Dickens's descriptive headings in the right order, and rewriting the short summary of the *Carol* found in the *Oxford Companion to English Literature* (and suggesting the student can improve upon it). Extended assignments include ideas for making a film version. Suggestions for further reading include other thrillers set at Christmas.

2213. Sibley, Brian, ed. *"A Christmas Carol": The Unsung Story. The Story Behind Dickens's Christmas Classic and the Original Story in Full.* Oxford: Lion; Sutherland, NSW: Albatross, 1994. 197.

This edition contains a wealth of supplementary material, divided into ten chapters and an epilogue. Sibley reviews the historical background (ragged schools, child labor, etc.), the history of Christmas in the church, the influence of Washington Irving, Dickens's celebration of Christmas, the composition of the *Carol* and its sources, the manuscript and publication, the illustrations by John Leech and later artists, the reception, sales, piracy, and translations, and the four succeeding Christmas books. Sibley offers a detailed and exhaustive survey of adaptations: parodies, film and radio versions, recordings, stage productions, ballets, operas—what Paul Davis (**2503**) calls the culture text. Unlike Davis, Sibley does not review the adaptations chronologically, so he does not offer an historical or cultural analysis of responses to the book. Although his comments on the different adaptations are useful and lively, the discussions are somewhat scattered. But he has uncovered many rare adaptations, including those in newspapers. A bibliography provides a good short listing of Dickensiana. The *Carol* appears in its entirety, with Leech's color prints. Printed on high-quality paper, with a huge selection of photographs and illustrations from the 150-year history of the *Carol*, this is a well-produced and interesting book that is unfortunately out of print and hard to find in libraries. Taking into account the vast number of books on the *Carol* and its adaptations, a reader might wonder why Sibley considers its story "unsung" in 1994.

2214. Dickens, Charles. *A Christmas Carol: With 45 Lost Engravings by Gustave Doré (1861) and 130 Other Victorian Illustrations.* Ed. Dan Malan. St. Louis: MCE Publishing, 1996. 176.

This unusual edition contains Doré's 1861 engravings for *A Christmas Carol* (first published in a French magazine) as well as his 1872 engravings from Blanchard Jerrold's *London, A Pilgrimage.* Also included are illustrations by John Leech, Hablot Knight Browne, Felix Darley, Sol Eytinge, George Cruikshank, E. A. Abbey, and Frederic Barnard. An introduction by Dan Malan, a Doré specialist, contains a great deal of useful information."Dickens and Doré" finds them to be kindred spirits with many friends in common, although there is no record that they ever met. "Dickens' Life and Works" focuses on "the illustrations in his original editions and how they contributed to his popularity," and it notes that the 1984 television adaptation of the *Carol* (**2340**) used illustrations from Doré's *London* to show the plight of the poor. "Doré's Life and Work" is followed by "Illustrated Editions of *A Christmas Carol*," which traces a shift in emphasis from Fezziwig to the spirits to Scrooge to Tiny Tim (first illustrated by Sol Eytinge in 1867). For a similar discussion of the illustrations see Davis (**2503**). Malan offers a useful survey of early engravings, illustrated parodies in British magazines, and comic book adaptations, as well as the history of Doré's illustrations. The text of the *Carol* is reprinted from the 1906–1908 National Edition, published by Chapman and Hall.

2215. Cusumano, Joseph D. *Transforming Scrooge: Dickens's Blueprint for a Spiritual Awakening.* St. Paul, MN: Llewellyn Publications, 1996. 170. Cusumano would not consider his book an "edition" of *A Christmas Carol* because the story is playing a supporting role to his psychoanalytical essay, rather than the other way around. But the complete text is here, with all of the original Leech illustrations. For Cusumano's commentary see Cusumano (**2500**).

2216. Dickens, Charles. *A Christmas Carol*. Ed. Jim Rimmer. New Westminster, BC, Canada: Pie Tree Press, 1998. 118.

Designed, illustrated, and printed by Jim Rimmer, this edition was published in a limited printing of 26, lettered A to Z, half-bound in leather, and issued in deluxe clamshell boxes. Another 100 copies were issued in cloth quarter bindings. In the introduction (pp. 7–8), Crispin Elsted finds the *Carol*'s appeal in its giving Scrooge a second chance. He concentrates on the illustrations for this richly produced edition, which he suggests makes us look at the story with fresh eyes because the production is uniquely designed and illustrated by one man. We are encouraged to be similarly individual in our reading of it. The illustrations, some in color and some in green and white, are stark and linear, with two of the ghosts an unhappy blend of female clothes with male bodies. More successful are some of the smaller images set into the text.

2217. ———. *A Christmas Carol*. New York: Scholastic Classics, 1999. 122.

An edition for schoolchildren with a brief introduction by Karen Hesse that touches on the *Carol* as a ghost story and as social criticism. Also contains an inaccurate short biography of Dickens.

2218. ———. *A Christmas Carol*. Ed. Suzanne Bosman. Paris: Editions Gallimard, 1999; New York: Viking Children's Books, 2000. 107.

An excellent children's edition (part of *The Whole Story* series), edited by Suzanne Bosman (the English edition translated by Barbara Brister). With illustrations by William Geldart (many of them after John Leech's), this nicely produced book includes a wealth of supplementary material for young readers on every page: information about Dickens, London, his times, Christmas customs, and references in the text, such as "Sir Roger de Coverley." Many of the added illustrations are old maps, engravings, photographs, and paintings. The biography of Dickens on the back flyleaf inexplicably has him born on 17 February 1812 in Edinburgh, but otherwise the notes seem to be fairly accurate.

2219. ———. *Dickens' "A Christmas Carol."* Ed. Allyson McGill. Foster City, CA: Hungry Minds, 2001.

Part of the "Cliffs Complete" series. Not seen.

2220. Dickens, Charles. *A Christmas Carol*. Broadview Literary Texts. Ed. Richard Kelly. Peterborough, Ontario, Canada; Sydney, Australia; Ormskirk, Lancashire, England: Broadview Press, 2003. 239.

A scholarly edition based on the text of the first edition with John Leech's original illustrations. This useful edition also contains annotations, a chronology of Dickens's life, and five appendices: extracts from other nineteenth-century writings about Christmas (Washington Irving's *The Sketch Book*, Thomas K. Hervey's *The Book of Christmas*, and Dickens's Christmas writings in *Sketches by Boz, Pickwick Papers,* and *Household Words)*; extracts concerning child labor, education, and the workhouse; extracts from Dickens's letters; extracts from contemporary reviews; and a listing of notable film, television, and radio adaptations. The cover photograph of ragged children at a Barnardos Home in 1875 emphasizes the social criticism of the *Carol.* Edited with an introduction by Richard Kelly (**2529**).

2221. Callow, Simon, ed. *Dickens' Christmas: A Victorian Celebration.* New York: Harry N. Abrams, 2003. 160.

This attractive edition for Christmas contains the complete *Carol* as well as many excellent colored and black-and-white illustrations (from Dickens and the Victorian age) and several sections of related text. "Dickens the Man" surveys Dickens's life with hardly any mention of his writings; "The Spirit of Christmas Past" provides an overview of Christmas in England from its pagan beginnings, concluding that for Dickens "Christmas was a living tradition" and his contribution was to the meaning of the season rather than the celebration. In "Dickens and Christmas" Callow considers "A Christmas Dinner" (from *Sketches by Boz*) and looks ahead to the social criticism of the *Carol,* the subject of "Dickens and *A Christmas Carol.*" "The Christmas Feast" discusses food in the *Carol* and in Victorian England. "New Traditions, Old Traditions" describes the Victorian celebration of the season and includes passages from Dickens's essay "A Christmas Tree" (misdated). In "Beyond Dickens' Christmas" Callow discusses Christmas in Sir Walter Scott and Washington Irving to argue (as does David Parker [**2546**]) that "the widely reported death of Christmas was greatly exaggerated." The tradition evoked (differently) by Dickens and Irving was well established. Callow then considers the influence of the *Carol* in America, Dickens's American visits, and his influence on the celebration of Christmas in America to the present day. Callow concludes that Dickens's Christmas "remains as potent a definition as ever of an aspect of the human condition" and a vital reminder to consider those who "have no place at the feast."

2222. Dickens, Charles. *A Christmas Carol.* Ed. Elliot Engel. New York: Pocket Books, 2003. xxiv + 148.

This good, cheap edition for children in the Enriched Classics series contains brief notes, eleven short critical excerpts from a range of critics from John Forster (**540**) to Fred Guida (**2373**), suggestions for further reading, and a brief biography of Dickens. In his lively introduction (pp. xi–xxiv), Elliot Engel credits Dickens with connecting Christmas with snow (pointing out that the eruption of an Indonesian volcano in 1815 caused more white Christmases than usual in

England in Dickens's childhood), with coziness, and with terror rather than sentiment. Engel wrongly credits Shakespeare as being the first writer to use the phrase "as dead as a door nail."

2223. ———. *A Christmas Carol.* New York: Aladdin Classics, 2004. 131. Foreword by Nancy Farmer. Not seen.

2224. ———. *The Annotated Christmas Carol. A Christmas Carol in Prose.* Ed. Michael Patrick Hearn. New York: W.W. Norton, 2004. 266. This expanded revision of Hearn's 1976 annotated edition of the *Carol* (**100**) contains a great deal of valuable new material. The introduction now contains a survey of Dickens's life and work prior to 1843, an extended discussion of Dickens's 1842 visit to America, and new material on the early dramatizations. Hearn now provides very useful information about the reception of the *Carol,* particularly abroad and in the United States. He extensively surveys the American newspaper and magazine reviews, noting that many reviewers had not forgiven Dickens for the recently published *American Notes,* and he describes an attack on Dickens that appeared as "Sequel to *The Christmas Carol*" in the New York newspaper *The New World* on 28 December 1844. Some of Hearn's already extensive annotations are further expanded (and printed in green), and the text of the *Carol* itself is printed in a much more readable font than in the earlier edition. In an appendix (not contained in the earlier edition) Hearn surveys Dickens's interest in the theatre, his amateur acting career, and the development of his public reading career, beginning in 1858 with the *Carol* (coinciding with the breakdown of his marriage, which Hearn discusses in detail.) Again Hearn usefully concentrates on the American audiences and reception of the readings, providing far more firsthand and newspaper accounts than have previously been made available. The appendix concludes with Dickens's reading edition of the *Carol,* published by Ticknor and Fields and illustrated by Sol Eytinge (**174**). This new edition contains many more illustrations than the 1976 edition.

2225. ———. *A Christmas Carol* and *The Christmas Angel* by Abbie Farwell Brown. Nashville, TN: Thomas Nelson, 2005. 301. First published by Elm Hill books, this combination of the *Carol* and Brown's *The Christmas Angel* has an introduction and afterword by Joe L. Wheeler. Not seen.

SCHOLARSHIP CONCERNING THE PIRACY OF
A CHRISTMAS CAROL

2226. Jaques, Edward T. *Charles Dickens in Chancery: Being an Account of his Proceedings in Respect of the "Christmas Carol" with Some Gossip in Relation to the Old Law Courts at Westminster.* Union, NJ: Lawbook Exchange, 2001. 95.

Reprint of the 1914 account of Dickens's lawsuit by a solicitor of the Supreme Court (**107**).

ABRIDGMENTS

Chronological Listing

2227. Dickens, Charles. *A Christmas Carol*. New York: Gilberton, 1948. 48. Number 53 in the Classics Illustrated series, this comic book version is illustrated by Henry Kiefer and abridged by George D. Lipscomb.

2228.———. *A Christmas Carol*. West Haven, CT: Academic Industries, 1984. 61.
A comic book version.

2229. ———. *A Christmas Carol*. In *The Faber Book of Christmas Stories*. Ed. Sara and Stephen Corrie. London: Faber, 1984. 50–89.
Illustrated by Jill Bennett. Abridged by Stephen Corrie, who notes at the end that he regrets having to shorten the story for inclusion. He thinks of it, however, as "one in which the full robust flavor of the original has been retained despite one or two changes in the wording and minuscule omissions of those entrancingly interminable embellishments which are part of the master's uniqueness."

2230. ———. *A Christmas Carol Pop-Up Book*. Ed. Betty Ren Wright. London: Methuen; Los Angeles: Intervisual Communications, 1986. [12]. This very abridged version is illustrated by Victor G. Ambrus. A young reader would have difficulty understanding Scrooge's transformation when Belle and Fanny are omitted from the story.

2231. ———. *A Christmas Carol. Being a Ghost Story of Christmas*. Abridged and illustrated by Mercer Mayer. New York: Macmillan, 1986. 38.
A good abridgment that retains much of the original text. The illustrations depict mice as the main characters, however, and the Ghost of Christmas Yet to Come is a crocodile (or possibly a dinosaur.)

2232. ———. *A Christmas Carol*. Ed. Jane Wilton-Smith. London: Blackie, 1986. 61.
Jane Wilton-Smith has simplified the vocabulary and omitted some major scenes. The illustrations by John Worsley include the Ghost of Christmas Present in a short dressing gown.

2233. ———. *A Christmas Carol*. Ed. Sheila Lane and Marion Kemp. Take Part Series. London: Ward Lock, 1987. 64.
This adaptation, illustrated by Robert Hales, is intended for group reading by children, ages 6 to 9, at different reading levels. The text

is completely rewritten and the children are intended to add sound effects.

2234. ———. *A Christmas Carol.* Edited and simplified by D. K. Swan and Michael West. London: Longman, 1987. 56.
Illustrated by Giles Waring. A stage-two reader with a 900-word vocabulary, this version simplifies the language but tries to keep to the original whenever possible. Contains a brief biography of Dickens, a description of Christmas in London in 1843, and questions on the story.

2235. ———. *A Christmas Carol. Easy Piano Picture Book.* Ed. Kenneth Lillington. London: Faber and Faber, 1988. Not paginated.
Abridged and rewritten for children, with illustrations after Leech by Annabel Spenceley and interspersed with eight traditional carols, transcribed for easy piano performance.

2236. *A Christmas Carol. Adapted from the Story by Charles Dickens.* Illustrated by Kareen Taylerson. London: Orchard; New York: Viking Kestrel, 1989. Not paginated.
A good edition for young children, well abridged and illustrated, with lift-the-flap and revolving picture additions that are based on Leech's original illustrations.

2237. Dickens, Charles. *A Christmas Carol.* Ed. Joanne Ryder. New York: Platt and Munk, 1989.
A children's adaptation with illustrations by John O'Brien. Not seen.

2238. ———. *A Christmas Carol.* Philadelphia: Running Press, 1990. 157.
This miniature adaptation (3'' by 2'') contains several color prints by Arthur Rackham and an excellent brief appreciation by Jane Parker Resnick.

2239. ———. *A Christmas Carol.* Gretna, LA: Pelican, 1990. 48.
A children's adaptation retold from Dickens's reading version and illustrated by James Rice. Not seen.

2240. ———. *A Christmas Carol.* West Haven, CT: Pendulum Press, 1991. 61.
A comic book version with illustrations by Jun Lofamia and cover art by Mark Hannon.

2241. ———. *A Christmas Carol.* Ed. Vivian French. London: Walker Books, 1992; Cambridge, MA: Candlewick, 1993. 44.
Illustrated by Patrick Benson. The text is extensively abridged and adapted. A dreadful portrait of Dickens forms the frontispiece.

2242. ———. *A Christmas Carol.* Oxford: Oxford UP, 1992. 73.
A Level 2 book in the Oxford Progressive Readers series (2100-word vocabulary). The intention is to improve vocabulary, so the story is rewritten with new words explained in the text and repeated ''for

maximum reinforcement.'' Chapter 11 of the twelve chapters is titled ''Tiny Tim is Dead.'' Questions and activities include language games based on the story. The illustrations are by Choy Man Yung.

2243. Manner, Carolyn S. *A Christmas Carol. Based on the Book by Charles Dickens.* Toronto: Prospero Books, 1992. 12.
A pop-up book for young children with illustrations by Samantha Carol Smith.

2244. Dickens, Charles. *A Christmas Carol.* Ed. Eric Kincaid. Newmarket: Brimax, 1992.
This adaptation for children was also published in French, Paris: Gründ, 1992. Not seen.

2245. ———. *A Christmas Carol.* Ed. Neil O. Connelly, Jr. New York: Ottenheimer, 1993.
A children's pop-up version, illustrated by Sergio Martinez.

2246. ———. *A Christmas Carol.* Ed. Joan Collins. Loughborough: Ladybird, 1994. 51.
A reprint of the 1982 children's edition (**140**), retold in simple language and illustrated by Chris Russell.

2247. Blishen, Edward. *Stand Up, Mr. Dickens. A Dickens Anthology.* London: Orion Books, 1995; New York: Houghton Mifflin, 1996. 29–42.
A selection of passages from Dickens which includes a slightly abridged reprinting of *A Christmas Carol* from Scrooge's taking ''his melancholy dinner'' to the end of Stave One. Blishen's short introduction explains Dickens's writing of the book and his love of public readings. Illustrated by Jill Bennett.

2248. Mould, Chris. *Charles Dickens' A Christmas Carol.* Oxford: Oxford UP, 1995. Not paginated.
This picture book for children is extensively but cleverly adapted. Mould's illustrations are part Gothic, part caricature, the cover design suggesting *Notre Dame de Paris.*

2249. Dickens, Charles. *A Christmas Carol.* Ed. Pamela Kennedy. Nashville, Tennessee: Ideals Children's Books, 1995. Not paginated.
A picture-book edition, illustrated by Carol Heyer and intended for ages five to eight, that can be read in 20 minutes.

2250. ———. *A Christmas Carol.* Ed. Carol Marsh. Kansas City: Hallmark Cards, Inc., 1995. Not paginated.
''Adapted for modern readers'' by Carol Marsh and illustrated by Gary Head, this lavishly bound version is hard to obtain.

2251. ———. *A Christmas Carol.* New Alresford, Hampshire: Hunt and Thorpe, 1996. Not paginated.
A pop-up edition for children, written by Linda Parry and illustrated by Alan Parry. Although the story is abbreviated (the Cratchits do not

appear in Stave IV), it is well done, and the clear plastic ghost pop-ups are effective.

2252. ———. *A Christmas Carol: Charles Dickens' Tale.* Ed. Shona McKellar. Deluxe Classics Edition. London: Dorling Kindersley; New York: Eyewitness Classics, 1997; Bolton, Ontario, Canada: Fenn, 1998. 64.

This useful edition for children is abridged from Dickens's reading version by Shona McKellar and illustrated by Andrew Wheatcroft. As well as the large illustrations for the story, this edition contains a good short introduction and several two-page spreads of illustrated facts about Dickens's London, Victorian society, Christmas in 1843, Dickens's life, and the history of *A Christmas Carol.* Each page of text is annotated with explanations and illustrated with photographs, stills from film versions of the story, and other pictures. Although the illustrations and annotations tend to dominate the story itself, the background information is useful and accurate, and the text of the *Carol* is abridged, not rewritten.

2253. ———. *A Christmas Carol. A Charles Dickens Story.* Ed Michael Lawrence. Oxford: Heinemann, 1999. 80.

Stage 4 in the Classic Novel series, adapted by Michael Lawrence and illustrated by Martin Cottam.

2254. ———. *A Christmas Carol.* Ed. Emily Hutchinson. Costa Mesa, CA: Saddleback, 1999. 79.

Adapted for grade 4 readers, ages 5 to 12.

2255. ———. *A Christmas Carol: A Pop-Up Christmas Classic.* New York: Playmore, Inc., and Waldman, n.d. Not paginated. Reprinted Bridlington, North Humberside: Peter Haddock, 2002.

Children's version well illustrated by John Patience.

2256. Wilding, Valerie. *Dickens Stories.* Illustrations by Michael Tickner. Top Ten Series. London: Scholastic, 2000. 240.

This "short cut" to long novels (the introduction assures its young readers that they are worth reading in full) includes *A Christmas Carol* as the tenth Dickens abridgement. "The X-Mas Files" tells the story in comic-book style. At a meeting of the Haunting Action Group, Jacob Marley tells his three friends about Scrooge's encounter with Bob Cratchit, Fred, and the charity gentlemen at the opening of the story. He enlists their help to reform Scrooge, and the rest of the story is told as their handwritten reports to the meeting. This amusing format remains fairly true to the original story. It concludes, for example, with Tiny Tim's hope that his presence in church would remind the people there of Christ's ministry.

2257. Dickens, Charles. *A Christmas Carol.* Ed. Jane Parker Resnick. London: Kingfisher; Philadelphia: Courage, 2000. 56.

This good abridgment contains 13 color plates and many excellent line drawings by Christian Birmingham. A large-size children's edition, it includes Dickens's preface.

2258. ———. *A Christmas Carol.* Ed. Clare West. Oxford Bookworm series. Oxford: Oxford UP, 2000. 72.

This retelling is illustrated by Ian Miller and contains a brief biography of Dickens. Intended for non-English-speaking school children, the text is simplified (Stage 3, 1000 headwords)—Ignorance and Want become Crime and Need, for example—but most of the scenes are included. Useful activities sections focus on vocabulary and plot as well as the broader issues of Christmas celebrations. Available on cassette (**2406**).

2259. ———. A Christmas Carol. Ed. Michael Dean. London: Penguin, 2000. 39.

A Level 2 reader (600-word vocabulary). The retelling is banal and at times surprising. Scrooge's remark that "every idiot who goes about with 'Merry Christmas' on his lips, should be boiled with his own pudding" becomes the more disturbing "I think I'd like to eat those people for Christmas dinner!" An activities section contains reading and writing practice and essay topics.

2260. ———. *Charles Dickens's A Christmas Carol.* Ed. Peter Leigh. Published in association with The Basic Skills Agency. London: Hodder and Stoughton, 2000. 28.

This Livewire Classics abridgment, with illustrations by Jim Eldridge, claims to retain "most of the original text and all of its magic." The text is set out in short lines, as in poetry, and although the story is abbreviated, this version does retain most of the important passages. Vocabulary and phrases are annotated in the margins. A teacher's resource book accompanies this edition (**2545**).

2261. ———. *A Christmas Carol.* Ed. Stephen Krensky. New York: Harper Collins, 2001. 60.

This attractive and well-abridged edition is intended for children aged 7 to 10. Dean Morrissey's color illustrations have the realism of photography, particularly in the faces. A Scottish influence is evident, particularly in the Ghost of Christmas Present's tartan tam and feather, but the young Scrooge looks decidedly American.

2262. ———. *A Christmas Carol.* Ed. David A. Hill. London: Penguin, 2002. 32.

This Level 4 reader (1400-word vocabulary), intended for children learning English, is nicely illustrated by Richard Hook. This retelling retains no hint of Dickens's language and reduces the plot to the giving of money. It contains a brief, unhelpful activity section and word search. Accompanying fact sheets for teachers and parents are available on the internet at Penguin.

2263. Dunbar, Polly. *Scrooge*. London: Scholastic, 2002. 28.

In the Hole Story Series, this board book for young children lets them look through a hole in each page to see the story unfold.

2264. Bradman, Tony. *Charles Dickens' A Christmas Carol*. The Classic Collection. London: Hodder Wayland, 2002. 46.

A retelling that includes the major scenes in some of the original language. Illustrated by Chris Hahner, with a good brief biography of Dickens.

2265. Dickens, Charles. *A Christmas Carol*. Toronto: Prospero Books, 2003. Not paginated.

The text in this pop-up book is so abbreviated as to make the story almost unintelligible, but it serves as an introduction to the story for very young children.

2266. Sims, Lesley. *A Christmas Carol. From the Story by Charles Dickens*. London: Usborne, 2003. 64.

Illustrated by Alan Marks and designed by Russell Punter, this children's version is rewritten and greatly abbreviated. Contains a brief and inaccurate biography of Dickens.

2267. Dickens, Charles. "The Cratchits' Christmas Dinner (from *A Christmas Carol*)." In *The Kingfisher Book of Classic Christmas Stories*. Selected by Ian Whybrow. Boston, MA: Kingfisher, 2004. 75–82.

This well-chosen selection of passages includes works by the Brothers Grimm, Louisa May Alcott, Kenneth Grahame, and L. M. Montgomery. In a short introduction, Ian Whybrow describes his own childhood Christmases and notes that the stories included here focus on the welfare of others. The *Carol* selection is illustrated by Susan Hellard.

2268. ———. *A Christmas Carol. A Family Classic. Original by Charles Dickens*. London: Evans, 2005. 46.

In the Fast Track Classics series, which claim to "lose none of the strength and flavor of the original." This retelling by Pauline Francis simplifies the original text. Illustrated with black-and-white line drawings and includes a short and inaccurate biography of Dickens.

READING ADAPTATIONS

Chronological Listing

2269. Dickens, Cedric. *Christmas with Dickens*. Stoneleigh, Somerset: Dickens Publishing, 1991. 41.

A very abridged version "specially edited to be read aloud over food and drink among friends." Five short passages (linked to a five-course meal) are interspersed with Dickensian recipes, games, and quotations from other Dickens novels. It is intended as a "guide to the creation of a wonderfully magical Dickensian evening." Assistant editors are David and Betty Dickens.

2270. Dickens, Charles. *A Christmas Carol in Prose. Being a Ghost Story of Christmas*. London: The Dickens House, 1993.

This new edition of the 1965 Dickens House edition of Dickens's reading version (**181**) was produced for the 150th anniversary of *A Christmas Carol*. It contains a preface by Michael Dickens Whinney, assistant bishop of Birmingham and great-great-grandson of Charles Dickens. A foreword by Cedric Dickens concerns the difficulties of reading aloud. An epilogue by Michael Slater gives a brief account of the popularity of *A Christmas Carol*.

2271. ———. *A Christmas Carol*. New York: Morrow, 1996. 56.

The text of this edition is Dickens's reading version at the Berg Collection in the New York Public Library (**172**). This large-format edition is illustrated by Carter Goodrich. In an Afterword Peter Glassman explains the genesis of Dickens's reading version.

2272. Engel, Elliot. *A Dickens of a Christmas*. VHS and DVD. Raleigh, NC: Media Consultants, 1997. 70 minutes.

Engel and Quinn Hawkesworth dramatize Dickens's influence on Christmas through a variety of readings including *A Christmas Carol*. First produced on cassette by the Raleigh, NC, branch of the Dickens Fellowship in 1994.

2273. Dickens, Charles. *A Christmas Carol. Scholastic Action* 23.6 (13 December 1999): 6–10.

This oral reading version for schools is so abbreviated that it is hardly comprehensible. It includes photographs from the TNT Hallmark film (**2362**). A "teacher's edition" in the same volume encourages teachers to link Scrooge with Dickens (both having unhappy childhoods and wanting to make money). There is also a student's edition with a quiz.

2274. *Christmas Glory from Westminster*. 2000 VHS and DVD. 60 minutes.

This recording of a Christmas concert at Westminster Cathedral in 1999 includes readings from *A Christmas Carol* by Richard Griffiths, filmed at Poets' Corner in the Cathedral.

2275. Barchers, Suzanne I., and Jennifer L. Kroll. "A Christmas Carol." In *Classic Readers Theatre for Young Adults*. Teachers Ideas Press. Greenwood Village, CO: Greenwood, 2002. 47–64.

This greatly abridged version for use in classrooms makes little use of Dickens's language. The introduction urges teachers to encourage students to paraphrase further.

2276. Dickens, Charles. *A Christmas Carol. In Four Staves*. In *The Annotated Christmas Carol* (**2224**). 213–56.
    The 1868 Ticknor and Fields edition of Dickens's reading copy (**174**).

COMMENTARY ON READING ADAPTATIONS

2277. Paschke, Jean. " 'A Christmas Carol' Retold." *British Heritage* 22.1 (December 2000/January 2001): 22–26.
    This interview with Gerald Dickens (great-great-grandson of Charles Dickens) discusses the writing of the *Carol* and Gerald's highly successful annual reading tours of the book in the United States. It includes photographs from the readings. Gerald Dickens's readings are available on CD (**2412**).

STAGE ADAPTATIONS
Chronological Listing

2278. Ball, David, and David Feldshuh. *A Christmas Carol. Dramatics* 60 (November 1988): 22–31.
    First performed at the Guthrie Theatre in Minneapolis in 1972. This version was replaced by Barbara Field's adaptation (**2281**) at the Guthrie.
2279. Ward, Ron. *Humbug! A Musical Play in Two Acts based upon Charles Dickens' "A Christmas Carol."* Stone, Staffordshire: Piper Productions, 1979. v + 43.
    Music by Tony Weston. Intended for youth theater and able to accommodate a large cast (a minimum of twelve actors is required.) There are thirty seven musical numbers. Production notes provide information on the characters, the use of ad-libbing and improvisation, and the use of a cyclorama for special effects. Ward recommends a fast pace. Originally produced at St. Wilfrid's Comprehensive School, Crawley, Sussex. The British Library holds the text and the musical score for five parts.
2280. Hischak, Thomas. *Mr. Scrooge's Christmas. From Charles Dickens' "A Christmas Carol."* Denver, CO: Pioneer Drama Service, 1980. 31.
    A short, basic version with brief production notes and property list. Marley begins the narration.
2281. Field, Barbara. *A Christmas Carol*. Minneapolis: Guthrie Theatre, 1982. 90 minutes.

A film of this stage adaptation was broadcast on The Entertainment Channel in 1982. It is now available on VHS (1997). Richard Hilger plays Scrooge with Marshall Borden as Charles Dickens (part narrator and part commentator) and J. Patrick Martin as Bob Cratchit. John Gielgud's pre-recorded voice is added as narrator. According to Guida (**2373**), the Guthrie has been staging this production since 1975.

2282. Manley, Andrew, and Jennifer Granville. *A Christmas Carol.* Typescript. 1983. 77.

This play was first performed at the Torch Theatre, Milford Haven, in 1983 with three actresses, six actors, and ten children. Notes stress the *Carol* as social criticism; Scrooge, a representative of ''the unfeeling, unscrupulous and exploiting capitalist class,'' has to be genuinely unpleasant, not just an old fool, because he is hard to convert.

2283. Barnett, C. Z. *A Christmas Carol: or The Miser's Warning!* Mission BC: Barbarian, 1984. xii + 49.

A limited edition of 350 copies, this fine edition of Barnett's 1844 stage production (**226**) is illustrated by E. N. Ellis. In an excellent introduction (pp. iii–xii), Joel H. Kaplan compares Barnett's version to the authorized Stirling version (**227**) and points out that Barnett brought his background in farce and melodrama to the story, making the characters more obviously black and white. He suggests that Barnett's Scrooge is akin to Douglas Jerrold's creditor-villains, while an added scene makes Fred (now Frank Freeheart) more obviously charitable.

2284. Majeski, Bill. ''Whatever Happened to Good Old Ebenezer Scrooge?'' *Plays* 44 (December 1984): 12–20, 36.

Reprint of children's version, first published in 1976. See Majeski (**417**).

2285. Holloway, Sister Marcella Marie. *A Christmas Carol.* Denver, CO: Pioneer Drama Services, 1985, 1995.

Reprints of her 1975 script (**286**). A one-act adaptation that includes musical interludes by Mary Ann Joyce that narrate parts of the story. Joyce's 21–page score with piano accompaniment is distributed in the United Kingdom by Hanbury Plays, Droitwich.

2286. Moore, Mavor. *A Christmas Carol: The Musical Version of Charles Dickens' Novel.* Woodstock, IL: Dramatic Publishing, 1996, and Chicago: Dramatic Publishing, 1997. 72.

This very successful version with incidental music by Stephen Woodjetts opened at the Carousel Theatre, Vancouver, BC, in 1988. It requires seven actors and four children.

2287. McGillivray, David and Walter Zerlin Jr. *The Farndale Avenue Housing Estate Townswomen's Guild Dramatic Society's Production of* A Christmas Carol. *A Comedy.* London: Samuel French, 1989. 72.

A farce, first produced at the Edinburgh Fringe Festival on 7 August 1987, in which an inept amateur dramatic group attempts to stage *A Christmas Carol*. It includes songs with music by Susan van Colle and Walter Zerlin Jr. and lyrics by David McGillivray. The script includes a furniture and property list, lighting plot, and effects plot.

2288. *A Christmas Carol*. Northern Ballet Theatre. DVD. Arthaus Musik. 2 hours 11 minutes.

This successful ballet version with music by Carl Davis (which incorporates well-known Christmas carols) and choreography by Massimo Moricone has been running in the north of England since 1991. It was broadcast on British television on Christmas Day, 1993. There is a recording on Naxos, *Twentieth-Century English Ballets: Cinderella, The Brontës, A Christmas Carol*. Northern Ballet Theatre Orchestra with John Pryce-Jones conducting. 86 minutes. For a review of the 1993 production see Edwina Porter in *Dickensian* 89.1 (Spring 1993): 65–66. Guida (**2373**) reviews the television production very favorably.

2289. *Scrooge The Musical*. Port Chester, NY: Cherry Lane Music, 1992.

This stage production based on Leslie Bricusse's 1970 film (**335**) opened at the Alexandra Theatre in Birmingham in November 1992, starring Anthony Newley as Scrooge. The soundtrack of this production is available on CD from Jay Productions. The musical has since been performed many times in Great Britain and the United States. It has been touring England every Christmas season since 2003 with Tommy Steele starring in the London Palladium performances. For the Christmas season 2006, Michael Barrymore took the lead role.

2290. Aylett, David. *Scrooge and the Spirits of Christmas. A Musical Play for Schools. Based on "A Christmas Carol" by Charles Dickens*. Typescript, copyright 1992, at the British Library. 22–page script, 16–page vocal score.

Includes notes for producers and suggested stage settings. This version adds two porters and their wives and requires about 33 actors.

2291. Ahrens, Lynn. *A Christmas Carol. The Musical*.

Directed by Mike Ockrent, with music by Alan Menken and choreography by Susan Stroman, this musical was first staged by Madison Square Garden Productions in New York in 1993. After running for ten years during the Christmas season in New York, it appeared as a film on NBC-TV in 2004 with Kelsey Grammer as Scrooge, Jason Alexander as Marley, Edward Gower as Bob Cratchit, and Jacob Moriarty as Tiny Tim. Available on DVD, with soundtrack from Jay Records.

2292. Lebow, Barbara. *Tiny Tim is Dead*. New York: Dramatists Play Service, 1993. Reprinted, New York: Applause, 1999. 60; and in *The*

Twelve Plays of Christmas: Traditional and Modern Plays for the Holidays. New York: Applause, 2000.

First produced by the Academy Theater in Atlanta, Georgia, in November 1991, this adaptation has been performed widely in the United States. A small group of homeless people find a copy of *A Christmas Carol* and re-enact it for the mute young son of one of the group.

2293. Holman, David. *The Play of Charles Dickens'* A Christmas Carol. Oxford: Heinemann, 1994. viii + 77.

Holman claims that it is possible to turn *A Christmas Carol* into a play without much alteration, and that he ''wouldn't attempt to improve'' upon Dickens's words. There is actually little of Dickens in this version, and some of the additions are unfortunate (Scrooge leads a conga line at Fred's Christmas party). The play includes carollers and a narrator. An introduction (pp. v–viii) by Lawrence Till includes an inaccurate short biography, and the book concludes with Questions and Explorations, and Further Activities for group and individual use.

2294. Fisher, Aileen. ''Mr. Scrooge Finds Christmas.'' In *Christmas Play Favourites for Young People.* Ed. Sylvia E. Kamerman. Boston: Plays, Inc., 1994. 207–225. Reprinted in *Plays* 66.3 (December 2006): 22–33.

A reprint of a short play originally published in 1960 (**276**).

2295. Reese, Kevin M. *A Christmas Carol.* Valley Center, Kansas: KMR Scripts, 1994.

A children's play, closely based on the original (''95% Dickens''), with 26 roles. Originally produced by Wichita Children's Theatre's Centerstage Company in 1993, produced by Monica Flynn and directed by J. B. Boldenow (who played Scrooge). This version runs for 70 minutes with Christmas carols, 55 minutes without. The script can be ordered on the internet through KMR Scripts.

2296. Mortimer, John. *Charles Dickens' A Christmas Carol.* London: Samuel French, 1995. 101.

First performed by the Royal Shakespeare Company at the Barbican Theatre, London, on 28 November 1994, directed by Ian Judge with music by Nigel Hess. Clive Francis played Scrooge with Paul Greenwood as Bob Cratchit. A chorus (consisting of any one actor not taking part at that moment) provides Dickens's narrative voice and advances the plot. Included is a list of the vocal music used in the Barbican production, a furniture and property list, a lighting plot, and an effects plot (clock chimes, fog, etc.) The play received mixed reviews. See, for example, Leslie Duguid, ''We Shan't Forget Tiny Tim.'' *Times Literary Supplement*, 16 December 1994, 20; and Paul Graham in *Dickensian* 91.1 (Spring 1995): 46–47.

2297. Smith, Mark Landon. *A Dickens' Christmas Carol: A Traveling Travesty in Two Tumultuous Acts.* Boston: Baker's Plays, 1996.

A spoof version using seven actors. The regular star of the annual production of the *Carol* calls off, so amateurs have to put on the play. A similar idea to the McGillivray adaptation (**2287**). Available also through samuelfrench.com.

2298. Schario, Christopher. *A Christmas Carol: Based on the Story by Charles Dickens*. New York: Dramatists Play Series, 1996.

A simple version for six actors accompanied by a fiddler. The play is framed by a child reading the *Carol* for the first time.

2299. Larson, Larry, and Eddie Levi Lee. *The Salvation of Iggy Scrooge: A Rock and Roll Christmas Carol*. New York and London: Samuel French, 1997. 63.

Scrooge is a misanthropic, failed superstar haunted by the ghosts of Buddy Holly, Bob Marley, and Elvis, who reform him with rock music.

2300. Mitchell, Reg. *A Christmas Carol. A Musical*. Timperley, Altrincham, Cheshire: New Theatre Publications, 1998. 54.

This two-act play with original music and lyrics by Reg Mitchell was first performed at the Royal Shakespeare Company's Swan Theatre, Stratford upon Avon, on 13 December 1998. The producer was Wilson Roberts. Dickens is narrator of this version, and while the narrative and dialogue are close to the original, the play emphasizes the social consequences of Scrooge's misanthropy. Four prostitutes, former employees of Scrooge whom he fired for minor offenses, sing about their dire circumstances as a result of his callousness.

2301. Horovitz, Israel. *A Christmas Carol: Scrooge and Marley*. In *The Twelve Plays of Christmas: Traditional and Modern Plays for the Holidays*. New York: Applause, 2000.

Reprint of the 1979 play (**290**).

2302. Sills, Paul. *A Christmas Carol: Adapted for the Stage by Paul Sills*. New York: Applause, 2001.

First published in *Paul Sills' Story Theater: Four Shows, with Theater Games for Story Theater by Viola Spolin*. New York: Applause, 2000. 57–100. In his introduction, Sills describes producing this version for the first time in 1994 in rural Wisconsin with an amateur cast of adults and children.

2303. Jones, Claire. *A Christmas Carol*. Timperley, Altrincham, Cheshire: New Theatre Publications, 2001. 40.

This two-act adaptation retains the original text through a narrator, but the play ends with Scrooge at the Cratchits' Christmas dinner, where he raises Bob's salary. Carols and songs are added throughout.

2304. Duncombe, Peter. *A Christmas Carol*. Lincoln: Pepper's Yard Playscripts, 2001. 59.

This adaptation for the stage is fairly complete and close to the original. Carols are interspersed throughout the play, and instructions on properties and special effects are copious and helpful. A useful introduction notes that Shakespeare's *The Winter's Tale* refers to ghost stories and explores a theme common to storytelling, "that a man's thoughts and deeds may haunt his present and shape his future." The introduction also notes the importance of Dickens as narrator in the original story, so in this version characters act as narrators as well as actors.

2305. Roberts, Belinda. *Scrooooooge: An Adaptation of "A Christmas Carol" by Charles Dickens.* Banbury: Beetleheart, 2001. 44.
This two-act verse spoof includes audience participation.

2306. White, D. F. *A Christmas Carol. A Pantomime by D. F. White. Adapted from the Novel by Charles Dickens.* Typescript, c. 2002. 37.
In the British Library. This slapstick version involves the audience and includes a visit to the North Pole to see Father Christmas. Loosely based on the *Carol*, it is brought up to date with contemporary references.

2307. Rowell, Steven A. *Tiny Tim: A Christmas Carol Revisited. A Full Length Holiday Play.* New York: Playscripts, 2002.
In 1899, Tim Cratchit, a cutthroat businessman in New York, is visited by several ghosts, including Scrooge and Teddy Roosevelt.

2308. Bartlett, Neil. *A Christmas Carol in Many Scenes and Several Songs from the Novel by Charles Dickens Adapted for the Stage by Neil Bartlett.* Absolute Classics. London: Oberon, 2003. 74.
This adaptation in two acts and thirty scenes was first performed at the Lyric Theatre in Hammersmith, London on 29 November 2002 (directed by Bartlett) and simultaneously at the Citizens Theatre in Glasgow (directed by Kenny Miller). At the Lyric, Scrooge was played by Tim Pigott-Smith, with seven actors taking on a variety of other roles. In a short introduction, Bartlett explains why he has retained Dickens's words; they "don't describe; they enact. When London freezes, the prose stamps and chatters; . . . When the story rises to its great emotional and moral climaxes, the prose tolls like a bell, rich in biblical echoes; it dances and blusters with the Fezziwigs." The text is thus used "as soundtrack, as setting, as rhythm, as atmosphere, as a conspiratorial game," interspersed with quotations (both spoken and sung) from Victorian carols that the audience will recognize and that further the story. Props can be minimal (a lightbulb is required) and the play's success relies upon the energy of the actors and their invention with the words. The effect should be playful. Robin Whitmore's set for the first run at the Lyric was based upon a Victorian toy theatre.

2309. Field, Barbara. "A Christmas Carol." In *New Classics from The Guthrie Theater.* Hanover, NH: Smith and Kraus, 2003. 1–46.

Field's *Carol* has been performed at the Guthrie Theater in Minneapolis annually since 1975. It includes a narrator (Dickens in the earlier productions) and draws attention to the Scrooge-Belle relationship as central to Scrooge's motivation.

2310. Oxspring, Andrew. *Mr. Humbug Sees The Light, or "Scrooge at School."* Rutland: Edgy Productions, 2004.

A seventy-five minute musical adaptation for school children, set at St. Ebenezer's School, where the Christmas-hating headmaster, Mr. Humbug, is taught a lesson by three ghosts. The script may be ordered from the website *www.edgyproductions.com/humbug/about.htm.*

2311. Durang, Christopher. *Mrs. Bob Cratchit's Wild Christmas Binge.* New York: Dramatists Play Service, 2005.

Not seen.

COMMENTARY ON STAGE ADAPTATIONS

2312. Bolton, H. Philip. "A Christmas Carol." In his *Dickens Dramatized.* London: Mansell, 1987. 234–67.

Provides a comprehensive listing of stage, screen, radio, and television adaptations from 1843 to 1984, many of them unpublished. In his introduction Bolton notes that despite the many immediate stage versions of the *Carol* it fell out of popularity until the second half of the twentieth century. See Sutcliffe (**2315**) on this point. His prediction that "we are presently (in 1984) somewhere near the crest of a wave of Christmas Carols" has turned out not to be true, as the wave has increased considerably since then. Bolton suggests that the *Carol* was not a popular drama in the nineteenth century because of the century's reticence about staging religious themes. His introduction includes a survey of BBC and other radio readings and dramatizations and notes that between 1950 and 1984 there were over 225 live stagings, filmings, radio, and television versions, most of them new versions to avoid copyright problems.

2313. Hughes, Leonard. "Dickenz in the 'Hood." *American Theatre* 11.1 (January 1994): 14–19.

Reviews Cornerstone Theater Company's dramatization of *A Christmas Carol*, titled *A Community Carol*, in Washington, DC, at Christmas 1993. Set in inner-city Washington, this adaptation remained faithful to Dickens's text but transferred the plot to contemporary America. Tiny Tim, or TT, is in a wheelchair, having been caught in street crossfire, and Scrooge is a black businessman. Dickens's moral vision was considered particularly relevant for this place and time.

Local children were included in the production, which was directed by Bill Rauch. See also Kuftinec (**2314**).

2314. Kuftinec, Sonja. *Staging America: Cornerstone and Community-Based Theater.* Carbondale: Southern Illinois UP, 1993. 161–65, 175–81.
Discusses the staging and reception of the 1993 adaptation *A Community Carol.* See Hughes (**2313**).

2315. Sutcliffe, Allan. "Pepper's Ghost and *A Christmas Carol.*" *Dickensian* 101.3 (Winter 2005): 225–32.
Sutcliffe has uncovered a large number of performances of *A Christmas Carol* in Birmingham between 1875 and 1900, which were staged by The Original Pepper's Ghost and Spectral Opera Company, managed by Fred Smith. Sutcliffe provides detailed descriptions of these performances that employed the so-called "Pepper's Ghost," a trapdoor and glass method that created the illusion of a ghost on stage, and is usually associated with *The Haunted Man* (**1224**). Sutcliffe quotes from contemporary reviews that praise the effectiveness of the ghost scenes. He concludes by pointing out that with 301 performances of the *Carol* in Birmingham alone, it was actually much more popular than *The Cricket on the Hearth*, contrary to received opinion. See Bolton (**2312**), for example.

2316. Weeks, Jerome. "What the Dickens?" *American Theatre* 17.10 (December 2000): 24–31.
Discusses various American stage versions of *A Christmas Carol* and includes interviews with the directors. Weeks discusses the importance of the narrative voice and the social commentary, often transferred to such American issues as racism. The article includes photographs from several American stagings.

FILM ADAPTATIONS

Chronological Listing

2317. *Scrooge, or Marley's Ghost* (**316**).
The first film adaptation of *A Christmas Carol* produced by R. W. Paul and directed by Walter Booth is now available on disc 1 of a 2–disc DVD set released by the British Film Institute and titled *Dickens Before Sound*. It runs for four minutes. See Davis (**2503**), Guida (**2373**), Petrie (**2378**), and Pointer (**2380**) for details of the original film.

2318. *A Christmas Carol* (**318**).
This 1910 silent film by Thomas A. Edison was released in 2001 on VHS and 2002 on DVD in *A Christmas Past: Vintage Holiday Films*

1901–1925, from the Paul Killiam collection, Kino Video. Reviewers comment that the pace is too fast, but the quality is quite good. A new musical score by Al Kryszak has been added. Also available on disc 2 of *Christmas Classics Collection* (Passport, 5 CDs, color). For a detailed commentary on the original film, see Guida (**2373**).

2319. *A Christmas Accident.* Edison, 1912. Silent. 15 minutes.

This rare film, now made available on DVD, is dubbed an early variation of the *Carol.* It stars William Wadsworth as a misanthropic old man who is taught a lesson by the family next door on Christmas Eve. Written by Annie Eliot Trumbull. Available on disc 1 of *Christmas Classics Collection* (Passport, 5 CDs) and on *A Christmas Past: Vintage Holiday Films 1901–1925,* from the Paul Killiam collection (Kino Video, 2002, DVD).

2320. *My Little Boy.* Bluebird Photoplays (U.S.A.), 1917. 5 reels.

Guida (**2373**) and Pointer (**2380**) list this film, partly based on *A Christmas Carol.* Guida notes that it was also inspired by Eugene Field's poem *Little Boy Blue,* not the nursery rhyme of that name (as indicated by Pointer.) Guida quotes from two 1917 reviews of the film. Scrooge (Uncle Oliver) has cut himself off from his nephew Fred when Fred marries, but he is transformed by a dream on Christmas Eve. Directed by Elsie Jane Wilson with screenplay by Elliott J. Clawson from a story by Rupert Julian. Uncle Oliver is played by Winter Hall.

2321. *A Dickensian Fantasy.* Gee Films (U.K.), 1934.

Listed in Guida (**2373**) and Pointer (**2380**) as a ten-minute film, directed by Aveling Ginever and produced by David Mackane. Lawrence Hanray plays a man who dreams about Scrooge and Bob Cratchit after reading Dickens.

2322. *Scrooge* (**325**).

The 1935 Paramount film, directed by Henry Edwards and starring Seymour Hicks as Scrooge, is available on VHS and DVD by a variety of companies as *Scrooge.* Also available on disc 1 of *Christmas Classics Collection* (Passport, 5 CDs, color) and *A Charles Dickens Christmas. Two Christmas Favorites* (DVD, 2006).

2323. *A Christmas Carol* (**326**).

The 1938 Edwin L. Marin film, starring Reginald Owen as Scrooge, was released on VHS in color by MGM/UA in 1988 and on DVD in color by Warner Home Video in 2005.

2324. *A Christmas Carol.* Gregory Markopoulos (U.S.A.), 1940. 5 minutes.

Guida (**2373**) lists this rare adaptation, made by Gregory Markopoulos in Toledo, Ohio, at the age of 11 or 12. Markopoulos appears as Scrooge. According to Guida, this film, made on an 8 mm Keystone home movie camera, is the first known amateur film version of the *Carol.*

2325. *Charles Dickens' The Christmas Carol.* Stokey and Ebert, 1949. 25 minutes.

This television version starred Vincent Price as narrator and Taylor Holmes as Scrooge. See Guida (**2373**) for details. It is now available on *A Charles Dickens Christmas. Two Christmas Favorites.* (DVD, 2006).

2326. *Scrooge* (**328**).

The 1951 Renown Pictures film, produced and directed by Brian Desmond Hurst and starring Alastair Sim as Scrooge, is now available on VHS and DVD in both black and white and colorized versions.

2327. *Mr. Magoo's Christmas Carol* (**333**).

Animated version of 1964, now available on VHS and DVD.

2328. *Scrooge* (**335**).

The 1970 Ronald Neame film, starring Albert Finney as Scrooge, is available on VHS by CBS/Fox video, on DVD, and on CED (Capacitance Electronic Discs.) For sheet music see Leslie Bricusse (**2430**).

2329. *A Christmas Carol.* Anglia Television, 1970. Animated. 58 minutes.

Produced, adapted, and narrated by Paul Honeyman. Still watercolor paintings by John Worsley are linked together in this version. The music is by Peter Fenn, sung by the Norwich Cathedral Choir. A rare VHS tape of this production (PAL, for British systems) appeared on eBay in early 2007.

2330. A Christmas Carol (**337**).

This animated version from 1971 by Richard Williams, narrated by Sir Michael Redgrave, with Alastair Sim and Michael Hordern, was released on video, New York: Fisher Price, 1992, and again in 1998. See Guida (**2373**) for a detailed description.

2331. *The Passions of Carol.* Ambar Films (U.S.A.), 1975. 76 minutes.

Directed by Amanda Barton (Shaun Costello) with Mary Stuart as Carol Screwge; a pornographic version.

2332. *The Stingiest Man in Town.* Rankin/Bass Productions, 1978. 90 minutes.

First broadcast on NBC-TV in December 1978. This animated version for children was produced and directed by Arthur Rankin, Jr. and written by Romeo Muller. Walter Matthau is the voice of Scrooge. According to Guida (**2373**), it was based on a 1956 live-action film that was broadcast on NBC-TV on 23 December 1956. Available on VHS.

2333. *Rich Little's Christmas Carol and Robin Hood.* Passion River DVD, 2006. 100 minutes.

This spoof on the *Carol* by Canadian impersonator Rich Little was first broadcast on CBC-TV in 1978, directed by Trevor Evans. Little impersonates a variety of famous people to portray the characters in the *Carol*: W. C. Fields as Scrooge, Paul Lynde as Bob Cratchit, Laurel and Hardy as the charity gentlemen, Richard Nixon as Marley, etc. For details, see Guida (**2373**), who considers this version inferior to Little's 1963 recording *Scrooge and the Stars*, on which the film is based. Guida also notes that a recording of the same title was released in 1979, and a shortened version that Little played on the Ed Sullivan Show is available on *A Classic Christmas from Ed Sullivan* (Buena Vista Home Video.) For this version, Jack Benny is Scrooge, George Burns is the narrator, and Ed Sullivan is a ghost.

2334. *Bugs Bunny's Looney Christmas Tales.* 1979. 25 minutes.
This children's animated film was first broadcast on CBS-TV on 27 November 1979. See Guida (**2373**) for details. A *Carol* adaptation with Yosemite Sam as Scrooge made up the first third of the program. Available on VHS.

2335. *An American Christmas Carol.* 98 minutes.
This version, directed by Eric Till, was first shown on ABC-TV in December 1979 with Henry Winkler as Benedict Slade, a miserly businessman in 1933 New Hampshire. For commentary see Guida (**2373**), who considers it "an interesting but flawed variation," one of the flaws being the evident artifice in trying to portray Winkler as an old man. Available on VHS and DVD.

2336. *A Christmas Carol.* Burbank Films (Australia), 1982. Animated. 75 minutes.
Produced by Eddy Graham. See Guida (**2373**) for details. Available on DVD and CED (Capacitance Electronic Discs.)

2337. *Mickey's Christmas Carol.* Walt Disney Productions (U.S.A.), 1983. Animated. 25 minutes.
Produced and directed by Burny Mattinson. Mickey Mouse plays Bob Cratchit to Scrooge McDuck, with Donald Duck as Fred and Goofy as Marley's ghost. For full details see Guida (**2373**). Robert Newsom (**2544**) notes "Foucauldian insights" in the Ghost of Christmas Present's lifting the roofs off the houses in his search for the Cratchits. The origin of this film was a Disney record of 1977 (**367**). Available in book form (**2447**), on CED (Capacitance Electronic Discs) and on DVD in *Walt Disney Treasures: Mickey Mouse in Living Color, Volume 2* (1993) and in *Classic Cartoon Favorites, Volume 9: Classic Holiday Stories* (2005). *Mickey's Christmas Carol* was also edited into *Mickey's Magical Christmas: Snowed in at the House of Mouse* (VHS and DVD, 2001), in which the Disney characters, snowed in on Christmas Eve, watch old cartoons to cheer up the grouchy Donald Duck. This recasting of the film is similar to Dickens's inventive Christmas numbers (especially *The Holly-Tree Inn*).

2338. *Alvin's Christmas Carol.* DIC/Bagdasarian Productions (U.S.A.). Animated. 1983. 23 minutes.

Produced by Ross Bagdasarian and Janice Karman. Written by Dianne Dixon. First broadcast on NBC-TV. For details see Guida (**2373**). A paperback version by Janice Karman, with cassette, was published by TimeWarner Audiobooks in 1994. Available on VHS.

2339. *The Gospel According to Scrooge.* Hope Productions International, 1983. 2 hours.

This popular musical play, directed by Mark S. Vegh and written by James P. Schumacher, was first broadcast in front of a live audience for the Christian Broadcasting Network in December 1983. Guida (**2373**) provides an extensive description and argues that this version's overtly Christian focus would have been viewed favorably by Dickens. Robert Buchanan played Scrooge, with Robert Whitesel as Bob Cratchit. The play is still performed widely in American churches. Released on VHS by Alpha Omega Publications (Bridgestone Media) in 1996.

2340. *A Christmas Carol.* Entertainment Partners (Great Britain), 1984. Directed by Clive Donner. Screenplay by Roger O. Hirson. 101 minutes.

This made-for-television version, starring George C. Scott as Scrooge, was first broadcast on CBS-TV 17 December 1984 and in theater release in the U.K. With Frank Finlay as Jacob Marley, David Warner as Bob Cratchit, and Susannah York as Mrs. Cratchit, this version has become one of the *Carol* film classics, praised for its fidelity to Dickens's text while being innovative. Scott is a complex, convincing Scrooge whose past is more fully explored than in previous versions. Scrooge's unsympathetic father, for instance, makes a brief appearance. Davis (**2503**) considers the film a "new-historical attempt to identify the sources of Scrooge's discontent in the economic ideology of his time and ours." Guida (**2373**) finds it "one of the most thoughtful and provocative *Carols* ever." It was filmed exclusively in Shrewsbury, England. See *A Christmas Carol: The Making of the Film in Shrewsbury* (**2369**). Sammon (**2381**) provides many little known facts about the film. It was released on VHS in 1995 and on DVD in 1999.

2341. *A Christmas Carol and Oliver Twist.* The Congress Video Group (U.S.A.), 1985. 30 minutes.

According to Guida (**2373**), this animated home video release uses "comic book style artwork" and is a "dull and tedious affair."

2342. *A Jetson Christmas Carol.* Hanna-Barbera Productions (U.S.A.). Animated. 1985. 22 minutes.

For details, see Guida (**2373**). First broadcast on television and now available on VHS, this version (one of a series about a space age community) has Mr. Spacely as Scrooge and George Jetson as Bob Cratchit.

2343. *Scrooged.* Paramount (U.S.A.), 1988. Produced and directed by Richard Donner. Written by Mitch Glazer. 101 minutes.

Bill Murray stars as Frank Cross, the Scrooge-like president of a television network that is presenting an international broadcast of *A Christmas Carol,* starring Buddy Hackett as Scrooge. This satire on the television age has been largely panned. See, for example, Guida (**2373**) and Sammon (**2381**), who find it humorless and mean-spirited and Cross's redemption unexplained. Davis (**2503**), however, analyzes it as an ''explosive deconstruction'' of the *Carol* in which the ''narcissistic world of images'' is torn apart by the dual plot: Cross's reformation that brings in earlier versions of the *Carol,* and the creation of a television production that is founded in the 1980s. Murray Baumgarten (**2370**) provides a very clear summary of the film. Available on VHS and DVD (1988).

2344. *Blackadder's Christmas Carol.* BBC-TV (England), 1988. Directed by Richard Boden. 43 minutes.

Written by Richard Curtis and Ben Elton. The ubiquitous Blackadder (Rowan Atkinson) begins as a kind-hearted benefactor who through a series of visions learns that his ancestors profited by being miserly and cruel, so he gives up his generous ways. This spoof on Victorian England (Queen Victoria is played by Miriam Margolyes, with Jim Broadbent as Albert) has little to do with the original *Carol.* Available on VHS by CBS-Fox, 1991, and on DVD, 2002. Also available on BBC audiobooks on CD and cassette, 1996. For commentary, see Guida (**2373**) and Sammon (**2381**).

2345. *The Spirits of Christmas.* Todd Rogers, 1990.

Guida (**2373**) lists this amateur production, produced by an American high school student. The setting is an urban housing project and Scrooge is a drug dealer.

2346. *A Christmas Carol.* Fuji Television/Saban International Services, 1991. Animated. 28 minutes.

Guida (**2373**) lists this home video as ''vulgar, offensive, and thoroughly unnecessary.''

2347. *Brer Rabbit's Christmas Carol.* Animated. Magic Shadows (U.S.A.), 1992. 1 hour.

First shown on television in 1992 and now available on DVD and VHS, this blending of Dickens and Uncle Remus is directed, produced and written by Al Guest and Jean Mathieson. The mean-spirited Brer Fox is taught a lesson when he inadvertently becomes a part of the animals' Christmas production of *A Christmas Carol,* a charity performance to raise money for Timmy Mouse. For commentary see Guida (**2373**).

2348. *The Muppet Christmas Carol.* Walt Disney/Jim Henson (U.S.A.), 1992. 86 minutes.

This film cleverly combines a real actor (Michael Caine as Scrooge) with Muppet characters. The Great Gonzo plays Dickens, with Kermit the Frog as Bob Cratchit and Miss Piggy as Mrs. Cratchit. For a detailed review see Sammon (**2381**). The original score by Miles Goodman with songs by Paul Williams is available on CD, Jim Henson records, 1992. Available on VHS and DVD.

2349. *Animaniacs: Helloooo Holidays.* Warner Home Video, 1999. 12 minutes.

A VHS version of the 1994 Animaniacs short spoof on the *Carol* in which Thaddeus Plotz, head of the Warner studio, is reformed by three ghosts. See Guida (**2373**) for details.

2350. *A Flintstones Christmas Carol.* Animated. Produced and directed by Joanna Romersa. Hanna-Barbera Cartoons (U.S.A.), 1994. 90 minutes.

Fred Flintstone stars as Scrooge in the Bedrock amateur production of the *Carol*, but in the process he becomes Scrooge-like in real life. This play-within-a-play format (see also *Brer Rabbit's Christmas* [**2347**]) allows the amateur cast to include Dickens's words overlaid by Flintstone jokes (the names are all stony: Marbley, Cragit, Ebonezer, Charles Brickons, etc.) Available on VHS. For commentary see Guida (**2373**).

2351. *A Christmas Carol.* Jetlag Productions (Goodtimes Entertainment), 1994. Animated. 48 minutes.

Reissued on VHS and DVD (2003). Guida (**2373**) calls this version "yet another lifeless, limited animation borefest." Written by Jack Olesker and directed by Toshiyuki Hiruma. Animation by Amisong Production.

2352. *Beavis and Butt-head Do Christmas.* DVD. 85 minutes.

First broadcast on MTV-TV in 1995; a spoof on the *Carol* occupies half of the DVD. Directed by Mike Judge. For comment see Guida (**2373**), who finds it deplorable.

2353. *Miracle at Christmas. Ebbie's Story.* VHS. 1996. 100 minutes.

Originally titled *Ebbie*, this version was first broadcast on the Lifetime Cable Network in 1995. It stars Susan Lucci as Ebbie Scrooge, an ambitious head of a department store, and Wendy Crewson as Roberta Cratchet. Like many of the adaptations in novel form, this updated version makes use of contemporary technology—microwave ovens, cell phones, computers—but Guida (**2373**) finds that it still adheres to Dickens's voice and is close to the 1951 film version (**2326**) in some of its scenes.

2354. *A Christmas Carol.* Pendulum's Video Classics, c. 1995. 50 minutes.

Guida (**2373**) lists this version as an "excruciatingly bad adaptation that uses comic book style artwork."

2355. *Ms. Scrooge.*
First aired 10 December 1997 on U.S.A. Cable Network. Wilshire Court Productions. Cicely Tyson plays Ebenita Scrooge, a loan shark, in this adaptation, directed by John Korty and produced by Julian Marks. For an interview with Tyson see M. S. Mason, *Christian Science Monitor* 90 (4 December 1997): 13. For cast list and commentary, see Guida (**2373**). Available on VHS.

2356. *A Christmas Carol.* DIC Productions (U.S.A.), 1997. Animated.
A children's musical version, directed by Stan Phillips, with Tim Curry as the voice of Scrooge and Michael York as Bob Cratchit. The Ghost of Christmas Present is read by Whoopi Goldberg and looks like her. This version stays fairly close to the original story but gives Scrooge a dog who undergoes a transformation as well. Available on VHS and DVD.

2357. *101 Dalmatians Christmas.* Walt Disney Studio. 22 minutes.
An animated version for children, first broadcast on ABC-TV on 20 December 1997, with Cruella de Vil as Scrooge. For details, see Guida (**2373**). Available on VHS.

2358. *Ebenezer.* Nomadic Pictures. First aired on TNT network, 25 November 1998.
This Canadian version made for television is set in the wild west around 1870 and stars Jack Palance as a cowboy Scrooge. Produced by Chad Oakes and directed by Ken Jubenvill. For an interview with Oakes, see *Alberta Report* 24 (5 December 1997): 27. For cast list and commentary, see Guida (**2373**). Available on VHS and DVD.

2359. *An All Dogs Christmas Carol.* Animated. Directed by Paul Sabella. Metro-Goldwyn-Mayer, 1998. 73 minutes.
Written by Jymn Magon, with score by Mark Watters and based upon the 1989 animated film *All Dogs Go To Heaven.* Carface (Scrooge, read by Ernest Borgnine) is a bulldog working for the evil Belladonna, who threatens to ruin Christmas in San Francisco. For details, see Guida (**2373**). Available on VHS and DVD.

2360. *A Christmas Carol.* Simitar Entertainment (U.S.A.), 1998.
This Armour Productions videotape is the film of a stage version performed in front of a live audience at Golden West College in Huntington Beach, California, in 1988. It would be hard to imagine a worse production than this one. The script bears little relation to Dickens's text. Directed by Charles Mitchell and Renata Florin, with Mike Owens as Scrooge and Stephen Silva as Bob Cratchit.

2361. *The Ghosts of Dickens' Past. (Les Fantômes du Passé de Dickens).* Quill Pen Productions. 1998. 96 minutes.
A feature-length film produced for television by Feature Films for Families (Utah) and CINAR (Quebec). Directed by Bruce Neibaur, it

stars Chris Heyerdahl as Dickens in a fictionalized account of the writing of *A Christmas Carol*, focusing on Dickens's sympathy with working children. Dickens is a Scrooge-like man, writing only for profit, until a young apparition shows him the error of his ways. Reviewers praise the authentic Victorian background. This film won the Best Feature Film Award and the Best Cinematographer Award at the Santa Clarita International Film Festival in 2000. Available on VHS and DVD (2003).

2362. *A Christmas Carol.* TNT Hallmark Entertainment Production (U.S.A.), 1999.

A television version, now available on VHS and DVD. Written by Peter Barnes, directed by David Jones, and produced by Robert Halmi, Sr. Patrick Stewart plays Scrooge with Richard E. Grant as Bob Cratchit. This somber film stays fairly close to Dickens's original text but opens with Marley's funeral and generally misses most of the humor of the *Carol*. Victorian sentiment is uppermost, so Bob's visit to Tiny Tim's deathbed is included. This film was the first *Carol* to use computer-generated graphics.

2363. *A Diva's Christmas Carol.* Paramount. Produced by VH1 Television and Viacom Entertainment. 13 December 2000.

Filmed in Montreal, this adaptation was written and directed by Richard Schenkman and produced by Patricia Clifford. Vanessa L. Williams plays Ebony Scrooge, a cold-hearted pop singer who comes to New York to star in a Christmas Day charity show and is visited by Marli Jacob, her former singing partner. Released on DVD, 19 November 2002.

2364. *A Christmas Carol.* ITV, 20 December 2000. 75 minutes.

A television adaptation in which Scrooge (played by Ross Kemp) is a modern-day loan shark. Screenplay by Peter Bowker, directed by Catherine Morshead, and produced by Joshua St. Johnson. For review see Jean Carroll, "Television and Theatre Reviews" in *Dickensian* 97.1 (Spring 2001): 72–73.

2365. *Maxine's Christmas Carol.* Animated. VHS. Hallmark (Shoebox), 2000. 30 minutes.

A grouchy Maxine is visited by ghosts from her past.

2366. *A Christmas Carol: The Movie.* The Film Consortium, Scala and MBP. Christmas 2001.

An educational CD-ROM accompanies this animated video for students aged 5 to 11. Directed by Jimmy T. Murakami and produced by Iain Harvey with the voices of Kate Winslet, Nicolas Cage, and Simon Callow. Reviewed by Jean Carroll, *Dickensian* 98.1 (Spring 2002): 63–64. For a "novelization" of the movie, see Dhami (**2446**). The soundtrack was released on CD by EMI in 2001.

2367. *A Christmas Carol: The Musical.* New York, NY: Hallmark Entertain-
      ment, 2004.
      Film version of the stage play. See Ahrens (**2291**). Available on DVD.
2368. *Doctor Who: The Unquiet Dead.* BBC-TV (Wales), 9 April 2005.
      43 minutes.
      This loose adaptation of the *Carol* story for the science fiction series
      Doctor Who was written by Mark Gatiss, produced by Phil Collinson,
      and directed by Euros Lyn. On Christmas Eve, 1869, a world-weary
      Charles Dickens gives a reading of *A Christmas Carol* in a Cardiff
      beset by some real ghosts. As he assists in the solving of the supernatu-
      ral mystery, Dickens's zest for life is renewed. Starring Christopher
      Eccleston and Billie Piper, with guest star Simon Callow as Dickens.
      Available on DVD from BBC Worldwide.

COMMENTARY ON FILM ADAPTATIONS

2369. *A Christmas Carol: The Making of the Film in Shrewsbury.* Shrews-
      bury: Shrewsbury Chronicle Publication, 1984. 31.
      This rare publication can be seen at the Dickens House Museum in
      London. It concerns the 1984 Clive Donner version (**2340**) and con-
      tains many photographs and commentary by the participants.
2370. Baumgarten, Murray. "Bill Murray's Christmas Carols." In *Dickens
      on Screen.* Ed. John Glavin. Cambridge: Cambridge UP, 2003. 61–71.
      Praises the 1988 film *Scrooged* (**2343**) for ridding the *Carol* "of the
      Victoriana customary to adaptations, bringing to twentieth-century life
      the experiences of healing and renewal commented on by Dickens's
      early readers." Baumgarten argues that the 1993 Bill Murray film,
      Groundhog Day, is also a *Carol* adaptation that takes up the story's
      "issues of time and identity" and in doing so is "perhaps truer to the
      central themes of Dickens's tale." Baumgarten provides an excellent
      overview of both films and relates them to Goethe's *Faust* in that "the
      vehicle of the moral education of the hero is the reconception of time."
      See also Baumgarten's article on the *Carol*·and Faust (**2483**).
2371. Guida, Fred R. "Charles Dickens' *A Christmas Carol.*" *Films in Re-
      view* 42.11/12 (November/December 1991): 362–69.
      This survey of some of the adaptations became incorporated into Gui-
      da's book-length study (**2373**). He begins with the adaptations by R. W.
      Paul (**316, 2317**) and Rupert Julian (**321**) and compares the 1951
      Brian Desmond Hurst version (**328, 2326**) to the 1935 *Scrooge,* star-
      ring Seymour Hicks (**325, 2322**), and the 1938 version, starring Regi-
      nald Owen (**326, 2323**), finding the Hurst version the most artistic and

truest to Dickens's intention. He praises Albert Finney's portrayal of Scrooge in the "very underrated" 1970 version (**335, 2328**), and he considers the 1984 film, starring George C. Scott (**2340**), the most important version. Of the television and animated versions, Guida singles out for praise the 1971 cartoon version, narrated by Sir Michael Redgrave (**337**), for using the voices of Alastair Sim and Michael Hordern and for imitating the effect of Victorian steel engraving in the colors. This useful survey ends with the suggestion that good films could be made of the other Christmas books and stories, especially "A Christmas Tree." Still photographs are reproduced from the 1938, 1951, and 1984 film versions.

2372. ———. "Merry Christmas from Charles Dickens . . . and Thomas Edison." *Films in Review* 45.11/12 (1994): 2–5.

An interesting discussion of the 1910 film (**318, 2318**), made by Thomas A. Edison and intended for home viewing. According to Guida, the director was John H. Collins, not Ashley Miller or J. Searle Dawley, as attributed elsewhere. Guida finds the film fairly true to the original story, although the ghostly scenes all take place in Scrooge's room, and Fred is at first rejected by his sweetheart, only to be accepted when the reformed Uncle Scrooge makes him a partner in the business. Guida quotes from several contemporary reviews of the film in the United States and England, where it was released in 1911.

2373. ———. A Christmas Carol *and Its Adaptations: A Critical Examination of Dickens's Story and Its Productions on Screen and Television.* Foreword by Edward Wagenknecht. Jefferson, NC: McFarland, 2000. xii + 264. Reprinted in paperback, 2006.   ·

This excellent compilation is the most complete and authoritative study and listing of the film versions of the *Carol*. Part 1 provides three excellent chapters on the background to the *Carol*: its roots in earlier Christmas traditions and literature and its relationship to Dickens's other writings about Christmas (and in particular the question of nostalgia); its political and economic roots; and its wider grounding in Dickens's religious faith. Part 2 surveys adaptations of the *Carol* from pre-cinema days, and so the fine chapter on stage productions and other pre-cinema adaptations extends Guida's study beyond his subtitle. Guida usefully discusses music hall versions and reading versions, including those by Dickens and Bransby Williams, and he offers an interesting detailed discussion of magic lantern shows. Chapters on the silent films, the talkies, and television survey in detail the major productions and include a wealth of background information and assessments from contemporary and later critics. Guida's assessments of the enormous range of versions are always well considered and succinctly expressed, comparing individual adaptations and placing them in the context of the *Carol* as "culture text," to use Davis's expression. See Davis (**2503**). In Part 3, Guida briefly surveys Christmas in Dickens's other writings, concentrating particularly on the later Christmases in *Great Expectations* and *The Mystery of Edwin Drood.* "Variations on a Theme by Dickens" surveys television shows and films that are loosely based on the *Carol*: skits, parodies, "deconstructions," or, as Guida puts it, "outright destruction." He includes in this category classics like *It's A Wonderful Life* and notes that the *Carol* is "a truly universal story—an utterly indestructible story." This chapter concludes with a discussion of *Carol* adaptations in print, from the first piracy to recent parodies, as well as an account of Christmas books by Thackeray, Ruskin, and others. The final section of the book is an annotated filmography: a chronological listing of films and television productions from the 1901 *Scrooge* to *Ebenezer*, a 1998 made-for-television western (**2358**). Guida's book is an invaluable resource for any *Carol* devotee.

2374. Keyser, Lester J. "A Scrooge for All Seasons." In *The English Novel and the Movies.* Ed. Michael Klein and Gillian Parker. London: Frederick Unger, 1981. 121–31.

An excellent account of the 1951 Brian Desmond Hurst film (**328, 2326**) that emphasizes Hurst's familiarity with Dickens. Keyser points out the influence of Leech's illustrations, especially the early pencil and wash drawings, on the composition and lighting. He notes that Hurst insisted on filming the Royal Exchange scenes on site, the first film to do so, and that he emphasizes the *Carol*'s origins in the Gothic morality tale and its concern with death. Tracing the film's fidelity to the text, Keyser also discusses its innovations, such as Mr. Jorkins, who seduces the young Scrooge away from Fezziwig, and the juxtaposition of Scrooge's failed love affair with Alice and his growing business success. Keyser argues that Hurst and Langley add "a new psychological pattern" by having Scrooge's mother die in childbirth, and that they cleverly make use of toys in the film. After praising the acting, Keyser regrets that this film version, a commercial failure from the start, will remain condemned to merely late night television reruns on Christmas evening.

2375. Mamet, David. "Crisis in Happyland." *Sight and Sound* 12.1 (January 2002): 22–23.

Discussing American films such as *It's a Wonderful Life* and *The Best Years of Our Lives*, Mamet sees them as following *A Christmas Carol* in promoting "Compassionate Conservatism": the privileged learn benevolence rather than the sharing of wealth.

2376. McCracken-Flesher, Caroline. "The Incorporation of *A Christmas Carol*: A Tale of Seasonal Screening." *Dickens Studies Annual* 24 (1995): 93–118.

Discusses the *Carol* as "culture text" (see Davis **2503**), in particular as "the Christmas narrative of corporate sales." McCracken-Flesher blames Dickens's care *not* to advocate overconsumption and extravagance for its popularity as a "a tool for corporate enrichment." She concentrates on Chrysler's "Shower of Stars" production on CBS-TV in the 1950s and Paramount's 1988 film *Scrooged* (**2343**), in which the viewer (in buying a ticket or renting a video) becomes a part of the usurpation of the *Carol* for a corporate agenda that denies charity.

2377. Norden, Martin F. "Tiny Tim on Screen: A Disability Studies Perspective." In *Dickens on Screen* (**2370**), 188–98.

Compares Dickens's portrayal of Tiny Tim with his representation in film, noting that Tim has become a much more important figure in film than he is in the book. (Davis [**2503**] shows how later illustrations of the text also emphasized him.) He identifies three areas in which the films depart from or extend Dickens's conception: Tim as the embodiment of absolute goodness; Tim as an object; and Tim's return to able-bodiedness. Norden finds these characteristics to be typical of representations of disability in films and on television, and he concludes by noting the disabled community's disdain for these stereotypes and for Tiny Tim as their apotheosis.

2378. Petrie, Graham. "Silent Film Adaptations of Dickens. Part I: From the Beginning to 1911." *Dickensian* 97.1 (Spring 2001): 7–21.

Describes the 1901 film *Scrooge, or Marley's Ghost* (**316, 2317**), the earliest still extant Dickens film (held at the British Film Institute), according to Petrie. It covers the whole story in five scenes and five minutes. Superimposed titles help to convey the plot but Petrie says that audiences would be expected to know the *Carol*. He also describes the 1908 Essanay film (**317**), now lost, and the 1910 Edison version (**318, 2318**), of which at least three copies are extant.

2379. ———. "Silent Film Adaptations of Dickens. Part II: 1912–1919." *Dickensian* 97.2 (Summer 2001): 101–15.

Describes the 1913 Zenith film (**319**) and the 1914 London Film Company version (**320**).

2380. Pointer, Michael. *Charles Dickens on the Screen: The Film, Television, and Video Adaptations.* Lanham, MD: Scarecrow, 1996, passim.

This comprehensive listing of film, television, and video adaptations of Dickens is divided into two sections: a chronological summary of Dickens on screen with important adaptations discussed in detail, and a chronological listing of all the adaptations with cast lists and other technical details but no commentary. In chapter 2, "The Wizardry of Boz," Pointer provides a detailed outline of the 1901 R. W. Paul version (**316, 2317**) and its connection to the 1901 stage adaptation *Scrooge* (**239**) by J. C. Buckstone. Later chapters briefly discuss the most important *Carol* film and television adaptations.

2381. Sammon, Paul. *The Christmas Carol Trivia Book: Everything You Ever Wanted to Know About Every Version of the Dickens Classic.* Secaucus: Carol Publishing Group, 1994. 237.

This entertaining paperback book, well illustrated with black-and-white photographs and intended for general readers, provides a light-hearted survey of the major film, television, and musical versions of the *Carol*. It also contains a brief biography of Dickens (that omits most of the major novels) and a section about the writing of the *Carol*, emphasizing Dickens's need for money. Other sections include "The Best Version" (the Brian Desmond Hurst film, **328, 2326**), "The Best Made-for-TV Version" (George C. Scott's 1984 portrayal of Scrooge [**2340**]), and "The Best Musical Version" (*Mr. Magoo's Christmas Carol* [333, **2327**]). Each section concludes with trivia questions which are answered at the back of the book. A useful section lists American suppliers of videotapes, audiotapes, and stills.

2382. Werts, Diane. "*A Christmas Carol*: Adapting a Dickens of a Plot." In her *Christmas on Television*. Westport, CT: Praeger, 2006. 145–55.

This badly written survey of *Carol* adaptations on television briefly discusses a handful of cartoon, sit-com, and fantasy (*Xena—The Warrior Princess*, *Quantum Leap*) adaptations, mostly on American television, and mostly episodes in serials, up to 2003. Werts also lists several made-for-television film versions, but her range is much more limited than Guida (**2373**), Pointer (**2380**), or Sammon (**2381**), and she does not include any production credits. Some of her selections are only loosely connected to *A Christmas Carol* and can hardly be considered adaptations. Guida, for example, dismisses the 1965 episode of *The Avengers* ("Too Many Christmas Trees") as "definitely not a *Carol* variation in any sense of the word." Werts offers no criticism of the *Carol* or comment on the reasons for its popularity other than to say that it is out of copyright and therefore popular with lazy producers.

RADIO ADAPTATIONS AND RECORDINGS
Chronological Listing

2383. *A Christmas Carol.* California: Mind's Eye, 1972. 1 cassette. 1 hour.
A reading performed by Rick Cimino and Bernard Mayes. Released as a vinyl recording by Jabberwocky Productions, directed by Bob Lewis, in 1973.

2384. *A Christmas Carol*. Prince Frederick, MD: Recorded Books, 1980. 2 cassettes or 3 CDs. 3 hours.
Unabridged reading by Frank Muller.

2385. *A Christmas Carol*. New York: Random House Books on Tape, 1984. 3 cassettes. 3 hours.
An unabridged reading by Richard Green.

2386. *A Christmas Carol*. Argo. 2 cassettes.
An unabridged reading by Daniel Massey, not readily available. Reviewed by Mary Postgate, *Gramaphone*, 63 (December 1985), p. 854.

2387. *A Christmas Carol*. BBC Audiobooks, 1988. 2 cassettes.
Narrated by Martin Jarvis and Denise Briars.

2388. *Sir John Gielgud reads* A Christmas Carol *by Charles Dickens*. Hodder Headline Audio Classics, 1988. Reissued by Hodder and Stoughton Audiobooks in 1994. 2 cassettes.
A one-hour abridgment.

2389. *A Christmas Carol*. Dove Audio, 1989. Reissued by New Millenium Audio, 2001. 2 cassettes.
An abridged edition (but three hours long) read by Paul Scofield.

2390. *Patrick Stewart Performs Charles Dickens'* A Christmas Carol. Simon and Schuster Audio, 1991. Reissued 2000. 2 cassettes or 2 CDs.
At just under two hours, this version is a little less abridged than Dickens's reading version. Stewart has been performing a one-man reading (in many voices) of the *Carol* in the U.S.A. and Britain since 1988. For an interview with Stewart, see Epstein (**2511**), pp. 193–97. Stewart performed charity readings of the *Carol* at the Marriott Marquis Theatre, New York, from 24–30 December 2001.

2391. *Charles Dickens. A Christmas Carol. A Musical Radio Play*. Austin, TX: Radio Theatre Productions, 1992. 2 cassettes. 57 minutes.
An adapted version with narration by Lynn Segall and the parts read by Shawn Sides, Craig Kanne, and Gail Threinen, with music and radio script by John L. Williams.

2392. *A Christmas Carol*. Random House Children's Books, 1992.
Read by Peter Bartlett and Barbara Bliss.

2393. *Charles Dickens. A Christmas Carol*. Ashland, OR: Blackstone Audiobooks, 1993. 3 cassettes. 3 hours 30 minutes.
An unabridged reading by Michael Low.

2394. *A Celebration of Christmas Classics: The Story of the Nutcracker, A Child's Christmas in Wales, and A Christmas Carol—Charles Dickens*. Harper Audio/Caedmon, 1994. 3 cassettes. 3 hours.
The *Carol* reading is a reissue of an earlier recording by Sir Ralph Richardson and Paul Scofield (**372**).

2395. *Charles Dickens. A Christmas Carol.* BBC Audiobooks, 1994. Reissued as a BBC Cover to Cover audiobook in 1998 and 2001. 2 cassettes. 3 hours.
An unabridged reading by Miriam Margolyes.

2396. *A Christmas Carol.* Abbey Home Media, 1995. 1 cassette.
An abridged reading by B. J. Meany.

2397. *A Christmas Carol.* HarperCollins Audio Books, 1995. 2 cassettes.
An abridged reading by Paul Scofield.

2398. *A Christmas Carol.* Hodder and Stoughton Audio Books, 1995. 2 cassettes.
In the "She" Children's Classics series.

2399. *A Christmas Carol.* The Classic Collection. Hodder and Stoughton Audio Books, 1995. 2 cassettes.
Read by Anton Rodgers.

2400. *A Christmas Carol and Other Charles Dickens Stories.* Minneapolis, MN: HighBridge Audio, 1996. 2 cassettes. 2 hours.
An abridgement, read by Sir Laurence Olivier, a reissue of an earlier cassette recording that was based on a radio broadcast of 1953 (**359**).

2401. *A Christmas Carol and Other Favorites as Told by Jim Weiss.* Charlottesville, VA: Greathall Productions, 1996.
A greatly abridged and completely rewritten version, intended to introduce children to the classics.

2402. *A Christmas Carol.* Puffin Classics. Penguin Children's Audiobooks, 1996. 2 cassettes. 3 hours 15 minutes. Reissued by Penguin Audiobooks in 1999.
An unabridged reading by Geoffrey Palmer.

2403. *Charles Dickens' Christmas Ghost Stories.* Soundings Audio Books, 1997. 10 cassettes.
Read by Nicholas Chadwin and based on Peter Haining's selection (**2852**). The lack of a contents page makes it difficult to find particular stories on the tapes. *A Christmas Carol* occupies sides 3 to 8. The cover suggests that Haining's introduction to the book version is included in the readings but it is not, leaving listeners unfamiliar with Dickens at a loss to understand the different narrators and situations of the stories.

2404. *Richard Wilson Reads* A Christmas Carol *by Charles Dickens.* Hodder and Stoughton Audiobooks, 1997.
This performance was broadcast on BBC Radio 4. Reissued in 2003 (**2419**).

2405. *A Christmas Carol.* Louisville, KY: American Printing House for the Blind, 1998. 1 cassette.
An abridged reading.

2406. *A Christmas Carol: 1000 Headwords.* Oxford Bookworms Library. Oxford UP, 1998. 2 cassettes.

Narrated by Clare West. In a series designed for "reluctant readers." See the print version (**2258**).

2407. *A Christmas Carol.* Adapted and read by Douglas Verrall. Privately published (St. Leonards-on-Sea, Sussex). 2 cassettes.

According to Brian Hick (*Dickensian* 94 [1998]: 144), Verrall's polished reading is tension-filled and full of variety. The sound quality is excellent.

2408. *A Christmas Carol by Charles Dickens.* Furicano Productions, 1999. 2 cassettes. Digital sound.

An unabridged reading by Daniel Philpott.

2409. *Charles Dickens A Christmas Carol.* Naxos Audiobooks, 1999. 2 cassettes.

An abridged version in 2 hours 30 minutes, read by Anton Lesser and edited by Perry Keenlyside.

2410. *A Christmas Carol.* Thousand Oaks, CA: Monterey Soundworks, 1999. 2 cassettes. 112 minutes.

Performed by the St. Charles Players, this reading incorporates original music and sound effects.

2411. *Charles Dickens' Christmas Carol.* CBC Radio. 1999. 2 cassettes.

Since 1990, members of the Canadian Broadcasting Company's staff have staged readings of the *Carol* at venues across Canada to raise money for charity. The reading recorded here took place in Toronto on 2 February, 1999. Produced by Judy Maddren, with Michael Enright, Shelagh Rogers, Bill Richardson, Russ Germain, Judy Maddren, and the Toronto Mendelssohn Youth Choir.

2412. *A Christmas Carol: Carols and Readings for Christmas.* CD. Herald, 1999.

Readings from Dickens include two extracts from *A Christmas Carol*, narrated by Gerald Dickens. For an interview with Gerald Dickens, see Paschke (**2277**).

2413. *Focus on the Family Radio Theatre Presents* A Christmas Carol. Focus on the Family Publishing, 1999; Wheaton, IL: Tyndale Entertainment, 2004. 2 CDs or cassettes.

This 90-minute reading by several voices is directed by Paul McCusker.

2414. *Sixty Greatest Old Time Radio Christmas Shows. Selected by Andy Williams.* Wallingford, CT: Radio Spirits, 2000. 30 hours. 20 cassettes.

Contains Sir Laurence Olivier's radio broadcast of the *Carol* (**359**) as well as Edmund Gwenn's 30-minute *Carol* for the Stars Over Hollywood on CBS-TV on 22 December 1951, and "A Modern Scrooge" with Lionel Barrymore on the Treasury Star Parade, Christmas Day

1942. This fifteen-minute radio broadcast was one of a series of advertisements produced by the Treasury Department to promote the sale
of war bonds in the U.S.A. Lionel Barrymore played Jeb Creeker, a
town grouch who refuses to buy war bonds until his dreams show him
the results of an underfunded military. The skit was narrated by Fredric
March and written by Noel Houston and Joseph Ruscoll.

2415. *Charles Dickens. A Christmas Carol.* Audio Book Connection, 2001.
2 cassettes. 90 minutes.
Read by Flo Gibson.

2416. *The Christmas Collection: And A Christmas Carol.* Naxos Audiobooks,
2001. 5 hours 30 minutes.
This compilation includes Anton Lesser's reading of the *Carol* (**2423**)
as well as reflections on Christmas by Christina Hardyment.

2417. *A Christmas Carol by Charles Dickens.* Multilingua, Inc., 2002. 2 cassettes.
Performed by Sir Laurence Olivier and others, with music.

2418. *Charles Dickens. A Christmas Carol.* Classics of Value. CSA Word,
2002.
Read by Martin Jarvis. Reissued by CSA in 2004 in *A Dickens Trilogy
II: A Tale of Two Cities, A Christmas Carol, Nicholas Nickleby.*

2419. *A Christmas Carol.* Hodder and Stoughton, 2003. 2 cassettes.
A reissue of an earlier radio broadcast by Richard Wilson (**2404**).

2420. *Jim Dale Performs* A Christmas Carol. New York: Random House
Listening Library, 2003; reissued 2006. 3 CDs. 3 hours.
An unabridged reading in which Dale employs a large range of differ-
ent voices.

2421. *Legends of Radio. Radio's Greatest Christmas Shows.* Wallingford,
CT: Radio Spirits, 2003. 10 CDs. 10 hours.
Contains *A Christmas Carol*, narrated by Orson Welles and read by
Lionel Barrymore and others, from the Campbell Playhouse produc-
tion. For a brief comment on Barrymore's readings see Peters (**2429**).
This production was also issued in St. Laurent, Quebec: LDMI, 1992.

2422. *Charles Dickens. A Christmas Carol.* Sound Room Publishing, 2003.
3 CDs and MP3 Audio.
An unabridged reading by Ralph Cosham.

2423. *A Christmas Carol.* Naxos Audiobooks, 2004. 3 CDs. 3 hours.
An unabridged update of Anton Lesser's 1999 abridged reading
(**2409**).

2424. *A Christmas Carol.* One Voice Recordings, 2005. 163 minutes.
In this unabridged reading, Doctor Watson is reading the *Carol* to
Sherlock Holmes.

2425. *A Christmas Celebration.* Naxos Audiobooks, 2005. 5 CDs. 6 hours.

This assortment of poems, stories, and essays contains *A Christmas Carol* read by Anton Lesser, with music by Corelli and Benjamin Britten as well as traditional carols.

2426. *A Christmas Carol.* Wallingford, CT: Radio Spirits, n.d. CD and cassette. 1 hour.
Read by Orson Welles and Arthur Anderson.

2427. *A Christmas Carol.* Azusa, CA: Audio Book Company, n.d. 2 cassettes. 3 hours.
An unabridged version read by Dan O'Herlihy.

COMMENTARY ON RADIO ADAPTATIONS AND RECORDINGS

2428. Giddings, Robert. "*Scrooge Blues* and *Not So Tiny Tim*, by Nicholas McInerny: BBC Radio 4, December 2002." *Dickensian* 99.1 (Spring 2003): 71–73.
A review of two radio broadcasts, directed by Peter Leslie Wild, that find Scrooge (read by David Hargreaves) a year after his reformation and married. In the first, Scrooge is tricked into signing over his business to Bob Cratchit. *Not So Tiny Tim* takes place fifteen years later, when the now miserly Tim Cratchit is reformed by the ghost of Scrooge. Giddings finds both adaptations disappointing, failing to achieve Dickens's remarkable blend of melodrama and comedy.

2429. Peters, Margot. *The House of Barrymore.* New York: Random House, 1990. 391, 470, 597.
Records that Lionel Barrymore missed his annual radio reading of *A Christmas Carol* on Christmas Day, 1936, because of his wife's death the previous day. His brother John replaced him and "managed to sound exactly like him." Reginald Owen replaced him for the 1938 Christmas Day broadcast. Peters notes that as Dr. Gillespie on film and Scrooge on radio, Lionel Barrymore "functioned as a symbol of courage and survival" during the war years.

MUSICAL ADAPTATIONS

2430. Bricusse, Leslie. *Scrooge: The Musical.* Port Chester, NY: Cherry Lane Music, 1996. 90.
Piano/vocal selections from the 1970 stage and screen version of the *Carol* (**335, 2328**). See also Bricusse (**379**).

2431. Deak, Jon. *The Passion of Scrooge or A Christmas Carol.* Innova Records, 2000. 1 CD.

Performed by the 20th Century Consort conducted by Christopher Kendall, with baritone William Sharp, this musical version has been described as a cross between concert drama, opera, and radio play. Ten musicians embody the *Carol* characters and moved to the front of the stage to accompany Sharp's singing. The CD is accompanied by three-dimensional stereograms by Preston Wright.

2432. Donnelly, Mary. *Scrooge, Scrooge, Scrooge.* Alfred Publishing, n.d. 12.
A choral octavo, arranged by George Strid. Also available on cassette and CD.

2433. Gould, Raymond. *Ebenezer Scrooge.* Oakville, Ontario, Canada: Leslie Music Supply, 1988. 8.
A two-part song, no. 75397 in the Leslie Choral Series.

2434. Leisy, Eberhard. *Scrooge.* Nashville, TN: Shawnee Press, n.d.
Arranged by Lambert. An operetta available as sheet music and in full performance cassette.

2435. Pogson, Steve. *Mister Scrooge: A Cantata for Young Voices.* London: Boosey and Hawkes, [1992]. 40.
Lyrics by George Simmers and German translation by Michael Obst, with piano accompaniment. Six songs are linked by short narratives.

MISCELLANEOUS ADAPTATIONS AND IMITATIONS

2436. Auchincloss, Louis. "Marley's Chain." In *Narcissa and Other Fables.* Boston: Houghton Mifflin, 1983. 95–108.
In this amusing short story, a wealthy American bachelor identifies himself with Scrooge after reading *A Christmas Carol* aloud to friends on Christmas Eve, 1936, and sets about trying to atone for his materialistic life.

2437. Baker, Lawrence. "A Christmas Carol Revisited: Mr. Robert Cratchit Many Years Later." *Worlds of Fantasy and Horror* 1.2 (Spring 1995): 35.
A three-stanza poem in which Bob Cratchit confesses that he is now a rich man, fifteen years after Scrooge's death, but he has sacrificed his family to amass his wealth.

2438. Bayard, Louis. *Mr. Timothy.* New York: HarperCollins, 2003. 384.
This post-modern novel tells the story of a grown-up Tiny Tim (the novel opens in 1860) who sets out to solve a murder mystery. Along the way he ponders postmodern questions of narrative, audience, and text while condemning the appropriation of his story by his father (now dead, and haunting him), and his Uncle Scrooge. This Tiny Tim claims never to have been the angelic child of the original.

2439. Bradley, Paul, and Pamela Bradley. "A Christmas Carol (with apologies to Mr. Charles Dickens." *Medical Education* 35.12 (December 2001): 1173–77.

An amusing parody in which Scrooge is a grumpy old-fashioned medical examiner who learns how to treat students humanely.

2440. Bueno de Mesquita, Bruce. *The Trial of Ebenezer Scrooge.* Columbus, OH: The Ohio State UP, 2001. 139.

It is 1856, Scrooge has died and is on trial for meanness at the Court of Heavenly Justice, defended by Tiny Tim and prosecuted by Professor Blight. Dickens is the key prosecution witness. The point of this defense of Scrooge is made clear in the epilogue, in which Bueno de Mesquita charges Dickens with the anti-Semitism that was prevalent in England in the 1840s. The defense rests partly upon the claim that Bob Cratchit was comparatively well paid and his family comfortably off. Scrooge, on the other hand, was the victim of a failing business and had to live on gruel.

2441. Chekhov, Anton. "The Exclamation Mark. A Christmas Story." In *Chekhov: The Comic Stories.* Trans. Harvey Pitcher. Chicago: Ivan R. Dee, 1999. 131–35.

First published in 1885. Lynne Truss drew attention to this little-known story in her popular book about punctuation, *Eats, Shoots & Leaves* (2003). Perekladin, a grumpy civil servant, goes to bed in a bad mood on Christmas Eve because earlier that evening a younger man accused him of not understanding punctuation. He is haunted by punctuation marks, culminating in an exclamation mark, who reminds him that he has had no occasion to use such a mark for forty years. Perekladin wakes to the realization that he has lived an emotionless life.

2442. Dailey, Janet. *Scrooge Wore Spurs.* Zebra Books. New York: Kensington, 2002. 346.

In this Western adaptation, rancher Eben MacCallister's hard heart is softened by having to look after four children. The story ends with a Christmas celebration and Eben's reunion with his estranged lover.

2443. Dalrymple, Andrew Angus. *God Bless Us Everyone! Being an Imagined Sequel to A Christmas Carol.* Illustrated by Mark Summers. Toronto: Methuen; New York: St. Martin's Press, 1985. 179.

This adaptation takes place in 1850. A wealthy Bob Cratchit has taken over the business and consigned Scrooge to Paradise Hall, a workhouse. Dickens comes to Scrooge's rescue, and Bob is shamed into reforming when Scrooge pretends to be mercenary again.

2444. Davies, Robertson. *A Christmas Carol Re-harmonized.* London: Penguin, 1995. 26.

The hero of this amusing adaptation is Dr. Fred Scrooge, the great-great-grandson of Fred, Ebenezer's nephew. As the philanthropic director of a museum he calls on the help of a Jinny to convert his Scrooge-like staff, but the attempts fail due to modern attitudes of political correctness. Dr. Scrooge concludes that the staff cannot be made happy because they are "without faith and therefore without joy." In a short concluding section entitled "Dickens and Music: A Coda to 'A Christmas Carol' Re-harmonized," Davies considers the references to music in Dickens's work, noting that the songs of Victorian family life are central to Dickens, rather than serious music. He finds musical adaptations of Dickens's novels unsatisfactory (including the operas based on *The Cricket on the Hearth* [**2587**]), and concludes that "Dickens' music is very deeply inherent in his prose and resists attempts to drag it to the surface."

2445. Davis, Patricia K. *A Midnight Carol. A Novel of How Charles Dickens Saved Christmas.* New York: St. Martin's Press, 1999. 198.

This unfortunate first novel tells a fictional story of Dickens's writing of *A Christmas Carol*, spurred on by the ghost of Oliver Cromwell, who wants Christmas to remain uncelebrated. The many inaccuracies and errors include an overstated emphasis on Dickens's poverty in 1843 and the machinations of his publishers to trick him out of the profits from the book. The *Carol* itself receives little mention.

2446. Dhami, Narinder. *Christmas Carol: The Movie.* London: Corgi, 2001. 75.

This book version of the animated film for children (**2366**) is framed by Dickens reading the story in Boston in 1867, interrupted by a mouse in order to justify the addition of mice in the story. In this adaptation, Belle is a nurse at a children's hospital that cares for Tiny Tim. The victims of Scrooge's money-lending are the hospital staff and children. The book concludes with a brief biography of Dickens.

2447. Disney, Walt. *Mickey's Christmas Carol.* Gallery Books. New York: W.H. Smith, 1988. 96.

A picture-book version of the Disney film (**2337**).

2448. Engel, Elliot. *The Night before Christmas Carol.* VHS and DVD. Durham, NC: Insight Productions, 1998.

Popular hour-long dramatization of Dickens's writing of *A Christmas Carol*, with David zum Brunnen as Dickens. Produced by ebzB productions, with an accompanying study guide.

2449. Eyton, Wendy. "The Ghost of Christmas Present." In *The Faber Book of Christmas Stories* (**2229**), 90–102.

Illustrated by Jill Bennett. In this short story, the fun-loving ghost of Ebenezer Scrimp plays tricks on some London neighbors. He delivers Christmas gifts and a turkey, but they all dissolve into powder.

2450. Forward, Toby. *The Christmas Mouse.* Illustrated by Ruth Brown. London: Andersen Press, 1996. Published as *Ben's Christmas Carol* in the U.S.A. New York: Dutton Children's Books, 1996. Not paginated. A delightful version for children. In Brown's excellent illustrations, the mouse story takes place behind the scenes of Scrooge's adventures, so children are introduced to the original story.

2451. Garner, James Finn. "A Christmas Carol." In his *Politically Correct Holiday Stories.* New York: Macmillan, 1995, 41–99.
The linguistic jokes are fairly obvious in this modern rewriting in which a modern-day Scrooge is visited by three "spiritual facilitators." Scrooge is unrepentant after the visits, only to be told by the Supervisory Spirit of Intercessory Therapeutics that he was given the wrong therapy. When she takes away all his possessions, he rediscovers Fred and his family.

2452. Gilmore, Robert. *Scrooge's Cryptic Carol: Visions of Energy, Time, and Quantum Nature.* New York: Copernicus, 1996. 251.
A modern-day Scrooge is haunted by the ghosts of Science Past (the spirits of energy and entropy), Science Present (the spirit of time), and Science Future (the spirit of quantum physics) in order to open his mind (and the reader's) about the underlying wonders of the natural world. A lively and entertaining book for physics students but has little about Dickens in it.

2453. Groom, Graham. *A Doctor Who Christmas Carol.* Privately published by Graham Groom, 23 Meadow Street, Darwen, Lancashire, 1999. 43.
In his introduction, Groom notes that he has retained much of the original dialogue and story because it cannot be improved upon. The *Carol* characters are recast as *Doctor Who* characters with Scrooge as The Master. According to Groom, the characters were easy to parallel: Doctor Bob Cratchit as the Fifth Doctor, Doctor Ghost of Christmas Past as the Third Doctor, etc.

2454. John, J. *More Than A Christmas Carol.* Rickmansworth, Herts: The Philo Trust, 2003. 32.
Design and illustrations by Pete Goddard and Bob Bond. Not exactly an adaptation, this small illustrated book by a well-known evangelist uses the *Carol* to teach children to become Christians. Drawings and photographs depict the *Carol*, as well as contemporary poverty and other social problems.

2455. Kaye, Marvin. *The Last Christmas of Ebenezer Scrooge: The Sequel to* A Christmas Carol. Holicong, PA: Wildside Press, 2003. 166.
Internet reviewers write fulsome praise of this sequel, in which life for the *Carol* characters improves because of Scrooge's redemption, and Jacob Marley is redeemed too. Not seen.

2456. "Kyd." [Joseph Clayton Clarke]. *Afterwards. Being a Somewhat Un-expected Sequel to 'A Christmas Carol.'* London: Jarndyce, 1993. 12. This is a facsimile edition of a handwritten manuscript of 1912. In 1993, 250 copies were printed to mark the 150th anniversary of the *Carol.* In this version, Scrooge is down on his luck because all the people he helped have become miserly rich people who turn him away. At the end the narrator laments the state of the world, wondering if civilization is breeding monsters. Clarke (1856–1937) was a watercolorist famous for his illustrations of Dickens characters.

2457. Le Maitre, Shawn. *A Caribbean Christmas Carol.* Darlington, England: Castle of Dreams, 2000. 10.
A children's book with no real connection to Dickens's *Carol.* God turns a saintly man into a Father Christmas figure after his death so that he can deliver gifts to children on Christmas Day.

2458. Levithan, David. *Marly's Ghost: A Remix of Charles Dickens's* A Christmas Carol. Dial Books. New York: Penguin, 2006. 176.
Unlike most modern adapters of the *Carol,* Levithan is concerned with Scrooge as a man who has rejected love rather than as a businessman. This Ben Scrooge is a teenager whose girlfriend, Marly, has died, leaving him cynical about love and isolated in his grief. In an Author's Note, Levithan explains that he wrote this Valentine's Day version with *A Christmas Carol* beside him, so many passages from the original are included verbatim and the ghosts have not been updated to the computer age, as in other retellings. Marly's charm bracelet is the chain that prevents Ben from connecting with others. This version takes up the *Carol'*s message of love, extending it particularly to a young gay couple, Tiny and Tim. The illustrations by Brian Selznick are based upon Leech's originals.

2459. Livingston, Joyce. *Bah Humbug, Mrs. Scrooge.* Uhrichsville, OH: Barbour, 2005. 170.
In the Heartsong Presents series of Christian romances, Eleanor Scrooge is a successful businesswoman trying to blot out her abusive childhood and failed early love affair with Bob Rachette.

2460. Machen, Arthur. "A New Christmas Carol." In *Christmas Ghosts.* Ed. Kathryn Cramer and David G. Hartwell. New York: Arbor House, 1987. 76–79.
A short story set ten years after the events of the *Carol,* in which the Ghost of the Christmas of 1920 shows Scrooge the misery caused by income tax.

2461. Morrow, James. "The Confessions of Ebenezer Scrooge." In *Spirits of Christmas: Twenty Other-Worldly Tales.* Ed. Kathryn Cramer and David G. Hartwell. New York: Wynwood, 1989. 203–09; New York:

Tor, 1995. Reprinted in James Morrow, *Bible Stories for Adults.* New York: Harcourt Brace, 1996. 151–61.

A short story set in 1846. Scrooge is visited again by Marley, who tells him that charity giving will not solve the ills of the world because in a capitalist system the benefactors' wealth comes from exploitation. Scrooge has to become miserly again to serve as a symbol for socialists and reformers.

2462. Mortimer, John. "Whatever Became of Tiny Tim?" *New York Times Book Review* 6 December 1992: 1, 37–38.

A short story in which Sir Timothy Cratchit, a successful but hard-hearted businessman, is visited by Scrooge on Christmas Day, 1894, and shown visions of world suffering in 1992. Scrooge and Tim agree that giving away turkeys cannot alleviate suffering, but that knowing about the miseries of others can change people like them for the better.

2463. Mula, Tom. *Jacob Marley's Christmas Carol.* Avon, MA: Adams Media Corporation, 1995. Reprinted 2006. 116.

Illustrated by Larry Wojick. Scrooge's redemption is seen from the point of view of its instigator, Jacob Marley. Mula performed this adaptation as a one-man show beginning in 1994. In his introduction, Mula admits to approaching the *Carol* "with fear and trembling" but reassured that the original "will remain pristine, unbesmirched by my muddy little footprints." Available in a two-cassette set with music by Larry Shanker and produced by Robert Neuhaus. Evanston, IL: Woodside Avenue Music Productions, 1996.

2464. Osmun, Mark Hazard. *Marley's Ghost.* Corte Madera, CA: Twelfth Night Press, 2000. 317.

Tells the story of Jacob Marley's troubled upbringing and dealings with Scrooge from the grave. Well reviewed by internet reviewers. Not seen.

2465. Powell, Dale. *Timothy Cratchit's Christmas Carol, 1917.* Lucasville, OH: Dickens World, 1998. Reprinted with the subtitle *A Sequel to the Charles Dickens Classic* in 2001. 116.

Tiny Tim, a wealthy citizen of Cincinnati at the end of World War I, is visited by three ghosts. I have not seen this sequel.

2466. Reed, Ishmael. *The Terrible Twos.* New York: St. Martin's/Marek, 1982. 178.

This postmodern novel satirizes contemporary American materialism, where "Scrooge" refers to the greed and selfishness of a people who act like two-year-olds. Christmas 1980 and 1990 are depicted, and the president undergoes a change of heart through the agency of St. Nicholas, who shows him America's past. Tiny Tim is an unnamed, disabled black orphan, and the "surplus population" of the *Carol* consists of black Americans. For a discussion of this novel, see Annegret Mack, "Dickens 'Postmodernised.' " *Dickensian* 97.1 (Spring 2001): 33–42.

2467. ———. *The Terrible Threes*. New York: Atheneum, 1989. 180.

This sequel to *The Terrible Twos* (**2466**) moves to Christmas 1994. Black Peter and St. Nicholas bring about a more just, less materialistic society. For a discussion of this novel see Annegret Mack, "Dickens 'Postmodernised.' " *Dickensian* 97.1 (Spring 2001): 33–42.

2468. Scarborough, Elizabeth Ann. *Carol for Another Christmas*. An Ace Book. New York: Berkley, 1996. 200.

In this unpleasant retelling, Scrooge returns through a computer to convert Monica ("Money") Banks, ex-IRS tax auditor and now CEO of a computer company.

2469. Sullivan, Daniel. *Inspecting Carol. A Comedy*. New York: Samuel French, 1992. 114.

Written in collaboration with the Seattle Repertory Company, this play is set in the Midwest United States, where a small company is putting on *A Christmas Carol* yet again and risks having their grant revoked.

2470. Sullivan, E. J. *A Redneck Christmas Carol*. Birmingham, AL: Crane Hill, 1997. 31.

Illustrations by Ernie Eldredge. Scrooge, a used-car dealer in the southern United States, sees Marley's face in the hood ornament of his new Cadillac. This satire on working-class America comes with a CD of the story, read with music and sound effects by Travis Tritt.

2471. Thornhill, Valerie. *The Tycoon's Tale. A Christmas Carol for the Millenium*. Beverley, England: Highgate, 1999. 94.

Jonathan Tytheson, an international financier, is forced to examine his priorities when he neglects his family for a jet-setting life at the end of the twentieth century. "Do I know the price of everything, but the value of nothing?" he comes to ask.

2472. Viola, Tom. "*A Christmas Carol*, Past, Present, Future." *Horizon* 27 (December 1984): 23–25.

Not seen.

2473. Watson, Carol. *Charles Dickens. A Christmas Carol*. London: Belitha Press, 1991. 32.

A children's edition told through Leon Baxter's illustrations with brief accompanying passages that incorporate lines from the original text.

2474. Willmott, Phil. *Uncle Ebenezer: A Christmas Carol. From the Novel by Charles Dickens*. Toronto: Hushion House, 2004. 71.

Based on a musical version by Willmott that played at the Battersea Arts Centre in London in 2000 with William Maxwell as Scrooge. In this version, Fred, a social activist, tells his family the story of his Uncle Scrooge's conversion.

2475. Worthington, Paul. "Another Christmas Carol." *British Medical Journal* 311 (23 December 1995): 1702–04.

In this short skit, Scrooge is a National Health Service Trust Chief Executive who is taught to spend more time in the hospital.

2476. Yow, John Sibley, and T. Stacy Helton. *A Redneck Christmas Carol: Dickens Does Dixie*. Atlanta, GA: Longstreet Press, 1997. 76.

Illustrated by David Boyd and set in an Alabama bait shop. Not seen.

STUDIES

2477. Ackroyd, Peter. *Dickens*. London: Sinclair-Stevenson, 1990. 407–17 and passim.

Ackroyd sees the *Carol* as becoming "almost a dream reworking" of *Martin Chuzzlewit* and also the first of Dickens's works to be infused with Dickens's childhood. Ackroyd finds Scrooge an exaggerated form of Dickens himself: his preoccupation with money, fear of poverty, and fear of being considered miserly. Like Parker (**2546**), Ackroyd corrects the mistaken impression that Dickens invented Christmas, arguing instead that he made the season more festive and closer to the ancient celebration that involved religious observance and pagan superstition. Ackroyd usefully discusses the importance of the story for Dickens and its evocation of the Victorian dichotomies of home and street, warmth and cold, comfort and anxiety: "The central idea is one of ferocious privacy, of shelter and segregation." Ackroyd also refers to Dickens's readings of the *Carol* quite extensively in this exhaustive biography.

2478. Allingham, Philip V. "The Naming of Names in *A Christmas Carol*." *Dickens Quarterly* 4 (1987): 15–20.

Allingham considers the aptness of Dickens's choice of names to be most apparent in the *Carol* because of their usefulness to the "homiletic nature" of the book. He concentrates on the name Ebenezer and its allusion to the stone "set up to commemorate the Israelites' victory at Mizpeh." Scrooge adheres to the stone of law, but the law of Malthus, not Moses, argues Allingham, and his transformation is analogous to St. Paul's on the road to Damascus. Allingham considers also the significance of the names Jacob Marley and Bob Cratchit, suggesting both "a whimsical fancy" and "to eat heartily" as derivations for the latter. Names in the *Carol* "work on us at a subconscious or associative level . . . giving the transformation of its protagonist particular seasonal significance."

2479. Andrews, Malcolm. "Christmas and Rejuvenation." In his *Dickens and the Grown-Up Child.* Basingstoke, England: Macmillan, 1984; Iowa City: U of Iowa P, 1994, 97–111.

Andrews briefly discusses Dickens's fondness for Christmas and its egalitarian spirit before analyzing Scrooge's retrieval of "the lost continuity whereby childhood is naturally linked to age," as in Wordsworth's poetry. Andrews usefully discusses the Ghost of Christmas Past and its representation of everything that Scrooge has shut out of his life.

2480. Augustine, Judith DeLeo. *A Guide for Using* A Christmas Carol *in the Classroom. Based on the Novel Written by Charles Dickens.* Westminster, CA: Teacher Created Resources, 1993; reprinted 2005. 48.

A teacher's resource book for grades 5 to 8, illustrated by Keith Vasconcelles.

2481. ———. *Literature Unit: A Christmas Carol.* Heatherton, Victoria, Australia: Hawker Brownlow Education, 2002.

A teacher's resource book for years 6 to 8 that takes the student through the text, with additional exercises intended to allow readers to "examine their own ideas and beliefs about Christmas" while experiencing Scrooge's story.

2482. Axelrod, Rise B., and Steven Gould Axelrod. "Dickinson's Dickens: 'Tim' and 'Dollie.' " *Emily Dickinson Journal* 11.1 (2002): 21–32.

The authors argue that Emily Dickinson based her "imaginary friend" or alter ego (invented around 1860) "Tim" on Tiny Tim, and that he represented childhood innocence (and the beginnings of the poet) for her. The Axelrods discuss Tiny Tim as the representation of goodness and examine his influence on the Cratchits and on Scrooge. Analyzing Dickinson's poem "We don't cry—Tim and I," they trace the influence of the *Carol* but find that while Scrooge achieves wholeness at the end, Dickinson's poems suggest the impossibility of such resolution. The Axelrods also discuss similar connections between Esther in *Bleak House* and Dickinson's poem "Dollie."

2483. Baumgarten, Murray. "Scrooge and Faust." *Dickensian* 97.1 (Spring 2001): 22–32.

Baumgarten does not suggest that Dickens was influenced by Goethe's *Faust* (although he shared Carlyle's admiration for Goethe); rather, he compares the two works to illuminate both as exemplifying a new view of time introduced by the Romantic movement. This view of private time as fluid and "reversible under certain conditions" was later established scientifically by Einstein. Connections between the *Carol* and *Faust* hinge on this view of time: both are ghost stories that incorporate illusion and "special effects"; in both, "the vehicle of the moral education of the hero is the reconceiving of time"; both heroes are imprisoned by "routinised behavior" and have to be literally shown time's flow. In an "augenblick"—a "transitory moment"—both heroes experience the present as containing past, present, and future that allows a "glimpse of the Eternal." This wide-ranging essay provides helpful references to Goethe on the subject of time. See also Baumgarten's essay on two films (**2370**).

2484. Billen, Andrew. *Who Was . . . Charles Dickens: The Man Who Invented Christmas.* London: Short Books, 2005. 100.
Despite its title, this biography for children (one of a series intended to accompany the English school curriculum) supports David Parker's view (**2546**) that the Victorians loved and celebrated Christmas. For Billen, Dickens's contribution in *A Christmas Carol* was "to capture the boisterous comedy of the British in a mood of over-the-top indulgence" while also drawing attention to the plight of the poor, especially poor children. Dickens and Christmas is the theme pursued throughout the biography, beginning and ending with Dickens's public readings of the *Carol* and mentioning in passing the other Christmas books and some of the Christmas stories. While the book would benefit from more careful editing, Billen's account of Dickens's life and interests is lively and full of anecdotes that children would enjoy. It concludes with twenty comic multiple-choice questions on the text.

2485. Bottum, Joseph. "The Ghost of Christmas Past." *Weekly Standard* 7 (24 December 2001): 29. Reprinted in *The Best Christian Writing 2002.* Ed. John Wilson. New York: HarperSanFrancisco, 2002. 38–50.
A delightful, wide-ranging article that uses the *Carol* to identify Dickens's magic as lying in his inventive and energetic use of language. Bottum briefly surveys some of the critical approaches to Dickens and points out their shortcomings.

2486. Bowen, John. "The Transformation of Scrooge." *English Review* 3.1 (September 1992): 38–40.
A brief overview of Scrooge's overcoming of his destructively selfish capitalist attitudes. Bowen points out that such a reformation is difficult to achieve, but that the supernatural means are close to psychoanalysis, and the story continues to offer hope for our own times. The article is illustrated with familiar images of Dickens, Scrooge, and the Cratchits.

2487. Brown, Dennis. "Did St. Louis Inspire Boz's *Carol?*" Supplement to *St. Louis Post-Dispatch* 22 December 1985: 5–6.
Not seen.

2488. Buckwald, Craig. "Stalking the Figurative Oyster: The Excursive Ideal in *A Christmas Carol.*" *Studies in Short Fiction* 27 (1990): 1–14.

Buckwald traces the significance of Dickens's description of Scrooge as being "secret, self-contained, and solitary as an oyster," finding the oyster image "a kind of master-trope for the story." Buckwald's analysis of Scrooge's character according to these three qualities is useful, concentrating on Scrooge's concealed inner goodness—the pearl within the oyster shell. He notes that the narrator is always sympathetic to Scrooge, and that "Dickens condemns Scroogism while he exemplifies an un-Scrooge-like mentality by showing Scrooge authorial kindness." At the end of the story, Scrooge is "the Christmas spirit personified, its pure essence." Buckwald is more successful than many commentators at identifying the source of the *Carol*'s popularity and appeal, comparing the story to the unwrapping of a Christmas present. "And so author and reader participate in the excursive sociality that *A Christmas Carol* celebrates."

2489. Burleson, Donald R. "Dickens's *A Christmas Carol.*" *Explicator* 50 (1992): 211–12.

Burleson finds in the first exchange between Scrooge and Fred "the covert presence, in each character, of an essential trace of the other." The language they use about Christmas reveals that Fred is more materialistic and Scrooge more generous than they appear to be.

2490. Burlison, Carlton L. "The Case of Ebeneezer [sic] Scrooge—A Walking Zombie." *Medical Hypnoanalysis* 4.1 (January 1983): 49–51.

A hypnoanalyst's interpretation of the story, finding Scrooge the patient and Dickens the hypnoanalyst, with the audience privy to both minds. Scrooge exemplifies the syndrome of zombiism: he dresses like a zombie, answers to Scrooge or Marley, and goes through zombie-like routines. Burlison finds in Scrooge's sessions with the ghosts clear evidence of Dickens's insight into the process of hypnoanalysis.

2491. Burnell, David. "Gad's Hill Place vs Hall Place." *Dickensian* 99.3 (Winter 2003): 213–22.

Argues that Hall Place, not Gad's Hill Place, was the site of Scrooge's school in the *Carol*. Burnell points out that Hall Place, a sixteenth-century building, was in use as a school between 1799 and 1870, whereas Gad's Hill did not become a school until 1924. Burnell goes through the description of the building in detail, and the article is well illustrated with photographs. Burnell was answered by Ann Everitt, headmistress of Gad's Hill School, in a letter to the editor. See *Dickensian* 100.1 (Spring 2004): 54–56.

2492. Butterworth, R. D. "*A Christmas Carol* and the Masque." *Studies in Short Fiction* 30 (1993): 63–69.

After establishing Dickens's knowledge of the masque genre (through the books in Dickens's library), Butterworth examines the significance of Dickens's calling the Christmas books "a whimsical kind of masque." He refers to Dickens's description of the Ghost of Christmas Present (mistakenly referred to as the Spirit of Christmas Past by Butterworth) as being both ornamental and symbolic. Scrooge is both participant and spectator, just as the spectators of the traditional masque often became participants in it. Ignorance and Want are anti-masque figures. Butterworth argues that the masque tradition allowed Dickens to "foreshorten character development," but that he transformed the conventions for his purpose as a social reformer. He sees this blending of masque and novel most clearly in the visit of Marley's ghost. The masque provided the festive elements necessary to lighten the serious message of Dickens's entertainment for Christmas. For another study of masques and the Christmas books, see Tracy (**2674**).

2493. Callahan, Charles W., Jr. "Tiny Tim: The Child with a Crippling Fatal Illness." *Dickensian* 89.3 (Winter 1993): 214–17.

Argues that Tiny Tim suffered from tuberculosis, the "single greatest cause of sickness and death in Europe" in Dickens's day. See also Chesney (**2496**) and Nelson (**2542**).

2494. Carter, A. J. "*A Christmas Carol*: Charles Dickens and the Birth of Orthopaedics." *Journal of the Royal Society of Medicine* 86 (1993): 45–48.

Carter credits Dickens with being the first writer to describe crippled children sympathetically and therefore with helping to change society's attitudes to their treatment. He argues that in *A Christmas Carol*, Dickens first drew attention to the connection between poverty and disease. He describes Dickens's influence on William Treloar, Lord Mayor of London, Queen Alexandra, and other philanthropists, as well as noting Dickens's support of the Great Ormond Street Children's Hospital and its staff.

2495. Černy, Lothar. "Dickens' *A Christmas Carol*: Revisiting and Reformation." *Connotations* 7.3 (1997/98): 255–72.

Concentrating on revisiting and its ties with memory, Cerny examines the *Carol* as enacting through the three Christmas ghosts Cicero's three-part definition of prudence: memory, understanding, and providence, or thinking about the future. Cerny sees Dickens's Christmas books as a whole as enacting Cicero's four parts of virtue: prudence, justice, fortitude, and temperance. He gives classical sources for Dickens's identification of memory with virtue and examines aspects of memory in the text besides Scrooge's own awakening of childhood memories. With the ghost of Christmas Yet to Come, Scrooge discovers that there is no memory value for others in his life as he has been leading it. By being visited by Marley and the ghosts, Cerny concludes, Scrooge learns to revisit and rejoin the human community.

2496. Chesney, Russell W. "Bah Humbug." *American Journal of Diseases in Children* 147.8 (August 1993): 818.

Chesney disagrees with Lewis's diagnosis of Tiny Tim's illness (**2532**), arguing that it was more likely to be tuberculosis or polio. He notes that the description of Tiny Tim is too scanty to offer many clues, and that Dickens might just have made up a condition. See also Callahan (**2493**) and Nelson (**2542**).

2497. Clark, Nicholas. "Dickens, Eric Crozier and Benjamin Britten: An Opera that Might Have Been." *Dickensian* 101.1 (Spring 2005): 27–28.

Explains how librettist Eric Crozier proposed to Benjamin Britten in 1954 that they write an opera in three short acts based on the *Carol*. Crozier excitedly notes that the story has "almost everything—intensity, humor (both grim and gay), pathos, and a small but finely contrasted set of characters." Clark regrets that nothing came of the suggestion, probably because of the pressure of other work.

2498. Collins, Philip. "*A Christmas Carol.*" In *Reference Guide to Short Fiction.* Ed. Noelle Watson. St. James Reference Guides. Detroit: St. James, 1994. Second edition, 1999. 785–86.

Collins finds the conversion of Scrooge mythical and magical, not a psychological process, and the book a celebration of a secular winter solstice festival. He still considers the book to be the unrivalled story of Christmas, however.

2499. ———. "The Reception and Status of the *Carol.*" *Dickensian* 89.3 (Winter 1993): 170–76.

Briefly surveys some of the critical responses to the *Carol* in this special 150th anniversary edition of the *Dickensian.* As well as discussing some of the contemporary opinions, Collins considers the criticism of Louis Cazamian, G. K. Chesterton, and Edmund Wilson and regrets that the institutional status of the book has caused many modern commentators to avoid it.

2500. Cusumano, Joseph D. *Transforming Scrooge: Dickens's Blueprint for a Spiritual Awakening* (**2215**), passim.

Cusumano explains that he is a psychologist specializing in psychospiritual growth, and that in his workshops he uses Scrooge as a role model for change. In his introduction he summarizes Paul Davis's book (**2503**), claiming his psychoanalytical reading as the next cultural interpretation of the story. Briefly, Cusumano's thesis, elaborated over eight chapters, is that Scrooge (like Dickens) was traumatized by abandonment and neglect, and the pain was left unresolved. He became an abuser himself until his defense mechanisms crashed, allowing for a sudden psychospiritual awakening. In chapter 4, "The Dysfunctional

Chakras of Scrooge,'' Cusumano ties Scrooge's problems to specific centers in the spine and head (chakras) that control the flow of the life force (kundalini energy) in the body and whose dysfunction accounts for his misanthropy. He compares Scrooge's experience to near-death and alien abduction stories. The book concludes with a warning for twenty-first-century Americans. Cusumano sees the *Carol* as Dickens's prophecy for the future because Ignorance, the deprived boy revealed by the Ghost of Christmas Present, will become violent if ignored. Cusumano sees such violence everywhere in modern society because America's children are neglected and grow up angry. By experiencing Scrooge's redemption ourselves (through letting repressed memories of childhood neglect surface), we can avoid damaging others.

2501. Davies, James A. ''The Sentimental Paternalist in *A Christmas Carol*.'' In his *The Textual Life of Dickens's Characters*. London: Macmillan; Savage, MD: Barnes and Noble, 1990. 75–86.

Davies begins his discussion of the limitations of the narrator by arguing that the illustrations extend the narrator's consistently limited view of the story. Noting that few critics have seen the story as a dramatic monologue in which the narrator speaks to a palpably present auditor, Davies argues that Michael Slater (**1415**) and Graham Holderness (**564**) oversimplify the narrative voice. Davies traces the narrator's defensiveness, his ''over-insistence on facts,'' and his refusal to take seriously the social conditions ostensibly being deplored. Even the figures of Ignorance and Want are undercut by the narrator's facetiousness, he points out. Arguing that the narrative stance is ''one of patronizing superiority,'' even callousness, Davies points to the depiction of the Cratchits and finds Tiny Tim's deathbed scene ''breath-taking in its evasive manipulation in the interests of narratorial wish-fulfilment.'' Fred's family, he argues, is manipulated to allow the sexually repressed narrator to fulfil his ''sensual-sexual fantasising.'' The narrator's lack of sympathy (and strained sentimentality at the end) thus subverts the *Carol*'s optimistic message that social change results from greater understanding; the illustrations, however, ''contribute to a sense of man's innate goodness'' by consistently showing Scrooge's latent benevolence. For another discussion of the narrator, see Parker (**2546**).

2502. Davies, Robertson. ''*A Christmas Carol*.'' In *The Enthusiasms of Robertson Davies*. Ed. Judith Skelton Grant. Toronto: McLelland and Stewart, 1979. 122–24. Reprinted from *Peterborough (Ontario) Examiner*, 15 December 1943.

In this brief celebration of the *Carol*, Davies quotes Dickens's children as evidence that Dickens was a ''fiery and tempestuous genius'' who never experienced the domestic happiness celebrated in the *Carol*. Davies humorously considers what the story would have been like if written by other hands. By Charles Morgan or John Steinbeck, for instance, the story "would have been a welter of pseudo-mysticism or weepy Marxism."

2503. Davis, Paul. *The Lives and Times of Ebenezer Scrooge*. New Haven: Yale UP, 1990. 283.

This fascinating book surveys the history of *A Christmas Carol* from its beginnings in 1843 as a Christmas book through its transformation into what Davis refers to as "culture-text," the Carol (unitalicized). He identifies six shifts in the cultural responses to the book, arguing that its meaning is recreated by each generation of readers. "Bringing Christmas to the City: The *Carol* in the 1840s" discusses the contemporary relevance of the story to Victorian readers as a story about the new industrial, urban England. "Founder of the Feast: *A Christmas Carol* as Secular Scripture" notes a shift in focus from Scrooge to the Cratchits later in the nineteenth century and also in Dickens's reading version. In analyzing the religious meaning of the book, Davis argues that the *Carol* is an analogue to Scrooge's experience and we are converted by it. With the Cratchits at the center, Tiny Tim reenacts the Christ child and the Cratchits represent the New Testament (redeeming Ebenezer Scrooge, a figure from the Old Testament). Noting that in illustrations, Tiny Tim on his father's shoulder became popular (Leech did not illustrate them), Davis argues that they replace the Madonna and child to reinforce the role of the father in realizing the kingdom of God on earth. "The Children's Hour" concerns the early twentieth century, when the *Carol* was no longer a "sacred text." Copyright had expired, Davis points out, so new illustrations abounded, adaptations appeared in music hall and film, and parodies and political cartoons made use of it. By 1900 everyone knew it, and for some it remained a children's book, belonging to an age of innocence no longer possible. Readers focused on the kindly grandfather Scrooge of Stave 5. In "Always a Good Man of Business: The Carol between the Wars," Davis argues that World War One made the children's *Carol* no longer possible. The versions of the 1930s articulated "a fantasy of liberation from the iron laws of economics," and the book offered readers an escape from the Depression. Several fine editions were produced as well as film and radio versions that favored the reformed businessman.

According to Davis, the Carol took off in America between the wars and was actually more popular there than in England. The American film versions (such as the 1938 version starring Reginald Owen [**326**]) departed from the more traditional British reading and became the dominant view. The film, echoed by Roosevelt and the New Deal, urged community service rather than the self-interest of Europe, so the Carol "became the Christmas manifesto for the brave New World." England in contrast was nostalgic for the old *Carol*: in the 1935 film (**325**), pages and illustrations from the text frame the movie, making the book "a kind of sacred object." "The Greening of Scrooge" continues to differentiate between the more traditional, Scrooge-centered British Carol and the American Cratchit-centered version that preferred adaptations to the original text. But Davis argues that the cultures became closer after World War Two when the class barriers began to be broken down in Britain and the Cratchits became more dominant in renditions of the story. According to Davis, postwar readers recognized Scrooge as a kind of Steppenwolf figure, with many contradictory selves. Psychological readings became popular, the best being the 1951 Alastair Sim film version (**328** and **2326**). This conflicted Scrooge "embodied the consciousness of the Sixties" as described in Charles Reich's *The Greening of America* and is evident in the 1970 film *Scrooge* (**335**). "Bread and Circuses: The Carol Now" brings the survey up to the 1980s, detailing its continuing (perhaps increasing) popularity in a wealth of different forms. Davis concludes that the book is not now seen as Christian, but as a secular treatment of the economics of Christmas. It remains relevant because contemporary America, like Victorian England, is two nations.

It is impossible to do justice to the contents of this remarkable book in a short annotation, but its strength lies not just in its comprehensive and entertaining survey of the multitude of adaptations, but also in its thoughtful analysis of the *Carol* itself, interspersed between accounts of the reception through the years. Davis also offers very valuable comment on the many illustrations that have accompanied the hundreds of editions of the text. For the illustrations see also the Gustave Doré edition (**2214**). Davis's book is lavishly illustrated with black-and-white drawings and photographs, and a chronological list of "some noteworthy versions of the Carol" follows the footnotes, which contain a wealth of references to material about the *Carol*. This book is one of the most readable and valuable sources of Dickensiana to be published in recent decades.

2504.   ———. "Retelling *A Christmas Carol*." *American Scholar* 59.1 (Winter 1990): 109–115.

This article appears as chapter 1 in Davis's *The Lives and Times of Ebenezer Scrooge* (**2503**). Here, Davis discusses the writing of *A Christmas Carol,* the early piracies and dramatizations, and Dickens's public readings that began the *Carol*'s transformation into the "Carol," a "culture-text."

2505. Davis, Philip. "Victorian Realist Prose and Sentimentality." In *Re-reading Victorian Fiction*. Ed. Alice Jenkins and Juliet John. London: Macmillan, 1999. 13–28.

In this defense of feeling (sympathy with the characters), Davis suggests that his essay is "really an introduction to reading *A Christmas Carol* as a central Victorian work." After discussing Elizabeth Gaskell, George Eliot, and Dickens, Davis points out that Scrooge learns how to feel about his own feelings by being allowed a double vision: his present self and his earlier self. Davis, like other commentators, sees the ghost as a therapist who leads Scrooge to re-experience his earliest feelings as a child. The *Carol* is seminal in showing that "so-called Victorian sentimentality, as its most powerful, is a normalized form of implicit or displaced or re-immersed *thinking*."

2506. DeGraff, Kathryn. "Charles Dickens and Christmas Traditions." *Caxtonian* 13.12 (December 2005): 1–4.

This useful and detailed account of *A Christmas Carol* begins with a reference to the Samuel Baldwin Bradford Dickens Collection at the DePaul University Library in Chicago, which contains almost one hundred editions of the *Carol* as well as over a hundred editions and adaptations of Dickens's other Christmas writings. This collection specializes in variant illustrations for Dickens's works. In placing the *Carol* in the tradition of Christmas celebrations in England, DeGraff credits it with becoming "the center on which Victorian Christmas observances found their focus." Dickens's contribution was "the personalizing of the experience of Christmas."

2507. Demme, Richard A. "Tiny Tim, Dickens, Renal Disease and Rickets." *American Journal of Diseases in Children* 147.8 (August 1993): 819–20.

Answering Lewis (**2532**), Demme argues that Lewis has diagnosed a very rare condition and that the more likely cause of Tiny Tim's condition is rickets, which affected 50%–80% of Northern European children and was caused by air pollution and latitude rather than diet. Demme notes that in the *Carol* manuscript Tiny Tim does not recover. See also Chesney (**2496**), Markel (**2533**), and Peterson (**2548**).

2508. Docherty, John. "A Christmas Carroll." *The Carrollian: The Lewis Carroll Journal* 14 (Autumn 2004): 3–8.

Noting the similarity between the opening of Carroll's *Through the Looking Glass* (which was published for Christmas 1871) and the opening of *The Cricket on the Hearth*, Docherty analyzes the railway carriage section of Carroll's story as a more complex version of *A Christmas Carol*. In both, a ruthless commercial attitude at the beginning is balanced by the rescue of a victim of this ruthlessness (in

Through the Looking Glass, the victim is the wasp in the wig from the chapter that Carroll did not include, on his illustrator John Tenniel's advice). Docherty argues that the sentimental love recommended by Dickens had died out by 1871, killed by the ruthless egoism of consumerism, so Carroll "attempts to bring Alice and his readers towards a higher Christian love." Where the *Carol* has only the unrepentant Scrooge, *Through the Looking Glass* provides different types of lovelessness in the three spheres of power (religious, economic, and political). Docherty works out an elaborate allegorical reading of Carroll's story based on his dealings with the church, and he concludes that Carroll dropped the wasp in a wig chapter to make his parody of *A Christmas Carol* less obvious, his criticism of Dickens being inappropriate in a work about love.

2509. Eastwood, D. R. "Melville's 'Bartleby' (An Essay in Old Criticism)." *Hypotheses: Neo-Aristotelian Analysis* 17 (Spring 1996): 21–30.
A discussion of compassion in Melville's story and *A Christmas Carol.* Not seen.

2510. Eigner, Edwin M. "On Becoming Pantaloon." *Dickensian* 89.3 (Winter 1993): 177–83.
Identifies Scrooge with Pantaloon, the old man of pantomime who undergoes two transformations in the "slapstick interlude called the Harlequinade or the Comic Business." Eigner focuses on the schoolroom scene and Scrooge's transformation from imaginative child into hard-hearted adult.

2511. Epstein, Norrie. "A Christmas Carol." In her *The Friendly Dickens.* New York: Penguin Viking, 1998. 174–97.
An amusing overview of the *Carol* and its redemptive power that includes a summary of the story and notes on its origins, Dickens's celebration of Christmas, and his influence on its celebration. "Caroliana" contains trivia about the book, including Lewis's diagnosis (**2532**) and other reactions to the book, especially in America. "Reading *Carol*" is an interview with Patrick Stewart (**2390**), and some of the film versions are discussed in a filmography of Dickens at the end of the book. The *Carol* chapter is illustrated with line drawings and photographs from the film versions.

2512. Erickson, Lee. "The Primitive Keynesianism of Dickens's *A Christmas Carol.*" *Studies in the Literary Imagination* 30.1 (Spring 1997): 51–66.
Cogently argues that Dickens was intuitively responding to the economic depression of Christmas 1843 and correctly recommended extravagant consumer spending as the solution. In calling this course of action a "primitive" version of the theories of John Maynard Keynes,

Erickson is referring to Dickens's reliance on personal generosity rather than the government programs advocated by Keynes. Erickson identifies Scrooge's problem to be hoarding cash (in order to have liquidity) because he fears a continuing economic downturn, and as a ''bear'' he has profited since Marley's death in 1836. Erickson also discusses the theories of Thomas Malthus and Thomas Carlyle's *Past and Present*, noting that Dickens's solution is much sounder than Carlyle's, and he concludes with a discussion of the disappointing profits made from the *Carol*, a result, Erickson argues, of Dickens's not realizing that his readership was the wealthy classes who could easily have paid more for it. Disagreeing with the attribution of the *Westminster Review*'s famous 1844 attack on the *Carol* (**460**) to Nassau Senior, Erickson attributes it to William Bridges Adams, a railway inventor.

2513. Feldmann, Doris. ''Victorian (Dis)Enchantments: Fantasy and Realism in the Visions and Revisions of Scrooge and Alice.'' *Anglistik & Englischunterricht* 59 (1996): 101–25.

Feldmann compares *A Christmas Carol* and *Alice in Wonderland* to later versions of them to argue that in the revisions the fantasy allows for unpopular views repressed in the *Carol* and *Alice* to emerge. The revisionist texts did not become popular because they revealed the sadistic and demonic underpinnings of Victorian society. The text she compares to the *Carol* is Mark Lemon's 1848 Christmas story *The Enchanted Doll* (**416**), which, she argues, ''uncovers the disenchanting structures within Dickens's text and within the society that extolled it by centering on the uncanny and punitive underside of *A Christmas Carol*.''

2514. Ferguson, Susan L. ''Dickens's Public Readings and the Victorian Author.'' *Studies in English Literature, 1500–1900* 41.4 (Autumn 2001): 729–50.

Describing Dickens's readings as ''monopolylogues'' that emphasized different characters and voices, Ferguson examines Dickens's alterations to the text of the *Carol* for his reading version to show that he deliberately cut out references to the narrator. In playing all the parts, Dickens distanced himself from the authorial narrator and thus joined with his audience in being the reader of the text. Ferguson sees this change as ''both violating the conventions of the playwright's role and challenging the Victorian tendency to associate narrator and author.'' She notes that this attitude to the audience (regarding his listeners as friends) was very different from Thomas Carlyle's didactic attitude in his readings.

2515. Fleissner, Robert F. ''Scrooge's Humbug Dissected.'' *Word Ways* 23 (1990): 200–204.

Using dictionaries of word origins as his sources, Fleissner speculates on the meaning of "humbug," tying it to humming (jesting) bugs, Hamburg (and a Jewish connection), and the Irish expression "uim bog" or "spurious coin." Other connections are stinging, old age, and ghosts ("bwg,"the Welsh word for "ghost.")

2516. Friedman, Stanley. "*A Christmas Carol*: Paradox, Puzzle, Exemplum." In his *Dickens's Fiction. Tapestries of Conscience*. New York: AMS, 2003. 47–60.

In this study of the way Dickens's artistry supports his moral vision, Friedman discusses the paradoxes in the Christmas book, in particular the question of whether the ghosts are supernatural or created by Scrooge's imagination; Friedman makes a good case for the latter. He provides a biblically based analysis of Scrooge's redemption and the salvation of his life and Tiny Tim's, finding the story's appeal in its working of a miraculous transformation through its double plot (a possible future that is averted). He notes that Scrooge's redemption is realistic because Dickens deliberately understates the harm Scrooge might have done through his miserly ways.

2517. Gilleland, Rebecca. *A Christmas Carol Study Guide*. Fall Creek, WI: Progeny Press, 2002. 60.

A student manual and book, intended for high-school students and written from a Christian perspective.

2518. Grossman, Jonathan H. "The Absent Jew in Dickens: Narrators in *Oliver Twist, Our Mutual Friend*, and *A Christmas Carol.*" *Dickens Studies Annual* 24 (1996): 37–57.

Looking at Dickens's representation of the Jew from the point of view of the narrators in the novels, Grossman takes issue with the view that Dickens proceeded "from an anti-Semitic stereotype to an apology." After discussing *Oliver Twist*, Grossman argues that Scrooge is a Jew, and that is why his conversion is incomplete, evidenced by "the persistence of Scrooge's dark sense of humor." Scrooge thus remains alien from his society, and his "silent" (because not stated) Jewishness "haunts" the narrator's discourse, defeating the conversion plot.

2519. Hagerty, Carol. *A Christmas Carol Study Guide*. Irvine, CA: Saddleback, 1998. 48.

A teacher's manual with suggestions, exercises, plot summary, and biographical notes. For use with Level 4 readers (grades 5 to 12) and adult ESL students.

2520. Hearn, Michael Patrick. "*A Christmas Carol:* Celebrating the Dickens Classic." *Gourmet* December 1993: 146, 234–38.

Summarizes the references to food and eating (and hunger) in the *Carol* as well as providing brief recipes.

2521. Hooper, Linda. *A Little Book about* A Christmas Carol *by Charles Dickens: On the Occasion of the 150th Anniversary of Its First Publication.* Dickens Project, University of California at Santa Cruz, 1993. Not seen.

2522. Huser, Glen. A Christmas Carol *by Charles Dickens: A Novel Study.* Edmonton Public Schools: Resource Development Services, 1998. 103.

A resource book for teachers of elementary-school age children containing background information, student activities, vocabulary lists, and recommended Internet sites.

2523. Irving, John. "Introduction." In the 1995 Modern Library edition (**2852**), pp. xi–xxii.

An excellent short appreciation that begins with the recollection of illiterate Hindu children—members of a circus troupe—enthralled by the Alastair Sim film (**328** and **2326**) in Gujarat in 1990. The children knew and loved the story.

2524. Jaffe, Audrey. "Spectacular Sympathy: Visuality and Ideology in Dickens's *A Christmas Carol." PMLA* 109 (1994): 254–65. Reprinted in *Victorian Literature and the Victorian Visual Imagination.* Ed. Carol T. Christ and John O. Jordan. Berkeley: U of California P, 1995. 327–344; and as "Sympathy and Spectacle in Dickens's 'A Christmas Carol' " in Audrey Jaffe, *Scenes of Sympathy: Identity and Representation in Victorian Fiction.* Ithaca: Cornell UP, 2000. 27–46.

Beginning with Guy Debord's definition of a commodity culture as a "society of spectacle," Jaffe examines the *Carol* as a circularity between "spectacular forms of cultural representation and . . . persons, objects, or scenes invested with ideological value and thus already surrounded in their cultural contexts with an aura of spectacle." Scrooge the spectator is led to identification with scenes that "are already spectacular in Victorian culture: invested with cultural value and desire." This identification leads to sympathy in Scrooge and the reader. Jaffe draws attention to the frames Dickens devises for the scenes—shop windows, for example—that "define the contents as desirable," and argues that these frames "turn out to be fully operative in the 'real' world," so reality becomes spectacle. Creating a space between the self and the image produces identification and sympathy. The vision of his death terrifies Scrooge because it indicates his "absence from culture, defined *as* representation." Jaffe concludes that in finding a spirit that can "walk abroad among his fellow-men," as Marley says, Scrooge gains a capitalist sensibility (that includes a conscience, and a knowledge of the implications of one's actions—a sense of the future). For another reading that concerns the visual, see Heady (**2656**).

2525. Jarvie, Paul A. " 'With what a strange mastery it seized him for itself':
The Conversion of the Financier in *A Christmas Carol.*" In his *Ready
to Trample on All Human Law.* New York: Routledge, 2005. 49–77.
Jarvie's starting place is that Dickens's critique of his society is
founded in "the difference between use-value and exchange-value,
and in the difference between productive circulations and mere accumulation." He sees a progression in Dickens's works from the early
novels, in which the evils of a money-based society are personal to a
character, through *A Christmas Carol,* in which individual generosity
is offered as a corrective, to the later novels, in which the evils of
capitalism are systematic. He sees the *Carol* as both criticizing financial capitalism and being a product in that system (as Dickens wrote
it both to criticize and to make money). This ambivalence gives rise
to an "anti-*Carol*" strain in the book that undermines any sense of
there being a solution to financial capitalism. Jarvie identifies the anti-
Carol in the passage about the shops in Stave 3, arguing that Dickens's
site of redemption (childhood and the child's point of view) contains
seeds of destruction and an underlying "fear of the immense power
and inevitability of the commoditizing marketplace." Jarvie traces this
doubleness in Marxist terms, seeing financial capitalism as "offering
a destabilizing, almost parodic, counterpoint to what is happening on
the surface of the story." Children are vulnerable and fearful (Jarvie
refers to "A Christmas Tree" here), but they are also dangerous,
"since childhood is shown to be inescapably infected with a sexuality
linking it with the non-generative, self-referential dynamics of exchange-value." Jarvie implicates the narrator in this subtext, referring
to the often-discussed passage at the end of Stave 2. He examines the
violence inherent in the "anti-*Carol*," arguing that Scrooge is aligned
to Jewish usurers and the hatred they inspired. At the end Scrooge is
still operating within a society based on financial capitalism which
(when the boy is equated with the turkey he is sent to buy) "is consum-
ing the very weapon the *Carol* is trying to use against it." Finally,
Scrooge's deathbed scene shows the entropy that is inevitable in the
system and can only be overcome by the act of faith on which
Scrooge's redemption rests. Jarvie concludes that in needing to make
money from the book, Dickens shared the dualism of the *Carol,* wanting its value to be "use-value" but being unable to avoid its "exchange-value."

2526. Johnson, Alan. "God Bless Tiny Tim: The Uses of Sentimentality in
A Christmas Carol." *Center Journal* 2 (Winter 1982): 101–14.
Johnson concentrates on Tiny Tim's threatened death as the most
important element in Scrooge's conversion. Noting how often the

Carol is criticized for its sentimentality (beginning with Thackeray's famous review [**458**]), Johnson argues that symbolism and allegory usually lie behind the sentiment. He sees Tiny Tim as a Christ figure through whom Dickens can attack the Malthusian doctrine espoused by the unconverted Scrooge.

2527. Johnson, Edgar, *"A Christmas Carol* Criticizes England's Economic System.*"* In *Readings on Charles Dickens.* Ed. Clarice Swisher. Greenhaven Press Literary Companion to British Authors. San Diego, CA: Greenhaven, 1998. 86–93.

Reprints extracts from Johnson's 1952 *American Scholar* article (**575**).

2528. Karson, Jill, ed. *Readings on "A Christmas Carol."* San Diego, CA: Greenhaven Press, 2000. 176.

This compilation designed for "young adults" contains extracts from the following critical works, "edited for content, length, and/or reading level": Robert L. Patten's 1972 essay, "Dickens Time and Again" (**621**); Harry Stone's 1979 book, *Dickens and the Invisible World* (**1421**); James A. Davies's *The Textual Life of Dickens's Characters* (**2501**); Elliot L. Gilbert's 1975 essay, "The Ceremony of Innocence: Charles Dickens's *A Christmas Carol"* (**545**); Edgar Johnson's 1952 essay, "The *Christmas Carol* and the Economic Man" (**575**); William E. Morris's 1965 essay, "The Conversion of Scrooge: A Defense of That Good Man's Motivation" (**609**); Joseph Gold's 1972 book, *Charles Dickens: Radical Moralist* (**547**); Catherine Waters's 1997 book, *Dickens and the Politics of the Family* (**2676**); G. K. Chesterton's *Appreciations and Criticisms of the Works of Charles Dickens* (**1358**); J. H. McNulty's 1937 essay "Our Carol" (**604**); D. B. Wyndham's essay "The Challenge of the Crib" (*The Universe*, December 9, 1949); Jane Vogel's 1977 book, *Allegory in Dickens* (**658**); Paul Davis's 1990 study, *The Lives and Times of Ebenezer Scrooge* (**2503**); and Donald Perkins's 1982 book, *Charles Dickens: A New Perspective* (**623**). Interspersed are short passages from essays by Don Richard Cox (**517**), Roger Rosenblatt (**635**), and Willoughby Matchett (**598**). "Charles Dickens: A Biography" (pp. 12–29) provides a lengthy but eccentric summary of Dickens's life. *The Old Curiosity Shop*, for instance, is described as a "travel story about an odd collection of characters." The book concludes with a chronology of Dickens's life and an inadequate listing of books for further reading.

2529. Kelly, Richard. "Introduction." In the 2003 Broadview Literary Texts edition (**2220**). 9–30.

A useful survey of the genesis, publication, and popularity of the *Carol*, focusing on Dickens's experiences as a child laborer and on the history of Christmas celebrations. Kelly argues that the two sides of Scrooge reflect a tension in Dickens, and in briefly tracing Scrooge's conversion Kelly discusses the use of tone and contrast in the book.

2530. LaBlanc, Michael L. and Ira Mark Milne, eds. *Novels for Students, Volume 10: Presenting Analysis, Context and Criticism on Commonly Studied Novels*. Farmington Hills, MI: Gale Group, 2001.

Not seen.

2531. LeFew, Penelope A. "Evidence of a Dickensian Gissing in 'Joseph Yates' Temptation.' " *English Language Notes* 26.3 (March 1989): 82–87.

Noting that other critics have noticed the influence of Dickens on Gissing's early works but have not provided specific examples, LeFew points to several close resemblances in characterization and plot between *A Christmas Carol* and "Joseph Yates' Temptation" (1877). LeFew argues that both stories preach the superiority of honest poverty over greedy wealth.

2532. Lewis, Donald W. "What Was Wrong with Tiny Tim?" *American Journal of Diseases of Children* 146.12 (December 1992): 1403–07.

Argues that Tiny Tim had distal renal tubular acidosis, a "potentially lethal, but implicitly reversible, crippling disease," based upon his shortness, his weakness and disability, and the treatments available in the 1840s. Lewis was answered by Chesney (**2496**), Demme (**2507**), Markel (**2533**), and Peterson (**2548**). Lewis then responded that he did the initial study to train his students in diagnosis and to introduce them to nineteenth-century medical conditions and treatments. See *American Journal of Diseases of Children* 147.8 (August 1993): 820–21. Epstein (**2511**) outlines the symptoms that led to Lewis's diagnosis.

2533. Markel, Howard. "On Tiny Tim, Charles Dickens, and Pediatrics." *American Journal of Diseases of Children* 147.8 (August 1993): 817.

Answering Lewis (**2532**), Markel does not dispute his findings but says he overlooks Dickens's fascination with humanity and his brilliance at describing illness and disease. See also Chesney (**2496**), Demme (**2507**), and Peterson (**2548**).

2534. McCaffery, James Manus. "A Kind Word for Ebenezer." *Mensa Bulletin*, December 1881: 18, 20. [No volume no.]

Listed in Hearn (**2224**).

2535. McCarthy, Patrick J. "Naming Tiny Tim: A Speculative Note." *Dickens Quarterly* 12.2 (June 1995): 73–74.

In response to an advertisement in *The New Yorker* (26 December 1994/2 January 1995) that claims to be reprinting a passage from Dickens's original manuscript of the *Carol*, McCarthy doubts the authenticity of the passage that would have Dickens contemplating "Little Larry," "Small Sam," and "Puny Pete" before settling on Tiny

Tim. After establishing that the handwriting in the advertisement is not Dickens's, McCarthy notes that an examination of the manuscript shows that Dickens did experiment with the name while writing the book.

2536. Miller, J. Hillis. "The Genres of *A Christmas Carol.*" *Dickensian* 89.3 (Winter 1993): 193–206.

This lively article examines the "stylistic verve" of the *Carol* in its overabundance of rhetorical devices (lists, hyperbole, personification, word play) and then considers how its hyperbole makes possible the abundance of genres into which the *Carol* can be classified—allegory, ghost story, dream vision, conversation narrative, novel. Miller argues for its status as primarily novel, and he concludes that its appeal is partly its "radical transformative power" over the reader.

2537. Miller, Robin Feuer. "Dostoevsky's 'The Dream of a Ridiculous Man': Unsealing the Generic Envelope." In *Freedom and Responsibility in Russian Literature. Essays in Honor of Robert Louis Jackson.* Ed. Elizabeth Cheresh Allen and Gary Saul Morson. Evanston, IL: Northwestern UP and The Yale Center for International and Area Studies, 1995. 86–104.

Traces the influence of *A Christmas Carol* on Dostoevsky's story. The many similarities include the following: both heroes are isolated and move from believing in the head to believing in the heart as a result of night time visions; both make a journey with a mysterious being; both stories incorporate motifs of light, darkness, and death. Miller refers to Dostoevsky's other writings about Christmas to argue that in borrowing from Dickens, Dostoevsky renders darker and "more stark" Dickens's comic or sentimental vision, but both writers seek to move the readers away from reason and into compassion.

2538. Moore, Julie. "The Child in *A Christmas Carol.*" *University of Dayton Review* 20.3 (Fall 1990): 127–34.

Moore traces Scrooge's redemption through his rediscovery of childhood. She examines the influence of Fred and Bob, who have childlike traits, as well as the influence of the children in the book. She also considers references to the Christ child. Unfortunately, Ebenezer is misspelled throughout the article.

2539. Mortimer, John. "Poorhouses, Pamphlets and Marley's Ghost." *The New York Times* 24 December 1992: 1, 37–38.

Concerns the manuscript of the *Carol.* Not seen.

2540. ———. "Meeting the Manuscript." In *A Christmas Carol: A Facsimile Edition of the Autograph Manuscript in the Pierpont Morgan Library* (**2202**). ix–xiii.

This excellent introduction begins with Mortimer's impressions of sitting with the manuscript in front of him, its crossings-out and hesitations showing the writer's thought processes that are now lost to writing on computers. He provides the historical background to *A Christmas Carol* and discusses its artistry, praising the fact that Dickens "writes as though he were speaking"; surprisingly, Mortimer does not mention the many public readings Dickens gave. Calling the method of the book "magic realism," he asserts that "nothing in the least like it has ever been written." He concludes by noting that the social ills depicted in the *Carol* are still with us.

2541. Nelms, Jeff. "Dickens's *A Christmas Carol*: A Possible Source for Browning's *Christmas-Eve*." *Studies in Browning and His Circle* 17 (1989): 84–90.

Nelms notes many structural and thematic similarities between the Christmas book and Browning's poem. The major difference—Browning's inconclusive ending and Dickens's unambiguous one—points to the difference between the two writers. Browning wanted to instill emotion in his readers through "a sense of uneasiness" whereas Dickens wanted to satisfy his readers' expectations. Nelms's knowledge of Dickens is shaky: he places Bill Sikes in *David Copperfield* and repeats the common error that the *Carol* sold out on its publication day.

2542. Nelson, Roxanne. "The Case of Tiny Tim; The Author of 'A Christmas Carol' Only Hinted at What the Dickens Ailed Tim Cratchit. But Medical Sleuths Have Ideas." *Washington Post* 24 December, 2002: F1.

Discusses the possible diagnosis of tuberculosis. See also Callahan (**2493**) and Chesney (**2496**).

2543. Newey, Vincent. "*A Christmas Carol*: Snatched?" In his *The Scriptures of Charles Dickens: Novels of Ideology, Novels of the Self.* Aldershot, Hants: Ashgate, 2004. 17–60.

Newey's argument is that Dickens played a part in the shift in Victorian society from faith in God to a liberal humanism, and that he wrote *A Christmas Carol* to bring readers into allegiance with "an evolving middle-class schema" in which a social hierarchy and a capitalistic system are still in place. Newey discounts the *Carol*'s Christianity, arguing that the book secularizes John Bunyan's *Pilgrim's Progress* and takes its rhetoric from it; thus the Cratchits' domesticity becomes "the site of a displaced religious sensibility." He concludes, however, that, unknown to Dickens, Scrooge fails to conform to his new role as "icon within a larger bourgeois iconography." Citing most readers' fondness for the unredeemed Scrooge, Newey argues that we have a "sneaking" respect for Scrooge's desire to be independent. As he explains in the introduction (pp. 1–15), the chapter's title refers to Jeremy Hawthorn's contention that we are "snatched" by ideologies because they are instilled in us; Scrooge therefore does not really awake to a freer life but rather "comprises in effect a lure and a construct for regulating thought and behavior." However desirable "hierarchical capitalism" may be, readers remain ambivalent about the story's conclusion because Scrooge could not choose his own path. Newey is, to my knowledge, the first critic to suggest that Scrooge is homosexual.

2544. Newsom, Robert. "Sentiment and Skepticism." In his *Charles Dickens Revisited*. New York: Twayne Publishers, 2000. 58–95.
In this chapter, which is concerned with Dickens's attitudes to faith and the spirit versus rationalism, Newsom sees the *Carol* as exemplifying Dickens's ambivalence about conventional Christian doctrine and the ease with which he allowed for both secular and religious interpretations of Christmas.

2545. Page, Philip, and Marilyn Pettit. *"A Christmas Carol": Teacher's Resource Book*. London: Hodder & Stoughton Educational, 2001.
A photocopiable (wire-o–bound) resource book for teachers in the Livewire Graphics series. Provides activities and related historical and cultural information to be used in conjunction with the Livewire Graphics edition of the *Carol* (**2260**). For students at Key Stages 3 and 4 (ages 11 to 16).

2546. Parker, David. "1843: *A Christmas Carol.*" In his *Christmas and Charles Dickens*. New York: AMS, 2005. 155–220.
Exasperated with the commonly held view that Dickens reinvented Christmas when it was all but dying out in English society, Parker sets out to correct this misconception in this brilliant study. In his first four chapters he thoroughly examines the celebration of Christmas in England from 598 to 1843, arguing that commentators have misinterpreted writers such as Robert Southey, who seemed to be lamenting the passing of Christmas ritual and custom. In the *Carol*, Dickens extolled the bourgeois Christmas that was celebrated all around him while deliberately rejecting a nostalgic view of the season. While inclined to belabor the point, Parker has still produced the most important book to date on the topic of Dickens and Christmas. This chapter on the *Carol* is quite simply the most complete and sensitive treatment of this extraordinary story available, written by the ex-curator of the Dickens House and a man who knows exactly how to write about Dickens. Placing the *Carol* in the context of Dickens's life and times (and after discussing Dickens's earlier descriptions of Christmas), Parker finds the book's roots partly in the ghost story but primarily in the

old English carol and its unique blend of mystery, the supernatural, miracle, and redemption. In explicating these topics through the story's plot and language, Parker argues that Dickens "made a popular festival mean more" by studying what the season meant to him. Tracing Scrooge's transformation, Parker sheds light on many topics, but he concentrates particularly on the complexity and flexibility of the narrative voices and the importance of the narrator as moral center, providing the values which Scrooge must regain. He traces the complex relationship between Scrooge and the narrator (especially in their attitudes to the ghosts), finding them sometimes similar in their playfulness and mischievousness, sometimes very different, and he argues that their near identification marks the end of the story. He concludes by comparing passages from *Nicholas Nickleby* and *Dombey and Son* to demonstrate the influence of Dickens's rendering of Scrooge's conversion on his art. Parker also discusses some of the other Christmas books (**2669**) and stories (**2802**). For another discussion of the narrator see Davies (**2501**).

2547. Patterson, Arthur P. "Sponging the Stone: Transformation in *A Christmas Carol.*" *Dickens Quarterly* 11.4 (December 1994): 172–76.

A personal response that traces Scrooge's redemption as a "transformation of consciousness" that can be undertaken by all readers. We must free ourselves from the sentimental recitation of this familiar story because "this story yearns to become our story." Similar in intent to Cusumano (**2500**) but much shorter.

2548. Peterson, Douglas C. "What Was Wrong with Tiny Tim?" *American Journal of Diseases of Children* 147.8 (August 1993): 818–19.

Responding to Lewis (**2532**), Peterson argues that Dickens crafted Tiny Tim's medical condition to fit the needs of the story and that it was beyond belief that he had observed the clinical course of a rare ailment. Dickens knew that poor children were more likely to die than rich ones, and that weak and crippled children (of which there were many in London) were the most likely to die. Peterson points out that film adaptations do not always adhere to Dickens's portrayal of Tiny Tim. See also Chesney (**2496**), Demme (**2507**), and Markel (**2533**).

2549. Petroski, Karen. " 'The Ghost of an Idea': Dickens's Uses of Phantasmagoria, 1842–44." *Dickens Quarterly* 16.2 (June 1999): 71–93.

Discusses the influence of the phantasmagoria (developed in France towards the end of the eighteenth century) on Dickens's art in *American Notes for General Circulation*, *Martin Chuzzlewit*, and *A Christmas Carol*. Petroski argues that Dickens uses the reader's disjunction between skepticism and belief when confronted with illusion to promote feelings of sympathy in the reader and to avoid self-absorption.

Her reading of the *Carol* analyzes the reader's sharing in Scrooge's experience of phantasmagoric images, mediated by the narrator. Just as Scrooge the child is affected by his reading, Petroski argues, Scrooge the adult recognizes the scenes he is shown as illusory but is affected by them, as is the reader. Illusion frees the reader from rational assessment, just as Scrooge and the narrator become less skeptical. Petroski concludes by aligning Dickens with Edmund Burke and their need to identify "the coherence of the notion of Englishness" (as mentioned in the opening passages of the *Carol*). Burke "described the nation as an ungraspable whole" whereas Dickens overcame the increasing fragmentation of society by "locating it . . . in moments of vision both transcendent and productive of sympathy." The modern reader, aware of having a "divided consciousness," recognizes the *Carol*'s lesson that "moments of private, individual insight" lead to sympathy. For another study of representation leading to sympathy see Jaffe (**2524**).

2550. Poe, Sue, and Hazel Jessee. "Staging a Literary Festival." *Virginia English Bulletin* 36 (1986): 149–152.

While teaching *A Tale of Two Cities* in a Virginia high school, Poe and Jessee staged a half-day literary festival featuring the children in scenes from *A Christmas Carol* and the novel. Elliott Engel appeared as a guest speaker.

2551. Rodas, Julia Miele. "Tiny Tim, Blind Bertha, and the Resistance of Miss Mowcher: Charles Dickens and the Uses of Disability." *Dickens Studies Annual* 34 (2004): 51–97.

Rodas traces a development in Dickens's attitude to disability by examining disability in *American Notes*, *A Christmas Carol*, *The Cricket on the Hearth*, and *David Copperfield* from the point of view of the satellite, a "nondisabled person who appears to construct his or her personal identity around a central nexus of disability, which is perceived as requiring mediation." After establishing Victorian attitudes to disability, Rodas discusses Dickens as satellite for Laura Bridgman, a deaf-blind child whom he describes in *American Notes*. Rodas finds Dickens trying to act as "spokesman for, and purveyor of" the child. Tiny Tim, Rodas argues, is equally stereotyped as a pitiable, helpless "product" who allows the ablebodied the luxury of feeling charitable. She notes that Tiny Tim has become the "poster child" in disability studies for the worst kind of attitudes to the disabled. Rodas goes on to argue, however, that Tiny Tim challenges his satellites, Bob Cratchit and the narrator, as evidenced by his "active little crutch" and his acting for himself. She reads the often quoted passage in which Bob explains that Tiny Tim hoped he would remind people of Christ as evidence that Tim does not regard himself as pathetic and needy;

rather, he aligns himself with divinity in a way that is smug and arrogant. Rodas sees Tim's "small defiance of the mediating presence" as indicating that Dickens increasingly realized that the disabled will speak for themselves. Rodas sees further defiance in *The Cricket on the Hearth* (**2605**).

2552. Rogers, Philip. "Scrooge on the Neva: Dickens and Tolstoj's *Death of Ivan Il'ič.*" *Comparative Literature* 40.3 (Summer 1988): 193–218. This interesting account of the influence of Dickens on Tolstoy is wide-ranging. Rogers makes use of Tolstoy's collection of Dickens's works, in which he had marked favorite passages. After a general overview of Tolstoy's association with Dickens, Rogers concentrates on the influence of Dickens on the central themes—"death, judgment, and brotherhood"—and the narration, genre, and rhetoric of "The Death of Ivan Il'ič." Rogers notes that Tolstoy edited a Russian translation of *A Christmas Carol* in 1886, two months after finishing the story, and he argues that Tolstoy altered the *Carol* to make it conform to "his own, more austere version," removing the Christmas ghosts and making Marley a figment of Scrooge's dream. After making some interesting stylistic and thematic comparisons among *The Cossacks,* "The Death of Ivan Il'ič" and *Little Dorrit*, (and Ivan and Podsnap from *Our Mutual Friend*), Rogers concentrates on comparisons with *A Christmas Carol*, notably the use of repetition, the handling of time, the use of irony, and the similarities between Ivan and Scrooge. He compares their attachment to respectability (arguing that Scrooge is obsessed not with wealth but with "the respectability of wealth") and their conversions, both men recovering their lost individuality. Rogers compares "The Death of Ivan Il'ič" to *Bleak House* on the theme of justice and class, and to *The Old Curiosity Shop* on the "discovery of the meaning in death," a theme he also finds in *A Christmas Carol.*

2553. Rowell, Geoffrey. "Dickens and the Construction of Christmas—Victorian Revival of the Religious Holiday." *History Today* 43 (December 1993): 17–24.
Rowell finds Christian meaning and imagery in *A Christmas Carol,* which is often criticized as having few Christian elements. He argues that like Coleridge's "The Rime of the Ancient Mariner" the book is "concerned with the spirit and life of Christianity." It signals the nineteenth-century shift "from a stress on the Atonement to a stress on the Incarnation." Arguing that the book influenced the way Christmas came to be viewed, Rowell concludes with a useful discussion of the church's celebration of Christmas from the seventeenth century to the nineteenth, and the role of the Oxford Movement in the revival of Christmas observances. In discussing the Christmas tree, he refers to

Dickens's 1850 Christmas number, and he provides a well-researched summary of the development of the Christmas carol. This article contains many useful references to nineteenth-century sources and valuable illustrations of Victorian Christmas scenes.

2554. Sable, Martin H. "The Day of Atonement in Charles Dickens' *A Christmas Carol.*" *Tradition: A Journal of Orthodox Thought* 22.3 (September 1986): 66–76.

While admitting that Dickens would be unlikely to have knowledge of Jewish prayer customs, Sable argues that Scrooge defies death through repentance and prayer and charity, the threefold Jewish Day of Atonement prayer that leads to a change of heart, and he compares Dickens's text with passages from the Additional Service of Yom Kippur and from the Old Testament.

2555. Sasaki, Toru. "Ghosts in *A Christmas Carol*: A Japanese View." *Dickensian* 92.3 (Winter 1996): 187–94.

In this good-natured, personal response, Sasaki begins with a brief overview of Dickens's popularity in Japan and the influence of Lafcadio Hearn on his reception there. He notes that in Japanese literature, two types of ghost are recognized—former human beings (like Marley) and non-human "strange creatures" (the Christmas Spirits). Although Dickens uses the terms "ghost" and "spirit" interchangeably, Sasaki argues that the Japanese distinction sheds light on the twofold nature of Scrooge's conversion, noting that Dickens does differentiate between ghost and spirit in the chapter headings. Focusing on hand imagery, Sasaki argues that the real conversion only comes with the spirits; Marley has merely a "weak imaginative hold" on Dickens. He also wonders why Marley is not accorded some peace in Heaven at the end of the story, as he would have been in a Japanese story of a "haunting human."

2556. Scott, James. *A Christmas Carol: Reproducible Teaching Unit.* Clayton, DE: Prestwick House, 1998. 40.

A resource book for teachers.

2557. Shainess, Natalie. "Charles Dickens: The First (Interpersonal) Psychoanalyst or—*A Christmas Carol*: A Literary Psychoanalysis." *American Journal of Psychoanalysis* 52.4 (1992): 351–62.

Similar to, although much less closely argued than, Cusumano's interpretation (**2500**), this reading identifies "Dr. Dickens" as the psychoanalyst who, with the help of Marley and the Christmas ghosts, leads Scrooge out of his alienated state. Whereas Cusumano blames Scrooge's father for the miser's problems, Shainess favors early toilet training problems, although she admits that there is no reference to toilet training in the story. The article has some factual problems, claiming that the Christmas book was started between *David Copperfield* and *Oliver Twist*, and that John Donne preceded Dickens by three centuries.

2558. Simmons, James R., Jr. "Scrooge, Falstaff, and the Rhetoric of Indigence." *English Language Notes* 32.3 (March 1995): 43–46.

Noting Dickens's fondness for Shakespeare's Falstaff, Simmons suggests that Falstaff's speech in Act I, scene 2, of *2 Henry IV* (when he pretends to think that the Lord Chief Justice's servant is a beggar) inspired Scrooge's famous "are there no prisons?" speech to the charity gentlemen.

2559. Slater, Michael. "The Triumph of Humour: The *Carol* Revisited." *Dickensian* 89.3 (Winter 1993): 184–92.

Slater addresses a surprisingly neglected aspect of the *Carol*–its humor—usefully applying Victorian attitudes to the terms wit and humor to the development of Scrooge's language from one to the other.

2560. Smith, Andrew. "Dickens' Ghosts: Invisible Economies and Christmas." *Victorian Review* 31.2 (January 2005): 36–55.

Starting from Mary Poovey's comment that money became less visible in the nineteenth century than it had been formerly (because new forms of financial activity were replacing landowning, and money was increasingly paper), Smith argues that the *Carol* "represents a fictional attempt to make money visible." He ties this analysis to Marx's account of "commodity fetishism," in which in a capitalist system objects become alive while the person creating them becomes increasingly objectified. Marx used Gothic language to convey this process, and Smith describes Scrooge's inner life as Dickens's attempt "to make visible the latent presence of labour within the system." Thus Marley's ghost (insubstantial) is attached to very visible cashboxes. Smith then argues that Scrooge's new perception generates a social conscience in him but not a perception of the economic system that created his wealth (for some reason Smith thinks Scrooge is a wine merchant). Like other Marxist critics, Smith faults Dickens for merely turning Scrooge into a better capitalist at the end, inviting the reader to accept the system as "potentially benign." He sees in the text "unresolved tensions" between the need for charity and the "unconscious acknowledgement that money cannot alleviate the problems it has created." Smith concludes by arguing that while Scrooge's consciousness cannot free itself from the dictates of the economic system, in his 1850 essay "A December Vision," Dickens reveals how the necessary scepticism can be developed in order to find an alternative to capitalism.

2561. Smith, Joanmarie. "The Religious Conversion of Ebenezer Scrooge." *Religious Education* 78.3 (Summer 1983): 355–61.

Smith argues that Scrooge's conversion is religious, according to John Dewey's distinction between religion and religious experience. She sees the conversion as relying upon Scrooge's dissatisfaction with his present state, and the aesthetic appeal of an alternative life.

2562. Stone, Harry. "Fairy-Tale Form in *A Christmas Carol.*"In *Readings on Charles Dickens* (**2527**). 74–81.

Reprints extracts from the *Carol* portion of Stone's chapter on the Christmas Books in his *Dickens and the Invisible World* (**1421**).

2563. ———. "A Christmas Carol: 'Giving Nursery Tales a Higher Form.' " In *Modern Critical Views. Charles Dickens.* Ed. Harold Bloom. New York: Chelsea House, 1987. 153–60.

Reprints the *Carol* section from Stone's chapter on the Christmas Books in his *Dickens and the Invisible World* (**1421**).

2564. ———. "A Christmas Carol: 'Giving Nursery Tales a Higher Form.' " In *The Haunted Mind: The Supernatural in Victorian Literature.* Ed. Elton E. Smith and Robert Haas. Lanham, MD: Scarecrow, 1999. 11–18.

Reprints the *Carol* section of Stone's chapter on the Christmas Books in his *Dickens and the Invisible World* (**1421**).

2565. Sutherland, John. "How Do the Cratchits Cook Scrooge's Turkey?" In his *Who Betrays Elizabeth Bennet? Further Puzzles in Classic Fiction.* Oxford: Oxford UP, 1999. 49–54.

Lists ten puzzles from the *Carol* that Sutherland posed to readers of the *Sunday Telegraph* at Christmas 1997. The title puzzle was provided to him by a class of schoolchildren in Bahrain, who point out that the Cratchits do not receive the uncooked turkey until noon on Christmas day. Sutherland suggests that there is a certain maliciousness in the reformed Scrooge's ensuring that his clerk will be late the next morning, following a very delayed Christmas dinner.

2566. Tambling, Jeremy. *Dickens, Violence and the Modern State. Dreams of the Scaffold.* London: Macmillan; New York: St. Martin's, 1995. 53–56, 66, 68–70.

Discusses *A Christmas Carol* in relation to *Dombey and Son* to argue that in both works change is shown to be impossible and the bourgeois world is heading towards its death. Scrooge's conversion into Fezziwig cannot happen (he would go out of business). The other ending is an anonymous death as offered by Scrooge's wiping his name from the tombstone. Scrooge "is destroyed as the embodiment of the business ethos of the bourgeoisie." Tambling notes parallels between the working people rifling Scrooge's death bed and Marx's reference to the bourgeoisie producing their own gravediggers (the proletariat). Later Tambling aligns Scrooge's death with that of Paul Dombey.

2567. Thomas, Ronald R. "Profitable Dreams in the Marketplace of Desire: *Alice in Wonderland, A Christmas Carol,* and *The Interpretation of Dreams.*" *Nineteenth-Century Contexts* 12.1 (Spring 1988): 35–45.

This reading applies Freud's view of the dream as a product created by the entrepreneur (the daytime thought) and the capitalist (the unconscious wish). Both Alice and Scrooge wish to own their threatening dreams, and they begin by taking control of language. According to Freud, wishes fulfilled in dreams are always the desires of the ego, so Alice seeks (and gains) the authority of adulthood that she desired, while Scrooge seeks to be not an altruist but a capitalist. Thomas bases this reading on the story's employment of economic terms, particularly in Scrooge's dialogue with the ghosts. Scrooge's dreams must be read as employing Freud's "secondary revision"; the more coherent the surface of the dream, the more disguised the ego's underlying desire. He points also to the shopping scenes to argue that the marketplace is celebrated, not condemned. With the last ghost, Scrooge makes the dream his own, and the story concludes with Scrooge still as miser, possessing his dream, and "possessing" the knowledge to "keep" Christmas.

2568. Tillotson, Kathleen. "A Background for *A Christmas Carol.*" *Dickensian* 89.3 (Winter 1993): 165–69.

Useful survey of some of the less well-known details of the genesis of the book, drawing on Dickens's letters from 1841–42 and Dickens's two (anonymous) defenses of Lord Ashley in the *Morning Chronicle.* Tillotson also discusses the influence of Dickens's father's improvidence on the writing of the book.

2569. Timko, Michael. "Why Dickens Wrote 'A Christmas Carol': Fancy and Fact." *World and I* 16 (December 2001): 300. Reprinted in *Current* 441 (March/April 2002): 22–27.

Timko's thesis is that Dickens's life was at odds with the admiration of domestic happiness and anti-materialism evident in the *Carol* particularly. But Timko seems to exaggerate Dickens's desire to be wealthy and his domestic unhappiness; a fairer account is provided by David Parker (**2546**), who argues that the early years of Dickens's marriage (including the time of writing the *Carol*) were happy ones. Timko concludes, however, by arguing that Dickens was a committed Unitarian whose works exemplified his commitment to social reform and moral growth.

2570. Traill, Nancy H. "Charles Dickens: Tradition and Transition." In *Possible Worlds of the Fantastic: The Rise of the Paranormal in Fiction.* Toronto: U of Toronto P, 1996. 46–73.

In tracing the rise of the paranormal in nineteenth-century fantasy (concentrating on Dickens, Turgenev, and de Maupassant), Traill sees a development in Dickens's fiction from the traditionally fantastic tales of *Pickwick Papers* to "The Signal-Man," a story of the paranormal. Calling *A Christmas Carol* "the richest of Dickens's traditional fantastic texts," she considers several elements of the fantastic in it besides the Gothic and fairy-tale effects: the role of the narrator, the nature of the ghosts, and the use of humor.

2571. Welch, Rosalynde Frandsen. "Culture Carol: Dickens's Influence on LDS Christmas Fiction." *Brigham Young University Studies: A Multidisciplinary Latter-Day Saint Journal* 40.3 (2001): 28–47.

Agreeing with Paul Davis (**2503**) that *A Christmas Carol* haunts the American cultural imagination, and that each generation recreates the story as a way of understanding collective anxieties and shared values, Welch examines the *Carol*'s influence on Latter Day Saints' Christmas stories in relation to LDS culture. She concentrates on the *Carol*'s social message and the importance of personal conversion in achieving a society based on familial rather than economic principles. LDS literature shares Dickens's belief that the written word can transform the reader, and for an LDS reader "Scrooge's overnight transformation simply represents in narrative form the lifelong process of transformation on which he embarks." LDS versions of the *Carol* do not employ the supernatural, transforming the villains through the act of giving itself.

2572. Zandvoort, R.W. "Mr. Fezziwig's Ball." In *Multiple Worlds, Multiple Words. Essays in Honour of Irène Simon.* Ed. Hena Maes-Jelinek, Pierre Michel, and Paulette Michel-Michot. Liège, Belgium: English Department, University of Liège, 1988. 303–07.

Reprint of his 1925 article (**668**).

2. THE CHIMES

COMMENTARY ON DICKENS'S READINGS

2573. Dickens, Charles. *The Letters of Charles Dickens* (**1**), VII, 131.

In a letter to Arthur Ryland, Dickens suggests *The Chimes* as the best reading for the Birmingham and Midland Institute in 1853 because he could make "the greatest effect" with it, and having read it privately he knows its power with an audience. Dickens chose *The Cricket on the Hearth* instead, despite feeling that Birmingham Town Hall was more suited to a "more dramatic, and forcible subject."

COMMENTARY ON STAGE ADAPTATIONS

2574. Bolton, H. Philip. "The Chimes." In his *Dickens Dramatized* (**2312**). 268–72.
   Notes that in the 1840s *The Chimes* was much less popular than *A Christmas Carol* or *The Cricket on the Hearth*, although it had nine early stagings. Bolton provides useful information about the Adelphi (**719**) and Stirling (**720**) productions. He lists 29 stage, film, and radio versions of *The Chimes*, some of which were never shown or broadcast.

FILM ADAPTATIONS

2575. *The Chimes* (**736**).
   Pointer (**2380**) provides a full cast list for this 1914 production and correctly identifies Trotty Veck as played by Warwick Buckland, mis-identified as Warwick Rutland in **736**.

RADIO ADAPTATIONS AND RECORDINGS

2576. *The Chimes*. Penguin Classics Audiobooks, 1996. 3 hours 30 minutes.
   An unabridged reading by Geoffrey Palmer.
2577. *The Chimes*. Colonial Radio Theatre on the Air, 2004. 1 hour 6 minutes.
   An abridged reading by Jerry Robbins with the Colonial Players. Available as a downloadable MP3 from Spoken Network. *www.spokennetwork.com.*

STUDIES

2578. Ackroyd, Peter. *Dickens* (**2477**). 440–48.
   Concentrates on the social criticism of the book, in which Dickens declares himself "a true radical, even revolutionary," his style deriving from Thomas Carlyle and Douglas Jerrold.
2579. Kurata, Marilyn J. "*The Chimes*: Dicken's [sic] Re-casting of 'Young Goodman Brown.' " *American Notes and Queries* 22 (September/October 1983): 10–13.
   Kurata's evidence for the influence of Nathaniel Hawthorne's story on *The Chimes* rests on the fact that both dreams revolve around three

encounters and that a woman is central to the characters' conversions.
The argument is unconvincing.

2580. ———. "Fantasy and Realism: A Defense of *The Chimes*." *Dickens Studies Annual* 13 (1984): 19–34.

Kurata argues that whereas in *A Christmas Carol* the fantasy was a "melodramatic device," in *The Chimes* it "functions as a narrative device that allows Dickens to retain a pattern of realism within the Christmas book format." Kurata notes that whereas in the other Christmas books Dickens's "naivete . . . can ascribe all rottenness to a few bad apples," in *The Chimes* Bowley, Cute, Filer, and the red-faced gentleman represent the terrifying indifference of the ruling classes. The nightmare vision that Trotty experiences is "the colorful raiment of reality," as Dickens's contemporaries recognized. The reality of the vision is prepared for by the "careful structuring" of the first two quarters, in which all the elements of the later dream vision are introduced. The visions depict the realism of life for the poor at that time and are also psychologically sound. Kurata concludes that because the dream portrays possibilities, the ending of the story is artistically and thematically satisfying.

2581. Orel, Harold. "Charles Dickens: Establishing Rapport with the Public." In his *The Victorian Short Story: Development and Triumph of a Literary Genre.* Cambridge: Cambridge UP, 1986. 56–78.

In this survey of Dickens's short-story work, Orel concludes that Dickens wrote short stories to please his readers, and for this reason he wrote stories for Christmas primarily. In his discussion of the Christmas books, Orel concentrates entirely on *The Chimes* as being typical of the series. He sees the book's attack on social attitudes rather than on individual misanthropy as marking "a crucial point in the evolution of Dickens's understanding of what had gone wrong in nineteenth-century life." Arguing that it was not just their propaganda that damaged the Christmas books as short stories, Orel finds that the transitions between dream and reality in *The Chimes* are not sufficiently marked, and Trotty Veck is inconsistent in both listening to his superiors but always knowing that his own class is worthy. Orel still finds the book "a fascinating version of the condition-of-England question."

2582. Pollin, Burton R. "Dickens's *Chimes* and Its Pathway into Poe's 'Bells.' " *Mississippi Quarterly* 51 (Spring 1998): 217–31.

Pollin presents evidence for Poe's having read *The Chimes* and used many elements of its form and language to turn the minor poem "The Bells" (1848) into a much more complex poem in the 1849 revision.

2583. Scheckner, Peter. "Gender and Class in Dickens: Making Connections." *Midwest Quarterly: A Journal of Contemporary Thought* 41.3 (Spring 2000): 236–50.

A badly written and researched essay that argues that in *The Chimes, Great Expectations, Hard Times*, and *A Tale of Two Cities*, women are aligned with the working classes and both are expected to be obedient and submissive to the ruling male classes and must be saved from themselves. Scheckner posits the question, how will Dickens be read in twenty-first-century American schools, which seek "to integrate issues of women and gender, race/ethnicity, class, and sexuality into the curriculum?"

2584. Smith, Sheila. " 'The ladies draw it in their books': The Picturesque in Some Victorian Literary Landscapes." *Journal of Garden History* 17 (1997): 208–13.

Smith examines two illustrations from *The Chimes* to show how Dickens uses the picturesque to advance the social criticism of the book. In Stanfield's portrait of Will Fern's cottage, she points out that Fern's presence in the seemingly picturesque scene denies the stereotype of the happy farm laborer. Both text and picture challenge the picturesque view that change could not come about through human means and that the relative positions or rich and poor are immutable. Fern's point of view is privileged over the spectator of the picturesque scene. Smith then discusses Leech's portrait of Trotty Veck, considering it urban picturesque in Trotty's similarity to Mr. Punch. Smith argues that this new urban version subverted the pomposity and complacency of the ruling classes. Thus in *The Chimes* "the poor insist on taking their place in the landscape of Victorian society."

2585. Terauchi, Takashi. "Dickens' Intentions in *The Chimes.*" *Studia Anglistica* 6 (September 1987): 10–20.

Provides an overview of Dickens's social criticism in the book, referring to Dickens's sympathy with the poor in the class conflict of the 1840s.

2586. Thurin, Susan Schoenbauer. "*Pictures from Italy:* Pickwick and Podsnap Abroad." *Dickensian* 83.2 (Summer 1987): 67–78.

Suggests that the social criticism of *The Chimes* was a response to the problems Dickens saw when he visited Genoa, and that the "paradoxical use of the bells" signifies both the passing of time and Dickens's sense that social problems are insurmountable. Thurin compares the description of the bells to Dickens's description of his visit to Ferrara immediately after finishing the Christmas book.

3. THE CRICKET ON THE HEARTH

STAGE ADAPTATIONS

Chronological Listing

2587. Mackenzie, Sir Alexander. *The Cricket on the Hearth* (**949**).
This opera was first performed in London in 1914. In 1995 Hyperion issued a compact disc (CDA 66764) that contains among other Mackenzie scores the overture to the opera. Notes to the selections, compiled by John Purser, discuss the "strongly Dickensian element in Mackenzie" as evidenced in this overture. The notes are reproduced in full in *Dickensian* 91.2 (Summer 1995): 140–41.
2588. Avery, Helen. *The Cricket on the Hearth.*
A one-hour stage adaptation for children, available on-line from *www.newplaysforchildren.com.*

COMMENTARY ON STAGE ADAPTATIONS

2589. Bolton, H. Philip. "The Cricket on the Hearth." In his *Dickens Dramatized* (**2312**), pp. 273–95.
Lists 180 stage, screen, and radio versions. Bolton suggests that the *Cricket* "may epitomize the process whereby the Yuletide brain-children of Charles Dickens were enshrined by theatrical means in the popular imagination of two nations," a reputation that most people would ascribe to *A Christmas Carol.* Bolton cites the popularity of the actors and directors involved: Dion Boucicault, the Keeleys, and J. L. Toole. According to Bolton, by 1850 the *Cricket* had been staged 33 times, and, unlike some of Dickens's other works, it remained popular throughout the nineteenth century with at least 111 stagings by 1900. Bolton also discusses the dearth of film and radio versions. See Sutcliffe (**2315**) on the popularity of *A Christmas Carol*, however.
2590. Davis, Jim. "The Importance of Being Caleb: The Influence of Boucicault's *Dot* on the Comic Styles of J. L. Toole and Joseph Jefferson." *Dickensian* 82.1 (Spring 1986): 27–32.
This interesting article argues that Joseph Jefferson in America and J. L. Toole in England became better actors for having performed the part of Caleb Plummer in Dion Boucicault's adaptation of *The Cricket on the Hearth* (**940**). Davis credits the range of humor and pathos required for the part, and he quotes several obscure contemporary reviews in support. Davis argues that the comedies written later for these actors

were more sophisticated to accord with their broader range of acting, exemplifying "the seminal influence of Dickens on comedy acting in the latter part of the nineteenth century."

FILM ADAPTATIONS

2591. *The Cricket on the Hearth* (**979**).
The first film adaptation of *The Cricket on the Hearth*, directed by D. W. Griffith and produced by Biograph in 1909, is now available on disc one of a 2–disc DVD set released by the British Film Institute and titled *Dickens Before Sound*. It runs for 14 minutes and has a voiceover commentary by Michael Eaton.
2592. *The Cricket on the Hearth* (**983**).
The 1923 Paul Gerson Pictures film, directed by Lorimer Johnson, is available on VHS.
2593. *The Cricket on the Hearth*. NBC-TV, 1952.
In the series *Kraft Television Theatre* with Grace Kelly and Russell Hardie. Listed in Pointer (**2380**).
2594. *The Cricket on the Hearth*. NBC-TV, 1967. Animated, 60 minutes.
In the series *The Danny Thomas Hour*, with the voices of Danny Thomas, Marlo Thomas, and Roddy McDowall. Available on VHS and DVD (2006).

COMMENTARY ON FILM ADAPTATIONS

2595. Petrie, Graham. "Silent Film Adaptations of Dickens. Part I: From the Beginning to 1911" (**2378**).
Describes the 1909 Biograph film, directed by D. W. Griffith (**979**). Petrie finds this version cinematically sophisticated (it has 25 short scenes, shot from different angles and distances), but viewers unfamiliar with the story would have trouble following it.
2596. ———. "Silent Film Adaptations of Dickens. Part II: 1912–1919" (**2379**).
Describes the 1914 Biograph film (**981**) as having too few descriptive titles and none of Griffith's flair with camera angles and editing (**979**).
2597. ———. "Silent Film Adaptations of Dickens. Part III: 1920–27." *Dickensian* 97.3 (Winter 2001): 197–213.
Describes a French version of 1922, directed by Jean Manoussi and starring Charles Boyer as Edward. This film is almost 30 minutes long and makes much more of Caleb and Bertha than did the earlier films.

Petrie also describes in detail the 1923 American version (**983**), which is 80 minutes long and contains some invented scenes. Bertha is central to this version, which Petrie finds ''stylistically undistinguished'' but ''well photographed and competently acted.'' Lorimer Johnson, the director, plays Tackleton.

2598. Pointer, Michael. *Charles Dickens on the Screen. The Film, Television, and Video Adaptations* (**2380**), passim.

Lists the film and television versions of *The Cricket on the Hearth* and places them in the context of the filming of Dickens's works generally.

RADIO ADAPTATIONS AND RECORDINGS

2599. *The Cricket on the Hearth.* Colonial Radio Theatre on the Air, 2004. 1 hour 20 minutes.

An abridged reading by Jerry Robbins with the Colonial Players. Available as a downloadable MP3 from Spoken Network. *www.spokennetwork.com.*

STUDIES

2600. Ackroyd, Peter. *Dickens* (**2477**). 483–85.

A biographical reading in which the Peerybingle marriage reverses Dickens's marriage: Catherine Dickens is the ''plodding'' husband, Dickens the quick-spirited Dot, beloved of everybody. Ackroyd suggests that Dickens was wanting to absolve himself of blame in his hypnotizing of Madame de la Rue and that he is present in the portraits of the loving father (Caleb) and the loving narrator.

2601. Gitter, Elisabeth G. ''The Blind Daughter in Charles Dickens's *Cricket on the Hearth.''* *Studies in English Literature* 39.4 (Autumn 1999): 675–89.

Gitter argues that Dickens exploits Bertha's blindness to gloss over the ''incestuous wishes and guilty desires'' of the elderly lovers Tackleton and John. Drawing on the theories of Freud, Lacan, Derrida, and others, she considers nineteenth-century attitudes to blindness and sexuality, and compares the Christmas book to other works including Hoffmann's ''The Sandman'' and Wilkie Collins's *Poor Miss Finch.* The blind girl ''embodies aspects of the other-worldly'' and is excluded from the communal dance at the end because she has served as ''a lightning rod for the guilt and aggression implicit in the January-May plot'' and as ''the repository of punishment for ocular crime.''

2602. Holmes, Martha Stoddard. "The Twin Structure: Disabled Women in Victorian Courtship Plots." In *Disability Studies: Enabling the Humanities.* Ed. Sharon L. Snyder, Brenda Jo Brueggemann, and Rosemarie Garland-Thomson. New York: Modern Language Association of America, 2002. 222–33.

Places *The Cricket on the Hearth* within a "pervasive trope in Victorian literature in which two women characters, one disabled and one nondisabled, are paired in a courtship plot that assigns them two very different physical, emotional, and sexual roles." Like Gitter (**2601**), Holmes focuses on Bertha's exclusion from the marriage plot, arguing that her intense emotion (her love for Tackleton that is revealed to be the result of a trick, and the transference of that love to her father) is marked as excessive and dangerous. Holmes goes on to argue that Bertha's exclusion from marriage is typical of Victorian society's attitudes to blindness and the belief that it was caused by sexual disease and could be transmitted from the mother to her child. The blind woman thus becomes "a historically terrifying figure." For a similar reading, see Klages (**2663**).

2603. Moncrieff, Scott. "*The Cricket* in the Study." *Dickens Studies Annual* 22 (1993): 137–53.

Arguing that *The Cricket on the Hearth* has been overlooked and undervalued, Moncrieff finds it a "complex, disturbing story" that is important in the development of Dickens's portrayal of love and marriage. He analyzes the plot, concentrating on the January/May relationships and the role of Dot, whose name (the dot of the i) reflects John's patriarchal attitude to her. Moncrieff comments at length on the role of Edward Plummer, who as the Stranger would have reminded Victorian readers of a contemporary and popular play about adultery. Unlike most critics, he credits Dickens with subtlety in examining Dot's subconscious doubts about her marriage, and he suggests that the enigmatic ending of the story points to Dickens's knowledge that the January/May marriage is a troubled one. Moncrieff also considers Caleb's misguided creation of a fantasy world for Bertha as imitating the role of the novelist in the story, and as supporting Dickens's view that the fantastic must be balanced with realism.

2604. Riach, Alan. "*The Cricket on the Hearth.*" In *Reference Guide to Short Fiction* (**2498**). 677–78.

This article appears only in the 1994 edition of the *Guide.* Riach provides a useful discussion of the book, finding its theatricality a virtue. He examines the role of imagination, considering "the ambiguous quality of the life of the imagination" to be Dickens's subject. Riach also discusses the "enigmatic sexuality" of the story and argues that the "sexual subjugation of women and the tyranny of the hearth lie underneath the blissful domesticity of home."

2605. Rodas, Julia Miele. "Tiny Tim, Blind Bertha, and the Resistance of Miss Mowcher: Charles Dickens and the Uses of Disability" (**2551**).
Continuing her discussion of the disabled person in relation to a satellite figure who acts as mediator and controller, Rodas sees Caleb as the arch-satellite, circumscribing his daughter Bertha's world and mediating her knowledge of it. She is disabled not by her blindness but by the benevolence of the narrator and Caleb. Rodas suggests that Caleb is actually self-serving in his care of Bertha because he is praised for his self-sacrifice and is gratified by it. Bertha seems to adhere to the stereotypes of the blind woman (an object of charity for her father and Dot, endowed with superior hearing and musical ability, employed in hand work, ignorant of sexual boundaries). But Rodas argues that Bertha "erupts out of the symbolic boundaries established by the satellite narrative" of Caleb and the narrator. Caleb is unable to control Bertha's feelings for Tackleton, which arise out of her own desire and "interpretive powers." The narrator too is thwarted because "Bertha refuses to reside passively within the enclosure constructed." She is gainfully employed, and her "expressions of erotic desire" are not quelled. In her dreams for the future, Bertha sees herself as a satellite to another disabled figure (her elderly father or husband). Rodas concludes that Dickens increasingly realized the impossibility of keeping the disabled within conventional boundaries. The essay then moves to a discussion of *David Copperfield,* in which Rodas argues that Dickens came to realize more fully the complex and shifting relationship involved in the disabled and the satellite.

2606. Stella, Maria. "Pip and Pinocchio: Dickensian Motifs in Carlo Collodi." In *Dickens: The Craft of Fiction and the Challenges of Reading: Proceedings of the Milan Symposium, Gargnano, September 1998.* Ed. Rossana Bonadei, Clotilde de Stasio, Carlo Pagetti, and Alessandro Vescovi. Milan: Unicopli, 2000. 301–17.
Notes parallels between *The Cricket on the Hearth* and *The Adventures of Pinocchio.* In both stories, a cricket undergoes a transformation and acts as a structural motif, and both stories are based upon a father/child relationship within an artisan context.

4. THE BATTLE OF LIFE

COMMENTARY ON STAGE ADAPTATIONS

2607. Bolton, H. Philip. "The Battle of Life." In his *Dickens Dramatized*
(**2312**). 296–301.
In his introduction Bolton points out that neither the Adelphi nor the
Strand dramatized *The Battle of Life*, possibly because *The Theatrical
Times* had been critical of dramatized Dickens. Bolton notes that there
were few versions after the 1840s. He lists 40 versions, including
a radio drama by David Willmott, broadcast on BBC-radio on 28
March 1957.

STUDIES

2608. Ackroyd, Peter. *Dickens* (**2477**). 512–15.
Concentrates on the significance of the title to note that Dickens upset
this favorite Victorian phrase for power and progress, using it instead
to signify self-abnegation.
2609. Allingham, Philip V. "*The Battle of Life* (1846) and the Prologue to
The Patrician's Daughter (1842)." *American Notes and Queries* 3
(1990): 165–68.
Notes an interesting similarity between the title of the Christmas book
and the Prologue that Dickens wrote for John Westland Marston's play
The Patrician's Daughter (1842). The lines were spoken by Dickens's
friend William Macready.
2610. Drew, John. *Dickens the Journalist.* Gordonsville, VA: Palgrave Macmillan, 2004. 109.
In discussing *Household Words* as the title for Dickens's new journal
in 1850, Drew notes that the "uncomfortable marriage" of battle
(Henry's speech at Agincourt, quoted in Dickens's motto) and domesticity is echoed in the Christmas book. He suggests that Dickens is
"celebrating and thus exposing two conflicting paradigms for man's
duty in society," the masculine one of competition and the feminine
one of family.
2611. Eigner, Edwin M. *The Dickens Pantomime.* Berkeley: U of California
P, 1989. 66.
Compares Marion's sacrifice with Wilhelm Meister's in Goethe's
novel but notes that Dickens missed Goethe's irony and executed a
"pious fraud" on the reader in *The Battle of Life*.
2612. Glancy, Ruth F. "The Shaping of *The Battle of Life*: Dickens' Manuscript Revisions." *Dickens Studies Annual* 17 (1988): 67–89.

A study of Dickens's writing of the story and his attempts to rectify the problems caused by a plot and theme too unwieldy to be handled without the supernatural agency employed in the other Christmas books. Changes made at manuscript and proof stage are examined.

2613. Stone, Harry. *The Night Side of Dickens: Cannibalism, Passion, Necessity.* Columbus: Ohio State UP, 1994. 236–40.

Finds the cannibalism motif central to *The Battle of Life* ("that stillborn novelette") in the metaphor of "the living battening on the dead," spelled out in the opening description of the village built upon the battlefield. Stone aligns this vision to Dickens's description of the Dedlock graves in *Bleak House* and to the graveyard in *Edwin Drood* as well as to James Joyce's *The Dead.* Stone sees an ambivalence in Dickens's motif of the living gaining sustenance from the dead: in the Christmas book the motif is not so much ghoulish as reflective, an image of "renewal and abundance" but with the overtones of the "dim, cannibal-haunted mists of his childhood conditioning." Stone is answered by Boborykina (**2644**).

5. THE HAUNTED MAN

THE HAUNTED MAN in Progress

2614. Dickens, Charles. *The Letters of Charles Dickens* (**1**), VII, 893.

Writes to Patric Park on 11 November 1848 that he is unable to visit him during the day, being "so occupied with my Christmas book (habitually walking out with the owls and other ill-omened birds.)"

SUBSEQUENT EDITIONS CONTAINING NEW INTRODUCTIONS

2615. Dickens, Charles. "The Haunted Man." In *Spirits of Christmas* (**2461**). 122–95.

In the introduction to this collection of ghost stories for and about Christmas (pp. 13–15), David G. Hartwell credits Dickens with linking Christmas to the "secular supernatural" and popularizing the form in his Christmas books and stories. *The Haunted Man* is included because its theme of remembering past sorrows in order to forgive "is one of the great themes of the whole Christmas ghost tradition" and shows Dickens arriving at "one of his seminal insights . . . that what is nobody's fault must be everybody's fault."

RECEPTION BY DICKENS'S CONTEMPORARIES

2616. Bulwer, afterwards Bulwer Lytton, Rosina Doyle, Baroness Lytton. *The School for Husbands; or, Molière's Life and Times.* 3 vols. London: Charles J. Skeet, 1852, I, iii.
Comments in the Preface, while complaining that people are influenced by critics, that were the critics "to assert that 'The Haunted Man!' was the finest Epic (!) in the language, we should have all St. James's da caponing the monstrous absurdity; and every little miss and mannikin in the kingdom inundating the press with diluted imitations of this ineffable trash."

COMMENTARY ON STAGE ADAPTATIONS

2617. Bolton, H. Philip. "The Haunted Man." In his *Dickens Dramatized* (**2312**). 302–05.
Lists 24 stage versions, noting that the story fell out of favor as a dramatization after the initial offerings.

MISCELLANEOUS ADAPTATIONS: MUSIC, RECORDINGS, AND PARODIES

2618. Holmes, W.H. "Milly's Consolation." London: J. H. Jewell, 1849.
See *The Letters of Charles Dickens. Pilgrim Edition* (**1**), VI, 145, for information about this song that was praised in the 13 July 1849 *Court Journal.*
2619. *Charles Dickens' Christmas Ghost Stories* (**2403**).
The Haunted Man occupies sides 9 to 15.

STUDIES

2620. Ackroyd, Peter. *Dickens* (**2477**). 553–55.
Briefly mentions this "strange and powerful book" in relation to the death of Dickens's sister Fanny and the writing of his autobiographical fragment.
2621. Allingham, Philip V. "The Illustrations in Dickens's *The Haunted Man and The Ghost's Bargain*: Public and Private Spheres and Spaces." *Dickens Studies Annual* 36 (2005): 75–123.

Examines the relationship between the illustrations and the text and between the artists and Dickens to argue that *The Haunted Man* was a "collaborative artistic endeavour" rather than just a "commodity text." Allingham analyzes the illustrations in detail, providing information about the style and strengths of the different artists involved (Leech, Tenniel, Stone, and Stanfield). He notes that Dickens apportioned the illustrations to suit the particular talents of the artists (emblem for Tenniel, architecture for Stanfield, character for Leech, and the spiritual Milly for Stone) in order to "maintain pictorial-narrative continuity" (not always possible, however). Throughout, Allingham argues that *The Haunted Man* was novel because through both text and illustrations it "valorizes the redemptive, succoring, and beneficent powers" of the woman's domestic sphere (Milly's) over the worldly or intellectual sphere of the masculine.

2622. Barsky, Robert F. "Re-vitalising the Memory through Narrative: Bakhtin's Dialogism and the Realist Text." *Discours Social/Social Discourse: Analyse du Discours et Sociocritique des Textes/Discourse Analysis and Sociocriticism of Texts* 3.1–2 (Spring-Summer 1990): 147–66.

After discussing *The Brothers Karamazov,* Barsky examines *The Haunted Man* as a "privileged locus" for the study of "how the story can play the role of an ever-active animated voice which sustains the cultural memory of a society, while at the same time acting [as] a disruptive force against lethargy, stasis or oppression of the status quo." He uses Bakhtin's concept of vitalism as being a way of understanding the dialogic relation between the mind and the world, and in a close reading of the story he analyzes Redlaw's interaction with his society before and after his loss of memory. Barsky is concerned with the realist novel's sense of being a "living text" and how *The Haunted Man* demonstrates the role of memory in connecting the mind to the world. He suggests that Dickens's source for the "metaphysics of language-life combinations" was Antoine Lavoisier and the law of thermodynamics (as providing " 'empirical' evidence for the life language connection"). He concludes that Dickens and Dostoevsky have written vitalist texts that fulfil Bakhtin's belief in the social importance of dialogism.

2623. Carse, Wendy K. "Domestic Transformations in Dickens's 'The Haunted Man.' " *Dickens Studies Annual* 23 (1994): 163–81.

Carse argues that while Dickens posits Milly as the antidote to Redlaw's evil influence as a man without a memory, the story ends enigmatically. Dickens has to defuse her power because it threatens to undermine "the very relationships—between classes and genders—that domesticity is constructed to contain and solidify." Carse analyzes the sources of Milly's supranatural power that is linked to her dead baby and concludes that at the end of the story Dickens has to take away the working-class woman's power and restore "a familiar hierarchy of both gender and class."

2624. Glancy, Ruth. "Dickens at Work on *The Haunted Man.*" *Dickens Studies Annual* 15 (1986): 65–85.

An examination of Dickens's meticulous writing and rewriting of the Christmas book in order to achieve coherence of plot and character development.

2625. Goeser, Robert J. "Memory, Evil and Transfiguration in a Neglected Work of Dickens." *Word and World* 13 (Spring 1993): 143–49.

Defends *The Haunted Man* from charges of sentimentality by finding in it "some of Dickens's most profound theological insights," which are woven into the narrative and dialogue. Goeser compares the juxtaposition of Millie's knowledge of the heart and Redlaw's knowledge of science (facts) to that of Sissy and Mr. Gradgrind in *Hard Times.* The Christmas book enacts grace and transfiguration.

2626. Gregory, Gill. "Editorial Authority: Charles Dickens." In her *The Life and Work of Adelaide Procter.* Aldershot, Hants: Ashfield, 1998. 192–250.

In comparing *The Haunted Man* to Procter's poem "The Requital" (1860), Gregory briefly (pp. 247–48) discusses the waif's attraction to Milly's house but senses that "a place there has not been entirely secured." She finds the image of Redlaw looking through the window at the waif (his alter ego) "resonant and disturbing," but notes that Dickens finds a happy resolution for the story, unlike the outcome in the meeting of woman and child in "The Requital."

2627. Moncrieff, Scott. "Remembrance of Wrongs Past in *The Haunted Man.*" *Studies in Short Fiction* 28 (Fall 1991): 535–41.

Noting Dickens's recurring motif of a man betrayed by his mistress and his best friend, Moncrieff argues that in this triangle the mistress and friend represent Dickens's parents, who betrayed him by consigning him to work in the blacking factory. He examines the relationships among Redlaw, his old friend Longford, and Longford's wife (Redlaw's former love) to show how through the betrayers' guilt and repentance Dickens was able to become the forgiver instead of the accuser, as he is in the autobiographical fragment written around the same time.

2628. Reed, James. "Dickens, Christmas, and the Baby in the Egg-Box." *Dickensian* 94.3 (Winter 1998): 165–71.

Taking as his starting place Dickens's description of seeing a dying baby in a poor Edinburgh house, Reed traces the development of Dickens's haunted Christmas men, from Gabriel Grub through Scrooge ("a brilliantly conceived pantomime villain") to Redlaw. Reed considers the waif in *The Haunted Man* as paralleling not only Redlaw's haunted condition but also his neglected childhood. Reed notes that the waif is still alone and wild at the end of the story, a Caliban to Redlaw's Prospero who learns that "the rarer action is in virtue than in vengeance."

2629. Shinoda, Akio. *Charles Dickens to Christmas mono no Sakuhingun.* Tokyo: Keishuisha, 1994. 142.

A study of the Christmas books. Not seen.

2630. Stone, Harry. *The Night Side of Dickens: Cannibalism, Passion, Necessity* (**2613**). 463–69.

Stone discusses the victimized child as central to *A Christmas Carol* and *The Haunted Man,* externally (sociologically) in the children Ignorance and Want (in the *Carol*) and the waif in *The Haunted Man,* but also internally (psychologically) in Scrooge and Redlaw. Stone sees these heroes as "unquiet ghosts of Dickens's haunted past," but whereas they are healed (and through unrealistic means: they have free will, but it is powerless without supernatural aid), Dickens remained haunted. Stone sees this haunting as culminating in "George Silverman's Explanation" (**2846**).

2631. Tabata, Tomoji. "Differentiation of Idiolects in Fictional Discourse: A Stylo-Statistical Approach to Dickens's Artistry." In *Approaches to Style and Discourse in English.* Ed. Risto Hiltunen and Shinichiro Watanabe. Osaka, Japan: Osaka UP, 2004. 79–106.

A stylistic analysis of the Christmas books that concentrates on *The Haunted Man.* Not seen.

2632. Tick. Stanley. "Autobiographical Impulses in *The Haunted Man.*" *Dickens Quarterly* 18 (2001): 62–69.

This reading of the Christmas book as autobiography is critical of the artistry of the story, finding the characters "lifeless and remote," the prose "erratic," and the story "uninspired when it is not mechanical." Only its links to the resurfacing of Dickens's past in the late 1840s make it interesting. Tick seems unaware of recent work on *The Haunted Man.* See Moncrieff (**2627**), for example, for a more interesting account of autobiographical impulses in the Christmas book. Tick's brief plot summary is inaccurate, and he does not take into account the death of Dickens's sister Fanny in 1847. See Stone (**1292**).

6. CHRISTMAS BOOKS

DICKENS'S LETTERS CONCERNING THE CHRISTMAS BOOKS

2633. Dickens, Charles. *The Letters of Charles Dickens. Pilgrim Edition* (**1**), IX: 556–57.

In a letter to the Rev. David Macrae written in 1861, Dickens says of his Christmas books that they have been ''imitated all over England, France, and America'' and that they cannot ''be separated from the exemplification of the Christian virtues and the inculcation of the Christian precepts. In every one of those books there is an express text preached on, and the text is always taken from the lips of Christ.'' Slater (**2857**) comments that this statement would be hard to illustrate.

COLLECTED AND SELECTED EDITIONS CONTAINING NEW INTRODUCTIONS

Chronological Listing

2634. Dickens, Charles. *Christmas Books*. Oxford World's Classics edition. Ed. Ruth Glancy. Oxford: Oxford UP, 1988. Reissued 1998. xxv + 486.

Contains a chronology of Dickens's life, explanatory notes, a list of further reading, and an introduction by Ruth Glancy (**2652**).

2635. ———. *Christmas Books*. London: Folio Society, 1988. xii + 403.

Drawings by Charles Keeping and introduction by Christopher Hibbert (**2658**).

2636. ———. *A Christmas Carol and Other Stories*. London: Reader's Digest, 1994. 287.

Contains *A Christmas Carol, The Chimes*, and *The Cricket on the Hearth*. Illustrated by Arthur Rackham, both full-page color and small line drawings, and Robert and Barbara Buchanan. The afterword (pp. 283–87) is adapted from A. Edward Newton's ''The Greatest Little Book in the World'' (**610**) and concerns only *A Christmas Carol*.

2637. ———. *A Christmas Carol* and *The Cricket on the Hearth*. Ed. Frank Green. Cheltenham: Thornes, 1995. 221.

Green's introduction contains an inaccurate short biography of Dickens illustrated with good pictures of Chatham in 1820 and the Marshalsea Prison. Green's short introduction to *A Christmas Carol* focuses on Dickens's financial problems and his worry that he was becoming obsessed with money. *The Cricket on the Hearth* is linked to

Dickens's marriage. This edition for children contains "fast forward" sections that let readers omit portions of text and read instead a "rewind" box that summarizes the skipped part. Each page contains a summary of the plot and a glossary. The Study Guide (pp. 103–09) contains questions on the plots and characters and suggestions for creative writing.

2638. ———. *The Christmas Books*. Everyman edition. Ed. Sally Ledger. With illustrations by John Leech, Richard Doyle, Daniel Maclise, Clarkson Stanfield, Edwin Landseer, Frank Stone, and John Tenniel. London: J. M. Dent; North Clarendon, VT: Charles E. Tuttle, 1999. xxxv + 500.

Ledger has provided much useful information for students and general readers, including a chronology of Dickens's life and times, notes, and suggestions for further reading. A section on Dickens and his critics surveys criticism of the Christmas books from 1843 to the present, finding the books more relevant than many recent commentators have given them credit for. Facsimiles of the title pages are included as well as all the original illustrations and prefaces. Ledger also provides a critical introduction (**2664**).

2639. ———. *A Christmas Carol. The Chimes. The Cricket on the Hearth.* New York: Barnes and Noble Classics, 2004. 304.

Introduction and notes by Katharine Kroeber Wiley. This edition also contains a comments and questions section and bibliography. Not seen.

RADIO ADAPTATIONS AND RECORDINGS

2640. *A Dickens Christmas Trilogy.* Salt Lake City, UT: Audio Books on Cassette, 1988.

A reading of *A Christmas Carol, The Chimes*, and *The Cricket on the Hearth* by Michael J. Bennett.

STUDIES

2641. Allingham, Philip V. "Dickens's Christmas Books: Names and Motifs." *English Language Notes* 29.4 (June 1992): 59–69.

This article follows the earlier discussion of names in *A Christmas Carol* (**2478**). Allingham looks at names in the other four Christmas books to argue that Dickens was using Ben Jonson's identification of name with character trait in order to make clear his message of social reform and spiritual renewal in the Hungry Forties. Some of his identifications are biblical (Toby from Tobit); others are literary (Caleb from

Godwin's *The Adventures of Caleb Williams*). That the names Swidger and Tetterby in *The Haunted Man* do not lend themselves to Jonsonian identification leads Allingham to conclude that at the end of the Christmas books Dickens's themes were becoming too complex for simple correspondences.

2642. Armstrong, Frances. *Dickens and the Concept of Home*. Ann Arbor: UMI Research, 1990. 33–34, 39–40, 55–56, 89–90, 130–31, 152.

Discussing homemaking for women and the connection between housekeeping and sexuality, Armstrong compares Dot's playful home-making to that of Ruth Pinch in *Martin Chuzzlewit* to argue that for both young women the game-playing is "a conscious device . . . to cope with the anxieties of the adult world" and "gain confidence." Whereas Dot only "plays" occasionally, Dora Spenlow (*David Copperfield*) lives in a play world. Armstrong finds in the Christmas books "a strong emphasis on the scope for action within the narrow sphere." *The Battle of Life* moves beyond the earlier books in showing that domestic acts have a "performative function" in the wider world, and even in a safe home, good acts are not always performed easily but require sacrifice and hard work. Armstrong links this theme to *Dombey and Son*. She finds *A Christmas Carol* the "high point of the celebration of the home," although she suggests that readers might mistrust the narrator's voice "and see Dickens writing what his audience wanted to hear."

2643. Barnes, James J., and Patience P. Barnes. "Solitude and Ghosts in Dickens's Christmas Books." *Dickensian* 89.3 (Winter 1993): 218–25.

The authors argue that Dickens's 1842 visits to the prisoners in solitary confinement in the penitentiaries of Pennsylvania led to his depiction of the haunting of solitary men in *A Christmas Carol*, *The Chimes*, and *The Haunted Man*.

2644. Boborykina, Tatiana A. *The Artistic World of Charles Dickens's Christmas Books: The Dramatic Principle in Prose*. St. Petersburg: Hippocrat, 1997. 199.

This delightful small book offers new insights into the artistry of the Christmas books from the perspective of a Russian academic and theater critic. Boborykina views the books as representing the turning point at which Dickens moved away from "humanistic illusions" towards a more pessimistic realism. The books operate on two levels, remaining fairy tales while harboring "a sense of tragic reality." Relating the imagery of the *Carol* to the dustheaps of *Our Mutual Friend* (and Dostoevsky's 1846 story "Mister Prokharchin"), Boborykina considers the structure of the book as a spiral in which Scrooge's fairy-tale redemption conceals a deeper and more realistic plot: "the *progressive degradation of man* under *the surface respectability of society*" (Boborykina's italics). This underlying theme gives the book its nightmarish quality and its drama, she asserts. In considering *The Chimes*, Boborykina focuses on Dickens's attack on false philanthropy, but her discussion is wide ranging. She finds parallels between Will Fern and Magwitch (in *Great Expectations*), between Lilian and Dostoevsky's Sonya (from *Crime and Punishment*), and between Edgar Allan Poe's "The Bells" and the Christmas book, arguing that, as in the *Carol*, a tragic story is the reality underlying the fairy-tale happy ending. Dickens's "Divine Idea of the World" (Fichte and Carlyle's phrase) is the ideal that rises above the tragedy and is found in the music of the bells. Boborykina's analysis of *The Cricket on the Hearth* finds this duality evident in the final vignette of a broken toy, and she argues that toys are central to our understanding of the characters. After outlining the main story, Boborykina looks closely at the tragedy underlying the Caleb/Bertha plot to argue that Caleb's fictional world is described symbolically, and in its tragic results for Bertha it contains Dickens's criticism of his own role as storyteller (for a similar reading of the toys see Hollington [**2660**]). She finds a foreshadowing of Maeterlinck's works in the story. Boborykina's defense of *The Battle of Life* is strikingly original. By concentrating on the battlefield motif, she explores an underlying tragedy that, she argues, is conveyed symbolically, through cinematographic techniques. That tragedy was the battle raging in "Great" Britain, through its wars overseas and its "laws and theories" and "cold professionalism" (represented by Snitchey and Craggs) at home in the philosophies of Malthus and Bentham: "Peeling away the veneer of the mediocre plot, we see the dramatic collision between the Christian Ideal of Sacrifice and the Anti-Christian Society's demand for victims." Boborykina makes several interesting comparisons between *The Haunted Man* and other literature (the Faust legends, Byron's "Manfred," Edgar Allan Poe's "The Raven," Hawthorne's stories, and *Dr. Jekyll and Mr. Hyde*), seeing Redlaw's condition as the modern man's split personality, one part dehumanized and without memory. She sees the story as thus foreshadowing later writers such as Orwell and Huxley, but, she argues, Dickens, like Dostoevsky, restores humanity through Christian belief. She concludes by referring to Bret Harte's parody "The Haunted Man. A Christmas Story" (**410**), arguing that Harte's re-creation of Dickens's spirit points to Dickens's presence in the Christmas book as the figure in the final portrait on the wall. Boborykina's book is well illustrated with a wide range of images from art and literature.

2645. Collins, Philip. "Charles Dickens." In *Reference Guide to Short Fiction* (**2498**). 180–84.

Collins inexplicably lists *A Christmas Carol* and *The Cricket on the Hearth* as short stories, but *The Chimes, The Battle of Life* and *The Haunted Man* as novels. He devotes only a paragraph to the Christmas books and finds only the *Carol* as worthy to be considered with the novels. The others engaged Dickens's talent, not his genius, he concludes.

2646. Daleski, H. M. "Seasonal Offerings: Some Recurrent Features of the Christmas Books." *Dickens Studies Annual* 27 (1998): 97–111.

Dismissing the Christmas books generally as potboilers, Daleski does credit them with "some arresting features" in their organizing mechanisms. These features are the contrast between the home (characterized by the hearth and the "angel" who presides over it) and the street, the threat of disaster and its avoidance, and the use of the supernatural. Daleski remains critical, finding the supposed death of Tiny Tim "bathetic in the extreme." He accuses Dickens of deliberately manipulating the reader's emotions and engaging in shameless deception (as in Dot's apparent intention to leave her husband for a younger man in *The Cricket on the Hearth*.) Daleski finds only Marley's ghost interesting because he represents Scrooge's double and therefore the uncanny rather than the supernatural, but he does not discuss Redlaw's ghostly double in *The Haunted Man*. Daleski concludes by noting aspects of the Christmas books that reverberate in the novels: Scrooge's coldness (Mr. Dombey), Ignorance and Want (Jo in *Bleak House*), Mr. Filer (Mr. Gradgrind).

2647. Dentith, Simon. "Literature and Political Economy: The Case of Mill and Dickens." *Il Testo Letterario e il Sapere Scientifico*. Ed. Carmelina Imbroscio. Bologna: CLUEB, 2003. 337–45.

Includes the Christmas books, particularly *The Chimes*, in this discussion of Dickens, John Stuart Mill, and Malthus. Not seen.

2648. Douglas-Fairhurst, Robert. "Introduction." In the 2006 Oxford UP edition (**2857**), pp. vii–xxix.

This lively and wide-ranging survey concentrates mainly on *A Christmas Carol* and the "strange and haunting power" of the style that conveys the Christmas book theme of generosity and connectedness. Douglas-Fairhurst is somewhat dismissive of the other Christmas books (quoting somewhat unfairly only from the most critical of early reviews), but he sees them as worth reading for their relationship to Dickens's writing—*The Cricket on the Hearth* and its concern with the writer as creator of fancy (like Caleb), for example. Douglas-Fairhurst concludes with Dickens's public readings, arguing that they took the place of the Christmas books and stories in allowing Dickens to "cosy up to his readers" as he does in sketches like "What Christmas Is, As We Grow Older." The introduction is enlivened by quotations (often unfamiliar ones) from Dickens's letters and from his associates and children.

2649. Fido, Martin. "The Christmas Books." In his *The World of Charles Dickens: The Life, Times and Work of the Great Victorian Novelist.* London: Carlton, 1997. 70–71.

Suggests that Dickens had some sympathy with Scrooge's antipathy to the charity workers because he was beset by friends and relations wanting handouts. Fido reminds readers that Dickens's Christmas celebrations in the *Carol* revolve around family games and fun, not "an orgy of spending and acquiring." He suggests that Trotty's Malthusian fear (in *The Chimes*) that the poor were responsible for their own plight was one not shared by many thinkers. *The Cricket on the Hearth* he finds sentimental (crickets indoors are annoying), and the story of supposed infidelity unsuited to the Christmas book ethos. *The Battle of Life* Fido dismisses as "a vapid love story no one in their right mind would read to children," the theme of renunciation in love having no place in a Christmas book. He considers *The Haunted Man* interesting in demonstrating that Dickens's sentimentality is based in his belief in shared sympathy, and that the book "makes sense of his willingness to make tear-jerkers of the poor and their children in so many otherwise sophisticated books."

2650. Gager, Valerie. *Shakespeare and Dickens: The Dynamics of Influence.* Cambridge: Cambridge UP, 1996. 91–94.

Argues for the influence of Daniel Maclise's painting *The Play Scene in 'Hamlet'*, exhibited in 1842, on the Christmas books and especially *A Christmas Carol.* Gager notes the similarity between the Ghost of Christmas Yet to Come and Maclise's portrait of the murderer pointing, and she argues that the three central phantom episodes of the *Carol* are a play within the human drama, a structure repeated in *The Chimes.* Gager suggests that the idea of the double (Scrooge and Marley's ghost; Redlaw and his phantom) was inspired by Maclise's representation of the murderer and his shadow.

2651. Giddings, Robert. *Student Guide to Charles Dickens.* Billericay, Essex: Greenwich Exchange, 2002. 165.

Includes the Christmas Books in a section concerning minor works. Not seen.

2652. Glancy, Ruth. "Introduction." In the 1988 Oxford World's Classics edition (**2634**), pp. ix–xxii.

Discusses the popularity and influence of *A Christmas Carol*, the social criticism of *The Chimes*, the fairy-tale and cinematic elements of *The*

Cricket on the Hearth, the reception and dramatizations of *The Battle of Life,* and similarities between the *Carol* and *The Haunted Man.*

2653. ———. "Charles Dickens." In *British Short-Fiction Writers, 1800–1880. Dictionary of Literary Biography.* Vol. 159. Detroit, MI: Gale Research, 1996. 84–105.

A survey of Dickens's short-story work from *Sketches by Boz* to "George Silverman's Explanation" that includes a summary of the stories' critical reception and bibliographies of Dickens's works and critical studies. The Christmas books are seen as contributing to Dickens's increasing sense of cohesiveness in plot and character development.

2654. ———. "The Christmas Books and Christmas Stories." In her *Student Companion to Charles Dickens.* Westport, CT: Greenwood, 1999. 57–71.

Provides a summary of the history, plots, and central themes of the Christmas books.

2655. Haywood, Ian. "The Retailoring of Dickens: *Christmas Shadows,* Radicalism, and the Needlewoman Myth." In *Famine and Fashion: Needlewomen in the Nineteenth Century.* Ed. Beth Harris. Aldershot, Hampshire: Ashgate, 2005. 67–86.

Argues that *Christmas Shadows,* an anonymous novel published in 1850 (**403**), was one of the needlewomen stories written by Chartists in the 1850s as a critique of capitalism.

Haywood demonstrates how the novel is a "minor masterpiece of retailoring," turning *A Christmas Carol* and *The Chimes* into a "culturally iconic narrative of female distress and economic exploitation." Scrooge becomes Cranch, an outfitter who exploits the women who sew for him. The visions he is shown of desperate seamstresses resemble Trotty's visions in *The Chimes.* The novel thus "feminizes" Dickens's stories at a time when women's rights were gaining interest and women readers were politically aware. Haywood discusses *The Chimes* in detail as coming in at the beginning of the "needlewoman mania" in politically motivated texts, but he argues that the dream vision and happy ending "distance the problem of needlework from contemporary reality," as happens also in *Nicholas Nickleby. Christmas Shadows* returns the needlewoman story to "its economic basis in capitalist relations."

2656. Heady, Emily Walker. "The Negative's Capability: Real Images and the Allegory of the Unseen in Dickens's Christmas Books." *Dickens Studies Annual* 31 (2002): 1–21.

Heady seeks to establish through *A Christmas Carol* and *The Haunted Man* that photographic imagery in narratives often questions rather than confirms the belief that images tell the truth. Dickens links the photographic with the phantasmagoric to remind us "not to believe what we see." Heady links this scepticism with Victorian audience's familiarity with illusory spectacles such as the magic lantern show, dioramas, and panoramas, which often had a didactic purpose and often used ghosts. She argues that Dickens's ghosts, like the phantasmagoric ghosts, redraw the boundaries between inside and outside, the mind and the outside world. We are asked to believe in what we know is a projection. Linking the books to photography, where "light and shadow can be seen as both authors and subjects of the photograph," Heady points out that the morality of the books is linked to the characters' associations with light and shadow. Shadows, like photographs, can make memories and upset notions of time; the "temporal hallucination" of the photograph allows Scrooge to live in the past, present, and future all at once. Memory, then, "both produces and is produced by the image," just as Milly in *The Haunted Man* is an angel in the house and also a producer of memories that bring healing. From Milly as image, Heady goes on to argue that just as the phantasmagoric ghosts seemed to have bodies, so Dickens is obsessed with the bodies of his characters in both Christmas books and the material nature of the visions. Agreeing with Jaffe's reading of *A Christmas Carol* (**2524**), Heady argues that the conversions in both books are made possible only through image, and Scrooge and Redlaw "must learn to identify with the set of representations that is culture if they are to continue to operate within the visual order put forward by Dickens's Christmas books." They must leave photography and enter metaphor, "where seeing correctly is predicated on seeing difference." The reader has to read the image's surface (the photograph) in order to find the significance (which, as in the phantasmagoria, is also in the viewer's mind). If the protagonists of the books are taught to read metaphorically, the reader cannot read literally (the turkey is a metaphor for Christmas spirit). Heady concludes by arguing that Ignorance and Want (in the *Carol*) exemplify the vision of the books by turning flesh into image and demonstrating "that metaphor has come to depend on the very illusions of materiality the image constructs." *The Haunted Man* goes further in the whole book's being an allegory about child deprivation, centered on the Waif. The books "incorporate photographic and phantasmagoric structures of vision to teach us ways to peel back the image's deceptive skin."

2657. Henson, Louise. "Investigations and Fictions: Charles Dickens and Ghosts." In *The Victorian Supernatural*. Ed. Nicola Bown, Carolyn Burdett, and Pamela Thurschwell. Cambridge: Cambridge UP, 2004. 44–63.

Henson's purpose is to discuss some of Dickens's ghost stories in the context of Victorian scientific and medical attitudes to apparitions, acknowledging Dickens's knowledge of and sympathy with rational explanations and psychological interpretations. Henson thus reviews the work of scientists such as Samuel Hibbert and David Brewster (who posited physical explanations for paranormal events) and their influence on Dickens when he was mesmerizing Augusta de la Rue. Henson discusses the apparitions in *A Christmas Carol* and *The Chimes* as deriving from the consciousnesses of the protagonists; the visions appear in a kind of "magnetic sleep" and are therapeutic, as were Dickens's sessions with Madame de la Rue. In temporarily giving up their conscious will, Henson argues, both Scrooge and Toby Veck are able to see the errors of their firmly held beliefs and act to redeem their futures. Surprisingly, Henson does not discuss *The Haunted Man.*

2658. Hibbert, Christopher. "Introduction." In 1988 Folio Society Edition (**2635**). vii–xii.

Hibbert begins with a good overview of Dickens's personal celebration of Christmas and the writing of *A Christmas Carol.* He finds the *Carol* "a pleasingly sentimental parable of redemption" and *The Chimes* interesting as social criticism. *The Cricket on the Hearth* he dismisses, and the failings of *The Battle of Life* he blames on Dickens's relationship with Mary Hogarth/Marion and Georgina Hogarth/Grace. He finds *The Haunted Man* interesting for its autobiography: the death of Dickens's sister Fanny and Dickens's rejection by his parents. Hibbert considers the books to be unsatisfactory compared to the novels.

2659. Higbie, Robert. *Dickens and Imagination.* Gainesville: U of Florida P, 1998. 69–71.

Concentrates on *A Christmas Carol* and *The Cricket on the Hearth* as extending Dickens's attempt in the earlier novels to make imagination lead to belief while opposed by reality. Higbie sees the narrator of the *Carol* as one who "purifies" the imagination and becomes its expression. It is thus more controlled than when it is found in the characters, and Dickens uses it to awaken belief in the reader, as he does in Scrooge. Scrooge represents the doubting materialist transformed by the ghosts, who "speak for the idealist imagination." Higbie finds *The Cricket on the Hearth* more ambivalent because of Caleb's "mistaken use of imagination" in creating a false world for Bertha. Higbie suggests that Dickens here is critical of his own use of the imagination in his earlier novels, which did not have the moral purpose of the *Carol*; the *Cricket*, he argues, shows that Dickens no longer sees the imagination as easily overcoming disbelief (as it had in the *Carol.*)

2660. Hollington, Michael. "Narrative Perspective and the Grotesque: *Master Humphrey's Clock*, the Christmas Books, and *The Uncommercial Traveller*." In his *Dickens and the Grotesque*. London: Croom Helm; Totowa, NJ: Barnes and Noble, 1984. 153–69.

This chapter deals with "the bizarre angle of vision of a grotesque outsider" in characters such as Master Humphrey (and Hollington notes European prototypes such as Quasimodo). Hollington relates this motif to the narrator of the *Carol*, first-person and ironically limited, like Scrooge, in his knowledge. The grotesque in the books allows characters and readers to see and understand the monstrosities of Victorian society. Discussing this motif in the *Carol* and *The Chimes*, Hollington dismisses the other books as "much less interesting" although he discusses toymaking in *The Cricket on the Hearth*, finding Caleb Plummer's making of grotesque toys a parallel to Dickens as a "grotesque satirist." Hollington concludes that in leaving the "synoptic vision" of the first two books, Dickens moved away from the idea of "transcendent height" bringing insight. For the importance of toys see also Boborykina (**2644**).

2661. ———. *Charles Dickens. Critical Assessments*. 4 vols. East Sussex: Helm, 1995.

Volume I, "Contemporary Assessments (Biographical and Critical) and General Assessments 1870–1945 (Biographical and Critical)" contains the 1844 *Westminster Review* comments on *A Christmas Carol* (**460**) and extracts from the following reviews: *Dublin Review*, December 1843 (**451**); *Dublin University Magazine*, 1844, of *A Christmas Carol*; *Christian Remembrancer*, 1845, of *The Chimes* (**785**); *Edinburgh Review*, 1845, of *The Chimes* (**789**); *Chamber's Edinburgh Journal*, 1846, of *The Cricket on the Hearth* (**1035**); *North British Review*, 1847, of *The Battle of Life* (**1154**); *Macphail's Edinburgh Ecclesiastical Journal*, 1849, of *The Haunted Man* (**1257**). Volume I, pp. 615–25, reprints G. K. Chesterton's "Dickens and Christmas" from his 1906 book *Charles Dickens* (**1357**). Volume II, "Assessments of Dickens's Early and Middle Work since 1870," contains the following essays: John Butt's "Dickens's Christmas Books" from *Pope, Dickens and Others* (**1352**); Stephen Prickett's "Christmas at Scrooge's" from *Victorian Fantasy* (**629**); Michael Shelden's "Dickens, *The Chimes*, and the Anti-Corn Law League" from *Victorian Studies* (**847**); Robert L. Patten's " 'A Surprising Transformation': Dickens and the Hearth" from *Nature and the Victorian Imagination* (**1404**); Katherine Carolan's "*The Battle of Life*: A Love Story" from *Dickensian* (**1166**); and Lucien Pothet's "Charles Dickens's *The Haunted Man*: A Secret and Its Disguises" from *Etudes Anglaises* (**1287**), translated by Michael Hollington.

2662. Kaplan, Fred. *Dickens: A Biography*. New York: William Morrow, 1988. 175–81.

Briefly discusses the Christmas books as moving away from the social message of the *Carol* and *The Chimes* into a genre that was unable to express Dickens's major themes of "displacement and tension." The Christmas books "increasingly embodied the misplaced benevolence or the antibenevolence of [Dickens's] own father," Kaplan claims, and through his role as purveyor of Christmas stories, Dickens "transformed Christmas spirit into financial profit" and healed himself while apparently acting as "Christ-like healer and provider."

2663. Klages, Mary. "Sentimental Posters." In *Woeful Afflictions: Disability and Sentimentality in Victorian America*. Philadelphia: U of Pennsylvania P, 1999. 56–78.

In this chapter Klages surveys Victorian fiction that was aimed at reminding able-bodied readers of their duty to care for the disabled, who appear in the marketplace "to reform the essential selfishness of economic relations." Finding *A Christmas Carol* to be the most famous fictional discussion of disability and economics, Klages argues that Tiny Tim "already knows his status as a cultural text" because he wants the people to be reminded of Christ when they see him at church (for a different reading of this scene see Rodas [**2551**]). Scrooge learns to replace economics with empathy by identifying with the scenes he is shown, particularly scenes involving Tiny Tim. Noting that Dinah Craik's *John Halifax, Gentleman* conveys the same theme, Klages then compares that novel with *The Cricket on the Hearth* to argue that in both works, blindness is "incompatible with any form of adult female sexuality, including motherhood" because the disabled are culturally enjoined from reproducing their defect" and they cannot be sites of both empathic feeling and of sexuality. Tackleton the businessman is also prevented from joining the domestic group because the Christmas book shows "the disastrous results of the intrusion of economic values into family life." For a similar reading of disability, see Holmes (**2602**).

2664. Ledger, Sally. "Introduction." In the 1999 Everyman Edition (**2638**). xxv–xxxv.

Ledger discusses the domestic ideal offered by the books, and the "transgressive feminine figures" who threaten it (in all the books except *A Christmas Carol*). She discusses the social criticism of the books, the role of children, and the role of memory in bringing about redemption. Ledger notes that the supernatural in the books indicates Dickens's contempt for utilitarian solutions to social problems.

2665. Marlow, James E. "The Dead Hand of the Past." In his *Charles Dickens: The Uses of Time*. Selinsgrove, PA: Susquehanna UP; London: Associated University Presses, 1994. 44–49, 202–04.

In this study of the importance of time past, present, and future in Dickens's works, Marlow positions the Christmas books as marking Dickens's shift from rejecting the past (in the early novels) to embracing it. Scrooge's denial of the past is utilitarian, Marlow notes, a flaw in his character that is addressed by the Ghost of Christmas Past. The subsequent books (although Marlow omits *The Cricket on the Hearth*) move towards the recognition (in *The Haunted Man*) that "the effort to obliterate the pain of the past . . . promotes the growth of evil from it." Later (pp. 91–92), Marlow argues that Dickens's vision of cannibalism and voracity in *Hard Times* came from the Christmas books and Dickens's attack on Malthus. Dickens's novels show "that the proper use of time can restore genuine security and comfort to the world."

2666. Muresianu, S.A. "Dickens's Christmas Books: A Vision of Coherency." In her *The History of the Victorian Christmas Book*. New York: Garland, 1987. xiv + 236.

This unedited reprinting of a 1981 Harvard doctoral dissertation places Dickens's books in the context of the genre. Muresianu briefly traces the influence of earlier Christmas writing on Dickens, including Sandys' carols and Washington Irving's *Sketch-Book*. She compares the world of Dickens's Christmas books to the universe of William Blake, both writers exploring "the fate of untainted human nature in a corrupting environment." Like Blake, Dickens reconciles opposites in a dialectical relationship of truth and fantasy, good and evil. After discussing Michael Slater's (**1415**) four characteristics of the Christmas books (intimacy of tone, the supernatural, overt social purpose, exaltation of family love), Muresianu considers three more: the motif of the double (for psychological and structural purposes, as the principal agent of conversion), the importance of food, and the illustrations (several are reproduced). She considers *The Battle of Life* and *The Haunted Man* as flawed because of their forced happy endings but interesting as revealing Dickens experimenting with description, form and rhythm, and character revelation.

2667. Ostry, Elaine. *Social Dreaming: Dickens and the Fairy Tale*. New York: Routledge, 2002. 220.

Discusses Dickens's use of fairy tale with regard to his social criticism in the novels, journalism, and Christmas books. Not seen.

2668. Page, Norman. "Christmas Books." In his *A Dickens Companion*. London: Macmillan, 1984; New York: Schocken Books, 1987. 253–62.

Provides an excellent brief overview (based largely on Michael Slater's Penguin edition, **1415**) of the books, taken together and then individually and concentrating on their critical and popular reception.

2669. Parker, David. "Christmas Books and Stories, 1844 to 1854." In his *Christmas and Charles Dickens* (**2546**). 221–82.

Parker concentrates on *The Chimes* and *The Haunted Man*, the only Christmas books other than the *Carol* that are set in the Christmas season. *The Cricket on the Hearth* and *The Battle of Life* he considers "exercises in melodrama," outside of the scope of this study but worth reading for their comedy and Dickensian touches. Parker considers *The Chimes* an inferior "supplement" to the *Carol*, a failed attempt to repeat the first book's achievement but deserving of attention for its powerful defense of the poor. He examines Dickens's "cranking up" in the second book, evident in Dickens's descriptions of his excitement in writing it, but he finds the narrator's emotions forced and lacking the inventiveness and flexibility of the *Carol*'s narrator. Similarly the supernatural elements of *The Chimes* are less complex than the ghosts because the moral crisis they are required to solve is more straightforward. Parker suggests that moving the story from Christmas to New Year deprived it of the wealth of associations and traditions that gave the *Carol* its greater depth. Parker finds *The Haunted Man* much more successful, rivalling the *Carol* in its creation of a sustained atmosphere and complex interplay between psychological realism and the supernatural through which "we are teased with the possibility of different explanations from the one ostensibly being offered." He sees Dickens's sensibilities in both Redlaw's brooding fixation with past sorrows, embodied by the ghost, and the openness and flexibility of Mr. Tetterby's discourse, which acts as a foil. Parker concludes that *The Haunted Man* is the most overtly Christian of the Christmas books, a sign that Dickens was becoming more devout at this time as evidenced in his early Christmas stories (**2802**). Parker devotes a separate chapter to *A Christmas Carol* (**2546**).

2670. Persell, Michelle. "Dickensian Disciple: Anglo-Jewish Identity in the Christmas Tales of Benjamin Farjeon." *Philological Quarterly* 73.4 (Fall 1994): 451–69.

In trying to account for Farjeon's idolization of Dickens and emulation of the Christmas books in his own Christmas tales, Persell argues that Dickens's books are secular and an "expression of voracious consumer demand" rather than Christianity, and are thus "the embodiment of desire created and shared by Jews and Gentiles alike who labor within the capitalist economy." She discusses *A Christmas Carol* and *The Chimes* in these terms.

2671. Pykett, Lyn. "Redemptive Fictions in 'a whimsical kind of masque': The Christmas Books, 1843–8." In her *Critical Issues: Charles Dickens*. Houndmills, Basingstoke, Hampshire: Palgrave, 2002. 89–97.
This brief overview of the Christmas books concentrates primarily on *A Christmas Carol*, suggesting that its blending of fantasy with social issues was to become Dickens's main method in his later novels.

2672. Reed, John R. "Dickens' Christmas Narratives." In his *Dickens and Thackeray: Punishment and Forgiveness*. Athens: Ohio UP, 1995. 154–68.
Reed traces the themes of forgiveness and repentance in the Christmas books. He notes the recurrence of the Scrooge pattern throughout Dickens's works in the "imperfect hero coming to a recognition of his limitations and amending them" and finds it a psychological parallel to the discovery and pursuit of the villain. In his analysis of *The Chimes* Reed argues that the punishment of the Bowleys, Cutes, and Filers is left for the future because a central tenet of Dickens's Christian beliefs was that the good must not actively bring about the suffering of the wicked. He considers Meg's withholding of forgiveness for Lilian until she has renounced her sinful life a pivotal scene whose power is often overlooked by modern readers. Meg is responsible for Lilian's redemption. In discussing secrecy, misunderstandings, and forgiveness in *The Cricket on the Hearth*, Reed argues that the ending of the story warns the reader that he or she too is prone to misreadings and rash judgments in condemning Tackleton. Had we "read more charitably," the ending would seem a fulfillment rather than a surprise. Tracing the forgiveness theme as central to *The Battle of Life*, Reed defends the book from charges of artistic failure by considering it as a successful parable that exemplifies the maxim "Judge not lest ye be judged." Clemency represents a "benign order" that underlies the apparent "battle." In this, Reed argues, the book is typical of Dickens's Christmas writings in favoring beneficence rather than punishment. *The Haunted Man* also illustrates this virtue.

2673. Swisher, Clarice, ed. "Entertaining Stories for Serial Publication." In *Readings on Charles Dickens* (**2527**). 67–93.
Despite the title of the chapter, this section reprints excerpts from Harry Stone's 1979 chapter on *A Christmas Carol* (**1421**), Louis Cazamian's 1903 chapter on the Christmas books (**501**), and Edgar Johnson's 1952 essay on *A Christmas Carol* (**575**). Swisher notes that the articles "may have been edited for content, length, and/or reading levels."

2674. Tracy, Robert. " 'A Whimsical Kind of Masque': The Christmas Books and Victorian Spectacle." *Dickens Studies Annual* 27 (1998): 113–30.

Tracy's study focuses almost entirely on *A Christmas Carol*, finding two qualities in the masque form (as exemplified by Ben Jonson and Inigo Jones) that influenced Dickens's books: the demonstration of virtue, and the use of machinery that allowed for elaborate stage effects. Tracy usefully traces the development of special effects in the nineteenth-century theater, particularly the sudden transformation of one scene to another, and examines Dickens's use of these effects to transform Scrooge. Scrooge is "an absorbed spectator at the drama of his own life" and is even allowed to rewrite his own story at the end. Tracy links this engagement in the drama to Dickens's methods as a novelist in the later works. In describing the Victorian love of spectacle in dramatic productions, Tracy refers to the dramatic versions of *No Thoroughfare* and *The Chimes*.

For a study of *A Christmas Carol* and the masque, see Butterworth (**2492**).

2675. Van Gogh, Vincent. *The Letters of Vincent Van Gogh.* Ed. Mark Roskill. London: Fontana, 1990. 316.

Van Gogh writes to his brother Theo at the beginning of April 1889 that he has been re-reading Dickens's Christmas books. He writes, "There are things in them so profound that one must read them over and over, there are tremendously close connections with Carlyle."

2676. Waters, Catherine. "Dickens, Christmas and the Family." In her *Dickens and the Politics of the Family.* Cambridge: Cambridge UP, 1997. 58–88.

Waters speaks collectively about the Christmas books throughout this essay, but she discusses only *A Christmas Carol* in any detail, just briefly mentioning the other four books. Her Marxist approach sees the celebration of Christmas as central to the Victorian middle-class ideology, and Dickens's books as instrumental in shaping that ideology of hearth and home. She sees the books as domesticating "Saturnalian impulses" from earlier times to make them palatable for their middle-class audience, so "all of the Christmas Books establish a woman's embodiment of the domestic ideal as the grounds for her sexual appeal to the male." After discussing the indoor/outdoor, private/public distinctions in the books, Waters argues that Dickens sees the answer to social problems as the general acceptance of a middle-class domestic ideal. David Parker (**2546**) takes issue with this interpretation.

2677. Weston, Nancy. "Dickens—The Voice of Authority." In her *Daniel Maclise: Irish Artist in Victorian London.* Dublin: Four Courts, 2001. 111–43.

In this survey of the relationship between Maclise and Dickens, Weston sees the illustrations for *The Chimes*, *The Cricket on the Hearth,* and *The Battle of Life* as contributing to their cooling friendship. Maclise's enthusiasm for working on *The Chimes* (evidenced by his praise of Dickens's private reading of it) was dampened by being given only the frontispiece and the title page. Weston records Maclise's unhappiness that his nude fairies (repeated in the frontispiece of *The Cricket on the Hearth*) were harshly criticized by the reviewers, compounded by his belief that Dickens did not adequately defend him. Maclise's letters to John Forster indicate his frustration at contributing illustrations for *The Battle of Life* because he felt unappreciated and, according to Weston, he was "disappointed with the wood engravings of his designs."

Part II. Christmas Numbers

CHRISTMAS NUMBERS OF HOUSEHOLD WORDS

1. THE CHRISTMAS NUMBER (1850)

EDITIONS OF THE 1850 CHRISTMAS NUMBER AND DICKENS'S CONTRIBUTIONS

Chronological Listing

2678. Dickens, Charles. "A Christmas Tree." In *Christmas Ghosts* (**2460**). 268–84.

In the introduction to this collection of Christmas ghost stories (pp. xiii-xv), David G. Hartwell discusses Dickens's popularizing of the ghost story at Christmas (a tradition from the eighteenth century, if not earlier). Unlike most Christmas ghost stories, the selections printed here are about Christmas as well as ghosts. Hartwell does not comment on "A Christmas Tree."

2679. ———. "A Christmas Tree." In *Charles Dickens. Selected Journalism 1850–1870*. Ed. David Pascoe. London: Penguin, 1997. 3–16.

Despite discussing the importance of the imagination to Dickens, Pascoe does not mention "A Christmas Tree" in his introduction but he does provide explanatory notes (pp. 595–97).

MISCELLANEOUS ADAPTATIONS

2680. *A Christmas Tree*. Rankin/Bass, 1972.

Guida (**2373**) and Pointer (**2380**) list this animated short film, in which an animated Dickens appears.

STUDIES

2681. Hennelly, Jr., Mark M. " 'Toy Wonders' in *Our Mutual Friend* (Part One)." *Dickens Quarterly* 12.2 (June 1995): 60–71.

In this analysis of "the grotesque perversion of foul play but also . . . the ultimate power and glory of fair play" in *Our Mutual Friend,* Hennelly discusses Dickens's descriptions of toys in "A Christmas Tree" and notes that despite the sketch's nostalgic remembrance of childhood's joys, it shares with the novel a sense of "the eternal playmate of Death" in the story of the Orphan Boy.

2682. Stone, Harry. *The Night Side of Dickens: Cannibalism, Passion, Necessity* (**2613**). 232–34.

Draws attention to cannibalistic overtones in Dickens's memories of childhood, including the "demoniacal Counsellor" with the wide-open mouth, damsel-eating giants, and the wolf in "Little Red Ridinghood." Stone suggests that Dickens "often became" both the Counsellor and the devoured.

2. EXTRA NUMBER FOR CHRISTMAS OF
HOUSEHOLD WORDS (1851)

STUDIES

2683. Andrews, Malcolm. "Christmas and Rejuvenation." In his *Dickens and the Grown-Up Child* (**2479**). 99–102.

Links "What Christmas Is, As We Grow Older" with Dickens's essay "Where We Stopped Growing" as exemplifying Dickens's belief that "maturity must include a sympathetic understanding of the child's world." Andrews compares the 1851 Christmas essay with Wordsworth's "Immortality" ode in its desire to recover a past sense of completeness in the present.

[3. A ROUND OF STORIES BY THE CHRISTMAS FIRE (1852). There are no new entries for this Christmas Number. See the Index for "The Child's Story."]

4. ANOTHER ROUND OF STORIES BY THE
CHRISTMAS FIRE (1853)

THE 1853 CHRISTMAS NUMBER IN PROGRESS

2684. Dickens, Charles. *The Letters of Charles Dickens* (**1**), VII, 142.

In a previously unpublished letter to Angela Burdett Coutts on 9 September 1853, Dickens writes that "it is dark now, and raining hard—good suitable circumstances in which to devise a Christmas number, which is my present employment."

5. THE SEVEN POOR TRAVELLERS (1854)

THE 1854 CHRISTMAS NUMBER IN PROGRESS

2685. Dickens, Charles. *The Letters of Charles Dickens* (**1**), VII, 475, 498–99, 770–71.
In a previously unpublished letter to the Hon. Mrs. Richard Watson on 1 December 1854, Dickens tells her that he will be busy all day Friday 8 December, the day before the printing of the number: "I have been so much disappointed in the nature of the Contributions as yet received, that it will require my utmost care and assistance." In the same letter he refers to the number as "this Christmas bull trying to toss me." On 5 January 1855 he tells Angela Burdett Coutts that 80,000 copies of the number have been sold, more than he had expected considering the Crimean War. Curiously, Dickens sent two copies of the number to her on 23 December 1855.

COMMENTARY ON STAGE ADAPTATIONS

2686. Bolton, H. Philip. "The Seven Poor Travellers." In his *Dickens Dramatized* (**2312**). 373–76.
Lists 14 stage adaptations between 1855 and 1875, and a BBC radio version of Eliza Lynn's "The Dead Witness" ("The Sixth" in the original number) in 1952.

RADIO ADAPTATIONS AND RECORDINGS

2687. *The Seven Poor Travellers.* Colonial Radio Theatre on the Air, 2004. 1 hour 6 minutes.
An abridged reading by Jerry Robbins with the Colonial Players. Available as a downloadable MP3 from Spoken Network. *www.spokennetwork.com.*

6. THE HOLLY-TREE INN (1855)

THE 1855 CHRISTMAS NUMBER IN PROGRESS

2688. Dickens, Charles. *The Letters of Charles Dickens* (**1**), VII, passim.
Prints for the first time a letter to Wilkie Collins on 30 September 1855 in which Dickens says he will tell him his plans for the Christmas

number "which will put you in train, I hope, for a story." Also includes Dickens's draft outline that was sent out to prospective contributors (**1548**). Referring to Dickens's letter to Wilkie Collins on 14 October 1855, the Pilgrim editors challenge Harry Stone's assertion that Dickens wrote the concluding portion of Collins's "The Ostler" (**1551**).

ABRIDGMENTS

2689. Dickens, Charles. *Charles Dickens's Boots at the Holly Tree Inn*. Published in association with The Basic Skills Agency. London: Hodder and Stoughton, 1999. 27.
Abridged by Peter Leigh and illustrated by Jim Eldridge. This Livewire Classic version includes a brief introduction to the story, which identifies Dickens as the narrator, and word glosses in the margins. The text is printed in very short lines, like verse, intended for reading practice.

FILM ADAPTATIONS

2690. *The Boots at the Holly Tree Inn*. BBC-TV (U.K.), 1957.
A fifteen-minute film in the series *Moira Lister Tells a Story*, listed in Pointer (**2380**).

COMMENTARY ON STAGE ADAPTATIONS

2691. Bolton, H. Philip. "The Holly Tree Inn." In his *Dickens Dramatized* (**2312**). 387–90.
Notes that interest in "The Boots" revived in the 1890s with Mrs. Oscar Beringer's productions (**1573**). Bolton also lists a BBC radio drama by Mollie Greenhalgh (Hardwick) in 1957, a BBC television film in 1957 and 1958 (whether of "The Boots" or something else is not recorded), and a reading of "Boots at the Holly Tree Inn" on 26 December 1966, read by Peter Cloughton.

7. THE WRECK OF THE GOLDEN MARY (1856)
THE 1856 CHRISTMAS NUMBER IN PROGRESS

2692. Dickens, Charles. *The Letters of Charles Dickens* (**1**), VII, 712; VIII, 195.

In a previously unpublished letter, Dickens writes to Wilkie Collins on 30 September 1855 about the 1855 Christmas number, telling him that he has postponed the shipwreck idea "for a year, as it seemed to require more force from me than I could well give it with the weight of a new start [*Little Dorrit*] upon me." Volume VIII, 195 contains Dickens's draft instructions for the number (**1598**). In the letter to the Rev. R. H. Davies of 24 December 1856, the Pilgrim edition restores words omitted from Forster's version (and the Nonesuch *Letters* [**1599**]), thereby removing the ambiguity that led critics to attribute Harriet Parr's "Child's Hymn" to Dickens.

EDITIONS

2693. Dickens, Charles. *The Wreck of the Golden Mary*. London: Hesperus, 2006. 129.
Foreword by Simon Callow. This edition contains the portions by Dickens, Wilkie Collins, and Harriet Parr. Not seen.

COMMENTARY ON STAGE ADAPTATIONS

2694. Bolton, H. Philip. "The Wreck of the Golden Mary." In his *Dickens Dramatized* (**2312**). 391–92.
Lists six versions. Bolton sees this dearth as evidence that the saturation point had been reached in staging the latest Dickens work. There were no later revivals either.

STUDIES

2695. Nayder, Lillian. "Dickens and 'Gold Rush Fever': Colonial Contagion in *Household Words*." In *Dickens and the Children of Empire*. Ed. Wendy S. Jacobson. Basingstoke, Hampshire: Palgrave, 2000. 67–77.
Discusses "The Wreck of the Golden Mary" in the context of *Household Words* essays written about working conditions for British sailors in the 1850s. While the articles support the sailors' claims of unfair treatment, Nayder argues that in the Christmas story Dickens transfers the sailors' class unrest to gold rush fever, replacing a political response with the more neutral "madness and disease." Despite the seemingly idealistic labor relations on the Golden Mary, Nayder detects an underlying unrest in the men, who desert their captain for the

gold fields of California. Nayder concludes her essay by asserting
that the Christmas story also reveals Dickens's sexism. The ship is
threatened not just by "unruly" sailors but by unruly women as well.
All are put in their place. Nayder's argument is fleshed out more fully
in her 2002 book (**2696**).

2696. ———. "Collins Joins Dickens's Management Team: 'The Wreck of
the Golden Mary.' " In her *Unequal Partners: Charles Dickens, Wilkie
Collins, and Victorian Authorship.* Ithaca: Cornell UP, 2002. 35–59.
Nayder's bias against Dickens, whose critics she charges with unfairly
denigrating Collins, is evident from the beginning of this study, which
opens with Collins's regret at losing a writing day in order to attend
Dickens's funeral. This revision of her 2000 article (**2695**) thus fo-
cusses more specifically on the working relationship of Dickens and
Collins to argue that the story's emphasis on "The Blue-Jacket Agita-
tion" (labor unrest among British sailors) derived from Dickens's
dealings with unruly and demanding contributors to his journals (especially, of course, Collins). She argues that Dickens defused the current
issue of labor unrest by setting the story in the notoriously lawless
California gold rush and by scapegoating a stereotypical Jew (Mr.
Rarx). He also recruited the potentially rebellious Collins on his side
as manager against "unruly women" who aspired to lead. Nayder
traces anti-feminism in *Household Words,* finding the journal particularly hostile to women who aspire to jobs at sea. In Nayder's reading,
the *Golden Mary* herself is a symbol of the dangers of female promis-
cuity when she betrays her loyal "husband" (the male captain and
crew). Nayder concludes with a discussion of Collins's contribution
to the number, arguing that Collins ended it "on a discordant note"
that undermines the captain's authority and proves that "an 'inimita-
ble' leader can prove expendable after all." She reiterates her thesis
that while Dickens continually repressed or diverted class conflict in
the Christmas numbers, Collins emphasized it.

2697. Trodd, Anthea. "Collaborating in Open Boats: Dickens, Collins,
Franklin, and Bligh." *Victorian Studies* 42.2 (Winter 1999–2000):
201–25.
An excellent, wide-ranging examination of the roots of the number in
the nautical literature and culture of the time, a background that provided a "model for collaboration": as Captain Ravender, Dickens
could be both self-sacrificing hero (prefiguring Sydney Carton) and
authority. Trodd discusses the number's defense of the British seamen
who had been charged with cannibalism in the Franklin expedition of
1845 and the influence of *The Mutiny on the Bounty* (1840) on the
story, noting that Dickens was incorrect in saying that Captain Bligh

warded off potential cannibalism by having the crew tell stories. Trodd traces Dickens's and Collins's love of sea stories and the nineteenth-century conception of the "Tar" as found in writers such as Frederick Marryat, James Fenimore Cooper, and Richard Henry Dana, and in contemporary culture. She places the Christmas story among the narratives designed to reestablish the sailor as hero in response to fears of mutiny and insubordination, noting the influence of melodrama on the national view of the sailor. Trodd's discussion of the collaborative writing of the number is valuable, noting that the number both extols collaboration and cooperation while suggesting the necessity for a leader: the ship founders on an iceberg when Mate Steadiman (Collins) takes over the helm. Nayder (**2696**) criticizes Trodd for overlooking both the labor unrest in the story and Collins's resistance to Dickens's authority.

8. THE PERILS OF CERTAIN ENGLISH PRISONERS (1857)

THE 1857 CHRISTMAS NUMBER IN PROGRESS

2698. Dickens, Charles. *The Letters of Charles Dickens* (**1**), VIII, passim.
Includes a previously unpublished letter to Emile de la Rue of 23 October 1857, criticizing "this wretched Lord Canning's maudlin proclamation about mercy." The Pilgrim editors note that Commissioner Pordage's words to Carton "are obviously a gibe at Canning." A previously unpublished letter to the Hon. Mrs. Richard Watson on 7 December 1857 repeats Dickens's comments to Angela Burdett Coutts on Dickens's wish to commemorate the bravery of the English women in India "without laying the scene there, or making any vulgar association with real events or calamities." In a previously unpublished letter to Lady Duff Gordon on 23 January 1858, Dickens confesses to being "overcome" every time he rereads the end of the story. Only when the printers needed the sheets could he "find it in [his] heart to look at them with a pen in [his] hand dipped in any thing but tears!" The whole number he considers "a very notable and happy piece of execution."

COMMENTARY ON STAGE ADAPTATIONS

2699. Bolton, H. Philip. "The Perils of Certain English Prisoners." In his *Dickens Dramatized* (**2312**), pp. 393–94.

Bolton assumes that, like the other Christmas numbers, the *Perils* was a collection of three different stories. He lists seven dramatizations.

STUDIES

2700. Brantlinger, Patrick. "The Well at Cawnpore: Literary Representations of the Indian Mutiny of 1857." In *Rule of Darkness: British Literature and Imperialism, 1830–1914.* Ithaca: Cornell UP, 1988. 206–08.

In this study of Victorian attitudes to imperialism, Brantlinger briefly discusses the racism of *The Perils of Certain English Prisoners*, which he considers "wildly inaccurate," and Dickens's "strangest—certainly his least compassionate—Christmas story." He sees Christian George King as representing Nana Sahib, the Indian leader responsible for the massacre at Cawnpore, and the story just a way for Dickens to extend his hatred of East Indians to all non-English races.

2701. Callanan, Laura. "The Dialectic of Scapegoat and Fetish: Failed Catharsis in Charles Dickens and Wilkie Collins's 'The Perils of Certain English Prisoners' (1857)." In her *Deciphering Race: White Anxiety, Racial Conflict, and the Turn to Fiction in Mid-Victorian English Prose.* Columbus, OH: The Ohio State UP, 2006. 76–95.

Callanan seeks to expand the discussion of Christian George King "as a scapegoat for public frustration over colonial unrest," as suggested by Nayder (**2706**), to the displacement of race, class, and gender distinctions through the pirates. She sees King as the vehicle through which Dickens expressed his anger over the Cawnpore Massacre, whereas Pedro Mendez, the central figure in Collins's section, reveals Collins's more complex reaction to the events in India. After explaining "scapegoat" and "fetish" in Marxist, Freudian, and contemporary theoretical terms, Callanan argues that the story attempts a cultural catharsis through King as scapegoat and Pedro Mendez as fetish. She compares Pedro to other literary depictions of pirates to argue that there is a "veiled homoeroticism" in his portrait, and that this transgressiveness takes the reader's attention away from the real issue of class in the story. Callanan concludes that the problem of Davis's class conflict remains unresolved because Mendez is not dealt with at the end, and the boundaries remain in place.

2702. Colley, Linda. *Captives: Britain, Empire and the World, 1600–1850.* London: Jonathan Cape, 2002. 373–74.

Identifies *The Perils of Certain English Prisoners* as an "unpleasant tale" in the captivity narrative genre. Colley finds the story an anachronistic rewriting for a Victorian imperialist audience: an English soldier would never have been rescued in such a situation. Citing Davis's racism, Colley argues that many Victorians were dismayed that the Indian Mutiny made it clear that they could not rely on native populations to bolster the British armed forces abroad.

2703. Hollington, Michael. " 'The Perils of Certain English Prisoners': Dickens, Collins, Morley and Central America." *Dickensian* 101.3 (Winter 2005): 197–210.

This original essay takes issue with Nayder's (**2707**) view that Dickens and Collins are at odds in the Christmas number. Hollington also defends Dickens against the frequently voiced charge of racism by pointing out that both Dickens and Collins were satirizing the views of the first-person narrator. Hollington provides an interesting overview of the Latin American background to the story by referring to contemporary articles in *Household Words*, particularly the series titled "Our Phantom Ship" to argue that the Christmas number shared the articles' sense of "dreamlike unreality." Gill Davis "experiences the trauma of captivity" and is often in a dream-like state, haunted by Christian George King. Hollington suggests that Davis be seen as "a study of psychological edge and twitchiness issuing forth in racial prejudice" and a consciously artistic creation rather than just a mouthpiece for Dickens's racism. He is akin to the captives described in Colley's book (**2702**). Hollington finds Carton's imperialism more problematic.

2704. Kaplan, Fred. *Dickens: A Biography* (**2662**). 379–80.

Suggests that Gill Davis is Dickens, rescuing Mary Hogarth and also Ellen Ternan.

2705. Moore, Grace. "A Tale of Three Revolutions: Dickens's Response to the Sepoy Rebellion." In her *Dickens and Empire: Discourses of Class, Race and Colonialism in the Works of Charles Dickens.* Aldershot, Hampshire: Ashgate, 2004. 113–34.

In tracing the development of Dickens's attitude to the Empire (which she argues is less racist than is usually assumed), Moore considers *The Perils of Certain English Prisoners* as being written at the "most Podsnappian of times for Dickens." In earlier chapters she argues that pre-1857 articles in *Household Words* are critical of British government in India and sympathetic to the Indians, but after the Cawnpore Massacre, Dickens took a much harsher view, especially evident in letters he wrote at the time. In the *Perils*, Dickens is still critical of the mismanagement of the East India Company through the ridiculous Pordages, but the story is essentially an attack on the sepoys and a defense of the English, especially the lower classes, represented by Gill Davis. Moore notes that the multiracial outlaws include the British,

but those British are convicts and therefore "not English." Arguing
that Collins is much more moderate in his section of the story, Moore
attributes Dickens's anger in the *Perils* to a simmering rage against
the British government throughout the 1850s (evident in *Bleak House*
and *Little Dorrit*, and in his frustration over the handling of the Crimean War). Moore notes Laura Peters's comment (**2709**) that Davis
and Christian George King are alike in both being marginalized, but
Moore argues that they are "different types of the colonized, both
oppressed by the English ruling classes." Davis, the decent English
working man, accepts his duty, while King and the sepoys he represents
rebel out of "sheer malice." Moore goes on to argue that Dickens's
rage was quickly tempered, and he aligned the sepoys and rebels with
the oppressed working classes of France and Britain in *A Tale of Two
Cities*. For a review article of Moore's book, see Patrick J. McCarthy,
"The Empire Strikes Back: Dickens on the Rioting Colonists," *Nineteenth-Century Prose* 32.2 (Fall 2005): 209–17.

2706. Nayder, Lillian. "Class Consciousness and the Indian Mutiny in Dickens's 'The Perils of Certain English Prisoners.' " *Studies in English
Literature* 32 (Fall 1992): 689–705.

Nayder compares Gill Davis to Jo in *Bleak House* to argue that whereas
in the novel Dickens blames imperialism for the neglect of children
like Jo, in the Christmas story he allows racism to displace class conflict. He is like the "telescopic philanthropists" that he satirizes in the
novel, using imperialism to prevent rather than promote social change.
Nayder compares his attitude to that of Cecil Rhodes, who saw imperialism as a way of solving class unrest. Davis's resentment against his
superiors is replaced by hatred for their mutual enemy, the pirates. At
the end of the story he is in a position of feudal gratitude to his
superiors, so the story "is socially as well as racially elitist; it justifies
the rule of the aristocracy over the masses at the same time that it
justifies the rule of whites over blacks."

2707. ———. "Class Consciousness and the Indian Mutiny: The Collaborative Fiction of 1857." In her *Unequal Partners: Charles Dickens,
Wilkie Collins, and Victorian Authorship* (**2696**). 100–28.

Essentially the same argument as in her 1992 essay (**2706**). Nayder
says that the attack is a class revolt caused by a proletarian mob
seeking silver, and their actions take the place of Davis's earlier desire
to mutiny against his superior officers. Davis then has to align with
the other Englishmen in defending "imperiled female virtue." All
become identified as manly workers rather than the idle upper classes.
Dickens then displaces Davis's "otherness" (his earlier sense of not
belonging to England) onto Christian George King. Dickens "thus

solves the problem of class resentment in the rank and file,'' a topic discussed in Nayder's chapter on ''The Wreck of the Golden Mary'' (**2696**). She goes on to discuss Collins's contribution to the number, arguing that he drew attention to the class differences among the Englishmen and criticized imperial practices and even suggested that ''their wrongdoing was partly responsible for the mutiny.'' The English privates and the Indians become aligned, and Collins ''suggests that social inequalities among the colonizers themselves may bring about an empire's fall.'' Discussing the third part of the story, Nayder argues that Dickens overrides Collins's ''subversive''section and returns Davis to a position of happy subservience. Miss Maryon, too, is put in her place, whereas in Collins's section she finds herself restricted by ''gender norms'' and appears as courageous and inventive, not just supportive. Nayder's argument is answered by Hollington (**2703**).

2708. Park, Hyungji. '' 'The Story of Our Lives': *The Moonstone* and the Indian Mutiny in *All the Year Round.*'' In *Negotiating India in the Nineteenth-Century Media.* Ed. David Finkelstein and Douglas M. Peers. New York: St. Martin's, 2000. 84–109.

Seeking a context for *The Moonstone*, Park briefly mentions Collins's role in *The Perils of Certain English Prisoners.* While finding it ''difficult to separate out Collins's views from his accession to Dickens's directives,'' Park notes that the hostility to Christian George King is more noticeable in Dickens's portions and is at odds with Ezra Jennings' nobility in *The Moonstone.*

2709. Peters, Laura. ''Perilous Adventures: Dickens and Popular Orphan Adventure Narratives.'' *Dickensian* 94 (Winter 1998): 172–83.

Peters discusses *The Perils of Certain English Prisoners* as one of many mid-nineteenth-century orphan narratives in which, despite the resourcefulness and nobility of the orphan hero, he is still denied class mobility by the country he is defending against foreign savagery. Orphan narratives also ''work to mythologise a bourgeois domesticity.'' Peters divides her discussion into two parts. In ''Victorian Attitudes to Empire in Response to the Cawnpore Mutiny'' she notes that Dickens's thirst for vengeance was shared by the popular press. In '' 'Perils' as an Imperial Tale'' she considers the character of Gill Davis, who as the writer of the story is attempting (and failing) to join the main discourse of England. Gill, an outsider in England, shares the marginal status of the natives whom he (and Dickens) despises. Discussing the final overcoming of Gill's resentment at his inferior status both in the English colony and at home, Peters argues that he remains alienated while also ''reconciled to symbols of British colonial authority.'' As colonial agent he is allowed to find a family in the

Navy, but he remains marginalized because of his illiteracy. Moore (**2705**) discusses Peters's position.

2710. ———. " 'Double-dyed Traitors and Infernal Villains': *Illustrated London News, Household Words,* Charles Dickens and the Indian Rebellion." In *Negotiating India in the Nineteenth-Century Media* (**2708**). 110–34.

Peters argues that the press played a major role in affirming the supremacy of the British during the Indian Rebellion, and that *The Perils of Certain English Prisoners* was a "moment of intersection between journalism and literary practice" that "also worked to legitimize attitudes to empire." In tracing the influence of the *Illustrated London News* on the *Perils,* Peters identifies the key issues in both publications as being the "imperial" role of both editor and press, the early criticism of the British administration in India, the construction of a British hero based on the degeneracy of the native peoples, and "a discourse of justice which quickly collapses into one of extermination." She notes that Dickens is critical of the British governors (in his portrait of the Pordages) but does not blame the administration for the rebellion. Rather, he emphasizes the heroism of the marines. Peters finds sources for the *Perils* in the *Illustrated London News* pieces such as eyewitness accounts by soldiers in the rebellion, which stress the personal treachery of the natives and the heroism of the British women. However, Peters notes that Dickens failed to include the eyewitness accounts' stories of natives who came to the aid of the British, and he "rewrites" the British soldiers' failure to protect the women and children in India. His portrait of Christian George King "revels in an excess which far surpasses these survivor letters" and reaffirms the "national and masculine myths" of superiority. Finally, Peters argues, Dickens shared the fear that the rebellion could spread throughout the empire, and that the rebellion was a religious war. With the purging of the demon Christian George King, the colonizers can return to their idyllic island paradise.

2711. Rance, Nicholas. *Wilkie Collins and Other Sensation Novelists: Walking the Moral Hospital.* Rutherford, NJ: Fairleigh Dickinson UP, 1991. 131.

In a brief mention of *The Perils of Certain English Prisoners,* Rance argues that Collins did not share Dickens's view of empire and was "unable to rise to [Dickens's] hysterical pitch." Collins's "cool and sardonic tone" does not accord with Dickens's sympathy for the English prisoners.

2712. Tambling, Jeremy. *Dickens, Violence and the Modern State: Dreams of the Scaffold* (**2566**). 187–93.

In a chapter on *Our Mutual Friend* Tambling argues that Dickens's sympathies border on the proto-fascist at times. He concentrates on Gill Davis as a double for Christian George King to argue that King's presence in Davis's dream reveals that the "perils" are actually the male Englishman's fear of homosexual rape, a fear created by bourgeois English ideology that rejects heterogeneity. Dickens's attempt to praise the British in India "does nothing more than try to sublimate feelings of envy, rancour and impotence" through a "self-justifying autobiography to maximise feelings of pity."

9. A HOUSE TO LET (1858)

EDITIONS

2713. Dickens, Charles, et al. *A House to Let.* London: Hesperus, 2004. 97. Contains the complete Christmas number. There is no introduction, but this edition includes annotations and biographical information for Dickens, Wilkie Collins, Elizabeth Gaskell, and Adelaide Procter, all of whom contributed to the number.

RADIO ADAPTATIONS AND RECORDINGS

2714. *A House to Let.* BBC-4 Woman's Hour. December 2006.
A dramatization of the number (excluding Adelaide Anne Procter's poem) by Martyn Wade, read by Marcia Warren, Alec McCowen, and Brian Croucher.

CHRISTMAS NUMBERS OF *ALL THE YEAR ROUND*

1. THE HAUNTED HOUSE (1859)

EDITIONS

2715. Dickens, Charles, and Others. *The Haunted House.* London: Nekta, 1998. 170.
This edition contains the whole Christmas number and an afterword by Peter Rowland (pp. 162–69). Rowland comments at some length on Dickens's editing of the number and discusses Dickens's quarrel with William Howitt on the subject of spiritualism. He offers some criticism of the contributed stories but does not discuss Dickens's

"The Ghost in Master B.'s Room" at all. He includes passages from "A Christmas Tree" and "A Haunted House" (*Household Words*, 23 July 1853) in his discussion of Dickens's views of spiritualism, concluding that Dickens definitely did not believe in haunted houses "except, of course, as a useful means of boosting the circulation of *All the Year Round*."

2716. Dickens, Charles, Wilkie Collins, et al. *The Haunted House.* Christchurch Dickens Fellowship, 2001.

A "compact, clearly printed booklet," which presumably contains the complete Christmas number. Not seen. For details, see *Dickensian* 97.3 (Winter 2001): 251.

2717. ———. *The Haunted House.* London: Hesperus, 2002. ix + 130.

This edition of the complete Christmas number contains biographical sketches of the contributors and a foreword by Peter Ackroyd (**2719**).

2718. ———. *The Haunted House.* Modern Library edition. New York: Random House, 2004. xxi +126.

Contains the whole number, a biographical sketch of Dickens and an amusing introduction by Wesley Stace, who provides background material on the writing of the number (from Dickens's letters) and the other contributors. He discusses the suitability of the contributed stories to Dickens's theme of the importance of memory and finds that Dickens's "The Ghost in Master B.'s Room" contains the only really frightening image in the number in the ghost that sleeps with the narrator. Stace makes some useful comments about Dickens's attitudes to ghosts and spiritualism and sees parallels between Dickens's contribution and *A Christmas Carol.*

STUDIES

2719. Ackroyd, Peter. "Foreword." In the 2002 Hesperus edition (**2717**). vii–ix.

Ackroyd puzzlingly confuses the Christmas books with the Christmas stories when he opens with the remark that *A Christmas Carol* had begun the "national institution" of the Christmas book, but "towards the end of [Dickens's] life he called in contributors to assist him in their composition." He mistakenly dates *The Haunted House* as 1862 instead of 1859, an error which somewhat diminishes his argument that the number reveals Dickens's melancholy "eight years before his own death." After misquoting a line from "The Ghost in Master B.'s Room," Ackroyd draws attention to the seraglio story as "in the worst possible taste . . . [it] smacks of mid-Victorian sentimentality at its most insidious, but it is curious and instructive nonetheless." He then links it to Dickens's relationship with Ellen Ternan, suggesting that Dickens may have been seeking some "protection from" adult love in "this story of childhood sexuality."

2720. Drew, John. *Dickens the Journalist* (**2610**). 148.

Drew gives the Christmas stories only passing mention, but he does discuss Dickens's argument with William Howitt and agrees with the latter that Dickens's attitude to spiritualism was perversely ambiguous.

2721. Baker, Fran, ed. "Introduction." *Bulletin of the John Rylands University Library of Manchester* 86.1 (Spring 2004): vii–cxxiv.

In her long introduction (pp. vii–cxxiv) to this edition of "The Ghost in the Garden Room," Elizabeth Gaskell's contribution to *The Haunted House*, Fran Baker discusses the origins of the number and Dickens's editing of Gaskell's story. Comparing the *Household Words* version to the manuscript, she argues that Dickens shortened the story to remove repetition but also to render "Bessy a more conventional and less combative heroine." Baker argues that Dickens also cut a passage from the end of the story to make it less disturbing and therefore more suitable for a Christmas number. In discussing the contributions by other writers, including Adelaide Anne Procter and Hesba Stretton, and noting that Dickens imposed a male narrator on Gaskell's story, Baker suggests that the contributions from women writers "provide a challenge to the masculine viewpoint of the male-penned pieces."

2. A MESSAGE FROM THE SEA (1860)

COMMENTARY ON STAGE ADAPTATIONS

2722. Bolton, H. Philip. "A Message from the Sea." In his *Dickens Dramatized* (**2312**). 413–15.

Discusses Dickens's attempts to secure the dramatic rights to the play by writing his own version for the stage (**1696**) and by opposing Hazlewood's production (**1697**). Bolton speculates that this opposition on Dickens's part contributed to the decline in dramatizations of his works in the 1860s as well as "a declining obvious theatrical appeal in his narrative manner." Dickens's public readings may have also contributed, he says. Bolton lists ten stage versions.

STUDIES

2723. Trodd, Anthea. "Messages in Bottles and Collins's Seafaring Man." *Studies in English Literature, 1500–1900* 41.4 (Autumn 2001): 751–64.

This wide-ranging discussion of *A Message from the Sea* concentrates on Wilkie Collins's contribution, chapter 4, "The Seafaring Man." Basing her discussion on the premise that the Christmas number is "a story about the healthful circulation of information and sympathy on which the progress of society depends," Trodd argues that Collins's chapter shows the younger writer departing from Dickens's narrative methods, encouraged by the success of *The Woman in White* and sharing that novel's exploration of characters who are ignorant of the rules of reading and writing (like the "unknown public" about whom Collins wrote in a *Household Words* article of that name in 1858). Whereas Dickens's Captain Jorgan is an archetypal Tar and skilled storyteller, Collins's Hugh is an attempt "to extend storytelling to the 'Unknown Public' by mimicking their supposed modes of thought and expression." Trodd's article also contains an interesting account of the use of messages in bottles for communication by the Admiralty and Reuters, and she suggests that *A Message from the Sea* was a response to the clearing of Sir John Franklin's name by a message in a bottle found in 1859. Hugh's father's name, she notes, is similarly cleared.

3. TOM TIDDLER'S GROUND (1861)

THE 1861 CHRISTMAS NUMBER IN PROGRESS

2724. Dickens, Charles. *The Letters of Charles Dickens* (**1**), IX, 430–31, 489, 548–49.
Previously unpublished letters include one to Arthur Helps on 25 June 1861 concerning Dickens's visit to James Lucas, a well-known recluse. Dickens writes to his printer Charles Whiting on the 15 November 1861 regarding revisions to the Christmas number. On 23 December he writes to Robert Lytton and Thomas Adolphus Trollope about the number and gives particular praise to Wilkie Collins's "wonderfully droll" contribution.

STUDIES

2725. Shatto, Susan. "Miss Havisham and Mr. Mopes the Hermit: Dickens and the Mentally Ill." *Dickens Quarterly* 2 (1985): 43–50, 79–84.
Shatto questions why Dickens is so critical of "Mad Lucas," the wealthy recluse suffering from paranoid schizophrenia whom he satirizes harshly in *Tom Tiddler's Ground*. Shatto notes his usual sympathy with the mentally ill and conjectures that he did not realize that

Lucas was ill. She suggests that Dickens unconsciously derived pleasure from the suffering of adults, and that Dickens's narcissism and jealousy of inherited wealth is evident in his persona, Mr. Traveller. Shatto also suggests that Dickens was getting revenge on Miss Havisham (who shared some similarities with Lucas) for her mistreatment of Pip in *Great Expectations*.

2726. Whitmore, Richard. "Encounter with Dickens (1861–1862)." In his *Mad Lucas: The Strange Story of Victorian England's Most Famous Hermit.* Hitchin, Hertfordshire: North Hertfordshire District Council, 1983. viii + 74.

This biography of the reclusive schizophrenic whom Dickens made the subject of *Tom Tiddler's Ground* provides a sympathetic account of his history, his encounter with Dickens, and his resulting notoriety.

4. SOMEBODY'S LUGGAGE (1862)

THE 1862 CHRISTMAS NUMBER IN PROGRESS

2727. Dickens, Charles. *The Letters of Charles Dickens* (**1**), X, 170–71, 182. Includes two previously unpublished letters to W.H. Wills. On 5 December 1862, Dickens writes that he is pleased that "young Jullien" liked "His Boots" and continues, "I *know* my Corporal to be true to the life,—as true as his garrison-town is." On 26 December he tells Wills not to bother altering a submission by Hesba Stretton (Sarah Smith) for the regular number; if it had been for the Christmas number Dickens would have given it more attention. He concludes that *Somebody's Luggage* is "a most signal hit."

STUDIES

2728. Den Hartog, Dirk. "Appendix B: The Taboo on Tenderness in 'Somebody's Luggage.' " In his *Dickens and Romantic Psychology.* London: Macmillan, 1987. 77–79.

At the end of a chapter examining *Dombey in Son* in relation to Wordsworth, in which he argues that Dickens increasingly attacked Nonconformists and others who denied tender feelings, Den Hartog discusses Mr. Langley in "His Boots" as exemplifying "an emotional malady" that was peculiar to the English gentleman. While Dickens does not explore this topic (blaming Langley's stiffness on a family quarrel rather than on his Englishness), Den Hartog finds the story typical of

Dickens's preoccupation with English attitudes, and he notes the story's affirmation of the restorative power of memory.

2729. Edgecombe, Rodney Stenning. "Dickens, Hunt and the Waiter in 'Somebody's Luggage.' " *Victorian Newsletter* 107 (Spring 2005): 25–28.

Finds a source for the waiter in Leigh Hunt's 1832 essay "The Waiter" from the *London Journal*, which Hunt republished in a collection titled *The Seer* in 1850. Edgecombe suggests that Dickens expands on Hunt's idea of waiters as a special breed but also departs from it by elaborating on the waiter's "piquant oddity" in speech. Dickens's waiter, Edgecombe argues, tries "to correct public 'misprisions' about the craft of waiting," mistakes made in Hunt's essay.

5. MRS. LIRRIPER'S LODGINGS (1863)

THE 1863 CHRISTMAS NUMBER IN PROGRESS

2730. Dickens, Charles. *The Letters of Charles Dickens* (**1**), X, 315, 325; XI, 137.

Includes several previously unpublished letters. Dickens writes to Edmund Yates on 15 November 1863 that Yates's dog story ("How the Second Floor Kept a Dog") "fits the design admirably" and that Dickens finished the number for press on the 14th. On 13 December Dickens writes to the Countess Cowley in response to one from her that had apparently criticized the excessive suffering inflicted on Mr. and Mrs. Duke Brownlow in Elizabeth Gaskell's "How the First Floor Went to Crowley Castle." Dickens admits to having felt "exactly the same uneasiness" when he corrected the proofs, but adds that Gaskell "has a way of rather abusing her strength, by making her victims unjustly unhappy sometimes." He refers to Mrs. Lirriper as his "respected friend." On 12 January 1866 Dickens writes to Henry Chorley that he would like to do a reading from Mrs. Lirriper but because she is the narrator "it must be done with little change of voice" and audiences are used to variety in Dickens's presentation. The Pilgrim editors' note (p. 137) that the Berg Library holds the only copy of the reading Dickens prepared is incorrect; see the British Library copy (**1754**).

EDITIONS

2731. Dickens, Charles. "Mrs. Lirriper's Lodgings." In *Mrs. Lirriper*. London: Hesperus, 2005. 1–127.

This attractive edition contains the complete Lirriper Christmas numbers, annotations, and biographical sketches of the contributors. In a brief foreword, Philip Hensher suggests that the numbers were written at a particularly happy time in Dickens's life, partly, he thinks, the result of the death of Dickens's mother in 1863. He finds the stories conventionally Victorian in their themes, characters, and obsessions (love, death, marriage, and sex) but Dickens's framework full of wit and Mrs. Lirriper's voice "a triumph of fantasy and observation."

MISCELLANEOUS ADAPTATIONS

2732. *Mrs. Lirriper's Lodgers* [sic]. Vitagraph (U.S.A.), 1912.
Directed by Van Dyke Brooke and written by W. A. Tremayne. It was released in October 1912 in the U.S.A. and in January 1913 in the U.K. Van Dyke Brooke played Major Jackman with Mary Maurice as Mrs. Lirriper, Courtenay Foote as Mr. Edson, and Clara Kimball Young as Mrs. Edson.
2733. *Mrs. Lirriper: Complete and Unabridged.* BBC Audiobooks, 1997.
Read by Miriam Margolyes.

STUDIES

2734. Ackroyd, Peter. *Dickens* (**2477**). 936–37.
Suggests that the kindly, sensible Mrs. Lirriper is Dickens's tribute to his mother on her death. Jemmy Jackman speaks like John Dickens, so the Dickens family becomes a "holy family" of orphan child raised by surrogate parents.
2735. Kaplan, Fred. *Dickens: A Biography* (**2662**). 438–40.
Asserts that Joshua Lirriper was based on Dickens's brother Frederick, and that Mrs. Lirriper's story was ironically written soon after the deaths of both his mother-in-law and his mother: "the perverse maternal legacy was commercially golden."

6. MRS. LIRRIPER'S LEGACY (1864)

EDITIONS

2736. Dickens, Charles. "Mrs. Lirriper's Legacy." In *Mrs. Lirriper* (**2731**). 129–254.
Contains the complete Christmas number with annotations.

MISCELLANEOUS ADAPTATIONS

2737. *Mrs. Lirriper's Legacy.* Vitagraph (U.S.A.), 1912.
Directed by Van Dyke Brooke and starring Mary Maurice as Mrs. Lirriper.

STUDIES

2738. Golding, Robert. *Idiolects in Dickens: The Major Techniques and Chronological Development.* New York: St. Martin's, 1985. 47–50.
Examines a passage from ''Mrs. Lirriper's Legacy'' to demonstrate ''how closely the rhythms of [Dickens's] fictional speech approach those of music,'' the passage beginning with a ballad-type rhythm and falling into a musical 6/8 time.

7. DOCTOR MARIGOLD'S PRESCRIPTIONS (1865)

THE 1865 CHRISTMAS NUMBER IN PROGRESS

2739. Dickens, Charles. *The Letters of Charles Dickens* (**1**), X, 109–10, 129.
A previously unpublished letter to George Russell on 14 November tells him that he will receive the new Christmas number in early December and that Dickens is ''rather proud and hopeful'' of Doctor Marigold. On 17 November he sends the number to Charles Kent, swearing him to secrecy and referring to ''a queer story of mine in the body of the No. 'To be taken with a grain of salt,' '' thus affirming Dickens's authorship of a story that has sometimes been wrongly attributed to Charles Collins. See *Doctor Marigold's Prescriptions* (**1794**). In a letter that does not appear in the Nonesuch edition (**1793**), Dickens writes on 31 December 1865 to Edward Bulwer Lytton thanking him for his praise of the number.

EDITIONS

2740. Cox, Michael, and R.A. Gilbert, eds. *The Oxford Book of Victorian Ghost Stories.* Oxford: Oxford UP, 1991. Paperback edition, 1992. Reissued 2003. xx + 497.
Contains ''To Be Taken With a Grain of Salt'' (pp. 55–64). In the introduction (pp. ix–xx) Cox and Gilbert provide an interesting history of the Victorian ghost story genre, arguing that in an age of transition

these stories linked the past with the present by offering a continuum between life and death. They see 1850 as the emergence of the anti-Gothic ghost story that was domestic in tone and somewhere between fact and fiction. While crediting Dickens with fostering the telling of ghost stories at Christmas, they do not discuss "To Be Taken With a Grain of Salt."

STUDIES

2741. Ackroyd, Peter. *Dickens* (**2477**). 969.
Identifies Doctor Marigold with Dickens, a performer who has to hide his emotions from the public. "Writing out of his own misery," Dickens was able to craft a brilliant public reading from the story.

2742. Holmes, Martha Stoddard. "The Twin Structure: Disabled Women in Victorian Courtship Plots" (**2602**). 231–32.
Notes that in *Doctor Marigold* a disabled woman is allowed to marry and bear children; however, unlike Bertha in *The Cricket on the Hearth* (**2602**). Sophy is not the emotional center of the story and therefore "does not evoke the discourse of woman as emotional and sexual danger." Holmes suggests that Victorian readers would be comforted that Sophy's child can hear.

2743. Long, William F. "John Galt's Mr. Snodgrass and Dr. Marigold." *Dickens Quarterly* 3 (1986): 178–80.
Long suggests that Dickens may have named his cheap jack after Dr. Marigold in John Galt's *Annals of the Parish* (1821).

2744. Traill, Nancy H. "Charles Dickens: Tradition and Transition" (**2570**). 61–64.
In her discussion of Dickens as a writer of fantasy, Traill places "To Be Taken with a Grain of Salt" as a transitional fantastic story that borders on the modern paranormal. It contains an enigma and its resolution, and the narrative works towards resolving the dilemma by making the narrator's psychological experiences credible. The story is both disjunctive and paranormal, she asserts, because while the narrator prepares us for "the possible expansion of the natural domain" (the paranormal), the murdered man acts like a stereotypical ghost. Traill finds the true paranormal in "The Signal-man" (**2773**).

MISCELLANEOUS ADAPTATIONS

2745. Montaño, Damian. "Suite from Ghost Stories." San Diego, CA: mp3.com, 2000.
This promo CD includes "The Trial for Murder."

8. MUGBY JUNCTION (1866)
THE 1866 CHRISTMAS NUMBER IN PROGRESS

2746. Dickens, Charles. *The Letters of Charles Dickens* (**1**), X, 253, 271–72, 280–81, 295.

Several previously unpublished letters relating to *Mugby Junction* include Dickens's instructions to the typesetter on 8 October, accompanying his contributions to the number, and a letter to W. H. Wills on 12 November noting that "the gentleman *from* Nowhere" should read "the gentleman *for* Nowhere." Others relate to Dickens's excitement over his proposed readings of "The Boy at Mugby" and "Barbox Brothers" (to George Dolby on 12 December), and his delight that by the beginning of January 1867 it had sold 256,000 copies.

EDITIONS
Chronological Listing

2747. Dickens, Charles. "The Signalman." In *Haunted Looking Glass: Ghost Stories Chosen and Illustrated by Edward Gorey.* 1959. New York: New York Review of Books, 2001.

Not seen.

2748. Johnson, Roy. "Charles Dickens, 'The Signalman.'" In his *Studying Fiction: A Guide and Study Programme.* Manchester: Manchester UP; New York: St. Martin's, 1992. 179–204.

"The Signalman" appears last in this discussion of short fiction (after stories by Arthur Conan Doyle, Katherine Mansfield, Thomas Hardy, Joseph Conrad, and D. H. Lawrence) because it is "so profoundly complex and enigmatic." The story is preceded by a good biographical note that briefly explains *Mugby Junction* (but does not mention the Staplehurst accident). After the story, Johnson poses several questions that point out the ambiguities of the story, and then offers two readings. A "common sense" reading asks if Dickens is commenting on the dehumanizing effects of industrial progress. A second reading considers the signalman's sensitivity and intuition posited against the rationality of the narrator. Finally, Johnson suggests an alternative interpretation—the narrator is the spectre—and offers supporting evidence. Self-assessment questions, essay questions, and suggestions for further reading (ending in 1985) follow. This guide is the most useful and thought-provoking of the editions intended for schoolchildren, although Johnson does not raise the question of the narrator's being Barbox in his lengthy discussions of the narrator.

2749. Dickens, Charles. *Mugby Junction.* London: Hesperus, 2005. x + 132.
Contains the whole Christmas number, with biographical notes on
Dickens and the other contributors and brief annotations. In a foreword
(pp. vii–x), Robert Macfarlane notes the influence of the Staplehurst
accident on Dickens's contributions, although he makes very little of
"The Signalman," referring to it only as "a gentle and affecting
story." Briefly discussing the railway as a force for good and evil,
Macfarlane suggests that in Dickens's sections "people are—metaphorically speaking—continually turning into trains, and trains into people" because Dickens refers to a character's "brooding carriage" or
his desire to "change his station in life."

ABRIDGMENTS

Chronological Listing

2750. Dickens, Charles. *Charles Dickens's The Signalman.* Published in association with The Basic Skills Agency. London: Hodder and Stoughton,
1999. 28.
Abridged by Peter Leigh and illustrated by Jim Eldridge. This Livewire
Classic version includes a brief introduction to the story and word
glosses in the margins. The text is printed in very short lines, like
verse, intended for reading practice. There is an accompanying cassette (**2759**).
2751. Dickens, Charles. *The Signalman.* London: Hodder and Stoughton,
1999. 32.
This study book, edited by Sue Hackman, includes a very abridged
version of the story with reading hints and glossary on each page.
Questions to encourage close reading are embodied in the text, and
pages of activities are interspersed. There is a brief biography of Dickens. The book is intended as basic skills support for levels 2–4 of the
English national curriculum (ages 7 to 9).

FILM ADAPTATIONS

2752. *The Signalman.* CBS-TV, 1953.
A 30-minute film for television written by Ben Radin, in the *Suspense*
series, with Boris Karloff and Alan Webb. Listed in Pointer (**2380**).
2753. *Le Signaleur.* RTF France, 1962.
Pointer (**2380**) lists this 18-minute film for television, written by Gerard Guilleumet and shown in Belgium on 2 July 1962.

2754. *The Signalman.* BBC-TV, 1976.
A 40-minute film for television, directed by Lawrence Gordon Clark
and starring Denholm Elliott, Bernard Lloyd, and Reginald Jessup.
Available on VHS and DVD.

RADIO ADAPTATIONS AND RECORDINGS

2755. *Bardell and Pickwick; Mr. Bob Sawyer's Party; The Signalman.* Argo
ZDSW or KZDSC 709–10. 2 records or cassettes.
Directed by Harley Usill, produced by Evdoros Demetrious, and nar-
rated by Roy Dotrice.

2756. *The Signal Man. By Charles Dickens.* Mystery Theatre, Volume 2.
ADW-1734. Toronto: Scenario Productions, 1999. From CBC-Radio
archives.
This dramatization was first broadcast in August 1968. Adapted and
produced by George Salverson, it is performed by Henry Comer as
the Signal Man, William Osler as Charles Dickens (cast as the narrator), and Glyn Morris as the Engineer. This adaptation removes some
of the essential details of the original (the signalman's past life, his
sense of helplessness in the face of another impending disaster, and
the engineer's reiteration of the narrator's unspoken thought, ''For
God's sake, clear the way!''). Dickens as visitor to the signalman
comes across as a priggish fool, exactly the type of person that Dickens
himself would have satirized. In an addition to the original story,
Dickens narrates the opening of *The Battle of Life* to the signalman,
who is horrified by the image of dead soldiers springing to life unexpectedly. The ending is marred by making the engineer impatient and
rude rather than respectful and subdued, as in the original story.

2757. *The Signal Man. Four Classic Dramas from the Golden Age of Radio.
Agnes Moorehead, First Lady of Suspense.* Glenview, IL: The Audio
File. AM 2401.
This radio dramatization from the ''Suspense'' series was first broadcast on 23 March 1953 and it contains the original advertisements for
Autolite electrical systems. Adapted to highlight Agnes Moorehead,
the narrator, the story is told by a magazine writer returning to the
railway line where as a child she had an obsessive dread of trains. She
goes down to interview the signalman, who identifies her as the spectre
he has seen on the line. Trying to prove to him that he has imagined
his fears, she walks down the line to the tunnel entrance. It is thus
Moorehead rather than the engine driver who calls out the warning
and covers her face as he is mown down. Available also as *Suspense:*

The Signalman; Around the World; the Great Train Robbery. Schiller Park, IL: Radio Spirits, 199–. Cassette.

2758. Dickens, Charles. *Mugby Junction.* Sandy, UT: Quiet Vision, 1999. CD.

A reading of the complete Christmas number.

2759. *Livewire Classics: The Yellow Wallpaper. The Signalman.* Hodder Arnold, 1999. One cassette.

Read by Jan Francis and Samuel West. Produced by Peter Leigh, who wrote an accompanying text (**2750**).

STUDIES

2760. Ackroyd, Peter. *Dickens* (**2477**). 992.

Finds Dickens reverting in the Barbox brothers story to "his most enduring fantasies and images" of disappointment and loss. The "murderous lust" of *Our Mutual Friend* and *Edwin Drood* is here "a sexless but powerful infantilism."

2761. Bonheim, Helmut. "The Principle of Cyclicity in Charles Dickens' 'The Signalman.'" *Anglia* 106 (1988): 380–92.

Bonheim applies a structuralist approach based on the presence of "recurring partials," elements of language, gestures, or plot segments that recur at intervals. He finds the story structured in three parts (the narrator's three visits to the railway line), with each part following the same pattern (arrival, recognition, greeting, etc.). Bonheim also discusses the story as an example of the journey to the underworld motif, and he analyzes the linguistic repetition of phrases and gestures (the warning shouts and arm gestures) in terms of classical rhetoric. His conclusion is that "the threefold pairing of spectre and calamity seems to carry a clear message": that the rational narrator's scepticism is misplaced and a supernatural event has in fact occurred. The reader is led to accept this conclusion by the cyclical structure of the story, which aligns it with folk tales and ghost stories. For another reading of the story's three-fold cyclicity, see Vescovi (**2776**).

2762. Caporaletti, Silvana. "Metamorfosi di un testo narrativo: *The Signalman* di Charles Dickens." *Strumenti Critici* 12 (January 1997): 33–60.

A reader-response approach. Not seen.

2763. Cockshut, A. O. J. "The Signalman." In *Reference Guide to Short Fiction* (**2498**). 1023–24.

Cockshut sets the story in the context of the railway age, arguing that "the idea of combining the inventions of the new industrial society

with a ghost story is peculiarly Dickensian." Finding human motives
more convincing here than in the "sentimental" Christmas books,
Cockshut praises the "pervasive downward movement," the powerful
description of place, and the signalman's sense of duty and work.

2764. Cooke, Simon. "Anxious Travelers: A Contextual Reading of 'The
Signalman.' " *Dickens Quarterly* 22.2 (June 2005): 101–08.

Argues that the story expresses the fears Dickens shared with his
contemporary readers after several serious rail disasters in the 1860s.
Noting that Andrew Halliday's contribution to *Mugby Junction* also
suggested danger, Cooke focuses on the railway literature of the 1860s,
the public's distrust of signalmen following the 1861 Clayton tunnel
disaster, and the contemporary fears, expressed in the literature, that
the nature of the position (isolation, stress, responsibility) led to mental
derangement. Witnesses to accidents (as Dickens's signalman is) were
also known to suffer from trauma, so the signalman is a case study of
two contemporary fears, the deranged signalman and the traumatized
witness. The story's horror is thus not inexplicable but very real. Cooke
provides excellent research from contemporary medical accounts (such
as *The Lancet*) in support of his reading.

2765. Day, Gary. "Figuring Out the Signalman: Dickens and the Ghost
Story." In *Nineteenth-Century Suspense from Poe to Conan Doyle*.
Ed. Clive Bloom et al. Basingstoke: Macmillan; New York: St. Mar-
tin's, 1988. 26–45.

Day begins by defining fantastic literature and finds the term as elusive
as the ghosts it often contains. His intention is not to identify "The
Signalman" as fantasy but to "see how it works as a text." Day's
reading becomes biographical, although the crux of his argument (that
the story enacts Dickens's oedipal guilt from his blacking factory days)
is told largely in footnotes and curiously hinges on "Dickens's close
relationship with his mother." Day relates the story to Dickens's autobiographical fragment, finding that in both, "everything 'means' both
more and less than itself" and "everything coincides or interpenetrates
with everything else." The signalman, the narrator, and the spectre
are all parts of the same split personality, just as Dickens's characters
are aspects of him. Day concludes that the story is a quest for unity
that cannot be achieved because the guilt goes unrecognized.

2766. Gilbert, Bernard. "The 'Signalman' de Dickens—ou le crime sans
châtiment." *Journal of the Short Story in English* 43 (Autumn
2004): 29–43.

Written in French, this Marxist essay analyzes the story as depicting the
destruction of the working-class signalman by a complacent, helpless
middle-class narrator.

2767. Graham, Paul. "Dickens, Spiers, and Pond. From the Birth of Anglo-Australian Cricket to the Death of the Missis of Mugby Junction." *Dickensian* 87.2 (Summer 1991): 111–20.

This entertaining article discusses Dickens's relationship with Felix William Spiers and Christopher Pond, Australian entrepreneurs who established the first English/Australian cricket series in 1862 and then invited Dickens to give a reading tour in Australia; after much deliberation he declined. Spiers and Pond moved to England, where they established refreshment rooms at many of the railway stations. An article in *All the Year Round*, 28 December 1867, credited them with freeing the British from the "tyranny" of the Missis, who ran the refreshment room at Mugby Junction.

2768. Greenman, David J. "Dickens's Ultimate Achievements in the Ghost Story: 'To Be Taken with a Grain of Salt' and 'The Signalman.' " *Dickensian* 85.1 (Spring 1989): 40–48.

After discussing the sources of Dickens's "gothic imagination" (his nurse's stories and popular periodicals), Greenman argues that the reader of "To Be Taken with a Grain of Salt" must do just that: in revealing that he himself has appeared in ghostly form during the story, the narrator is admitting to the reader that he has made the whole story up to cure his own boredom. Greenman then argues that the narrator of "The Signalman" is also a ghost, rejecting the clear connection made at the beginning of the story between the narrator and Barbox, the unghostly narrator of the *Mugby Junction* framework. In this reading he is following Stahl (**1887**). Greenman, however, agrees that if the narrator is a real man the ending is perhaps even more powerful because we sympathize with his guilt over not preventing the accident, a realization that concludes the story.

2769. ———. "The Alienation of Dickens's Haunted Businessmen." *Dickens Quarterly* 7 (1990): 384–92.

Greenman compares Tom Smart (in *Pickwick Papers*) and Scrooge to the narrators of "To Be Taken with a Grain of Salt" and "The Signalman" to argue that in his later stories Dickens's alienated businessmen can no longer overcome their isolation.

2770. Justin, Henri. "The Signalman's Signal-Man." *Journal of the Short Story in English* 7 (Autumn 1986): 9–16.

Justin offers a Freudian interpretation of the story, following on from Jacques Carre (**1870**) in seeing the narrator and the ghost as doubles of the signalman. The narrator fails to act as interpreter between the signalman and his warning spectre because he is a Victorian, a rationalist who has romanticist leanings but does not know how to communicate between the two types of experience or make sense of the romantic (irrational) part of the mind. Justin concludes that "Dickens was following the realism of deep psychology" and "experimenting with the notion that the dark forces of the psyche might well have their language too." The narrator thus becomes the central figure in a narrative about reading signs.

2771. Matus, Jill L. "Trauma, Memory, and Railway Disaster: The Dickensian Connection." *Victorian Studies* 43.3 (2001): 413–36.

Matus makes an excellent case for "The Signalman" as a story born out of Dickens's post-traumatic stress after the Staplehurst railway accident. Matus traces the development of the diagnosis of trauma from its beginnings in the 1860s (due in large part to technological accidents like train wrecks) to Freud's work on shell shock during World War One. She argues that Dickens recognized trauma for what it is and made use of the ghost story genre "to articulate what the nascent study of trauma at this time was not quite yet poised to formulate." The signalman exhibits what are now recognized as classic symptoms of trauma: the uncoupling of event and cognition, belatedness, repetitive and intrusive return, and a sense of powerlessness at impending disaster. Matus usefully discusses altered states of mind and the effect of trauma on the memory as well as Dickens's interest in mesmerism and the unconscious. The ghost story, she argues, has much in common with the trauma narrative, and "The Signalman" allowed Dickens to articulate his own trauma in a way that was "uncannily prescient of the direction and emphasis that trauma studies would take in the next century." Matus sees the ghost as "an articulation of the signalman's traumatized consciousness" and the narrator, signalman, ghost, and engine driver as being "bound together" in a series of overlapping and repeated occurrences that go beyond the confines of the narration.

2772. Pope, Norris. "Dickens's 'The Signalman' and Information Problems in the Railway Age." *Technology & Culture* 42.3 (July 2001): 436–61.

This interesting examination of Victorian railways and the accidents caused by early signaling problems relates "The Signalman" to two earlier accidents: the Clayton Tunnel disaster of 25 August 1861, and the Staplehurst accident of 9 June 1865. Although the article is concerned with history rather than literary analysis, Pope ties the character of the signalman—his isolation, sense of responsibility, and dependency on a communication system that was in its infancy—to the real events of the times.

2773. Traill, Nancy H. "Charles Dickens: Tradition and Transition" (**2570**). 67–73.

Traill considers "The Signal-man" the best developed of Dickens's stories of the paranormal, although "its play of questions and answers betrays its mystery story origins.'' Concentrating her study on the narrator, she argues that the spectre is a paranormal phenomenon, authenticated by the independent experiences of the other characters. Traill concludes that ''both the signal-man's and the narrator's psychologies are subtly etched in the personal nature of their cognitive experiences'' and are proof that Dickens understood psychology.

2774. Tytler, Graeme. ''Dickens's The Signalman.'' *Explicator* 53.1 (Fall 1994): 26–29.

Argues that the signalman is suffering from lypemania (or monomania), a type of mental illness caused by sadness, unease, guilt, and night watching that was first identified by J. Esquirol in 1810. Symptoms include hallucinations, a haggard appearance, a ''fixed look,'' an obsession with words, and rationality in speaking about the hallucinations. Tytler argues that Dickens is intending to suggest that the apparitions are connected to the breakdown in human communication, with the railway being a metaphor for society as a vast signaling system. Tytler analyzes the story as illustrating the idea of language as a universal signaling system based on class differences. The reader has to become a signalman because the story is ''par excellence a story to be read'' with punctuation and other signs (such as parentheses) there to be interpreted as portents of the signalman's death. The narrator misreads the signalman's apparent rationality because he too is superstitious, as his language reveals. He may ''be exposing the roots of Victorian man's susceptibility to the supernatural.'' The ghost's gestures and words are ''merely expressions of a partially insane signalman's unconscious, wherein lie stored up memories of all the codes of social behavior he has ever acquired.''

2775. ———. ''Charles Dickens's 'The Signalman': A Case of Partial Insanity?'' *History of Psychiatry* 8.3 (September 1997): 421–32.

A similar article to Tytler's 1994 essay (**2774**) in arguing that the signalman is suffering from some form of partial insanity. In this article, however, Tytler focuses on Esquirol's description of the symptoms and causes of monomania as fitting the signalman's case. He notes that Dickens was very knowledgeable about mental illnesses, but he concludes that the story's ending is ambivalent enough to provide the thrill required of a ghost story.

2776. Vescovi, Alessandro. ''The Bagman, the Signalman and Dickens's Short Story.'' In *Dickens: The Craft of Fiction and the Challenges of Reading: Proceedings of the Milan Symposium, Gargnano, September 1998* (**2606**). 111–22.

Vescovi compares an early story from *Pickwick Papers* with ''The Signalman'' to show the evolution of Dickens's short-story technique.

He notes that while both stories deal with the uncanny, "The Signalman" includes social engagement as well. It is also more complex in its structure with a cyclical format that is repeated three times. Vescovi's reading stresses the way the narrative guides the reader's response and forces an analeptical reading, a technique that he compares to the ballad in the use of repetition and the deferring of meaning (as in a detective story). The story can then blend the ghost tradition with a Marxian protest against the alienation of the signalman as a result of his working conditions. Finding it curious that other commentators have not tried to answer the question why the signalman does not clear the way, Vescovi suggests that his alienating work is the cause: an interpreter of signals fails to recognize the human sign that could have saved his life. The reader adds the ghostly element at the end of the story because he has been filling in the gaps in the narrative throughout. For another reading that stresses the threefold cyclical structure see Bonheim (**2761**).

2777. ———. "Dickens's 'The Signalman' and Rubini's *La Stazione.*" In *Dickens on Screen* (**2370**). 53–60.
Analyzes the parallels between Dickens's story and Rubini's 1990 film, which was based on a play and released in 1991 as *The Station* in English-speaking countries. Likening the debt to Chaplin's *City Lights'* debt to *The Cricket on the Hearth*, Vescovi says the film borrowed the railway setting, the cross-class encounter, and various details and incidents. The film, however, employs comedy that is lacking in the story, and that resembles some of Dickens's other work (according to Vescovi, the station-master is like Sam Weller). Both story and film have Marxist overtones in the alienation of the worker, he argues, and both exemplify the dangers of technology.

9. NO THOROUGHFARE (1867)
EDITIONS

2778. Dickens, Charles, and Wilkie Collins. *No Thoroughfare.* Christchurch Dickens Fellowship, 2001.
I have not seen this "compact, clearly printed booklet." For details, see *Dickensian* 97.3 (Winter 2001): 251.

STUDIES

2779. Bump, Jerome. "Parody and the Dickens-Collins Collaboration in 'No Thoroughfare.' " *Library Chronicle of the University of Texas at Austin* 37 (1986): 38–53.

Argues that the collaboration disproves the Romantic view that creativity can be achieved only in isolation. Bump finds self-parody and mutual parody in the dramatic version, especially in the overuse of melodrama, and he also refers to the satire on the story published in *The Mask* in 1868 (**1940**). Creativity can thus be a "collective as well as an individual phenomenon," and parody can stem from admiration. This article contains several good illustrations related to Dickens, Collins, the play, and the *Mask* parody from the Harry Ransom Humanities Research Center at the University of Texas, Austin, which holds a copy of the play with annotations by Richard Herne Shepherd (**1935**). Nayder (**2782**) says that Bump in misled by Shepherd into thinking that Dickens wrote portions of the play. But see, for instance, Collins's autobiographical fragment (**1905**) in which he writes that he wrote the play in collaboration with Dickens and Charles Fechter.

2780. Gray, Beryl. "Dickens and Dogs: 'No Thoroughfare' and the Landseer Connection." *Dickensian* 100.1 (Spring 2004): 5–22.

In this interesting and well-illustrated article, Gray laments the absence of dogs from the alpine scenes in *Little Dorrit* and notes that Dickens makes no mention in the novel of Landseer's 1820 painting *Alpine Mastiffs Reanimating a Distressed Traveller*, a copy of which hung in the Great St. Bernard Hospice. The balance, she argues, was redressed in *No Thoroughfare*, in which rescue dogs play a vital role. Gray finds the story melodramatic and wooden, but the dogs "reanimate the story, and introduce some authenticity into its mechanisms." She notes that the dogs were omitted from the dramatic version of the story. Gray discusses the parody of the story that appeared in *The Mask* (**1940**) and reprints the cartoon that accompanied it, noting the prominence of the dogs.

2781. Hollington, Michael. " 'To the Droodstone,' or, From *The Moonstone* to Edwin Drood via *No Thoroughfare*." *QWERTY* 5 (1995): 141–49.

Hollington's intriguing argument is that John Jasper's murder of his nephew Edwin Drood enacted Dickens's murderous jealousy of his former collaborator and friend, Wilkie Collins, with Rosa Bud representing the adulation of the British public for which both writers were vying. Angry at Collins's success with *The Moonstone* and the dramatization of *No Thoroughfare*, and antagonistic to Collins's brother (Dickens's son-in-law), Dickens added the murder of Nancy to his public reading repertoire at this time. Hollington's interest in *No Thoroughfare* is in the light it sheds on the plot of *The Mystery of Edwin Drood* in relation to *The Moonstone*. Links between the three works include a central female character and her circle of uncles and would-be suitors, the heroine's flight with a solicitor to a place of refuge, the

marking of the heroine's maturity by an anniversary, and the importance of wills. Hollington also finds an oedipal (and autobiographical)
thread in all three works, in which the detective searching for the
murderer finds him in himself. In *No Thoroughfare*, Wilding's wine
vault both prefigures the crypt in *Edwin Drood* and recalls the recasting
of Dickens's early blacking factory experience as David Copperfield's
at Murdstone and Grinby. Hollington goes on to elaborate the effects
of opium and the resulting ''fragmentation of text and consciousness''
in these three detective stories, citing Vendale's fragmentary words
spoken at his ''death'' in the mountains as a key link between the
motif as it appears in the two novels. Hollington then elucidates Dickens's move away from *The Moonstone* and into his fascination with
murder and identity: the split personality and the problem of knowing
who one is. Again he cites *No Thoroughfare* (and Dickens's portion
in particular) as asking ''whether identity is in fact only constituted
through the narratives of others.'' The Christmas story and *Edwin
Drood* both move beyond the linear detective story narrative of *The
Moonstone* to a circular meditation on identity and death that works
at the level of myth.

2782. Nayder, Lillian. *Unequal Partners: Charles Dickens, Wilkie Collins,
and Victorian Authorship* (**2696**). 139–162.
Continuing her argument that Collins continually fought against Dickens's racism and misogyny, Nayder compares Dickens's interests in
''No Thoroughfare'' with Collins's by examining their contributions.
On the question of illegitimacy, Nayder claims that Dickens posits
women as transgressors who violate rules, rather than victims (as they
were required to be by the rules of the Foundling Hospital, which took
the babies only of seduced and deserted women). In Dickens's portion
of the story, the claims of mothers to their children are illegitimate,
and Dickens not only excludes biological mothers from the story but
''more generally disparages female autonomy and women who assume
the prerogatives of men.'' Collins, Nayder argues, tries to return the
story to women's ''exploitation and dependency.'' Drawing on contemporary descriptions of alpine exploits that posit the English moun-
taineers as ''patriarchs and imperialists'' conquering a ''savage,
feminine'' landscape, Nayder compares Dickens's treatment of Obenreizer to Collins's, arguing that Dickens makes him a combination
of peasant and savage, conflating both ''class resentment and racial
antipathy.'' In the dramatic version, written primarily by Collins, Obenreizer becomes a tragic figure. Nayder is critical of Dickens's portrayal of Marguerite also, arguing that despite her bravery and strength,
she is also depicted as subservient, and the story concludes with the

autonomous woman defeated and patriarchy restored. Nayder argues that in act 4, Collins deliberately questions "the power of fathers to legitimate." She suggests that the passage describing Maître Voigt in pastoral terms was written by Dickens (and resembles his description of his Swiss Chalet in the garden at Gad's Hill Place). Collins, in contrast, "implicates him in the abuses of patriarchal power."

2783. Taylor, Jenny Bourne. " 'Received, a Blank Child.': John Brownlow, Charles Dickens, and the London Foundling Hospital—Archives and Fictions." *Nineteenth-Century Literature* 56 (December 2001): 293–363.

Concludes this long study of the Foundling Hospital and the shifting attitudes to illegitimacy in Victorian England with a discussion of "No Thoroughfare." Taylor argues that in failing to find his own identity, Wilding eludes all the meanings projected onto the foundling child. Usefully touching on all the doublings in the story, Taylor sees Wilding as progressing further than the divided consciousnesses of Oliver Twist and Tattycoram (in *Little Dorrit*). The revelation that Vendale is the real Wilding "allows the last traces of the bastard as absolute Other to remain intact" while at the same time "detach[ing] these traces from the dual identity of the Foundling Hospital child."

STAGE ADAPTATION BY DICKENS AND COLLINS

2784. Dickens, Charles, and Wilkie Collins. *No Thoroughfare. A Drama. In Five Acts* (**1906**).

Published by the office of *All the Year Round*, this script is now available on the internet, with an introduction by Beppe Sabatini. http://home.earthlink.net/~bsabatini/Inimitable-Boz/

CHRISTMAS STORIES

COLLECTED AND SELECTED EDITIONS

2785. Dickens, Charles. *Christmas Stories*. Ed. Ruth Glancy. Everyman Edition. London: J. M. Dent; North Clarendon, VT: Charles E. Tuttle, 1996. xxxvi + 843.

Contains all of Dickens's contributions to the Christmas numbers of *Household Words* and *All the Year Round* as well as his linking passages to the omitted stories by other writers. Contributions by Wilkie Collins that are essential to the numbers (such as chapter 2 of *The*

Perils of Certain English Prisoners) are included. This edition also includes all the illustrations that were produced for the Charles Dickens edition of 1871 (**1962**) and the Illustrated Library edition of 1876 (**1963**). The stories are annotated. Other sections include information on the public readings, the publishing history of the Christmas stories, and the manuscripts. There is a chronology of Dickens's life and times and biographical notes on Dickens's contributing authors. Introduction by Ruth Glancy (**2792**).

RADIO ADAPTATIONS AND RECORDINGS

Chronological Listing

2786. *Charles Dickens' Christmas Ghost Stories* (**2403**).
        Dickens's portions of "The Haunted House" occupy sides 1 and 2. "The Signal Man" is on side 16. "Ghosts at Christmas" from "The [sic] Christmas Tree" is found on side 17.
2787. Dickens, Charles *The Christmas Stories*. Blackstone Audio, 2006. 4 hours.
        An unabridged reading of Dickens's portions of the *Household Words* Christmas stories, narrated by Robert Whitfield. Downloadable from Spoken Network. *www.spokennetwork.com.*

STUDIES

2788. Allingham, Philip V. "Dickens's Aesthetic of the Short Story." *Dickensian* 95.2 (Summer 1999): 144–53.
        Allingham seeks to address what he sees as "a century of neglect" of Dickens's short stories by establishing Dickens's view of the story as different from the novel. Allingham seems unaware of the many recent studies and editions of the short stories. He briefly mentions some of the Christmas stories, "George Silverman's Explanation," and *Holiday Romance*, and concludes that for Dickens the greatest power of short fiction was "its power to move" a large audience to laughter, tears, or dread.
2789. [Anon.] "Christmas Books." *The Academy* 55 (3 December 1898): 375.
        This review of new publications for Christmas 1898 includes a note on Chapman and Hall's reissue in pocket volumes of the complete Christmas numbers. Calling the books "handy and pretty," the reviewer regrets that the stories are still anonymous (with the exception

of *Mugby Junction*), noting that the contributors' names are "carefully given" in the large green one-volume edition published by Chapman and Hall.

2790. Bowen, John. "Bebelle and 'His Boots': Dickens, Ellen Ternan and the Christmas Stories." *Dickensian* 96.3 (Winter 2000): 197–208.

Links *Somebody's Luggage*, the Lirriper numbers, and *Mugby Junction*, as well as some of the *Uncommercial Traveller* pieces, with Dickens's and Ellen Ternan's hidden relationship in France at that time. Bowen finds evidence in the stories to support the claim (made repeatedly over the years but never substantiated) that Ellen bore Dickens's child.

2791. Collins, Philip. "Charles Dickens." In *Reference Guide to Short Fiction* (**2498**). 180–84.

In a paragraph Collins surveys the Christmas stories, which he finds disappointingly mawkish: "Dickens was unaffected by the short story art then being created by Poe and others." He singles out "The Signalman" as one of Dickens's best supernatural stories.

2792. Glancy, Ruth. "Introduction." In the 1996 Everyman edition (**2785**). xxi–xxxiii.

Explains the genesis and intentions of the Christmas numbers, stemming from Dickens's "*Carol* philosophy" and his belief in the beneficial effects of autobiographical storytelling.

2793. ———. "Charles Dickens." In *British Short-Fiction Writers, 1800–1880. Dictionary of Literary Biography* (**2653**). 84–105.

Places the Christmas stories in the context of Dickens's life and work, concentrating on their related themes of confession, isolation, and memory.

2794. Gregory, Gill. "Editorial Authority: Charles Dickens." In her *The Life and Work of Adelaide Procter* (**2626**), passim.

Surveys Procter's contributions to the Christmas numbers to argue that Procter's poems show her resisting Dickens's authorial control by introducing figures (especially excluded ones such as children and single women) and emotional states that are at odds with Dickens's frameworks and conclusions. Gregory begins with Dickens's introduction to Procter's *Legends and Lyrics* to argue that Dickens valued Procter's humor and "sterling noble nature" but disliked the melancholic strain in her poetry. In *Another Round of Stories by the Christmas Fire*, Gregory finds that Procter's "The Angel's Story" and Dickens's "The Schoolboy's Story" and "Nobody's Story" all convey the tensions of being excluded or included, especially for children. Dickens finds a "precarious" resolution in the Christmas fireside framework that "The Angel's Story" resists. In *The Seven Poor Travellers*, Gregory finds Dickens teasing Procter and the other contributors because he is identified with the "rich" editor and proprietor while they are the "poor travellers." Noting the centrality of Dickens's contribution, "The Story of Richard Doubledick," Gregory argues that Procter's contributions question this dominance. She points to similarities between the child in "The Sailor Boy" and Goethe's Mignon to argue that both narratives reveal a young woman whose creativity and emotions are blocked, a topic generally avoided by Dickens, although Gregory notes that Dickens had explored such repression in Louisa Gradgrind in *Hard Times* that year (and punishes Louisa by not allowing her to marry and have children). Gregory sees Procter as both masking strong emotions in her poetry and enjoying the performative aspects of writing, a side of her that Dickens admired. For Gregory, this side is evident in Procter's second contribution to the 1854 number and may show that Dickens "unwittingly" accepted both sides of Procter, the repressed and the expressive. Both poems subtly challenge Dickens's dominance. Gregory sees Procter's poems for *The Holly-Tree Inn* and *The Wreck of the Golden Mary* as mirroring the anonymity forced on Procter by the framework and by Dickens's authorial control. In 1858, however, Procter's "narrative voice is in direct opposition to the solutions which Dickens provides for the single woman depicted in his frame narrative." In her poem, Gregory argues, Procter resists Dickens's neat overcoming of the problem of deprivation at the end of the number. Gregory suggests that Dickens may have derived the framework idea for *A House to Let* from Bryan Procter's essay "The Story of the Back-Room Window," published in 1838. Gregory analyzes Procter's contribution to *The Haunted House* at length in an earlier chapter in the book and here discusses Dickens's teasing of Procter in the framework (as Belinda Bates) and the similarities between "The Ghost in Master B.'s Room" and Procter's poem in their recollection of childhood play and early erotic feelings.

2795. ———. "Dickens and Adelaide Procter." *Dickensian* 96.1 (Spring 2000): 29–40.

Essentially an abbreviated version of the discussion of the Christmas numbers contained in Gregory's *The Life and Work of Adelaide Procter* (**2794**).

2796. Heath, Catherine. "Sensations of a Very Queer Small Boy: Childhood Selves in Dickens's Journalism and Short Fiction." *Australasian Victorian Studies Journal* 5 (1999): 35–50.

Heath includes "A Christmas Tree," "What Christmas Is, As We Grow Older," "The Child's Story," "The Schoolboy's Story," "The Ghost in Master B.'s Room" (from *The Haunted House*), "The Guest" (from *The Holly-Tree Inn*), "His Leaving It Till Called For" (from

Somebody's Luggage), and "Barbox Brothers" and "Barbox Brothers and Co." (from *Mugby Junction*) in this perceptive discussion of Dickens's exploration of childhood, memory, and imagination in his short prose and fiction. Heath considers the creation of the "childhood *self* in relation to the adult self" and the consequences of its displacement into the narrative imagination. She considers the ambiguities of this relationship and discusses the moral and aesthetic values that Dickens attributes to childhood, concluding that Dickens's narrators confine their childhood selves in narrative because they "threaten to overwhelm rationality and linearity."

2797. Henson, Louise. "Investigations and Fictions: Charles Dickens and Ghosts"(**2657**). 55–61.

In a section titled "Haunted Houses and Haunted Men," Henson discusses *The Haunted House*, "The Signalman" (from *Mugby Junction*), and "To Be Taken With a Grain of Salt" (from *Doctor Marigold's Prescriptions*) as revealing Dickens's engagement with contemporary debates about paranormal experiences. "The Ghost in Master B.'s Room" (from *The Haunted House*) "draws on the spectral illusion theory" in which the ghosts are the creation of the mind. Henson sees "The Mortals in the House" from the same number as exemplifying contemporary theories of "expectant attention, where the mind provokes a physiological response and the individual's own unconscious agency is taken for that of a supernatural power." Henson sees this theory at work in "The Signalman," as well as spectral illusion and clairvoyance, and she argues that the narrator's ambiguous attitude to the signalman's concerns reflects the contemporary confusion over the boundary between sanity and madness. Henson also discusses the relationship between the signalman's mental processes and his role as interpreter of technological signs which he cannot fully comprehend.

2798. Hollington, Michael. *Charles Dickens: Critical Assessments* (**2661**), Vol. 3, 791–807, 811–21, 825–36.

Reprints Percy Fitzgerald's "Charles Dickens in the Editor's Chair" (**1995**), Helmut Bonheim's "The Principle of Cyclicity in Charles Dickens's 'The Signalman' " (**2761**), and Raymond Tschumi's "Dickens and Switzerland: *No Thoroughfare*" (**1956**).

2799. Nayder, Lillian. *Unequal Partners: Charles Dickens, Wilkie Collins, and Victorian Authorship* (**2696**), passim.

Nayder concentrates on the Dickens/Collins collaborations in *The Wreck of the Golden Mary* (**2696**), *The Perils of Certain English Prisoners* (**2707**), and *No Thoroughfare* (**2782**), but she also comments on the other numbers to argue that Dickens "often uses the relationships among the characters to self-consciously represent and justify his authority over his contributors, whose debt and subordination to their editor became unspoken subjects in the stories.'' Thus in *The Seven Poor Travellers* and *The Holly-Tree Inn* Dickens's character is the only gentleman while Collins's is respectively a disreputable lawyer and an ostler. Nayder argues that Collins's gradual withdrawal from Dickens's journals was caused by Collins's dissatisfaction with being cast as the ''right hand'' in their Christmas collaborations and by their differences of opinion. In the numbers written between 1858 and 1861, she argues, Collins's contributions were at odds with Dickens's themes and reflected instead Collins's ''continuing concern with class and gender inequities, and with imperial wrongdoing.'' Thus in *A Message from the Sea*, Collins's persona's refusal to narrate a story reflects Collins's antagonism to Dickens's instructions. Nayder believes that Collins's contributions to *The Haunted House* and *Tom Tiddler's Ground* contradicted Dickens's intentions in the numbers.

2800. Orel, Harold. ''Charles Dickens: Establishing Rapport with the Public'' (**2581**). 56–78.

In this survey of Dickens's short-story work, Orel concludes that Dickens wrote short stories ''when he thought his public wanted them; he stopped writing them when he believed they preferred novels.'' For this reason he wrote stories for Christmas primarily. Orel deals only with *Mugby Junction* in any detail when discussing the Christmas Stories. He briefly mentions ''The Boy at Mugby'' as being a sketch and the boy a voice, not a character. ''The Signal-Man'' he considers Dickens's best story and the delineation of the signalman's emotional state particularly well done. Orel does not recognize the narrator as being Barbox, however, and faults him as a narrator for failing to identify any relationship between himself and the stories. Orel concludes that Dickens's short stories resemble Dickens's novels more than they resemble other short stories of the time.

2801. Oulton, Carolyn W. de la L. *Literature and Religion in Mid-Victorian England: From Dickens to Eliot*. Basingstoke, Hampshire, and New York: Palgrave Macmillan, 2003. 37–38, 57–59.

In discussing Dickens's view of manliness as a Christian virtue, Oulton argues that Wilkie Collins did not share Dickens's linking of virtue with physical prowess. She finds ''The Story of Richard Doubledick'' from *The Seven Poor Travellers* as evidence of Dickens adopting the Evangelical position that military patriotism was linked to religious commitment. She notes that the violence in *The Perils of Certain English Prisoners* is found only in Dickens's portions, Collins's violence being ''purely psychological.'' In *The Wreck of the Golden Mary*, Oulton argues, heroic sacrifice rather than military strength is emphasized, and she finds both Dickens and Collins to be critical of Evangelicalism and its tendency to selfishness in the portrait of Mr. Rarx. In

No Thoroughfare, Oulton finds Collins's interest in moral rather than physical strength overwhelmed by Dickens's stress on "moral victory through physical prowess." Oulton goes on to examine the two writers' views on manly Christianity in *The Frozen Deep*.

2802. Page, Norman. "Christmas Stories." In his *A Dickens Companion* (**2668**). 263–64.

Page finds the stories lacking in interest for modern readers with the exception of Mrs. Lirriper's "verbal inventiveness." He notes the stories' popularity for Dickens as public readings.

2803. Parker, David. "Christmas Books and Stories, 1844 to 1854." In his *Christmas and Charles Dickens* (**2546**). 221–82.

Parker discusses Dickens's contributions to the Christmas numbers of 1850 to 1854, arguing that Dickens then deliberately moved away from Christmas as a topic because of his increasingly unhappy marriage. Concentrating on the narrative voice in "A Christmas Tree" (as he had in his discussion of the *Carol*), Parker closely analyzes the flexibility and range of mood and point of view in the piece, a diversity that is balanced and coherent in its depiction of the importance of Christmas. No other text, he argues, "more strikingly demonstrates [Dickens's] capacity for mixing the comic and the grave to profound and thrilling effect." Parker sees "A Christmas Tree" as the culmination of Dickens's examination of what Christmas meant to him and how it affected his life and art. "What Christmas Is, As We Grow Older" Parker considers a "skillful" summary of Dickens's views, powerful in religious conviction but lacking complexity, mere "pious affirmation." Parker concludes his chapter on the Christmas books and stories with *The Seven Poor Travellers*, finding it less intense, with "no sense of Christmas as a key to understanding human destiny."

2804. Peters, Catherine. *The King of Inventors: A Life of Wilkie Collins.* London: Secker and Warburg, 1991, passim.

Briefly discusses Collins's contributions to the Christmas numbers. Peters misdates *The Perils of Certain English Prisoners* and states incorrectly that the original idea for the number was Collins's. She finds the story, and especially Collins's contribution, "unpleasantly racist" and suggests that he drew on Henry Morley's "Our Phantom Ship: Central America" (*Household Words*, 22 February 1851, volume 2, not 17 as given in Peters) for his section.

2805. Reed, John R. "Dickens' Christmas Narratives." In his *Dickens and Thackeray: Punishment and Forgiveness* (**2672**). 154–68.

After discussing the Christmas Books (**2672**), Reed surveys Dickens's religious themes (especially forgiveness) in the Christmas stories, including "A Christmas Tree," "The Schoolboy's Story," "The Story of Richard Doubledick'' (from *The Seven Poor Travellers*), *The Holly Tree*, *Somebody's Luggage*, *Mugby Junction*, the Lirriper numbers, and *No Thoroughfare*. He notes that even in the stories that involve wickedness or natural disaster (*The Perils of Certain English Prisoners*, *The Wreck of the Golden Mary*, and *No Thoroughfare*) the ''overwhelming mood is redemptive.'' Reed discusses the secret forgiveness in ''The Story of Richard Doubledick'' as being more acceptable to modern readers than overt forgiveness because it is unwitnessed and therefore sincere. In *The Holly Tree*, the narrator ''forgives where there was no injury'' and thus feels self-righteous. In telling the story, he rights this wrong. Reed concludes the chapter by finding in *No Thoroughfare* the clearest exemplification of ''the moral scheme that regularly guides Dickens' narrative decisions.'' Rather than having the villain Obenreizer punished by another character, Dickens manipulates the plot so that he is hoist on his own petard, cast out of the narrative by the author/providence.

2806. Rem, Tore. ''Fictional Exorcism? Parodies of the Supernatural in Dickens.'' *Dickensian* 96.1 (Spring 2000): 14–28.

Includes *The Haunted House*, ''A Christmas Tree'' (misnamed ''Ghosts at Christmas''), ''The Signal-man'' from *Mugby Junction*, and ''To Be Taken With a Grain of Salt'' from *Doctor Marigold's Prescriptions,* as well as ''To Be Read at Dusk'' and other ghost stories by Dickens to argue that Dickens believed in ghosts and was fascinated by the supernatural. Rem does not discuss the Christmas books because the ghosts in them are used allegorically. Examining Dickens's mesmeric powers and attitudes to them, Rem argues that because Dickens frequently laughed about supernatural or irrational occurrences he ''must have believed in the occurrences of ghosts and the real forces of a liquid running through the universe.'' Dickens makes fun of the supernatural as a defense against being ridiculed for believing in it. Because the Mugby Junction stories are serious, Rem says little about them, and he follows Haining (**2852**) in wrongly attributing ''The Goodwood Ghost Story'' to Dickens and misnaming ''Well-Authenticated Rappings'' as ''The Rapping Spirits.'' Rem's carelessness with sources and failure to include some of Dickens's well-known statements about the supernatural (such as his remark to Elizabeth Gaskell that most supernatural occurrence can be rationally explained with the removal of one small detail in the story) undermines his argument that Dickens feared the power of ghosts and therefore exorcised them through parody and humor.

Part III. Separately Published Short Fiction

TO BE READ AT DUSK

STUDIES

2807. Glancy, Ruth. "To Be Read at Dusk." *Dickensian* 83.1 (Spring 1987): 40–47.

Provides some information about the manuscript (held at the Royal Library in Windsor) and discusses the influence of Dickens's experiences as a mesmerist with Madame de la Rue on the first of two included stories. Glancy notes that the first story deals with female sexual passion, a topic usually not dealt with explicitly in Victorian fiction. The second story is compared to a ghost story by Daniel Defoe and again illustrates Dickens's interest in unusual states of consciousness.

2808. Henson, Louise. "Investigations and Fictions: Charles Dickens and Ghosts"(**2657**). 51–53.

Discusses "To Be Read at Dusk" as engaging "with contemporary anxieties about the effect of superstitious belief on mental health." Henson relates the story to Dickens's mesmerizing of Madame de la Rue.

2809. Traill, Nancy H. "Charles Dickens: Tradition and Transition" (**2570**). 58–61.

Traill regards "To Be Read at Dusk" as telling two transitional fantastic stories, where the paranormal begins to emerge. There are Gothic conventions too, but the stories employ clairvoyance and precognitive dreams, both aspects of the modern paranormal.

HUNTED DOWN

"HUNTED DOWN" IN PROGRESS

2810. Dickens, Charles. *The Letters of Charles Dickens* (**1**), IX, 43–44, 60, 89, 141.

Includes Dickens's letter to Robert Bonner on 29 March 1859, not included in the Nonesuch Letters (**1440**) but mentioned in Mackaness (**2066**), agreeing to write a story for the *New York Ledger*. A footnote quotes Bonner's advertisement in the *New York Times* on 25 April for the upcoming story, and a letter from one of Bonner's staff members to W. H. Wills on Bonner's agreement to the story's being published in *All the Year Round*. Previously unpublished letters include one to a New York lawyer on 3 May acknowledging payment for the story and to Robert Bonner on 7 July, enclosing the corrected proofs. Dickens tells Bonner that he has divided the story into five sections, "feeling that the effect is heightened thereby," and telling him that when he read the story to some friends "it took strong possession of them." A footnote quotes a letter from Bonner to Dickens, acknowledging his satisfaction with the story. In a letter to Forster on 24 October, Dickens complains that an article in the *Bath Chronicle* has taken Sampson's belief in physiognomy as Dickens's.

EDITIONS

Chronological Listing

2811. *Hunted Down: The Detective Stories of Charles Dickens.* Ed. Peter Haining. London: Peter Owen; Chester Springs, PA: Dufour, 1996. Reprinted 2005. 223.

This edition of "Hunted Down" (pp. 174–96) contains an illustration by E. G. Dalziel of the murderer confronted. Other extracts are taken from *Pickwick Papers*, *Martin Chuzzlewit*, *Bleak House*, *Household Words*, *All the Year Round*, and *The Uncommercial Traveller*. Introduction by Peter Haining (**2815**).

2812. Cox, Michael, ed. *Victorian Tales of Mystery and Detection.* Oxford: Oxford UP, 1992.

This selection includes "Hunted Down" but it is not mentioned in the introduction (pp. ix–xxvi).

FILM ADAPTATIONS

2813. *Hunted Down.* CBS-TV, 1952.
Broadcast in the *Suspense* series, with John Baragrey. Listed in Pointer (**2380**).

STUDIES

2814. Allingham, Philip V. "Dickens's Unreliable Narrator in 'Hunted Down.' " *Studies in Short Fiction* 29 (1992): 85–93.
Allingham finds Sampson unreliable because he deliberately hides information from the reader and is essentially playing "mind games" as a result. He compares Dickens's technique to that of Wilkie Collins in his mystery novels, finding Collins's method more interesting and his villains more fascinating than Slinkton. Allingham suggests that Slinkton's betrayal of his nieces may reflect Dickens's sense of his mother's betrayal when he was sent to work in the blacking factory.

2815. Haining, Peter. "Introduction." In the 1996 Peter Owen edition (**2811**). 7–21.
Haining discusses Dickens as the pioneer of the detective story, but he concentrates chiefly on Dickens's detectives rather than on the story as a genre. He notes that Meltham in "Hunted Down" hired rooms in the Middle Temple, where R. Austin Freeman was later to place Dr. Thorndyke, the "greatest medico-legal detective of all time." Haining quotes Ellery Queen on "Hunted Down": "True, the character who plays the role of the detective cannot be claimed by any modern school: he is not a dilettante or scientist whose forte is deduction: nor is he the tough hombre of the hard-boiled species; yet in motives and actions, he is undeniably a realistic sleuth."

2816. Jenkins, William D. "Hunting Down *The Speckled Band.*" *Baker Street Journal* 41 (1991): 37–38.
Speculating that "Hunted Down" was the inspiration for *The Speckled Band*, Jenkins considers that Arthur Conan Doyle "knew that he made a silk purse out of a sow's ear." Jenkins quotes Doyle (who admired Dickens very much) as saying that like the other great novelists, Dickens "left no single short story of outstanding merit behind him."

2817. Motion, Andrew. *Wainewright The Poisoner.* New York: Alfred A. Knopf, 2000. 258–60.
Briefly compares Slinkton to Jonas Chuzzlewit and Rigaud (in *Little Dorrit*), whom Motion claims were also partly modelled on Thomas

Griffiths Wainewright, to argue that Dickens was fascinated rather than just repelled by Wainewright. Motion notes that Dickens kept this fascination firmly in the background of his fictions, however.

2818. Ruth, Jennifer. "The Self-Sacrificing Professional: Charles Dickens's 'Hunted Down' and *A Tale of Two Cities.*" *Dickens Studies Annual* 34 (2004): 283–99.

Places the story in the context of the shift in mid-Victorian England from the professional as businessman to the professional as disinterested public servant whose sphere of influence was the home rather than the marketplace. Ruth argues that this shift was not a return to the "noblesse oblige" of the old aristocracy but a whole new ideology based on the self-sacrificing model of the "angel in the house." This new male moral authority made itself an essential intervener in the family unit, as the lawyer Sydney Carton is the only person who can save the Darnay family in *A Tale of Two Cities* (written contemporaneously with "Hunted Down"). Ruth sees "Hunted Down" as similarly positing a professional whose value can be affirmed only by his death. Dickens chooses an actuary for his hero (Meltham) because the life insurance business was particularly concerned to prove its disinterested professionalism. The villain is Slinkton, who embodies the previous saviour models of clergyman and uncle. Sampson, the life insurance manager, is also unable to intervene because he is cannot free himself from business practices and become truly disinterested. Meltham (and Carton) must be disinterested to the point of sacrificing their lives for others.

HOLIDAY ROMANCE

HOLIDAY ROMANCE IN PROGRESS

2819. Dickens, Charles. *The Letters of Charles Dickens* (**1**), XI, 343, 394–95, 403, 410, 420, 438.

Contains several previously unpublished letters. Dickens writes to J. R. Osgood on 29 March 1867 promising "four little papers expressly designed" for *Our Young Folks*, the payment to be 1000 pounds and the length not less than *Hunted Down* and possibly more "if I find that the series would suffer by condensation within those limits." He promises to deliver the story by the end of October. He writes to J. T. Fields on 12 July that Mr. Dolby is bringing *Holiday Romance* to the American publisher in both manuscript and typeset and he does not know how the American audience "will humour the delicate little joke'' which Dickens expects to "be a great success here." He notes that the story lends itself to illustration, but while it might be "expedient" not to illustrate it in *Our Young Folks*, they could republish it in a book "with as much illustration as you please, if you can find (*I* can't!) a fanciful man." At the request of Ticknor & Fields, on 25 July Dickens sends a proof of the story to William Thomas, a prospective artist for it. On 9 August he writes to Wills that John Forster read the stories and finds them "the quaintest, wisest, most charming, most comical, in all ways most delightful, things" he has ever read. Sending proofs to Charles Kent on 3 September, Dickens writes that in the stories he "wanted oddly to combine a child's mind with a grown up joke." To Kent's enthusiastic reply, Dickens answers on 26 September that he is not surprised that Kent enjoyed the stories: "you and I love children and flatter ourselves that we know something about them." The Pilgrim edition does not contain a letter to Charles Kent of 2 October 1867 held in Yale University Library (**2074**).

EDITIONS

Chronological Listing

2820. Dickens, Charles. "The Magic Fishbone." In *Victorian Fairy Tales: The Revolt of the Fairies and Elves*. Ed. Jack Zipes. New York: Methuen, 1987. 91–99.
   Includes John Gilbert's original illustration for the story. Zipes, a professor of German, provides a fine overview of the genre, including the reasons for its early flowering in Germany and France rather than in England, and the reasons for its popularity in the nineteenth century. Discussing "The Magic Fishbone" (pp. xxi–xxii), Zipes sees the story as depicting Dickens's favoring of fancy over reason as the solution to society's problems. The conventional logic of the patriarch is no match for the creativity and moral soundness of the child.

2821. ———. "The Magic Fish-Bone." In *The Victorian Fairy Tale Book*. New York: Pantheon; Edinburgh: Canongate, 1988; reissued 1990. 106–15.
   Includes John Gilbert's original illustration for the story. An excellent introduction by Michael Patrick Hearn reviews the history of the fairy tale since Roman times. Hearn considers Victorian England the golden age of the fairy tale, or "tale of enchantment," where it was cleansed of earlier savagery and ethical ambiguity. As a mock fairy tale, "The Magic Fish-Bone" succeeds by combining the naïveté of its child

narrator with a clear moral: the villain is poverty. Hearn argues that the stories included in this edition "reflect Victorian England better than most of the earnest novels and social tracts from that era."

2822. ———. "The Magic Fishbone." In *The Oxford Book of Modern Fairy Tales*. Ed. Alison Lurie. Oxford: Oxford UP, 1993. 99–108. Reprinted 2003.

In her introduction (pp. xi–xviii), Lurie briefly mentions "The Magic Fishbone" as a burlesque based on "a scatty Micawber-like (or Dickens-like) family."

2823. ———. *Holiday Romance and Other Writings for Children*. Everyman Dickens. London: J. M. Dent; North Clarendon, VT: Charles E. Tuttle, 1995. xxix + 480.

Holiday Romance occupies pp. 397 to 437 and includes Sir John Gilbert's illustrations for the four parts and G.C. White and Sol Eytinge's initial letter designs (reproduced on one page). The "Dickens and his Critics" section includes a passage from F. J. Harvey Darton's *Children's Books in England* (1932; republished 1982). Introduction by Gillian Avery (**2826**).

FILM ADAPTATIONS

2824. *The Magic Fishbone*. NBC-TV (U.S.A.), 1958.

A one-hour film in the series *Shirley Temple's Storybook*, directed by Oscar Rudolph. Listed in Pointer (**2380**).

STUDIES

2825. Allingham, Philip V. "The Original Illustrations for Dickens's *A Holiday Romance*." *Dickensian* 92.1 (Spring 1996): 31–48.

Allingham provides an interesting overview of the composition of the story and its American illustrations. James T. Fields, the American publisher, oversaw the illustrations and engaged the artists: John Gilbert, an English magazine editor, provided a plate for each of the four chapters; and Field's own illustrators, G. C. White and Sol Eytinge, illustrated the opening page of each chapter, incorporating the initial letter of the first sentence. Allingham points out that these illustrations are not well known, although they are now reproduced in the Everyman edition of the story (**2823**). Allingham speculates that the unsigned portrait of Dickens at the beginning of the story was by Sol Eytinge, and he notes its "abstracted and brooding" look. Although Allingham cannot establish what control, if any, Dickens had over the illustrations, he discusses in detail the children's magazines of the time and Gilbert's extensive reputation in England. Comparing the illustrations to the text, Allingham notes the attempts of the artists to translate English setting and humor for American children; an English lamppost, for example, becomes an American fence, and the dress is also American. The scenes depicted in the illustrations preceded their appearance in the text. One of Gilbert's plates even appeared with the text of another story in the magazine. Allingham finds Gilbert a careless reader of the story, failing to notice that "Redforth" and "the Pirate-Colonel" are one boy, not two, and mistaking humor for melodrama in the same plate. He suggests that both Dickens and the illustrators "suffered a want of imagination" in the conclusion, but in the first three parts the illustrations aid the child reader in understanding the story.

2826. Avery, Gillian. "Introduction." In the 1995 Everyman edition (**2823**), pp. xix–xxviii.

Considers *Holiday Romance* "subversive" by Victorian standards because it dealt with a taboo subject: childhood love. Noting that American children's literature sometimes included lovesick boys (such as Tom Sawyer), Avery sees the story as foreshadowing Kenneth Grahame in England in the "archly ponderous style" and the division between imaginative children and plodding adults. She also sees its influence on Edith Nesbit and J. M. Barrie. Avery suggests that there is much of Dickens's own childhood in the story but does not elaborate.

2827. Bacile di Castiglione, Claudia. "*Holiday Romance:* Children's Dreams of Omnipotence in Dickens's Last Fiction." In *Dickens: The Craft of Fiction and the Challenges of Reading: Proceedings of the Milan Symposium, Gargnano, September 1998* (**2606**). 153–65.

This analysis of Dickens's evocation of children's voices and thought processes finds *Holiday Romance* "perhaps the most concise and brilliant of Dickens's texts" and evidence of his "post-modernist sensibility." Bacile di Castiglione's starting place is Dickens's lifelong defense of childhood imagination, but in this late story, she argues, he depicts not child victims but children who can "challenge the adult world, exploiting and overturning the literary patterns and modes of behavior that they had learned in their 'stultifying' books." The children are capable of offering a "new balance in social relationships." The analysis concentrates on the four different child narrators and their employment of the elements of romance, fairy tale, and pirate stories (by Defoe and Melville) to stress the children's independence and sense of power. Bacile di Castiglione also discusses the importance of dolls in the stories as indicators of social status.

2828. Higbie, Robert. *Dickens and Imagination* (**2659**). 157–58.

Sees *Holiday Romance* as demonstrating that, as in *Our Mutual Friend,* Dickens appears to have reached the conclusion that imagination does not lead to belief. Higbie notes that even the children in *Holiday Romance* have trouble believing in the imagination. Alice, representing the "submissive, female side of imagination," overcomes the masculine or rebellious male side, represented by Robin, and urges the children not to rebel openly against the reasoning adults. The imaginary is thus not "real" and cannot be taken seriously.

2829. Moss, Anita. "Varieties of Children's Metafiction." *Studies in the Literary Imagination* 18.2 (Fall 1985): 79–92.

Considers *Holiday Romance* and E. Nesbit's 1899 novel *The Story of the Treasure Seekers* as "works in which the imagined process by which the story is created becomes a central focus" because they have child narrators and they explore "the nature and function of children's literature generally." Moss argues that *Holiday Romance* fails as literature because Dickens's purpose was to remind adults about the necessity of romance and imagination in children's literature (at a time when children's literature was primarily moral and didactic). Moss finds only Alice a convincing child narrator with an interesting story to tell because she alone chooses the fairy tale; the other narrators are unconvincing and their stories dull. According to Moss, Nesbit, writing later with the fairy tale no longer needing to be defended, created a more convincing child narrator in Oswald and a new kind of children's story.

2830. Ostry, Elaine. *Social Dreaming: Dickens and the Fairy Tale.* New York: Routledge, 2002. 220.

Includes *Holiday Romance* in this discussion of Dickens's use of the fairy tale for social criticism. Not seen.

GEORGE SILVERMAN'S EXPLANATION

"GEORGE SILVERMAN'S EXPLANATION" IN PROGRESS

2831. Dickens, Charles. *The Letters of Charles Dickens* (**1**), X, 342.

Contains some previously unpublished letters. On 29 March 1867 Dickens writes to J. R. Osgood that if the publisher to whom he had promised "George Silverman's Explanation" (Benjamin Wood) does not produce the payment on the agreed date Ticknor and Fields can have it for 1,000 pounds. Wood failed to pay and the story passed to the American publisher.

EDITIONS

2832. Dickens, Charles. *George Silverman's Explanation*. Edited with introduction and notes by Harry Stone. Illustrated by Irving Block. California State University Northridge Libraries: Santa Susana, 1984. xxxv + 44.

Published in honor of the twenty-fifth anniversary of California State University, Northridge, this fine edition was limited to 26 lettered and 300 numbered copies. Irving Block's delicate line drawings, decorating nearly every page, complement the narrator's hesitant style and acute sensitivity. Their Gothic elements, heightened by being black and white, contribute to the almost morbid self-effacement of Silverman and complement his sense of having lived life "always in the shadow looking on." This is the only edition of the story in book form, and the only illustrated edition. It contains a note on the text and an introduction by Harry Stone (**2844**).

RADIO ADAPTATIONS

2833. "George Silverman's Explanation." BBC Radio 4, 1 May 2003. 45 minutes.

This adaptation by Michael Eaton was directed by Sebastian Graham-Jones. Paul Scofield read the adult George Silverman, with Alan Cox as the young George, David Warner as Brother Hawkyard, Gemma Jones as Lady Fareway, and Katherine Heath as Sylvia and Adelina. Music by John Tams. For a brief review, see Donald Hawes, *Dickensian* 99.2 (Summer 2003): 177–78.

STUDIES

2834. Ackroyd, Peter. *Dickens* (**2477**). 996–97.

Speculates that in George Silverman's story there is "an echo of Dickens's life as it might have been if it had gone altogether wrong." Ackroyd sees Dickens's self-justification of his relationship with Ellen Ternan in George's confession, and he suggests that the name Hoghton Towers may have been a reference to Houghton Place, former home of Ellen and her mother.

2835. Bock, Carol A. "Miss Wade and George Silverman: The Forms of Fictional Monologue." *Dickens Studies Annual* 16 (1987): 113–25.

Argues that "George Silverman's Explanation" is "perhaps the bleakest reflection of the author's diminishing faith in the power of the individual to transcend the damaging effects of his personal past." George's "neurotic need for self-renunciation," which in *David Copperfield* had led to the hero's salvation, now prevents the hero from overcoming guilt and learning how to love. Bock suggests that George's description of Hoghton Towers as an objective correlative for his "state of mind" is analogous to Dickens's identification of "a privately felt dilemma" with George's situation. The story is thus closer to T. S. Eliot's "The Love-Song of J. Alfred Prufrock" than to the dramatic monologues of Browning. Bock sees this "mask lyric" style as allowing Dickens to go beyond the ironic, objective narrative of Miss Wade in *Little Dorrit*.

2836. Butterworth, R. "Hoghton Tower and the Picaresque of 'George Silverman's Explanation,'" *Dickensian* 86.2 (Summer 1990): 93–104.
    After summarizing the history of Hoghton Tower and its condition when Dickens visited it in 1867, Butterworth discusses its importance in Silverman's moral development. Seeing the crumbling tower—man's work—surrounded by eternal nature, Silverman learns a new sense of "something beyond the here and now" and the futility of "worldly" ambitions. Silverman becomes a man "whose behaviour is self-effacing and high-minded, but who is also unable to be happy in this world." Butterworth then examines the unusually large number of settings for such a brief short story and explains their presence in terms of the picaresque elements of Silverman's ascendancy of the social scale. He maintains, however, that Silverman reaches his moral worthiness at Hoghton Tower and that his tragedy lies in continually aspiring to a higher plane.

2837. Cunningham, Valentine. *Everywhere Spoken Against: Dissent in the Victorian Novel.* Oxford: Clarendon, 1975, passim.
    Briefly discusses Dickens's attack on nonconformism in "George Silverman's Explanation" in her study of the topic in Victorian fiction.

2838. Forsyte, Charles. "The Sapsea Fragment—Fragment of What?" *Dickensian* 82.1 (Spring 1986): 12–26.
    Argues that the fragment of text that John Forster found and that has always been assumed to be intended for *The Mystery of Edwin Drood* was actually written earlier, and led to "George Silverman's Explanation." Forsyte notes similarities between the fragment and the story and finds "George Silverman's Explanation" to be highly autobiographical. Forsyte's comments on the Penguin edition of *The Mystery of Edwin Drood* are answered by its editor, Arthur J. Cox, in *Dickensian* 82.3 (Autumn 1986): 178–79. See also Longley (**2842**).

2839. Glancy, Ruth. "Charles Dickens." In *British Short-Fiction Writers, 1800–1880. Dictionary of Literary Biography* (**2653**). 84–105.

Discusses the story in the context of Dickens's other short stories, seeing Silverman in relation to Dickens's earlier isolated narrators, Master Humphrey and Barbox (from *Mugby Junction*).

2840. Jay, Elisabeth. *The Religion of the Heart: Anglican Evangelicalism and the Nineteenth-Century Novel.* Oxford: Clarendon, 1979. 26–27.

Briefly mentions Brother Hawkyard as one of Dickens's dissenting preachers who "demonstrate an awareness of the enmity and jealousy felt by the Dissenter for the Anglican." Dickens's Anglican Evangelicals, Jay argues, are more "frighteningly powerful" than his greedy Dissenters. She is answered by Oulton (**2843**).

2841. Kaplan, Fred. *Dickens. A Biography* (**2662**). 537–38.

In discussing Dickens's identification with the murderer Bill Sikes during his public readings of the murder of Nancy in *Oliver Twist*, Kaplan suggests that "George Silverman's Explanation" is "his most concentrated psychological portrait of the mono-identity of the pursuer and the pursued."

2842. Longley, Katharine M. "Letter to the Editor." *Dickensian* 82.2 (Summer 1986): 84–85.

Agrees with Charles Forsyte (**2838**) that the Sapsea fragment was not related to *The Mystery of Edwin Drood* but suggests that it related not to "George Silverman's Explanation" but to an 1868 Christmas number that never materialized. Forsyte replied in *Dickensian* 83.1 (Spring 1987): 48–49. Ackroyd (**2477**) also sees the fragment as abandoned plans for a Christmas number.

2843. Oulton, Carolyn W. de la L. *Literature and Religion in Mid-Victorian England.* Basingstoke, Hampshire: Palgrave Macmillan, 2003. 48–50.

Includes the story in her discussion of Dickens's religious views to suggest that he took an increasingly seriously view of Dissent because it had become a more powerful force in society. Oulton disagrees with Jay (**2841**) to argue that Hawkyard is a much more dangerous influence than Stiggins in *Pickwick Papers*.

2844. Stone, Harry. "Introduction." In the 1984 California State University, Northridge, edition (**2832**). vii–xxxiii.

Stone's introduction expands upon his 1958 *Studies in Philology* article (**2138**) and provides an excellent biographical overview and critical commentary. Stone is more sympathetic to Silverman than are the many commentators who find his confession egotistical and distasteful. Stone usefully compares Silverman to other children from deprived backgrounds in Dickens's fiction, particularly Pip and Magwitch from *Great Expectations* and Arthur Clennam and Miss Wade from *Little*

Dorrit. Stone discusses the psychological complexity of Silverman's inability to extricate himself from his feelings of guilt in terms of the artistry of the story—the confessional mode of narration, the symbolism of scene and setting, the use of repetition and parallelism, and the significance of names. Stone concludes that the story has universal power because it tells us "that we are all prisoners, in great or small degree, of forces we did not make and cannot control."

2845. ———. "The Long Chain." In his *The Night Side of Dickens: Cannibalism, Passion, Necessity* (**2613**), pp. 433–538.

For Harry Stone, "George Silverman's Explanation" is the work that most clearly and artistically depicts the "dark corners" of Dickens's mind and explores the question of necessity and free will. This long chapter is essentially an expanded version of the introduction in Stone's 1984 edition of the story (**2832**); many passages are virtually identical. What is added here is a much more detailed analysis of the autobiographical background, both Dickens's childhood (as told in the "Autobiographical Fragment" printed first in John Forster's biography), and his relationship with Ellen Ternan. Stone argues that the story reveals Dickens's crippling guilt and his inability to renounce it (unlike George Silverman, who gives up Adelina, the Ellen figure in the story). This chapter also considers in greater depth Dickens's developing explorations of necessity and free will in his fiction, finding it tragic that George has no option but to make the choices he does because of his early experiences.

2846. Tambling, Jeremy. *Confession: Sexuality, Sin, the Subject.* Manchester and New York: Manchester UP, 1990. 151–55.

Concludes a chapter on confessional modes in novels from 1848 to 1868 with a Freudian analysis of "George Silverman's Explanation" in relation to *Great Expectations* and the effect of misplaced guilt on Pip and George. In analyzing the circularity of George's narrative, Tambling also refers to Dickens's autobiographical fragment to argue that "the novelistic narration—overtly confessional or not—only begins to cover the unconscious material that is ready to surface."

Part IV. Mixed Editions and Guides, Indexes and Compendiums

EDITIONS

Chronological Listing

2847. Dickens, Charles. *The Signalman and Other Ghost Stories*. Gloucester: Sutton, 1984. x + 138.

Besides selections from the novels and other works not included in this bibliography, this edition contains "The Trial for Murder" from *Doctor Marigold's Prescriptions*, "The Signalman" from *Mugby Junction*, "To Be Read at Dusk," and an excerpt from "A Christmas Tree." There is a detailed biographical note by Sheila Mitchell that does not discuss Dickens's short-story work. Reissued in 1990 (**2849**).

2848. ———. *A Christmas Carol and Other Christmas Stories*. Ed. Frederick Busch. New York: New American Library, 1984. 223. Reprinted New York: Signet Classic, 1999.

Contains *A Christmas Carol* and "A Christmas Tree" as well as "A Christmas Dinner" from *Sketches by Boz*, selections from *Pickwick Papers*, and a select bibliography of Dickens's works and criticism. In his excellent introduction (pp. 9–28), Busch suggests that the Christmas books reveal Dickens's "double vision," caused by his early childhood experiences. Christmas to Dickens is not just cheer but also the remembrance of past cruelties leading to forgiveness. "It is a way of being Christian and wrathful at once." Tiny Tim represents Dickens's childhood threat of dying from neglect. Busch traces this theme in the portrayal of Scrooge, arguing that in depicting Scrooge as an abandoned child Dickens is afraid that he too could share Scrooge's fate. Busch also discusses the artistry of the *Carol*, finding parallels between Scrooge and Macbeth and between the three people at

Scrooge's deathbed and the witches. In his comments on "A Christmas Tree," Busch again finds Dickens's double vision, and he argues that the Christmas stories suggest that Dickens died a metaphorical death as an abandoned child. Scrooge's recovery and the Christian ending of "A Christmas Tree" cannot overcome Dickens's feelings of exile; "always at Christmas time he recollects what he had, or wished to have, as a paradise that is lost."

2849. ———. *The Signalman and Other Ghost Stories*. Gloucester: Sutton, 1990. Reprinted 1995, 1996, 2001. xiv + 256.

This reissue of the 1984 volume (**2847**) has added *The Haunted Man* and *The Haunted House* ("The Mortals in the House" and "The Ghost in Master B.'s Room") as well as an introduction by Paul Webb. Webb compares *The Haunted House* to Thomas Hood's poem of the same name, and he considers *The Haunted House* to be Dickens's most interesting story. This edition is marred by lack of textual information (the stories are undated and their original sources often unacknowledged) and major printing errors.

2850. Dalby, Richard, ed. *The Mammoth Book of Victorian and Edwardian Ghost Stories*. New York: Carroll; London: Robinson, 1995. 573.

Contains "The Signalman." A brief introduction (pp. xi–xiii) notes Dickens's influence on the ghost-story genre and finds "The Signalman" Dickens's best story.

2851. Dickens, Charles. *Charles Dickens' Christmas Ghost Stories*. London: Hale; New York: St. Martin's, 1992. Reprinted in paperback 1994. 256.

This odd selection is introduced by Peter Haining, who makes some serious mistakes in attribution. The contents are as follows: an excerpt from "A Christmas Tree," here titled "Ghosts at Christmas"; "The Goblins Who Stole a Sexton" from *Pickwick Papers*; "The Mother's Eyes," an (altered) excerpt from *Master Humphrey's Clock* that includes the story "A Confession Found in a Prison in the Time of Charles the Second"; *A Christmas Carol*; *The Haunted Man*; "The Rapping Spirits," said by Haining to be written for the December 1858 edition of *Household Words* but which is actually "Well-Authenticated Rappings" from 20 February 1858; "The Mortals in the House" and "The Ghost in Master B.'s Room" from *The Haunted House*; "The Signal Man" from *Mugby Junction*; and "The Last Words of the Old Year" from *Household Words* (4 January 1851). Haining also includes a story he titles "The Goodwood Ghost Story." In his introduction, Haining claims that Dickens's authorship of this story is disputed but that Ernest Rhys "was convinced" it was by Dickens when he included it in his collection *The Haunters and the Haunted* (1921). Rhys, however, places the story in "Ghost Stories from Local Records, Folk

Lore, and Legend" rather than in the "Ghost Stories from Literary Sources" section, and he prefaces the story with the words "Doubtfully attributed to Charles Dickens." Haining claims that the story appeared anonymously in *All the Year Round* in December 1862, but this bibliographer has been unable to find the story in this or any other number of *AYR* and considers it highly unlikely that it is by Dickens. Curiously, Haining does not include "To Be Taken With a Grain of Salt" from *Doctor Marigold's Prescriptions.* The volume closes with Dickens's review of Catherine Crowe's *The Night Side of Nature; or, Ghosts and Ghost-Seers* from *The Examiner*, 26 February 1848. Haining claims that Dickens knew Crowe because "she had written three stories for his magazine, *Household Words*" (which began publishing in 1850). There is a sound recording of this collection (**2403**). Haining's introduction (pp. 1–13), which contains many inaccuracies, credits Dickens with popularizing the white Christmas and Christmas ghost stories.

2852. ———. *A Christmas Carol and Other Stories.* New York: The Modern Library, 1995. 339.

Also contains *The Chimes* and *The Haunted Man,* a good short biography of Dickens, and an introduction to *A Christmas Carol* by John Irving (**2523**).

2853. Hudson, John, ed. *Dickens' Christmas.* Stroud, Glos: Sutton, 1997. 122.

This well-illustrated edition begins with an introduction (pp. 1–8) that places Dickens in the history of the celebration of Christmas. Hudson finds only *A Christmas Carol* memorable among Dickens's writings for Christmas. Extracts are included from the following works covered by this bibliography: *A Christmas Carol, The Chimes, The Cricket on the Hearth, The Haunted Man,* "A Christmas Tree," and "What Christmas Is, As We Grow Older." The volume also contains excerpts from other Victorian writers such as Washington Irving and Elizabeth Gaskell. A wide range of illustrations includes some of the original illustrations from the Christmas Books.

2854. Dickens, Charles. *Short Stories by Charles Dickens.* Cheltenham, Glos: Stanley Thornes, 1997. 90.

This edition for high school students includes "The Signalman" from *Mugby Junction* and "The Trial for Murder" from *Doctor Marigold's Prescriptions.* Editorial matter by Mike Royston includes a biographical sketch with pictures, and brief notes about Dickens and the ghost story and the supernatural. Text boxes on each page contain commentary on the plot and a glossary. A good Study Guide includes questions to be considered after reading a few pages and suggested activities for individual and group work. An overview at the end provides activities that involve all four stories. The questions are challenging and interesting.

2855. ———. *Best Ghost Stories.* Ware, Hertfordshire: Wordsworth, 1997. x + 273.

Contains *A Christmas Carol*, *The Haunted Man*, "To be Read at Dusk," "The Mortals in the House" and "The Ghost in Master B.'s Room" (from *The Haunted House*), "The Trial for Murder" (from *Doctor Marigold's Prescriptions*), and "The Signalman" (from *Mugby Junction*). In the introduction (pp. v–x), Christine Baker discusses Dickens's attitude to the supernatural, arguing that his "natural inclinations towards drama, the macabre and the lurid made him a superlative teller of ghost tales."

2856. ———. *A Christmas Carol and Other Christmas Writings.* Ed. Michael Slater. London: Penguin, 2003. xxxvii + 288.

Contains *A Christmas Carol*, *The Haunted Man and the Ghost's Bargain*, "A Christmas Tree," "What Christmas Is, As We Grow Older," and "The First" and "The Road" from *The Seven Poor Travellers.* Appendices provide Dickens's prefaces for the first cheap edition (**1299**) and the Charles Dickens edition (**1301**) of the Christmas Books as well as Dickens's descriptive headlines for *A Christmas Carol* and *The Haunted Man* from the Charles Dickens edition. A third appendix provides a useful account of Dickens's references to *The Arabian Nights.* Annotations for the selections follow. In his excellent introduction, Michael Slater places Dickens in the context of the English Christmas to argue that although he didn't "invent" Christmas Dickens was "hugely influential" in the new emphasis on charity and kindness in the celebration of Christmas in the nineteenth century. After surveying the history of the selections and their thematic interest (especially the role of memory), Slater concludes by affirming Dickens's strong belief in the ministry of Christ.

2857. ———. *A Christmas Carol and Other Christmas Books.* Ed. Robert Douglas-Fairhurst. Oxford: Oxford UP, 2006. 496.

Contains the five Christmas books and "What Christmas Is, As We Grow Older," as well as facsimile pages from Dickens's reading version of *A Christmas Carol* (**172**). This useful edition also contains annotations, a bibliography, and twenty black-and-white illustrations from the original Christmas books. Introduction by Robert Douglas-Fairhurst (**2648**).

RADIO ADAPTATIONS AND RECORDINGS

2858. *Charles Dickens Christmas Set.* Ashland, OR: Blackstone Audio, 2006. 4 CDs.

A Colonial Radio Theatre production, with Jerry Robbins, Jeffrey Gage, Mark Vander Berg, and the Colonial Radio Players. Disc 1 contains *The Chimes*, disc 2 contains *The Cricket on the Hearth*, disc 3 contains *The Seven Poor Travellers,* and disc 4 contains *A Christmas Carol.* Not seen. The cover claims that the selections are unabridged.

GUIDES, INDEXES, AND COMPENDIUMS

2859. Bentley, Nicolas, Michael Slater, and Nina Burgis. *The Dickens Index.* Oxford: Oxford UP, 1988; paperback, 1990. xii + 308.
Originally compiled by Nicolas Bentley but rewritten and completed by Slater and Burgis on Bentley's death in 1978, this useful compendium briefly identifies characters in Dickens's fiction, including the Christmas books, stories, and separately published short fiction (omitting "To Be Read at Dusk," although there is a general entry for this story). It also identifies biblical, literary, topographical and other sources and provides plot summaries for individual novels and stories. Vocabulary and references unfamiliar to modern readers are defined. A useful time chart relates events in Dickens's life to contemporary historical and literary events.

2860. Davis, Paul. *Charles Dickens A to Z. The Essential Reference to His Life and Work.* New York: Checkmark Books, an imprint of Facts on File, 1998. ix + 432. Published in Great Britain as *The Penguin Dickens Companion: The Essential Reference to His Life and Work.* London: Penguin, 1999. xii + 546.
Contains short entries for all the stories with extended descriptions of each of the five Christmas books that include a plot summary, brief commentary, and some references to criticism and adaptations.

2861. Hawes, Donald. *Who's Who in Dickens.* London: Routledge, 1998. xxv + 278.
Useful short descriptions of the characters in Dickens's works, including the Christmas books, Dickens's contributions to the Christmas numbers, and the separately published stories. Hawes includes quotations from the stories and information relating to possible sources. Characters are listed by work at the beginning. Hawes's excellent introduction provides an overview of the vast subject of Dickens's characters.

2862. Newlin, George, comp. and ed. *Everyone in Dickens.* 3 vols. Westport, CT: Greenwood, 1995. xlix + 839; xxxix + 840–1725; lvi + 704.
Vol. I contains the five Christmas Books, each listed separately and chronologically. The entry for *A Christmas Carol,* for example, begins

with a "Précis," a list of the illustrations from the work that are
reproduced in the following pages, a list of characters, and then the
descriptions themselves of "The Protagonist" (Scrooge), "Other Principals," "Supporting Roles," "Others," and "Walk-ons" (such as
Ali Baba and the Undertaker and the Undertaker's man).

Under the heading "The Christmas Stories" in volume II, an "Introduction," II, 957–59, lists and provides brief descriptions of the twenty
titles from "A Christmas Tree" (1850) to "No Thoroughfare" (1867).
The titles listed are of the segments by Dickens for the earlier Christmas Numbers (thus two are listed for 1852 and 1853—"The Poor
Relation's Story" and "The Child's Story" for 1852, and "The
Schoolboy's Story" and "Nobody's Story" for 1853) and the title for
the Number for the rest. For these entries the structure is not as elaborate as for the Christmas Books. Generally speaking, for each Christmas Number, a complete list of stories, with their authors, is provided,
but the only characters listed are those in the stories by Dickens.
Sometimes the characters are listed separately for each story by Dickens (as in the entry for "Mugby Junction") and sometimes, as in
the single entry for "Mrs. Lirriper's Lodgings" and "Mrs. Lirriper's
Legacy," the characters are combined in one list—by type of character
as "Principals," "Supporting Characters," etc.).

For the separately published short fiction, a précis is followed by a
list of characters, and then brief descriptions (in quotations from the
work) of the individual characters.

2863. ———, comp. and ed. *Every Thing in Dickens: Ideas and Subjects
Discussed by Charles Dickens in His Complete Works: A Topicon.*
Westport, CT: Greenwood, 1996. lviii + 1102.

Includes quotations from the Christmas Books and Christmas Stories
and separately published short fiction on a huge range of topics.

2864. Oppenlander, Ella Ann. *Dickens' All the Year Round: Descriptive Index and Contributor List.* Troy, NY: Whitston, 1984. 752. Reprinted
2005, 764.

This index has always been very hard to find but has recently been
republished in paperback. It includes an introduction containing the
origins of *All the Year Round*, a short history of weekly publications,
a comparison of *All the Year Round* and *Household Words* (Dickens
had less personal involvement in the former), and sections on the
audience, contributors, editorial policies, and business practices. There
are four indexes: Table of Contents, Contributors, Titles, and Key
Words. At the time of compilation, Oppenlander says that "of the
approximately 2,500 titles published in *AYR*, more than one quarter
of the authors have been identified." The sources for attributions are

various and are given in the Contributors List. Oppenlander's bibliography contains some rare nineteenth-century items and is useful for anyone interested in Dickens as an editor.

2865. Schlicke, Paul, ed. *Oxford Reader's Companion to Dickens*. Oxford: Oxford UP, 1999. xxiii + 654.

Invaluable guide for anyone interested in Dickens and his times. Each of the Christmas books has its own entry with a brief plot summary and survey of the writing and reception. The Christmas stories are covered in one entry, but there is a short entry for each of the four separately published short stories covered by this bibliography. Other items in the *Companion* are helpful for readers of the Christmas works and other short fiction (ghost stories, Christmas, fairy tales, public readings, etc.) as well as entries for his collaborative writers such as Wilkie Collins and Elizabeth Gaskell.

Name and Subject Index

INDEX

(For names of people and works mentioned in Ruth F. Glancy's "Dickens's Christmas Books, Christmas Stories, and Other Short Fiction: An Annotated Bibliography, Supplement I: 1985–2006," see special index, pages 485–96.)